Crimes Of the FBI-DOJ, Mafia, & Al Qaeda

2nd Edition

Captain Rodney Stich

Library of Congress Catalog Card Number: pending

Stich, Rodney—Author

This book: *Crimes of the FBI-DOJ, the Mafia*, and al Qaeda, 2nd ed.

ISBN: 978-0-932438-59-1
Digital ISBN 978-0-932438-60-7

Published and distributed in the United States of America by Silverpeak Enterprises, a Nevada Corporation, PO Box 4, Alamo, CA 94507 and offices in Nevada.

America's Housing & Financial Frauds	(978-0-932438-54-6)
Blowback, 9/11, and Cover-ups,	(978-0-932438-15-7)
Congress and Other Cesspools	(978-0-932438-29-4)
Crimes of the FBI-DOJ, Mafia, & al Qaeda	(978-0-932438-19-1)
David vs. Goliath: 9/11 & Other Tragedies	(978-0-932438-25-6)
Defrauding America, 4th ed. Vol. One	(978-0-932438-18-8)
Defrauding America, 4th ed. Vol. Two	(978-0-932438-19-5)
Disavow: A CIA Saga of Betrayal	(978-0-932438-17-1)
Drugging America, 2nd ed.	(978-0-932438-11-9)
Explosive Secrets of Covert CIA Companies	(978-0-932438-23-2)
FBI, CIA, the Mob, and Treachery	(978-0-932438-24-9)
History of U.S. Aviation Disasters—1950 to 9/11	(978-0-932438-65-2)
Iraq, Lies, Cover-ups, and Consequences,	(978-0-932438-22-5)
Japanese and U.S. World War II Plunder	(978-0-932438-69-0)
Lawyers and Judges: American Trojan Horses	(978-0-932438-16-4)
Lockerbie to 9/11: Massive Fraud & Conseq.	(978-0-932438-67-6)
Medical Industry's Death Panels: Greek Trag..	(978-0-932438[73-7)
Subverting America, Vol. One	(978-0-932438-20-1)
Subverting America, Vol. Two	(978-0-932438-21-8)
Terrorism Against America,	(978-0-932438-14-0)
Those Ugly Americans: 20th & 21st Centuries	(978-0-932438-01-0)

Table of Contents

In Appreciation

The author has great appreciation and admiration for the many courageous people who contributed to the information that is in this and his other books. They are the former government agents, including FBI, CIA, ONI, DEA, Secret Service, Customs, the former drug smugglers, and the former Mafia figures. They had nothing to gain by providing this information and had much to lose. And some did lose, as a result of their efforts to help. These books, and the efforts behind it, are dedicated to, among others:

- Those courageous people who went public with information on the arrogance and corruption that they found, attempting to inform and motivate the American people to respond to their responsibilities, to help fight the mutating corruption and resulting tragedies that are partly described within these pages.
- To the memory of those who became victims of the corruption and arrogance, victims of the cover-ups, and victims of those who could have helped and prevented the resulting harm.
- To the many thousands of American GIs who were killed or maimed, or otherwise adversely affected, and their families, who were victims of the serial lying, the cover-ups, and those who supported the liars.
- To the hundreds of thousands of killed, maimed, wounded, and adversely affected Iraqis who were also victims of the serial lying, the cover-ups, and those who supported the serial lying. They have provided insider information to the people that if the people would read and understand, and show some element of courage, the continuing series of human tragedies can be greatly changed. They are the *real* heroes in the United States.

This, and each of my other books, is dedicated to those courageous, and surely foolish, people who sought to stop the arrogance and corruption in government, only to suffer great personal and financial harm.

Bravo goes to those who sought to expose the serial lying by White House and congressional politicians seeking to halt the parade to war with Iraq, only to suffer the standard indignities. And condolences are shown to the thousands of American military personnel killed, maimed, or otherwise harmed as certain American politicians, with the support of a majority of the American people, pushed to start the war that all knew would result in thousands of killed and maimed Iraqis.

Introduction

This book provides facts and documented evidence showing:

- FBI personnel involved in murders of U.S. citizens.
- FBI-DOJ personnel involved in misconduct that enabled to occur a series of catastrophic terrorist attacks upon U.S. targets.
- "Deep-Sixing" of information from al Qaeda source about planned terrorist attacks on U.S. targets that did occur.
- A New York Mafia soldier acting as a mole inside a key al Qaeda cell headed by Ramzi Yousef, the mastermind behind the 1993 bombing of the World Trade Center and the planned bombing of 11 U.S. airliners departing Far East locations.
- Years of prior FBI-DOJ misconduct that enabled to occur a continuing series of preventable aviation disasters and other tragedies from high-level misconduct being covered up.
- Corrupt misuse of FBI and other U.S. Department of Justice facilities to retaliate against present and former government agents to discredit their reports of high-level corruption.
- Cover-up of serial murders by FBI agents acting secretly with organized crime and Mafia groups.
- A culture in the FBI and other Department of Justice divisions that constitutes the greatest internal threat, and the source of greatest harm, to the American people. Some of the conduct described within these pages highlights what is described in far more detail in some of the author's other books, including *Defrauding America* and *Drugging America.*
- Many of these conditions are totally foreign to most people. It is almost surreal, like looking into a crystal ball. But these conditions *do* exist, and they daily inflict great harm upon innocent people. When properly understood, it can be seen that the America we think exists has been subverted by corrupt individuals, and that the so-called freedom, justice, constitutional protections, are PR slogans to placate the masses.
- Don't think you can't be the next victim. If you aren't *directly* affected, you are indirectly affected as the entire nation suffers from these matters.
- "Thanks" to the culture of cover-ups by members of Congress, by the media, and by the political pundits, the people are kept from hearing about these matters, and suffering the consequences.

A Fact of Life Unrecognized by Most Americans

A poem was written by Martin Niemoller that depicts a fact of life that most Americans have yet to learn, though they are experiencing the consequences of it:

First they came for the Jews and I did not speak out because I was not a Jew. Then they came for the Communists, and I did not speak out, because I was not a Communist.

Then they came for the trade unionists, and I did not speak out, because I was not a trade unionist. Then they came for me, and there was no one left, to speak out for me.

Pastor Martin Niemöller

Pastor Martin Niemöller (1892-1984) first supported the rise of Adolf Hitler, and then upon learning the truth, and objecting, he was imprisoned. He wrote a poem about the state of denial of Germans about what Hitler was doing. Probably no better example could be shown than what has been done to the American people, in their name, while they lazily ignored the outrages, some of which are detailed in this book, and many more in related books

About the Author

Captain Rodney Stich became an activist against corruption in government after discovering, as a key federal airline safety inspector, a culture of arrogance and corruption responsible for a series of major aviation disasters. In his many unusual attempts to circumvent the universal cover-ups in government, seeking to halt the continuing and deadly corruption, he exercised a multitude of other attempts. These included publishing informational books, appearing as guest and expert on over 3,000 radio and television shows since 1978, filing lawsuits seeking to make additional records of the corruption and the consequences.

The publicity from these various actions caused him to become a central point for other government agents and insiders, providing him for the past 20 years with evidence of other hardcore corruption of people in virtually every major area of overt and covert government operations.

Aviation Background Started Before the Pearl Harbor Attack

Stich's background started while he was in the U.S. Navy during World War II. He was in the Navy on December 7, 1941. During his naval career he was an instructor in the PBY Catalina seaplanes, a Patrol Plane Commander in the Liberators and Privateers, and believed to be the youngest Patrol Plane Commander during that war.

Worldwide Commercial Airline Experience

After World War II, Stich flew for the airlines, flying as captain in domestic and international operations. He was checked out as captain on virtually every type of plane flown by U.S. airlines, including the double-deck Boeing Stratocruiser, Lockheed Super Constellation, DC-4, DC-3, Martin 202, Convair 340, Curtis C-46, Lockheed Electra, DC-8, and Convair 880.

He was one of the first pilots licensed by Japan as an Airline Transport Pilot, holding Japanese Airline Transport Pilot license number 170. He was also one of the first captains for Japan Airlines, during which time his copilots were former Japanese military pilots from World War II, against whom he had formerly been in combat.

The *Saturday Evening Post* had written a series of three articles in 1950 about the pilots at his primary airline, Transocean Airlines. The articles were titled, "The Daring Young Men of Transocean Airlines."

In those days, flying overseas, especially in the Middle East, were pioneering experiences, encountering situations that no airline pilot today encounters. In one instance, in 1953, he found himself at the center of a revolution in Iran, which he later learned was engineered by the CIA. He flew Muslim pilgrims to Mecca and Medina on the Hajj during the Muslim holy period. He may have been the only pilot to take pilgrims to Medina, where he landed in the desert outside of the holy city. He resided in Jerusalem, Ramallah, Beirut, Tehran, and Abadan, visited Palestine refugee camps, and associated with the residents who were, in those days, friendly to the Americans.

He had his share of in-flight emergencies, including engine failures, engine fires, sudden closing of virtually all airports at his destination, serious icing problems on the North Atlantic, sudden shortage of fuel when the head winds over long over-water flights became more adverse than forecast.

Aviation Safety Inspector-Investigator for Federal Government

Eventually he left airline flying and became a federal aviation safety agent for the Federal Aviation Administration (FAA). He was responsible for conducting flight checks of airline pilots, evaluating their competency, issuing government ratings, evaluating safety matters and preparing reports on safety problems and recommended corrective actions.

Assignment to Halt Worst Series of Airline Disasters in U.S. History

Eventually, the federal government gave him the assignment to correct the conditions causing the worst series of airline crashes in the nation's history. It was here that he discovered the deadly politics of air safety and corruption in government offices. To circumvent the blocks preventing the federal government from carrying out its aviation safety responsibilities, Stich exercised legal remedies in ways that had never before been done.

In desperation, seeking to halt the continuing brutal airline disasters, he acted as an independent counsel, conducting hearings to obtain testimony and additional evidence that showed the deep-seated culture in the government's aviation safety offices that enabled countless numbers of preventable aviation tragedies to occur. The events of September 11, 2001, would be one-day's consequences of these serious matters.

Unable to correct the deep-seated corruption, Stich left government services and then engaged in other activities seeking to bring the corruption to light. Like a magnet, these activities caused other former and present government agents and insiders to provide him with additional information and evidence of corruption in government offices far beyond the aviation field. These were agents from the CIA, DEA, DIA, FBI, Customs, Secret Service, drug smugglers, and organized crime figures.

Trojan Horse Corruption and David Versus Goliath Battles

The magnitude of the corrupt and Trojan Horse-like criminal and subversive activities, and the harm resulting from them, caused Stich to spend the remainder of his life fighting the escalating corruption in the three branches of government. No other government agent, or whistleblower, revealing hardcore corruption in government offices, had suffered such great harm, as he engaged in years of escalating David versus Goliath battles to protect national interests and halt the harm being inflicted upon the people.

Over 3,000 Radio and Television Appearances

He has appeared as guest and expert on over 3,000 radio and television shows since 1978, throughout the United States and in Canada, Mexico, and

Europe. He published numerous books, including among others *History of Aviation Disasters: 1950 to 9/11*, *Defrauding America*, and *Drugging America*.

In addition, Stich was a successful entrepreneur, having acquired and developed over $10 million in real estate properties (valued today at $17 million. His properties included motels, hotels, truck stops, golf courses, rental properties, and land holdings. He used these assets to fund his exposure activities.

The detailed information in these books reveals a pattern of deep-seated corruption in the three branches of government that played key roles in the success of the terrorists on September 11, 2001, and is responsible for many areas of human tragedies, including the sham imprisonment of tens of thousands of men and women. That corruption is another form of terrorism that continues to inflict far more harm upon America and its people in a Trojan horse fashion.

The information he provides in these books can be a very valuable tool to fight the widespread and unpublicized, unknown, corruption throughout government and in many non-government operations, including the media.

Stich has paid a heavy personal and financial price for seeking to protect important national interests by exposing these matters.

For more information put "Rodney Stich" into Internet search engines such as www.google.com and www.defraudingamerica.com.

Rodney Stich in the 1990s

CHAPTER ONE

History of Corrupt Culture In the FBI-DOJ

The greatest threat to the people of the United States is the deep-seated culture of the lawyers in the United States Department of Justice (DOJ). It adversely affects national security and the lives of America's people. No form of reorganization will correct this problem without exposing the pattern of criminal and even subversive activities that I and my dozens of government insiders discovered during hundreds of years of *cumulative* experience.

Forget everything you were taught or felt about integrity, honesty, guilt or innocence in the FBI and other divisions of the U.S. Department of Justice. Forget everything you may have heard about people sentenced to prison deserving what they got. The integrity of many who have been sentenced to federal prison is far greater than many Justice Department prosecutors whose misconduct constitutes major crimes and would be punishable if they were ordinary citizens.

Deeply Embedded Justice Department Culture

The Justice Department culture is political, corrupt, and extremely dangerous to the people. The people in control of the awesome Justice Department power are responsible for human tragedies far beyond anyone's comprehension. The Justice Department, under the U.S. Attorney General, includes the Solicitor General, Federal Bureau of Investigation (FBI), the U.S. attorneys, Drug Enforcement Administration (DEA), Immigration and Naturalization Service (INS), U.S. Marshals (USMS), and Bureau of Prisons (BP).

The Justice Department is a political animal and covers up for the crimes of presidents who appoint many of its top officials and for the president's allies. The crimes of Ronald Reagan and George H.W. Bush in the October Surprise and Contra gun and drug smuggling activities were covered up and not prosecuted. The crimes of federal judges and top government officials are routinely covered up. The consequence has been great harm to national security and the lives of countless numbers of people.

In 1989, when U.S. Attorney General Edwin Meese was testifying in a criminal trial, he was asked, "Is it not true that your focus was not the focus of an attorney general wearing the attorney general's hat but basically to gather information to protect the President and deal with the political problem brewing in Congress?" Meese replied, "Yes." As usual, the Justice Department's 1986 probe into the sale of arms to Iran was not to find the facts but to protect President Reagan who appointed him. This is the normal Justice Department obstruction of justice, which is kept from the public by a compliant media that aids and abets the obstruction of justice.

When the Justice Department investigates itself or political allies, it usually selects "investigators" who are politically appointed staff members. It diffuses congressional investigations by stating the matters are under Justice Department investigation—which never comes to fruition and eventually the matter passes on.

Since attorney generals are political appointees, it would be unrealistic in light of the complicity of the government and media checks and balances to expect them to honestly investigate the corrupt activities of the people who are responsible for their high position!

The prosecutor in the Justice Department has more control over the amount of human tragedies that the government can inflict upon America's men, women, and families. He can file false charges, pay for informants to provide perjured testimony, release to the media information about people or corporations being investigated, interview friends and neighbors seeking information, determine who to be arrested and who to be protected, and use one-sided information to get a grand jury to indict a person or corporation.

There are a reported 3,000-plus criminal offenses on the books. They can be used against anyone as a tool by the Justice Department to silence any criticism or exposure of high-level corruption in government. Under the creative Justice Department, almost any act can be made into a criminal act, including the conspiracy statute and the mail and wire fraud statutes. Prosecutors have a virtual unlimited authority to determine who will or will not be investigated, who will or will not be called before a grand jury, who will or will not be prosecuted. Prosecutors will frequently ignore serious criminal activities for political considerations or favoritism.

Raw Power That Controls Media and Corporate Silence

Any corporation, including broadcast and print media, can be seriously harmed and even put out of business by a unit of government that is easily controlled by Justice Department lawyers. The great number of regulations affecting a corporation can be the basis for false or even real but minor charges, putting them at risk. An airline, for instance, with thousands of records and hundreds of requirements, can easily be charged with record violations and fined huge amounts of money. Or put out of business. The public perceives such charges as indicative of serious safety problems. But similar violations in thousands of required records could be found at any airline and are often of minor consequence.

Members of Congress are especially prone to misuse of Justice Department power. Leaks to the press that a particular member of Congress is being investigated can have a devastating influence on his reelection. The influence would be even worse if false charges were filed against the member of Congress. With the vast amount of political donations that is a part of their daily life, it is not difficult to find a basis for conducting an investigation.

Organized Crime in the U.S. Justice Department

"Organized Crime in the U.S. Justice Dept" was the heading in the Forum section of the *Sacramento Bee* (October 27, 1991), accurately reflecting the decades of criminality in the most misnamed agency of the federal government:

> "Indications...point to a widespread conspiracy implicating government officials in the theft of Inslaw's technology." Inslaw, bad as it was, constituted only the tip of the iceberg.

Inslaw is described in detail in *Defrauding America*, and consisted of Justice Department attorneys forcing a company into bankruptcy so they could steal its computer software called PROMIS. The attorneys had an interest in a company that would be bidding on a lucrative government contract worth a half-billion dollars to install a computer program in Department of Justice offices.

DOJ Blocked Every Effort to Halt
Crash-Related Corruption in the Aviation Field

For 30 years, Justice Department attorneys blocked every attempt I and other government agents made to report high-level corruption that we discovered as part of our official duties. If my reports, or those by other government agents, of criminal activities had received the reaction required by law, there would not have been the extent of government corruption that now exists (and which is largely unknown to the majority of the public).

Responsibilities of Justice Department Employees

Under federal law, the responsibility for ensuring that the laws of the United States are properly enforced belongs to the United States Department of Justice, which is under the control of the U.S. Attorney General, and in turn, the President of the United States. In practice, the politically appointed Attorney General routinely has used the Justice Department to cover up corrupt and criminal acts involving high-level government personnel or corrupt covert activities of the CIA and other covert agencies—including CIA drug trafficking.

These problems occurred during the Reagan and Bush administrations and were especially prominent during the Clinton presidency, as Attorney General Janet Reno protected him and the Democratic Party. Occasionally the checks and balances work as intended, and the person in that position of trust goes to prison. Attorney General John Mitchell, for instance, went to prison, as did Webster Hubbell and other attorney generals. Subsequent attorney generals have committed federal offenses involving far more serious crimes, and were never prosecuted or called to task by the poorly functioning checks and balances in government and the media.

Responsible for Protecting the Civil Rights of American Citizens

Within the U.S. Department of Justice are numerous divisions. These include, for instance, the Federal Bureau of Investigation, responsible for investigating the many crimes that I reported to it; the civil rights division, with the responsibilities to investigate the civil rights violations that I reported to them; the criminal division, responsible for preventing the many criminal activities that I reported to them (including those perpetrated by Justice Department personnel seeking to block my reports); the U.S. Trustee, who is responsible for preventing the rampant fraud in bankruptcy courts that I and others reported to that office; the Drug Enforcement Administration (DEA), responsible for preventing the massive drug trafficking, including that committed by the CIA and DEA.

This is the Justice Department that has persecuted me continuously since mid-1987, retaliating against me for reporting the federal crimes that I uncovered; who retaliated against me for exercising lawful and constitutional protections to halt the barrage of civil and constitutional (and criminal) violations inflicted upon me. Every one of these divisions has been routinely used to commit the federal crimes that they have a duty to prevent.

Succession of Corrupt Attorneys General

A succession of Attorneys General have been implicated in corrupt acts and federal crimes, but have escaped prosecution because they held the highest law enforcement position in the United States. Subsequent Attorneys General have committed federal offenses involving far more serious crimes, and were never prosecuted or called to task by the checks and balances in government.

Attorney General Edwin Meese, a former California lawyer and Alameda County District Attorney, was prominently associated with an escalation of the sleazy and corrupt activities in government. He was implicated in the 1980 October Surprise scheme that helped bring the Reagan-Bush team into power. As a reward, or to protect the Reagan-Bush team from prosecution in that scandal, the Reagan-Bush Administration appointed Meese U.S. Attorney General. Meese was then used to protect Reagan and Bush from the October Surprise scandal and others that followed.

When the stench from Meese's activities forced him to resign, he was replaced by Richard Thornburgh, who continued the criminal activities of Inslaw, the obstruction of justice activities, and the persecution of whistleblowers and informants. Thornburgh left the Attorney General position in 1991 to run for the Senate seat vacated by the death of Senator John Heinz in a plane crash in Philadelphia. A Pennsylvania newspaper identified Thornburgh as the "Harrisburg Mafia."

President George H.W. Bush, who had a long-time relationship with the CIA, then appointed[1] William P. Barr as U.S. Attorney General. Barr was General Counsel of the CIA while Bush was Director of the Agency. From the very beginning, Barr blocked investigations into the major scandals that were surfacing almost daily, including those that directly involved the Justice Department and the CIA. Barr has a long history of CIA relations.

Barr blocked an investigation of the part played by Justice Department officials in the Inslaw affair, denying the request by the House Judiciary Committee for an Independent Prosecutor.[2] Barr refused to appoint a special prosecutor to investigate the White House's funding of Iraq's military build-up. Barr refused to appoint an independent prosecutor to investigate the White House's role in the Bank of Lavoro scandal. He refused to appoint an Independent Prosecutor to investigate Inslaw. The House and Senate Judiciary committees had requested the Attorney General to request appointment of an independent prosecutor in each of these matters.

Decades of Obstruction of Justice

It has been a common practice to appoint someone to the highest law enforcement position in the United States who has been involved in criminal activities, and act as damage control. Before William Barr was appointed U.S. Attorney General by President George Bush, he was legal counsel for the CIA's Southern Air Transport, and former CIA operative Terry Reed said that he personally saw Barr in drug-related activities. Another source, Gene Tatum, also personally encountered Barr in similar activities.

This same general practice is applied to the political selection of federal judges who then act to block any prosecution or revealing civil actions. Bush was heavily involved in the overall drug smuggling activities, acting with Oliver North and other drug traffickers, and it would be only "normal" to put one of their own at the head of the nation's top law-enforcement agency. Further, U.S. Attorneys are selected to insure that this plan works. This problem reflects one of the major flaws in our constitution. It was visibly reflected during the presidency of Ronald Reagan, George Bush, and Bill Clinton.

Threat to Any Member of Congress

The mere investigation by the FBI arm of the Justice Department can cause a member of the U.S. Senate and House to lose an election. The Justice Department can easily fabricate charges, especially conspiracy or misprision of felony offenses, by stretching facts clearly out of proportion to reality. Possibly the fear of what the Justice Department can do was one of the reasons every member of the U.S. Senate from 1991 to 1993 refused to respond to my multipage petition to investigate the corruption I brought to their attention. But this was no excuse for them aiding and abetting the criminal activities. They had a

---

[1] October 27, 1991.
[2] Sometimes called independent counsel.

duty to perform. When they accepted their position, they assumed the responsibilities that went with the pay, the perks, and the prestige.

Pattern of Criminal Activities by Justice Department

For thirty years I have been intimately connected with the criminal acts committed by Justice Department officials and their various divisions. Their misconduct in the 1960s, which I initially discovered while a federal investigator, had devastating consequences in the aviation areas that I brought to their attention. Since then, as these pages reveal, the criminality in the U.S. Department of Justice has increased many times over, very possibly making it the key cog in the pattern of racketeering activities against the American people.

If Justice Department personnel did, in fact, do any of the acts described within these pages, these same personnel would have to misuse the power of the federal government and of the Justice Department to block the reporting of these crimes.

These Justice Department lawyers have made it standard practice to misuse Justice Department facilities to falsely charge dozens of informants and whistleblowers with federal offenses to block their reporting of crimes implicating federal officials.

Outrageous Prison Sentences

America reportedly has the greatest percentage of its population in prison of any country in the world. Outrageous prison sentences are imposed for often-minor offenses, such as filling in swamps on one's own property or being found with small quantities of drugs. Minor drug offenders are sentenced to twenty or more years in prison for a one-time offense while vicious killers are often released in a fraction of the time. Often the drug offender is a person simply filling the demand created by a drug-crazed society, which may arguably share a greater blame than the person responding to the demand.

These outrageous prison sentences are legislated by the same members of Congress who have committed crimes associated with their cover-up of the criminal activities described within these pages. These congressional felonies are often worse than the offenses that place thousands of people in prison for years of confinement.

Army of Informants Looking for Victims—
Another Growth Industry

Government agencies, and especially the various divisions of the Department of Justice, have thousands of agents and informants who must find offenses committed by people. They search public and financial records looking for technical errors that they can charge as federal crimes—and the list is endless, including matters committed by almost any adult.

They set up elaborate pseudo criminal enterprises and look for people they can entice into them in such a way that criminal charges can be filed. The coalition of government agents, informants, and prosecutors are quite imaginative. Anyone trapped into one of them doesn't stand much of a chance against this coalition with unlimited funds and juries that will believe virtually anything the "government" charges.

One example: a government informant may induce a "patsy" to assist him in undercover work, falsely encouraging him to assist in bringing about the arrest of alleged drug traffickers. The patsy is told to contact certain people—who are actually undercover government agents—and to gain their confidence by bragging about past drug trafficking activities. The patsy doing the bragging may never have been near drugs or involved in any drug offense, but he is told it is a chance to work for the government and be well paid.

Unknown to the patsy, he is telling these tall tales to government undercover agents who arrest him after his fabricated drug-trafficking statements are recorded. Based simply upon these statements—no drugs are involved—the patsy who is no match for this government conspiracy, is charged, tried, and then naive jurors find him guilty.

Chalk up another "win" for the public and Congress' tough-on-crime stance. The jurors have a "feel-good" attitude, and government agents receive bonuses. Oh yes, the patsy may get life in prison with no chance of parole.

Agents Transferred to Undesirable Locations if No Arrests

During an April 1999 phone call with a former ATF and DEA agent, Michael Don Stewart, he described the quota-system that requires ATF agents to fabricate cases against innocent people. "If you go two months without making an arrest, a search warrant, a seizure, or open or close an investigation, you are transferred to some place where they need you, and where you don't want to go, such as Detroit, East LA, little Cuba—Miami."

I responded, "This practice encourages agents to file sham charges, doesn't it." Stewart replied, "You are exactly right; most people aren't aware of that." He said that agents, to avoid being transferred, look for technical paper violations to justify opening an investigation. The agents go to pawnshops, gun shops, and other places looking at records and seeking some technical mistake—no matter how innocent or minor—which permits them to conduct an investigation and make sham charges against the person.

Searching Records for Targets to Destroy

A practice similar to that had been described to me many years ago by CIA asset Gunther Russbacher. CIA and other government personnel look for people and companies that can be forced into involuntary bankruptcy. Then, the rampant corruption in bankruptcy courts seizes and loots the assets. (Details in *Defrauding America.*)

Adding Conspiracy Laws to Feel-Good Tough-On-Crime Self-Serving Legislation

Not to be outdone by the other political party, politicians pushed through—just before election time—*another* law showing them as being tough on crime: the drug conspiracy statute. The conspiracy statute greatly expanded the number of people ensnared by the draconian minimum sentencing law. Now, almost *anyone* can be sentenced to a long prison term—or even life without parole; no drugs even need be present to convict as a major drug kingpin.

In real life, as applied by Department of Justice prosecutors, men and women have been sent to prison with long prison sentences—even life in prison—who were guilty of no crime, and who are in prison because of the fertile imagination of career-obsessed attorneys in the United States Department of Justice. This law, as members of Congress knew, targets innocent people who have no connection to drugs, who had never entertained any drug-related thoughts, and to this day can't understand why they are in prison.

American men and women in prison now exceed the combined population of Alaska and Wyoming. In 1998, for instance, a dozen European countries making up the European Union, whose population exceeds the United States' by over 100 million, had only one third as many people in prison (*San Francisco Examiner,* May 10, 1999).

The Catchall Conspiracy Charge That Can Put *YOU* in Prison

Congress' drug conspiracy laws have put more people in prison than any other statute. A man or woman doesn't even need to possess drugs, handle any drugs, or play any role in any drug transaction. For the prosecutor and informant, the "beauty" of it is that they can send someone to prison for years or for life who doesn't even know what he had done!

A "Dry" Conspiracy

A "dry" conspiracy or "no drug conspiracy" is the name given to a conspiracy where there is no evidence of any drugs. All it requires for conviction is a government-paid witness testifying to something that he claims you said. You might have even been bragging, without ever having done anything you claim, but you end up with a long prison sentence. Thousands of men and women are serving long prison sentences because they talked about importing or selling drugs or were present when others did, and which never occurred.

How DOJ Attorneys Improve Their Performance Record

The conspiracy legislation permits a prosecutor to sit behind his desk and let his imagination wander. With a little mental calculation, he can concoct the type of conspiracy to charge against our Joe or Jane target, which needs no relationship to reality. Great business for defense attorneys! Almost any business person or someone active in the business world can be charged with some type of conspiracy. Anyone can be approached by a government informant and sucked into a conspiracy scheme concocted by your friendly government agents. No evidence is needed!

A Conspiracy of One—Another DOJ Trick to Imprison People

Attorneys in the Department of Justice have even expanded on the conspiracy statute. A conspiracy requires two or more persons. No problem; Justice Department prosecutors now charge single persons with a conspiracy when there is no other person involved.

Very Few Countries Have Conspiracy Laws

Former counsel to the U.S. House committee on the Judiciary, Eric E. Sterling, said that very few countries have conspiracy laws as exist in the United States because "they can be so badly abused." He added:

Our conspiracy law is such that long after you've dropped out of the conspiracy, you're still responsible for things that you may have done way in the past. The criminal organization marches forward. You've gone straight. But when the chain gets connected all the way to the back, you can still be held liable for things that you had no responsibility for and you could not foresee. It's a terrible problem, the way in which conspiracy is being used in these cases.

Another Growth Industry—DOJ's-Paid Perjurers

Perjury-for-sale is the type of growth industry that an insider could associate with the culture in the Department of Justice. This practice greatly increases the number of people sent to fill new prisons or crowded into old ones. DOJ prosecutors routinely compensate witnesses who testify before grand juries and trial juries, as they want the witness to testify.

Some of them are paid on an occurrence basis. Others are on a monthly salary. Some are in prison, willing to say anything to bring about their release. Others may be charged with a criminal offense and are offered to have charges dropped for parroting what the prosecutor wants said. And they have another advantage: they have the Department of Justice protecting them against being charged with criminal perjury, regardless of the extent of their lying under oath.

The Liars Club

Another name for this group is "Liars Club." Some are professional perjurers who travel around the country testifying for DOJ prosecutors. The Liars Club includes prisoners, some with life sentences, who read newspapers to learn or fabricate facts about people recently arrested, most of whom they had never seen, heard of, or dealt with. Their expertise at fabricating testimony to use before grand juries and during trial is their greatest value.

"Jumping on the Bus"

A term defining the process is "jumping on the bus." Prisoners obtain information from other prisoners—even buy the information—and then contact DOJ prosecutors and offer their services to testify against a person prosecutors want arrested, or who had just been arrested and is waiting for trial.

The best liars for DOJ prosecutors are prisoners and people charged with criminal offenses. The longer their sentences, the more willing they are to fabricate testimony exactly as requested by the DOJ attorneys. They also know the lingo and the ropes.

A release-from-prison promise in exchange for perjured testimony does not take into account the crime for which the person is in prison. He may be a brutal murderer, a major drug kingpin, and someone who will return to his prior crimes once he is released.

And even more bizarre, there is no limit to the bizarre angles involved. The target against whom testimony is being "paid" may be guilty of a very low offense, or even no offense. One answer is that the new conviction increases the prosecutor's conviction record; the hell with justice!

Working the System

The real hard-core incarcerated drug trafficker works the system. He thinks to himself, "What do I have to do to get out of prison?" He asks the prosecutor, "What do I have to say? Who do I have to testify against? How much drugs do I have to say that he discussed?" With the government backing the liar, most naive jurors believe the witness called by the government.

The liar is sitting with the government at his side. The government presents the liar in the court. Is the average juror going to doubt the integrity of the United States? Surely you can believe your own government! [Forget again the history of government lying for the past 50 years.]

Another problem facing the defendant is that judges will often bar a lawyer from presenting a certain defense, the very one most applicable to show the person's innocence.

Major Drug Kingpins Get Released Through Fabricated Testimony

Often, a high-level drug kingpin will give testimony against a low-level participant in a drug operation—or someone totally innocent—and the drug kingpin gets released from prison. "Big fish" are given their freedom to provide testimony against minor offenders. It's like the food chain; major drug dealers snitch on low-level dealers and go free, while innocent or low-level people end up with long prison sentences.

Like Crooked Cops Holding the People Hostage

Other criminal statutes are often simultaneously violated when this crime occurs, including falsely accusing a person of a crime, conspiracy, and obstruction of justice, among others. But who is going to prosecute the prosecutor? It's like having a department of crooked cops holding the citizens hostage.

Worse than Hitler's Gestapo

When I was growing up in the late 1930s, as Hitler came to power, I remember the many media articles decrying the culture of informants or neighborhood spies that Adolph Hitler's Gestapo used to get neighbors to spy on neighbors. The United States Congress and Department of Justice have gone far beyond what Hitler initiated. Now, family members testify against each other, children testify against their brothers or sisters, children testify against parents. This is what the attorneys in the Department of Justice have brought upon America as their slime permeates throughout government, industry, and society.

Encouraging Someone to Give False Testimony is a Crime

Under federal criminal statutes, the prosecutor is guilty of a crime if he procures another person to commit perjury. When a law-enforcement officer commits this crime, it is far worse than when done by someone else. The law says:

> Title 18 U.S.C. § 1622. Subornation of perjury. Whoever procures another to commit any perjury is guilty of subornation of perjury, and shall be fined... or imprisoned...

The evidence is overwhelming that Justice Department attorneys responsible for prosecuting people for subornation of perjury routinely perpetrate this crime. They hold themselves above the law, with one standard for the people, and another for themselves.

Compensation for Testimony is a Federal Offense

Under federal criminal statute, Title 18 USC Section 201, it is a criminal offense for *anyone* to give any form of compensation to a person providing testimony, whether it is before the fact or after the fact. Title 18 USC § 201(c)(2) says:

> Whoever...directly or indirectly, gives, offers or promises anything of value to any person, for or because of the testimony under oath or affirmation given or to be given by such person as a witness upon a trial, hearing, or other proceeding, before any court...authorized by the laws of the United States to hear evidence or take testimony...shall be fined under this title or imprisoned for not more than two years, or both. That statute does not require that the testimony be proven false; only that some type of compensation be promised for a witness's testimony.

Section 201(b)(3) of the same title addresses the matter of compensation given to *influence* the testimony. DOJ prosecutors have been violating both of these statutes for years and continue to do so.

American Bar Association Rules of Professional Conduct (Section 3.4(b) says: A lawyer shall not (b)... offer an inducement to a witness that is prohibited by law. The theory against paying for testimony was reflected in a Florida case (*The Florida Bar v. Jackson*, 490 So.2d 935 Fla. 1986):

The very heart of the judicial system lies in the integrity of the participants. Justice must not be bought or sold. Attorneys have a solemn responsibility to assure that not even the taint of impropriety exists as to the procurement of testimony before courts of Justice. It is clear that the actions of the respondent in attempting to obtain compensation for the testimony of his clients...violates the very essence of the integrity of the judicial system and the disciplinary rule and the code of professional responsibility, the integration rules of the Florida Bar and the oath of his office.

In another example, the lawyer who paid $50 for a police officer to testify truthfully for his client was suspended from practice for 18 months. (*In re Kien*, 372 N.E.2nd 376 (111.1977))

Legal Challenge to DOJ Compensated Testimony

Such bribery is common and was challenged during a 1998 trial in Denver. DOJ prosecutors charged Sonya Singleton and Napoleon Douglas with money laundering and conspiracy offenses. Before trial, DOJ prosecutors offered to drop charges against Douglas if he testified against Singleton as they wanted him to testify. This offer was made despite the statute barring payment for testimony. With this compensation and freedom against perjury, Douglas accepted the prosecutor's offer. Singleton was convicted solely on the basis of this compensated testimony.

It is possible neither one was guilty of the charges. But for one of them to be assured freedom from prison, maybe from a life-in-prison sentence, it paid Douglas to fabricate lies, especially when the prosecutor protected him against criminal perjury charges. It was another "he-said she-said" type of trial, with Douglas having the benefit of the government of the United States alongside him. The naive jurors received the impression that he was probably telling the truth, despite the fact that DOJ prosecutors routinely solicit and pay for perjured testimony.

Denver attorney John "Val" Wachtel appealed Singleton's conviction based upon the fact that the sole witness against Singleton was paid to testify, and that this violated the clear wording of the federal statute. Three judges[3] in the Court of Appeals Panel at Denver heard the appeal.

OK for DOJ Prosecutors But Not for Defendants' Lawyers

Justice Department prosecutors argued that it was legal for them to pay or compensate people for testimony during grand jury and trial jury proceedings even though it was *not legal* for defense lawyers to do so. The prosecutor has the advantage of being able to free a prisoner or drop charges; the defense lawyers cannot do that. The DOJ attorneys argued that Title 18 USC § 3553(e) permitted them to request a reduction of sentence or dropping of charges for those who provide testimony that prosecutors wanted. That section says:

Upon motion of the Government, the court shall have the authority to impose a sentence below a level established by statute as a minimum sentence so as to reflect a defendant's substantial assistance in the investigation or prosecution of another person who has committed an offense. Further, USSG § 5K1.1 provides for reduction of sentence. They also sought support in Federal Rule of Criminal Procedure Rule 35(b):

> The court, on motion of the Government made within one year after the imposition of the sentence, may reduce a sentence to reflect a defendant's subsequent, substantial assistance in the investigation or prosecution of another person who has committed an offense...

The three-judge Court of Appeals decision denied the government's position, holding that *assistance* did not include *purchasing* testimony. They held that reduction in sentence could be provided for *information*, but not for *sworn testimony*:

---

[3] Judges Paul J. Kelly, David M. Ebel, and Chief Judge Stephanie K. Seymour.

Each of these provisions of law authorizes only that substantial assistance can be rewarded after it is rendered; none authorized the government to make a deal for testimony before it is given, as the government did with Mr. Douglas. [The paid witness against Singleton.] However § 201(c)(2) prohibits even the rewarding of testimony after it is given; it prohibits anything of value to be given, offered or promised because of "testimony" given. 18 U.S.C. § 201(c)(2). The sentencing provisions may thus appear to conflict by authorizing something of value (a motion for and grant of sentence reduction) to be given because of testimony rendered.

We believe the statutes can be read together in this way: in light of § 201(c)(2), "substantial assistance" does not include testimony. Congress enacted the sentencing provisions against the backdrop of its general prohibition against giving anything of value for or because of testimony... Our reading of the statutes will not impair the substantial assistance provisions, because a defendant can substantially assist an investigation or prosecution in myriad ways other than by testifying.... In the circumstances before us, the appropriate remedy for the testimony obtained in violation of § 201(c)(2) is suppression of its use in Ms. Singleton's trial.

The appeal panel held that the statute's plain words barring any type of compensation for testimony meant what it said, and applied both to government agents and the public. The Court of Appeals decision reversed the conviction of Singleton, requiring the prosecutor to retry the case without using compensation-tainted testimony. (U.S. v. Singleton, 144 F.3d 1343 (1998)) The decision made sense.

A similar district court decision was made in Miami on August 4, 1998 by U.S. District Judge William J. Zloch in the case of U.S. v. Lowery. In that decision, Judge Zloch held that the deal for a co-defendant's testimony gave him "every reason to fabricate, falsify or exaggerate his testimony in an attempt to curry favor."

Motion for *En Banc* Rehearing by All 12 Judges

After the three-judge Court of Appeals panel overturned the Singleton dismissal, Department of Justice attorneys filed a rarely used motion for the entire 12-judge Court of Appeals to hear the matter *en banc*, which it did. On January 8, 1999, the 10th circuit Court of Appeals rendered a decision overturning its three-judge panel, holding that the word, "Whoever," in Title 18 USC § 210, applied only to the public and did not apply to DOJ prosecutors!

Therefore, DOJ prosecutors continue paying compensation to their witnesses, even though the statute clearly prohibited it. Defense attorneys were barred from doing the same, and innocent people could continue to be imprisoned in this manner. (Many of the Court of Appeals judges were former Department of Justice attorneys.)

Forfeiture Laws, Another Feel-Good Self-Serving Tough-On-Crime Legislation That Boomeranged on the Public

Another feel-good legislation passed by members of Congress that destroys previous constitutional safeguards is the forfeiture statute. Members of Congress passed the forfeiture statute in 1976 and broadened it in 1984, making it possible to take anyone's property without charges and without a hearing. The wording appeared innocent enough, as it states the right to seize "all real property which is used, or intended to be used, in any manner or part, to commit, or to facilitate the commission of a violation of the act." However, as usually occurs, the application of that statute is outrageously unconstitutional, and as usual, no reaction from the victimized public.

As applied, the seizure laws inflict serious financial losses upon people who are innocent of any crime, who are often never charged, or the seizure of assets whose values are often totally out-of-proportion to the real or imaginary offense. The seizure of assets has been expanded to include those who have never been charged with any offense and who don't get the property back. Rather clever, don't you think!

Property that had been loaned, or rented to someone else, may be seized for an offense that the owner could not foresee or have any control over. An example of this occurred to an elderly couple in their eighties, whose home in Hamden, Connecticut was seized and sold because a grandson staying in the house had marijuana and cocaine in his possession.

For some people, the loss of the asset may be that person's primary asset. The property may have been accidentally seized, or seized without justification. The value of the property seized could be totally out of proportion to the offense. An aircraft worth many millions of dollars can be seized and forfeited if a few marijuana seeds are found—or planted by government agents or informants.

A couple of drinks before or with a meal may have raised your blood alcohol level to the legal level of as low as .08. In some jurisdictions, this relatively low blood-alcohol level results in seizure of your car. For some people barely surviving financially, this seizure can be catastrophic.

Many asset seizures can occur from even minor technical violations, and the list of offenses is growing as government personnel continue to take away rights that had existed for the first 200 years of this country's existence. A passive public makes this possible.

Representative Henry Hyde wrote a book about the constitutional outrages arising under the forfeiture statute in which he wrote:

Federal and state officials now have the power to seize your business, bank account, records and personal property, all without indictment, hearing or trial. Everything you have can be taken away at the whim of one or two federal or state officials operating in secret. The more they seize, the more they get for their own official use."

License to Steal Approved by Supreme Court Justices

"License to Steal" was the heading on an article in San Francisco's legal newspaper, *Daily Journal* (March 18, 1996). The subtitle said, "In Supreme Court Ruling, Rights of the Innocent Are Forfeited." The article made reference to the Supreme Court's March 1996 decision upholding the right of government agencies seizing property from innocent people. The article stated in part:

> The U.S. Supreme Court has given its stamp of approval to states that steal property from innocent people. Such forfeiture doesn't violate the constitutional protections of due process, the high court said... Chief Justice William Rehnquist...writes opinions as if he were writing algebraic formulas—they make no reference to the lives they affect...The high court just issued Michigan and other states a license for theft...Justice Ruth Bader Ginsburg wrote a concurring opinion that in effect apologizes for the decision—yet supports it.

A *Wall Street Journal* article (December 29, 1997), titled, "The Dangerous Expansion of Forfeiture Laws," stated:

> Asset forfeiture laws have been spreading like a computer virus through the nation's statute books.... more than 100 federal laws authorize federal agents to confiscate private property allegedly involved in violations of statutes on wildlife, gambling, narcotics, immigration, money laundering, etc. The vast expansion of government's forfeiture power epitomizes the demise of property rights in modern America.
>
> Federal agents can confiscate private property with no court order and no proof of legal violations. Law-enforcement officials love forfeiture laws because a hefty percentage of the takings often go directly to their coffers.
>
> A federal appeals court complained in 1992: "We continue to be enormously troubled by the government's increasing and virtually unchecked use of the civil forfeiture statutes and the disregard for due process that is buried in those statutes."
>
> A September 1992 Justice Department newsletter noted: "Like children in a candy shop, the law enforcement community chose all manner and method of seizing and forfeiting property, gorging ourselves in an effort which soon came to resemble one designed to raise revenues."
>
> **[Innocence is Irrelevant in Forfeiture of Property]**
>
> In many forfeiture cases, innocence is irrelevant. The Supreme Court further tilted the legal playing field against ordinary people last year in a decision in a case involving the innocent co-owner of confiscated property. John Bennis stopped on his way home from work to dally with a prostitute in his Plymouth; Detroit police descended on the scene and seized the car, whose co-owner was Mr. Bennis's wife, Tina. The court ruled 5-4 that the seizure did not violate the wife's constitutional rights even though she clearly was not complicit in her husband's illicit behavior.

Chief Justice William Rehnquist wrote:

"The government may not be required to compensate an owner for property which it has already lawfully acquired under the exercise of government authority." By asserting that the government had already "lawfully acquired" the Bennises' car simply because it had a law authorizing seizure of the car, Justice Rehnquist basically granted government unlimited power to steal: If it wants to "lawfully acquire" private property without compensation, all it needs to do is write more confiscatory laws.

The article, written by James Bovard, author of *Lost Rights: The Destruction of American Liberty*, described how Justice Department employees strip a defendant of the funds needed to defend himself or herself. Referring to a bill pushed by Representative Henry Hyde, chairman of the House Judiciary Committee, said:

The new bill greatly expands the power of the prosecutor to seize people's assets before trial (thereby potentially crippling a person's ability to hire defense counsel), makes it much more difficult for citizens to get summary judgments against wrongful seizures, and greatly increases the number of crimes for which government can seize a person's or a corporation's assets.... "Virtually any business that has any substantive inventory and is extensively regulated by the government is in danger of having its goods seized—even for non-criminal regulatory infractions."

Your Property is Seized, Now What?

After seizure, government employees don't have to tell you how to get it back. And major steps must be taken to even *try* to get it back. The time limit for taking these steps is usually very short, sometimes only ten days after seizure, before the average person even recognizes what happened. Then, the person must find an attorney to take the case, have the money to pay the attorney, and post a bond. Many people cannot meet these requirements, or find the legal costs too expensive to bother.

Who Benefits by Seizing Your Property?

In many cases, property seized by a government agency remains the property of that agency. Government agents sometimes occupy homes that are seized. Cars or airplanes that are seized are often used by the seizing agency. Or the proceeds from the sale of the assets go to the seizing agency. Where government informants are involved, they get a percentage of the asset value. The more assets that a person has, the greater the incentive for government agents and government informants to file sham charges and seize the assets. Even though innocent, failure or inability to promptly take the necessary legal steps means the assets are lost. The following cases are examples of people who suffered the consequences of the tough-on-crime legislation that can happen to almost any man or women in the United States, including you.

Make A Casual Drug-Related Remark—Go to Prison!

Someone in your group says, maybe in jest, "Let's get some cocaine and sell it; we'll make a lot of money." Nothing else may ever be said or done. But by being present when that statement was made, criminal charges can be filed against you or anyone else who was present. The person being charged may not have done a thing after that statement was made. The charge is conspiracy to engage in drug trafficking. Your length of imprisonment depends upon how boastful the drug statement was.

The person making that casual statement may be a government informant and looking for a target—it could be you. The next step, a paramilitary group breaks down the door to your home several days later, with guns drawn, hollering obscenities, slams you and your wife to the floor, holds a large-caliber gun to your heads that could at any moment accidentally—or purposely—discharge. After you are arrested, your assets are seized. If you have a business, that is shut down. If you have a job, you lose it. If your wife is also charged, your children may end up in foster homes. Surprise; this is part of Congress' tough-on-crime laws.

> These attacks clearly violate Fourth Amendment protection which states: "The rights of the people to be secure in their persons, houses, papers, and effects, against unreasonable searches and seizures, shall not be violated." But this protection is openly violated every day of the week as paramilitary forces break down the doors of homes and threaten and even kill innocent people.

Exercise Your Legal and Constitutional Defenses And Be Charged with Obstruction of Justice

Your assets are seized, so you have to rely upon a government-provided attorney—who doesn't want to offend the government people who hired him—and he raises a lackluster defense; or is incompetent. A naive jury believes the prosecutor and believes the "government" would not make these charges against you if they were not true. It finds you guilty. In addition, since you were uncooperative by insisting on a trial, the judge adds years to your sentence for alleged "obstruction of justice" or perjury.

The jurors usually have no idea what their guilty decision means for the defendant in length of imprisonment. Maybe you are lucky, and it may only be ten or twenty years. Your children are placed in foster homes. Think it can't happen to you? Think again; many others felt the same way. You become another victim who ignored warnings about government corruption.

Offer Merchandise for Sale—Go to Prison

How many people would suspect that offering merchandise—a car or real estate—for instance, could result in a long prison term? Tens of thousands of government agents and informants are looking for victims to carry out this next trick. Let's look at a few examples. Understanding how this is done can save you from a prison sentence

In 1989, German citizen Helmut Groebe, wanted for crimes in four countries, was hired by Department of Justice personnel as an informant. At that time, he had defrauded his new wife, defrauded several other women, and even defrauded his daughter and her husband by stripping their company of its assets. Just the type of person compatible with DOJ culture!

Because of his criminal convictions in other countries, Groebe was not eligible for citizenship in the United States. DOJ personnel offered him citizenship in the United States and then set him loose to prey upon individual Americans. DOJ personnel eventually paid him over $600,000 for perjured testimony that was used against the victims.

Wolfgang von Schlieffen —one of the victims of this DOJ-inspired conspiracy—told me in 1996, while he was in prison, what happened. Groebe, looking for his next victim or prey, contacted Von Schlieffen, who owned a car dealership in Miami. Groebe, knowing that Wolfgang had a Rolls Royce car and a condominium for sale, falsely told Wolfgang that he had two friends interested in buying his automobile. This was a Justice Department-approved lie.

During a meeting to close the deal, Wolfgang concentrated on describing the car. The pseudo buyers periodically interjected that they were drug dealers. Not being familiar with this, Wolfgang didn't know he was being set up for prison.

A tape of the conversation showed Wolfgang telling them he had no interest in drugs and what they were doing was wrong, that this meeting concerned a car deal. Caught off-guard and not familiar with this common Justice Department entrapment scam, Wolfgang didn't know he was in a trap. The government agents put $10,000 on the table as a down payment, and when Wolfgang picked it up, government agents pulled out their guns and arrested him.

DOJ prosecutors charged Wolfgang with conspiracy to launder drug money through the sale of the car and the condominium. He was guilty of nothing except being the prey in another Justice Department scam, far worse than a financial scam that merely strips a victim of money.

During the subsequent trial, the unsophisticated jurors believed the charges by the prosecutor and the perjured testimony of the professional con artist, finding Wolfgang guilty. The years of work acquiring a business were all lost. Groebe, who had a history of swindling innocent people, was paid a tidy sum by the Department of Justice for carrying out this DOJ scheme.

"How could something like this occur in America?"

From prison, after losing his business, his assets, his freedom, and his good name, Wolfgang wrote, "How could something like this occur in America?" He didn't know the America that *once* existed is now in an advanced stage of corruption, with the DOJ culture spreading like a cancer through government and society.

After Wolfgang was released, he filed a lawsuit against the Justice Department on the basis of the false charges. Justice Department prosecutors turned around and filed other criminal charges against Wolfgang, and he ended up back in prison. What a system!

Groebe and DOJ Preying on a Lonely Widow

During the trial against Wolfgang, DOJ prosecutors withheld from the defense several important facts about Groebe's background. In one case, Groebe defrauded a woman, Elena Abuawad, who he had promised to marry. After defrauding her, he set her up for prison as part of a DOJ scheme by promising to repay her in cash. She was trying to sell a condominium, and Groebe said he had someone who would buy it, and the purchase price would be paid in cash.

DEA Special Agent Lucas, along with several other DEA agents, all part of the scheme against this lady—unsophisticated in the undercover tricks of the Department of Justice—then arrived to pay her cash. Lucas casually told her the money came from drug deals; the legal implications of that statement were far beyond her understanding—as it would be to 99 percent of the public. That statement didn't mean anything to her. She knew nothing about drugs, and was simply trying to sell a piece of real estate.

Within minutes, DEA agents arrested her, handcuffed her, and put her in a jail cell. DOJ prosecutors then charged this twice-defrauded woman with a drug-related conspiracy, using the con artist that defrauded her earlier to carry out the scam! She had no criminal record and probably never would have thought of doing anything illegal. The only participants were government agents and the professional con artist hired and paid by the government agents who set up and carried out the scheme.

Would you, your wife, or your parents, have been sophisticated enough, and quick-witted enough, to have known what to do if such a statement was casually made out of the blue?

Again, a dim-witted jury held her guilty while approving the conduct of the Justice Department-con artist conspiracy.

"I was in love," the Victimized Widow Later Said

The woman later said: "I was in love. I wanted to get married, and I wanted to have a home again. If he asked me to do something, I was going to do it because I didn't want to lose him." The woman's attorney later filed an appeal, stating in it:

> It is difficult to imagine misconduct more egregious, more immoral, more unfair or more improper than that of the government using and paying an informant to falsely profess his love to a woman with no prior criminal record, to violate her person by making love to her, under the pretense that he has romantic feelings for her to become involved in a criminal offense by playing on and with her emotions and taking advantage of her psychological vulnerability.

America's Gun Owners Beware—
Prison May Be Your Next Stop

Millions of gun owners who purchased guns that were legal at the time of purchase can end up in prison and be financially destroyed, solely at the whim of a bureaucrat from the Bureau of Alcohol, Tobacco and Firearms (ATF) or Justice Department. I first heard from W.J. Chip Stewart in 1997, whose home was Springdale, Arkansas, after he had been charged with a federal offense by the ATF for having in his possession two semi-automatic handguns.

The guns were legal to own when he purchased them, a small 22 caliber and a 45 caliber semi-automatic pistol made by the Holmes Firearms Company, similar to those owned by millions of other people. ATF bureaucrats decided, after many of these guns were sold, that the widely sold semi-automatic guns could be converted by a gunsmith to become an automatic weapon and were therefore illegal.

Government agents had gotten Stewart's name from the gun manufacturers' registration records. ATF agents notified Stewart that the (legally purchased) guns were now unlawful. Stewart voluntarily turned the guns over to them. Eight months later, Justice Department prosecutors obtained a grand jury indictment against him.

Stewart, who owned an auto wrecking business and was a permanent member of the community, could have been served peacefully with the warrant for his arrest. Instead, sixteen heavily armed ATF and FBI agents and local sheriff's department personnel converged upon his home, breaking down the door. Fortunately for Stewart, he wasn't home. Otherwise, he could have met the deadly fate of Scott, the Weavers, the Branch Davidians, or the many others who were killed by the "brave" men of ATF and FBI.

ATF and Justice Department attorneys assisted by the typical naive jurors, unsophisticated to the corrupt culture in the Department of Justice, caused Stewart to be sentenced to federal prison for twenty-seven months. As a result of his imprisonment, Stewart lost his business, his wife (who didn't wish to be inconvenienced by his imprisonment), his credit worthiness, and his money.

Imprisoning a Doctor on Perjured Testimony

In 1997 I started receiving information from a physician who had been targeted in a similar gun-charge. Dr. Jed Cserna was an MD with a private practice in Ely, Nevada, and a Lt. Colonel in the Idaho National Guard, with 16 years of military service behind him. His problems started in Ely, Nevada, where he was a physician. Cserna told me that while he was treating a patient, Doris Gratzer, she told him, "If I'm ever shot, Steve [her husband] did it." Dr. Cserna told this to the hospital staff and they said that she always had problems, and this occasion was no different than others. A week later, she was found dead, killed by a bullet wound to the head.

Cserna said her husband, Steve Gratzer, was influential in the town, especially with the sheriff, who was responsible for conducting an investigation into his wife's killing. Cserna was now a danger to Gratzer. According to Cserna, false statements were made by a government informant seeking to justify his informant's pay and for government payments that resulted in a raid by ATF agent Doreen on his doctor's office. His home was broken into and possessions disappeared. Participating in the ATF raid was the sheriff who he referred to as Burnie (Ronero), who would soon participate in sham charges filed against the doctor.

Government agents arrested Cserna a short time later and charged him with possession of a machine gun and a short-barreled rifle. The guns in question were an AR-15 that was not an automatic, and a Uzi 9 mm that had been sold to him with a folding stock and various barrels. He had used both guns two and three times a week at the local police firing range and was never questioned about their legality.

Inflammatory Statement by DOJ Prosecutor

Witnesses testified that the guns were legal and in common use by gun hobbyists. By misrepresenting the facts, the prosecutor convinced a jury that the doctor did in fact commit a federal offense and that it was their duty to find him guilty. Inflaming the jury in his closing argument, the prosecutor said, just before the jurors recessed, "Either this gun nut will take his machine gun and kill you and your kids or he'll sell it to someone who will."

The jury came back in 21 minutes with a guilty verdict. With that verdict, Dr. Cserna, an MD who spent nearly ten years to get his license and who had devoted long hours to his medical practice in a small town, lost his right to practice medicine in the United States.

DOJ Retaliation Because of Refusing Ruby Ridge Participation?

Cserna told me about an event that happened in Idaho while he was the physician assigned to the Idaho National Guard air wing holding the rank of Lt. Colonel. During the Ruby Ridge attack that killed Mrs. Weaver and her son, ATF agents had gone to the Idaho National Guard base and told the Commander of the helicopter division, "We are ordering you to activate your choppers to go north and strafe Ruby Ridge." The Colonel refused, stating, "This is against the law, the constitution. And finally, Randy Weaver is an Idaho citizen. Either you get out or I'll have you thrown out."

According to Cserna, the ATF wanted to take out their frustration on *any* high-ranking Idaho Guard member. Everyone of rank who lived in Idaho was fairly well secure in the state. But Cserna lived in Nevada and didn't have the long-standing connections the other officers had. Cserna thought this could have played a role in why the ATF then went after him. The charges against Cserna were similar to what I learned over the years from other gun owners who were also falsely charged under similar circumstances. Cserna's evidence relating to Doris Gratzer's murder was blocked by filing false charges against him.

"I was guilty of believing in the United States"

Upon release from prison in 1998, Cserna left the United States and settled in Switzerland. In one of his letters he wrote, "I was guilty, not of the charges, but instead, of believing in the United States."

Decades earlier I first learned the frustration of the corroding of quality of life in California by the legal and judicial fraternity, and how I thought about what a group, in control, can do to corrupt an area. The same legal and judicial fraternities are now corrupting life on a national scale. Over the years a number of my sources have left the United States because of this same pattern of corruption.

Tsunami Expert Set Up as Patsy: Goes to Prison

George Pararas-Carayannis was known for his expertise on major tidal waves known as tsunami that are triggered by earthquakes. He was director of the Tsunami Information Center in Hawaii. He also had a small jewelry store as a side business to his government job. He would shortly be one of the thousands of victims of Department of Justice fraud who was put in prison without having committed any offense, another victim to a DOJ-con artist conspiracy.

Federal agents had earlier arrested a Canadian, Lauri McEwen, in Honolulu on drug charges, and offered to drop charges if she could get evidence against others. McEwen carried out the fraudulent sting operation by becoming friendly with Pararas, falsely representing herself as an interior decorator and head of an escort service.

The young and attractive McEwen, wearing stunning clothes, feigned a love interest in Pararas. After getting into his confidence, she asked Pararas to run credit card charges from her "escort" business through his credit card machine at the jewelry store. He made no money out of it and was simply doing a favor for someone he thought was his girl friend. He promptly turned the money over to her after it was credited to his account.

Federal prosecutors then accused Pararas of money laundering resulting from processing money from a prostitution ring through his merchant credit card account. When Carayannis next saw his lady friend, she no longer had the low-cut dresses and loving smile.

Federal prosecutors offered to reduce the charges if he pled guilty to one of them. He refused. He wasn't guilty of anything. Fighting the power of the government with its unlimited funds and ability to intimidate jurors, Carayannis lost everything after a jury decided he was guilty and the judge sentenced him to three years in prison. As a result of the false charges, he was fired from his government job in 1995. He later said, "I had faith in this system. I thought with this kind of evidence and due process, I would be acquitted." Having already suffered several heart attacks, prison was difficult for him.

Apply for Loan: Be Charged with Drug Money Laundering

Beryle Johnston, from Papillion, Nebraska, was offered a deal by undercover government agents to refinance his farm. They instructed him to meet the lenders in Florida to complete the transaction. During the discussion, government informant Jerry Woody told Johnston that the people putting up the money for the loan were members of the Cali Cartel. That did it. Johnson, like most people, didn't know the significance of that DOJ statement, that it was a standard trick used by Department of Justice attorneys to incarcerate another victim. What came next? You guessed it; DOJ prosecutors charged him with drug money laundering.

During the trial, FBI agents perjured themselves, falsely stating that Woody owned a bank and had handled billions of dollars. The truth was, Woody didn't have any bank. He didn't have any money. He was living off his girlfriend's credit cards. The government agents knew this. Based upon the DOJ perjury, a jury convicted Johnston. Woody later admitted his testimony was perjured. But it was too late to save Johnston or the farm the government seized. The legal and judicial system has made government agents immune from suit to where neither they—nor the government—could be sued for their criminal misconduct.

Hire A Lobbyist—Go to Prison

Lobbyists and bribery go hand in hand when dealing with members of Congress. But it is a different scenario for non-government small fry, even when they are innocent. For example, William Moore's company developed an optical scanning device that he tried to sell to the U.S. Postal Service. He publicly criticized the postal service for sticking to an inferior product. A government undercover agent advised Moore to seek a lobbyist to promote his device with the postal service. He hired lobbyist John R. Gnau, Jr., who, unknown to him, had been passing bribes with William Spartin to a member of the Postal Service's board of governors, Peter E. Voss. All three of them were being investigated by the DOJ. All of this was unknown to Moore.

Tearing Up Immunity Agreement for Refusing to Lie

DOJ employees had made a written agreement with Spartin that if he cooperated in the prosecution of Gnau and Moore he would not be prosecuted. Spartin was willing to testify about Gnau's bribing, but said that Moore knew nothing about it. For refusing to commit the requested crime of perjury, the DOJ prosecutor tore up the immunity agreement and said he would prosecute Spartin.

Spartin's attorney then asked the prosecutor for another chance, after which Spartin "refreshed" his memory and stated that Moore did know about the bribes, which everyone knew was a lie. The prosecutor then marched Spartin into the grand jury room and asked Spartin if he had told postal inspectors that Moore knew about the bribes. Spartin replied in the affirmative. The corrupt prosecutor never told the jurors that Spartin had said over a dozen times in earlier questioning that Moore did *not* know.

DOJ Requesting Others to Commit Perjury

That was not the end of the prosecutor's misuse of prosecutorial power. He prepared a statement for one of Moore's employees, Frank Bray, to sign, stating that Moore knew about the bribes. When the employee refused to sign, the DOJ prosecutor threatened to charge him with perjury.

Moore, one of America's naive public, said: "I did not believe this could happen to somebody like me in America. I'm a patriot, businessman. I got to the pinnacle of my success and these guys used criminal statutes to bring me down when I hadn't done anything." Moore lost his company and was put into a state of poverty.

True to form, the DOJ Office of Professional Responsibility held that the prosecutor's conduct was acceptable. Robert Bennett, one of Moore's attorneys (who later represented President Bill Clinton) called the DOJ conduct "an outrageous and shameful exercise of prosecutorial power, frighteningly abused."

Moore's Attorney Sued the Government

Moore was fortunate in finding a law firm that was willing to sue the government on a contingency fee basis. The Cleveland firm of Jones, Day, Reavis and Pogue agreed to file suit on a contingency basis, filing the case in a Texas court seeking $30 million in damages. The lawsuit charged that the DOJ prosecutor, Valder, brought the suit because Moore had criticized the government.

The lawsuit charged the DOJ prosecutor and postal inspectors with multiple offenses: pressured witnesses to give perjured testimony; withheld evidence showing Moore's innocence; provided false, misleading, or incomplete evidence to the grand jury, and concealed or destroyed exculpatory evidence. The lawsuit charged that the federal prosecutor told postal inspectors he didn't care if Moore was guilty or not, and wanted to obtain a high-profile indictment to further his own career.

In response, the DOJ argued that the government was absolutely immune for its conduct, no matter how illegal or corrupt. This argument was upheld by the judge protecting the system.

I think back to how I offended powerful people in government. First, as an FAA inspector I tried to expose a pattern of criminal misconduct at United Airlines and within the FAA related to a series of fatal airline crashes. Later, as I sought to expose other criminality documented in my other books, raw government power was criminally misused against me to silence me and to retaliate against me for exposing the crud.

Preying on Financially Strapped DeLorean

DOJ personnel use these corrupt schemes to prey on those vulnerable due to severe financial problems. They did this with financially ailing carmaker, John DeLorean. DeLorean had no interest in drugs, but government agents set up a scheme and then induced or pressured him to cooperate. At one point, when DeLorean did not want to go along with the government's scheme, one of the Justice Department's agents seeking to induce him to continue, said, "John, I want you to understand something. If you don't cooperate, your daughter's head will be brought to you in a paper bag!" (Attorneys in the Department of Justice were never known to have any recognizable finesse.)

Fortunately for DeLorean during the 1986 trial, the jury recognized the scheme and acquitted him on the basis that he would not have considered committing a drug offense if government agents had not induced him into it. The jury felt that government agents went after a desperate man to commit an act that he would not otherwise have committed. Bravo for a rare intelligent jury!

Introduce Two People to Each Other—Go to Prison

For arranging a meeting between a drug supplier and a drug dealer, Clarence Aaron was arrested and sentenced to three consecutive life-in-prison sentences. Aaron had no drugs. He had no money. He simply arranged a meeting. For giving testimony against Aaron, DOJ prosecutors dropped charges against the people actually dealing in drugs. If DOJ prosecutors had filed charges against the actual drug traffickers and none testified for the government, they might have been acquitted. But by having the *real* drug traffickers testify against an innocent person, at least the Justice Department employee could get a guilty verdict that improves his status and pay.

Watch Your Friends

A drug sting instigated by a friend who faced federal prosecution for another drug offense caused an 18-year-old boy, Joey Settembrino —who had never committed an offense—to be sentenced to ten years in prison without parole. His friend had been arrested earlier, and the DOJ prosecutor offered reduction in charges if he would implicate others. Settembrino became the target. The friend asked Settembrino to get him LSD, which was done, and a DEA agent was waiting to arrest him. The joint conspiracy using the DEA agent worked: Settembrino went to prison, the DEA agent got his reward, and the friend who was into drugs had charges dropped.

DOJ Paying Witnesses to Engage in a Conspiracy to Lie

DOJ agents paid former lobbyist Ron Cobb, who had been arrested on drug charges in 1989, $4000 a month and a $150,000 bonus if he could assist in targeting state legislators in South Carolina. Cobb then lied in an effort to bring about the conviction of several targeted legislators. Cobb lied to a federal grand jury with full knowledge of Justice Department prosecutors. U.S. District judge Falcon Hawkins dismissed the charges in 1997, stating:

The breadth and scope of the government's misconduct and the involvement of the FBI during this entire incident was and is shocking. Most offensive to this court is that the government sat silent when it knew that its silence would not only fail the efforts of the defendants to fully develop defenses to which they were entitled, but would misrepresent facts to both the grand jury and the trial court, and mislead the court to such an extent as to affect its rulings. This silence is subornation of perjury.

Violate a Technical Business Requirement—Go to Prison

Anything placed in the mail invokes the mail fraud statute if any of the thousands of government technical requirements are violated. Eugene Kent learned about this the hard way. Mail fraud charges were filed against him for co-mingling money in a self-insurance fund his insurance company had set up for a number of South Dakota banks. No money was lost or misplaced; it was *technical violation.* Kent hadn't done anything vicious or with the intent to defraud. Company funds were casually placed in the same account as the reserve funds. The jurors acquitted Kent of all charges except the mail fraud, and this opened the door for a prison sentence.

He might not have been indicted except for the fact that during grand jury testimony a government agent gave perjured testimony. The lying government agent did not suffer any consequences. When Kent later discovered this fact and filed a motion for a new trial, the judge refused to grant it, stating that the information withheld from him by the DOJ should have been raised during the trial. Kent went to prison, and this was followed by the usual financial and personal tragedies, including family breakup.

Employee Charged for Crimes Committed by Boss

Another way that your world can come tumbling down is to be an employee in a business where, unknown to you, there is drug activity. The boss is arrested and given a chance to implicate others, thereby giving the prosecutor a witness to back up the charges. Suddenly, *you* are charged with being a drug kingpin based upon the perjured testimony of the *real* drug kingpin!

Here is another example. Norberto Guerra and Ramon Jimenez worked on a boat that brought drugs into the United States. They suspected something like that was going on but had no role in it. DOJ prosecutors first charged their bosses—who were bringing in the drugs—with drug-related offenses. When the evidence against the real drug traffickers was difficult to track down, DOJ prosecutors made the real drug traffickers a deal. Justice Department prosecutors used the known perjured testimony of the actual drug traffickers—Raul Sanchez who brought tons of cocaine into the United States and also confessed to two murders, and convicted murderer, Leonardo Alvarez—against the two employees. They were charged with being the kingpins responsible for bringing almost four tons of cocaine into the United States.

DOJ Fraudulently Withholding Exculpatory Evidence

Despite repeated requests by defense attorneys to turn over information about their witnesses, the requests were improperly refused. DOJ attorneys fraudulently stated they had no information. Sanchez failed a lie-detector test, which was withheld from defense attorneys. It was later learned that DOJ agents and prosecutors had destroyed hundreds of pages relating to interviews and data on their key witness, Sanchez. During trial, Sanchez falsely stated that he had not received any promise of leniency in return for his testimony. That was perjury, and the DOJ personnel hearing it aided and abetted it by remaining silent.

Don't Anger Department of Justice Employees

Lawyer Patrick Duffy said, as he defended archaeologist Peter Larson in South Dakota, "Don't anger the Department of Justice." Larson had obtained authorization from a property owner to search for what he found, the skeleton of a fossil. He had paid the ranch owner for the find and then *donated* it to the Black Hills Institute of Geological Research. DOJ prosecutors then stepped in, claiming the person who gave Duffy permission to search for fossils had placed his property in trust with the federal government and the government agents now claimed the fossil belonged to the government.

That fossil would never have been found except for the diggings by Duffy. Duffy appealed this claim to federal courts, without success. For having fought the matter in court—which Duffy warned could result in DOJ retaliation—DOJ prosecutors charged Larson with a federal offense that ended up with a two-year prison sentence. For a fossil!

Escort Service Owner Refuses to Conspire With DEA—Goes to Prison for Ten Years

Robin Marie Head ran an "escort service" in Austin and Houston, Texas, the type found in large cities throughout the United States, which most police departments ignore. She was approached by ATF, DEA and FBI agents seeking to have her become an informant and give them the names of her clients. They wanted to blackmail political figures and judges, influence elections and court cases, and engage in extortion. The agents were particularly interested in obtaining information on critics of President Bill Clinton. Further, they wanted to become co-owners with her in her business.

Head told them the only way she could reveal the names would be through a court order. Angered at this defiance, federal agents started harassing her, making threatening phone calls, and finally after a year of this, federal agents charged her with operating an organized criminal activity (i.e., running an "escort service").

Head said that they went after her son, and made life miserable for him. After she was sent to prison, her phone lines were taken over by government agents who lured her former customers to another escort service controlled by government agents.

Several of my deep-cover sources have told me over the years that many escort services (and adult movie or porn shops) are fronts for the CIA and other government agencies. They particularly described their contacts with escort services in the San Francisco area and adult movie operations in San Diego.

Head described how undercover agencies "lure young naive females into doing overseas drug smuggling in order to bust them, thereby holding these young ladies under submission."

She said one of the ATF agents, Mike Taylor, who was involved in the attack upon the Waco Davidian group, threatened her. She said her court-appointed attorney sabotaged her defense, warning her that he would file habitual criminal charges against her if she did not plead guilty. She said that her attorney repeatedly said, "I will see that you get the life sentence that you deserve." She explained:

This is a very tight organization of old time good-old-boys. It is very elite and includes all the heavies and power people. They want more power; i.e. election fraud, more judicial control, etc. This clique is greedy and vile to the core. They will kill, or pay to have someone killed.

This elite gang also includes attorney Richard Racehorse Haynes and the like. They are the backbone of Texas, true power, and they want more. In describing the arrogance of the ATF agents, she described an incident in which they shot the owner of a topless club because he demanded they pay the $5 cover charge, and then put the owner in jail, which was followed by getting the IRS after him.

Government-Entrapped Victim Received Greater Sentence Than Murderer Who Killed His Wife on Their Honeymoon

Out of a job, a government informant named Scott had been busted on drug charges. DOJ prosecutors offered him a reduction in sentence if he could find someone else to charge. Scott then pressured a friend, Staufer, to find LSD for him, something that Staufer had not done before. Staufer had no money to finance such a transaction, but government agents took care of that.

At first, Staufer could not get enough LSD to satisfy the prosecutor who was seeking to send him to prison for a much longer term. The informant kept pressuring Staufer until he was able to find a supplier who would sell him the larger amount on consignment. Staufer was then arrested by the government agents who developed, funded, and coordinated the entire conspiracy.

A Los Angeles judge sentenced Michael Staufer to the mandatory 12-year prison sentence. The judge lamented that the Court of Appeals had just overturned a life sentence that he gave to a man who killed his wife by throwing her overboard on a honeymoon ship cruise. He was now required, by law passed by Congress, to give the 21-year old Staufer a longer sentence than the murderer received.

Casual Statement to FBI Agent on Beach—Go to Prison

U.S. Attorney Joseph Russoniello of San Francisco charged U.S. District Judge Robert P. Aguilar (June 1989) with misusing his judicial position in a racketeering enterprise (RICO) and obstructing justice. What were the charges based upon?

- He allegedly made false statements to an FBI agent while Aguilar was sitting on the beach in his swimsuit at Waikiki during a Hawaiian vacation.
- He gave legal advice to an attorney friend to use in defending Aguilar's brother-in-law.
- He told his brother-in-law not to call him because the brother-in-law's phone might be tapped.

The *real* reason for prosecuting Aguilar for these relatively minor matters was that Aguilar often disagreed with the Justice Department prosecutors in judicial proceedings. Aguilar halted the deportation of refugees that Justice Department attorneys wanted deported. He also once engaged in a heated argument with U.S. Attorney Russoniello in open court, threatening Russoniello with contempt of court.

Accountant Makes an Error on *Your* Tax Form: *You* Go to Prison

Another judge targeted by Justice Department prosecutors (1986) was U.S. District Judge Harry Claiborne in Las Vegas. Prosecutors charged Claiborne with bribery and other offenses related to failure to properly show expenses on his income tax statement. Claiborne's accountant had failed to list the profit made on one of several real estate transactions on Claiborne's income tax report. Claiborne had rendered decisions unfavorable to the Justice Department in the past. This retaliatory prosecution removed Claiborne from a position where he could oppose DOJ prosecutors. It also sent a warning to other judges who might not be cooperative with DOJ prosecutors.

Justice Department prosecutors used Nevada brothel owner Joseph Conforte, who had been sentenced to prison, to testify against Claiborne. In return, DOJ prosecutors promised Conforte that charges would be dropped against him. Conforte had been sentenced for income tax evasion, compounded with bail-jumping charges for fleeing to Brazil where he was presently located. By giving false testimony, Conforte would have his prison sentence dropped, would retain his otherwise forfeitable assets, and be granted immunity for perjury.

DOJ Threat Against Members of Congress

The mere investigation by the FBI, DEA or any other division of the Department of Justice can cause a member of the U.S. Senate or House to lose an election. Justice Department employees can easily fabricate charges, especially conspiracy charges, which can be almost fabricated out of thin air, and a career and life are destroyed.

Possibly the fear of what Justice Department employees can do was one of the reasons every member of Congress to whom I brought evidence of government corruption during the past 30 years refused to respond. But this was no excuse for aiding and abetting the criminal activities. They had a duty under federal criminal statutes and by their position to perform their congressional oversight duties or responsibilities. When they accepted their position, they assumed the responsibilities that went with the pay, the perks, and the prestige. If they were too cowardly to perform, they should have resigned. Dream on!

Dangerous for Defense Lawyers to Vigorously Defend Clients Against the Justice Department

In the San Francisco area, Justice Department prosecutor Anthony White, displeased with lawyer Clarence Hallinan's vigorous defense of his clients against Justice Department charges, used one of Hallinan's clients, Ciro Wayne

Mancuso, to make false charges against the attorney. Mancuso had been convicted earlier of income tax fraud and fled to South America.

Justice Department prosecutors offered Mancuso a deal: release from the prison sentence, dropping of forfeiture actions against $600,000 in a Swiss bank account, and Mancuso could keep over $4 million in property that would otherwise have been seized. In exchange, Mancuso would have to testify as DOJ prosecutors wanted him to testify, against Hallinan. An additional plus for Mancuso: DOJ would immunize him against the perjured testimony. He couldn't lose.

Jurors with Greater "Street Smarts" Than Most

Fortunately, the jury in Reno had more street smarts than most jurors, especially middleclass jurors who shield themselves from unpleasant realities. They didn't believe the DOJ prosecutor, and they didn't believe the DOJ's paid witness. The jury found Hallinan not guilty (*United States v. Hallinan*, CRN-39-HDM Nevada). In 1996, Mancuso's lawyers appealed his sentence claiming that DOJ's prosecutor White had promised that he would not get any prison time if he testified against Hallinan.

Apply for Loan, Embellish Details—Go to Prison

Here is a trick by which Justice Department employees can prey on almost any adult and put almost *anyone* in prison. You submit a loan application and somewhere in the many details you exaggerate your income, your length of employment, your assets, or some other information. People are prosecuted and sentenced to prison on this minor matter all the time.

It doesn't matter that you have made your payments on time, that no one suffers any loss that the lender is happy, or even that the loan has already been paid off. Any ambitious prosecutor, government agent, or informant, can go over old loan records and find where you or your wife, or anyone who co-signs with you, even your aged parents, exaggerated some part of your application, and charge all of you with offenses that can send each of you to prison.

Let's add a little more reality to the above scenario. You've already committed this "crime," maybe 20 years ago. During the night, a paramilitary force breaks down the door to your home, the thugs terrorize your family, ransack your home, and destroy furniture. If you happen to suspect they are criminals and appear with a gun, you may be shot dead. You are hauled off in chains, and your neighbors think you are guilty of some major crime; they think, *surely* the government wouldn't do something like this if you weren't guilty of a heinous offense! This is not far-fetched.

Tens of thousands of people who falsified their incomes to obtain subprime loans were prime candidates for prison, enabling prosecutors to greatly improve their job advancement.

Threatening an Aged Parent or Wife to Obtain Confession

This culture preys on everyone. If you refuse to plead guilty, they have another trick to play on you. Your wife, mother, or some other member of your family is threatened with criminal charges if you don't plead guilty. It doesn't matter that you are innocent; that's the last thought that would enter the minds of the Department of Justice gang. The "government" that you previously thought would *never* do such things has been doing them for years. Wake up; it happens all the time. And it happens because the uninformed and apathetic Americans let it happen.

Refuse to Lie for DOJ Prosecutors—Go to Prison!

A federal judge sentenced a young lady to federal prison (1989) for failure to remember details of stock transactions that happened several years earlier while she was a stockbroker for Drexel Burnham Lambert (which incidentally had CIA connections). Lisa Jones, a 24-year-old dropout and runaway who became financially successful at the Wall Street investment firm of Drexel, was one of the first witnesses called by Justice Department attorneys investigating insider trading and other security violations at Drexel. Her sense of honesty and integrity prevented her from fabricating the testimony requested by Justice Department attorneys. And for refusing to lie, she paid a heavy price.

In retaliation for refusing to lie, Justice Department attorneys charged *her* with perjury and obstruction of justice, resulting in an eighteen-month prison sentence. She was paraded in chains from prison to prison, a standard humiliation inflicted by government personnel misusing the raw power of government. Prison transportation for a woman is especially hard, traveling in chains and the subject of leers and snide remarks by male inmates.

After all this, Drexel's attorneys sued the young lady for payment of legal fees that Drexel had agreed to pay. In response to Drexel's claim that they would sue Ms. Jones for the amount of money that they had advanced, San Francisco attorney Daniel Bookin stated:

It is inconceivable to me that Drexel would sue Lisa after all that she's gone through, and in view of her serious psychological problems. All issues of compassion and decency aside, however, one simple fact seems certain: Lisa has virtually no assets; she could not even begin to repay the cost of her legal representation."

Sacramento Real Estate Developer Refused to Lie: Goes To Prison

Another example in the same judicial district: Justice Department prosecutors charged a Sacramento area real estate developer, Marcel Cordi, with a federal crime for refusing to falsely testify against a bank officer whom Justice Department prosecutors wanted to convict. Sacramento U.S. Attorney David Levi wanted Marcel to testify against a bank official and alter the facts in his testimony. Marcel was willing to testify, but would not lie to enable Justice Department prosecutors to falsely convict the person. In retaliation for refusing to commit perjury, U.S. Attorney Levi charged Marcel with fraud based upon an incorrect statement on a prior loan application relating to his length of employment.

Contempt of Court for Reporting Government Corruption

Levi charged me with criminal contempt of court in 1987, retaliating against me for filing an action in the U.S. District Court at Sacramento seeking to report to a federal judge serious criminal activities that I and several of my CIA assets had discovered. This report to a federal judge (or other federal officer) is mandatory under the clearly worded requirements of federal criminal statute, Title 18 USC Section 4.[4]

Levi and Judge Milton Schwartz refused to receive the evidence of criminal activities that I and the other former government agents sought to report. Some of the criminal activities were involved in a series of fatal airline crashes, and would at a later date have ripple effects in the hijacking of four airliners on September 11, 2001. This relationship is described in two of my books: *History of Aviation Disasters: 1950 to 9/11*; and *Blowback, 9/11, and Cover-Ups.* (Available at amazon.com.)

In retaliation for seeking to make such reports, they charged me and prosecuted me for criminal contempt of court for seeking to present such evidence, based upon an earlier order that barred me from federal court for the remainder of my life: an obviously unlawful and unconstitutional order. In the process, they also violated the constitutional right to a jury trial.

The combination of corrupt U.S. Attorney and federal judges constituted a Kangaroo Court. They held me guilty and at the age of 67, I was sent to federal prison for six months (for attempting to report criminal activities that were periodically resulting in fatal airline crashes, information that I first discovered during my official duties as a key federal air safety inspector-investigator.

Levi's conduct may have played a role in his appointment in 1992 to a federal judgeship, where he is now a U.S. District Judge in Sacramento. It is standard practice to appoint Justice Department officials who "cooperate" to the federal bench, increasing the probability of Justice Department prosecutors prevailing in court.

Aircraft Broker Sells Airplane, Refused to Lie—Goes to Prison

A Memphis aircraft broker sold an aircraft to a customer who later used it to fly drugs. The aircraft broker had no way of knowing the background of the buyer or how the plane was to be used—nor was he required to become an investigator. Later, when federal authorities arrested drug traffickers and were building a case against the suspects, they requested the aircraft broker to fabricate testimony to assist in obtaining convictions.

The broker was willing to testify, but had enough integrity that he wasn't going to lie. Justice Department attorneys retaliated, charging him with mispri-

---

[4] Title 18 U.S.C. § 4. Misprision of felony. Whoever, having knowledge of the actual commission of a felony cognizable by a court of the United States, conceals and does not as soon as possible make known the same to some judge or other person in civil or military authority under the United States, shall be fined under this title or imprisoned not more than three years, or both.

sion of a felony (Title 18 USC Section 4) on the basis that he failed to report to federal authorities the aircraft was to be used in unlawful activities. (Strange, I was charged with contempt of court for reporting high-level government corruption that I sought to report under the same statute!)

The aircraft broker was subsequently put on trial with 32 other defendants, some of whom *were* guilty of drug-related offenses. Without competent legal counsel to provide an adequate defense, and unsophisticated, lazy, or naive jurors who accepted the "government's" charges as true, the aircraft broker was held guilty under the conspiracy statute and sentenced to five years in federal prison. He never committed a crime. He, and the others listed here, and the thousands of others not listed here who were innocent, provided figures showing the "success" of the Congressional legislation and the public's "feel-good" response to crime.

Suicide Induced by Federal Tactics

There were other unfortunate consequences to that case. When that broker was in a county jail near Memphis waiting for trial, he witnessed the fatal consequences of these outrages. His cellmate, Mike Scarlett from Texas, had been enticed by federal agents into making the controlled substance "speed." Knowing that Scarlett was having serious financial problems supporting his family, he was excellent prey. Federal agents encouraged him to produce the drug, taught him how to produce it, financed the operation, and set him up with the equipment and a location.

On the first day Scarlett started to make it, federal agents arrested him, charging him with manufacturing amphetamines that they had induced him to make—and which he would not have made without their coaxing, pressure, assistance, and equipment. He would never have committed the offense if government agents and informants hadn't set it up.

While in prison, Scarlett discovered that his wife was sleeping with one of the federal agents who set him up. The aircraft broker told me that Scarlett was very distraught-looking after phoning his wife. He described how the inmate wrote what was later discovered to be a suicide note. Scarlett hung a bed sheet over the prison bars, as if he wanted privacy for sleeping. Behind the sheet, Scarlett stepped onto the rim of the toilet and tied a strip torn from a bed sheet to a grill near the ceiling. Scarlett then stepped off of the toilet and hung himself.

Forcing Wife into Sex to Avoid Federal Charges

A DEA agent in Northern California reportedly forced a wife to have sex with him and then testify against her husband, according to an action filed in the U.S. District Court at San Francisco by attorney J. Tony Serra who specialized in cases involving the underdog. John Dalton was indicted in 1996 for involvement in a marijuana-related conspiracy in the heavy marijuana growing area of Northern California.

Testifying against him was his wife, who reportedly had sex with DEA agent Mark Nelson. The DEA agent reportedly encouraged her to tape record her husband's comments about marijuana while they were in bed together. The DEA agent reportedly threatened the woman with money laundering charges if she did not cooperate.

Killing a Nearly Blind Rancher: "Success" in the Drug War

A screaming paramilitary force burst into the home of a wealthy and nearly blind rancher, Donald Scott, near Malibu, California (October 2, 1992). Federal personnel had tried to buy the ranch to expand the adjacent Santa Monica Mountains National Recreation Area, but Scott, a recluse, partially blinded by recent cataract surgery, didn't want to sell.

The multi-agency drug task force of over two dozen heavily armed California and federal agents[5] mounted a military-type assault upon Scott's home late at night. They used the excuse that an informant said there was a field of marijuana spotted from a plane flying over the 200-acre property in the hills above Malibu called Trail's End.

Instead of going to the ranch in a peaceful manner with a search warrant, they conducted a commando-type raid, breaking into Scott's home while he was sleeping, and killed him as he came out of his bedroom. No marijuana plants or drugs were found on his property. There was no reason for this commando-type raid, as there was no need for the element of surprise. If Scott had actually been growing fields of marijuana, he could not suddenly dump it down the toilet. The peaceful serving of a search warrant was all that was necessary.

Investigation showed that the *real* motive was not a search for drugs, but a desire to seize Scott's ranch under federal forfeiture laws. Scott's wife had been a former drug user and if the slightest speck of drugs could be found on the property, the five million-dollar ranch could be seized under the draconian federal forfeiture laws.

Subsequent investigation revealed that federal agents had obtained a property appraisal before invading Scott's home, showing the value of adjoining property and indicating the desire to seize the property. Federal personnel in charge of the raid advised the attacking agents to look for evidence of drugs so as to justify seizing the property. None of the killers were ever punished.

Multiple Life Sentences for Someone who Never Saw any Drugs

Peter Hidalgo escaped from Cuba to the United States in the late 1960s and become a boat builder and racer. He, his wife, and small daughter lived in a modest cottage and felt they were in paradise compared to what they left. But that would change in late 1992 as they joined the endless list of victims of Congress' feel-good legislation and DOJ fraud.

Hidalgo had not been part of any drug operation. He had no involvement with drugs. He knew nothing about them. Drug traffickers, who had already been arrested, were offered release if they implicated someone else. Through

---

[5] The invaders were from the Los Angeles County sheriff's department, the Los Angeles Police Department, the U.S. Drug Enforcement Administration, National Park Service and California National Guard.

fabricated testimony, they testified that Hidalgo was the drug kingpin. Now, Justice Department prosecutors had people willing to testify, so a conviction was more certain and easier to obtain. The people used by DOJ prosecutors to testify against Hidalgo were major drug traffickers and killers. Hidalgo lived a modest life style raising a family.

The DOJ prosecutor reportedly paid one witness $500,000 to testify, as the prosecutor wanted him to testify. Another witness against Hidalgo bragged to his cellmates that he had received a substantial reduction in his prison sentence in exchange for lying during trial. One witness, not happy with lying, told his sister he feared for his safety for not being willing to lie. He was found dead shortly thereafter, probably murdered to keep the DOJ scheme from being exposed.

False Confidence by State-of-Denial Jurors

Hidalgo felt confident that he would be found innocent. His name never appeared in any of the many taped telephone conversations, suggesting his innocence. But Hidalgo didn't realize that it didn't matter that DOJ prosecutors knew he was innocent; they would prosecute anyone to show another conviction on their record.

In 1999, in Leavenworth federal prison, Hidalgo was reported to have said, "These people have broke me financially; they broke up my family. The only thing they won't be able to break is my dignity and my principle. If they get me a new trial, I'm gonna show what the government has done, that it's out of control." Lots of luck, Hidalgo, you'll need it!

Sending Senior Citizen to Prison:
$4 Million in Taxes Not Enough

Justice Department prosecutors charged Leona Helmsley with evading income taxes and sentenced her to four years in federal prison, leaving behind her 81-year-old husband who, at his age, could be dead before her release date. Helmsley's accountants had claimed on her tax returns business expenses that Justice Department attorneys considered not business related. Helmsley had paid over $4 million federal income taxes in the disputed tax year, and the amount owed by the disputed charges was a very small percentage of that amount. Much of the media—who were simultaneously covering up for much of the corruption in government—jeered this 72-year-old lady.

Seeking Incarceration for Playing Chess

Justice Department prosecutors found time in December 1992 to investigate and indict[6] Bobby Fischer for playing a chess game in Yugoslavia, charging him with violating a presidential order barring business relations with communist countries. At the same time, government agents were engaging in all types of criminal activities: gun smuggling, undermining governments,

[6] Fisher violated a June 1992 executive order by President George Bush restricting commercial relations with Yugoslavia. The indictment subjected Fisher to ten years in prison and a fine of as much as $250,000. Is it any wonder the United States has the highest percentage of its citizens in prison?

smuggling drugs into the United States, and much more. These matters are detailed in my books, *Defrauding America* and *Drugging America*.

Mother Given a Ten-Year Prison Sentence for Not Reporting One Side of Telephone Conversation Relating to Drugs

On December 7, 1990, U.S. District Judge Samuel Conti sentenced a young black girl from Oakland, California—the mother of two infants—to ten years in prison on a drug-related conspiracy charge. The young girl had a telephone conversation with another person concerning the sale of drugs. The conversation never went any further, but federal agents, monitoring the phone call, charged the girl with conspiracy to traffic in drugs.

She was in tears when U.S. Marshals drove her back from the federal courthouse in San Francisco to the Dublin Federal Detention Center after Judge Conti sentenced her to ten years in a high security prison. As described in the latest edition of *Defrauding America*, this same judge played a major role in blocking my exposure of CIA drug trafficking and other criminal activities.

Pushed Into Government Conspiracy—Go to Prison

In one case, government agents pressured Lorenzo Naranjo for months to purchase cocaine that he would never have done. Naranjo finally succumbed to the pressure and obtained a small quantity. Because the DEA agent wanted the target to be charged with a greater offense, he pressured Naranjo to accept a gun in exchange for the cocaine. The law reads that if a gun is available during a drug offense, the penalty is doubled.

The gun was not used in carrying out the offense, and would not have been there except for the action by the conspiring undercover agents. DOJ employees brought about the crime, provided the gun, and arguably, should have been charged with conspiracy, drug offenses, and the gun offense. Naranjo was charged and a jury convicted him. The DEA agent looked good. The prosecutor chalked up one more conviction. But for Naranjo, his wife, and children, the personal and financial tragedies destroyed the family.

Guilty of Nothing—Ten Years in Prison for Mother of Five

A mother of five children in Texas drove her boyfriend's van into Mexico and upon returning to the United States she was arrested at the border. Her boyfriend had *hidden* cocaine in her van without her knowledge. The jury, assuming that Justice Department officials would not prosecute an innocent woman, rendered a decision holding her guilty, causing her to receive a 10-year mandatory minimum sentence. She knew nothing about being used as a "mule."

Force Companies into Bankruptcy— Seize and Loot the Properties

Brief reference is made here to a practice described in *Defrauding America* and *History of Aviation Disasters: 1950 to 9/11*. That is the practice of forcing companies and people with lots of assets into involuntary bankruptcy and then looting everything. The practice of targeting people and companies for the purpose of seizing their assets, by forcing them into bankruptcy, is widely used by

CIA operatives who operate jointly with the corrupt attorneys, law firms, Justice Department trustees, and judges, and is rampant throughout the United States.

Government Agents Report Government Corruption—Go to Prison

All of my books describe government agents who reported high-level government corruption and are then fraudulently charged with criminal offenses. These victims included agents of the FBI, CIA, DEA, INS, Customs, FAA, among others. The felonious retaliation carried out by Department of Justice attorneys against government inspectors and covert agents constitutes obstruction of justice, retaliation against witnesses, and other criminal offenses.

For example, a highly decorated Vietnam War helicopter pilot, Richard Taus, and a ten-year veteran of the FBI, was falsely charged with criminal offenses after he contacted members of Congress about criminal activities that he discovered that involved key government officials and his FBI superiors wanted him to falsely deny existed. His story is told in two of my books: *FBI, CIA, the Mob, and Treachery*. And in *Crimes of the CIA-DOJ, and the Mafia*.

In another of many examples, former agent of U.S. Customs, John Carman, was falsely charged by DOJ prosecutors to silence his exposure of massive drug shipments coming into the United States via railway cars from Mexico, which his superiors blocked from being investigated. Carman has a web site, www.customscorruption.com, which described these corrupt activities.

DOJ Lying to Have Sister Testify Against Brother

DOJ prosecutors charged James Rounsavall and his sister, Mary Ann Rounsavall, with drug-related offenses in 1994. DOJ prosecutor Bruce Gillen tried to get Mary Rounsavall to testify against her brother. When she wouldn't, the prosecutor told her that her brother was dying and that he would be dead within a short time, so she might as well testify against him. Further, she would be recommended for a sentence reduction.

Reluctantly, based upon her brother's imminent death, she testified, using testimony given to her by the prosecutor. Her brother was then sentenced to life in prison, their assets seized, and the sentence reduction that she had been promised never came. She was sentenced to 20 years in prison. She later learned that her brother was *not* dying.

Rancher Fills in Mosquito-Breeding Hole—Goes to Prison

Justice Department prosecutors sent Allen Kafkaesque to prison for filling in a mosquito-breeding low spot on *his* 103-acre ranch. He allowed two loads of dirt to be dumped in the spot as a base for a shed. Federal officials then charged him with filling in "wetlands," which has been made a crime by members of Congress seeking the votes from far-out environmentalists (probably trying to save from extinction some type of cockroach!). DOJ prosecutors sought to have him imprisoned for 27 to 33 months. When the judge reduced the sentence to six months, Justice Department prosecutors appealed, seeking to have Kafkaesque imprisoned for almost three years!

Farmer Files a Crop-Loss Claim—Goes to Prison

A farmer in Illinois, James Catton, filed a crop insurance claim following a very dry year in which his crops suffered heavy damage. The insurance provisions allowed this claim. A DOJ prosecutor charged Catton with fraud, and during the trial, a government employee testified that the claim was fraudulent. After the trial, and after the jury convicted Catton, he learned that the government "expert" had never seen his farm—or the adjacent one which suffered the same damage and for which a similar claim had been paid during the same period. This critical information was withheld from the defense and from the jurors. The fraudulent prosecution caused Catton to lose his farm in bankruptcy.

Another Conspiracy Sham—Dentist Ends Up in Prison

In 1980, Dr. John W. Newton, a dentist, was arrested in front of his patients and charged with drug conspiracy. I received a call from a mother who told me how her dentist son was targeted by a DOJ informant. She explained that he had never been anywhere near drugs. Fortunately for him, the jurors were not rubber stamps for the prosecutor and handed down a not-guilty verdict. However, the dental board revoked his license, solely on the word of a government-paid informant in collusion with a DOJ prosecutor. For the next 15 years Newton worked at odd jobs to support his family while undergoing serious financial problems.

In 1996, he managed to get his dental certification back. It was his mother, Margaret Newton, living in Apex, North Carolina, a feisty lady in her eighties who tried to wake up people to the threat posed by government agents, especially in the Department of Justice. She wrote to me stating, "Americans are too indifferent and too lazy to be concerned." She was active in promoting the information written in *Defrauding America*. At 80 years of age, she had more courage and character than most people in the United States. A few people like her gave me the inspiration to continue the almost hopeless task of waking up even a small percentage of the American people.

Government Targets Wife of CIA Asset Gunther Russbacher

Rayelan Russbacher, while she was the wife of one of my key CIA sources, Gunther Russbacher, described how she was targeted in a drug-sting operation that would probably have succeeded if she hadn't been far more sophisticated and aware of the Department of Justice fraud than most people.

She had been very vocal as a speaker in helping to expose several major government scandals that are described in *Defrauding America*, starting with her exposure of the October Surprise scandal. She explained how the drug scam was carried out. Rayelan was called on the phone and asked to meet certain people at a nearby Denny's restaurant who told her they had information about government misconduct that she would want.

She met two men who, during the conversation offered to help her financially if she would sell something for them. She immediately sensed they were talking drugs. Outraged, she got up and said, "If you want me to sell drugs I'll have nothing to do with it!" She got up from the booth and left the restaurant. If she had stayed, even out of politeness, and allowed the talk to go into drugs, she would probably have been arrested on a drug conspiracy charge. It is *that* easy to prey on innocent people and put someone in prison in these United States!

Jurors with Inadequate Knowledge and Comprehension

Federal grand juries usually consist of 23 people, often people with no understanding of what really goes on in the Justice Department and the criminal justice system. (The same applies to trial juries.) Their low level of understanding legal and criminal matters forces them to rubber-stamp whatever the prosecutor wants.

With one or more shills on the jury, the prosecutor can manipulate the jurors to do whatever the prosecutor wants. It takes only a simple majority to bring about an indictment against the person the U.S. attorney seeks to prosecute. Federal prosecutors have great power and can act irresponsibly knowing that they will not suffer any retaliation for lying and corrupt activities.

Deputy Attorney General Arnold I. Burns, during President Reagan's tenure, said, "The federal grand jury is no longer a protection of the person who is suspected of crime, it is a vicious tool. The grand jury process today is as far afield from what it was intended to be as it could possibly be."

Grand Juries are Prosecutors' Tools

Grand juries are not as grand as the title sounds. They are tools, often composed of legally unsophisticated people, manipulated by the politically-appointed prosecutors to hand down the indictments that the jurors often don't understand but do what the prosecutors wants. A common reference to grand juries is that they will indict a ham sandwich if requested by the prosecutor.

During grand jury hearings, where a person is asked to testify, he cannot have legal counsel in the room, cannot produce evidence showing his innocence, and does not have the right to cross-examine his accusers. The grand jury can take hearsay evidence. It is often used as a political tool, where Justice Department lawyers use known perjured testimony.

Congress and DOJ Making Prisons into Future Burial Places

Many people, given life-in-prison sentences, will die in prison. This includes many people who never committed the crimes fabricated against them by DOJ attorneys. They don't realize they are considered prey by DOJ and similar agencies.

Judges Protecting DOJ Corruption

Former New York State prosecutor Bennett Gershman, who taught law at Pace University in New York, wrote the 1997 book, *Prosecutorial Misconduct*. He wrote that federal judges had done nothing about the prosecutorial misconduct that continues to inflict grave harm on people in all walks of life. "They are now simply a rubber stamp," he said, asserting that federal prosecutors know that no matter how bad their misconduct, it is almost impossible for a criminal defendant to sue a federal officer or prosecutor, and this came about due to judicial decisions that subvert civil rights statutes. He said judges know what is going on and excuse their conduct by saying it was the jury's decision, not the judge's.

Prosecutor's Sham Immunity From Civil, Constitutional, And Criminal Violations Against Americans

The San Francisco and Los Angeles area legal newspaper, *Daily Journal*, carried an article (September 22, 1994) stating in part:

> Prosecutorial misconduct is encouraged–if not indirectly condoned–by pervasive judicial abstention and "buck passing." Although appellate courts sometimes threaten to dismiss a case based on prosecutorial misconduct, they rarely do so, either finding the wrongdoing "harmless" or suggesting alternative remedies such as contempt.
>
> It is well-documented that in reality there often is no effective sanction for prosecutors who engage in unethical conduct....This misconduct included violation of grand jury rules, violation of defendants' Fifth and Sixth Amendment rights, knowing presentation of false information to the grand jury, and mistreatment of witnesses. The report documents the fact that the Justice Department effectively ignored the courts' findings of governmental abuse, and that not one of the individuals involved was sanctioned, thereby raising "serious questions regarding what the Department considers 'prosecutorial misconduct.'"
>
> There is virtually nothing that an aggrieved party [defendant] can do when a court declines to sanction unethical government conduct, because prosecutors are absolutely immune from suit. In *Imbler v. Pactman*, 424 U.S. 409, 431 (1976), the Supreme Court ruled that a Los Angeles deputy district attorney who intentionally suborns perjury cannot be sued by the defendant who is wrongfully convicted...leaves the genuinely wronged defendant without civil redress against a prosecutor whose malicious or dishonest action deprives him of liberty. The Supreme Court, quoting an earlier case, decided that it is "better to leave unredressed wrongs done by dishonest officers than to subject those who try to do their duty to the constant dread of retaliation."
>
> Similar reasoning is used by judges to hold themselves immune from their wrongful and oftentimes criminal acts. They argue that to hold judges liable for unlawful acts would dampen the judicial spirit. Federal statutes have priority over judge-made case law, and give citizens the right to sue *anyone* who violates their rights. And in the English language, that includes judges.
>
> People have been fraudulently sent to prison, even for life, on the basis of perjured testimony given by a person who is protected against the perjury by the prosecutors who often reward the perjurer for making the false statements demanded by the prosecutor.

The reward for perjured testimony may be release from prison, dropping of charges, or placement in the witness protection program with long-term income provided. The witness giving false testimony need not fear being charged for perjury, as the prosecutor responsible for such charges is orchestrating the perjury.

Occasional Judicial Protest Against Prosecutorial Misconduct

Occasionally, a judge will express concern about the abuses with DOJ use of purchased testimony. In one Ninth Circuit Court of Appeals case at San Francisco, the three-judge panel said in their opinion:

> What we find most troubling about this case is not the assistant U.S. Attorney's initial transgression, but that he seemed to be totally unaware he'd done anything at all wrong, and that there was no one in the United States Attorney's office to set him straight. [Could it be that they were all corrupt!] Nor does the government's considered response, filed after we pointed out the problem, inspire our confidence that this kind of thing won't happen again.

How can it be that a serious claim of prosecutorial misconduct remains unresolved—even unaddressed—until oral argument in the Ninth U.S. Court of Appeals? Surely, when such a claim is raised, we can expect that someone in the United States Attorney's office will take an independent, objective look at the issue. Yet, the United States attorney allowed the filing of a brief in our court that did not own up to the problem, a brief that itself skated perilously close to misrepresentation.

Prosecutor's Shocking Immunity from Civil Rights and Criminal Violations

Federal judges—many of them former DOJ prosecutors—have rendered decisions holding that federal prosecutors are immune from the consequences of their acts. This is not what the civil rights statutes say, which have priority over case law, but it is what federal judges have done to protect the system. The San Francisco area legal newspaper, *Daily Journal,* carried an article (September 22, 1994) stating in part:

> Prosecutorial misconduct is encouraged—if not indirectly condoned—by pervasive judicial abstention and "buck passing." Although appellate courts sometimes threaten to dismiss a case based on prosecutorial misconduct, they rarely do so, either finding the wrongdoing "harmless" or suggesting alternative remedies such as contempt.
>
> It is well documented that in reality there often is no effective sanction for prosecutors who engage in unethical conduct.... This misconduct included violation of grand jury rules, violation of defendants' Fifth and Sixth Amendment rights, knowing presentation of false information to the grand jury, and mistreatment of witnesses. The report documents the fact that the Justice Department effectively ignored the courts' findings of gov-

ernmental abuse, and that not one of the individuals involved was sanctioned, thereby raising "serious questions regarding what the Department considers "prosecutorial misconduct."

There is virtually nothing that an aggrieved party [defendant] can do when a court declines to sanction unethical government conduct, because prosecutors are absolutely immune from suit. In *Imbler v. Pactman*, 424 U.S. 409, 431 (1976), the Supreme Court ruled that a Los Angeles deputy district attorney who intentionally suborns perjury cannot be sued by the defendant who is wrongfully convicted ... leaves the genuinely wronged defendant without civil redress against a prosecutor whose malicious or dishonest action deprives him of liberty. The Supreme Court, quoting an earlier case, decided that it is "better to leave unredressed wrongs done by dishonest officers than to subject those who try to do their duty to the constant dread of retaliation."

Similar reasoning is used by judges to hold *themselves* immune from their wrongful and sometimes criminal acts. They argue that to hold judges liable for unlawful acts would dampen the judicial spirit. Federal statutes have priority over judge-made case law, and give citizens the right to sue *anyone* who violates their civil or constitutional rights. And in the English language, that includes judges.

DOJ Prosecutors Grinding Up People

Former U.S. Attorney General Ramsey Clark said that the impact of prosecutors withholding exculpatory evidence is especially bad because it impacts defendants who can't pay for high priced lawyers to uncover withheld evidence. Both Gershman and Clark said that this prosecutorial misconduct has gotten worse over the years, which parallels the worsening government corruption that I have documented for the past 30 years. Clark said, "It is really tragic how we grind up poor people in these situations."

Misnamed Division—DOJ Office of Professional Responsibility

Another misnamed government office, a division of the Department of Justice, is its Office of Professional Responsibility (OPR), has the responsibility of investigating misconduct in the Department of Justice. Instead of meeting that trust, it has functioned to *cover up* such misconduct, aiding and abetting it, and in some cases, it constitutes obstruction of justice. To insiders, that office is a farce.

Extension of Legal Fraternity Culture into Prosecutor Role

Decades of experience working with attorneys, in and out of government, part of it detailed and documented in my other books, makes it easy to understand how the sleaze in the legal fraternity surfaces in the prosecutor's office. With an almost unlimited power to inflict harm upon people, the prosecutor's position provides the power to satisfy the mentality of many attorneys.

Among the Congressmen Openly Approving These Outrages

Almost all members of Congress openly or tacitly approve the outrages described in this and my other books. Congressman Bill McCollum, one of many covering up for CIA drug smuggling during the 1980s, said as he approved of these outrages:

> I am much more concerned about the loss of life to drugs and to the crime that's going on out there and the need to stop it and protect our innocents and our citizens than I am about anybody's concern over [the abuses arising from] informants.
>
> I have no problem with the judicial system in regard to what we're doing. We're trying to lock up people, most of them very bad people who are causing a problem. Ninety-three percent of those who are in our state prisons for drug dealing are there because of violent offenses or they're there for multiple offenses, and almost all of the people who are there in the system for cocaine trafficking are there for large quantities. So I think we're doing the right thing by what we're doing in our federal law enforcement system.
>
> There are very few people in jails today in the United States who didn't deal in large quantities of the drugs. Occasionally you'll run into somebody that's in there on a conspiracy charge because that's the easiest way to get them convicted, but that doesn't mean they haven't committed multiple offenses. They're violent offenders with a long track record—look at their histories. There are very few people in there who did not have substantial drug trafficking histories before they were ever put away, and for those that are there, they're there usually because the prosecutor has tried to get them to cooperate and they've refused to squeal on somebody who is higher up.

Senator Jeff Sessions (R-Ala), former U.S. Attorney, said of the drug laws, and with a straight face: "I think what we tried to do is give the taxpayers the best return on their dollar. The prosecutors do a good job."

In response to the question, "Isn't it a problem that conspiracy law allows innocent people to be convicted on testimony alone?"

That's a theoretical problem; that's not reality. People do not testify against innocent people; they only testify against guilty people. I have not found that to be a problem. Innocent people are not getting convicted under this on any kind of routine basis.

Double Standard between the Public and Those in Power

One of Senator Richard Shelby's constituents, Jerry Lundy, wrote a letter to the senator asking for his help on behalf of Lundy's son who was sentenced to 30 years in prison on drug charges when the son never had any drugs, never was near any drugs, and sentenced solely on the purchased testimony coerced by DOJ prosecutors. That witness later recanted his testimony and made out an affidavit describing how he was coerced and threatened by DOJ prosecutors to provide the perjured testimony. The father was seeking the senator's help. Senator Shelby responded with the standard form letter:

> We must take a strong stand against drugs, and I support strict punishment for individuals involved in the possession or distribution of illegal drugs. I believe that our nation's drug problem is serious enough to warrant harsh sentences.

But when it came to his own son, his position took a complete reversal. The senator's son, Claude Shelby, was arrested upon arriving by plane at Atlanta's Hartfield Airport with 13.8 grams of hashish. Shelby applied the proper pressure in the right places and instead of a long prison sentence the charges were reduced to a simple misdemeanor and ordered to pay a $500 administrative fine. Without the senator's involvement, his son would probably be a prison inmate with a long prison sentence.

Series of *Pittsburgh Post-Gazette* Investigative Articles

The *Pittsburgh Post-Gazette* ran a ten-part series of articles written by investigative journalist Bill Moushey in November and December 1998 titled, "Win At All Costs—Government Misconduct in the Name of Expedient Justice." The titles on these articles tell much about what was found during the two-year investigation. The paper wrote a synopsis of what was discovered during the past year and printed in the articles:

> About this series: Hundreds of times during the past 10 years, federal agents and prosecutors have pursued justice by breaking the law. They lied, hid evidence, distorted facts, engaged in cover-ups, paid for perjury and set up innocent people in a relentless effort to win indictments, guilty pleas and convictions, a two-year Post-Gazette investigation found.
>
> Rarely were these federal officials punished for their misconduct. New laws and court rulings encourage federal law enforcement officers to press the boundaries of their power while providing few safeguards against abuse. Victims of this misconduct sometimes lost their jobs, assets and even families. Some remain in prison because prosecutors withheld favorable evidence or allowed fabricated testimony. Some criminals walk free as a reward for conspiring with the government in its effort to deny others their rights.

Air Force Veteran Discovered America's Domestic Enemies

In the first article, Moushey describes the plight of Air Force veteran, Loren Pogue, who was sentenced to 22 years in prison on a drug conspiracy and money laundering charge. Pogue had never used drugs. He was never near them. He did not buy or sell them. It was another setup preying on people unaware of the scheming tactics by Justice Department attorneys.

Pogue had sold land to a government informant who later testified that Pogue knew he was a drug smuggler, which was a lie. DOJ prosecutors then used the drug smuggler's testimony to charge Pogue under the catchall feel-good drug conspiracy and drug money laundering statutes. A jury found him guilty. But he was guilty of nothing!

The government agents involved in the conspiracy—and a conspiracy is a federal crime—escaped punishment and received bonuses for their corrupt activities. Pogue, sentenced to prison at the age of 65, will probably die in prison, never again to see any of his 15 adopted children. Pogue is baffled that the government for whom he served in the military for 30 years would betray him like that.

It is long overdue for millions of American vets to wake up to the threat from within that is inflicting *more harm* on people in the United States than any foreign country has ever done. It is time for them to start doing something helpful for the country rather than parading around in military gatherings or having reunions!

Apply for Government Contract—Go to Prison

In one of the cases described in the *Pittsburgh Post Gazette* series, FBI agent John Clifford, using the alias of Hal Francis, approached Dale Brown, a small manufacturer offering products for sale to the government in the space industry. The FBI agent told Brown that he had developed a product that NASA might want to buy which he described as an ultrasound device.

The FBI's scheme was to trap small business people seeking to sell products to the government space program. The FBI agent told Brown and several other manufacturers that the product was proven reliable and provided pictures and documents to support that statement. Everything looked professional and on the up-and-up.

When Brown and several others entered into an agreement with the undercover FBI agent to promote the device, FBI agents filed charges against them for trying to sell a known phony device to the government. After indictments were handed down by the grand jury against the 15 defendants, FBI agents pressured all but two to plead guilty, warning them that if they tried to fight the charge they would end up with long prison terms, large fines, property seizures, and family humiliation.

FBI Agent Francis testified that Brown (and the other defendant who fought the charge) knew that the device he was trying to sell to the government was phony and this amounted to fraud against NASA for trying to win contracts for a bogus product. The undercover agent paid Brown $500 for expenses to promote the product and then fraudulently claimed this was bribe money that Brown accepted.

Serious Physical Consequences of False DOJ Charges

In fighting the charges, Brown suffered a massive heart attack requiring complex surgery, and was on life-support system the day he was indicted by DOJ agents. Brown said, "I lost my fiancée, my health, my cars, my house, was forced into bankruptcy and underwent two open-heart surgeries, intestinal surgery and brain surgery because of a massive stroke due to the stress." Quite a change from a former skydiver and athletic person. Brown explained, "The government agents intentionally and methodically drove our companies and personal bank accounts to zero and drove our reputation to ruin."

Brown filed a lawsuit against the government, which a federal judge promptly dismissed, claiming federal "law enforcement" officers are immune from civil lawsuits, despite the gravity or illegality of the actions perpetrated by the federal employees.

DOJ Prosecutors Providing Perjured Testimony to Mob Figure

The *Pittsburgh Post-Dispatch* described the case of crime figure John Pree who admitted, FBI agents approached him and asked him to lie to help win indictments against more than a dozen reputed Detroit-area gangsters. Pree described how government agents provided him information concerning several crimes and the murder of a Detroit gangster so that he could plead guilty to being part of them, bring about the conviction of others, and then he would quietly be released from prison shortly thereafter.

Pree said government agents promised him a new identity, monthly compensations, and cash. He admitted he had never met some of the people with whom he was to have committed the crimes and against whom he would be testifying. Pree failed several polygraph tests given to him by DOJ employees before the trial, but they used him anyhow. During the trial, he failed to identify one of the defendants with whom he allegedly committed some of the crimes.

DOJ Generating Crimes Where None Would Otherwise Exist

The *1998 Pittsburgh Post Gazette* articles described how government agents set up crime scenes that generate "crimes" when they otherwise would not exist. Government agents—under control of DOJ personnel—brought sham charges against innocent people and exaggerated charges against others. The series said, "Time after time, former criminals, con artists, dope smugglers, perjurers, and killers were employed to help catch suspects in exchange for reduced sentences or even six figure payoffs. With straight faces, prosecutors insist in court that none of these witnesses have an incentive to lie."

Human Tragedies from Lying Government Informants

Paramilitary forces break into homes based upon false information given by government informants who must justify their compensation. This happened to Don Carlson in 1992 as a military-like force invaded his San Diego-area home after an informant, being paid $2000 a month, made up a story about drugs. When the agents stormed Carlson's home in the middle of the night, he shot through the door, thinking they were criminals. The government agents shot back, shooting him in the back.

The *Pittsburgh Post-Gazette* article described government agents joining the criminal activities of their informants:

That arrangement [between confidential informants] can prove slippery.

This investigation found dozens of cases where agents became so close to their informers that they crossed the line—sometimes assisting them in their criminal activities or protecting them, or even joining them and sharing in the profits of their crimes.

Released Murderers-Drug Traffickers Returning to Old Habits

The one-year investigation by the *Pittsburgh Post Gazette* revealed criminals released from prison under the Witness Protection Program have gone on to commit hundreds of crimes, many of them violent, and over 20 murders. The study showed that most criminals released from prison under this program revert to their old habits. And this includes murder.

PBS Series Documented the Personal Tragedies

In the latter part of 1998, PBS ran a television documentary entitled "Snitch," describing the conspiracy between government agents and government informants. The human tragedies followed along the line exposed in the *Pittsburgh Post-Gazette* series.

District Attorneys Lie and Conceal Evidence to Win Cases

A January 11, 1999, article in the *Chicago Tribune* was titled, "Study: DA's Lie, Conceal Evidence to Win Cases" and stated:

> Of 381 verdicts overturned, 67 defendants had faced execution. With impunity, prosecutors across the country have violated their oaths and the law, committing the worst kinds of deception in the most serious of cases. They have prosecuted black men, hiding evidence the real killers were white. They have prosecuted a wife, hiding evidence her husband committed suicide. They have prosecuted parents, hiding evidence their daughter was killed by wild dogs. They do it to win. They do it because they won't get punished. They have done it to defendants who came within hours of being executed, only to be exonerated.
>
> In the first study of its kind, a *Chicago Tribune* analysis of thousands of court records, appellate rulings and lawyer disciplinary records from across the United States has found repeated instances of prosecutors hiding evidence showing the defendant was innocent, allowing them to receive long prison sentences or even death sentences.

National Law Journal Investigation

An investigation continuing for almost a year, and reported in the *National Law Journal* (NLJ), stated:

> Abuses by informants and law enforcement threaten the rights and the safety of innocent people, as well as the integrity of the courts. The war on drugs is the engine driving this development. New forfeiture laws have made drug busts a law enforcement prize, generating lots of cash both to pay informants and to increase their own operating budget. Mandatory sentencing laws and crushing prison terms adopted in the 1980s have created powerful incentives for criminals to go to any lengths to avoid jail.

The NLJ study showed the federal government paid over $100 million a year to informants, making this a cottage industry exceeding the outrages inflicted by Adolf Hitler's SS Guards. It was rare that Hitler's informants were motivated by profit and lying, as exists in America today.

Judicial Warning About DOJ Witnesses

U.S. District Judge Stephen S. Trott on the Ninth Circuit Court of Appeals in San Francisco, said during a lecture to federal prosecutors:

> Criminals are likely to say and do almost anything to get what they want, especially when what they want is to get out of trouble with the law. This willingness to do anything includes not only truthfully spilling the beans on friends and relatives, but also lying, committing perjury, manufacturing evidence, soliciting others to corroborate their lies with more lies and double-crossing anyone with whom they come into contact.
>
> Career criminals acting as informants are remarkably manipulative and skillfully devious, playing on the investigators' inexperience, laziness or unchecked ambition to generate cases that will get them off the hook.

U.S. District Judge Marvin Shoob in Atlanta said, "Informants are sometimes worse criminals than the defendants on trial." Former veteran DEA agent Celerino Castillo said about the informants he had known:

> Informers are running today's drug investigations; not the agents. They are paid two or three times as much as the agents, and agents have become so dependent on informers that the agents are at their mercy....All of the federal law agencies, and DEA in particular, have been hiring agents out of college with no previous investigative experience. These are people who have never been street-trained on how to deal with informants. That's where the problem is coming from.
>
> The federal agents have allowed the informants to take over investigations, and the agents don't make a move without getting approval from their informants. Our rights as citizens and the United States Constitution are now in the hands of a group of about 15,000 wild out-of-control informants. If you get in their way, they will take you down, and the agents are ignorant enough or lazy enough to let them do it.

***Frontline* Interviews**

The television program, *Frontline,* questioned U.S. Attorney J. Don Foster in the Southern District of Alabama, concerning the use of paid informants. Without batting an eye, the Justice Department prosecutor said he would continue to use purchased testimony as long as it was truthful. But prosecutors usually coach witnesses on what to say, making it clear that if they don't make those statements under oath, they will not receive any compensation.

When asked, "How do you know that they are testifying truthfully," the prosecutor replied with a straight face: "We try to evaluate based on experience and based on careful examination, based on corroboration." When asked, "Does the jury know that they are benefiting from their testimony," the prosecutor answered, with tongue in cheek no doubt: "It's hard to make up a story that fools twelve people."

As to the practice of allowing witnesses to share the same prison cell prior to testifying, so as to compare notes and synchronize their stories, the prosecutor responded: "If the judge tells them not to talk and they talk, they're in violation of the judge's order, and the judge does tell them not to talk with each other, does tell them not to tell each other what they have testified to." Either Foster had been living on another planet since birth, or he is a gifted liar. My belief is the latter.

Prisoners Seeking Release on Perjured Testimony are Honest?

When the questioner asked in disbelief, "You count on this admonition," Foster replied: "I think that's a very important admonition. I think federal judges make an impact on witnesses. And witnesses try to do the right thing. And they try to obey the judge's orders, I believe."

A particular case was mentioned, in which a person received a life sentence based solely on the uncorroborated testimony of a paid witness. The witness stated that he delivered nine kilograms of cocaine, with no evidence other than that. Based on this type of "evidence," anyone in the United States can be imprisoned for life, on perjured and purchased testimony. It happens all the time!

Informant Admits what Everyone Knows—They Lie for DOJ

Appearing on a *Frontline* documentary was an informant using the alias, Tony, with his faced blacked out. He admitted lying to get out of prison. He admitted the Department of Justice prosecutor told him the testimony he would have to give against the defendant. He stated that when he initially refused to give the false testimony, the Justice Department arrested his mother and brother.

After this was done, he then gave the perjured testimony that the prosecutor wanted him to give. Tony admitted the people he testified against were absolutely innocent. But he said, given the alternative of 30 years to life in prison, he was forced to do this, another crime that would not have been perpetrated if Department of Justice attorneys had not brought it about.

Which of Two Defendants will Lie to Avoid Life in Prison?

Another informant, Ronald Rankins, appeared on the show, describing how DOJ prosecutor Donna Barrows pressured him to give false testimony. He and his co-defendant, Algernon Lundy, were drug users, not dealers. During the part of the taping that was aired, Rankins said prosecutor Donna Barrows told him:

> One of you is going to receive a life sentence, Mr. Rankins. Now, it don't matter to me which one of you receives a life sentence. I can assure you the federal government have a 98.6 conviction rate, and if I tell you you're going to receive a life sentence, you can call your family and tell them to break you plate because you won't be coming home again.

Rankins asked, "Let me ask you a question. If you were faced with a life sentence right now, and they tell you, 'Well, Miss Oprah, if you don't testify on this guy, your next-door neighbor, that you saw him selling drugs, we're going to make you part of this conspiracy, and give you a life sentence,' what are you going to do? You're going to take that life sentence?"

Rankins gave false testimony against Lundy to avoid life in prison. Later, he wrote letters, claiming his testimony was coerced, to Attorney General Janet Reno, President Clinton, Oprah Winfrey, *60-Minutes*, *Hard Copy*, *New York Times, Mobile Press*, and many others. None responded.

Recanting Doesn't Help the Victim

Where informants have admitted, years later that they lied to bring about the imprisonment of someone still in prison, and who will remain there until he dies, judges and lawyers say, "Are you lying now, or did you lie then? Are you trying to help somebody get out of jail or help somebody with their appeals?" Recanting seldom helps the victim of earlier perjured testimony.

Over $1 Million for Testimony

A *New York Times* article on March 8, 1995, stated the FBI paid $1,056,000 to Emad Salem for his testimony against Sheik Omar Abdel who was charged with others in planning to bomb the Holland and Lincoln tunnels under the Hudson River between New York and New Jersey and the United Nations building. (In other pages it is shown how Justice Department cover-up led to the bombing of the World Trade Center building and events that happened on September 11, 2001.)

Routine DOJ Practice of
Releasing into Society Dangerous Killers

DOJ personnel frequently release dangerous killers into society, regardless of the threat they pose to people who may be their next victim. A *Sacramento Bee* article dated April 17, 1999, reported an El Dorado County grand jury near Sacramento indicted a former member of the federal witness protection program who had been living in Cameron Park under the name of Robert Rameses. The article said: "Rozier, an admitted seven-time murderer, was living under the name of Robert Rameses, the identity given him under the federal witness program."

19 Murders: DOJ Arranges Freedom and Money

In the John Gotti case, Salvatore "Sammy the Bull" Gravano, who admitted to involvement in 19 murders, was given his freedom for providing testimony against Gotti, and allowed to keep over $8 million in illegally gained assets. This tradeoff was a distorted use of the federal Witness Protection Program.

People in Phoenix, Arizona discovered they had a serial killer in their neighborhood. A June 26, 2001 article in the *New York Times* described how Gravano left the witness protection program in 1998 and established a Southwest chapter of La Cosa Nostra in Arizona that purchased Ecstasy pills from a

Brooklyn supplier with ties to the Israeli mob. This large-scale operation based in Phoenix involved his entire family, including Gravano's wife and daughter. Gravano was charged with federal crimes in New York and state crimes in Arizona. His wife and daughter were charged with Arizona offenses.

Gravano pled guilty in Phoenix, Arizona, on June 20. 2001, to state drug and racketeering charges for his role as the mastermind of Arizona's largest ecstasy drug ring, which included drug dealing, money laundering, participating in a criminal syndicate and weapons violations, and sentenced to 20 years without parole. A month earlier, he pled guilty in federal court at New York City for similar offenses. He would be serving his state sentence concurrent with his federal sentence. Gravano's wife and two children were involved and made plea agreements in Maricopa County Superior Court.

Releasing Mass Murderer for Assistance In Incarcerating Covert Government Agent

In the book, *Drugging America*, I describe the Justice Department's actions that brought about the release from prison of Jimmy Ellard, a partner with infamous Colombian drug lord Pablo Escobar. Ellard played a key figure in the placement of a bomb on a Colombian airliner that killed 110 people, and had admitted bringing tons of cocaine into the United States.

His release was based on testifying against Rodney Matthews, an undercover contract agent for U.S. Customs who had learned too much about the government's involvement in drug trafficking and the diversion of drug money to a political party. Ellard became a darling to DOJ prosecutors and was paid for giving perjured testimony that blocked the exposure of high-level government corruption. This relationship reflects the low priority given by Justice Department personnel to those whose crimes result in catastrophic aviation disasters.

Public Obsessed with Released "Child Abuse" Offenders and Indifferent to Murderers in Their Midst

The public is obsessed with people released into their neighborhood who were once convicted of "child abuse," which could be simply touching someone in the wrong place. The same people who are terrified of that person are oblivious to the murderers released into their midst under the Witness Protection Program.

Blackmail Members of Congress to Block Corrective Actions

It is well known that FBI Director J. Edgar Hoover was skilled at obtaining incriminating and embarrassing information on political figures, and had a file on almost every member of Congress. In *From the Secret Files Of J. Edgar Hoover*, author Athan Theoharis describes Hoover's interest and ability in gathering scandalous information about prominent political figures. The CIA and other government agencies have similar activities to exert control over key politicians, media personnel, and publishers.

Good People, Remaining Silent, Allow These Conditions to Occur

You say this can't happen in the United States? Good people, remaining ignorant or too cowardly to speak out, allow these tragedies to happen. Wake up; things have changed in America. It *is* happening, and it *is* getting worse. And it is getting worse because good people are not getting informed and not exercising a little courage. Good people, failing to speak out, made Adolf Hitler's rise to power possible, and the horror that followed. Some form of that tragedy will happen to America.

Consequences of Corruption, Fraud, and Public Indifference

Another of the thousands who were either set up, or who played a minor peripheral role in drugs, was David Correa. He was the fall guy in the usual Justice Department trade of using testimony from major drug pushers for the easy prosecution of a peripheral one-time player.

Correa's parents fled Cuba when Fidel Castro came to power. He obtained a Bachelor of Science degree from the New Jersey Institute of Technology and was an engineer for the National Aeronautics and Space Administration (NASA). He was a pilot for Eastern Airlines until the day of his arrest. (Eastern Airlines top management who knew their airline was being used for drug trafficking never were prosecuted by federal prosecutors. See details in *Defrauding America* and *Drugging America*.)

Correa told me he was set up by the Rickabough family from Altoona, Pennsylvania, who were reportedly involved in gambling, prostitution, drug trafficking, and stolen motorcycles. Correa said the group gave testimony against him in exchange for charges being dropped against them. They had a long criminal record and Correa had none. They went free and Correa received a life-in-prison sentence with no chance of parole.

Former Airline Pilot Wanting to Die

Correa wrote in an April 25, 1999, letter that he wanted to die—now! He said:

> It looks like I will die in prison. I and many like me, including people who are older than me who are also first time, non-violent drug violators with draconian sentences, would rather that the government kill us and get it over with, rather than endure all the mental cruelty of watching our families suffer. Allow us to die.
>
> We are not suicidal, but people like me are very tired of this way of being and if we are condemned to die in prison for no just reasons, then we choose to die now. We want to be able to choose our own method of expiration because we do not want to have to suffer any further! It's been ten years in prison and I am just tired of this way of being with no hope of ever going home.

Donate to Charity and End Up in Prison

Consider the following example of two men sentenced to prison at San Francisco in July 2001. They had donated boats to a charity under the IRS 501(c)(3) tax deduction program. The U.S. attorney in San Francisco charged Gregory Jampolsky, a Sausalito yacht broker, and Stanley Wild, a marine surveyor, with engaging in a conspiracy to defraud the United States.

They had donated boats to the Vallejo Foundation, a tax-deductible organization that provided maritime education to children. Justice Department prosecutors, looking for people to prosecute, charged that they claimed a value for tax-deductible purposes that were higher than the boats were subsequently sold for by the Vallejo Foundation.

The fact that this is a standard practice, deducting the fair market value for an item donated, which may be higher than the charitable organization eventually sells the item for, didn't phase these Justice Department personnel who routinely cover up for crimes on a national scale perpetrated by government personnel and in covert government operations. The prosecutor claimed that the purpose of the scheme was to obtain large tax deductions for the owners of the boat.

Virtually Unrecognized Catastrophic Ripple Effects

Corrupt and cover-up culture by people in the FBI-DOJ made possible the conditions that enabled terrorists to carry out their scheme to bomb the World Trade Center in 1993 (as described in *Defrauding America*). The same culture enabled terrorists to carry out the scheme to hijack four airliners on 9/11. The blowback or ripple effects from the FBI-DOJ culture killed nearly 3,000 people and set in motion events that mushroomed into even worse consequences.

Strange, and so obvious to those knowing the facts, how seemingly localized areas of corruption and cover-ups can have such far-reaching and deadly consequences. It is the same with the corruption I discovered, documented, and reported to the public for the past 40 years.

Weaver Family Against ATF And Justice

At an isolated mountain-top home in Idaho 400 heavily armed ATF and FBI agents, U.S. marshals, local law enforcement agencies (supported by military vehicles and tanks), surrounded a small house occupied by Randy Weaver, a former Green Beret, his wife, and their four children. Weaver was on the Justice Department's hit list for refusing to cooperate in an undercover operation against a group of local skinheads. Weaver had been asked to infiltrate the group, but after attending a few meetings, he didn't want anything to do with the plan.

ATF and FBI personnel instituted a plan to retaliate against Weaver. An undercover agent of the Bureau of Alcohol, Tobacco and Firearms pressured Weaver to sell him sawed-off shotguns, which Weaver at first refused to do. After ATF persistence, Weaver finally did what he was requested to do, selling two of them that were allegedly 1/4 inch short of the minimum legal length.

Justice Department prosecutors charged Weaver with violating federal firearms law, and ordered him to appear in federal court. When Weaver failed to appear (due to an error in the reporting date made by the court clerk), six heavily armed U.S. marshals in camouflaged clothing sneaked onto Weaver's mountaintop property. Weaver's dog spotted the intruders and started barking, after which a family friend, Kevin Harris, and 14-year-old Samuel Weaver went to investigate.

As the dog approached the intruders, they shot and killed the animal. The young boy cried out, "You've killed my dog." At that point Randy Weaver came out of the house and hollered for his son to come back. Sammy hollered, "I'm coming, Dad." As the boy ran toward the house one of the marshals fired seven shots at him, hitting him in the back. The boy lay there, suffering, and eventually died.

Harris, who had gone with the young boy to investigate, witnessed the killings and shot back, killing the marshal that murdered Sammy. The remaining U.S. marshals then retreated, returning with a force of over 500 heavily armed, battle-ready, FBI and other federal personnel, bravely massed to do battle against the father, the mother, three children, and a friend.[7] Included in this armada against the family under siege were tanks and other weapons of war.

The FBI took charge and ordered the small army to shoot anyone seen outside the house. During this siege the father went to a storage building adjacent to the house to view the body of his slain son. A sharpshooter from this small army then shot him in the back. His wife, Vickie Weaver, was standing in the opened doorway holding her infant daughter, when a federal agent shot her with a large caliber rifle, splitting her head apart. Blood spurted from her wound as Weaver pulled his wife inside and laid her down on the kitchen floor. Frightened, Weaver and his children lay on the blood-splattered floor, expecting to die at any moment. For eight days they waited in fear, as the U.S. taxpayer-financed army threatened to kill them all.

Although only a small percentage of Americans cared, outraged neighbors and people from all over the country converged on the site, protesting the slaughter. Several members from a concerned citizens group in Hawaii arrived, as did people from throughout the state. Their presence may have saved the remaining hostages from being murdered as happened to young Weaver and his mother.

According to a *Wall Street Journal* article,[8] an internal FBI report shortly after the siege commenced, justified killing Mrs. Weaver and her son, asserting that they had put themselves in harm's way. The article stated:

> Court records show that while the woman's body lay in the cabin for eight days, the FBI used microphones to taunt the family. "Good morning,

[7] *Spotlight*, September 25, 1992.
[8] *Wall Street Journal*, January 10, 1995.

Mrs. Weaver. We had pancakes for breakfast. What did you have?" asked the agents in at least one exchange.

No shots were ever fired from the cabin.

Justice Department prosecutors obtained an indictment against the remaining Weaver family from a rubber-stamp federal grand jury in Boise (September 16, 1992), charging the victims with federal crimes. The indictment against the Weaver family (including the children) read in part:

> Vicki Weaver and other members of the family did unlawfully, willfully, deliberately...shoot, kill and murder one William F. Degan.

That indictment, as worded, included the infant whose mother had been killed.

Promoting Killers

The jury in the subsequent trial held Weaver innocent of the charges filed by Justice Department officials, but held him guilty of a relatively minor offense; failure to appear in court for a hearing. Despite the trauma of having witnessed the killing of his wife and son, Weaver served a prison term for failing to show up for a court appearance.

Justice Department officials launched an investigation, issuing a 542-page report in 1995 recommending criminal prosecution of federal officials. Assistant attorney general for civil rights, Deval Patrick, refused to take this action, claiming that the murders of Sammy and Vicki Weaver were justified.

On January 6, 1995, Freeh issued oral and written reprimands (big deal) to several of the people responsible for the killings, and then promoted several of them, including Larry Potts, who was appointed to the second highest position in the FBI. Eugene F. Glenn became head of the Salt Lake City FBI office. E. Michael Kahoe became head of the FBI's Jacksonville, Florida office.

Freeh said that the shot that killed Mrs. Weaver, while she was holding her baby, was a "tragic accident." Freeh absolved the sniper of blame in that murder. This FBI mindset was blasted by attorney Gerry Spence who labeled Freeh's actions as:

> A total whitewash. The censure means nothing. The promotion means everything. The clear message is: "It's all right to kill innocent women; we'll stand behind you; we'll even promote you."

Despite this example of the vicious mindset of Justice Department officials, very few Americans saw the threat to themselves and others, to constitutional rights, and the dangerous mindset in government. As usual, Congress did nothing about this misuse of a federal agency over which they had supervisory responsibilities.

The U.S. Marshall Service, on March 1, 1996, gave to those who murdered members of the Weaver family its highest award for, would you believe, valor. The award mentioned "their exceptional courage, their sound judgment in the face of attack, and their high degree of professional competence during the incident." The award called the men "heroes."

Eventually, after a lawsuit was filed, the U.S. Department of Justice paid the surviving Weaver family members $3.1 million to settle the case. A press release by the Justice Department stated:

> The settlement reflects the loss to the Weaver children of their mother and brother. By entering into a settlement, the United States hopes to take a substantial step toward healing the wounds the incident inflicted.

Enlargement on the Murderous Weaver Attacks

The Weaver tragedy received very little press coverage, even though it indicated a very dangerous mindset by ATF and Justice Department officials. By ignoring it, as in every other form of corruption implicating federal officials, the pattern continued and worsened. On Sunday morning, February 28, 1993, about one hundred heavily armed Alcohol, Tobacco and Firearms agents (ATF) invaded the residence of a religious group in Waco, Texas, attacking the building with loud shouts as if they were attacking a drug cartel. There were about a hundred people inside the residence, primarily women and children.

The religious group resided in a large building on property known as Mount Carmel, owned by a religious group known as Branch Davidians. They were a relatively peaceful group, harming no one, wanting to be left alone. As is common in Texas, to earn extra money, the group frequented gun sales and had accumulated a large cache of various types of weapons. They also knew about the Weaver tragedy and others, and didn't want the same to happen to them. They were more aware of the government arrogance than most Americans.

Upon hearing the shouting hoard of heavily armed paramilitary group descending upon them, the religious group locked the doors and braced for an attack. ATF agents broke windows and shot into the residence, killing eight people inside, including a two-year-old girl. As heavily armed agents started breaking windows and entering the building, the Branch Davidians naturally shot back, killing four of the assaulting ATF agents. Firing then stopped, and the paramilitary force retreated, followed by a nearly two-month standoff.

The residents placed bales of hay against the gaping holes in the walls and where the windows were knocked out. Federal agents ordered electricity cut off to the compound, forcing the residents to use kerosene lanterns for illumination, creating a high fire risk. Government agents blasted the occupants twenty-four hours a day with loud noises, and shook the building with the movement of huge military tanks. Several of the besieged residents gave up and left the building, at which time they were immediately arrested and charged with conspiracy and murder of the four ATF agents who had invaded their residence.

The ATF agents were joined by FBI agents and National Guard troops, equipped with heavy attack vehicles and tanks, surely the envy of many Third-

World military leaders. They were brave men, ready to do battle with the frightened religious group consisting mostly of women and children.

If the besieged residents had any hope that public pressure would bring a halt to the siege, they were sadly mistaken. As in Hitler's Germany, the government misconduct didn't directly affect them. The government's Wurlitzer-like manipulation of the media sought to make the besieged victims the culprits.

The large building in which the occupants were trapped was an old wooden building and highly flammable. A fire starting inside the structure could be expected to spread rapidly, especially if the winds were blowing hard as they often do on the Texas prairie. Once fire started inside, escape would be very difficult.

Apocalyptic Assault

Early in the morning on April 19, 1993, while the lanterns burned inside the building, the war-ready heavily armed military force commenced an attack, using armored vehicles and tanks, knocking down walls that fell inward upon the residents. Inside the building, sections of sheetrock and wood rained upon the frightened occupants, knocking burning lamps onto the piles of hay, causing them to ignite. As if this weren't enough, over 200 tear gas canisters were thrown into the building.

The leader of the religious group rushed through the building handing out gas masks and instructing the people to put them on immediately. The wind was blowing at over thirty miles an hour, roaring through the holes ripped in the building by the tanks, fanning the flames started by the overturned lanterns. Inside, the residents were trapped, scared, and unable to escape. The blackness of the early morning hours, the heavy smoke, the eye irritation caused by the tear gas, and the piles of debris in the hallways, made escape impossible for most of the residents. Eight managed to flee the searing heat, some of them with their clothes on fire.

Once the fires took hold, they spread in firestorm fashion, insuring the fiery death of everyone inside. Many of the frightened women and children huddled in fear, feeling the effects of the searing heat. Suddenly, as the flames reached the butane fuel escaping from a ruptured tank, an explosion sent flames hundreds of feet into the air, an event seen throughout the world on television screens. Possibly never in the history of the civilized world had such an arrogant government attack upon a group of religious people occurred, permitting the horrible consequences to be watched by a largely apathetic nation.

Oiling Up the Disinformation Machinery

The Waco tragedy had the potential of waking up the American public to the mindset of their leaders. This danger required oiling up the nationwide misinformation network controlled by various federal agencies; it appeared to work, except for those people who were informed about this form of government arrogance.

The same federal agents who inflicted that great tragedy upon the religious group sought to absolve themselves of blame, stating they saw the residents starting the fires. They sought to support this far-fetched statement on allegedly seeing someone in the building bending over. It is very possible that the person bending over was trying to put out the fires started when the lanterns were knocked over; or it was totally fabricated.

Federal officials reported that many of the bodies had bullet holes in them, implying the leader of the religious group shot them to prevent them from escaping the flames. Texas coroner Dr. Nizam Peerwani, heading the Tarrant County Coroner's office in Fort Worth, stated:

There is absolutely no evidence of that,
as far as we are concerned at this stage.

Interviewed on *Good Morning America* on April 23, 1993, the coroner stated that because of the condition of the bodies it would be difficult to determine bullet wounds and that the immense fire left very little of the bodies to examine. He added, "When a corpse is exposed to such intensive heat, the head will often explode."

The mainstream media, which had kept the news of the Weaver tragedy from the American people, couldn't hide the Waco tragedy as they did the Idaho assault. But they did report as fact, over and over again, that the group had committed suicide; that the blame for the holocaust was upon the victims and not upon the attacking military force.

Eight members of the religious group escaped the inferno and were immediately arrested. When questioned separately by their attorneys, each of them described what happened inside the building. The survivors described the chaos in the building as the tanks inflicted heavy damage. They described how the kerosene lamps had been knocked over by the tanks crashing into the building, and the resulting fires, the difficulty of moving about because of debris from the collapse of the walls and the heavy smoke and tear gas. The smoke caused total darkness inside the building. "You couldn't see your hand in front of your face," stated attorney Dick Kettler, speaking for one of the religious group members, Remos Avraam.

Attorney Dick DeGuerin stated that his client told him "there was pandemonium, they knew they were trapped. It was difficult to move around even before the fire started because the tank battering had damaged the inside of the compound."

After hearing the facts stated by the survivors, President Clinton repeated during an April 23, 1993, press conference what he had stated several days earlier: that the victims were responsible for their deaths. "I do not think the United States government is responsible for the fact that a bunch of fanatics decided to kill themselves." Clinton used the disinformation given by Justice Department agents to support his statements, even though they were contradicted by the independent statements of the survivors and by common sense.

Start of Another Congressional Cover-Up

Appearing on the *Larry King Live* television show within a few days of the holocaust, Senator Dennis DeConcini said he would head a senate investigative committee investigating the Waco affair. DeConcini repeated the statements of the Justice Department and President Clinton placing the blame for the deaths on David Koresh, the leader of the group. This dogmatic statement indicated his pre-judgment of the matter and his determination to protect government personnel. His statement blaming one of the victims came after there was overwhelming evidence showing Justice Department agents to be lying.

DOJ "Investigators"

Never at a loss to find people willing to assist Justice Department mischief, a team of "investigators" came upon the scene several days later and defended the onslaught, stating the occupants themselves decided to set the building and themselves on fire. The wife of the team's leader, Paul Gray, worked for the same people who started it all, the Bureau of Alcohol, Tobacco and Firearms. Gray taught at the ATF's academy, and had been selected by the ATF to conduct the investigation. Gray confirmed, "This fire was intentionally set by persons inside the compound." Most of the gullible public believed this tale.

Subsequent Report

In response to pressure from groups of concerned citizens, Treasury Secretary Lloyd Bentsen called for an independent review to determine what really happened. In September 1993, the Treasury Department released its report, defending the use of the paramilitary force on the residence occupied mostly by women and children. The report admitted that there was a pattern of deception by senior officials in the aftermath of the bungled operation. Simultaneously, Department of Justice officials released a report clearing Attorney General Janet Reno and other federal officials (who had given approval to the attack), blaming the tragedy on field personnel.

Long Prison Term for Survivors

The jury found the survivors innocent of most charges, except aiding and abetting. U.S. District Judge Walter Smith handed down sentences (June 17, 1994) of as much as forty years to eight survivors of the Waco holocaust. The aiding and abetting charges, which would more appropriately apply to many federal personnel, permitted Judge Smith to render long prison terms for those who had suffered so greatly. As usual, most of the public was indifferent to the crime perpetrated upon this religious group.

Several of the survivors started corresponding with me in 1994, and gave me details of the vicious attack upon the group. It was obvious that the charges used to "justify" the attack upon the compound were the usual fabrication.

Financial Loss If Public Defender Offends
The Justice Department or Federal Judges

On the state and federal levels, private attorneys are selected to represent defendants who lack sufficient money to hire their own attorneys. The income of the court-appointed attorneys arising from representing defendants is often either the sole or a major source of income. If the attorney incurs the wrath of the Justice Department or federal judges, these attorneys can find themselves without any court-appointed cases, and literally find themselves out of business.

Rewarding Major Drug Smugglers

Cases have been cited[9] where major criminals are not charged by Justice Department prosecutors on the basis of information that they gave relating to other drug operations, often enabling Justice Department prosecutors to obtain many other convictions of lesser figures. There are hundreds of peripheral drug players in prison facing long mandatory prison terms while those government officials (and of course judges) guilty of far more serious drug offenses are free, primarily because they were able to snitch on others.

Long prison terms for drug offenses become even more preposterous when it is realized that the CIA and DEA have engaged in large-scale drug trafficking operations into the United States for decades.

Misprision of Felony

A frequent charge for sentencing innocent people to prison is charging them with the federal crime, misprision of felony. Anyone who knows of a federal crime and who does not promptly report it to a federal judge or other federal tribunal is guilty of this crime. This statute has no exclusions and applies to members of Congress, White House officials, Justice Department personnel, the media, judges, all of whom have committed this crime. In practice, punishment for this crime is reserved for citizens, excusing those in the inner circle of government corruption.

Buying and Selling Human Lives

Judges, prosecutors and lawyers often buy and sell cases and human lives as if they were commodities. Judges are paid off to rule favorably on particular cases. A clerk can lose a key file or piece of evidence. The court reporter can change the transcript to indicate the reverse of what is actually in the record.

Lawyers often sabotage their own clients, allowing them to be convicted to satisfy a debt to their adversary's legal counsel or to placate a judge who may want the other party to prevail. Trading of human life in court is like kids trading marbles. Prosecutors will let a defendant go free in exchange for the life of another man. Criminal lawyers will plead a man guilty just to pay back a prosecutor for not prosecuting another client. Prosecutors will lie to imprison an

---

[9] Including a December 26, 1990 article by Harry Hellerstein, Assistant Federal Public Defender in San Francisco, in the *Wall Street Journal*.

innocent person or to cause his incarceration for years longer than the law provides for the offense that was actually committed. Cases are fixed by paying judges, prosecutors, police, and others.

Some Justice Department lawyers justify their lying, using the argument that the defendant lies so why shouldn't they do likewise. But a defendant may lie to avoid prison. Prosecutors lie to imprison innocent persons or to greatly increase the length of sentence for the purpose of making their record look good, regardless of the human tragedy it brings.

The public doesn't perceive this misconduct as a threat to themselves. When the Justice Department prosecutes a party for an alleged crime, the average person, including unsophisticated members of the grand jury, assumes that the party is guilty. Otherwise the accused would not be charged, or so they think. I fell into that trap in the past until I learned that Justice Department lawyers lie and cheat as a standard tactic.

Justice Department lawyers win year-end bonuses and personal-recognition awards for putting people in prison, guilty or not.

Dismissing U.S. Attorneys That Expose High Level Corruption

A common method for covering up evidence of the ongoing criminal activities is to dismiss investigators who report evidence of the crimes. For instance, when the investigative activities of the U.S. Attorney in Philadelphia threatened too many politicians involved in political corruption, President Carter reportedly pressured the Justice Department to remove U.S. Attorney David Meese "Dave" Martson from office. Speaking before the Washington National Press Club (January 25, 1978), Martson stated:

> If a single Congressman can remove his hometown prosecutor who's actively investigating public officials, with a single call to the President—if that can happen, and that's what did happen—our federal criminal-justice system won't work. No amount of rhetoric will ever convince the bagmen and the fixers that they can't pull strings in Washington, because they're sure that strings got pulled in Washington.
>
> The Justice Department—controlled by the United States Attorney General, who is appointed by the President of the United States—investigated President Carter and his political friend, Attorney General Griffin Bell, for possible obstruction of justice. Is it any wonder the Justice Department cleared their boss of any wrongdoing?

As I wrote in *Defrauding America*, those same tactics were used by Justice Department officials against Assistant U.S. Trustee Gregg Eichler in the San Francisco area when his investigations exposed the part played by federal judges and Justice Department officials in the corrupt Chapter 11 courts. I had given Eichler information on the criminal activities that I experienced in Chapter 11, implicating federal judges, federal trustees, and law firms. Eichler was dismissed from government service in late 1991, after he exposed the corruption by trustee Charles Duck, and as he was going after the judges.

Some years later, during President George Bush administration, that tactic was duplicated in over a dozen cases.

Justice Department officials fired one of their investigators in retaliation for testifying in the Inslaw affair. Justice Department officials arranged for the removal of Chapter 11 Judge George Bason from the District of Columbia bench after he ruled in favor of Inslaw, and then arranged for the Justice Department's lawyer defending against the Inslaw charges to replace Judge Bason. By packing the courts in this manner, corrupt Justice Department officials gain control over the judicial process, wherein they protect themselves.

Investigator Lloyd Monroe was forced to quit the Justice Department after he discovered connections between the savings and loan scandal and the CIA-related Southmark Corporation in Dallas.

Justice Department officials reprimanded Assistant U.S. Attorney Dave Howard in the San Francisco office after he filed a highly sensitive eleven-page report on July 11, 1990, describing the judicial corruption in Chapter 11. Howard recommended the appointment of a special counsel to investigate the corruption by federal judges and trustees in Ninth Circuit Chapter 11 courts. Instead of acting on the report, Justice Department officials censored Howard for preparing the report. Details in the book, *Defrauding America*.

Jack Blum, on Senator Terry Sanford's committee, was forced to resign when he pursued the investigation of BCCI corruption when the committee wanted to drop it. After Sanford's committee blocked the investigation into BCCI, Blum went to Manhattan's District Lawyer Robert Morgenthau with his evidence, resulting in criminal prosecution against powerful lawyers who sold their country down the river for financial wealth. Justice Department officials repeatedly blocked the exposure of the BCCI corruption, just as they blocked the exposure of every other scandal described in these pages.

Wholesale Dismissal of DOJ Prosecutors to Obstruct Justice

During the George W. Bush administration there was a wholesale dismissal of U.S. Attorneys to either block prosecution of Republican politicians or to file charges against Democratic politicians. Eight U.S. attorneys were fired to halt prosecution of Republican members of Congress.

The FBI has its own way of dealing with whistleblowers. The former head of the Los Angeles FBI office, Ted Gunderson, said[10] that he had been harassed by the FBI to suppress his reports of drugs smuggled into the United States in the bodies of dead GI's sent back from the Vietnam War. Gunderson retired from the FBI in 1979, becoming a private investigator, during which time he obtained evidence of widespread drug dealings at Fort Bragg, North Carolina. Numerous CIA assets have given me data confirming this sordid practice. Gunderson told the United Press reporters that the FBI and Justice Department had tapped his business phone and smeared his name.

---

[10] *United Press*, February 22, 1986.

Deaths of Those Exposing Justice Department Corruption

Mysterious deaths of people exposing Justice Department and CIA corruption have been repeatedly reported throughout these pages. One of the main murders, closely associated with the Justice Department's criminality in the Inslaw matter, was the widely publicized death of Danny Casolaro. The September 10, 1992, Congressional Inslaw report addressed this link, reporting that there was a need for a further investigation into Casolaro's death and the link to the Justice Department officials.

Arrogance on an International Level

The mindset rampant in the Justice Department has no bounds. Justice Department lawyers have sanctioned and ordered the seizure in foreign countries of foreign citizens. Many of these people had never been in the United States, or the acts that may have been legal in the country where they were committed, did not occur in the United States. Under law, the Justice Department had no jurisdiction over them.

In one instance involving a resident of Mexico, Dr. Humberto Machain, Justice Department personnel paid bounty hunters $50,000 to kidnap him and bring him into the United States to stand trial. He had allegedly assisted in torturing a U.S. DEA agent in Mexico. Civilized international law procedures require that extradition be requested of Mexican officials.

Applying this tactic to other nations, there is far more "justification" for other nations to kidnap American citizens based upon the crimes inflicted in their country by the CIA and other U.S. dirty-trick squads. Using this reasoning, hundreds of federal officials, especially those in the CIA, could be seized for the crimes that they caused to be inflicted as they invaded the sovereignty of foreign countries such as Vietnam and Nicaragua, or undermined the lawful governments of other countries.

Iranians could justifiably sneak into the United States and abduct American citizens to stand trial in Iran for having committed crimes under Iranian laws, including interference in Iranian governmental activities, or the shooting down of an Iranian airliner by a trigger-happy U.S. Navy crew that had invaded Iranian waters. The Vietnamese government could sneak into the United States and abduct American officials for their part in causing the deaths of tens of thousands of Vietnamese in the Phoenix program.

The U.S. invaded Panama, killing hundreds of Panamanian citizens, to capture the head of a foreign country (who has never committed a crime in the United States), for having trafficked in drugs in Panama. Making the seizure of Manuel Noriega more bizarre, he was formerly on the payroll of the same CIA, engaging in drug trafficking in partnership with the Central Intelligence Agency's sanctioned operations.

Supreme Court Approval of Unlawful Seizure

A federal judge in Los Angeles threw out the indictment against Dr. Humberto Machain after a declaration was entered into the court records by a Mexican informant. That declaration stated that another doctor, Fidel Kosonoy, was responsible for administering the drugs that kept an American DEA agent, Enrique Camarena, alive so that the agent could be tortured in an effort to obtain additional information. Kosonoy was the personal physician of Rafael Caro Quintero, a Mexican drug trafficker. Justice Department prosecutors withheld this declaration that contradicted their charges against the Mexican doctor.

The Justices of the U.S. Supreme Court upheld the right of Justice Department officials to invade a foreign country and seize their citizens in this manner. There was an exception: Justice John Paul Stevens called the decision "monstrous," which it was. The United States has given federal bounty hunters carte blanche to violate a widely held principle of international law, implying that foreign countries can do the same to U.S. citizens.

Chief Justice William Rehnquist upheld this violation of international law on the basis that "the treaty says nothing about the obligations" of the two countries "to refrain from forcible abductions." Using this rationale, U.S. bounty hunters can kill foreign citizens in foreign countries if the extradition treaty says nothing about that issue.

The Supreme Court Justices held that it was legal for American bounty-hunters to invade the sovereignty of a foreign country, using force if necessary, including killing foreign citizens, bringing them to the United States for trial, with Justice Department-appointed "defense" lawyers. These are the same Justices who obstructed justice when I repeatedly brought the corruption described within these pages to their attention via petitions, appeals, and letters.

Foreign nations and their media strongly criticized the United States Supreme Court for this position. Chile's most important newspaper, *El Mercurio*, reacted to the Supreme Court's ruling with the heading "Caramba! They've legalized terrorism." The June 23, 1992, editorial summarized the arrogance:

> The decision promotes contempt for the rule of law and the right of due process, violates national sovereignty and opens the door to acts of reprisal among nations. And what happens if U.S. agents—or people cooperating with the U.S.—clash with police in Mexico, Colombia or some other country, with gunfire that may even injure or kill innocent bystanders?

Chilean Socialist leader Marcelo Schilling said of the Supreme Court rule that it was "the law of the jungle in which the weaker countries will lose out." Guatemalan President Jorge Serrano called the Supreme Court's ruling an "unacceptable judicial monstrosity."

When asked what he thought of the kidnapping doctrine, legal adviser to the State Department, Judge Abraham Sofaer, testified before Congress in 1985, stating:

> *How would we feel if some foreign nation...came over here and seized some terrorist suspect in New York City, or Boston, or Philadelphia...because we refused through the normal channels of international, legal communications to extradite that individual?*

In 1989, the Assistant Attorney General in charge of the Office of Legal Counsel, William P. Barr, held that the FBI could legally seize suspects in foreign countries, even though they had never been in the United States and had never committed any offense in the United States.

Referring to the first President Bush, the heading in the Mexico City newspaper El Financiero read "Bush and the Culture of Terrorism," and described the "new world disorder in which the United States...can kidnap, torture and assassinate citizens from other nations."

On November 11, 1990, the United Nations Convention Against Illicit Traffic in Narcotic Drugs came into force and passed a resolution stating in clear text that a treaty party "shall not undertake in the territory of another Party the exercise of jurisdiction and performance of functions which are exclusively reserved for the authorities of that other Party by its domestic laws."

It was the invasion of Mexico under orders of Justice Department officials that required this restatement of international law. The resolution was introduced by Canada and Mexico and approved by the United Nations group. The United States ratified that convention agreement in 1990 and then promptly violated it by seizing a Mexican citizen in Mexico in 1992.

In response to the U.S. kidnapping of a Mexican citizen and the U.S. Supreme Court upholding that act, the Mexican senate approved an amendment to the Mexican criminal code imposing a 40-year sentence on anyone who kidnaps Mexicans on behalf of the United States or any other foreign authority who may wish to duplicate America's invasion of a foreign country's sovereignty to kidnap foreign citizens. So intense was Mexican anger toward the United States that the bill was approved unanimously and then approved by President Carlos Salinas de Gortari. This new law was Mexico's response to the U.S. Supreme Court ruling in June 1992 that approved the 1990 kidnapping of the Mexican doctor from Mexico.

DEA -DOJ After Pain-Relief Doctors

"Party of Pain" was the title to an article in the *New York Times* (January 21, 2006) by John Tierney, stating what I had discovered from physicians who have been victimized. The article stated:

> A Handcuffs-happy D.E.A. prolongs unneeded suffering. D.E.A, and federal prosecutors have been prosecuting doctors for prescribing painkillers like OxyContin, even where there's no evidence of any of the drugs being resold on the streets. It doesn't matter that the doctor genuinely believed that the patient needed the drugs and was not abusing them. It doesn't matter that the patient was in pain.
>
> Doctors are now going to prison merely for prescribing more pain pills than the D.E.A. and prosecutors deem a "legitimate medical purpose." These drug warriors are not troubled by the enormous range in the level of pain medication that different patients need. They don't even seem to worry much about the potency of the pills, just the number. They want enough

> pills of any dosage to make a good photo, like the bag of pills that Tandy held up at a press conference celebrating one doctor's conviction.
>
> The doctors who matter are the small number of specialists in pain treatment who prescribe opioids. Ronald Libby, a professor of political science at the University of North Florida, estimates that 17 percent of those doctors were investigated during one year by the D.E.A., and an even greater number of others were investigated by local and state authorities, typically in concert with the drug agency. That means a pain specialist might have a one-in-three chance of being investigated for prescribing opioids.
>
> Faced with these odds, doctors are understandably afraid. As noted in The New England Journal of Medicine this month, the D.E.A. has made doctors reluctant to give opioids to desperately ill patients, even when these drugs are the most effective pain treatment. The article warned that a victory for the Bush administration in the Oregon case, besides affecting terminally ill patients in Oregon, could cause doctors across the country to abandon patients and their families in their moment of greatest need.
>
> The Supreme Court's decision is a victory for patients and their doctors, including, I hope, some of the ones in prison for violating the federal legal theory that has not been rejected by the court. The doctors should go free, and Republicans in the White House and Congress should restrain the drug warriors who locked them up.

The reference to the recent Supreme Court decision was the Supreme Court upholding the Oregon law that authorized doctors to prescribe whatever pain medication was necessary for relieving the pain of patients.

Personal Knowledge of Incredible Pain Suffered by Dying

My father had suffered greatly from pain from terminal cancer, and for politicians to deny relief from such pain is intolerable.

Another DEA-DOJ Scheme Against Doctors

There are so many schemes used by government prosecutors to imprison innocent people that it would take an entire book devoted just to that subject to give the subject justice. Another tactic used by DEA-DOJ people was revealed by a *New York Times* article (January 24, 2006) written by John Tierney:

Sex, Lies and OxyContin

Jennifer Riggle, a drug addict, was a star witness in the trial of her doctor, Bernard Rottschaefer. She testified that he had fondled her breasts in the examination room and then given her prescriptions for OxyContin and Xanax in return for sex. In testimony in federal court two years ago, Riggle quoted the doctor as saying, "You satisfy my needs and I'll satisfy yours."

Rottschaefer denied the allegations but was convicted and sentenced to six and a half years in prison. The "drugs for sex" trial in Pittsburgh appeared to be a triumph for the Drug Enforcement Administration, which had helped investigate the doctor. But now it looks more like a frightening example of what's wrong with the D.E.A.'s war against doctors.

The drugs-for-sex case was based on the testimony of Riggle and three other women. All were in trouble with the law and had something to gain by cooperating with the D.E.A. agents who interviewed them.

Riggle's former boyfriend, angry at her for dumping him, produced a batch of letters he had received in prison from her; in them, she said she had never had sex with the doctor. She explained to her boyfriend that she was committing perjury because she faced drug charges that could have sent her to prison for six years. "They're saying he was bribing patients with sex for pills," she wrote, referring to the doctor, "but it never happened to me. D.E.A. said they will cut my time for good testimony. I don't want to be a snitch but what should I do?" After she cooperated, she received probation instead of prison time for the drug charges.

In the letters to her boyfriend, she fretted about being caught for perjury and urged him to destroy the incriminating letters. She worried she might have to take a polygraph test. She berated herself for having told another inmate about her perjury.

"See babe, the reason why I've been so down is cause you know that big secret I told you about the doctor? Well, I told someone about it way back and I am scared to death that she will reveal it and I'd never go home." Later that inmate would indeed come forward and say that Riggle had confessed to making up the story about sex with the doctor.

Justice As it Might Once Have Been

In a long-ago decision, when corruption was not as endemic as it became, U.S. Supreme Court Justice Sutherland, in a written decision in *Berger v. United States*, [11]wrote:

> The United States Attorney is the representative not of an ordinary party to a controversy, but of a sovereignty whose obligation to govern impartially is as compelling as its obligation to govern at all; and whose interest, therefore, in a criminal prosecution is not that it shall win a case, but that justice shall be done.
>
> As such, he is in a peculiar and very definite sense the servant of the law, the twofold aim of which is that guilt shall not escape or innocence suffer. He may prosecute with earnestness and vigor- indeed, he should do so.
>
> But, while he may strike hard blows, he is not at liberty to strike foul ones. It is as much his duty to refrain from improper methods calculated to produce a wrongful conviction, as it is to use every legitimate means to bring about a just one.

---

[11] *Berger v. United States*, 295 U.S. 78, 88, 55 S.Ct. 629, 633 (1935)

Bribing of Judges

Another source of harm inflicted upon innocent people by the legal and judicial fraternities is the bribing of judges. Just as with the common bribing of members of Congress, most of it is done discretely to where it is difficult to obtain evidence. Occasionally the "safeguards" fail and either the briber or the judge receiving the bribe is caught. In Operation Greylord, many Chicago judges were charged with taking bribes.

Prominent national trial lawyer Richard F. Scruggs was indicted (Nov. 29, 2007) by a federal grant jury in Oxford, Mississippi for offering a $50,000 bribe to a Mississippi state judge, seeking a favorable ruling on a fee dispute with another lawyer over litigation relating to Hurricane Katrina.

"Sobbing ex-judge gets can for graft" was the title in a *New York Post* article (June 6, 2007) relating to a New York judge:

> Disgraced former judge Gerald Gerson broke down yesterday as he was slapped with three to ten years in prison for accepting favors, cash and cigars from a crooked lawyer he'd taken under his wing.
>
> Referring to the hours of videos shown to the jury at his trial, tapes in which Garson is seen taking bribes and engaging in sophomoric banter with the lawyer, Paul Siminovsky, he added, "As I watched the surveillance tapes, I was appalled, embarrassed and ashamed of my demeanor."
>
> The harshest words for Garson came from Sigal Levi, the Brooklyn woman whose agonizing divorce case provided the backdrop for the ugly drama. "Mr. Garson, you stole my children," she said, referring to a decision granting custody of the two oldest boys to her husband. "You stole them from their two sisters and their younger brother. You stole them from their grandparents, their aunts and uncles. I didn't get what I deserved in your courtroom, but I hope and pray that you get what you deserved in this courtroom today."

Just One Side of Department of Justice Culture

There are many other sides to the culture of those who have controlled the Department of Justice for many decades. In my various books, including *Defrauding America* and *Drugging America*, I give many instances of DOJ personnel actively involved in criminal activities, which continue to inflict great harm upon innocent people and upon the security of the United States.

Justice for Sale

"Justice for Sale" was the title to a *Wall Street Journal* article (Nov. 15, 2007) written by U.S. Supreme Court Justice Sandra Day O'Connor. The Justice described how special interest money corrupts the judicial process:

> Motivated interest groups are pouring money into judicial elections in record amounts seeking to sway the voters. Whether or not they succeed in their attempts to sway the voters, these efforts threaten the integrity of judicial selection and compromise public perception of judicial decisions.

The final four candidates running for open seats on the Supreme Court of Pennsylvania raised more than $5.4 million combined in 2007, shattering fund-raising records in Pennsylvania judicial elections.

Most of this money comes from special interest groups who believe that their contributions can help elect judges likely to rule in a manner favorable to their causes. Nine out of ten Pennsylvanians regard judicial fund raising as evidence that justice is for sale, and many judges agree.

False Evidence: Another Ingrained FBI Culture

In 2007, the FBI announced that it was discontinuing forensic examinations using bullets to associate the lead bullets at the crime scenes with bullets found in suspect's bullet supply, holding that the tests were found to be erroneous. However, many people were sent to prison for years on those suspected tests. In addition, as I describe in other books, the FBI and DOJ prosecutors routinely fabricate evidence, use known false testimony, and pay for such false testimony, resulting in thousands of innocent people going to prison.

But this is a culture in government as people seek to promote their own status. For instance, as came out in the 1980s, the Department of Transportation had sent many of the blood, urine, and body-tissue samples from transportation crashes to the FAA Oklahoma City medical unit for testing. Accuracy is obviously important in this testing area. It was in this area that another FAA scandal surfaced. The FAA medical laboratory routinely falsified alcohol and drug test results.

A detailed article in the *Wall Street Journal* dated July 31, 1987 described the falsification of alcohol and drug tests conducted by the FAA medical unit at Oklahoma City. Officials in the FAA and other government agencies knew serious problems existed, but they all covered up. The problems came to a head after the Conrail and Amtrak collisions near Baltimore:

> The public was clamoring to know if the Conrail engineer had any drugs in his system. Because of the importance of the tests in accident investigations, the Transportation Department used the FAA laboratory at Oklahoma City, on the assumption that the FAA test results would be more reliable than those from a private testing laboratory. Because of the importance of the test in this most disastrous of train accidents, swarms of federal officials were at the FAA facility waiting for the results.
>
> Biochemist Delbert Lacefield and his assistant worked throughout the night to come up with the report that should have taken a relatively short time to complete. There was a problem: Neither biochemist Lacefield, nor anyone else in the lab, knew how to use the sophisticated equipment needed to perform the test.
>
> Lacefield reportedly submitted a fuzzy and contradictory report that raised questions about the integrity of the testing. In the Philadelphia Amtrak crash, CAMI's workers reached conclusions using improperly calibrated equipment, which they did not know how to operate. They lost, or

destroyed, the computer data that backed up their findings. Therefore their work could not be verified. The FAA laboratory squandered the entire blood sample taken from the engineer soon after the train accident, preventing further testing by a competent lab.

The engineer's urine sample was split, and a sample sent to a private lab. This tested positive for marijuana. But lab experts say that without the more precise blood test, there is no way of knowing whether the engineer was drug-impaired at the time he pulled his Conrail engine in front of a fast moving Amtrak train carrying 600 people.

A year earlier, in June 1986, the Armed Forces Institute of Pathology reported to FAA officials that the FAA laboratory lacked safeguards, that the personnel were unqualified, that their tests were inaccurate, and that proficiency training and tests by an outside group were necessary. The FAA ignored these warnings, and protected those fabricating the test results.

Even CAMI's own employees tried to alert higher FAA authorities to the lab's incompetence and falsifications. FAA supervisors rebuffed medical technologist Claudia Ryan when she reported the lack of quality control to Mr. Lacefield's supervisors. This caused her to remain quiet and not report the falsification of reports. She chose not to become a "whistleblower." During the subsequent investigation, three of the lab's four laboratory technologists testified that they complained to FAA officials about numerous problems without result.

An investigative team from the Federal Railroad Administration investigated the Civil Aeromedical Institute (CAMI), and made startling discoveries. The investigators discovered that the laboratory fabricated the results of seventeen blood tests during a nine-month period.

Federal Railroad Administrator John Riley downplayed the gravity of the falsified tests. But the problems at the lab were actually much worse than publicly admitted, as high FAA officials covered up for the fraud. It turned out that FAA supervisory personnel knew of the problems nearly a year earlier, but they refused to take corrective actions. Instead, they protected the FAA officials falsifying the test results. It wasn't until the Philadelphia Amtrak tragedy that public attention focused on the fraudulent lab reports.

In a 1984 airplane crash near Laredo, Texas, CAMI reported that the pilot had a blood alcohol level of .406, a condition that is close to death, and far beyond a pilot's ability to even try to fly. A nearby hospital found only about a quarter of the amount of alcohol reported by the FAA laboratory, which was still serious.

When the railroad administration picked CAMI to run its post-accident testing program, they knew that the FAA lacked a device called a gas chromatograph/mass spectrometer that is necessary for sophisticated blood testing. The FAA promised to subcontract blood tests to a nearby nongovernmental laboratory, but it never did. None of the FAA employees knew how to extract a test sample from blood plasma, which was a necessary first step before an outside lab could analyze the fluid. The FAA simply falsified and fabricated the test results. The head of the lab had worked at CAMI for 21 years, continually operating in this manner, fraudulently fabricating test results.

Despite the fraud involved in these years of tests, and the knowledge of the fraud by FAA officials, no one was punished. The Transportation Department shut down the FAA lab, and transferred all post-accident railroad and airline testing to a non-government laboratory. The government protected its own.

In later pages, falsified FBI forensic evidence is shown related to the prosecution in the Pan Am explosion over Lockerbie.

You May be the Next Victim of the FBI-DOJ Culture

Although the law was intended to require that a person being charged with a crime had the intent to commit a crime, prosecutors and informants have ignored that major due process requirement. In this way they increase their status and pay by charging anyone with a crime for unknowingly violating any of the thousands of laws members of Congress called a crime. A *Wall Street Journal* article (September 29, 2009), titled, "You Commit Three Felonies a Day," described the felonies committing unknowingly by the average person every day:

Boston civil-liberties lawyer Harvey Silverglate calls his new book "Three Felonies a Day," referring to the number of crimes the estimates the average American now unwittingly commits because of vague laws. New technology adds its own complexity, making innocent activity potentially criminal.

This problem is compounded by a trend that has accelerated since the 1980s for prosecutors to abandon the principle that there can't be a crime without criminal intent.

Mr. Silverglate is a persistent, principled critic of overbroad statutes. … [Referring to the prosecution of a banker resulting in] reversal of his criminal conviction on vague charges of obstruction of justice.

These miscarriages are avoidable. Under the English common law we inherited, a crime requires intent. This protection is disappearing in the U.S. As Mr. Silverglate writes, "Since the New Deal era, Congress has delegated to various administrative agencies the task of writing the regulations," even as "Congress has demonstrated a growing dysfunction in crafting legislation that can in fact be understood."

> **[Destroying Targeted Individuals]**
>
> Prosecutors identify defendants to go after, instead of finding a law that was broken and figuring out who did it. Expect more such prosecutions as Washington politicians and bureaucrats adds more regulations.
>
> Americans should expect that a crime requires bad intent and also that Congress and prosecutors will try to create clarity, not uncertainty. Out legal system has a lot of catching to do to work smoothly [and honestly] with the rest of our lives.

In this way, as in any third world country, employees in control of the U.S. Department of Justice, either on their own or as used by such politicians as President George W. Bush, selectively attack particular people, as clearly shown thoroughly this book and most of my others.

CHAPTER TWO

DOJ Cover-Up of Murders Involving Boston FBI Agents

For years, several CIA assets had given me the names of FBI agents involved in assassinations. I could never get myself to write about what they were telling me. It was too bizarre to comprehend that FBI agents, entrusted with protecting people, would be engaged in murdering them. And that higher FBI and DOJ officials were protecting the murders.

However, criminal proceedings and civil lawsuits filed in the Boston area in the 1990s provided proof that some FBI agents secretly worked with crime figures in murders and other crimes. Investigative newspaper reports and criminal proceedings provided the details of these happenings in the Boston FBI offices, and implicated high FBI and DOJ officials in Washington.

FBI Corruption and Murders in Boston Office Indicated Deep-Seated Culture Throughout FBI and DOJ

Over the years the instances of corruption involving FBI personnel had been kept off the public radar, but this would change in the 1990s when decades of FBI involvement in murders and other criminal acts were exposed by courageous media people in the Boston area. Media outlets elsewhere kept the lid on this scandal. This attention was brought about by the large number of murdered victims in the Boston area associated with the FBI-criminal relationship.

If it weren't for determined investigative reporters at the *Boston Globe* and the *Hartford Courant,* the murderous conduct would probably still be functioning as it had for the past 20 years. Helping to expose these matters were two reporters for the *Boston Globe*, Dick Lehr and Gerard O'Neill. They authored the book, *Black Mass: The Irish Mob, the FBI and a Devil's Deal.* The following was revealed by affidavits, testimony, court proceedings, and government records.

FBI Boston Office a Criminal Enterprise— Sanctioned by Washington FBI and DOJ Officials

The courageous media reporting and court proceedings revealed decades of FBI agents misusing their FBI positions to protect the murderous Boston-based crime group known as the Winter Hill gang headed by James "Whitey" Bulger and his partner, Steven "The Rifleman" Flemmi. Under the pretext of using Bulger and Flemmi as confidential informants, FBI agents, and particularly FBI Agent John Connolly, protected the crime group against state and federal prosecution and provided them insider information about wiretaps and pending indictments so they could protect themselves.

FBI agent Connolly's corruption began in 1976 when he accepted gifts from Bulger and returned the favors by giving Bulger inside information. FBI agents provided Bulger and Flemmi with information about wiretaps placed upon their phones by state and federal agencies, and with information on pending indictments.

FBI agents knew that Bulger and Flemmi were committing murders, some of which occurred after FBI agents leaked information about FBI confidential informants to Bulger. Bulger was involved in numerous criminal activities and needed the FBI to protect him whenever a state or federal agency threatened him.

The alleged purpose for this cozy arrangement was for the FBI to receive information from the Winter Hill gang on the activities of rival gangs. However, the information provided to the FBI by this relationship was relatively minor, while the benefits to the Bulger group were of immense value. By providing information to the FBI about Winter Hill's competitors in criminal activities, the gang was able to not only murder their competition in other criminal groups but also to take over their racketeering activities.

Another valuable benefit to the Winter Hill gang was that the FBI agents provided information about FBI informants, who were then tortured and murdered. This information permitted the Winter Hill gang to murder many government informants—with the full knowledge of the FBI agents and the Justice Department official in Washington—including FBI director J. Edgar Hoover.

Bulger was not only a living legend in Boston, but also had strong political connections in Massachusetts. His younger brother, William "Bill" Bulger, was powerful in the Massachusetts Senate, and later became president of the University of Massachusetts. While president of the University of Massachusetts, William Bulger refused to testify in December 2002 before a congressional committee investigating the FBI's conduct associated with the Winter Hill gang and William Bulger's brother. Referring to William Bulger, a *New York Times* article (April 10, 2003) stated:

In December, Mr. Bulger refused to testify at a hearing of the committee [House Government Reform Committee], in Boston, pleading his Fifth Amendment right against compelled self-incrimination. In December it was revealed that Mr. Bulger had told a federal grand jury looking into misconduct by F.B.I. agents in Boston, "I had an honest loyalty to my brother. I don't feel an obligation to help everyone to catch him." Mr. Bulger also disclosed that he had spoken with Whitey Bulger by telephone shortly after he went into hiding and had not advised him to give himself up.

Who Was Using Whom?

The FBI-Bulger connection made Bulger the undisputed crime king in New England, without any significant competition, and using the FBI for protection against prosecution for the dozens of murders committed. It was not the FBI using Bulger but rather Bulger using the FBI. The FBI was Bulger's enabler, paving the way for an already powerful murderous organized crime group to become even more powerful.

The incestuous relationship between the biggest crime group in New England and the FBI started in the 1960s for Flemmi, and 1975 for Bulger. This relationship continued until the turn of the century. During this period, FBI agents socialized with Bulger and Flemmi, having dinner at each other's homes, exchanging gifts, and in several cases, the FBI agents received cash from the crime group.

FBI Blocking State Police Investigations

When the Massachusetts state police sought to indict Bulger and other members of his criminal organization for murders and other crimes, FBI agents provided protection. The FBI informed Bulger of investigations, removing their names from indictments, disclosing wiretaps, and refusing to cooperate in joint task force investigations. This made possible the continuation of the murders, drug smuggling, and other racketeering activities that could have otherwise been prevented.

One Agent Exposed the Links, and High Level Cover-Up

FBI Special Agent Robert Fitzpatrick repeatedly told his superiors that Bulger was committing murders and other crimes and should be terminated as an FBI informant. He also advised his bosses that FBI Special Agent John Connolly was passing confidential FBI information to Bulger, and that this information assisted Bulger to avoid certain areas where telephone and other taps were in place. The decision was made at high FBI levels, including Washington, to continue this relationship with Bulger, knowing that people were being murdered and that racketeering activities were continuing to flourish.

Two of the many murders perpetrated by Bulger and Flemmi involved young women, Deborah Hussey and Debra Davis. Flemmi was living with his common-law wife, Marion Hussey, starting this relationship when Deborah, her daughter, was only five years old. As Deborah grew older, Flemmi started a sexual relationship with her, in addition to what he had with her mother.

When Deborah decided to end the sexual relationship, Flemmi and Bulger strangled her. Before disposing of the body, to prevent identification, they cut off Deborah's fingers and toes and knocked out all of her teeth.

While Flemmi had sexual relations with Marion Hussey and her daughter, he also had a sexual relationship with Debra Davis. She had foolishly entered a relationship with Flemmi at the age of 18, lured partly by the gifts lavished upon her. Several years later, when she announced an intention to end the relationship, Bulger and Flemmi strangled her in a house owned by Flemmi's mother. Flemmi and Bulger feared she would reveal what she learned about the criminal activities during her relationship with Flemmi. She was buried under a railroad trestle in Quincy, Massachusetts.

As the information became known about how Bulger and Flemmi had murdered their daughters, the girls' mothers filed civil actions against Flemmi and several FBI informants and agents. On February 26, 2001, Deborah's mother, Marion Hussey, filed a lawsuit and on March 7, 2001, Olga Davis filed hers.

Protection from Other Government Offices

While the FBI protected Bulger and Flemmi, protection came also from other DOJ offices—which would be ordered at the Washington level. Although it was common knowledge in the community that Flemmi and Bulger were murderers and protected by the FBI, William F. Weld, the U.S. Attorney in Boston from 1981 to 1986, did nothing to interfere. Nor did he do anything when he subsequently became governor of Massachusetts. And this protective stance continued after Weld left the governorship and became Assistant Attorney General in Washington, D.C.

In 1984, while Weld was U.S. Attorney, the DEA planned to use wiretaps against Flemmi and Bulger to obtain additional evidence of their drug crimes. The DEA asked Weld if the FBI wanted to get involved in a joint operation. Weld asked the head of the FBI Boston office, James Greenleaf, if he wanted to cooperate. Greenleaf refused. The DEA then proceeded without FBI assistance, but their subsequent wiretaps were rendered useless when FBI agents tipped off Bulger and Flemmi about the location of the wiretaps and bugs.

When U.S. Attorney Robert Mueller was responsible for the Boston office, he also covered up for the relationship. He later became director of the FBI to defend the United States against crime in the presidency of George H.Bush (Jr.). While Mueller was U.S. attorney in San Francisco, I made his office aware of considerable corruption that I and a group of other former federal agents had uncovered, much of it in Mueller's immediate jurisdiction. Mueller and his office chose to cover up for the criminal activities.

This entire FBI-Winter Hill gang partner-in-crime relationship was known to FBI Director J. Edgar Hoover for many years, and nothing was done to halt the incestuous and criminal relationship. Hoover, the FBI, and the Justice Department became complicit in the murders made possible by FBI misconduct. In my book, *History of Aviation Disasters: 1950 to 9/11*, I described writing to FBI Director J. Edgar Hoover—while I was a federal agent for the Federal Aviation Administration—accusing him of criminal cover-ups. A federal agent does not get away with such accusations unless they are true.

When a secret federal indictment against Bugler occurred in 1994, FBI agent Connolly immediately informed Bugler, enabling him to flee. He is still on-the-run. Senator Bugler stated he was unaware of his brother's criminal career, which no one, of course, believed.

***Local* Media Exposure Finally Forced Justice Department Action**

The *Hartford Courant* and the *Boston Globe* ran a series of articles on the sordid relationship between FBI agents and the Bulger gang, while most of the national media kept the lid on the scandals. One such article was the following:

As the State of Massachusetts was about to hand down indictments against Bulger, Flemmi, and other members of the Winter Hill gang, FBI Agent Connolly alerted Bugler, who then fled, along with a female companion.

James Bulger was shown on the Internet web site of the Massachusetts State Police as being wanted by the State of Massachusetts and the DEA, offering one million dollars reward for information leading to the arrest of Bulger. The Internet site listed Bulger under Most Wanted, and "Wanted for 19 counts of murder." The Internet site lists his female companion for harboring a fugitive: Catherine Elizabeth Greig (aka Helen Marshall and Carol Shapeton).

Defense Argument: Murders Perpetrated with FBI Permission

Defense lawyers for defendants Bulger and Flemmi argued before U.S. District Judge Mark L. Wolf that the charges should be dismissed because the government tacitly gave Flemmi and Bulger permission to commit the crimes they committed while they were acting as FBI informants. They also argued that the FBI knew of the crimes being committed and looked the other way.

FBI Aiding and Abetting Revealed in Testimony

In one of Flemmi's affidavits, he stated that FBI agents had a practice of alerting him to avoid certain places where the FBI had placed bugs; that FBI agents told him of impending indictments, and gave him the names of government informants, who were then murdered.

Those statements were supported by John Morris, former supervisor of Boston's Organized Crime Squad, who testified that he told FBI Agent Connolly about an informant who would be testifying against Bulger in the murder of a New England Jai Alai operator, Roger Wheeler. A short time later, the informant was killed.

The informant, Edward Brian Halloran, had information showing that Bulger killed Wheeler, and asked the Boston FBI office to allow him to testify and to put him in the government's witness protection program. Despite the fact that this information could solve one or more murders, the FBI refused. Halloran's name was given to Bulger, knowing that Holloran would be killed shortly thereafter.

Another FBI Agent Exposed in the Murderous Boston Office

According to testimony by a Mafia boss and a government informant, Boston FBI Special Agent H. Paul Rico was also heavily involved with criminal elements. He reportedly helped kill a gangster, and framed others for murders that they did not commit.

FBI Agent Taking Cash from Murderous Crime Group

Former FBI agent John Morris, testifying under a grant of immunity, admitted taking cash on several occasions from two informants, totaling $7000, and that the money came from Bulger and Flemmi. FBI Agent Connolly, who was Bulger's handler—or the other way around—repeatedly refused to answer questions, invoking his Fifth Amendment right against self-incrimination.

Thirty Years in Prison For Crime the FBI Knew He Didn't Do

A May 4, 2001, *Boston Globe* headline read, "Man Imprisoned 30 Years for Crime FBI Knew He Didn't Commit:"

> Due to the withholding of evidence, Salvati was sent to prison in 1967. A Massachusetts father of four, Joe Salvati, was convicted of murder and served 30 years in prison—while the FBI, including Washington headquarters, knew he was innocent and knew the murder was committed by one of their paid informants. The known perjured testimony of an FBI informant led to his conviction and imprisonment.

Foreign News Service Reporting FBI Corruption

A June 20, 2001, R*euter's* article, titled, "FBI Agent Accused In Corruption Inquiry," referred to an FBI agent in nearby Providence, Rhode Island, accepting expensive gifts from criminal elements. The article stated:

> An F.B.I. agent has been suspended over accusations that he accepted gifts from a mob associate's former wife ... the Providence Journal reported today. The newspaper said the Federal Bureau of Investigation confirmed that the special agent, David DiLustro, has been suspended with pay.
>
> The gifts Mr. DiLustro received included a bath house at an exclusive beach resort ... The F.B.I. is investigating Mr. DiLustro's relationship with Gail-Ann Calenda, who bribed city officials to get property-tax reductions in 1998. Two tax officers and a lawyer were convicted in the case. Mayor Vincent Cianci and five others have been indicted on corruption charges as a result of the inquiry.

Dying in Prison for Crimes They Didn't Commit: Courtesy of Justice Department Personnel

Two of the men convicted with Salvati died in prison for a murder they did not commit and which the FBI knew they didn't commit. Salvati remained in prison for 30 years until a rare lawyer's persistence produced documents withheld by the FBI and Boston police. It took years for Salvati's lawyer, Victor Garo, to obtain documents proving FBI agents and Boston police prosecuted Salvati to protect the identities of several FBI informants who would possibly be exposed if the real murderer were identified.

Congressional Hearings—and Then the Usual Cover-Up

A hearing was held on May 4, 2001 before the House Government Reform Committee concerning the FBI's involvement in covering up for several of their informants who were involved in a Boston murder and how the FBI withheld information so as to convict an innocent man and father of four of murder.

After listening to what occurred, Representative Christopher Shays tearfully told Joe Salvati:

> *Your story of faith, your story of family, your story of courage and perseverance is a gift to your nation. And we cherish it. Your testimony will insure on one else has to endure the outrageous indignities and injustices you, Mr. Salvati, Marie, and your family, have suffered." [Don't count on this PR statement!]*

"Truth be dammed."

Testifying before the committee, Victor J. Garo, a lawyer, said: "It was more important to the FBI that they protected their prized informants than it was for innocent people [to be sent to prison]. The truth be dammed. It didn't matter about the truth."

FBI Agent's Arrogance

In response to a question from a committee member whether FBI Special Agent H. Paul Rico felt any remorse for his role in the case, he defiantly shouted, "What do you want, Tears? It'll be probably a nice movie or something."

Documents Showed FBI Director Implicated in Crimes

Documents presented during the criminal trial proved that FBI Director J. Edgar Hoover knew of the criminal misconduct, false testimony, murders perpetrated by protected FBI informants, sending innocent people to prison, and did nothing to stop it.

Connolly's tip to Bulger of his indictment occurred in 1994 and enabled Bulger to flee. Many people connected to the case believe that the FBI does not want to capture Bulger so as to cover up its own decades of criminal involvement. Burger was finally discovered on a tip from a neighbor in June 2011, living in Santa Monica with his companion, Catherine Greig.

Long Overdue Federal Indictments

Federal indictments were also finally handed down against FBI agent John Connolly, who was arrested on Christmas Eve, 1999, and charged with racketeering. The trial of John Connolly took place in an atmosphere that implied his innocence. Connolly was permitted to sit in the audience with his family rather than at the defense table. U.S. District Judge Joseph A. Tauro saw no problem in that arrangement.

Sitting in the courtroom was the new FBI director, Robert Mueller, who many believe was appointed FBI director because of his capacity to cover up governmental scandals. He followed the profile of many past FBI Directors, including former FBI Director William Sessions who rose from a lowly federal district court Judge in Texas to the FBI Directorship after he cooperated with President Reagan and his Attorney-General Dick Thornburgh in the 1980's.

In politics, rewards are handed out to those that cooperate. During the 1980s AUSA, Robert Mueller in Boston kept the lid on the FBI scandal involving the criminal group headed by Bulger. He was appointed United States Attorney in Boston, insuring that information was kept from the Boston Police

Department about the crimes perpetrated by the Bulger group and by FBI agents.

Boston Police Department complained bitterly that both the Justice Department and the FBI interfered or prevented their investigations into known mob operations. Watching Connolly's trial in May and June of 2002 was Massachusetts State Senator William Bugler, who was also the president of the Massachusetts senate. William Bulger was the younger brother of mobster James "Whitey" Bulger, who headed a powerful organized crime group in Boston, in which FBI Special Agent Connolly was involved.

Media Publicity Forced Prosecution of FBI Agents

On May 23, 2002, Assistant U.S. Attorney John Durham filed charges against Connolly, who at that time was retired from the FBI. The charges stated that Connolly "functioned as a member of a criminal enterprise;" racketeering and obstruction of justice; leaking confidential information to people in the Bulger organized crime group that resulted in the killing of three witnesses; taking bribes; active participation in sending innocent men to prison; role in murdering witnesses against the mob; covering up crimes committed by the criminal elements; and tipping off James "Whitey" Bulger, the powerful head of a Boston crime group.

Jury Finds Connolly Guilty of Lesser Charges, With Federal Judge Proposing Leniency

The jury found Connolly guilty of racketeering, obstructing justice, and lying to an FBI agent, and innocent on the conspiracy to murder charges. Following this verdict, senior U.S. District Judge Edward F. Harrington wrote a letter to the sentencing judge requesting leniency for Connolly.

In 2002, Connolly was sentenced to ten years in prison for his conduct that resulted in FBI informants being murdered, in conduct converting the FBI offices into a racketeering enterprise, and other crimes. The sentence was less than countless numbers of men and women received for peanut quantities of drugs or no-drug conspiracies in which government agents and government informants falsely testify about drug evidence. The system protects their own!

In criminal trials against the non-government criminal defendants, one of Bulger's brothers pleaded guilty (April 15, 2003) in U.S. district court at Boston for perjury and obstruction of justice arising from lying to federal grand juries.

Rico was charged with the 1965 murder of Tulsa businessman Roger Wheeler, a murder that Rico committed after retiring from the FBI and working for Wheeler as a security consultant. Rico murdered Wheeler at a Tulsa country club because Wheeler had discovered Rico had embezzled funds from Wheeler's company, World Jai Alai. It could be assumed that the FBI's tolerance of Rico's criminal conduct while in the Boston office emboldened Rico to kill Wheeler, thinking he was immune from prosecution. While waiting to go to trial, Rico died in January 2004 at an Oklahoma state prison in Tulsa. His death prevented further information about FBI misconduct from being revealed during trial.

Subsequent Trial Nets FBI Agent Connolly 40 Years in Prison

A Miami jury convicted former FBI agent John Connolly of second-degree murder in the 1982 shooting death of World Jai-Alai president John Callahan and a judge sentenced him to 40 years in prison. Six civil lawsuits were filed, with another ten expected, from family members of people who were murdered due to Connolly's actions.

Media Blackout Despite the Grave National Implications

The evidence showed a major scandal with national implications, but national media exposure was limited, and only a few local newspapers provided the public with details on this sordid FBI drama. These were the *Boston Globe* and *Hartford Courant,* running a series of articles that commenced in 1988. The rest of the nation's media covered up for the sordid and widespread misconduct in the FBI. This is the FBI that would be counted upon to detect terrorists and other threats to national interests!

A *CBS "60-Minutes*" broadcast in April 2001, provided an abbreviated account, showing mob boss James J. "Whitey" Bulger, as being a paid FBI informant for over 20 years and protected against investigation and prosecution while he and his gang engaged in murders, drug dealings, and other crimes.

An April 6, 2001, *Dateline* program revealed that Robert Fitzpatrick, who was an Assistant Special Agent in charge of the FBI's Boston Field Office in the 1980s repeatedly told his superiors that Bulger should be terminated as an FBI informant after learning of the numerous murders he committed. Fitzpatrick also said he warned top FBI officials that former FBI Agent John Connolly was leaking confidential information to Bulger. So successful was the media cover-up that I could not find a single person, including talk show hosts, who knew about the Boston FBI scandal.

Many More Involved at State and Federal Levels

Many more people in state and federal government positions were involved, either directly or through cover-ups, who escaped prosecution. One name that wasn't mentioned in this scenario was former Massachusetts Governor Bill Weld.

Weld headed the Boston U.S. Attorney's office during much of the time Bulger & Flemmi were engaging with the FBI in a racketeering enterprise. Nor was any mention made of U.S. Attorney Robert Mueller, who was responsible for prosecutions in the Boston FBI office during part of the time these FBI crimes were ongoing.

High FBI Officials Implicated, Making Cover-Up Urgent

Among the high-ranking figures that surfaced at Connolly's trial were Robert S. Mueller, III; former FBI Director J. Edgar Hoover, and the former president of the Massachusetts senate, William Bulger. FBI Director Mueller was an assistant U.S. attorney in Boston, in charge of the Criminal Division, and for a period of time was the acting U.S. attorney, while Connolly was involved in murderous misconduct with a criminal group headed by James Bulger. Mueller never acted to halt Connolly's misconduct.

Mueller covered up for numerous criminal activities[12] that I reported to him while he was with the FBI office in San Francisco.

Diverted Congressional Hearings

The publicity forced the U.S. House of Representatives' Committee on Government Reform to conduct hearings. But not to address the corruption within the FBI that went to Washington and included DOJ officials. The hearings were primarily on the advisability of using government informants!

"An institution in dire need of reform."

An outspoken member of the committee was Congressman Bill Delahunt of Massachusetts. He said, "What happened in Boston is not just a John Connolly rogue street agent problem. What we have revealed here is an institution in dire need of reform, with no accountability, no transparency, and a total lack of controls." Representative Delahunt spent 20-years as a local district attorney and claimed his own investigations of Whitey Bugler were undermined by FBI protection of the mobster.

As far back as 1965, FBI Director J. Edgar Hoover was told that four innocent men had been sent to prison for life for a murder which the FBI knew was committed by one of the FBI's informants. The murder of Edward Deegan in 1965 was committed by FBI informant Vincent Flemmi. The U.S. Attorney Boston investigated whether other FBI agents were involved. In an attempt to cover its own involvement in the murders and other crimes committed by Connolly, officials in FBI Washington headquarters sent a team to investigate some of these accusations back in 1997. FBI Agent Charles Prouty and a team from the FBI and Justice Department looked into the situation discovered by U.S. District Court Judge Mark L. Wolf.

Standard Government Whitewash

Within five weeks, Prouty and his team released their report, which found *no* wrongdoing within a five-year statute of limitations period. Further hearing by Judge Wolf unearthed the misconduct that was eventually cited in the Connolly trial. For protecting the FBI's role in the crimes, Prouty was promoted to the head of the FBI Boston Field Office as its new Special Agent-In-Charge.

While the Justice Department's Criminal Division prosecuted Connolly, the civil law suits against him were being vigorously *defended by* the Justice Department's Civil Division. The U.S. Department of Justice was willing to defend Connolly in these civil lawsuits because the FBI was also being sued. The standard of proof in a civil suit is much lower than in a criminal case. Here ju-

---

[12] I offered to provide evidence to Mueller while he was in the FBI San Francisco office, and the criminal activities that I offered to report were those that I described in my book *Defrauding America*. They consisted of drug smuggling by people in the FBI, rampant corruption of federal judges and others in the bankruptcy courts; and others, all of which involved people in government positions. He never responded.

rors base their findings on only a preponderance of evidence, not proof beyond a reasonable doubt.

Huge Civil Judgments Resulting From FBI-DOJ Criminal Conduct

Referring to the victims of the FBI corruption in Boston, an Op-Ed article in the *Wall Street Journal* ((August 2, 2007) by Richard Moran addressed the problem of prosecutors knowingly filing false charges against innocent people:

Last week, Judge Nancy Gertner of the Federal District Court in Boston awarded more than $100 million to four men whom the F.B.I. framed for the 1965 murder of Edward Deegan, a local gangster. It was compensation for the 30 years the men spent behind bars while agents withheld evidence that would have cleared them and put the real killer—a valuable F.B.I. informant, by the name of Vincent Flemmi—in prison.

Most coverage of the story described it as a bizarre exception in the history of law enforcement. Unfortunately, this kind of behavior by those whose sworn duty is to uphold the law is all too common. In state courts, where most death sentences are handed down, it occurs regularly.

My recently completed study of the 124 exonerations of death row inmates in America from 1973 to 2007 indicated that 80, or about two-thirds of their so-called wrongful convictions resulted not from good-faith mistakes or errors but from intentional, willful, malicious prosecutions by criminal justice personnel.

Yet too often this behavior is not singled out and identified for what it is. When a prosecutor puts a witness on the stand that he knows to be lying, or fails to turn over evidence favorable to the defense, or when a police officer manufactures or destroys evidence to further the likelihood of a conviction, then it is deceptive to term these conscious violations of the law as merely mistakes or errors.

Mistakes are good-faith errors—like taking the wrong exit off the highway, or dialing the wrong telephone number. There is no malice behind them. However, when officers of the court conspire to convict a defendant of first-degree murder and send him to death row, they are doing much more than making an innocent mistake or error. They are breaking the law.

Since so many wrongful convictions result from official malicious behavior, prosecutors, policemen, witnesses or even jurors and judges could themselves face jail time for breaking the law in obtaining an unlawful conviction.

The term "wrongfully convicted" is technically correct, and also has the potential to be misleading. It leads to the false impression that most inmates ended up on death row because of good-faith mistakes or errors committed by an imperfect criminal justice system—not by malicious or unlawful behavior.

Falsified FBI Forensic Evidence Reports

Referring to forensic evidence, the article stated that "The best trained and most honest forensic scientists can only examine the evidence presented to them; they cannot be expected to determine if that evidence has been planted, switched or withheld from the defense." The article referred to FBI laboratory technicians making positive reports of crime evidence that they falsified, sending many innocent people to prison.

Another article referring to the FBI corruption in those Boston cases (*New York Times*, Aug. 5, 2007) described the harm suffered by the families of those men wrongly convicted. Louis Greco, Sr. died in prison. His wife, depressed, started drinking heavily and abandoned the children. A son, Louis Greco, Jr., depressed, committed suicide. Others suffered personal and financial tragedies due to the corruption in the FBI and Department of Justice.

FBI Agent's Involvement in Murder of Telex Corporation CEO

Appearing on CBS's *60-Minutes* show (January 6, 2008), one of the mass killers for the Winter Hill gang, John Martorano, admitted to murdering over 18 people, and was a government witness. He admitted killing the CEO of Telex Corporation, who also owned World Jai Alai, Roger Wheeler. Martorano stated, as he had previously testified, that Boston FBI Special Agent Paul Rico provided the logistical information to carry out the murder.

In another murder, Martorano stated that FBI Special Agent John Connolly advised him and Bulger that one of their associates, John Callahan, was about to expose him for murdering Wheeler. With this information Martorano then murdered Callahan.

When asked on the show, "Do you think that John Connolly knew that you were gonna kill Callahan?" Martorano replied, "Sure. He said it. 'We're all going to go to jail the rest of our life if this guy doesn't get killed.'"

CHAPTER THREE

DOJ Retaliation Against FBI Agent Exposing Corruption

In the past, several FBI agents have revealed serious corruption problems within the Justice Department, adding to the knowledge I acquired during 30 years of combat with various Justice Department divisions. Starting in 1997, another and still more important FBI source became known to me.

Richard Taus had been a Special Agent for the FBI from 1978 to 1988. During this time he was assigned to organized crime and foreign counter-intelligence operations, and acted as a relief Supervisory Special Agent (SSA). Among his additional duties in the Bureau, Taus was a Pilot-In-Command (PIC) flying missions for the FBI New York Field Office. The *New York Times Reference Book* for the Year 1988 lists Taus under "FBI Events." In the 1980s he conducted an undercover operation from a squad consisting of 17 special agents. He also held the rank of Lieutenant Colonel in the aviation branch of the U.S. Army Reserve.

Taus had uncovered and reported evidence of major criminal activities, some of it involving CIA and other government operations. When his reports exposed CIA or White House involvement in these activities his supervisors ordered him to halt his investigations, often using the familiar excuse that they were national security matters. When Taus sought to circumvent the cover-ups, government power was misused to silence him. After I contacted him, he initially felt that the gravity of the government corruption had to be exposed, but he was unsure he could do so without suffering retaliation because of his prior FBI position.

I advised Taus that in my opinion the national welfare, Supreme Court decisions, and federal criminal statutes, required that any government employee, regardless of any secrecy agreement that he or she might have signed, had an obligation to report government corruption. Because of the heavy involvement of high-level officials, including those in the Justice Department, in the criminal activities and the cover-ups, I felt that an imaginative use of the law and other means must be used to meet these responsibilities.

I suggested using the book route to force government and non-government checks and balances to address the corruption that he and other conscientious people were trying to expose and correct. Failure to do so could only make possible the continued infliction of great harm upon the United States and its people.

It wasn't as if we were exposing secret operations or operatives engaging in lawful activities. We were exposing criminal and subversive activities that if not stopped, could bring about the internal collapse of the United States.

Since the government retaliation effectively silenced Taus, he decided that the national interest dictated that he and I would work together to expose and correct the corruption in government that we had discovered.

A Brief History

During two tours of duty flying combat missions in Vietnam, Taus received three Bronze Star Medals and seven Air Medals, as well as several decorations for meritorious service. In 1967-68, as an Armed Forces Courier officer, Lt. Taus fought in the Tet Offensive and flew in the siege of Khe Sanh. In 1970-71, as a Helicopter Unit Commander for the First Cavalry Division, Taus, then Captain, flew Boeing CH-47 Chinook helicopters directing rescue-and-recovery operations.

On his first tour, Taus adopted a Vietnamese orphan whom he brought back to the United States and who now bears the name, David Taus. This adoption was rather historic. It required obtaining specific approval and assistance from President Thieu and President Johnson, amending U.S. Immigration and Naturalization laws. This adoption received global media attention. David Taus would later work for the FBI in the mid-1980s as a personnel analyst in the New York Field Office.

CIA Drugging of American GIs

While he was a helicopter unit commander and pilot in Vietnam, Taus reported to his supervisors the widespread drug trafficking by the Central Intelligence Agency. Taus described how the CIA carried drugs that were sold to American GIs in Vietnam and Laos, causing over a third of the armed forces to become drug addicts. These GIs were often too drugged out to either fight or defend themselves. In addition, in that condition they often killed their own officers, a practice known as "fragging."

Taus described an incident that occurred while he was on a helicopter mission in Vietnam. He heard a radio distress call from the pilot of an Air America C-46 as the plane was about to make a crash landing. (Air America was one of many CIA airlines.) Taus landed at the crash site, offering to fly the unharmed pilots to their base of operations, but the Air America crew refused to leave the aircraft, saying they would wait for Air America people to arrive. The reason for refusing to leave the aircraft was suggested by the nature of the cargo, which consisted of about 4,000 pounds of heroin.

Upon return to base, Taus made a written report to his military unit describing the heroin on the Air America plane. He also sent a letter to his New York congressman concerning the drug smuggling by the CIA. A congressional "investigation" followed, which covered up for the CIA's drug smuggling. The final report stated that the heroin on the Air America aircraft was not for the

CIA but for the personal use of the crew. Four thousand pounds of heroin for the personal use of the crew?

Reports that I have received over the years from many military and CIA people made it obvious that the military was heavily involved in drug trafficking. It is ironical, and this is surely a mild word for it, that the public is paying billions of dollars a year for CIA, DEA, Customs, and the military (among others), to stop the flow of drugs into the United States, while these same government entities are actually involved in drug trafficking. The implications of this are, of course, horrendous. But who's going to tell the people? And will they listen?

CIA Infiltrating the FBI

Taus explained how the CIA had infiltrated the FBI and discovered the names of FBI agents and informants, and investigations that could expose covert and criminal CIA operations. The CIA knowingly gave false information to FBI agents, jeopardizing FBI missions and misleading top Justice Department and White House personnel. Most of this false information is still in FBI records.

FBI's Assassins

For years I had been told by some of my CIA contacts that the FBI had assassins in their employ, and I found this hard to believe. Although CIA assassinations were admitted to me by my CIA contacts—at least two of whom participated in assassinations early in their CIA careers—I had difficulty accepting the fact that the FBI would stoop to this level. Hearing it from Taus, an FBI veteran gave support to what other deep-cover operatives had told me in the past. One of the FBI names that were frequently repeated as an assassin for the FBI was Chuckie Peters.

"I never thought the FBI would do something like this"

Taus said the third assassination, of Steve Lopez, was conducted by FBI agents, and received media attention in *The Staten Island Advance* and the *New York Post*. Taus said, "I never thought the FBI would do something like this." Taus said that he reported these assassinations to his FBI supervisor, Manny Gonzalez, who replied he "could do nothing to assist me with these revelations." In 1993, Gonzalez was appointed by Louis Freeh to be an Assistant Director-In-Charge of the Federal Bureau of Investigation.

CIA Arming the IRA

Taus described discovering that the CIA provided arms to the IRA. In *Defrauding America* I mentioned Stephen Crittenden, the head of a covert CIA airline, who described to me flying a C-130 into Ireland with a load of arms for the IRA. Based upon his vast FBI background, Taus wrote about the Mafia's infiltration of government:

There is a sanctioned Mafia organization that works within our government and industries. I know. I have discovered it under the veneer of the surface "street gangsters" such as Gotti, Scarpa, Bonanno, etal, who answer to an appointed Godfather (the late Paul Castellano). In turn, Paul takes orders from his first cousin Vito Castellano who works for the Governor of New York in Albany, N.Y. Incredible? I do not know who is boss now. Taus told me about his informant who had revealed the CIA drug route that was associated with the Pan Am Flight 103 disaster over Lockerbie.

The Enterprise Involving the CIA, NSC, and Oliver North

The K-Team had a front operation with the patriotic-sounding name, National Freedom Institute, and called its operations the "Enterprise." Taus said that this was the "Enterprise" that repeatedly surfaced in the Iran-Contra congressional hearings that involved Ollie North.

During this investigation Taus' team discovered that the K-Team was a CIA operation and that it was engaging in drug trafficking, looting of savings and loans, and activities related to what later became known as Irangate and Iraqgate. Taus' team discovered in 1983 that K-Team members arranged for Iraq to obtain U.S.-backed loans for agricultural products and that the money was used to purchase war material. These loans and the purchase of war material continued until Iraq used the military weapons to invade Kuwait.

The "Enterprise" involved among others, Lt. Col. Oliver North, Navy Vice Admiral John M. Poindexter, and Air Force Major General Richard V. Secord. Several years before the public heard about that operation, Taus was reporting their illegal activities in FBI reports.

A clue leading to the disclosure of the commodity fraud was the FBI's discovery that one of the Iraqi players in the US loans for commodities was a major arms dealer. Officials in the Reagan White House in 1983 knew that Fadhil Al-Marsoumi, Baghdad's largest weapons dealer, was behind the 1983 request for U.S. commodities credits. The Reagan-Bush team knew of the diversion of U.S. funds for military use years before the 1989 Iraqi invasion of Kuwait and made possible the invasion by providing funds, intelligence, and help in acquiring equipment and chemicals.

As the investigation continued, it was learned that the Iran and Iraq scandals were not only a CIA operation, but that high level federal officials were implicated, including Vice President George H.W. Bush.

Investigating the CIA-Front, the K-Team

In the 1970s, the FBI started receiving reports of criminal activities involving a group known as the "K-Team " operating out of Freeport, Long Island. Taus' FBI superiors ordered him in 1981 to start an undercover operation to investigate this group. The cover for this FBI investigation was the Freeport Soccer Club, and enabled the FBI to infiltrate the K-Team operation. During that investigation, Taus discovered the K-Team operations included several CIA operatives.

Foreign Media Circumvented U.S. Media Cover-Up

Foreign newspapers started exposing the Iran-Contra activities, circumventing the U.S. media cover-up. The foreign exposures forced Congress to address the issues, at least the outer fringes. Taus wrote:

When the revelations occurred in November 1986, the Team became increasingly desperate. The FBI files were being filled with misinformation about the "Enterprise" and its team members. There were assassinations.

I was instructed by my FBI supervisor, Patrick Groves, to "eliminate" my informants and cooperatives who were no longer interested in cooperating with the K-Team's own investigation. The FBI case agent on the " K-Team" case, Carmine Rivera, told me that I would be seriously hurt by my continuing investigation into Oliver North's Enterprise. Finally, supervisory FBI officials warned me "to desist or you will be in great trouble."

The FBI was doing everything possible to cover up for the criminal activities that independent prosecutor Lawrence Walsh was empowered to investigate. Taus wrote that the FBI cover-up was in part unnecessary, as Walsh covered up for the hard-core criminal aspects associated with the Iran-Contra affair, as did members of Congress.

Walsh had received boxes of hard evidence on the drug trafficking from state and federal investigators, and from sources sending him evidence, including the evidence that I sent to him. Taus identified this cover-up as he wrote, "Walsh conducted his investigations into the Irangate affair using the same FBI agents who tried to cover up the matter at the direction of the CIA." Taus wrote that a young staff lawyer for Walsh, Jeffrey Tobin, was continually stifled by the FBI under the umbrella of the phony "national security" label. (Tobin wrote a book, *Opening Arguments*, about these cover-up problems.)

Pizza Connection

As an FBI special agent working under Assistant U.S. Attorney (AUSA) Louis Freeh, and during the investigation culminating in the well-publicized Pizza Connection, Taus discovered CIA involvement in organized crime's drug trafficking. During these investigations Taus discovered that pizza parlors and cheese factories were fronts for organized crime's drug trafficking operations. This became known as the Pizza Connection, and propelled Louis Freeh to prominence in the FBI.

The discovery of CIA drug trafficking by Taus and other FBI agents with whom he was working came about as a result of their investigations into organized crime activities, including the Pizza Connection cases. Their discovery was aided by the report of the Pennsylvania Crime Commission Report on drug trafficking among the pizza and cheese industries. The Pennsylvania report described extensive interstate and international drug-trafficking involving Mafia figures throughout the United States and Canada, and the heavy involvement of the CIA in these activities.

It was Taus' belief that there was a conflict between the Sicilian Mafia drug activities and that of the American Mafia, and that the CIA's connections were with the American Mafia. He felt that the selective crackdown on organized crime drug trafficking was initiated against the Sicilian Mafia because it was creating friction and competition with the CIA-backed American Mafia drug activities.

Also, the Pizza Connection drug charges focused on the lower level Mafia figures while protecting high-level personnel in industry and government. Taus explained the obstacles blocking prosecution by well-placed political figures, judges, and others. He explained how AUSA Freeh blocked the issuance of subpoenas for such companies as Cremosa and Drexel-Castle, which had CIA connections.

He explained that the American Mafia was an entrenched third generation and that the Sicilian Mafia, which was more violent, was creating not only competition in the drug business but also causing too much friction.

Making Taus' revelations especially valuable is that I was receiving insider information from the daughter of Albert Carone, a Mafia figure who had been concurrently working for the CIA and the New York police department. I was also receiving additional insider information from several CIA operatives concerning the relationship between the CIA and organized crime in the New York and other areas. This information provided even more support to what I had already learned about the decades of CIA working relationship with organized crime in drug smuggling and other racketeering activities.

The media showed Louis Freeh as being responsible for developing the Pizza Connection case, but Taus explained that the credit goes to the Pennsylvania Crime Commission. At that time, Freeh was a new assistant U.S. Attorney (AUSA).

Discovering Other CIA Drug Connections

During the investigation, Taus discovered that several of those involved in the drug trafficking were members of the CIA's secret group in Freeport, Long Island. One was Sal Imbergio, who ran for mayor in that town. Several of the CIA K-team operation were associated with a nearby CIA-related firm called Drexel Company, which later changed its name to Castle Securities after its CIA-controlled Cayman Island parent, Castle Bank.

Taus explained that the Drexel Company was connected to the larger business firm of Drexel, Burnham, Lambert, a junk-bond securities company with Mafia associates and high-ranking political connections in New York state. He explained that he tried to show Freeh the connections between the Drexel firm and the drug activities of the Pizza Connection, but Freeh refused to act on the information, concentrating instead upon certain segments of the Mafia. Freeh was protecting the Mafia segments that had current CIA drug trafficking relations. Taus explained, "Other known figures with connections or associations to the CIA escaped federal prosecution."

Mafia, Drugs, Savings & Loans, and the CIA

Taus listed many of the Mafia figures involved in drug trafficking, including Carmine Persico, a member of the Colombo crime family; Salvatore Piga, a Luchese crime family member; Mario Renda, a Mafia untouchable heavily involved in looting of savings and loans during the 1980s; Angelo Ruggiero, a member of the Gambino crime family; Giuseppe Lamberti and Salvatore Mazzurco, partners in the Mafia-controlled Pronto Demolition Company.

Piga went to First United Company in Garden City, Long Island, a brokerage house dealing in credit exchanges, which was owned by Mario Renda. Renda had numerous foreign operations, some of which were shell companies to confuse investigators and for diverting funds. Taus explained that some of these were associated with Oliver North's Enterprise operation in Central America.

One of Renda's firms, Amalgamated Commercial Enterprise (ACE), played an important role in the weapons and drug shipments from Central and South America to Florida. ACE was also doing business with and supporting Southern Air Transport's missions involving arms and drug shipments that were part of the White House's National Security Council and CIA operations.

Taus explained the two echelons of the Mafia, the street Mafia represented by the five crime families in New York and the higher-level Mafia imbedded in blue-chip Fortune 500 corporations and in high government positions.

Southern Air Connection to Drugs and the CIA

Taus described how his investigations took him to Florida and discovery of Southern Air Transport's relationship to the CIA and drug trafficking, which provided more corroboration to what was revealed to me by my many CIA sources over the last decade. He also discovered National Security Council's Oliver North's involvement in drug trafficking, which takes us right up to the steps of the White House. Taus' statements about CIA drug trafficking, the involvement of Southern Air Transport, for instance, coincided with what several of my deep-cover sources told me, and as described in part in earlier pages.

Taus described what appeared to be a two-tier Mafia, in which the Sicilian drug trafficking in the Pizza case was interfering with other government drug-routes and supplies from the Middle East through Lebanon, Syria, Bulgaria and Turkey. It was this competition that caused Justice Department officials to eliminate the Sicilian's drug business. In other investigations, Taus discovered the involvement of CIA operatives in the K-Team operations at Freeport, Long Island.

More Evidence of CIA Looting of Savings and Loans

In addition to the vast amount of evidence given to me by various CIA operatives describing the CIA's looting of savings and loans, Taus described the same problems that he uncovered during his FBI investigations. As he explained to me, "The [Freeport] CIA station was involved in financial fraud with unsecured loans, unauthorized securities, dummy shell corporations, and the bilking of numerous savings and loans."

He described the CIA's unlawful participation and meddling into areas handled by other government agencies, such as the State Department, Defense, and Commerce. He described how Irangate and Iraqgate were some of the consequences of the illegal CIA activities.

He explained how the CIA had numerous shell companies, proprietary airlines, ship and land transportation resources to get products to market. Of course, the Korean, Vietnam, and Nicaraguan conflicts in which the CIA was involved, provided additional logistics for drug shipments to the United States.

Details of everything that Taus found during his FBI investigations had been told to me by my CIA and other deep-cover sources, some of whom were carrying out these activities under orders of their superiors or handlers.

Working Under FBI Supervisory Agent Lindley DeVecchio

Taus, with worldwide experience as a war veteran and in covert operations before joining the FBI, worked under the younger Lindley DeVecchio, who had joined the FBI out of college.

DeVecchio received his promotion from Special Agent to Supervisory Agent on the basis of his work in prosecuting CIA agent Edwin Wilson. Wilson had sold weapons to Libya and supplied arms to the Contras in the 1980s, as part of covert CIA operations that were secretly authorized by White House politicians.

Among DeVecchio's top-level informants was a Colombo capo named Gregory Scarpa, Sr., who had been previously terminated because of the murders he was suspected of carrying out.

DeVecchio was put in charge of the Bonanno organized crime (OC) squad in 1983, and Taus worked that assignment. But after Taus was accumulating evidence to file charges against various members of the Bonanno group, DeVecchio quickly transferred Taus out of the office, in October 1984, to the FBI's Foreign Counter-Intelligence Division. This transfer occurred about a week after one of DeVecchio's informants, Gregory Scarpa, Sr., murdered a government informant, Mary Bari.

FBI Supervisor DeVecchio Blocked Investigations

Taus described how his immediate supervisor, R. Lindley DeVecchio, refused to act on his reports of CIA-related drug trafficking. The reason why his FBI supervisor did *not* act on the CIA and American Mafia drug trafficking surfaced several years later. In late 1996, DeVecchio was charged with aiding Gregory Scarpa, a member of the Colombo organized crime family. The corrupt relationship between a Colombo mafia capo and DeVecchio started surfacing in the early 1990s.

Instructed to Falsify Reports

Taus explained that one of the events that triggered retaliation against him was his refusal to falsely sign the FBI's yearly statement requiring FBI agents to certify that they know of no unreported criminal activities. The form requires agents to report on that form any criminal activities that they know to exist. His supervisors wanted him to sign that he knew of none, when in fact he knew of a great amount of criminal activities that his supervisors wanted covered up.

When Taus refused to falsely state on that yearly form that he knew of no criminal activities, his Supervisory Special Agent warned him that he wasn't on the team. That warning, and his reporting of the criminal activities and the FBI's cover-up of them to FBI Director Sessions and Congress, was followed by the false charges against him that resulted in a virtual life sentence.

Terminating the FBI Investigation and Informants

Shortly before the 1988 presidential elections, Taus' supervisors, including Lindley DeVecchio, instructed him to shut down the undercover FBI operation and terminate the informants working for him. Three of the FBI informants failed to remain silent and sought to give their stories to the media. In 1988 and 1989, they were *really* terminated. One was an electrician, Ritchie Roberts, acting like the "plumbers" in Nixon's Watergate, rigging electrical devices such as bugging equipment, and also deactivating security alarm systems.

Another informant who refused to remain quiet was Thomas Ziegler (alias Charles Schering), a carpenter, who worked with Roberts. Both lived in Queens, New York. Roberts and Ziegler, working for the CIA's K-Team, broke into the Grenadian Mission at the United Nations building in New York, obtaining documents, and planting evidence to falsely discredit people. Taus said that CIA agents assassinated them.

Circumventing the FBI Obstruction of Justice

Outraged at the FBI's cover-up of the CIA drug trafficking, the corruption leading up to the arming of Iraq through sham agricultural loans, the cover-up of assassinations, and other crimes, Taus wrote to FBI Director William Sessions, reporting the criminal activities that his group had discovered, and the cover-up by his FBI supervisors. When Sessions did not respond, Taus wrote letters to members of Congress. None responded, a reaction that I repeatedly encountered during the 40 years, starting while I was a federal agent, of reporting major corruption to members of Congress. To me, they are the nation's top obstruction of justice group.

CIA Assets in Congress

Taus wrote, "Some of our infamous congressional leaders are either former CIA agents, such as Congressman Henry J. Hyde, or stooges for them, such as Arlen Specter, Charles Schumer (now a senator), Alfonse D'Amato and even my own representative, Peter King of Nassau County."

Using a Standard Prosecutor Obstruction of Justice Tactic

On November 4, 1988, shortly before the presidential elections where George H.W. Bush was seeking reelection, it became necessary to silence or discredit FBI agent Taus. He was arrested by his own FBI associates on sham charges, thereby eliminating any threat of exposing Bush's involvement in the criminal activities. The FBI charged Taus with using a government credit card to obtain nine dollars worth of fuel for his car. Taus had used the credit card during a criminal investigation when a government car was not available and he had to use his personal car. The other federal charge involved sexual allegations allegedly occurring almost a year earlier.

The arrest was obviously intended to discredit Taus and the reports that he had been making. Taus' letters to FBI chief William Sessions and to Congress about the criminal activities of the CIA and White House personnel required that he be silenced or discredited. The enormous power of the federal government and government offices were then exercised.

Using People in State Agencies to Obstruct Justice

State prosecutors and judges routinely work with federal prosecutors to assist in silencing or ganging up on a particular individual. And this was done in Taus' case. Federal prosecutors wanted to move the case against Taus into state court, apparently to avoid Taus claiming that the federal charges were retaliation for reporting high-level criminal activities.

Using State Agencies in the Conspiracy

After the federal charges had been filed, a political New York state prosecutor filed criminal charges against Taus, alleging sexual misconduct with several young boys who were members of the Freeport Soccer Club, the organizational structure used by the FBI for two undercover cases.

After these state charges were filed, federal charges were then dropped. Bail was set by the Nassau County district lawyer and cooperating state judge at an unprecedented $2,500,000, insuring that Taus would not be free to report the government corruption.

By getting a state prosecutor to carry out the scheme, there was less chance of associating the charges with efforts to silence his reporting of criminal activities on the federal level.

Judge Blocked Presentation of Exculpatory Evidence

Taus explained how New York State Judge Edward Baker refused to allow the jury to hear any testimony or disclosures about the government's motivation for arresting him. Judge Baker refused to allow evidence to be presented showing that the boys who made the charges had first denied that there were any sexual violations.

Prosecutors Threatening the Alleged Sexual Victims

Judge Baker also refused to allow testimony showing that the families of the boys had been earlier charged with criminal offenses and that the charges were dropped after the boys testified as the prosecutors wanted them to do. Also, that the boys were themselves threatened with incarceration if they did not testify as prosecutors wanted. There were other judicial violations that denied Taus a fair trial.

The trial record included sworn testimony by senior FBI supervisory agents stating that "Taus was involved in highly sensitive national security cases," and that "his arrest was ordered at the highest level in Washington."

The charges against Taus to silence him were a joint effort between the FBI-DOJ and the Nassau County district attorney. The need to get Taus immediately out of the FBI office was accomplished by charging Taus with a sham federal offense: using a government-issued credit card to put nine dollars of fuel into the private automobile he was using to carry out government surveillance activities while the government-issued car was being repaired. Then, with apparent behind-the-scene coordination between the Department of Justice officials and District Attorney Denis Dillon, the sham improper sexual conduct charges were made.

The district attorney then did what is often done; he pressured teen-age witnesses, their parents, some of whom were threatened with criminal violations, to testify, as the prosecutor wanted them to testify.

Violating Taus' Due Process Rights and Protections

FBI 302 Interview forms and other material that the FBI turned over to the Nassau County district attorney, that included 24 witnesses who said Taus was innocent, was withheld from Taus' defense lawyers, and not discovered until ten years later by his appellate attorney, with the names redacted. Attempts to obtain the names of those blacked out were denied by Washington Department of Justice officials.

The withheld material showed that Taus was innocent, and the withholding of that evidence was not only a corrupt act by the prosecutor but also violated Taus' due process rights to a fair trial. FBI Special Agent Ron Mchaffrey attended Taus' trial and told Taus' attorney that certain material documents and interview statements were missing.

Help from Old Friends

MIT Professor Noam Chomsky tried to help Taus by referring him to John Kelly, the former U.S. Assistant Secretary of State for Near Eastern and Asian Affairs. Kelly wanted to do a story about the FBI cover-up on his 1994 Public Broadcasting Series (PBS-TV), *Inside the FBI*, but Taus declined, fearing possible violations of the Secrecy Agreement Act. Kelly later testified before Congress after the "surprise" Iraqi invasion of Kuwait, explaining that the State Department was unaware of Iraq's intentions. The CIA knew what was coming, as did the National Security Council. There is little doubt that the FBI was left in the dark or simply supplied with misinformation by the CIA.

32 to 90 Year Prison Sentence Insured Taus' Silence

Psychiatrists and psychologists hired by the prosecutor admitted that Taus told them that there was a major cover-up and conspiracy involving the Iran-Contra scandal, told them of the CIA drug trafficking activities and that it reached into the highest office in the country, and included Vice President George Bush. They testified that Taus described the cover-up of high-level criminal activities, adding that in their many years of experience they felt Taus was telling the truth. The jury, probably believing that surely the government would not be charging Taus with the offenses if he weren't really guilty, held Taus guilty in November 1990, and Judge Baker sentenced Taus to prison for 32 to 90 years!

That sentence was outrageous even if, for argument, Taus *had* been guilty of improper sexual encounters. Contrast this with the refusal to prosecute (or the relatively minor charges against) the hundreds of Catholic and other priests who actually preyed on boys. Over a period of years I discovered that sham child molestation charges are common tactics to silence or discredit state or federal agents who blow the whistle on high-level government corruption.

Removal of His Accusers for Sex and Other Offenses

After Taus was convicted and sentenced, nearly all of his opponents were fired or resigned. The prosecutor and Deputy Chief District Attorney J. Kenneth Littman, who prosecuted Taus for alleged sexual violations, was ousted by the District Attorney for soliciting sex with a minor in the Nassau County courthouse.

A November 6, 1993, New York *Daily News* article addressed the matter with the title, "Prober A Heel: Long Island Teen." A November 5, 1993, article in *Newsday* was titled, "Prosecutor Ousted." Taus' trial judge, Edward Baker, retired under questionable circumstances while making front-page headlines in the August 13, 1993, issue of *Newsday*.

FBI Director Sessions and FBI ADIC Fox Were the Next Ones Fired

FBI Director William Sessions was later fired by President Clinton after Sessions stated he would make an investigation of government corruption. The Assistant Director-In-Charge of the FBI's New York office, James Fox, who was present when Taus was falsely arrested, was suspended shortly before he was to retire. He refused to retract a statement that he made to the media declaring the innocence of another government agent being falsely charged to silence his exposure of high-level drug activities and political bribery: Immigration and naturalization Agent Joseph Occhipinti.

Occhipinti is described in other pages. Occhipinti had sought to expose Dominican drug trafficking and drug money bribes to U.S. politicians and ended up being charged by DOJ prosecutors with violating the civil rights of a bodega operator. The stress on Fox may have contributed to his subsequent demise.

Confirmation of His FBI Reports on Criminal Activities

In seeking to obtain evidence revealing the probable retaliatory acts originating from within the Justice Department, Taus requested under the Freedom of Information Act files concerning him and his reports of criminal activities involving Iraq, Iran, and CIA drug trafficking. The FBI replied in an October 1995 letter that the FBI had over 2,400 pages containing both his name and matters relating to Irangate, but refused to give him copies. Taus had no copies of the records that he prepared as an FBI Special Agent, and as he said, if he *had* kept copies, they would have been seized when the FBI ransacked his home after the false charges were made.

Encouraging Taus to Report FBI-DOJ Corruption

I explained to Taus that there was a U.S. Supreme Court decision rendered about 15 years earlier stating that a federal employee had a greater duty to report criminal activities by his superiors than a duty to cover up for such crimes because of an employee secrecy agreement. I also explained that in my opinion, the statutory requirement to report federal crimes, such as required by federal criminal statute Title 18 U.S.C. § 4, superseded any secrecy agreement required to be signed by government employees or agents. Taus said he did all he could to report these federal crimes, but the cover-up was too pervasive, reaching senior FBI officials such as ADIC Oliver "Buck" Revell, who had earlier stalled and stopped legitimate FBI investigations concerning both the Irangate and Iraqgate scandals.

Continued Disclosures

Taus wrote about the mysterious death of William Sullivan, Assistant Director of the FBI, who resigned from the FBI after more than 36 years of service. He quit because of the cover-ups by the FBI, including the cover-ups by former FBI Director J. Edgar Hoover. Sullivan was responsible for Taus' entry into the FBI and the two of them had a close relationship. Sullivan's attempt to expose some of the FBI's cover-up activities was halted by his suspicious death in a 1977 hunting accident.

Taus explained how the CIA engaged in "plausible deniability," adding that responsibility cannot be avoided legally, as an agency relationship exists in all their operations, whether conducted by their bona-fide special Agents or operatives.

Limited Media Exposure

An article in the October 28, 1991, issue of *Time* was titled, "Reagan Knew Everything." An October 26, 1992, article in *US News & World Report* was titled, "Cover-Up." An informative article on the K-Team activities was found in the December 4, 1992 issue of *Washington City Paper*.

Other disclosures of what Taus discovered were later contained in an article by Ben Bradlee appearing in *Guts & Glory*. The media reported the existence of the K-Team that Taus and other FBI agents discovered to be a CIA operation in Freeport, and that it was the home of the infamous "Enterprise" operated by the National Security Council's Oliver North.

The K-Team carried out the secret operations of CIA-Director William Casey and the NSC's Oliver North when the Reagan Administration fueled the war in Nicaragua, undermining the government that had replaced the brutal CIA-backed Somoza regime. The CIA reacted to this publicity with the standard practice of releasing a report with some truth to it and then building on it with false information, denying that it had any part in the K-Team operation.

Federal Bureau of Investigation

RICHARD M. TAUS
Special Agent

95-25 Queens Blvd.
Rego Park, NY 11374

(212) 459-3140

Taus boarding his helicopter in Vietnam

The following is an affidavit prepared by former FBI Special Agent Richard Taus relating to corruption that he discovered.

Affidavit of Richard M. Taus

I, Richard M. Taus, declare and state: I am a former Special Agent for the Federal Bureau of Investigation assigned to the New York Field Office and the Brooklyn-Queens Metropolitan Resident Agency from July 1978 to November 1988. I was assigned to both the Foreign Counter-Intelligence Division and the Criminal Division.

During this period of time, my investigations into these matters revealed criminal activities and operations which I reported and documented to my superiors in the FBI, as follows:

The involvement of officials, agents and operatives of the Central Intelligence Agency (CIA) with organized crime members and drug-trafficking activities. And the participation by members of the CIA who engaged in the looting of the Savings & Loan (Thrift) Industries, financial scams and fraudulent securities transactions.

The involvement of people from the National Security Agency Staff and Council and the White House in criminal activities associated with funding the acquisition of military supplies and equipment, arms and ammunition which were referred to as the Iran-Contra Area Initiative, known as Irangate, and the Iraqi Scandal, known as Iraqgate.

The association between known and suspected members of the Mafia and CIA agents in conducting drug-trafficking activities and financial frauds

I was ordered by my supervisors in the FBI to halt these investigations, destroy my written reports, terminate my informants and make no reference to these criminal and subversive activities implicating high-ranking government officials, politicians, Mafia and business leaders who controlled and manipulated government agencies and operations

Without any support from my superiors at the FBI New York Field Office, I then sent a letter describing what I had discovered in my official status as an FBI Special Agent to the FBI Director, William Sessions, and this was ignored. I proceeded to write Congressional officials, among them Senators Arlen Specter, Alfonse D'Amato, John Kerry and Congressman Norman Lent, Charles Schumer, and many others who were on both the Senate and House Intelligence Oversight Committees. None of the above officials or representatives provided any support or assistance in exposing the CIA-White House corruption and the obstruction of justice tactics by my FBI superiors.

I declare and affirm under penalty of perjury that these statements are true to the best of my knowledge and belief. Executed this 13th day of August 1997, in the County of Clinton, State of New York.

Linda O'Connor Richard M. Taus

Notary seal

Making Friends in Prison with Pakistani CIA Asset

Taus was sentenced to prison and incarcerated at the state prison in Dannemora, New York. In prison, Taus met another inmate who was a former Pakistani air force captain, Mian Farooq. Farooq knew one of the terrorists who would be involved in the 9/11 hijackings, Mohamed Atta. In one of Taus' letters to me he wrote:

Farooq said that in 1996 he met Mohamed Atta at JFK International Airport dressed in an airline captain's uniform. He knew Atta and asked him why he was so dressed and Atta replied that he owned a flight school operation in Florida. His story about his acquaintance with Atta indicated he was very friendly with Atta. Repeatedly, prior to the 9/11 disaster, he often mentioned that we Americans do not know the depths of hatred and ill feelings toward us by Middle Easterners.

He was indeed expecting something to happen. Prior to 9/11, he approached me to contact trusted FBI agents to give his story, but it was not until the 9/11 tragedy that he finally spoke about some of his knowledge. He felt it could and should have been prevented, though he said there would be terrorist attacks.

In short, working for the CIA, he knew that attacks were being planned and he was stunned when 9/11 occurred, saying to me, that it was Mohamed Atta and his associates that did the awful deed.

I immediately notified prison officials as to the value of this information and they were cooperative. I said I would contact my law enforcement friends on the outside, since NYS DOCS was unsure about how to handle the information.

My friends, such as NYPD Captain Rudy Blaum, spoke directly to the FBI New York Field Office on everything and requested FBINYO to interview the Pakistani and me. It was not until after the first national alert of another pending attack [weeks later] that two "country-club" agents finally interviewed me. They were arrogant, uninterested and ill prepared for the interview. In fact, when they later interviewed the Pakistani, the Pakistani said they were incompetent! They knew nothing about terrorist or foreign counter-intelligence work!

[FBI Incompetence Related To Terrorist Plans]

He then refused to give them any further information, especially after they tried to disparage me. (That I deeply resented since I served this nation in war and peace with honor and courage. I found the Pakistani to be more honorably and respectful of me than the incompetent FBI agents who knew of my military and FBI service!)

[CIA Handler Warned Him Not To Disclose Knowledge]

Later, within a week, probably in late September or early October 2001, the CIA agent that handles the Pakistani came here and warned him not to say anything to anyone. Again in confidence, he told me about their implied threats to him.

After the second national alert, probably in October or November 2001, the Pakistani again shared some information, asking me to see if the FBI would do anything. With no response from FBI Headquarters, the Pakistani decided to wait until something positive happened with his own criminal appeal. Finally, when FBI SA Rowley spoke out, the Pakistani asked me to arrange an interview with her. Again, I advised prison officials who let me proceed, mailing her information and phoning her. I explained to Rowley that she should call the Superintendent and fax them reasons why she wanted to interview the Pakistani, which was exactly what I was told to do by prison officials here.

The Pakistani says he has not heard from Rowley. I feel the reason is that CIA is claiming a working relationship with him, whether former CIA agent or source, and thereby preventing the FBI from interviewing him, a sort of "gentlemen's agreement" on using informants.

There is no doubt that his revelations would also confirm the information I had told the FBI about, as long ago as 1986(!), that the FBI was not paying any attention to their investigative duties and responsibilities. Herein is the FBI complacency, if not complicity in these terrible events. As I often said the FBI is deliberately ill equipped, under-trained, and disinterested in doing its most important investigations. Even FBI Director Mueller commented on the shambles of archaic and assorted computer equipment that the Bureau is still using.

From my experience, the FBI has been set up to be ineffective in doing its FCI and counter-terrorism tasks. And the FBI's failure to address the information from the Pakistani and me, in a timely fashion and with proper resources (interviewers) proves this real conspiracy against all Americans who rely upon their law enforcement efforts. (I could easily get into the many other minor cases that the FBI pursues, but I will bite my tongue for now).

The United States government is more concerned about who gave the Iraqi the NBC (nuclear, biological and chemical) capacity. Isn't it the same government that supplied both sides in the Iranian-Iraqi War with weapons! Now it is all coming back to haunt U.S. intelligence, just as CIA-trained Osama bin-Laden has done. When the U.S. government engages and works with criminals, psychopaths and evil men, we can expect the worse.

Referring to Farooq, Taus wrote, "I believe he has been truthful and that he knows much more, but is fearful of CIA reprisals."

Blocking Report on Terrorist Activities from Atta's Friend

After the 9/11 attacks, FBI agent Coleen Rowley sent a letter (May 21, 2002) to FBI director Robert Mueller complaining about the poor response to agent's reports. For that, *Time* magazine named her one of the three women of the year. Some might wonder why she didn't do that before the 9/11 attack, and did it only after it was safe to complain.

Taus described how he had sent Coleen Rowley a 40-page report describing what the Pakistani was willing to tell her or any other FBI agent. He included details about what he had earlier discovered about terrorist activities while head of an FBI investigative group, about his discovery of the funding and arming of Iraq through the U.S. Department of Agriculture loan guarantee program, and the CIA-drug smuggling, among other corruption in key government offices. Despite her alleged courageous speaking out, she ignored this additional information from a Pakistani who knew Atta, the main pilot in the 9/11 hijackings.

FBI Indifference To Information From Atta's Close Friend

Referring to the refusal of FBI agents to pay attention to the Pakistani, with contacts in al Qaeda cells, willing to provide information about terrorists that he knew, Taus wrote in an earlier letter:

> He and I, separately, have been interviewed by FBI agents from the Plattsburgh Resident Agency Office of the FBI. FBI SAs Steven Weisknopf and Thomas Longerhan were not interested in hearing our stories. They conducted the interviews only because there was another national alert and the FBI already had egg-on-its-face from the 9/11 WTC tragedy.
>
> Farooq was also interviewed by a CIA agent here who, in the past, told him to "clam-up," otherwise the CIA would not help him with his appeal. I told him that if the CIA were going to do anything to help him, he would have already been out on bail. For whatever reason, the CIA let him go through the trial, although he possesses sensitive information on the terrorist investigations.
>
> Finally, after the abortive interviews and lack of any relief for him from the CIA or anyone else, he said he would speak to FBI SA Coleen Rowley, and only her. [Rowley was the FBI whistleblower that was given widespread media attention for sending a letter to the media complaining about FBI inaction—something known for decades.]
>
> I should also note that prison authorities have been very cooperative with me since this information affects Homeland Security.
>
> **[Refusal to Obtain Terrorist Information]**
>
> I can only speculate as to the reasons the FBI did not contact the Pakistani for his information. He was a key source, a friend of Atta, a former Pakistani pilot, and an intelligence officer in Pakistan. He could have been a gold mine of information for preventing further terrorist activities. No competent intelligence entity would ignore such a source and such information. Refusal to obtain the Pakistani's information could be due to (1)

danger of focusing attention on how the FBI silenced Taus when Taus was exposing CIA drug smuggling, (2) unlawful funding and arming of Iraq by the Reagan-Bush administrations; (3) incompetence; or (4) other unknowns.

Former FBI Agent Describing FBI Director's Dubious Past

Taus described the role played by FBI Director Mueller in protecting the Winter Hill organized crime activities in Boston, including the FBI's involvement in numerous murders and assassinations. (That subject is described in later pages.) Taus wrote (August 23, 2002):

> Getting back to FBI Director Mueller. He's implicated in the Boston FBI cover-up and trial of former FBI agent John Connolly back in May-June 2002. Mueller was the acting US Attorney in Boston when the FBI continued its cover-ups of Mafia and other mobsters, most notably Whitey Bugler.
>
> Because of former acting US attorney Mueller involvement, the Boston police department stated that the FBI has for more than 30 years protected the mobsters and stymied their (BPD) investigations. The Boston FBI case is similar to my case with the Supervising FBI SAR, Lindley DeVecchio who covered for Mafia Capo Gregory Scarpa.

Mueller's History of Cover-ups

Mueller was the U.S. Attorney in San Francisco where I reported to him in 1997 areas of documented criminal activities described in *Defrauding America*. These include, for instance, the criminality in the government's aviation safety offices, the FBI, the bankruptcy courts, the federal courts, and the actions by federal judges blocking the reporting of criminal activities.

The criminal activities, and his cover-up of them, assisted in making possible the continuation of the great harm upon national interests, including national security. On the basis of his obstruction of justice in these matters, it is natural to assume that he would continue the cover-ups in the ultra political office of U.S. Attorney General. If he had acted, or any of the other people that I notified had acted, actions could have been started that most probably would have prevented the successful terrorist acts on September 11, and very possibly have discouraged terrorists from plans for more attacks upon U.S. interests.

Other Areas of Cover-up by Mueller

Mueller was involved in the prosecutions related to the bombing of Pan Am flight 103 and surely knew of the false charges against the Libyans and knew the Syrian terrorists who actually placed the bomb on Pan Am under an Iranian contract in retaliation for U.S. forces shooting down an Iranian airliner that killed 290 people.

He was in the U.S. Attorney's office during the massive bankruptcy court corruption involving Justice Department trustees, judge-appointed trustees, and federal judges, and which continues to this date. These matters are detailed in the third and later editions *of Defrauding America* and *Unfriendly Skies: 20th & 21st Centuries.* (Replaced by *History of Aviation Disasters: 1950 to 9/11.*)

He was acting U.S. Attorney in Boston during the time that the Boston FBI office was protecting organized crime figures and murderers in the Winter Hill gang. He came to the U.S. Attorney's office in San Francisco in 1976 after leaving his lawyer role at the San Francisco law firm of Pillsbury Madison and Sutro, which are believed to have close ties to the CIA.

He was in the U.S. Attorney's office responsible for prosecuting people involved in the BCCI bank scandal that was more of a cover-up than prosecution. Charles Schumer, a U.S. representative from New York at that time, made a report claiming Justice Department personnel were refusing to pursue the case. Schumer stated "There is possibly a cover-up or conspiracy," saying the failure to pursue the criminal activities was because there were too many prominent politicians that had connections to BCCI.

The Manhattan District attorney, Robert Morgenthau, who conducted his own investigation of BCCI, accused the Justice Department of failing to pursue the case and refusing to share material evidence to prosecute the guilty. BCCI was one of the world's largest banking scandals that caused people throughout the world to lose their life's savings. This is detailed in *Defrauding America.*

Muller Covering Up For Criminal and Subversive Activities Detailed In *Defrauding America*

Mueller also covered up for the criminal activities that I brought to the attention of FBI agents in the San Francisco office while Mueller was in charge of that office. Mueller also refused to respond to the certified letters that I sent to him in that San Francisco position, after he became director of the FBI prior to September 11, 2001, and the certified letters that I sent to him after the success of 19 hijackers on that date. (Described in *Defrauding America.*)

Mueller Cover-Up In BCCI Scandal

A *Wall Street Journal* editorial (May 31, 2002) stated of Mueller's handing of the BCCI scandal:

> Prior to his appointment [to FBI director], we raised questions about his handling of the BCCI scandal while he was head of the Criminal Division in the early 1990s. In [the New York U.S. attorney's] attempts to prosecute the case, the Manhattan District Attorney felt the same kind of frustration with main Justice that Agent Rowley now feels about FBI headquarters. His appointment, we wrote, put the Bureau "in the hands of someone who will turn over no rocks and rock no boats."

Soft-Glove Criticism of the FBI

During the kid-glove investigation of events that made possible the success of the 9/11 hijackers, considerable media and congressional attention was paid to FBI agent Coleen Rowley who had written a letter to the joint congressional committee complaining about her frustration and roadblocks within the FBI—a complaint she didn't voice until it was safe to do so, after 9/11. It was also a complaint that I and other government agents had raised for years, with no action taken, except against the person making the complaint.

Talk Show Host Described FBI Cover-Up

In April 1997, radio host David Bresnahan contacted me and described how a senior FBI Special Agent from Washington had conveyed information to him of another cover-up. The agent was part of a team of 75 Special Agents and 125 clerical staff investigating criminal activities implicating former commerce secretary Ron Brown and business executives, some of who had ties to Chinese and Indonesian interests. The FBI agent confided to Bresnahan that indictments were about to be handed down involving 54 top business executives.

This FBI source said that a group of Justice Department agents barged into the offices occupied by the FBI investigative team and ordered everyone to leave the premises. The FBI investigative group was searched as they left the building to be sure that they did not take out any revealing documents.

From outside the glass-paneled offices, the FBI agents saw the Justice Department group shredding the evidence that they had accumulated and which supported the indictments that were about to be issued. As I have witnessed for over 30 years, this cover-up and obstruction of justice is routine, and no government official or employee ever goes to prison for perpetrating these crimes.

Senior FBI Agent in Charge, Los Angeles

One of my friends and sources for many years was retired FBI agent Ted Gunderson, who had been in charge of the Los Angeles office. He devoted his retirement years to exposing FBI misconduct, especially the cover-up of pedophile activities involving prominent people and government officials. In 1997 he started a campaign to reorganize the FBI, seeking to correct the many problems that he, Taus, many others, and I, discovered of that government agency.

Complicity of FBI and Other Justice Department Personnel

Starting while I was a federal aviation safety agent, and while acting as an independent counsel in the FAA, I made my charges of deadly federal criminal misconduct known to FBI agents and several U.S. attorneys, along with the head of the Department of Justice. I encountered the standard refusal to receive evidence that implicated federal personnel.

I encountered Justice Department block when I circumvented the block and appeared before a federal grand jury in Denver while I was a federal agent. I encountered their blocks when I filed federal actions under the federal crime reporting statute (18 U.S.C. § 4) seeking to report the Trojan-horse-like corruption in government offices. In 1986, Justice Department prosecutors charged me, a former federal agent and witness, with criminal contempt of court for attempting to report criminal activities, including those that created the conditions enabling terrorists to seize four airliners on 9/11.

I had notified FBI chief Robert Mueller of the criminal activities while he was in the U.S. attorney's office in San Francisco, and then after he became head of the FBI, followed by the usual cover-up. The same notification was sent to U.S. Attorney General John Ashcroft and prior U.S. Attorney Generals. They refused to receive the evidence that I and other former government agents sought to report related to other areas of corruption implicating government officials and other government personnel.

Justice Department personnel prosecuted the head of a multi-agency task force that focused on the drug operations of people in the New York-New Jersey areas, including the Jersey City terrorists who the following year bombed the World Trade Center in 1993. The prosecution of that agent halted the investigations and sent a message to other government agents not to proceed with the investigations. That obstruction of justice tactic enabled the Jersey City terrorists to proceed with the bombing of the World Trade Center a year later, in 1993.

The same culture was shown by the FBI's support for organized crime in the Boston area, with William Bulger and others, wherein FBI agents—with Washington approval—provided the names of government informants to organized crime figures, causing the informants to be murdered. I have acquired information from organized crime insiders that the same conditions existed in the New York City area, showing the widespread culture in the FBI, which obviously is not compatible with protecting U.S. interests. Considerable other evidence is available to show the depravity of this culture. I offered this information to members of Congress and the Justice Department; none responded.

As I detailed in several of my books, some of the other areas in which Justice Department personnel obstructed justice, with serious and sometimes catastrophic consequences, included the following:

- Acting in a manner that enabled terrorist group to obtain possession of large numbers of surface to air missiles in 1995.
- Filing sham criminal charges against a highly respected Customs agent and head of a multi-agency drug task force that was targeting the money source for Jersey City terrorists, which caused the investigations to end. These terrorists subsequently exploded a bomb in the World Trade Center in 1993. Ramzi Yousef, for instance, escaped and planned to place bombs on 11 U.S. airliners departing Far East locations. He also had knowledge of the planned hijacking of U.S. airliners and ramming them into buildings.
- Filing criminal contempt of court charges against me, a former federal air safety agent, for attempting to report corruption within the government's aviation safety offices, which was being reported under the mandatory requirements of the federal crime reporting statute, Title 18 U.S.C. § 4.
- Filing sham criminal charges against a former Mossad agent and head of an international investigative firm who filed a report describing the terrorists who actually placed the bomb on Pan Am Flight 103.

- Filing sham charges against a covert DIA agent who provided evidence showing a CIA-DEA drug pipeline that facilitated the placement of the bomb on Board Pan Am Flight 103 that exploded over Lockerbie.
- Filing sham criminal charges against a covert CIA agent who had provided testimony in a court proceeding about the U.S. personnel involved in paying bribes to Iranian terrorists involved in the scheme known as October Surprise.
- Filing sham criminal charges against a counter-terrorism expert, Keith Idema, who had discovered, while training Russian and Lithuanian government and military personnel, the theft of suitcase nuclear bombs and other nuclear material from Russian arsenals, and learned about FBI and CIA agents who were giving U.S. secrets to the Russians. The false charges blocked discovery of how the nuclear material was being stolen, blocked discovery of who had already received the suitcase nuclear bombs and nuclear material, and blocked discovery of the identities of the spies in the CIA and FBI.
- Filed sham criminal charges against a covert CIA agent for testifying about the U.S. personnel he saw in Europe who were involved with the scheme that bribed Iranian terrorists to delay the release of U.S. hostages held in Iran, the intent being to alter the 1981 presidential elections.

Complicity of Many Members of Congress

For several years prior to September 11, 2001, I repeatedly notified members of Congress (some by certified mail) of the serious corruption that I and other government agents had discovered in the government's aviation safety offices, within the Justice Department, and the Central Intelligence Agency. I repeatedly requested that they receive testimony and evidence from me and other former and present government agents. Our offers were repeatedly ignored.

The serious matters that I sought to report included, for instance, reports of (a) surface to air missiles being acquired by terrorists, made possible by actions of FBI and CIA personnel; (b) suitcase nuclear devices being smuggled from the former Soviet Union through Lithuania, and which will surely be used in American cities at some future date; (c) drug smuggling into the United States by people acting under cover of government positions and covert operations; (d) Soviet spies in the FBI and CIA offices, made known prior to their discovery; (e) retaliation against FBI agents seeking to report criminal activities of CIA personnel; and (f) other matters inflicting harm upon national interests.

Never Were my Charges Disputed

No one ever denied the validity of my charges. Nor would they be in a position to have done so. Initially, when the corruption was related primarily to the FAA, some members of Congress admitted the gravity of what I charged, but then refused to act on the excuse that these matters were not in their area of responsibilities. (Tell that to the families of the 9/11 victims!) The matters *were* in their areas of responsibilities. They also had the option of requesting the General Accountability Office, the congressional investigative body, to receive my evidence. They also had a responsibility under the federal crime reporting statute to receive my evidence of federal crimes.

Many Letters from Richard Taus

During the years I received many letters from Taus with inside information about the FBI culture and also mob activities. Based on this information, information provided by Gregory Scarpa, Jr. with whom I had a book contract in 2002, and other mob sources, I wrote an earlier book called, *FBI, CIA, the Mob, and Treachery*.

The following are miscellaneous comments made by Taus in these letters. In an April 4, 2006, letter to me, Taus wrote about his former supervisor, Lindley DeVecchio:

> DeVecchio was my supervisor back in 1983-84 on an FBI Criminal Division Bonanno Organized Crime (OC) squad working out of the Manhattan FBINYO. He must have previously been assigned to the Colombo OC squad to have inherited Gregory Scarpa Sr. as his informant. Obviously, the Bonanno OC squad would have dealt strictly with Bonanno Mafiosi figures, along with some Gambino OC members since both the Bonanno and Gambino families were very close.
>
> It also stood to reason that DeVecchio would want to work on another squad instead of the Colombo one in order to gain information that he handed over to the Colombo Capo Scarpa. It is apparent that whatever information DeVecchio's Bonanno squad collected that might be detrimental to the Colombo organization was quickly delivered to Scarpa. This could explain why two of my criminal cases, while I was on DeVecchio's squad, were closed, despite their importance.
>
> At this point, I have some difficulty in not believing that a greater force was behind DeVecchio's work for the Mafia. Given Scarpa's involvement with covert activities as far back as the mid-1960s, it stands to reason that DeVecchio did not conceive of this idea of protecting the Mafia alone and only based upon his own greed.
>
> It was Caproni thru U.S. District Court Judge Reena Raggi that dismissed Gregory Scarpa Jr.'s testimony and evidence against Ramzi Yousef. It was Judge Raggi who refused me bail in late 1988 and who, later, in 2005 refused to recuse herself from the 3-judge panel that heard my federal habeas corpus petition in the U.S. Court of Appeals for the 2nd Circuit. Judge John Walker was the Chief Judge on that panel, who also denied me. Walker was involved in other nefarious decisions.
>
> I always felt that DeVecchio purposefully prevented my further investigations of Asaro and Esposito. But DeVecchio accommodated me with my Freeport case which originated off of SSA Many Gonzalez' Bonanno OC squad.

Asaro was contacted by Taus, warning him against carrying out the contract against FBI SA Joe Pistone

When DeVecchio transferred me from his Criminal Division squad to a Foreign Counter-Intelligence squad, I was quite upset. And as I later discovered, that transfer was to the very squad that had CIA Station Chief and front-company President Dan Priscu as a phony FBI FCI informant.

I doubt that DeVecchio knew about Priscu and his CIA employment. But perhaps, someone higher in the FBI did and so assigned me.

There is this invisible power or force that seems to be calling the shots. From all the information I have at this time, it appears that DeVecchio was either duped by higher-ups to reopen the Scarpa informant file in 1980 (which was closed with prejudice against Scarpa since he engaged in criminal activities while an FBI informant), or, that DeVecchio was deliberately told to reopen Scarpa and use him. For nearly 11 years or more, DeVecchio did so and jeopardized his job.

Judge Jack Weinstein, in January 2004, rejected Gregory Scarpa Jr.'s testimony about Ramzi Yousef. Weinstein wrote a lengthy written 24-page decision that was worse than what NY Nassau assistant district attorney ever said about me! I find it not coincidental that three of the four federal judges that heard my appeal in 2005 were also involved in all the other aspects concerning DeVecchio, Scarpa, and Yousef.

Despite four arrests made by the FBI and MI6 (British Intelligence), after Farooq and I named Al-Qaeda suspects, we were never thanked by anyone. Sounds like the powers in charge really did not appreciate our efforts, but had little choice but to make the arrest.

In an April 6, 2006, letter, Taus wrote about the criminal investigations that were suddenly cancelled by DeVecchio:

During the time that I worked for DeVecchio, I knew that there were problems since he closed several of my Mafia cases without good reason.

New York police detective Joe Simone was on the joint task force with FBI Special Agent Chris Favo (who was on DeVecchio's Bonanno squad) and leaks to the Mafia were blamed on Simone, when they were made by DeVecchio, according to FBI agent Favo.

I still maintain that these "turf wars" (or so they appear to be) between the NY US Attorney's office/DOJ and the State DAs are controlled by higher powers (White House, CIA) who for political reason precipitated them.

Greed alone might have motivated DeVecchio, but it was sanctioned since DeVecchio was permitted (or told) to reopen Scarpa's closed informant file after it was closed with prejudice due to Scarpa's criminal activities as an informant. I believe that DeVecchio may not even be aware of how he was used in this matter.

> In the end, DeVecchio was "outed" because of Mafia friends on-the-outside who wanted their associates in federal prison freed. Greg Scarpa Junior knew the terrible truth about DeVecchio and was speaking out.
>
> The Brooklyn DA, Charles Hynes, pursued DeVecchio because his constituents, all from Brooklyn and most with Mafia ties, demanded action and ignoring they would lose their votes at the next election.

In an April 8, 2006, letter, Taus wrote about DeVecchio restoring Scarpa to Top Informant status:

> There was a greater power and reason behind DeVecchio's opening of Scarpa's closed FBI Informant file back in 1980. Someone high in the government wanted Scarpa back on its payroll, probably to defeat rival Mafia families that were engaged with the Pizza Connection case and the renegade Sicilian faction that was raking in huge profits from drug trafficking.
>
> Recall that I identified the CIA as the major "party" in this activity. The CIA removed any competition from its "sanctioned drug-trafficking." Scarpa eliminated competition for his government and for personal reasons; he had a government license to kill.

In other letters, Taus wrote about a CIA agent who supplied the FBI with false information:

> Files in the FBI have misinformation or disinformation supplied by agents and operatives of the CIA for the past 50-plus years as I had initially discovered back in the early 1980s. CIA Station Chief and Castle Securities president (circa 1983-88) was Dan Priscu, a former OSS WWII agent who merged into the fledgling CIA in 1947. He continuously supplied FBI agents with false informant information to mislead their investigative efforts.
>
> In addition, Priscu, George Hebert and Michael (or David?) Studer all admitted that they provided the FBI with false information. (Studer's security trading license was revoked by the Securities and Exchange Commission in 2004 for fraudulent financial transactions.)
>
> And the CIA had its own people in the employ of the FBI to further monitor their independent investigations. In that way, CIA avoided any legal pitfalls or legal turmoil resulting from a diligent agent's efforts. FBI SA Thomas Pierce certainly fit that profile when, as my assistant case agent, he failed to do the taskings I gave him. And so too did DeVecchio who foiled my promising Mafia cases on several occasions as they drew close to CIA operations.
>
> The internal jealousy and friction between the FBI and CIA were both real and contrived. Neither agency, along with other intelligence agencies, worked together in the best interest of all Americans. There were "turf-wars" nearly similar to the Mafia families' conflicts, but without apparent bloodshed, all in the CIA's efforts to mask its illegal activities and opera-

tions, many of which were unlawfully conducted in the US contrary to their congressional charter.

As an FBI Special Agent assigned to the FBI New York office Criminal Division, I found file after file of Mafia subjects who extorted, murdered, drug-trafficked, and other criminal activities, with impunity during the time I served in Vietnam. Those Mafiosi figures weren't indicted, prosecuted or imprisoned by my former FBI colleagues during the last 1960s and early 1970s.

An example is the Casamento Brothers who were finally prosecuted in the Pizza Connection case. During the time I served in combat, they were operating drug-trafficking activities in the states. Since that information was recorded in their old FBI files, why were there so few indictments?

I felt obligated to those who died fighting for this country, to do my part as an FBI agent and take these and other criminals off the streets. The Pizza Connection case finally did that, but only to a select fraction of those involved in such crimes. Drug trafficking, money laundering, extortion, financial frauds, and other crimes, persisted despite some valiant efforts by some FBI agents and other law enforcement officers and departments. The problem is that many such organized crime groups are sanctioned either by political, governmental, business, or organized crime leaders or a coalition of these groups.

I knew that the CIA was involved in drug trafficking overseas and even instituted the war in Vietnam. My prior experiences in Latin America confirmed that complicity. And my FBI investigations, especially under SSA Lin DeVecchio, further fortified that the CIA was involved with the Mafia and other organized crime groups.

The early 1981 investigation, the genesis of the Pizza Connection case, concentrated on the pizza and cheese industry with various wholesalers in the New York area. Cremosa Cheese company in my hometown of Freeport was frequented by several known Mafiosi figures. Disturbingly, both the FBINYO's Criminal Divisions and its Foreign Counter-Intelligence (FCI) Division had two separate investigations on a company called Drexel in Freeport.

Drexel later changed its name to Castle Securities, a CIA front dealing in financial instruments, dummy corporations, illegal international weapon transfers and sales, drug –trafficking and money laundering. Yet, neither the Criminal Division nor the FCI Division was aware of the other division's investigative efforts.

When I was later assigned to DeVecchio's OC squad, several of my promising cases were closed or stymied by him. In particular, Al Embarrato, aka Al Walker, who in 1982 was promoted to a Capo status, and Danny Asaro, another Capo, neither investigation was encouraged by DeVecchio despite successes which could have led to indictments.

There was CIA involvement in the Freeport case as clearly reflected in my investigations and from other reliable and credible researchers, including LTC Oliver North himself.

Despite all the efforts at disclosing these criminal violations, my case was stymied and delayed by the FBINYO and FBIHQS. When I refused to sign the biannual US Senate and House Intelligence Committees acknowledgment form (that I knew of no unreported crimes or activities), I was arrested on false charges the week prior to the November 1988 presidential elections. Events about DeVecchio sadly reflect a culture of cover-ups, conspiracies, and complicity and complacency by the FBI and other government agencies.

Scarpa was used by the FBI until 1975 when his file was closed (he was murdering too many people). But in 1980, DeVecchio reopened his file and Scarpa went to work again, this time killing off rival Mafia associates.

Mary Bari was murdered on September 24, 1984, and a week later I was transferred from under DeVecchio to the FBI's Foreign Counter Intelligence unit.

DeVecchio's files are periodically reviewed by his superiors, who would include the Supervisory Agent in Charge (ASAC) and by the SAC of the FBI Criminal Division in the New York offices. The mere fact that the FBI reopened the Scarpa file after knowing that he was involved in murders was an example of the culture in that agency.

The federal courts are trying to whitewash DeVecchio since his conviction [for criminal activities with Scarpa Sr.] will result in the overturning of several Mafia figures' convictions. The indictment against DeVecchio is just the tip-of-the-iceberg concerning his "misadventures" and the terrible price Americans are paying. (May 4, 2006) DeVecchio retired in 1996 after a phony FBI internal affairs (OPR) investigation cleared him!

After DeVecchio's defense attorneys asked the federal district court in New York to take over the case under federal law that says he acted "under the color of law," I believe that the feds will again try to cover up this mess.

At the time of this writing, Richard Taus, remains in prison, falsely prosecuted and given a long prison sentence, serving as a reminder to other government personnel the consequences of revealing high-level corruption. In May 2012, Taus's mother, Yolanda, died, waiting for her son to return home.

At this time, Taus can be contacted by writing to him at the following address:

Richard Taus, 91A1040 LH
Clinton C.F. POB 2001,
Dannemora, NY 12929-2001.

CHAPTER FOUR

False DOJ Charges Aided Terrorist Money Sources

INS agent Joseph Occhipinti was a key figure in fighting drug traffickers and drug cartels in the New York-New Jersey area, part of which funded terrorist activities. He spent over 20 years with the U.S. Immigration and Naturalization Service, primarily in drug-related investigations.

During that time he earned over 70 commendations and awards, including three from the U.S. Attorney General. Because of his outstanding work, he was promoted to chief of the Anti-Smuggling unit for the New York City area. In that position he gained considerable knowledge about the operation of Dominican and Middle East groups trafficking in drugs. After he discovered drug smuggling among Middle East and a CIA-front company, personnel of the U.S. Department of Justice filed sham charges against him. These tactics, duplicated many times over, would have a catastrophic effect on September 11, 2001.

Testimonial to Corrupt Politicians and DOJ Personnel

As Occhipinti brought about the arrest of many politically connected criminal elements, politicians and Justice Department personnel blocked further investigations and prosecutions. In addition, and working in unison, all three groups retaliated against him and brought an end to his long and outstanding government career. His family suffered severe hardships, and Occhipinti ended up in prison for allegedly violating the civil rights of drug traffickers—something that had never happened before.

Project Intercept

One of several multi-agency task forces Occhipinti coordinated was the 1987 operation called Project Intercept, and included personnel from the Drug Enforcement Administration (DEA), Port Authority Police Department (PAPD), and the Immigration and Naturalization Service (INS). The purpose of bringing agents from the various agencies into one group was to coordinate their investigations, evidence, and prosecution of criminal activities.

That operation was credited with identifying Dominican and Middle East groups that were involved in drug trafficking, money laundering, and alien smuggling activities. Occhipinti's group had a high arrest and conviction rate and was so successful that Project Intercept became the subject of congressional hearings.

It was so successful that—after the politically powerful Dominicans and drug traffickers complained—the INS District Director terminated it within a year of its startup. Occhipinti was then ordered to concentrate instead upon filing reports against employers who hired illegal aliens, a group that did not have the political clout of the drug traffickers and the large Dominican population.

Project Resurrect

Starting in 1988, Occhipinti coordinated another multi-agency undercover operation called Project Resurrect, involving agents from the New York City district attorney's office, Postal Inspection Service, and the U.S. Department of State. This project resulted in the successful prosecution and conviction of over two dozen Dominican organized crime figures in the New York City area.

The project exposed the role of a group known as the Federation of Dominican Merchants and Industrialists of New York, otherwise known as The Federation. This group operated bodegas, money transfer businesses, travel agencies, boutiques, loan companies, and an assortment of other businesses. (Bodegas is the term used by people in the Spanish community for grocery stores.) One of the people arrested and convicted was a key member of the federation, Executive Board member Martha Lozano.

Discovering Theft Ring at JFK Airport

One of Occhipinti's investigations focused on a high-level smuggling operation at New York's John F. Kennedy Airport. Due to a shortage of government agents, the Immigration and Naturalization Service hired private agencies to do some of its routine tasks. Wells Fargo was one of the companies hired, being responsible for placing illegal aliens, caught by INS agents, on board aircraft to be sent back to their country of origin. The company engaged in a "shell game" that protected illegal immigrants from being deported.

Corrupt employees of Wells Fargo developed a profitable scheme. When an illegal alien was arrested, his or her relatives would be contacted, and for a price, an impostor would replace the illegal alien. The impostor—who was legally in the United States—would be placed on board the aircraft and flown out of the United States. He or she would then fly back as a legal or documented alien. The illegal alien would meld into the community and most likely succeed in remaining in the United States.

Operation Red Eye

In 1989, Occhipinti was involved in another multi-agency task force called Operation Red Eye. It was composed of agents from the DEA, Port Authority, Amtrak Police Department, and INS. Its goal was to interdict at major New York City transportation centers illegal aliens smuggled into the United States via Mexico and the Canadian border.

The project was successful in apprehending alien drug couriers employed by the Dominican drug cartels and other ethnic crime groups. The operation was shut down when the U.S. Attorney's office in New York (SDNY) complained that the interdiction stops were based on racial profiling. It was irresponsible to shut down an operation aimed at Dominican crime groups on that basis when a large percentage of drug smugglers were Dominicans.

U.S. Attorney Sabotaging Drug Investigations

Over a period of time, Occhipinti found that personnel in the U.S. Attorney's office was repeatedly blocking the actions of the multi-agency task force, thereby allowing large quantities of drugs to enter the United States.

Investigating Drug-Related Murder Exposed Other Crimes

The murders (October 18, 1988) of two New York police department (NYPD) officers, Michael Buczek and Christopher Hoban, in the Washington Heights section of New York City, caused the police department to ask for Occhipinti's assistance because of his expertise in Dominican organized crime activities. (Washington Heights had turned into a major Dominican neighborhood where Dominican organized crime groups based many of their operations, and which had one of the highest homicide records.)

When I was growing up many years ago on the New Jersey side of the Hudson River across from Washington Heights, it was considered a desirable middle-class neighborhood. As a result of this investigation, the murderer was reported to be Dominican drug lord Daniel Mirabeaux.

During this investigation, Occhipinti discovered a major Dominican drug operation controlled by Freddy Antonio Then, who established training camps in the Dominican Republic teaching people how to traffic in drugs. He reportedly smuggled these people into the United States from Mexico and then arranged for these aliens to be married to U.S. citizens, and thereby obtain permanent resident status with the arranged marriage.

Occhipinti learned that Then was buying local grocery stores, bodegas, which were used for various illegal activities, such as drug trafficking and drug money laundering. Occhipinti arrested Then several times on various charges, including illegal gun possession. Then's prominence in the Dominican population and as a key member of the Federation would shortly be used against Occhipinti.

Project Bodega

Another 1989 multi-agency task force in which Occhipinti was a member was called Project Bodega. It was composed of agents from the DEA, Customs service, FBI, New York Police Department, Manhattan district attorney's office, and INS. It investigated activities at the many bodegas in the New York City area where certain known criminal activities were prevalent.

Manhattan District Attorney Supported the Task Force

Because of its many discoveries of criminal activities, the Manhattan district attorney's office was so pleased with the group's work that it assigned several of its prosecutors, including John F. Kennedy, Jr., full time to prosecute the cases that were generated.

The task force discovered a widespread pattern of criminal activities involving Middle East and Dominican groups in the New York-New Jersey area; some of them associated with bodega grocery stores operated mostly by Dominicans, Cubans, and Middle East people. During *consensual* searches of bodegas, the task force discovered evidence of drug trafficking, drug money laundering, food stamp fraud, food coupon fraud, loan sharking, and smuggling of illegal aliens.

Involvement of CIA-Front Company: Sea Crest Trading Company

Investigators discovered that many bodega activities involved Sea Crest Trading Company. That company was incorporated in Connecticut and had its main office in Greenwich, with another office in New York City. Closely tied to Sea Crest was Capital National Bank in New York, and included numerous CIA operatives from the Bay of Pigs fiasco. Sea Crest started operations in 1984, and during the 1980s and 1990s was extensively used by the CIA in various activities. It was a CIA proprietary.

Years earlier, several of my CIA sources, primarily Gunther Russbacher, described Sea Crest and Capital National Bank as CIA-front companies, and recipients of DOJ protections. The president of Capital National Bank, Carlos Cordoba, a Cuban national, was convicted in 1992 of bank fraud. Despite the seriousness of the offense, he received only a token probation sentence—which would be routine if the bank was in fact a front for the CIA.

A confidential source in the New York Police Department (NYPD) Special Investigations Unit uncovered evidence of arson and other criminal activities at Sea Crest. He discovered Sea Crest had key political connections that were protecting it against prosecution. As with other city, state and federal agents, he was intimidated and harassed by higher-ups. During the investigation, he discovered a conflict of interest between Christopher Lynn, a lawyer and member of the NYPD Civilian Complaint Review Board. Lynn defended those involved in Sea Crest's illicit activities. The confidential source reported the disappearance of critical evidence on Sea Crest's drug activities from the police department records.

An affidavit executed on March 1, 1994, by Domingo Antonio Lovera, described the growth of Sea Crest over the years in usurious loans, using Dominicans and Cubans to obtain and collect loans from bodega operators. Lovera described how Sea Crest used Capital National Bank to launder the money obtained from various illegal operations. Investigations showed that this CIA-front company made a practice of putting Dominicans into bodegas and then forcing them into various unlawful activities. Because of the high-interest and usurious loans (permitted where Sea Crest was incorporated Connecticut), and high monthly payments, bodega operators found they had to engage in criminal activities to keep from losing their businesses.

Sea Crest and Bodegas in Connecticut

In a two-part series (August 1998), the *Hartford Courant* described the activities of Sea Crest Trading Company, the Dominican-run bodegas, and various criminal activities. The articles described drug dealers ducking into bodegas immediately after making drug sales and giving the cash to the bodega operators, and drugs being purchased from the operators. Quoting Hartford police Detective Robert Lawlor:

The bodegas provided a meeting place and the cover of a legitimate business. It hasn't reached the point here that it has in New York, but it's only a matter of time.

The newspaper article made reference to a 1997 classified report by the U.S. Department of Justice on Dominican drug trafficking and said dealers "move proceeds by disguising them in the financial records of travel agencies, boutiques, grocery stores and other Dominican-run businesses." Despite the Justice Department's knowledge of Sea Crest's activities, the CIA-connected company appeared to have a get-out-of-jail card that kept them from being prosecuted; another sign of being a CIA-front or having CIA connections.

Dominican Revolutionary Party (PRD) Funding Presidential Candidates

According to an article in Puerto Rico's *El Vocero* newspaper, Dominican Revolutionary Party (PRD) members, including Simon Diaz and Pablo Espinal, contributed money to President Clinton's reelection campaign during a fund-raiser at Coogan's Irish Pub in New York's Washington Heights. The article stated that this drug-tainted money was linked to the Dominican Revolutionary party. Vice President Al Gore posed for pictures with Diaz and Espinal.

The article identified Simon Diaz as vice president of a New York City chapter of the PRD and that he was currently under investigation by the Drug Enforcement Administration (DEA) and anti-narcotic agencies concerning PRD's "alleged nexus with international drug cartels."

Private Investigator Also Uncovers Similar Criminal Activities

A concurrent investigation by a private investigator uncovered considerable evidence of criminal activities at bodegas that the multi-agency task forces were discovering, especially as it related to food coupon fraud. Private investigator Ben Jacobsen, a retired New York detective, was working as chief investigator for the A.C. Nielson Corporation, which administered the food coupon program for many large companies selling to grocery stores. Corporations estimated that they were losing over $200 million a year in fraudulent coupon redemptions. Jacobsen's investigation uncovered canceled checks and other evidence showing Sea Crest Trading Company and one of its associate companies, Control Book Keeping, to be behind this practice.

The food coupon fraud worked like this: People involved in the fraud brought into a central location newspapers and magazines containing food coupons that were intended to be used to purchase a particular food item. The coupons were clipped, put into a barrel or some other device that dirtied them to look like Customers had handled them. The coupons were then distributed to different bodegas that sent them to coupon redemption centers. When the checks were sent to the grocers for these coupons, the checks were either endorsed over to Sea Crest Trading Company or cashed, and the money sent to Sea Crest. At the center of the scam was the CIA's Sea Crest.

Repeated High-Level Blocks to Investigation of Criminal Activities

Occhipinti told me that he and Jacobson, acting independently of each other, had tried repeatedly to interest various federal state and even local law enforcement authorities to follow through on investigations of Sea Crest. "But always the investigations go nowhere." Lenny Lemmer, a detective sergeant with the New York City Police Department, said in a sworn statement that he has encountered similar dead-ends in probing Sea Crest and its alleged drug cartel connections.

Repeated FBI Blocks (i.e., Obstruction of Justice)

Lemmer said he was called to meet several times with FBI agents and federal prosecutors, who tried to intimidate him into abandoning any leads he might uncover about Sea Crest or anything exculpatory about Occhipinti. Lemmer said he was aware of "concrete evidence" about alleged Sea Crest money laundering activities in Bogotá, Colombia, and conveyed this information to an FBI agent.

Funding the 1993 Bombing of the World Trade Center

In an interview after the 1993 World Trade Center bombing, Jacobson confirmed that proceeds from coupon fraud paid for the World Trade Center bombing, and that Sea Crest had received redemption checks signed over by Middle Eastern and Dominican grocers suspected of participating in such fraud. The conspiracy was so loose that money could be siphoned off to terrorists without the parties involved in the original loan-shark-coupon scams being aware of it, according to investigators.

Cover-up of Criminal Elements Related to WTC Bombing

FBI Special Agent Lionel Baron of the FBI's New York City terrorist unit obtained from Ben Jacobsen the names of his informants with the expressed intention of infiltrating Sea Crest. Despite receiving considerable evidence showing that criminal activities did exist, Baron and the FBI never went forward with any prosecution.

Lying by FBI Agents

When *New York Post* reporter Al Guart requested access to Baron's investigative notes under the Freedom of Information Act, the FBI replied there were no notes and no investigation. This false statement by the FBI was made despite the fact that Baron had interviewed a number of witnesses, including Cesar Cabral, Hector Rodriguez, Alma Camarana, Peter Navaro, Luis Rodriguez, and Detective Raul Anglada, proving that an investigation *had been made*. Rodriguez had even given a sworn affidavit to the FBI relating to a usurious loan from Sea Crest. Guart discovered many of the alias corporations used by Sea Crest.

Investigation of Sea Crest Blocked at All Levels

Guart's continuing investigation into Sea Crest's activities, including interviews with law enforcement agents, confirmed to him that in every case, investigations and prosecutions were blocked by high-level state and federal people. In *Defrauding America* and *Drugging America* I give numerous examples of this type of cover-up.

Guart interviewed Bronx Borough President Fernando Ferier regarding Sea Crest's operations in the Bronx with the intent of getting the Bronx district attorney to investigate the company. Ferier denied knowing anything about Sea Crest, but said he would set up an appointment with the Bronx district attorney.

When Guart conducted a Lexus check, he discovered a *New York Times* article (August 13, 1993) in which Ferier assisted Sea Crest in procuring a special ordinance to rebuild the building that had mysteriously burned in the Bronx. In the article, Ferier was quoted as referring to the president of Sea Crest, Mr. Berkovitz, as "my good friend Bernie."

A DEA report (October 16, 1992) provided by Occhipinti alleged that Sea Crest was reportedly responsible for over $500 million in money laundering operations from the Washington Heights section of New York City.

***New York Post* Cover-up of Covert Criminal Activities**

Guart prepared four articles on Sea Crest that were to be published. Suddenly, his editor told Guart the newspaper was afraid to publish the articles. Earlier, when the *New York Post* ran a series of articles, "The Framing of a Cop," which made reference to bodegas and Sea Crest, the newspaper received bomb threats, and threats from the Dominican Federation that they would boycott the *New York Post* in the Washington Heights section of New York.

The Federation

The multi-agency task force discovered that members of the Federation were frequently involved in criminal activities, that major drug groups were using the federation businesses as fronts, and that the Federation's influence extended into political offices, including New York City Mayor David Dinkins. The Federation started putting pressure on political figures, seeking to disband the task forces led by Occhipinti.

Customs Investigation Halted by CIA Pressure

A confidential source in the New York Police Department Intelligence Unit knew about the Dominican Federation's involvement in criminal activities following a prior joint investigation with U.S. Customs (Customs Case # NY 02AR8NY003). Targets in that investigation included Pedro Allegria and Federation Vice President Erasmo Taveras, who had been indicted in 1989 and later convicted of a $70 million money laundering and loan sharking scheme. According to the confidential source, the CIA ordered Customs to drop the pending indictments against several of the Dominican drug traffickers, who then continued to engage in money laundering activities—with the protection of the

DOJ—despite evidence presented to the U.S. Attorney by Staten Island Borough President Guy Molinari in 1992.

Bergen County Investigation Halted

Under-sheriff Jay Albert of the Bergen County, New Jersey, sheriff department authorized a criminal investigation into Sea Crest and the Federation's infiltration into that county. The investigation was turned over to detectives Juan Lopez and Wayne Yahn, who gathered evidence substantiating the involvement of Sea Crest and the Federation. Their investigation was terminated on the basis of an alleged jurisdictional dispute with the Bergen County prosecutor's office.

Project Esquire: Investigating U.S. Attorney's Office

During the Project Bodega investigations, the group discovered from a police informant, Alma Camerena, that a former assistant U.S. Attorney and his law partner were allegedly part of Then's drug cartel operations and involved in political corruption. According to Camerena, the former U.S. Attorney was attending sex and drug parties with his former colleagues in the U.S. Attorney's office and receiving favored treatment in criminal cases involving his clients. Occhipinti said, "I found the allegations to be credible for a variety of reasons."

DOJ Terminating Investigation After Evidence Proved the Existence of Criminal Activities

Occhipinti reported these allegations to Assistant U.S. Attorney David Lawrence, who was the Deputy Chief of the Criminal Division, with whom Occhipinti had previously worked. Lawrence then arranged to debrief Camerena. After questioning Camerena, and determining that the charges were true, instead of addressing the matter, Project Esquire was terminated.

Search of Dominican Bodegas

Occhipinti's task force had multiple investigations going simultaneously. Focusing on the criminal activities in the bodegas, the task force sought additional court-admissible evidence by conducting consensual searches of several dozen bodegas in the Washington Heights section during the last half of 1989 and early 1990. In conducting consensual searches, the owner or operator is asked to sign a consent form agreeing to have their properties searched. Otherwise, a search warrant must be obtained.

In one search of the Then's Brothers Grocery Store, the task force discovered $131,000 in cash bundles destined for Sea Crest. This money was later judicially forfeited as drug proceeds by the U.S. District Court in Manhattan. In another bodega owned by Richard Knipping in the Bronx, the task force discovered hundreds of newly issued government food stamp books. Knipping could provide no explanation for how he acquired them.

These seizures and related criminal charges started major retaliation efforts against Occhipinti by various members of the Federation, Dominican criminal cartels, the black Mayor, David Dinkins, and the U.S. Attorney's office in New York City.

Drug Smugglers & Immigrants Reacted with Demonstrations

The politically powerful Dominican drug traffickers, the Federation, and Mayor David Dinkins orchestrated demonstrations against Occhipinti in the drug-infested Washington Heights area of Manhattan. Rather than support the head of the multi-agency task force, Project Bodega was terminated, despite the heavy concentration of drug and other criminal activities discovered during the bodega searches. Drug trafficking then escalated.

During Dinkins reign as mayor of New York City, murders and other crimes were escalating. The murder rate and other crimes dropped dramatically when Dinkins was voted out of office and Rudolph Giuliani became mayor and William Bratton became police commissioner. (Bratton received so much publicity for his crime-reduction efforts that Giuliani removed him from that position.)

Blaming the Other Political Party

Mayor Dinkins issued a statement claiming the search of the bodegas was a "Republican Conspiracy" intended to sabotage the 1990 census and intimidate immigrant voters from going to the polls. Dinkins was referring to the large numbers of illegal aliens in the area, many of whom voted for him in the prior election that resulted in the slim majority that won him the election.

What Dinkins was probably afraid of was that the increased police activities would keep illegal aliens from the voting booths where he had a large following in the Dominican community. Dominicans constitute a large voting block in the New York and other urban areas in the Northeast. Figures indicate there were over half a million Dominicans in New York City alone, and that they would outnumber all other Hispanic groups within a few years. Dinkins had been receiving large contributions from the Federation and the Dominican crime figures, being another reason for wanting to shut down the investigation of criminal activities involving mostly Dominicans.

Consensual Searches Violated Their Civil Rights?

The Federation, the immigrants, the drug traffickers, and Mayor Dinkins, claimed that the searches violated the civil rights of the bodega operators. They focused their charges against Occhipinti, even though he was only one member of the task force. It was necessary to focus the attacks on one individual in order for the planned scheme to succeed.

The U.S. Attorney then filed criminal charges against Occhipinti, claiming he violated the civil rights of the bodega operators on the basis that the signing of the consensual forms occurred *after* their bodegas were searched. This charge had never been done before against a government agent on the basis of an alleged technical violation.

Several members of the multi-agency task force told the U.S. Attorney that there were no violations of anyone's civil rights during the task force's search of the bodegas. IRS Special Agent Ronald Nowicki was present during the search of Knipping's bodega and stated there were no violations of search procedures. DEA agent John Dowd was also present during the search of Knipping's bodega and stated that the search was legal. But this wasn't what the DOJ prosecutors wanted to hear.

Reporting Threats Against Occhipinti to U.S. Attorney

Alma Camarena, the legal secretary in the law offices of former AUSA Jorge Guttlein, and Andres Aranda, overheard the lawyers discussing ways to eliminate the threat that Occhipinti posed to their Dominican and drug trafficking clients. Upon hearing these threats, Camarena went to the U.S. Attorney's office to report what she heard, and was interviewed by Assistant U.S. Attorney Jeh Johnson.

Camarena said, "Mr. Aranda told Mr. Guttlein that he would like to have Mr. Occhipinti eliminated." Camarena added that Guttlein didn't like that idea and said he would think up another plan. After she gave this information to the U.S. Attorney's office, Johnson, or someone else in the U.S. Attorney's office, gave this confidential information, and the name of the confidential witness, to Camarena's boss, who was the target of the charges! (Jorge De Jesus Guttlein, Guttlein & Associates.)

U.S. Attorney Indicted Occhipinti, Thereby Protecting Drug Crimes, a CIA Operation and Middle East Terrorists

Instead of protecting a respected government agent who was bringing about the arrest of people subverting major national interests, the U.S. Attorney filed criminal charges *against* Occhipinti. Those charges were based upon the perjured statements of the bodega operators—most of who were engaging in criminal activities and who were continuing their unlawful activities.

The Department of Justice indictment charged Occhipinti with failure to obtain written consent of the bodega operators *before* searching the premises, relying upon their verbal consent. They also claimed that Occhipinti kept money seized by the task force group (During trial, the jury held him not guilty of that charge, and at a later date some of the bodega operators who made that charge admitted that they lied.)

This was the same U.S. Attorney's office that had been covering up for the criminal activities that Occhipinti and his task force had been exposing. It was the same office that had covered up for the CIA-Mafia drug trafficking reported by one of their own FBI agents, Richard Taus, during this same time period.

He was also subjected to sham charges after he reported in a letter to members of Congress the corrupt activities of a CIA-front company, the repeated blocking of investigations by his supervisor, Lindley DeVecchio. Taus' story is described in the book, *FBI, CIA, the Mob, and Treachery*. I had been experiencing this culture of FBI-DOJ retaliation and obstruction of justice, starting while I held a key federal positions involving airline safety, and continued to document the pattern for the next 40 years.

Peculiar Comparisons

Compare these civil rights "violations" with the common practice of DEA and ATF agents breaking down the doors of peoples' homes, throwing the residents to the floor, shoving loaded pistols in their faces, and occasionally shooting and killing innocent people. These agents have the full support of the Department of Justice and federal judges. But when a federal agent interferes with powerful drug traffickers and a covert CIA operation, the law is applied in reverse!

Withholding of Exculpatory Evidence by DOJ Prosecutors

Transcripts of the grand jury proceedings showed DOJ witnesses lying when they testified they did not have prior criminal records. DOJ prosecutors withheld this perjury from the grand jury members and from the defense during the Occhipinti trial. Also withheld from the grand jury and jury trial was the fact that the task force had discovered contraband and illegal activity at each of the locations that they searched.

Black Activist Federal Judge with Strong Ties to Democratic Mayor Dinkins and the Federation

Selected to be the judge for Occhipinti's trial was U.S. District Judge Constance Baker Motley. She was the first black woman appointed to the federal bench, and had a radical and biased reputation. Federal court procedures required assignment of judges to a particular criminal trial be done on a normal rotation process, and is normally done by the court clerk. Judge Motley was pre-selected instead of chosen at random. Instead, she was picked out of sequence. Occhipinti said U.S. Attorney Jeh Johnson's face reflected joy and he gave a "thumbs-up" sign when Judge Motley's name was announced as being the trial judge.

Motley had close political ties to black mayor of New York City, David Dinkins. She was a protégé of Raymond Jones, a powerful black leader of Tammany Hall who was also an associate of David Dinkins in the Harlem Carver Democratic Club.

A Mafia Don would Have Been Pleased with That Lineup

A *New American* article (February 21, 1994) stated that during Motley's Senate confirmation hearings, evidence was presented showing Motley to be an ardent Young Communist League organizer who established student cells at New York University. The records showed that Constance Baker, her maiden name, was training for the Red Underground. Despite this record, Senator Edward Kennedy nominated Motley to become America's first black female federal judge. Other senators, looking for as many black votes as possible, quickly endorsed her.

The prosecutor, Jeh Johnson, was a former law clerk for the judge, and it was said that he was her "Godson." The article raised another problem that should have been the basis for a change of judges:

> There was bad blood between [Johnson] and Occhipinti as a result of the Project Esquire investigation of corruption within [Johnson's] office. Further, some of Johnson's associates alleged that he had boasted that an Occhipinti conviction would land him a high-paying private sector job-a pre-

diction that was fulfilled. Today, Johnson's office walls at the prestigious New York law firm of Paul, Weiss, Rifkin, Wharton and Garrison are adorned with artists' renderings of the Occhipinti trial, which Johnson regards as "trophies."

Record of Overturned Decisions

Judge Motley had more decisions overturned on appeal than any other judge in that circuit, indicating she was either legally ignorant, contemptuous of the law, or rendering decisions based on personal interests or money under the table.

Pre-Trial Problems for Occhipinti

Making matters worse for Occhipinti, his lawyer, Norman Mordkofsky, was suffering a nervous breakdown. The heavy media publicity and street demonstrations, and the loss of his legal practice, caused the trial lawyer to suffer severe stress before the trial. Occhipinti sought substitution of another legal counsel. Mordkofsky explained his serious problems to Judge Motley and filed a motion to be excused so that Occhipinti could obtain another lawyer. Judge Motley denied the request, calling the lawyer a liar. Occhipinti ended up with inadequate legal representation.

A week earlier, New York Supreme Court Judge Anthony Scarpino removed Mordkofsky from a murder case because of his bizarre behavior. The judge publicly admitted that there was no question that Mordkofsky was suffering some kind of psychological problem. After Occhipinti's trial, the lawyer was admitted to a hospital for psychiatric care.

Some time afterwards, Occhipinti wrote to me, stating:

> During my trial, he talked about committing suicide on several occasions. Judge Motley demanded that he go to trial. On the trial records, Mordkofsky demonstrates before the jury bizarre behavior as well as his failure to call very much needed defense witnesses or go through the counts of the indictment. It was also determined that his breakdown was attributed to the termination of his law practice.
>
> His two partners were criminal defense lawyers who represented many Dominican organized crime figures I was investigating, including some of Freddy Then's drug associates. Clearly, I had won several crucial criminal cases which made Mordkofsky's two partners look bad. Another important fact I later learned that Mordkofsky's next-door neighbor was a lawyer who incorporated many of the Dominican Bodegas with suspected ties to the Federation and Sea Crest.
>
> In fact, it was this very same lawyer who represented the Then Brothers grocery store on the $131,000 forfeiture case. I truly believe that there was immense pressure on Mordkofsky, which resulted in his nervous breakdown. There are medical and hospitalization records to document this breakdown.

Occhipinti's Fate

How did Occhipinti fare after his many years of dedicated government service? After 22 years of federal service, after receiving many awards, he was forced to retire on a disability pension. He suffered from post-stress trauma, hypertension, heart disease, and gastrointestinal disorders, surely brought on or worsened by his years of fighting crime and government cover-ups. Occhipinti wrote:

> I will always cherish my many law enforcement accomplishments and my efforts to protect our borders from drugs. Unfortunately, I realize now that my dedication to duty was in vain. I was very naive. I believed in the criminal justice system and the alleged war against drugs. I realize now that we have lost the war against drugs.
>
> Moreover, how politically powerful foreign drug lords are in the United States. I was getting too close to the major players in the drug world and had to be eliminated. Fortunately, I wasn't murdered like journalist Manuel De Dies. Instead, the drug lords sent a more powerful threat to law enforcement; they can now manipulate and misuse to their advantage, important civil rights laws that can imprison and intimidate dedicated law enforcement officers.
>
> At present, due to my landmark civil rights prosecution, which never involved police brutality, racial bias or corruption, drug interdiction in many jurisdictions has been terminated. The police assigned to drug interdiction often rely upon consent searches and will not subject themselves to possible imprisonment and loss of a career due to an allegation of an unlawful search and seizure. My only regret is that I took away precious time from my family and subjected my loved ones to tremendous hardships simply because I wanted to do my sworn duty.

DOJ Prosecutor Threatening Witnesses

During another telephone conversation, Occhipinti told me about how Justice Department prosecutors threatened witnesses who wanted to testify on his behalf. During the conversations Occhipinti explained:

> The Manhattan district attorney's office, which provided the staff for the multi-agency task force, included three Assistant district attorneys and a team of investigators. They wanted to testify on my behalf. They knew the project was lawful and had proper predication. In fact, Ann Rudman, chief of the Asset Forfeiture Program, tried to convince INS not to close down the project.
>
> Yet, these district attorney officials never came forward. According to Jacobson and others, the Manhattan district attorney's office was threatened by SDNY prosecutors that if they came to my aid, they might subject themselves to federal prosecution since they jointly worked on the task force with me.

Also, in the documented setup of another NYPD police officer, Louis Dellapizzi, on fabricated civil rights charges, Lawyer Andres Aranda was never indicted for the setup because of reported influence by SDNY prosecutors. If Aranda had been indicted, many suspect that as part of a plea-bargain deal, he would have confirmed my setup and exposed the official corruption at the US Lawyer's office.

Common Judicial Chicanery

During the trial, Judge Motley refused to allow the defense to introduce information about the criminal background of the Dominicans witnesses who claimed Occhipinti violated their civil rights, despite the fact that this information was relevant to assess the witnesses' credibility. Motley made numerous rulings that kept any information about CIA and criminal activities from being heard by the jurors.

DOJ Withholding Exculpatory Evidence

Many of the bodega operators who filed civil rights complaints against Occhipinti were suspected of dealing in food coupon fraud or drug activities, and continued to be suspected of violations after the trial had ended. This information was known to the prosecutor who unlawfully withheld the information throughout the trial proceedings. Federal law requires that the prosecutor provides the defense with all exculpatory evidence known to the prosecutor; this requirement is routinely violated by the Justice Department lawyers, who never suffer any retaliation for it.

Prosecutorial Deception

There were numerous prosecutorial errors before and during trial, all intended to insure that the jury decide Occhipinti to be guilty. To obtain the indictment from the federal grand jury, U.S. Attorney Johnson withheld exculpatory evidence and made inflammatory statements against Occhipinti. The prosecutor threatened and intimidated witnesses who would be testifying in Occhipinti's defense. One official with the NYPD admitted to Jacobsen that NYPD officers involved in Project Bodega were being threatened with indictment if they came to Occhipinti's defense.

Outraged Lawyer Filed Court Affidavit

During the trial, lawyer Angel Nunez, who had been observing the proceedings, became outraged by the prosecutorial and judicial misconduct, submitted an affidavit into court records detailing the numerous trial irregularities. Nunez interviewed those who filed the complaint against Occhipinti, and in 55 undercover taped conversations they admitted the searches were legal in their estimation, contradicting their grand jury and trial testimony.

Nunez tried to submit an affidavit into the trial relating to these findings, showing a conspiracy against Occhipinti and that the witnesses were lying. Judge Motley refused the request. When Nunez tried to admit the tapes and transcripts into the hearing, the judge again refused, compounding her refusal by seizing the tapes, thereby preventing them from being used elsewhere.

When the judge heard that Occhipinti reported these irregularities to the media, she put a "gag order" on Occhipinti, preventing him from speaking out, another unconstitutional act.

The jurors from the area that Occhipinti's group had targeted handed down a guilty verdict against Occhipinti on June 12, 1992, on the charge of conspiracy to violate the civil rights of the bodega operators.

First Law Enforcement Officer Sentenced To Prison for *Alleged* Technical Error

Never before in American history had a federal law enforcement officer been criminally prosecuted in a case where there was no violence involved and where the officer had done a routine consensual search, and merely involved an "alleged" technical violation. Even if, for argument, Occhipinti, a key agent in U.S. Immigration and Naturalization Service, had actually violated some technical search procedure that would not subject the officer to prison.

Instead, the evidence obtained in a faulty manner would be excluded and administrative action possibly taken against the officer. It had always been, and still is, government policy to conduct an administrative hearing, and certainly not file criminal charges. The FBI never conducted any hearing. The question is, why did the Department of Justice file the sham charges?

Ending a Successful Drug-Fighting Career

Judge Motley sentenced Occhipinti to 37 months in a maximum-security prison where Occhipinti would be surrounded by convicted drug dealers that he helped put in prison.

Justice Department Retaliating Against FBI Supervisor

FBI Special Agent in Charge (SAC) of the New York office, James Fox, had replied to media questions, stating the FBI had evidence showing Occhipinti was innocent of the charges and that the government was withholding the evidence. In retaliation, the FBI suspended him—two months prior to his planned retirement.

Occhipinti filed a motion for a new trial, based upon Fox's statements, but Judge Motley denied the motion. (Fox died of cancer in 1998.)

Fallout from Justice Department's Misconduct

There were several consequences to the Justice Department's charges against Occhipinti:

- Government agents were put on notice not to go after politically connected criminal elements in the Dominican community.
- Caused other government agents to ignore politically connected criminal activities.
- Established an "acceptable" procedure for retaliating against government agents who threaten politically connected criminals.
- Emboldened larger and well-connected drug traffickers to continue or escalate their criminal activities, knowing they would be protected by DOJ per-

sonnel. Small-time drug traffickers, with no political or CIA connections, would receive DOJ attention.

- Protected Jersey City terrorists who received some of their funding from the drug activities that Occhipinti was targeting. These were the terrorists who later bombed the World Trade Center in 1993.

Perilous Drop in Investigations—and 1993 WTC Bombing

A 1993 report by the president of the New Jersey Police Benevolent Association said that in the year before Occhipinti's conviction the local Drug Enforcement Agency conducted 2,700 investigations, and that the year *after* Occhipinti's conviction, that number dropped to 500. The reason given was that agents feared being sent to prison for carrying out their drug investigations. This impediment to investigations surely contributed to the success of the 1993 bombing of the World Trade Center.

The president of the New York-New Jersey Port Authority Police Union said that their officers had ceased all consensual searches and drug interdiction activities in the ports of New York and New Jersey, out of fear of being charged with civil rights violations (of politically-connected criminal groups).

Sgt. Lenny Lemmer of the NYPD-DEA drug task force gave testimony to Congress stating that during a 1992 criminal investigation they discovered evidence at Sea Crest of a conspiracy against Occhipinti. The U.S. Attorney's office in New York ordered Lemmer to remain silent about this information, giving the sham excuse that there was an ongoing investigation. The Justice Department prosecutors chose to use the obviously biased statements from major drug traffickers over the statements of any of the government agents. Evidence showed overwhelmingly that Sea Crest was a CIA operation.

Threat of Violence by Ethnic Groups
Affected Occhipinti's Appeal Process

With a new lawyer, Stephen Frankel, Occhipinti appealed his conviction. Oral arguments were scheduled (June 1992) at the Second Circuit Court of Appeals and included in the appeal issues was the ineffective assistance of counsel, prosecutorial misconduct, and judicial errors. The appeal brief and appendix exceeded 750 pages. (This is the same court of appeals that covered up for my attempts to report the criminal activities that enabled terrorists to hijack four airliners on 9/11. Information in *History of Aviation Disasters: 1950 to 9/11*; and in *Lockerbie to 9/11: Massive Fraud and Consequences*.

Trying to intimidate the judges, the Dominican Federation staged a noisy demonstration in front of the courthouse. The noisy group carried signs warning of riots in Washington Heights if Occhipinti's trial decision was overturned, and then packed an overflowing courtroom where oral arguments were heard.

Often, appellate court judges take weeks or even months before they issue a decision after an oral hearing, but in Occhipinti's case, the decision was rendered within one hour of the hearing, quieting the Dominican immigrants, drug traffickers and bodega operators.

Risks of Violence in Prison

His appeal rejected, Occhipinti was ordered to turn himself in on June 12, 1992. The day before he was to turn himself in, Occhipinti appeared on a New York television show, the "Jackie Mason Show," explaining what really happened. Judge Motley retaliated, ordering the U.S. Marshal to immediately arrest Occhipinti. The marshal ignored her order and told Occhipinti to surrender the next morning. As is customary, Occhipinti was placed in leg irons and body chains and sent by prison plane to El Reno, Oklahoma. The greater distance from New York insured he would have difficulty getting publicity or using other legal remedies.

Virtual Impossibility of Getting the Public to React

If Occhipinti thought the public would react, he was sadly disappointed. I had appeared on over 3,000 radio and television shows since 1978, detailing the corruption that I discovered during my official duties that caused or enabled to occur a series of major airline disasters. To this day, not one of the millions of people who heard or saw me on radio and television made any effort to help, including the families of the next of kin.

Recognized by Prisoners He Previously Arrested

As Occhipinti entered the general prison population at El Reno, Oklahoma, he was recognized by some of the prisoners from New York whose incarceration came about as a result of Occhipinti's task force. Fortunately, sympathetic prison guards, made aware of the risk, put Occhipinti into solitary confinement. While this protected him from physical harm, the isolation resulted in a breakdown. DOJ prison officials blocked every attempt by Occhipinti to be transferred closer to his family, realizing that he and his supporters would be working to bring about his release and publicize the misconduct by Justice Department prosecutors.

**Many People Protested the Outrage and
DOJ Protection of Politically Connected Criminals**

A few courageous people who knew Occhipinti expressed outrage at sentencing him to prison for having reported the criminal activities in the New York area. Staten Island Borough President, Guy V. Molinari, heard about Occhipinti's plight, and even though Occhipinti was not one of his constituents, Molinari started an investigation, acquiring several affidavits from key people that proved Occhipinti's innocence.

U.S. Attorney and FBI Blocking Investigation

Molinari's actions seeking to reveal the truth behind the DOJ's prosecution of Occhipinti started an all-too-common DOJ retaliation. Assistant U.S. Attorney Valerie Capone and FBI Special Agent Jarrett investigated Molinari's staff on the excuse the evidence the staff had uncovered was fabricated. Capone also threatened NYPD Detective Lemmer with potential prosecution for providing Molinari with exculpatory evidence relating to the Occhipinti setup and cover-up of criminal activities in the New York area.

Misusing DOJ Power to Obstruct Justice

The DOJ, through its FBI agents, then tried to entrap Molinari, using a woman wearing a wire-recorder, seeking to trap him with false charges. They also charged Molinari with compensating a person for giving testimony. An article in the *New York Post* (April 26, 1995) made reference to the misuse of the FBI's powers against Molinari: "Guy Molinari Fumes: FBI tried to set me up." The article stated in part:

> Staten Island Borough President Guy Molinari angrily charged yesterday that two FBI agents sought to entrap him in a criminal scheme with the help of a "wired" government informant. "It's outrageous," Molinari said. "If they will do this to me, an elected official, I hate to think what they might do to a member of the general public."
>
> Molinari came under FBI scrutiny during his relentless efforts to prove the innocence of Joseph Occhipinti, the Immigration and Naturalization officer who was convicted and imprisoned on charges of conducting illegal searches of drug locations in upper Manhattan. Occhipinti, the most decorated officer in INS history, served seven months of a 37-month prison term before relief came.
>
> Molinari, who had never heard of Occhipinti, became involved only two days before the agent was sentenced. He was so appalled at what he saw at the sentencing that he and his staff launched an independent probe. Molinari concluded that Occhipinti had been framed and convicted on the perjured testimony of drug dealers. Molinari's efforts on behalf of the beleaguered agent—who is not even a constituent—are among his finest hours in a long career of public service. But those efforts started his problem with the FBI.
>
> "When a small team of FBI agents working out of Queens arrived at my office, it became clear to me that the focus of their investigation was not the evidence we had produced but the involvement of me and my office in the matter." Molinari told me yesterday. "Here was I, a law-abiding citizen, seeking to redress what I believed to be a miscarriage of justice, and finding that I had become the target of the FBI probe. They tried to get me to commit a crime. It's outrageous."
>
> Molinari's evidence against the FBI includes a sworn affidavit from Alma Camarena, a former law clerk who first informed the government that Dominican drug lords were planning to frame Occhipinti. [With Justice Department assistance!] In the affidavit, Camarena swears:
>
> On or about January or February of 1993, I was contacted by [an FBI] agent to come to their office in Queens. I agreed. At that interview, they said that they wanted me to set up Mr. Molinari by my wearing a wire against him. I said, "Yes only because I was afraid."
>
> Camarena said she overheard the agents planning the operation. "They were bragging how they would get a helicopter to circle Mr. Molinari's of-

> fice to overhear my conversation with him," she swore. "They said when Mr. Molinari agreed to get me a job on the wire, they would arrest him."
>
> Camarena said she called Molinari, but "I never said what the FBI wanted me to say. The FBI agents appeared upset because I didn't repeat everything they wanted." Molinari told the FBI's Office of Professional Responsibility that the agents seemed more interested in investigating him than in the criminal conspiracy or the perjury against Occhipinti. Molinari said: The Occhipinti case is very significant. It is part of a new phenomenon in which law-enforcement officers are being convicted on the perjured testimony of drug dealers.

Complaining to FBI's Office of Professional Responsibility

Molinari complained to the FBI's Office of Professional Responsibility (OPR) about the scheme to file false charges against him. Almost a year later, the FBI responded, using the standard off-the-shelf tactic:

> There is insufficient evidence to find that the allegations made by you and supported by Alma Camarena are substantiated. While it appears that on August 28, 1992, the agents discussed with Camarena the possibility of her wearing a wire in some type of cover action against you, and that she agreed to do so, the idea was not endorsed by the agents' supervisor and was flatly rejected by Department of Justice lawyers.

President George H.W. Bush Sr. Pardons Occhipinti

After acquiring considerable evidence and affidavits clearly showing how drug traffickers and DOJ personnel set up Occhipinti, Molinari requested President George H.W. Bush to commute Occhipinti's sentence. Other concerned people also contacted Bush. On January 15, 1993, shortly before the senior Bush left office, he signed a commutation for Occhipinti. However, he refused to give Occhipinti a full pardon, which left Occhipinti with a felony conviction.

During the 1980s, Bush was heavily involved in CIA activities in which Sea Crest played an important role. Bush was also involved in or knew of other CIA activities, some of it being drug trafficking, especially during the Contra affair. I describe these matters in the books, *Defrauding America* and *Drugging America*.

Cover-Ups Because of High Political and CIA Links

After Occhipinti was released from prison as a private citizen, he presented evidence concerning many criminal activities to various law enforcement agencies that had jurisdiction and responsibilities in those areas. During a February 2, 1993, meeting in the office of the Bronx district attorney to discuss Sea Crest and Dominican crime activities, attended by district attorney personnel, Occhipinti described the evidence that the task force group had acquired. Before leaving, an unnamed investigator privately told Occhipinti that no investigation would be conducted because of the high political links to the CIA and Dominican organized crime operations.

Brooklyn District Attorney Joins Cover-Up

Brooklyn District Attorney Charles J. Hynes had meetings with Occhipinti in 1993 concerning the evidence Occhipinti's group had acquired, which was in his jurisdiction and area of responsibility. Hynes stated he would authorize an investigation into Sea Crest. But that investigation never occurred.

Some years later, the same District Attorney Charles Hynes came to the rescue of FBI-DOJ personnel when he suddenly dropped murder charges against a key FBI supervisor, Lindley DeVecchio. More about that in other pages. As of this writing, the public doesn't know how the cover-ups of those murders played a major enabling role in a series of successful terrorist attacks, including those that occurred on September 11, 2001.

Bronx DA Halts Investigation

During a January 12, 1994, meeting with Assistant District Attorney Edward Friedenthal in the Bronx, Friedenthal told Occhipinti that an investigation would be conducted into Sea Crest, based upon information provided by Occhipinti's task force. Again, the block to investigating the corruption occurred, involving both federal and state "law enforcement" personnel.

New Jersey Investigation Halted by Department of Justice

A conference took place on July 21, 1994, with Sgt. Jim Mulholland of the New Jersey police intelligence unit, Occhipinti, and several high-ranking deputy attorney generals from New Jersey. That meeting was arranged by former New Jersey Attorney General Robert Del Tufo. A week earlier, on July 13, 1994, Occhipinti and several New York City law enforcement agents testified before the New Jersey Senate about Dominican organized crime operations in New Jersey. New Jersey law enforcement personnel planned to act upon the information—until Justice Department personnel contacted them.

Postal Service and ATF Cover-up

Federal agents from the U.S. Postal Inspection Service and the Alcohol Tobacco and Firearms Bureau interviewed Occhipinti in December 1994 concerning these criminal activities. According to a confidential source, Postal inspectors and the Organized Crime Strike Force for Newark, New Jersey, had indicated an interest in Sea Crest Trading Company. That investigation was also stopped, indicating again that a powerful force in the federal government was involved.

Congressman Traficant Seeking Congressional Hearing

Complaints of the criminal activities and government cover-ups were brought to Representative James Traficant's attention. He obtained a confidential June 1992 DEA report that corroborated reports of a special interest group protecting Sea Crest corrupt activities. The DEA report said that Sea Crest laundered over $500 million dollars a year from Washington Heights.

Traficant placed into the Congressional Record (September 27, 1996) affidavits and other evidence showing the existence of the CIA and Dominican drug offenses in the United States. He also referenced Justice Department's actions blocking the exposure of these activities.

Dominican Diplomat Confirming Dominican Criminal Activities

Ramon Antonio Grullon, a former Dominican diplomat, prepared two affidavits (March 10, 1994) that were entered into the Congressional record by Traficant. In the affidavits, Grullon said he had been recruited by Federation members Pedro Allegria and others to participate in a conspiracy against Occhipinti, and that the motive for these acts against Occhipinti was to halt Occhipinti's investigation of Sea Crest and the Federation's bodegas. Grullon described the criminal activities of Sea Crest and the involvement of Richard Knipping and Jose Liberato in the illicit operations. Grullon also described being present when drug money was given to certain elected officials.

Congressional Resolution That Went Nowhere

A resolution was entered into the Congressional Record on April 28, 1993, by Representative Dick Zimmer seeking the appointment of a special or independent prosecutor to investigate the matters that Occhipinti discovered. The resolution stated in part:

> Whereas, there is voluminous evidence that in 1991 and 1992 Mr. Occhipinti may have been the target of a well orchestrated conspiracy by Dominican drug dealers, leading to his prosecution on civil rights charges under 18 U.S.C.§§ 241 and 242; (1)
>
> This House memorializes the President and Congress of the United States to appoint a special or independent prosecutor to investigate the case of Mr. Joseph Occhipinti, including an investigation of the alleged drug cartel conspiracy against Mr. Occhipinti, and, further, of the alleged Justice Department cover-up in the handling and prosecution of the Occhipinti case. The President is memorialized further to grant, if the investigation warrants, a full pardon so Mr. Occhipinti can clear his name.
>
> This House further memorializes the President and Congress of the United States to seek a congressional investigation examining the extent of Dominican crime operations in the United States especially in New Jersey.

Congress Unwillingness to Offend Dominican Constituency

Despite the gravity of the criminal activities in the New York area uncovered by the various law enforcement agencies, and despite the obstruction of justice activities by DOJ personnel, few in Congress wanted to investigate the problems. Some were covering up for the Justice Department and others were too scared and cowardly. An investigation would alienate the large Dominican political constituency.

A full investigation would reveal, for instance, the decades of CIA drug trafficking; drug money going to both political parties; the most recent examples of drug money going to the Democratic party and President Bill Clinton.

DOJ Retaliation Against Congressman Traficant

In a not-unusual sequence, federal prosecutors then charged Traficant with federal crimes, sending him to prison and forcing him out of office. It also served as one more example to members of Congress what can happen if they expose corruption in the nation's top law enforcement office.

Seeking Congressional Relief for Occhipinti

Further information supporting Occhipinti's innocence and the DOJ-organized crime coalition against him was provided by an affidavit placed into the Congressional Record (E1734) on September 27, 1996, by William Acosta, which stated in part:

> I am former thirteen-year law enforcement official who successfully infiltrated the Medellin and Cali Colombian drug cartels. I am considered an expert on the Colombian and Dominican drug and money laundering operations in the New York City area.
>
> **[Political Corruption Involving John F. Kennedy]**
>
> In 1987, I was previously employed as an undercover operative for the United States Customs Service, wherein I was assigned to route out corruption at John F. Kennedy International Airport. In 1987, I was the principle undercover agent on "Operation Airport 88," which resulted in the prosecution and conviction of seventeen government officials for bribery corruption and related criminal charges. I was then promoted to Special Agent and reassigned to the Los Angeles District Office.
>
> **[Evidence of New York City Police Corruption]**
>
> In 1990, I was appointed to the New York City Police Department as a Police officer. In view of my Colombian heritage and confidential sources close to the Colombian cartel, I was eventually assigned to the Internal Affairs Unit. During my undercover activity, I generated evidence of police corruption for the Deputy Commissioner of Internal Affairs, which was later corroborated by the "Mollen Commission" hearings, which investigated police corruption.
>
> **[Drug Cartel Conspiracy Against Occhipinti]**
>
> On January 14, 1992, Manuel De Dios, a close personal friend and world-renown journalist executed the attached notarized affidavit, wherein, Mr. Dios corroborated the existence of a drug cartel conspiracy against Mr. Occhipinti. The orchestrators of the conspiracy were major Dominican organized crime figures connected with the "Dominican Federation" which is the front for the Dominican drug cartel.
>
> The Federation is the principle drug distributors in the United States for the Colombian cartel. Unfortunately, Mr. De Dios was assassinated before he could bring forward his sources who could prove the drug cartel conspiracy against Mr. Occhipinti. After Mr. De Dios' assassination, I too became fearful of my personal safety and never made public the evidence on the Occhipinti case.
>
> **[Corroborating the Federal Conspiracy]**

It should be noted that I personally assisted Mr. De Dios in this investigation of the Occhipinti case, which corroborated the Federation conspiracy. In fact, I personally accompanied Mr. De Dios to the Washington Heights area where we secretly taped recorded Federation members who confirmed the drug cartel conspiracy. Those tapes still exist and can exonerate Mr. Occhipinti. In essence, Mr. Occhipinti was set up because of his increased enforcement efforts on Project Bodega which was exposing and hurting the Dominican Federation's criminal operations in New York City, which included illegal wire transfers, drug distribution, gambling operations, food stamp fraud, and food coupon fraud, among other organized crime activity.

[Criminals Protected by High-Level Government Officials]

My investigation also determined that Mr. Occhipinti was exposing a major money laundering and loan sharking operation relating to the Federation, which was controlled by the Sea Crest Trading Company, of Greenwich, Connecticut. Sea Crest also maintains an office at 4750 Bronx River Parkway in the Bronx, New York.

Sea Crest was using the Capital National Bank in order to facilitate their money laundering operations. In 1993, Carlos Cordoba, the President of Capital National Bank was convicted in Federal Court at Brooklyn, New York for millions of dollars in money laundering and he received a token sentence of probation. My investigation confirmed that Sea Crest, as well as the Dominican Federation, are being politically protected by high-ranking public officials who have received illegal political contributions, which were drug proceeds. In addition, the operatives in Sea Crest were former CIA Cuban operatives who were involved in the "Bay of Pigs." This is one of the reasons why the intelligence community has consistently protected and insulated Sea Crest and the Dominican Federation from criminal prosecution.

[Dominicans and Colombians Partners in Drug Activities]

At present, there are nine major Colombian drug families, which control drug operations in the New York City area. These drug families often referred to as the "Nine Kings." The Dominican Federation are part of their drug trafficking and money laundering operations. I possess documentary evidence, as well as video surveillance tapes of their drug operations. In addition, the New York City Police has investigative files to corroborate this fact.

I have also uncovered substantial evidence of political and police corruption, which has been intentionally ignored. In fact, it is my belief that former New York City Police Internal Affairs Commissioner Walter Mack, who I directly worked for, was intentionally fired because of his efforts to expose police corruption. I plan to make public this evidence to the United

States Congress, as well as key members of the media in order to preserve this evidence in the event I am assassinated like Mr. De Dios.

[Common Obstruction of Justice by DOJ Personnel]

It should also be noted that criminal Investigators Benjamin Saurino and Ronald Gardello of the U.S. Attorney's Office in Manhattan similarly ignored the evidence I brought forward to them on the Nine Kings and Dominican Federation. These two investigators were credited for convicting Mr. Occhipinti and they made it clear to me they didn't want to hear the evidence I had on the Federation which could have exonerated Mr. Occhipinti.

They were only interested in corruption cases I had brought to their office. In fact, I recall a conversation, wherein, Investigator Saurino asked me about my involvement with Manuel De Dios and if I knew anything about the Occhipinti case. He then stopped and referred to Occhipinti in a derogatory manner, by saying "He's no [redacted] good." Realizing his bias and lack of interest in investigating the Federation and Nine Kings, I changed the subject of conversation.

[Rampant Corruption in New York Police Department]

In April 1995, I resigned from the New York City Police Department Internal Affairs Unit after it became evident that my efforts to expose police corruption were being hampered. The same reason why I believe Commissioner Walter Mack was fired. It became evident to me that my life was in eminent danger and I could be easily set up on fabricated misconduct charges like Mr. Occhipinti. In fact, they brought departmental charges against me in 1995 and I won the case. The trial judge also admonished the department on the record for perjury. Often, I found myself isolated and in constant danger working alone in the worst neighborhoods of the city without a backup.

Today, I possess substantial evidence to prove that the NYC Police Department media campaign to demonstrate that they could independently police themselves and route out corruption was simply a media ploy to avoid having an independent counsel to oversee their internal affairs unit. In reality, corruption is still rampant in the department and high-ranking police brass are intentionally terminating viable corruption investigations in order to avoid future scandals exposed by the Mollen Commission. I also possess a consensually monitored tape conversation, which implicates a high-ranking police official who received bribes from the Dominican Federation.

[Drug Cartels and U.S. Politicians]

I am willing to testify before Congress as to the allegations set forth in this affidavit. In addition, I am willing to turn over to Borough President Molinari and Congressman Traficant the documentary evidence I possess on the Dominican Federation, the Nine Kings and the Occhipinti drug cartel conspiracy. There are other important pieces of information relating to drug cartel operations and political corruption that I have not made public in this affidavit in order to protect my sources as well as ongoing media investigations that I am involved with. In addition, I am willing to submit to a polygraph examination to prove the veracity of my allegations.

William Acosta

Veteran Police Officer Who Knew the Ropes

Acosta, with over 12 years in law enforcement, had come to the United States from Colombia and became a police officer, working undercover with state and federal agencies in bringing about the arrest and conviction of numerous criminals. As a Colombian, he had a better understanding of the drug smugglers and their method of operation, and better able to infiltrate their ranks.

During this time he received numerous commendations and medals. His work gained him attention in articles appearing in the *New York Times*, the *New Yorker*, *Newsday, George Magazine*, and the *Village Voice*. ABC's television program, "*Nightline*," showed Acosta as "The Good Cop" on a segment, with one of the guests saying he took the oath of an officer "too literally." As a result of carrying out his duties, Acosta suffered retaliation, he was threatened, he was shot at, he was attacked, and financially ruined.

Another Witness Came Forward

In the same Congressional record, Manuel De Dios, former editor of *El Diario/La Prensa* and editor of a weekly newspaper known as *Canbyo*, gave an affidavit that was published several years later in the Congressional Record (September 27, 1996). The affidavit stated:

During the course of my work for Canbyo I understood to write an expose concerning criminal complaints brought against an Immigration and Naturalization Service Supervisory Special Agent named Joseph Occhipinti by various members of the Federation of Dominican Merchants and Industrialists of New York. During the course of my investigatory work in researching the article, I interviewed numerous individuals who are members of the Federation of Dominican Merchants and Industrialists of New York.

These individuals confided to me that Mr. Occhipinti had been set up by the Federation and that the complaints against him were fraudulent. These individuals have indicated to me that they are in fear of their safety and as a result would not go public with this information. I would be more than willing to share my information with any law enforcement agencies or Courts concerned with these matters and would cooperate fully in any further investigations.

Expose DOJ-Protected Corruption and Be Murdered

In an all-too-common scenario befalling people who expose DOJ corruption, De Dios paid the price. He was gunned down and killed on March 11, 1992.

Assistant U.S. Attorney John F. Kennedy, Jr.: Profile in Cowardice

An article in *The New American,* titled, "Profile In Cowardice," described a prominent New York socialite who contacted Congressman James Traficant (December 2, 1993) and provided information on one of the actions taken by DOJ officials, using Assistant U.S. Attorney John F. Kennedy, Jr., to frame Occhipinti. The witness was identified in the article as "A.R.," and identified as a friend of John F. Kennedy, Jr. That witness stated details of a conversation that he had during a June 11, 1991, conversation with John F. Kennedy, Jr. the night before Kennedy was to testify for the Department of Justice against Occhipinti. The article stated in part:

> He testified that Kennedy bemoaned the fact that the next day he would have to testify against an innocent man. According to J.R., Kennedy stated that he was being "forced" to testify for political reasons and that he was being "used" to prejudice the jury.
>
> The object was to use Kennedy's testimony to influence the jury, even though Kennedy had never heard of the Occhipinti case. Occhipinti's defense team had the witness undergo a polygraph examination for determining his truthfulness, which he passed.

Several years later, Kennedy died in a private plane crash when he was flying from New Jersey to Nantucket. The crash was due to Kennedy's lack of piloting experience during marginal night visual conditions.

Dominican Republic Diplomat Supported Occhipinti

A *New American* article (February 21, 1994) described a witness, identified as "R.A.G," who held several diplomatic positions for the Dominican Republic, including that of consul general and ambassador to Jamaica. The witness gave two highly sensitive affidavits (August 19, 1993) that provided more details about the conspiracy against Occhipinti. One affidavit stated in part:

> On or about the end of 1989, I was personally told by Dominican businessmen Jose Delio Marte, Silvio Sanchez, Pedro Allegria, and Ernesto Farbege that they needed my political assistance in eliminating former Immigration officer Joseph Occhipinti. They explained to me that Occhipinti was a threat to their illegal businesses, which included loan sharking, gambling, drug distribution, and the employment of illegal aliens.

In his second affidavit, the witness stated in part:

> I have confirmed why government witness Jose Liberato, a complainant against Mr. Occhipinti at trial, had falsely testified against Mr. Occhipinti and participated in the conspiracy. Mr. Liberato, a bodega owner, is a ma-

jor participant of Sea Crest Trading Company and its illegal activities. In his affidavit he also named the person who delivered drug-related money from the Federation and Sea Crest to the Dinkins political campaign. CIA money going to Dinkins?

DOJ Witnesses Arrested Again

Most of the witnesses used by DOJ prosecutors against Occhipinti had criminal records. After the trial, they continued to engage in criminal activities and continued to be arrested. An example: *New York Daily News* headline (June 17, 1993) read:

Vice Cops Bag 3 in Bribes. Two of the people named were brothers, Jose and Joaquin Checo, who had filed charges against Occhipinti and had been arrested by the New York Police Department for gambling and bribery offenses at their bodega. In the same article, New York Police Department spokesman, Raymond O'Donnell, referred to the two brothers as members of a Dominican organized crime organization known as The Federation.

"We're going to do to you like we did Occhipinti!"

The immigrants learn fast. As the brothers were being handcuffed, one of the police officers, Sgt. Frank Perez, heard an employee holler, "You can't get away with this. We're going to do to you like we did to Occhipinti!"

More Information Showing Connections Between Sea Crest, CIA, DOJ, and White House Politicians

Occhipinti described to me during a telephone conversation (October 11, 1997) the findings of his multi-agency task force while investigating criminal activities in New York while working with AUSA Louis Freeh:

Let me explain to you why things happened, in connection with my case, and why I think they prematurely suspended James Fox, the FBI Director. There is a company called Sea Crest Trading Company in Greenwich, Connecticut. Now we know, and its been established that they've been the target of as many as ten federal and local investigations. And in each and every case, the investigations were ordered terminated by the Justice Department.

[CIA, Capitol National Bank, Dominican Criminals]

The company was being run by certain Cubans who were involved in the Bay of Pigs. And they had, as part of their money laundering operations, they were dealing with Capitol National Bank in New York, being run by Carlos Cordoba, another CIA operative. I understand that, in Dominican organized crime, it's probably one of the most vicious ethnic crime groups in the United States.

And what they do is, they basically intermingle and usually work hand in hand with the Cuban organized crime network, particularly in the gambling operations. So what happens, without realizing it, I stumbled into this Operation Bodega, never realizing that the Dominican bodegas that I was hurting was part of this Dominican Federation which is actually the front of an established Dominican cartel and that the fact that they were using in their money laundering operation, the Sea Crest Trading Company.

I was the Chief of Immigration and Naturalization Service. I was working mostly drug cases, and I was probably the most expert on Dominican organized crime. Nevertheless, all in all, I thought that I was being set up simply because I was hurting Dominican organized crime and that I knew the federation was a very politically powerful organization. And I just believed the time that they went to Mayor David Dinkins, convinced him that I was a racist and that I was hurting their operations, and Dinkins, who attributed his win in the 1988 election to the Dominican Federation, which is a front, called for a federal civil rights investigation.

Now, what happened, I uncovered evidence into this cartel that I was investigating, that their chief legal counsel was a former Assistant United States attorney in the southern district of New York; and that according to my source who is a credible informant and who was willing to wear a wire, she alleged that this former Assistant U.S. Attorney was the legal counsel for the Dominican Federation.

[Top Criminal Job to CIA-Front and Drugs]

And he said to me, this guy's name was David Lawrence, who was chief of the criminal division. David Lawrence said to me, 'I want to interview this woman." So I brought her in. Not only was she credible, she actually had documents in her possession that could put this guy, this former Assistant U.S. Attorney and his partner, away in jail for a variety of drug trafficking, money laundering violations.

[U.S. Attorney Exposing Government Informant]

What happened is, a week after I brought her in, her information was leaked to this former assistant for whom she worked in that law firm saying, "I know what you did; my people told me, and the U.S. Attorney is trying to set me up, and he said he put a contract on Camarena." It's clear I went to the U.S. Attorney with viable evidence and he refused to work on it.

What they actually told me was, "Leave the investigation alone; leave it alone." At that time I simply said, Well, you know what it is; the U.S. Attorney is very much concerned about their prestige. What happened was, in the southern district a year earlier, FBI had arrested an assistant U.S. Attorney for drug possession, and his name was Pearlmutter. [Daniel N. Pearlmutter]

[DOJ Blocking Exposure of Crime Activities in New York]

What I thought at the time was, well, they're blowing New York simply because they had a scandal two years earlier and they're trying to avoid a potential scandal, and they're only concerned about their image. But when David Lawrence told me to leave this investigation alone, I was angry. A New York City police officer was murdered and I'm on the trail of a major Dominican cartel. That's when I started my Operation Bodega, knowing that I wasn't going to get any support from the Justice Department.

[NYC Prosecutor Circumventing DOJ Cover-Up]

So I went over to Morgenthau office [Robert M. Morgenthau, New York District Attorney] and he was convinced that Operation Bodega not only would net the cartel but also expose the money laundering operations as well as the alleged corruption. He assigned three assistant district attorneys to my case and within a ten-month period we began to develop substantial evidence not only on the Dominican federation but Sea Crest Trading Company.

[DOJ Protecting Bribe of Law Enforcement Officer]

And I knew I was getting close to the operation because two, actually three bribery offers were made to me and immediately I went back to the FBI, the supervisor in the corruption unit. And I told him everything I uncovered on Sea Crest and on this former federal prosecutor. And he was convinced; he wanted to do an undercover investigation. He was so convinced that he actually assigned a case agent. And the goal was for me to accept bribes, set them up and take them down, and squeeze them and find out who's corrupt.

[U.S. Attorney Blocking Investigation]

What happened is, when we get to my meeting in the southern district of New York, which is the criminal division, I get told by them that the southern district would not go with the undercover operation. He said to me specifically, he said, "Something smells." So I realized that several months before that they told me they didn't want to do Operation Esquire.

[Drug Cartels Demand Shutdown of Investigating Unit]

I had worked previously in the corruption unit and I had some confidence in them, so when the Dominican Federation held their press conference on the steps of City Hall demanding that my operation be closed down and that I be investigated for federal civil rights investigation, at the time I didn't have knowledge of all the facts.

I just simply thought I was hurting a drug cartel; they needed to try to make it into a racial issue with politicians, with the Republican thing, and that's what happened. So, at that the pieces to the puzzle weren't being put together. What happened was, they simply thought that I would be prosecuted and convicted and be taken away. And no one would even listen to me. But what would ultimately happen was that I was a credible person, and every time the media investigated my case, they found out that I was innocent and that I had been set up by drug lords.

[Drug Lords and U.S. Attorney's Office]

And that the drug lords influenced the U.S. Attorney's office to selectively prosecute me. Now we know that because several PD undercover operations were done where they went actually into the same bodegas who testified I conducted unlawful searches and capture them on national TV involved in criminal activity. What happened was, I was in prison, and the pressure was so much on the White House that they had to do something. My case was getting a lot of notoriety.

My Years of Observing DOJ Obstruction of Justice

I had seen for years the cover-ups and obstruction of justice by people in the U.S. Department of Justice, but this was getting even more serious. I asked Occhipinti, "What charges did they make?"

"They charged me for federal civil rights violations. The first officer in American history to be charged under the federal civil rights with illegal consent search. The claim was, yes his signature was on the consent, but they claimed they didn't sign the consent form until after the search. The first officer to be prosecuted; it's an administrative violation under the exclusionary rule. If a judge thought a search was illegal, they'd just throw the case out of court. I was the first one to ever be prosecuted.

The bottom line was, President George [H.W. Bush], under intense pressure and because of his relationship with Staten Island president Molinari told him there was so much evidence for my innocence, he gave me clemency—he didn't give me a full pardon but he gave me clemency and got me out of jail.

What happened was, in January I get my retirement because I had 22 years in the government, and I'm a credible witness. Very credible, and what everyone basically puts it up to is, this is an illustration of how powerful the struggles are in our United States, and secondly how they're able to manipulate the civil rights to their advantage.

At that point I became not only hero to American law enforcement but even some of the civil rights groups have been convinced that my case was a clear case of how the drug cartel was using civil rights laws to their advantage. Right now I have a lot of friends, a lot of credibility. What I thought I could put together was the following.

[Occhipinti Supported by FBI SAC James Fox]

I started to realize when witnesses came forward that James Fox was one of my biggest supporters. While I was in jail, James Fox publicly stated that there was evidence of my innocence despite the fact that the FBI was refusing to release the evidence. What we believe happened was the following:

We believe, while I was in jail, the Justice Department conducted an investigation. And they cut James Fox out of the loop for one reason or another. We believe James Fox realized that I was being framed and he asked one of the agents who conducted the investigation what happened. We believe when he saw what happened he publicly announced he was to retire in a couple of months.

[Motion for New Trial]

Now when these public statements were made, we made an application for a new trial based on newly discovered evidence from the drug cartel. We specifically made mention that James Fox made public statements, and I know that the U.S. Attorney was very upset with him. Cause they called him down and they asked him to give a deposition saying that his public statements were taken out of context. He refused to do it, and he was fired; he was terminated about three months before his retirement.

In response, I asked, *"What's the status of that? Has he taken any legal action?"*

Basically he left and became one of the heads of security for a major bank; he passed away about 3-4 months ago. Let me tell you what we uncovered. A major investigator for a clearing house that deals in food coupons; you know those coupons when you go shopping. He brought to my attention that terrorist groups were using coupons as a way to front international terrorism. He explained that it was a 200 million-dollar-a-year operation. And they were using bodega supermarkets. Sea Crest Trade Company was to do the money laundering.

[Involvement of Middle East Terrorists]

Most of your Middle East terrorist groups were using several ways to raise money for terrorism. One was food stamp fraud, the second was food coupons, and the third was pirating of films that was sold out of supermarket bodegas that was controlled by the Federation. And they were using the bodegas as a clearinghouse for Sea Crest Trading Company, which explains why I was getting them a little nervous. But he said to me, "Joe, you're missing the picture here. The Dominicans are involved with the Cubans, but don't you realize what really happened here?" And this is what he explained.

[Bodega Money to Terrorist Groups]

When Ben Jacobson began his investigation into the food stamp fraud and coupon fraud, he was the chief investigator for E. C. Nielson Company that administers food stamps in the coupon program. In his investigation he said that what really was happening was that much of the coupon redemption would be concentrated at a little grocery store. And when he became suspicious that the monies were going to terrorist groups, he reported his findings to the FBI.

But what happened was, the President had given me clemency, and I knew that I had been set up. The evidence clearly showed it. We believed I had been set up solely by the Dominican drug lords and that I was easily prosecuted because I wasn't perceived as a team player because I was attempting to expose corruption. So what happened was, Ben Jacobson opened my eyes and he explained to me what happened. And he's a credible guy. Not only is Ben Jacobson a retired New York City detective; he's also a college professor that teaches at Rutgers University. He is also the chief investigator for E. C. Nielson Company. And this is what he proceeded to explain:

[IRS Retaliation—Another Standard Trick]

Ever since he started his investigation at Sea Crest, he became the focus for retaliation by the IRS and others; he was basically told to leave the investigation alone. He couldn't understand why. What he was able to connect was that Sea Crest, based on documents he obtained; they're called Buck's; Universal Commercial Code. Let me explain; if I lend you a thousand dollars I fill out a promissory note that you registered with the county clerk on a form that's called the CC.

[DOJ Personnel Protecting Middle East Terrorists]

With this investigation he started to notice that many of the people who were tied into Sea Crest were from the Middle East, managing stores that he suspected, supermarkets, mini-markets, that he suspected had ties to terrorism. And he reported his findings to the FBI. He provided them evidence of the funding for terrorism. What happened was, the FBI, just like the other investigations by the IRS, were ordered by the Justice Department to terminate it. And this is why he believed that happened.

They needed a way, a mechanism to launder the money. So it was decided that they would bring in the Mujaheddin principals into the United States, set them up in mini-markets and supermarkets and utilize Sea Crest Trading Company as a way to funnel money to the Dominican Republic, and then back. And the money was earmarked for arms.

[World Trade Center Bombing Facilitated by FBI-DOJ and CIA Personnel]

What happened, he thinks, is while the government may have had a legitimate reason for using Sea Crest Trading Company, which was being run by former CIA operatives, Cuban Nationals, they never realized that the terrorist groups were using the money. And when Ben Jacobson provides them with that intelligence and they closed it down because they were told to, we believe, the bombing of the World Trade Center resulted.

Now if you look at the convicted people on the World Trade Center Bombing, one fellow is Salam Abdel-Rahman. He owned a mini-market in Jersey City. If you pull the UCC [report], it comes back "Sea Crest Trading Company." So what happened was, the Justice Department and the CIA were afraid that if this information was ever exposed, it would show that the FBI was alerted that these monies through the food and coupon fraud actually funded the bombing of the World Trade Center, and that the FBI failed to take any action.

There would be a major scandal. Now we believe this is one of the reasons why James Fox knew what was happening. He was the one who spearheaded the entire FBI investigation into the bombing of the World Trade Center. So listen to this very carefully.

[DOJ Shuts Down Congressional Investigation]

Congressman Traficant begins a series of inquiries into Sea Crest under the Freedom of Information Act, and almost immediately they close it down. They refuse to give any information, quoting national security. So what I think we have here, the real scandal is, the CIA realized the federal agency was being set up in order to protect their operation, they allowed me to go to jail.

But the real story was that the CIA used Sea Crest Trading in order to facilitate money for Mujaheddin [terrorists] during which time it inadvertently got into the hands of suspected terrorists. They were alerted of that fact; they failed to take any action; the bombing occurred, and they've got to do damage control. They were afraid if the American public learned about this it would be a major scandal.

[Drug Cartels Funded Clinton's Election Campaign]

To further compound this now, what's been happening with the White House? We've now learned that the Dominican Federation is a front for cartels and Sea Crest Trading Company was behind many, many fundraisers for the Clinton-Gore campaign. Now this is published in the New American magazine. What I'm saying here is published also in the Congressional Record. I think this guy Richard Taus, and what he says was accurate and what was happening in the New York FBI office.

[CIA Practice of Secret payments to Media Personnel]

Now the guy who broke the story, the guy who came up with the evidence, is a reporter for the *New York Post* by the name of Al Guart. But the paper refused to print it; apparently the CIA must have a lot of influence in the media. The Post refused to allow him to break the story. There's another guy, Karl Ross.

He does investigative reports for some of the largest magazines and newspapers, and also the *Washington Post*. And they're refusing to allow him to break his story on Sea Crest. The point I'm trying to make here is, this is what was happening. This is what we could prove. That viable local and federal investigations into the Sea Crest Trading Company have been suspiciously terminated by the Justice Department. Why?

[CIA Sea Crest Operation Funding Afghan Terrorists]

I just wanted to let you know that the Sea Crest Trading Company appears to have been a CIA operation; it was being run by the Cuban mob that was involved in the Bay of Pigs. We know their connection with the Colombian and Dominican cartels. But as I said, apparently that was used as a front to money launder the money for the Mujahedeen when, during that process, monies were actually diverted to actual terrorist groups and the FBI knew about it, was told not to do anything and then, when the bombing occurred, there was a big scandal there.

Nostalgia Writing of Occhipinti's Tragic Downfall

It was sad to write about how powerful and corrupt people have inflicted upon Occhipinti and his family, and upon many other dedicated government personnel who suffered retaliation for carrying out their duties. It reminded me of what I went through, first as an FAA air safety inspector and then later what I experienced as I sought to expose other areas of government corruption. It is very probable that Occhipinti and I, and others like us, were fools, trying to protect a public who didn't care enough to get informed or show any responsibility. During a discussion with Occhipinti in March 1999, he said that almost every reporter who exposed the DOJ corruption has had the IRS after him.

Radio and Television Appearances

Upon being released from prison, Occhipinti appeared as guest on several hundred radio and television shows, exposing the crime and drug cartels, and their political influence, and how the FBI and CIA protected terrorists. His grueling schedule caused him to collapse on board an airliner (November 21, 1993), followed by four days of hospitalization. Since 1978, I appeared as guest on over 3000 radio and television shows and it can be especially tiring, especially when on a tour and doing seven or more shows a day.

Pattern of DOJ Obstruction of Justice

In one of his writings, Occhipinti explained to me some of the problems associated with government agents' attempts to fight powerful ethnic crime groups:

> I have seen dozens of viable federal and local investigations into Dominican organized crime groups prematurely terminated by federal authorities. Why? In July 1997, the FBI published a confidential intelligence report on Dominican organized crime operations in the United States, which confirm what I have known for the past twenty years. There has been much speculation that many of these investigations were prematurely terminated due to possible national security reasons, or maybe, the principals were government informants that had to be protected.
>
> It is important to note that the biggest crime threat facing the American public is the growth of international drug syndicates in the United States. Foreign drug lords and organized crime have adapted very well in setting up criminal operations in the United States for a variety of reasons. Foreign drug lords and ethnic organized crime groups have learned the essence of American politics and know how to manipulate the political and criminal justice systems.
>
> **[Principal Distributor of Colombian Drugs]**
>
> For instance, U.S. law enforcement sources have developed convincing evidence that the Dominican drug cartel is the principal distributor of nar-

cotics in the United States on behalf of the Colombian drug cartel. In addition, they are credited for laundering billions of dollars in drug proceeds, both here and abroad. Yet, we rarely see media reports that publicize Dominican organized crime. Why?

[Dominican Drug Cartels Politically Powerful]

Many ask me why the Dominican cartel has become so politically powerful in the United States. I explain that they will often operate as a legitimate political action group, often making unlawful political contributions to elected officials and having become successful in conducting widespread election fraud. Clearly, the ability to deliver campaign contributions and needed votes to win an election can understandably influence most political candidates.

[Organized Ethnic Crime Groups]

Hopefully, you can better understand why foreign drug cartels have become politically powerful in the United States. It also explains that when ethnic organized crime groups become the targets of law enforcement scrutiny, they seek immediate political intervention in hopes of terminating a criminal investigation or inquiry. In many cases, elected officials are successful in influencing authorities to terminate a criminal investigation by often alleging officer misconduct, or that the investigation was racially motivated.

[Most Crimes Committed by Ethnic Crime Groups]

In the United States, statistics will show that the majority of organized crime activity in the United States is being committed by organized ethnic crime groups. Yet, the Justice Department's "Organized Crime Strike Forces" continues to target and prosecute traditional Italian organized crime groups, which represent less than one percent of organized crime activity in the United States. Why? Is it because it has become "politically" incorrect to target these other ethnic crime groups? Or, are these foreign drug lords being protected by elected officials or the intelligence community?

[Ethnic Groups Taking Over Criminal Activities]

Partly because of naïveté, partly because of American's gullibility, partly because of Americans who are willing to sabotage America's interest for money from special groups, ethnic groups are taking over all types of criminal activities that make all of America suffer. Even the Japanese version of the U.S. Mafia: "yakuza." has taken advantage of America's love affair with drugs.

Many Colombian and Mexican drug traffickers, and the yakuza, set up businesses along the Mexican-U.S. border after NAFTA came into being. Little is known in the United States about yakuza activities, or even its existence. Years ago, CIA agent Gunther Russbacher described his dealings in the Midwest with the yakuza, most of which I left out of my books for another day. It was reported to me that a company with packinghouses in

Mexico along the U.S. border, Fruitiko, is associated with the Japanese yakuza.

Al Qaeda Terrorists Obtain Funds from Local Drug Activities for 1993 World Trade Center Bombing and 9/11

Evidence not publicized by the Justice Department, Congress, or the mainstream media shows a relationship between the World Trade Center bombing and the criminal activities government agents sought to report, which DOJ employees blocked. And these activities would again affect the World Trade Center on the fateful day of September 11, 2001. Money to fund the terrorist bombing of the World Trade Center came from the very same criminal activities that Occhipinti and other government agents sought to halt: and DOJ employees protected!

Money acquired by Sea Crest, a CIA operation, funded terrorists. FBI and CIA people were identified by the 9/11 Commission as failure to act on known terrorist activities. But what the commission withheld from the report was that these people actively assisted and protected terrorists, for years.

Financing World Trade Center Bombing With Bodega Food Coupon Fraud and Drug Money

A New Jersey news service, *Golden State News Service*, distributed to newspapers on October 1995 the following in-depth interview with several key New York area law enforcement officers relating to the bombing of the World Trade Center:

> The terrorist bombing of the World Trade Center was financed with drug and other racket money laundered and leveraged through small ethnic grocery stores. What's more, terrorists even now are siphoning off more such funds. The real leader in the World Trade Center bombing has been allowed to flee capture, and all this is happening under the apparent protection of the Central Intelligence Agency.
>
> According to Jacobson, it was the monies generated from the Sea Crest food coupon redemption fraud scheme that financed the bombing of the World Trade Center. According to Jacobson, Sea Crest is suspected of being the source of a two hundred-million-dollar a year food coupon redemption scheme ... Jacobson alleges that Sea Crest has been protected by the Justice Department because of an alleged CIA operation that utilized that firm....
>
> Occhipinti says he and Jacobson, acting independently of each other, have tried repeatedly to interest various federal state and even local law enforcement authorities to follow through on investigations of Sea Crest. "But always the investigations go nowhere." Lenny Lemmer, a detective sergeant with the New York City Police Department, said recently in a sworn statement that he has encountered similar dead-ends in probing Sea Crest and its alleged drug cartel connections...

Lemmer said he was called to meet several times with FBI agents and federal prosecutors, who tried to intimidate him into abandoning any leads he might uncover about Sea Crest or anything exculpatory about Occhipinti. Lemmer said he was aware of "concrete evidence" about alleged Sea Crest money laundering activities in Bogotá, Colombia, and conveyed this information to an FBI agent.

[CIA's Sea Crest Operation Funded WTC Bombing]

In a recent interview, Jacobson confirmed that proceeds from coupon fraud paid for the World Trade Center bombing, and that Sea Crest had received redemption checks signed over by Middle Eastern and Dominican grocers suspected of participating in such fraud. The conspiracy is so loose that money may be siphoned off to terrorists without all parties involved in the original loan-shark-coupon scams being aware of it, according to investigators.

[History of Funding Terrorists and Paying Afterwards]

The United States funneled over three *billion* dollars to the Mujahedeen in the 1980s, and provided training in the use of weapons and terrorist activities. This was done despite the known hatred of the Mujahedeen for the United States due to its one-sided support for Israel. The knowledge that these acquired terrorist tactics and weapons would eventually be used against the United States was ignored, with dire consequences for many terrorist victims in the United States.

Congressional Bill to Address Culture of Corruption In U.S. Department of Justice: Fair Justice Act of 2000

Slightly more than a year before the nation's most catastrophic terrorist events in the nation's history—greatly enabled by widespread corruption of people in the U.S. Department of Justice, Representative James A. Traficant. Jr. of Ohio introduced a bill to set up a government agency responsible for continuously monitoring the conduct of employees in the Department of Justice.

The Fair Justice Act would have the power to subpoena Justice Departments employees, investigate their conduct, and to prosecute. One of the main areas of DOJ misconduct was in the New York FBI-DOJ offices. Because of the unseen power of the Justice Department controlling culture, there was little chance the legislation would pass.

Hearings were commenced on July 25, 2000, and right off the bat, Representative Jerald Nadler, whose constituency included the upper west side of Manhattan, including Washington Heights, where the Dominican Republic drug cartels were flourishing, blocked the proceedings and ridiculed respected witnesses.

The primary witness in favor of the legislation, and with the most specific information on Justice Department misconduct, was Joseph Occhipinti, a former chief of the anti-drug task force in the New York City area. I had written about his years earlier in my book, *Drugging America.*

Federal judges—many of them former DOJ prosecutors—had held in case law decisions that prosecutors whose misconduct inflicts great personal or financial harm on individuals and families were immune from prosecution.

Among the introductory statements made by Representative Traficant were the following:

> Numerous incidents over the past several years have made it painfully clear that the Justice Department cannot effectively police itself. The American people expect the Justice Department—more than any other federal agency—to be beyond reproach when it comes to ethics and responsible behavior.
>
> I was prompted to introduce the legislation after years of analyzing cases of Justice Department misconduct that were not properly investigated by the Justice Department. In recent months, I have been presented with evidence alleging that FBI agents currently working in Youngstown have been on the payroll of organized crime. I have also been presented with evidence that FBI agents pocketed thousands of dollars in informant payments. I also have been presented with evidence that an FBI agent in Youngstown asked an informant to commit murder. I know for a fact that the U.S. Attorney's office in Cleveland, Ohio has been aware of these allegations for at least two years.
>
> The first witness I am presenting is Joseph Occhipinti, a graduate of Brooklyn College. He joined the United States Department of Treasury as a customs patrol officer in 1972. In less than 5 years, Mr. Occhipinti compiled the highest felony arrest and contraband seizure record in Customs Service history. After working undercover for the Justice Department's Organized Crime Strike Force in New York, he was promoted to the Chief of the New York City Anti-Smuggling Unit.
>
> Mr. Occhipinti has been described as one of the most decorated Federal agents in U.S. History. He has received three Attorney General Awards and 78 commendations for meritorious service and valor. In 1995, he established the National Police Defense Foundation, which has become one of the largest police foundations in the United States.

The following are excerpts from both the testimony and also the submitted material by Occhipinti:

> **Testimony of Joseph Occhipinti, Executive Director, National Police Defense Foundation, Manalapan, NJ**
>
> In essence, I come here because of the concern on behalf of the entire law enforcement community. We are held to a certain standard by the government, and unfortunately injustice occurs not only against criminals and citizens but also law enforcement officers. And yet we find an increase in

prosecutorial misconduct and that same standards that apply on police officers unfortunately are not applied on prosecutors.

In 1988 a New York City police officer was murdered in New York City. I was requested to investigate the homicide because of my expertise. I am one of the country's leading experts on international crime syndicates. I was able to solve the homicide, and during the course of the investigation I identified a major Dominican drug cartel that was implicated in the murder of the police officer.

[Sex and Drug Parties in U.S. Attorney's Office]

During that investigation, I uncovered serious allegations of alleged misconduct at the U.S. Attorney's Office. The cartels were holding private sex and drugs parties for prosecutors. I immediately brought the case to the attention of the chief of the criminal division as well as my superiors, who I thought were going to support the need for an undercover investigation. I found the informant very credible because she was willing to go undercover and corroborate much of the evidence that she was alleging.

In any event, I was told the investigation would not go forward. I continued my efforts to target the drug cartel who had been implicated in the murder of a police officer. With the cooperation of the State prosecutors including, by the way, John F. Kennedy, Jr., who was assigned to help me in the investigation, I started an operation called "Operation Bodega," because we determined that this cartel were buying up Spanish grocery stores and using them to facilitate drug trafficking and money laundering activity.

Within months, the operation was a home run, a success, getting arrests, defendant convictions. In fact, we had three full-time State prosecutors assigned to us. I know we were getting very close to the cartel because we started to expose more corruption. And what did I do? I went to the FBI and they agreed this was a case that warranted an undercover investigation, and I myself was willing to go undercover because some bribery overtures had been made to me, and that is one of the things that organized crime does: to try to neutralize the officer to see if they can bribe you.

[FBI Cover-Up: Exclude Other Law Enforcements Groups]

But unfortunately, a week later, the group supervisor of the FBI corruption unit told me they don't want to do the investigation, the same prosecutor's office where the misconduct was alleged. All of the sudden, I find out that the Dominican Federation, which is a proven front for the Dominican cartel, held a press conference alleging that my Operation Bodegas was a Republican conspiracy to sabotage the 1990 Census.

[Combining Obstruction of Justice with Retaliation]

Immediately the Justice Department terminated my investigation despite protests from State prosecutors, and a year later I was the sole defendant in a multi-count indictment that alleged I conducted illegal searches. I became the first law enforcement officer in American history to be charged for Federal civil rights violations despite the fact that there was no brutality, no racial bias, and no corruption.

This piece of paper here is what they claim. The complainants who testified were Dominican Federation complainants. And despite their signatures [approving the searches] which appeared on a government Consent to Search Form in Spanish, of which I speak Spanish fluently, I was indicted.

What we learned, it was a classic railroad job. Everybody who investigated this case, including your colleague, former colleague, Guy Molinari, a Pulitzer winner, Mike McAlary of the New York Post, all realized this was a well-orchestrated conspiracy by international drug lords to set me up.

The TV show "Inside Edition" went undercover almost 2 years after my conviction and captured on national TV the same complainants who were portrayed by prosecutors as being law abiding, they have engaged in ongoing criminal activity. In fact, the producer confronted one of the key witnesses who testified against me, and he admitted before the American public that his perjured testimony was responsible for my conviction.

Ladies and gentlemen, I was shackled with leg irons and body chains and placed into the general prison population. My roommate was a convicted Dominican drug dealer. My landmark case has had adverse implications on the entire law enforcement community.

As I speak today, drug interdiction is not in effect in many jurisdictions, because when you do drug interdictions you rely on Consent to Searches. But everybody said, why was this man convicted?

If you take a moment and look at my statement, I have named over 20 high-ranking law enforcement officials, government agents who were on searches with me who came forward to the prosecutor with evidence of the drug cartel conspiracy. For example, a New York city police detective came and admitted that 18 months before my indictment, he reported to the same prosecutor who prosecuted me, evidence that they overheard the drug cartel setting me up. And you know something? The prosecutor in the sworn statement never denied the fact. He simply said, I don't recall.

A New York City Internal Affairs investigator who I invited in on one of these operations and had the entire conversation monitored on tape went to the prosecutor and said, "You have made a grave mistake here. Something is wrong. Listen to the tape. The man got permission." and I can go on and on and on.

But you know something? When the Staten Island borough president, Guy Molinari, pushed for an independent investigation, when the New Jersey General Assembly and the New York State Senate said this is a grave injustice, let's get an independent prosecutor, the Justice Department said, justice has been served, and they rubber-stamped the court opinion.

[DOJ "Investigating" It's Own Obstruction of Justice]

And one thing further. When the Justice Department compromised and said we will take a look at the Occhipinti case, did they assign a group of agents outside of the jurisdiction? No. They assigned a local FBI agent that answers to the same prosecutors who did an in-house investigation. And you know what we learned—and it is in the Congressional Record—that this agent went over the line, and I represent Federal agents. He tried to set up Guy Molinari and when Mr. Molinari brought that to the attention of the Justice Department they apologized.

I brought my case to every legal expert and I have here Professor Gershman, one of the leading experts on prosecutorial misconduct, whose consensus was this was the worst case he has ever seen.

But if I violate the civil rights of any person or defendant or citizen, a law enforcement officer is subject to criminal prosecution. Yet, this prosecutor, well-documented evidence of prosecutorial misconduct, is exempt from prosecution. That means people who go to jail, who are falsely convicted, that prosecutor is immune from prosecution. And what I learned is something further.

[Referring to the executive clemency order]

In January 15, 1993 President George Bush granted me executive clemency. Despite that, I went ahead and applied for a new trial based on newly discovered evidence, which meant I could go back to jail if I was convicted again. That is how strong I felt about the case. And again, my application was denied by the court and OPR said it would do an independent investigation and they came back and said they could not find any credible evidence of any conspiracy or any prosecutorial misconduct.

And that is very important because Jim Fox, who was the FBI Director of New York, he publicly stated—this is the man who was on every night news when the bombing of the World Trade Center—he told the media that there was evidence of my innocence. And when we tried to get a new trial based on those statements, he reportedly was told by prosecutors to execute an affidavit saying his statements were taken out of context. They did not like it, and a month before his retirement after 30 years he was suspended.

There are many that believe the conspiracy was sanctioned by the intelligence community to protect certain CIA operations and assets under the disguise of national security.

Wherein, others are convinced there is widespread corruption in the Justice Department and I had to be eliminated due to my increased enforcement efforts that would ultimately expose the drug cartel operations and official corruption.

I would like to conclude by saying we have lost the war against drugs and we need this important till to have basic oversight authority over the Justice Department. My colleagues in law enforcement tell me every day that they are more afraid of being prosecuted and railroaded by our own Justice Department, then by putting their lives in harms way.

Congressman Nadler Protecting His Dominican Supporters

Protecting his constituents of heavily Dominicans, the judge, and the Department of Justice that had been so "tolerant" and accommodating, Nadler, criticized the highly-acclaimed drug task force leader that has been so successful in drug interdiction. Nadler continued to discredit Occhipinti as he stated:

Mr. Chairman. I want to read from the sentencing memorandum of the Southern District of New York in Mr. Occhipinti's case, which I will ask to put in the record, and I will ask Mr. Occhipinti a question based upon what I am about to read. The sentencing memorandum says that:

"On June 28, 1991 the Defendant Occhipinti was convicted, after trial by jury, of one count of conspiracy to violate civil rights, ten counts of violation of civil rights, and six counts of making false statements in Immigration and Naturalization Service Reports.

"The evidence at trial showed that in a series of unlawful searches which he organized, Mr. Occhipinti repeatedly and without consent, engaged in warrantless searches, unlawfully seized property, and falsified reports of the searches and seizures to cover up his unlawful conduct. These searches were conducted with no prior information of illegal activity and none of the searches uncovered any narcotics or cash linked to a drug cartel. Mr. Occhipinti's conduct involved the intimidation of persons in the areas searched and targeted many victims. The victims of Mr. Occhipinti's actions were persons who are particularly vulnerable to civil rights violations—recent immigrants. The evidence further indicates that Mr. Occhipinti repeatedly and deliberately engaged in this conduct, despite his knowledge of the law.

"Mr. Occhipinti's pattern of misconduct is not limited to the present case. During one of the unlawful searches for which he was convicted, Mr. Occhipinti unlawfully seized a handgun from a store and obtained a false confession from the storeowner, Miss Altagracia Crucey. Mr. Occhipinti then prevailed upon the Manhattan District Attorney's Office to charge Altagracia Crucey with illegal possession of the gun, despite the fact that Ms. Crucey's sister Eusabia Crucey, had given Mr. Occhipinti a statement that she owned the gun and that her sister had been unaware of its presence in the store.

In a state court hearing, Mr. Occhipinti wilfully failed to disclose Eusabia Crucey's statement that she owned the gun and allowed Altagracia Crucey to be unlawfully convicted. He also perjured himself in the state court hearing by falsely stating that he obtained permission to search the store. After the jury verdict in this case, the Manhattan District Attorney's Office moved to vacate Altagracia's illegal conviction that resulted from Mr. Occhipinti's perjury and unlawful search.

"As the evidence shows, Mr. Occhipinti is not now before the court as the result of one isolated incident. Rather, Mr. Occhipinti is an experienced law enforcement officer who had previously been found to violate the

Fourth Amendment in the United States v. Cruz," citation, "and who deliberately, flagrantly, and repeatedly engaged in criminal conduct as shown by the evidence in this case."

"Since his conviction, Mr. Occhipinti has attempted to persuade the court and public to disregard the jury's finding that he was guilty of serious criminal conduct. This court will not do so. The jury in this case heard more than four weeks of evidence and found, beyond a reasonable doubt, that Mr. Occhipinti engaged in the conduct alleged. Mr. Occhipinti has produced no new evidence since the trial pointing to his innocence, and the jury chose to believe the testimony of numerous witnesses who contradicted Mr. Occhipinti's depiction of the events in this case."

The following are excerpts from the prepared statement submitted into the congressional record by Occhipinti:

Prepared Statement of Joseph Occhipinti, Executive Director, National Police Defense Foundation, Manalapan, NJ

Dear Mr. Chairman, Committee Members and Invited Guests, my names is Joseph Occhipinti and I am the Executive Director of the National Police Defense Foundation (NPDF), which is a Congressionally recognized and IRS approved 501c (3) non-profit foundation that protects and supports the efforts of the national law enforcement community.

I founded the National Police Defense Foundation in 1995 after it became evident that many dedicated law enforcement officers from around the country were being unjustly victimized by the same criminal justice system they serve.

Today, the NPDF speaks for the interest of thousands of Federal Agents, Police Chiefs, State Troopers, Sheriffs and local law enforcement personnel in the United States and abroad. The NPDF funds two important law enforcement initiatives. The first one is the Congressionally recognized "Safe Cop" program that post a $10,000 for pubic information leading to the arrest and conviction of any one who shoots a law enforcement officer. The second NPDF initiative is the "Operation Kids" program that distributes free child fingerprint kits to parents, posts rewards for missing children and arranges for life saving heart operations for critically ill children.

I am a retired federal agent who was the former Chief of the Immigration & Naturalizations Service's Anti-Smuggling Unit at New York City. During my twenty-two years of unblemished federal service with both the Department of Justice and Treasury Department, I became a leading government expert on international crime syndicates and drug cartel operations.

I am one of the most decorated federal agents in United States history having received over 78 official commendations, including three Attorney General Awards. I worked almost five years undercover infiltrating the

Dominican drug cartel that resulted in the prosecution of major organized crime figures, as well as one of the largest drug seizures ever recorded in our country.

I come here today to testify in support of the passage of H.R. 4105, the "Fair Justice Act of 2000" that will create a new agency to investigate any official misconduct or corruption by Department of Justice personnel. I support this bill for personal reasons that I hope can be effectively described in the foregoing statement.

My problems started on October 18, 1988, when Dominican drug lords in New York's Washington Heights, savagely murdered NYC Police Officer Michael Buczek. The NYPD had arrested the wrong suspect and their Chief of Detectives formally requested my assistance in the homicide task force due to my expertise in Dominican organized crime.

I was instrumental in helping to solve the murder, as well as in identifying the Dominican drug lords responsible for the officer's death. During the course of this homicide investigation, I developed credible evidence that Dominican Drug Lord Freddy Antonio Then was buying up Spanish grocery stores called "Bodegas" in Washington Heights in order to facilitate his drug trafficking and money laundering activities.

[Former Federal Prosecutor Working for Drug Lords]

At that time, a registered police informant told me that the Then cartel had on their payroll two Dominican attorneys, one of whom was a former federal prosecutor at the Southern District of New York (SDNY). It was alleged that the cartel was holding private sex and drug parties for some prosecutors in exchange for favorable court dispositions. Unfortunately, despite the credibility of the informant who agreed to wear a wire against the attorneys, the Chief of the Criminal Division (SDNY) refused to authorize "Operation Esquire."

In August of 1989, I continued my investigation of Mr. Then and started "Operation Bodega." Within a few months the operation developed into a highly successful multi-agency task force resulting in numerous felony arrests, defendant convictions and contraband seizures. However, due to the lack of cooperation by SDNY federal prosecutors, I went to the Manhattan District Attorney's Office who assigned me three Assistant District Attorneys, one of whom was John F. Kennedy Jr. It was clear that federal prosecutors were unhappy with my actions and continued investigation.

On April 4, 1989, the "Dominican Federation," an established front for the Dominican drug cartel according to the NYPD, held a press conference at City Hall calling Operation Bodega a "Republican Conspiracy" that was sabotaging the 1990 census. Also, they accused the operation of violating the federal civil rights of hard working Dominican merchants.

One year later, I became the sole defendant in a multi-count conspiracy indictment for alleged civil rights and related violations. The SDNY had conducted an unprecedented "in-house" investigation rather than refer the case to the FBI, as required by law. According to a published report, an unidentified Justice Department source alleged that federal prosecutors were afraid that the FBI would lie for Occhipinti.

A review of the indictment disclosed that the majority of the complainants openly committed perjury before the Grand Jury with respect to their criminal past and continued involvement in organized crime activity. In fact, two years later, the TV show "Inside Edition" went undercover into the very same Bodegas and captured the same complainants and their employees involved in ongoing criminal activity. One complainant, when confronted by the producer on national TV, admitted his perjury helped to convict a federal agent.

In another TV documentary, the jury foreman openly admitted that the trial jury realized the perjury by the complainants. However, they convicted me because they misunderstood the law. The jury was led to believe by the prosecutor that an Immigration Officer had no authority to search for narcotics, which is clearly not the law. Congressman James Traficant immediately brought this matter to the attention of Attorney General Janet Reno who unfortunately refused to overturn the conviction, alleging it is not relevant whether or not the jury understood the law.

[DOJ Personnel Protecting CIA-Politically-Connected Criminal Drug Activities]

It should be noted that my landmark prosecution had adverse implications on the entire law enforcement community, as well as drug interdiction operations. For example, today drug interdiction in the States of New York and New Jersey and other jurisdictions has been terminated since agents utilize consent searches in those operations and are fearful that fabricated allegations could land them in jail.

[First Law Enforcement Officer Prosecuted Under Civil Rights Laws Relating to Search Approval]

I became the first law enforcement officer in United States history to be prosecuted under federal civil rights laws for an allegation of an unlawful search and seizure. There were no acts of police brutality, corruption or racial bias! It is not uncommon for drug suspects or their defense attorneys to allege that an officer's search, seizure or arrest was unlawful. It is the general practice that these allegations are handled administratively by the courts or by the agency. Not in my case!

After my indictment, I solicited and received the aide of the Dominican community, as well as some civil rights leaders who knew my commitment to protect the community from drugs. Dr. Angel Nunez, a local Dominican immigration lawyer and legal counsel for the National Hispanic Coalition, agreed to conduct his own independent investigation into the allegations. Dr. Nunez later executed a lengthy sworn statement that was entered into the Congressional Record that not only confirmed the drug cartel conspiracy, but also documented some outrageous acts of prosecutorial misconduct.

[Proof That No Civil Rights Violations Occurred]

As part of his investigation, Dr. Nunez conducted taped interviews of all of the Bodega owners I investigated, including the Federation complainants. In essence, Dr. Nunez determined that the non-Federation Bodega owners all admitted the consent search were lawful, wherein Federation complainants testified they never gave permission. However, after careful questioning, many of the Federation complainants finally admitted on tape they gave permission.

In addition, some members of the Dominican community volunteered to work undercover by making controlled buys of contraband from the Federation complainants in order to prove their involvement in ongoing criminal activity. The goal of this defense undercover operation was to convince the jury of the drug cartel conspiracy. A total of 55 undercover tapes were made, which was later ordered by the court to be turned over to prosecutors for transcription. Unfortunately, the prosecutors intentionally delayed the process, which precluded the defense from presenting those tapes to the jury, which would have impeached the credibility of the Federation witnesses.

In an effort to better understand why I was railroaded into a conviction, it's important to note the many acts of alleged prosecutorial misconduct that was never properly investigated by the Office of Professional Responsibility. For that reason, I have prepared the following brief synopsis of the alleged misconduct and unprofessional behavior that has been well documented in the Congressional Record, the District Court, the Second Circuit of Appeals, and the Department of Justice.

[Standard DOJ Denial of Defense Evidence]

A defense prosecutor is required to turn over to the defense during the discovery stage any written document or contemporaneous work product memorializing an interview that is considered exculpatory. It is the defenses contention that the following law enforcement agents provided critical exculpatory evidence, which was unlawfully withheld from the Grand Jury and defense.

[References provided.]

A. Walter Connery, NYC Asst. District Director of Investigations, INS.
B. William Glinka, Regional Commissioner, INS.
C. Lt. John Brown, NYPD Commanding Officer, 52nd Pct.
D. Rita Kardesman, Congressional Aide, Congressman Charles Rangle Office, NYC.
E. Detective Edmundo Rivera, NYPD, 52nd Pct.
F. Scott Blackman, NYC Deputy District Director, INS.
G. Captain Salvatore Blando, Commanding Officer, NYPD Manhattan North Homicide.

H. William Slattery, Deputy Commissioner, INS.
I. John McAllister, Deputy District Director, INS.
J. Chief Patrick Harnett, NYPD Chief of the Department.
K. Captain Joseph Reznick, NYPD Commanding Officer, 34Pct.
L. Detective Harold Hilderbrand, NYPD.
M. Chief Charles Ferrigno, Organized Crime Drug Task Force, INS.
N. Chief ADA Ann Rudman, Manhattan District Attorney's Office
O. Senior Special Agent John Dowd, DEA.
P. Lt Kidd, NYPD Internal Affairs Supervisor.
Q. Detective Stefanie Rich, NYPD Internal Affairs Unit.
R. Special Agent Richard Lauria, INS.
S. Special Agent Nicolas Minervini, INS.
T. ADA John F Kennedy Jr, Manhattan District Attorney's Office.
U. Special Agent Ronald Nowick, Internal Revenue Service, CID.
V. Special Agent Michael Capasso, DEA.
W. Special Agent Michael Agrifolio, DEA.
X. Supervisory Special Agent Vincent Wincelowitz, FBI Corruption Unit.
Y. Detective Ronnie Stripp, NYPD.
Z. Assistant United States Attorney Larry Brynes.

[Among the Errors During Trial]

AUSA Jeh Johnson failed to advise the Grand Jury and defense of exculpatory information he received from NYPD Detective Raul Anglada relative to the proposed drug cartel conspiracy.

AUSA Jeh Johnson should have recused himself as the prosecutor for conflict of interest since he was intimately involved in the Operation Esquire and Freddy Then drug investigations, both of which alleged official corruption at the SDNY.

AUSA Jeh Johnson should have recused himself due to his admitted social relationship with the judge and her family. Also, that he was the judge's former law clerk. During the trial it appeared that AUSA Johnson had some ex-parte communications with the judge, without the approval of the defense.

[Improper Selection of Federal Judge]

It appears that it was extremely convenient that this same judge was selected without being picked out of the "wheel", which is the proper procedure in federal courts for designating a trial judge. The prosecutors expressed unprofessional jubilation at the arraignment when the judge was selected. According to an unconfirmed Justice Department source, the judge was pre-selected. I noted my objections on the court record.

[Denial of Competent Legal Counsel][13]

---

[13] As was done with Ronald Rewald when he was made the scapegoat to cover up for CIA-political corruption, the federal judge barred famed attorney Melvin Belli from

During the trial, Dr. Angel Nunez volunteered to be co-counsel in light of the nervous breakdown of my attorney. AUSA Johnson conveniently told the court that Dr. Nunez could not be my attorney since he would be called as a government witness. Dr. Nunez was subpoenaed but never called as a witness.

[DOJ Personnel Withholding Impeachment Tapes]

During my trial, AUSA Johnson reportedly took full advantage of my attorney's mental state by debriefing him on a daily basis for defense strategies. This is how AUSA Johnson learned about our "Impeachment" tapes that recorded the undercover buys from the Federation witnesses. The prosecutors then pressured the court to have them released to their custody under the ruse they wanted to make transcriptions. The prosecution conveniently held the tapes while the Federation complainants testified and returned them once their testimony was completed. The defense was prevented from impeaching the witness's testimony because the tapes were not transcribed and available to the court.

During trial, the prosecutors took blatant advantage of my attorney's mental state by often taunting him with insults, pranks and derogatory gestures. For example, they would surreptitiously hide important "Brady" material on a cluttered defense table knowing he was disorganized to read the material and prepare for next days cross examination of prosecution witnesses.

The prosecutors learning of the perjury by the Federation complainants made representations to the jury that these witnesses were not testifying under any plea bargain cooperation agreement. Moreover, the prosecutor led the jury to believe these witnesses would be prosecuted for their admitted crimes. No prosecutions ever materialized.

The prosecutors told the jurors that INS Special Agent Stafford William, an un-indicted co-conspirator, would not be prosecuted for alleged civil rights violations in exchange for his testimony against me. They also told the jury that the plea bargain cooperation agreement did not guarantee him his job.

According to testimony entered into the Congressional Record, INS Deputy Commissioner William Slattery stated that prosecutors tried to intimidate the INS in not firing the agent. When that failed, the prosecutors reportedly attempted to get the agent another law enforcement position in US Customs.

According to Department of Justice regulations, federal prosecutors are obligated to report all felony violations involving witnesses to the appropriate federal and state law enforcement agencies. Staten Island Borough President Molinari confirmed from the IRS District Director that prosecutors never informed them of the admitted income tax evasion by Federation complainants. Similarly, prosecutors reportedly never notified any other law enforcement agency of their admitted felony crimes.

[DOJ Employees Threatening Defense Witnesses]

---

representing Rewald, forcing a just-graduated and unqualified lawyer as his legal counsel. See *Explosive Secrets of Covert CIA Companies*.

Department of Justice regulations prohibit prosecutors from coercing, intimidating or harassing any defense witness. According to testimony entered into the Congressional Record, my defense witnesses were routinely confronted in the defense witness room by prosecutors who demanded to know their testimony. These defense witnesses, many of who were younger law enforcement officers, felt very intimidated of potential retribution.

According to Federal Court procedures, a court-designated interpreter must be unbiased and must properly translate to the court all testimony. In my trial, the prosecutors influenced the judge to use as the "court interpreter" the same Spanish interpreter they had used for over a year to debrief the Federation witnesses, both during the grand jury and pre-trial process. Despite using the interpreter in court, they used her as one of their expert witnesses, who openly admitted before the jury her bias towards me. A Hispanic journalist in the court reported to the defense that he overheard the interpreter intentionally rephrasing defense questions and failed to provide correct translations to the court. This action was highly prejudicial to the defense and was reported to the court.

On one operation, I was convicted for conducting an illegal consent search solely upon the testimony of an INS agent who I previously disciplined for misconduct. At trial, the prosecutor never called the actual complainant to testify. Instead, he relied solely upon the testimony of the agent.

According to testimony entered into the Congressional Record by John McAlister, the INS Deputy District Director, he reported to prosecutors that the agent committed perjury. The agent had asked him to backup his court testimony that he had reported the alleged misconduct to his supervisor, which never occurred.

[DOJ Ignoring Evidence of Innocence]

In addition, I learned after the trial that this particular operation had been monitored by the NYPD Internal Affairs Unit. I had requested their presence because of allegations of police corruption. According to Lt. Kidd, the NYPD Internal Affairs supervisor, he went to the prosecutor and produced the undercover police tape confirming the legality of the search. This critical evidence was intentionally ignored and never turned over to the defense.

According to Patrick Harnett, who retired as the NYPD Chief of the Department, he met with prosecutors and attempted to convince them of my innocence. Chief Harnett confirmed that the genesis of Operation Bodega was the homicide investigation of PO Michael Buczek.

He also verified that the NYPD was aware of its operations and fully endorsed it. This was critical since prosecutors misled the jury to believe I invented the operation without a predication for my own personal gain. A copy of Chief Harnett's affirmation was placed in the Congressional Record.

According to an official memorandum entered into the Congressional Record, DEA Senior Special Agent John Dowd was reportedly threatened by prosecutors with potential prosecution after he confirmed that one of the searches enumerated in my indictment was lawful. The DEA agent and IRS agent were present during the search when permission was given. In any event, the prosecutor ignored the evidence and the fact that the complainant was a major Dominican organized crime figure under investigation by numerous federal and local agencies. Once the agent reported the incident to his supervisor and executed a memorandum memorializing the incident, the prosecutor agreed to dismiss that count in the indictment. The memorandum was never turned over to the defense.

After my conviction, many noteworthy journalists and radio personalities began to champion my cause. On one occasion, AUSA Jeh Johnson called up the WABC early morning show to criticize the show host for supporting my cause. On another occasion, SDNY prosecutors put out a formal press release criticizing Pulitzer Prize journalist Mike McAlary who published a series of investigative articles that exposed the drug cartel conspiracy. This type of action by federal prosecutors is unprecedented and not sanctioned by the Justice Department.

As you can see, it is virtually impossible for me to outline every documented act of prosecutorial misconduct or to convince you of the drug cartel conspiracy. Instead, let me represent that my landmark prosecution has been closely scrutinized by many, as well as independently investigated by numerous media entities, journalists, elected officials, police officials, legal experts, the New Jersey General Assembly and Civil Rights Groups. It was their general consensus that I was the target of a well-orchestrated drug cartel conspiracy. Moreover, my prosecution was politically motivated and there were many outrageous acts of prosecutorial misconduct.

One case in point, a New York Judge privately brought my case to the attention of Professor Bennett Gershon, a law professor at Pace Law School in New York who wrote a book on prosecutorial misconduct. In essence, Professor Gershon believes my prosecution is one of the worst cases of prosecutorial misconduct he has ever seen during his career.

[Stuck with Lawyer Suffering Mental Breakdown: Repeat of DOJ Tactics with Ron Rewald]

Professor Gershon was particularly outraged that my attorney of record, who suffered a nervous breakdown prior to trial, was refused permission to be replaced by substitute counsel. The prosecutors believed my attorney was lying about his nervous breakdown, despite the fact we have documented medical evidence reflecting the attorney was hospitalized and tried to commit suicide on two occasions. In addition, a New York State Supreme Court Judge came forward and confirmed that a week earlier he excused my attorney on a murder trial for what appeared to be severe depression and bizarre behavior. A few years later my lawyer was disbarred for threatening a judge at a side bar.

[President George H.W. Bush Provided Partial Relief]

Finally, former President George Bush showed the courage to go against his own Justice Department by granting me Executive Clemency on January

15, 1993. This is the first time a sitting president reportedly had taken that action.

For almost two years after my release, I filed an application for a new trial based upon newly discovered evidence, which meant if I was convicted again, the clemency would no longer be valid and I could be returned to prison.

[Two Years of Congressional Cover-Ups: What Else is New!]

For almost two years, I worked closely with distinguished [distinguished!] members of Congress, the United States Senate, New Jersey General Assembly, New York Senate, among others to have Congressional Hearings in my case. In fact, the New Jersey General Assembly, both Republican and Democrat, unanimously passed a resolution calling upon the Justice Department to appoint a Special Prosecutor. In addition, legislative resolutions were put forward in the New York Senate and New York City Council.

Unfortunately, these requested congressional hearings failed to materialize due in part to the resistance of the Justice Department and the fact President George Bush granted me Executive Clemency. Instead, the Justice Department convinced my supporters that an unbiased investigation by the Department of Justice, Office of Professional Responsibility (OPR), as well as the FBI, would be conducted into my case.

As for OPR, it is an extremely small unit with a tremendous backlog of cases that prevented them from conducting a thorough investigation. This investigation, if conducted properly, would have included the interviews of over seventy-five witnesses, as well as the review of volumes of defense investigative files. It is unfortunate that OPR failed to interview critical witnesses and basically rubber-stamped the court of appeals decision that no prosecutorial misconduct occurred.

[Standard DOJ Office of Professional Responsibility Cover-Up]

*For example, as previously noted, OPR failed to interview NYPD Detective Rau*l Anglada who confirmed that one year *prior* to my indictment, AUSA Jeh Johnson ignored critical information of the proposed drug cartel conspiracy. The detective is very credible; he was physically present when the informant told the prosecutor that she overheard the Dominican Attorneys Jorge Guthlein and Andres Aranda conspiring to set me up on fabricated civil rights charges. What is compelling is that AUSA Johnson in a sworn statement to the court, *did not* deny the allegations of being told, but conveniently said he did not remember the conversation.

[FBI Investigating Themselves]

As for the FBI investigation, it seems highly unprofessional that the FBI would assign local FBI agents to conduct a misconduct investigation involving federal prosecutors in the same judicial district where the agents work. Normally, the FBI would assign an OPR agent or a team of agents from another district office.

As for the promised "unbiased" FBI investigation, the case agent concluded that there was no credible evidence of the drug cartel conspiracy. According to sworn statements entered into the Congressional Record, the FBI Agent allegedly intimidated many witnesses, both civilian and law enforcement.

The following is a brief synopsis of alleged misconduct involving the FBI Case Agent who many believe engaged in an unprofessional and shabby investigation.

1. The investigative staff of Staten Island Borough President who spearheaded a two-year investigation into my case furnished the FBI with full access to the informants. It was their critical undercover activities that helped to expose the drug cartel conspiracy, as well as the extent of organized crime activity by the Federation and others. Mr. Molinari encouraged the FBI to conduct their own independent undercover investigation, which could have resulted in numerous federal RICO prosecutions, which he refused.

[DOJ Culture Fitting of Criminal Racketeering Group]

When the FBI refused to do the undercover drug buys from the Federation complainants, Borough President Molinari convinced Customs Commissioner Raymond Kelly, the former NYC Police Commissioner to do their own undercover operation. However, on the day of the planned drug buys, the NYPD detectives were reportedly told the operation was terminated at the request of federal authorities.

The FBI agreed to interview me during my imprisonment in order to obtain background information regarding the Project Esquire and related corruption investigations. The interview never materialized and instead they interviewed my brother-in-law and sister who had no idea of the cases I worked as a federal agent.

[Standard Practice by FBI Employees Threatening Witnesses in Obstruction of Justice Tactics]

The FBI Case Agent reportedly threatened the entire investigative staff of Borough President Molinari with potential criminal prosecution for fabricating the evidence of the drug cartel conspiracy. The agent even referred the case to the Eastern District of New York for a Grand Jury investigation. No prosecution ever took place and it is believed the action was intended solely to intimidate Mr. Molinari and his staff from continuing with their investigation.

The FBI Case Agent reportedly threatened NYPD Police Sergeant Lenny Lemer who was assigned to the DEA Task Force that was investigating the Dominican Federation for money laundering activity. Sgt. Lemer had come forward with evidence of the drug cartel conspiracy and reported to his superiors. According to his sworn affidavit that was entered into the Congressional Record, Sgt. Lemer was similarly threatened with potential prosecution for attempting to expose the conspiracy.

[FBI Employees Setting Up Scheme to File False

Charges, As Part of Obstruction of Justice Tactics][14]

The FBI case agent unlawfully attempted to setup Borough President Molinari on obstruction of justice charges through an informant who reportedly was intimidated by the case agent. When Mr. Molinari learned of this sting operation by the informant, he immediately reported the matter to the Justice Department and OPR. In response, the Justice Department made a written apology for the unprofessional and illegal actions of the case agent.

FBI Special Agent Lionel Baron convinced Dr. Angel Nunez and the undercover informants involved in my case that he was willing to help prove my innocence, as well as develop a criminal case against the Dominican Federation and others. However, the informants must be fully debriefed regarding their undercover activity on my case and be willing to work exclusively for the FBI. After their initial debriefing, the FBI Agent never did any follow-up activity. A FOIA request by New York Post Reporter Al Guart, among others disclosed no written record of any such investigation by the agent.

According to William Acosta, a former U.S. Customs and NYPD Internal Affairs officer who dedicated his entire career in exposing corruption, he furnished the Justice Department with critical evidence confirming the drug cartel conspiracy and the fact the Dominican Federation had reported ties to our intelligence community.

Mr. Acosta executed two sworn affidavits that reflected he learned of the drug cartel conspiracy from his joint investigations with Manuel De Dios, a world renowned journalist who was exposing the Dominican Federation and other crime syndicates. You may recall that Mr. De Dios was the first American journalist in this country to be assassinated by drug lords.

[Convenient Murder Protecting Corrupt DOJ Employees]

There are many law enforcement sources who believe that Mr. Dios was conveniently murdered a week after he executed a sworn affidavit wherein he agreed to testify before Congress regarding the drug cartel conspiracy, as well as Federation witnesses. Both, Mr. De Dios and Mr. Acosta's sworn affidavit has been entered into the Congressional Record. Why didn't the FBI case agent feel it important enough to debrief Mr. Acosta?

[Evidence on Top of Evidence Showing DOJ Employees Feloniously Obstructing Justice]

It should be evident that the intended goal of this FBI Agent was to intimidate the witnesses, as well as discredit the overwhelming evidence of the conspiracy. The FBI which has jurisdiction to investigate such federal crimes as drug distribution, RICO violations, loan sharking, interstate gambling, etc. failed miserably in their responsibility to investigate and prosecute crimes we

---

[14] The standard practice of DOJ employees setting up a scenario to file sham criminal charges against innocent people, especially government agents, is repeatedly shown in such books as *Defrauding America*; *Unfriendly Skies: 20th & 21st Centuries*, *Drugging America*, and others.

brought to their attention. The FBI ignored a golden opportunity to effectively use our intelligence, evidence and access to our defense undercover informants to infiltrate and prosecute the Dominican Federation, and others.

It should be noted that everything I said about the Dominican organized crime groups, such as the Federation, was officially corroborated in a 1997 one hundred page Department of Justice intelligence report entitled "The Dominican Threat, a Strategic Assessment of Dominican Drug Trafficking."

[Respected Government Agents Not Immune From
Culture of Criminal Retaliation and Obstruction of Justice]

I am sure you recall Jim Fox, the former FBI Special Agent in Charge at NYC who spearheaded the World Trade Center bombing case. We all saw him almost every night on the national news. Well, Mr. Fox proved to be a very courageous FBI official who was not easily intimidated or afraid to tell the truth to the public or the Justice Department. Mr. Fox publicly admitted that the FBI possessed certain evidence of my innocence. It was those public statements that my defense team used in order to support my application for a new trial.

Mr. Fox was unfortunately severely penalized for making those statements. According to published reports, it was alleged that federal prosecutors in my case directed Mr. Fox to prepare an affidavit reflecting that his comments were taken out of context. He reportedly refused and was later suspended one month prior to his scheduled retirement after 30 years of unblemished service with the FBI. A clear message that no matter who you are, or your position, you do not cross the Justice Department.

**[DOJ Tactics Protected Drug Income of Drug Cartels And
Muslim Terrorists in New York-New Jersey Area]**

In conclusion, I can only say that during the past ten years I have noticed a pattern of abuse by the Justice Department involving any organized effort by law enforcement to aggressively target the Dominican drug lords or their crime syndicates. Instead of supporting their efforts, it appears the agents are pressured to prematurely terminate viable investigations through intimidation and coercion. If the agent is uncooperative, he will find, like myself, that they have become the targets of a Justice Department probe.

There are many sources who believe that these Dominican organized crime investigations are being protected by Special Interest groups for a variety of reasons: pressure from our intelligence community, political intervention, official corruption or perhaps it has simply become politically incorrect for the Justice Department to investigate ethnic organized crime groups. No matter what the reason, dedicated agents should not be made the scapegoats.

Over the past ten years I have obtained personal knowledge that the following criminal investigations involving Dominican organized crime may have been prematurely terminated for some of the reasons noted above. Moreover, many of the case agents involved were reportedly pressured and intimidated to prematurely terminate their investigations. When the agents refuse, they conveniently become potential defendants for alleged civil rights prosecution.

A DEA investigation by S/A John Dowd involving the Sea Crest Trading Company.

- An IRS investigation by S/A Ronald Nowicki involving the Sea Crest Trading Company. In addition, a confidential source confirmed that IRS Agents in Connecticut were similarly being pressured to terminate their investigation.
- A Manhattan District Attorney investigation by NYPD Detective Ronnie Stripp involving the Sea Crest Trading Company.
- An U.S. Customs investigation (Case # 02AR8NY003) into alleged money laundering by the Dominican Federation.
- A DEA investigation by Sgt. Lenny Lemer involving the Dominican Federation and the Sea Crest Trading Company.
- A Manhattan District Attorney's Office criminal prosecution was reportedly terminated against Dominican Attorney Andes Aranda for allegedly conspiring to set up NYPD Police Officer Louis Della Pizzi on fabricated civil rights charges. According to many sources, these two attorneys who were the subject of the "Project Esquire" corruption probe have similarly escaped other criminal prosecutions.
- A DEA investigation involving Dominican Attorney Andres Aranda, who was allegedly implicated in the Jheri Curls drug organization. According to published reports, he was captured on tape accepting drug money from the head of this drug organization, who was convicted for drug distribution.
- A NYPD Internal Affairs investigation by former Deputy Commissioner Walter Mack into Sea Crest Trading Company and the Dominican Federation.
- A Bronx District Attorney's Office investigation by Assistant District Attorney Edward Friedenthal into the reported illicit activities of the Dominican Federation, the Freddy Then drug cartel, Sea Crest Trading Company, Dominican Attorneys Jorge Guthlein and Andres Aranda.
- A New Jersey State Police investigation by Detective Sergeant Jim Mullholland into the Dominican Federation and Sea Crest Trading Company. This inquiry was predicated upon my testimony before the New Jersey Senate Crime Committee investigating the infiltration of Dominican organized crime operations in the State of New Jersey.
- A Brooklyn District Attorney's Office investigation authorized by District Attorney Charles Hynes into the Dominican Federation and Sea Crest Trading Company.

- A FBI investigation that was predicated upon evidence furnished by retired NYPD Detective Ben Jacobsen of the A.C. Nielson Company into organized coupon fraud involving the Sea Crest Trading Company.
- A NYPD/US Customs money laundering investigation by Lt. R. Rose into the Dominican Federation and Sea Crest Trading Company.
- An U.S. Postal Inspection investigation by Inspector J.V. Barrett into the Sea Crest Trading Company.
- A Bergen County (NJ) investigation by Detectives Juan Lopez and Wayne Yahn into the Dominican Federation and Sea Crest Trading Company.
- The dismantling of DEA Group 33 at NYC that had the highest arrest and seizure record involving the Dominican cartels. The agents were later reassigned and investigated by SDNY federal prosecutors for alleged civil rights violations. The agents were never prosecuted and later filed a civil suit against the government.
- The dismantling of an elite NYPD anti-crime unit in Washington Heights who had the highest arrest and seizure record involving Dominican organized crime. This elite unit was investigated by SDNY federal prosecutors for alleged civil rights violations. One of the officers was prosecuted for alleged perjury since the prosecutors felt he was uncooperative. The conviction is on appeal and Congressman King (NY) has championed his case and has requested an OPR investigation into allegations of prosecutorial misconduct.
- The dismantling of an elite Pennsylvania State Attorney General's Narcotics Unit that was investigating the distribution of heroin in Philadelphia by Dominican Drug Lords from Washington Heights. The investigation disclosed that million of dollars in suspected drug proceeds were being delivered to a presidential candidate in the Dominican Republic.

[No Limit to Extent of Complicity]

When the agents began to make inquiries with the State Department and CIA, they were reportedly pressured to terminate their investigation, as well as reveal the identity of the informant. The agents reported the incident to the Senate Intelligence Committee who commenced a hearing into the allegations. Almost immediately, the agents were relieved of their duties pending a Justice Department and FBI investigation involving alleged civil rights violations. Almost two years later, the agents were cleared of any wrongdoing and the investigation still remains inactive. The agents have filed a civil suit against the PA State Attorney General, the United States Attorney in Philadelphia, the State Department and CIA, which is scheduled for trial this year.

There has been a lot of controversy surrounding my landmark prosecution and many theories as to why the Justice Department may have gone to great lengths to prosecute a highly decorated federal agent for an alleged consent to search form infraction. There are many that believe the conspiracy was sanctioned by the intelligence community to protect certain CIA operations and assets under the disguise of national security. Wherein, others are convinced there is widespread corruption in the Justice Department and I had to be eliminated due to my increased enforcement efforts that would ultimately expose the drug cartel operations and official corruption.

Or was this simply a case of an over zealous federal prosecutor with a personal agenda who engaged in widespread prosecutorial misconduct to gain a conviction and secure a position in a prestigious law firm. Another case scenario is that there are a few elected officials who have been unwittingly corrupted by crime syndicates, such as the Dominican Federation who reportedly made substantial campaign contributions to certain elected officials, as well as helped to win certain elections through organized election fraud.

The American public and criminal justice system holds the police to a higher standard wherein they are subjected to more civil suits, criminal prosecutions and imprisonment for alleged misconduct than any other profession. Yet, using that same criteria, federal law includes federal prosecutors and other Justice Department personnel who knowingly violate the civil rights of a defendant to be completely immune from prosecution. Hopefully, your bill will change that dual standard.

I would strongly recommend that the committee consider contacting Staten Island Borough President Guy V. Molinari, as well as Congressman James Traficant who can turn over to the committee volumes of defense case files, undercover tapes and related evidence that establish substantial misconduct on the part of the Justice Department. Moreover, that a dedicated federal agent was betrayed by the very same government he proudly served.

Thank You

Joseph Occhipinti, Executive Director
Along with numerous attachments

Another witness testifying was John Culbertson, Director, Center for Reform, Washington, D.C. Excerpts from his prepared statement included the following:

> This pattern of selective investigation coverup is precisely the reason why a new oversight agency must be considered. Problems like those exhibited at DOJ will not go away with a new Attorney General, administration or promises to do better in the future. They are institutional in nature, as those who embarked on the pattern of abuses must continue to obfuscate and cover up, protecting themselves at the expense of the innocent.
>
> I have worked on numerous cases where the Department of Justice has refused defendants access to evidence in violation of Brady. They have invoked national security or cited other ongoing investigations as reasons for

denying defendants access to evidence and information they are entitled to under the Constitution.

Facts are made to fit the case, rather than the case developed to discover the facts. The Department of Justice continues to amass considerable power without proper checks and balances.

The Department of Justice has continued to whitewash, stonewall or selectively investigate serious allegations of wrongdoing

At the conclusion of testimony, questions were then asked by panel members. Representative Nadler, whose constituents included the drug smugglers and Dominican groups, then asked Occhipinti:

The point is your conviction was upheld by the Second Circuit. Is it true that you were released from jail because your sentence was commuted by President Bush? Who requested the President to commute your sentence to time served?

Occhipinti replied, *"Staten Island Borough President Guy Molinari, among leaders from the black and Hispanic community and law enforcement agencies."*

Nadler Giving Criminals More Credibility Than Respected Members of Law Enforcement and Society

Ignoring the fact that this large group had more credibility than the largely Dominican jurors that convicted Occhipinti, and were blocked from receiving massive amounts of contradicting evidence from throughout the law enforcement community that did not have the self-serving interests or uninformed status of the jurors, Nadler stated:

Okay. Mr. Chairman, I would simply submit I don't know why the President decided to commute this sentence and I am not going to criticize that. There may have been good reasons to do so. I don't know. I would submit on the basis of the court record Mr. Occhipinti is a perfect example of the kind of misconduct by people in prosecutorial and law enforcement positions that supposedly we are here to try to figure out how to prevent.

Mr. Occhipinti, according to the finding of the court by various unlawful actions, including perjury, prejudiced the rights of other people, got them illegally convicted, I find him hardly a credible witness as to malpractice against him.

First of all, sir, that sentencing memorandum was based upon testimony from Federation witnesses."

Occhipinti replied: *"Federation. Federation witnesses. Those bodega owners were members of the Dominican Federation, which were proven by the police officers to be a front for the cartel."*

Nadler stated, *"The court [the judge that blocked evidence from multiple respected people] didn't believe they were fronts for the cartel, did it?"*

Occhipinti replied:

> One of the things of the prosecutorial misconduct, sir, is when I was indicted, people from the community came forward to help me and we had to prove that their testimony was perjured because they were portrayed as being law abiding. People that were not professional informants went undercover into the bodegas, captured them on tape involved in ongoing criminal activity.
>
> And for example, Dr. Angel Nunez, an attorney of the National Hispanic Coalition even interviewed and tape recorded many of those complainants who indicated that in fact their testimony was not credible, that permission had been granted. We attempted at trial to turn in 55 tapes which impeached their credibility that showed their perjury of the tapes. When the government found out about the tapes, they directed that we turn over those impeachment tapes to the government.
>
> We were precluded from using the tapes because they told the court, the prosecutors, they were making transcriptions. Well, every Federation witness testified, okay. We could not cross-examine them to impeach their credibility. So, sir, what I am saying that memorandum you read was based upon perjured testimony and the fact that the jury never heard all of the facts in the case.

Ignoring the fact that appellate judges—who I had repeatedly found and documented as corrupt—Nadler stated: "I assume, sir, that all of the contentions you are now making were in your appeal, that you appealed on this basis, among others, to the Second Circuit."

Occhipinti added:

> I would like to remark, sir, if you will allow me with respect to the appeal. Yes, sir, we did file an appeal brief and appendix well in over of a thousand pages. On the day the oral arguments occurred there were a group of Federation people in front of the courthouse protesting. When my attorney and Mr. Molinari was there, took the podium to argue my oral arguments, these Federation members with signs, they came into the courtroom. In fact, they threatened that if the Occhipinti conviction was overturned there would be rioting in Washington Heights.
>
> The point was they interrupted him when he was making oral argument. It was established fact that they were out there protesting because I was told by U.S. Marshals—
>
> However, it was said that if the conviction was overturned there would be rioting in Washington Heights. What is very unusual from legal experts, sir, is that less than one hour after oral arguments, the Court of Appeals said the conviction was upheld.

Nadler responded mockingly:

So your testimony then is that this trial was controversial, that there were elements in the community that were very much supporting you, that there were elements in the community that were very much supporting the allegations against you, that one or both sides demonstrated outside of the courtroom, that some of those people were allowed to come inside, but not demonstrate inside, all of which is perfectly typical of the way things happen in New York, and other places

I assume, and that the Second Circuit, having heard the arguments of your attorney, who I presume made the arguments that you made here a few minutes ago, within an hour disposed of this. One can assume since they disposed of this so quickly that they thought there was no substance to it or very little and upheld the appeal? That is what you are telling us, right?

Occhipinti added: *"It was said that if the conviction was overturned there would be rioting in Washington Heights. What is very unusual from legal experts, sir, is that less than one hour after oral arguments, the Court of Appeals said the conviction was upheld."*

Nadler responded:

So your testimony then is that this trial was controversial, that there were elements in the community that were very much supporting you, that there were elements in the community that were very much supporting the allegations against you, that one or both sides demonstrated outside of the courtroom, that some of those people were allowed to come inside, but not demonstrate inside, all of which is perfectly typical of the way things happen in New York, and other places I assume, and that the Second Circuit, having heard the arguments of your attorney, who I presume made the arguments that you made here a few minutes ago, within an hour disposed of this. One can assume since they disposed of this so quickly that they thought there was no substance to it or very little and upheld the appeal? That is what you are telling us, right?

Occhipinti replied: "Absolutely."

Department of Justice Whitewash Team

Department of Justice sent their representatives to testify that everything in the Department of Justice was fine. David Margolis, who was Special Attorney for the Justice Department's Organized Crime Force in Boston—while FBI agents engaged in years of murders with the organized crime group headed by Bulger: and John Keeney, Deputy Assistant Attorney General of the Criminal Division of the Department of Justice. Excerpts from their sworn testimony included the following:

The Department objects to the proposed legislation which would in effect create a standing independent counsel for the Department of Justice.

> Our demonstrated record of success in pursuing allegations of internal misconduct establishes that the proposed legislation is neither necessary not well advised, and represents a solution in search of a problem.
>
> The system of checks and balances currently in place, I believe, assures the effectiveness of our present system. The Department's various institutional components foster public confidence. The Department of Justice has in place several components that work independently of each other, but which produce a coordinated response to allegations of professional or criminal misconduct within our ranks.

That legislation was blocked from proceeding. The vast power of the Department of Justice people could possibly have been circumvented if Traficant had brought forth more witnesses that could have testified about hard-core corruption of people in the Department of Justice besides Occhipinti. The information surrounding him was of great importance, but the addition of many of those insiders that I had acquired over the years would have shocked the nation into finally doing something.

Nadler's Cover-Up Tactics and Impending Catastrophic Events

It is possible that if Nadler and others had not impeded that legislation to address major misconducts among employees of the U.S. Department of Justice, nearly 3,000 people would not have died 18 months later on a single morning in New York City. Fortunately for Nadler, he had plenty of others doing the same cover-up.

Endless Series of Congressional Cover-Ups

For two years, Occhipinti testified before members of Congress on these serious criminal activities upon the part of employees in the U.S. Department of Justice. One such appearance was on July 27, 2000, before the House Judiciary Committee, during which Occhipinti presented dozens of affidavits, including those from respected people in law enforcement and the community that supported what Occhipinti had been stating. The usual cover-up occurred.

For years, I had documented to cover-ups by that and other congressional groups. Many of my letters sent to them for over 40 years identifying specific corrupt acts affecting national security were brought to their attention. See *www.defraudingamerica.com.*

Congressman Traficant Suffered the Standard Off-the-Shelf Reaction from Department of Justice Employees

That proposed legislation never went anywhere and shortly thereafter federal prosecutors filed criminal charges against Congressman Traficant, causing him to lose his congressional position and end up in prison. That not uncommon reaction would be why members of Congress look the other way when corrupt and criminal activities of people in the Department of Justice is reported to them. With most or all members of Congress involved in blatant bribes (aka political contributions) and resulting legislation and perks for "contributors," any of them can be easily charged with a crime by Justice Department prosecutors.

CHAPTER FIVE

CIA-Protected Assets In Local Terrorist Cells

Since 1990, several of my CIA sources explained how Sea Crest—a CIA front—laundered money to obtain military equipment and provide training for the Mujahedeen in Afghanistan during the 1980s. Occhipinti's task force, with no connection to my CIA sources, also discovered this funding, and that some of the money was going to terrorists in the United States. Former FBI agent Richard Taus also discovered this relationship during his duties in the FBI's New York City offices.

A key figure in one of the terrorist groups funded by the CIA Sea Crest operation was Sheik Omar Abdel-Rahman. He was convicted by a New York jury for his role in planning the bombing of the World Trade Center building and sentenced to life in prison, and nine co-conspirators were sentenced to long prison terms.

CIA Granting Visa to Known Terrorist

Despite his known terrorist activities, including his involvement in the plot to assassinate Egypt's Anwar Sadat in 1981, a CIA agent in the U.S. consulate office in Khartoum, Sudan, issued a one-year visa for Sheik Omar Abdel Rahman to enter the United States in May 1990. He arrived in New York City in July, and a few months later the State Department revoked his visa. U.S. Immigration and Naturalization Service (INS) were informed of this fact, but deportation was blocked by high-level sources in government. This pressure caused the INS to issue a green card to Sheik Omar several months later.

The people who funded Sheik Omar's entry into the United States included Mustafa Shalabi (Director of Alkifah, a support fund for Mujahedeen fighters based in Brooklyn); Muslim Brotherhood member and CIA asset from Afghanistan, Mahmud Abouhalima, and El Sayid Nosair, an Egyptian. They had received training, funding, and arms from the CIA.

U.S. Army Training Afghan Terrorists

Besides receiving CIA training, Nosair and Abouhalima had been earlier trained by the terrorist, Abu Nidal. During the Soviet presence in Afghanistan the U.S. Army provided training to recruits for the Mujahedeen, which would be another example of the blowback consequences suffered by the United States from intervention in foreign affairs. The people the U.S. called "freedom fighters" would turn their U.S.-acquired terrorist skills against the United States.

FBI Cover-up of Terrorist Activities

Nosair was suspected of the 1990 murder of Rabbi Meir Kahane, a Jewish militant in New York City. Following this murder, the FBI obtained a search warrant and seized terrorist material from his Jersey City apartment. Included in this material were bomb-making materials, a list of people marked for death, including Rabbi Meier Kahane, bomb-making instructions, and pictures of targeted buildings, including the World Trade Center! The FBI made no arrests, and withheld this information from New York City prosecutors seeking to arrest those responsible for Kahane's murder. This withholding of evidence played a key role in his December 20, 1991, acquittal.

DOJ Cover-up Helped Plan Airliner Bombings

Money for Nosair's defense was obtained from criminal activities associated with Sea Crest Trading Company. Many of these activities were under the supervision of Ramzi Yousef, an Afghan terrorist who came to the United States and became part of Sheik Omar's group in 1992.

Mastermind of 1993 World Trade Center Bombing

Ramzi Yousef was the mastermind behind the 1993 bombing of the World Trade Center. After the bombing, he fled to Manila, and planned to bomb 12 U.S. airliners departing Far East locations. That plot was given the name of Bojinka. Yousef tried out one bombing of a Philippine Airline 747 as a rehearsal. It did not down the aircraft, but the bomb killed one passenger.

While working with explosives in his Manila apartment in 1994, a fire occurred, causing Yousef to flee before police arrived. He then fled to Pakistan where he was later arrested and brought to the United States to await trial on the Bojinka plot. If that accidental fire had not occurred, it is possible that the Bojinka plan would have succeeded, killing thousands of air travelers.

Advance Warning of Plans to Fly Airliners Into Buildings

Abdul Hakim Murad was arrested before he could also flee. He was a pilot who received his pilot training in the United States. Under questioning, Hakim revealed that al Qaeda cells planned to crash U.S. airliners into buildings in the nation's capital at Washington. A search of Yousef's computer files provided information on other terrorist plans, further showing plans to hijack U.S. airliners and fly them into buildings. This information was given by the Philippine National Police (PNP) to the U.S. consulate in Manila. They passed the information to the FBI.

Yousef was seized in Pakistan in 1996 and flown to the United States, where he was convicted in late 1996 of involvement in the conspiracy to place bombs on U.S. aircraft in the Far East. That conviction occurred despite the favored treatment given by U.S. District Judge William Schlesinger to Yousef's lawyer, William Kunstler.

WTC Bombing Made Possible by DOJ Cover-ups

Without funding from Sea Crest Trading Company, and without Justice Department personnel blocking prosecution of Dominican drug traffickers and Sea Crest, it is very probable funding to carry out the terrorist activities would have been lacking. That 1993 bomb killed six people, injured over a thousand others, and did over $500 million in damage in the February 26, 1993, World Trade Center bombing. The imprisonment of Sheik Omar, following the World Trade Center bombing, did not destroy the group's ability to conduct further terrorist acts in the United States. That would become apparent on September 11, 2001.

Dominican Drug Money Helped Elect U.S. President

Reports indicated that U.S. and Dominican Republic politicians were receiving substantial money from Capital National Bank, Sea Crest Trading Company, and the Dominican Federation. An in-depth *The New American* article (April 28, 1997), titled "Dominican drug money may have helped elect our President," stated in part:

> A report from Puerto Rico suggests that the Clinton White House has accepted drug-tainted contributions linked to the Dominican Republic's radical Dominican Revolutionary Party (PRD). PRD members ... made campaign donations last September during a Democratic National Committee fund-raiser at Coogan's Irish Pub in Washington Heights [in New York City]. PRD members Simon Diaz and Pablo Espinal supported the campaign of U.S. President Clinton....
>
> Both Diaz and Espinal reportedly posed for pictures with Vice President Al Gore, according to PRD leaders. Diaz is vice president of a New York City chapter of the PRD and president of a group of party-affiliated businesses. He is also currently under investigation by the Drug Enforcement Administration (DEA) and various other anti-narcotics agencies with regard to the PRD's "alleged nexus with international drug cartels" as El Vocero reported....
>
> Furthermore, although U.S. federal officials were aware of the links between PRD and the drug cartels, "for reasons that remain unclear, these officials exerted pressure to derail active investigations in the matter."
>
> Despite his known drug and crime connections, Jose Francisco Pena-Gomez, the PRD's leader and Dominican Republic presidential candidate was President Bill Clinton's choice in the Dominican elections held in 1994 and 1996. This recommendation followed the campaign contributions received by Clinton and Al Gore.

Luck of President Bill Clinton and Al Gore

On May 10, 1998, another potential witness and threat against President Bill Clinton and Vice President Al Gore died. Former Dominican Republic presidential candidate Jose Pena-Gomez was a potential threat to them because of the drug money Gomez and his drug-related groups gave to the Clinton-Gore campaign and because of the Clinton administration's protection of Dominican drug trafficking and other crimes. Pena-Gomez died from pulmonary edema.

Parallel Blocks in Pennsylvania

Four agents from the Pennsylvania Bureau of Narcotics Investigation office (BNI) were experiencing similar problems with Dominican drug traffickers, high-level cover-ups, and retaliation. Agents John R. McLaughlin, Charles A. Micewski, Dennis J. McKeefery, and Edward Eggles, working as a team, discovered evidence of widespread criminal activities by the Dominican Revolutionary Party and Dominican crime figures. They also suffered retaliation that insured the continuation of the drug smuggling and funding of terrorist activities.

The BNI narcotic agents discovered that drug money was gathered and distributed at fund raisers held in Pennsylvania and that various government agencies were actively aware of these facts. They also discovered drug money funneled to U.S. politicians and to the U.S.-backed candidate for the presidency of the Dominican Republic, Jose Francisco Pena Gomez, who was being supported by the Clinton Administration.

Ties to Colombian Drug Traffickers

McLaughlin described what he found about Colombian connections to Dominican drug traffickers:

> *While at an intelligence meeting, I received a document from Interpol that described an organization of Dominican drug traffickers with ties to the Cali cartel in Colombia dating back to at least 1991, and also documents hundreds of kilos of cocaine seized as well as approximately 100 people either arrested or having outstanding arrest warrants. This organization has ties to the Dominican Revolutionary Party headed by Jose Francisco Pena-Gomez who was being backed by the U.S. Department of State in the last election.*

Pennsylvania Attorney General Protecting Drug Traffickers

On May 10, 1996, McLaughlin notified the Deputy Attorney General of a major heroin shipment due to arrive from New York and a large amount of drug-money being laundered. Harrisburg Attorney General's office refused to allow a bust to occur. The surveillance team was called off and the heroin sale occurred that evening at 7:45 p.m., with Dominicans taking over $100,000 to New York.

Shortly thereafter, over 116 overdoses from heroin were reported from using the heroin brand, "Dead Presidents." Numerous drug overdoses and deaths were reported from using another form of Dominican heroin called "Super Buck." BNI agents were ordered not to interfere with these sales that were occurring at various Philadelphia street corners.

Dropping Charges Against 85 Drug Traffickers

McLaughlin was told that from April 16 to November 19, 1996, the Philadelphia district attorney's office dismissed 85 defendants who were caught with $879,000 worth of heroin, $47,000 worth of crack, $148,000 worth of cocaine, and large sums of money, vehicles and weapons. In addition to protecting the major drug trafficking, this sent a message to other government agents that they should not investigate any of the Dominican drug traffickers, drug-money launderers, or drug-money-related political contributions.

Retaliation Against Effective Agents

Shortly thereafter, on April 16, 1996, Arnold Gordon, First Deputy District attorney for Philadelphia, met with the Attorney General and charged that there was a problem with the BNI agents in the Philadelphia office. This was followed by a series of adverse actions against the four agents that halted their drug investigations into the politically connected drug traffickers.

Part of their removal was related to information provided by Darlene Novinger, as I described in *Defrauding America* and *Drugging America.* These books provide considerably more information about the matters in these pages, which further prove the corrupt culture in the various offices of the Justice Department and the CIA, and the effect of that culture upon national security.

The Pennsylvania Attorney General's office took McLaughlin off drug cases on the sham excuse that McLaughlin made a grammatical error on an affidavit. McLaughlin stated "the" informant instead of "an" informant, an error that was meaningless in light of the details in the report, and could be made by anyone without any unfavorable results. It was clear; the Pennsylvania Attorney General's office was protecting drug traffickers from arrest.

Lawyer Advising Client to Lie

On January 13, 1997, a confidential informant (CI 902-96) told BNI agents that a prominent defense lawyer, Guy Sciolla, was telling his Dominican clients to falsely report that BNI narcotic agents skimmed money from them when they were arrested. This was the same false charge used against Occhipinti by two Dominican drug traffickers. McLaughlin reported this to the district attorney's office and again, the Pennsylvania prosecutor refused to act against the lawyer.

Fearing for the Life of an Informant

During a March 27, 1996, BNI meeting at Philadelphia headquarters, attended by CIA agent David Lawrence, McLaughlin and Regional Director John Sunderhauf, Lawrence wanted the name of one of BNI's key informants who was disclosing highly sensitive information about Dominican drug trafficking. Recognizing that the state Attorney General's office was blocking the investigation and prosecution of known drug traffickers, McLaughlin, fearing for the life of the informant, refused to reveal the informant's identity.

FBI Pressuring Informant to File False Affidavit

McLaughlin reported (July 8, 1997) that a Confidential Informant (Nr. 910-95) called BNI agents about FBI agents from the Federal Corruption Probe Task Force pressuring him to sign an affidavit containing derogatory statements about BNI agents that weren't true.

Retaliatory Reassignment

In May 1996, State Attorney General Tom Corbett announced that McLaughlin and the three other BNI agents working on Dominican-related cases were removed from their drug assignments and reassigned to a less meaningful task. Despite the agents' request for information as to what they had done wrong, no reason was given. They were reassigned and given menial and often degrading tasks.

I know the tactic. While I was with the FAA, reporting deadly air safety and criminal violations related to a series of fatal airline crashes, I was transferred to an undesirable assignment. My predecessor on that same assignment, who reported similar air safety misconduct, was transferred to Puerto Rico, an undesirable location.

On June 3, 1996, the BNI agents were told that they could no longer get information from the New York DEA office, thereby depriving the BNI of important drug-related information. On July 18, 1996, the Pennsylvania district attorney's office advised the narcotic agents that the office would accept no more cases from them. On August 21, 1997, U.S. Customs agent John Malandros told McLaughlin that he was ordered to drop the investigation into the Revolutionary Dominican Party.

Media Aiding and Abetting Drug Traffickers and Cover-ups

Within a few days, the media started printing and airing a series of stories critical of the narcotic agents and protective of the drug traffickers and government retaliation. On April 23, 1996, Philadelphia's *Channel 3 News* did a lead story, comparing the BNI agents to a group of Philadelphia police officers who created false crimes and wrongfully accused people in the 39th Precinct. That misleading television story was followed by others, including derogatory stories in the *Philadelphia Inquirer* and the *Philadelphia Daily News*.

For reasons unknown to the agents, Supervisor Lou Gentile in the Pennsylvania Attorney General's headquarters in Philadelphia, ordered the narcotic agents not to correct the false media stories. These media sources had enough access to insiders to know the true story. They chose to mouth the official government line. Former Attorney General Tom Corbett told agents to "take it on the chin," and that he wouldn't correct the false media reports.

ACLU Protecting the Criminals

ACLU lawyers stated that they intended to seek monetary damages for the Dominicans arrested by the BNI agents. State Senator Vince Fumo from Philadelphia, urged convicted Dominican drug dealer Felix Torres to seek vengeance against the BNI agents: "Sue them, bankrupt them, take their houses from them. That's the only time they're going to get the message."

Reporting the Problems to Senate Investigators

McLaughlin described these activities to investigators from the Senate Intelligence Committee, including chief counsel John Bellinger, Janice Kephart, and Al Cummings. He informed Randy Scheunemann on the staff of John Bellinger the National Security Advisor.

McLaughlin called Senator Arlen Specter's office on October 15, 1996, concerning the Dominican Republic drug trafficking and the Justice Department's protection of their drug activities. The Senate Select Committee on Intelligence asked McLaughlin to testify behind closed doors about the drug trafficking and other criminal activities, and the obstruction of justice at the state and federal levels.

Blocking Congressional Investigation into Drug Trafficking

Seeking to prevent McLaughlin from testifying to Congress about the criminal activities and their cover-ups, the Pennsylvania Attorney General's office sent him a memo on November 7, 1966, barring him from testifying. The Attorney General also sent a fax to Senator Specter that McLaughlin was not to appear before the Senate Intelligence Committee. No reaction from Specter concerning this obstruction of justice.

Threats if He Testified Before Congress

John Kelly, Regional Director for the Pennsylvania Attorney General office, threatened McLaughlin with termination if he testified before Congress. Under federal law, this obstruction of justice threat was a criminal act. (Title 18 USC Section 1505, 1512, 1513 and the related obstruction of justice statutes)

McLaughlin *did testify* in a secret executive session to the U.S. Senate Select Committee on Intelligence on January 29, 1997. No action was taken, despite the serious implications of the testimony. Congress took no actions when Occhipinti and his group described the serious problems, after testimony by the Pennsylvania agents, or the many other government insiders described within these pages and in my other books. Members of Congress had covered up for major criminal and even treasonous and subversive activities detailed to them by government insiders. Instead of acting as required by their positions, they joined the cover-ups. I experienced and recorded 40 years of congressional cover-ups.

Filing a Civil Rights Complaint Against Government Officials and Drug Traffickers

In response to the obstruction of justice and retaliatory actions by Pennsylvania and federal officials, the four agents filed a lawsuit in late 1997 in the U.S. District Court for the Middle District of Pennsylvania under the Civil Rights Act and as a *Bivens* complaint. The complaints, filed by Pennsylvania lawyers Don Bailey from Harrisburg and Samuel Stratton from West Chester, charged the defendants with conduct that was criminal, subversive, and related to aiding and abetting the smuggling of drugs into the United States. The introductory statement in the Complaint stated in part:

> This is a civil rights complaint brought to redress, inter alia, the deprivation of the plaintiffs' federally guaranteed interests in free speech and property. This is also a Bivens' complaint, the gravies of which is that a Dominican drug organization, through the protection of certain persons in the State Department and the

CIA, was effective in having the plaintiffs' law enforcement efforts stopped and their careers destroyed.

The plaintiffs began gathering evidence on the PRD, a Dominican political party supported by the United States, which indicated that illegal drugs were being prolifically sold at will in the United States to our Black and Hispanic populations. This money was being put into American elections.

Plaintiffs contend that they discovered a highly organized Dominican group organized as the Revolutionary Dominican Party (PRD), a political party seeking power in the Dominican Republic, that was, and is, protected and sanctioned, unlawfully, by agencies of the United States government, to include the CIA and the State Department, enabling the Dominicans to distribute illegal drugs at will to the Black and Hispanic populations of the Eastern Seaboard.

Plaintiffs also allege that in furtherance of the unlawful policy of protecting the large-scale distributors of illegal narcotics to largely captive center city populations, the defendants have utilized the offices of the United States attorney for the Eastern District of Pennsylvania, and the FBI, to pursue an oppressive threatening investigation of the plaintiffs in an effort to destroy their Credibility and silence them.

These tactics include the ferreting out of plaintiffs' information sources so that they may be silenced [killed] through the mechanism of a federal grand jury. They ask this Court to appoint, or urgently request, a special prosecutor, independent of the Justice Department and either political party, to investigate the cover-up they allege in order that they and some of their sources can be saved from more abuses ... ask this court to issue an order forcing federal authorities to protect Confidential Informant "P-Man," 902-96, who is now known to them, immediately.

General Allegations

In the Complaint, the four narcotic agents charged that the defendants in various combinations engaged in conspiracies to:

Block government agents from halting the flow of illegal drugs into the United States.

Allow the flow of illegally procured money from the sale and distribution of drugs in the United States into the political coffers of Francisco Pena Gomez of the PDR in the Dominican.

Prevent disclosure and/or further discovery by the plaintiffs of the flow of illegally procured money from the sale and distribution of drugs by the PRD to black and Hispanic Americans.

Discredit the plaintiffs in order to destroy their credibility and thus their ability to participate in the prosecution of drug traffickers.

Protect the proceeds (money) of Dominican drug dealers and traffickers from exposure and prosecution.

Protect the government conspirators, both named and unnamed, from criminal prosecution for their role in aiding and abetting the illegal sale and distribution of drugs in the United States.

A mid-1998 *New York Times* article titled, "Dominicans Now Dominant in East Coast Drug Trade," provided further support for that fact.

Undercover ONI and CIA Agent Speaks Out

On December 12, 1994, James Ridgeway de Szigethy executed an affidavit admitting that Sea Crest had been a CIA operation, a fact that he had learned from his activities as an informant for the Naval Intelligence Service, as well as from his CIA associates. Szigethy also revealed that the assassination of Prince Chitresh "Teddy" Khedker in New York City was committed by CIA operative George Cobo.

According to Szigethy, the prince was a CIA operative involved in the Sea Crest operation in Canada and that Cobo was a Cuban national trained by the CIA. Szigethy provided Congressman Traficant with other affidavits and documents regarding Sea Crest and the Occhipinti conspiracy. Szigethy was previously polygraphed with respect to another affidavit he executed and found to be truthful.

DOJ Drops Criminal Investigation of Drug Fighters

U.S. Attorney Michael R. Stiles issued a statement on February 18, 1999, announcing the closing of its investigation into suspected criminal activities against the four Pennsylvania narcotic agents! No mention of any investigation into the drug traffickers and the evidence accumulated against them.

Gravity of the Implications

The Occhipinti and McLaughlin cases provided additional evidence of widespread drug and other criminal activities involving a segment of the population largely composed of immigrants to the United States. Key people in this group had connections to the CIA, explaining why Department of Justice personnel repeatedly protected drug dealers, Middle East terrorists, while prosecuting anyone exposing these criminal activities.

There were repeated cover-ups and obstruction of justice by almost every level of the state and federal criminal justice system, and a pattern of retaliation against those few government agents with the courage and integrity to carry out the responsibilities of their jobs. That pattern had to be orchestrated and protected by a powerful source in government. That would be people in control of the U.S. Department of Justice.

Agents Form Group to Protect Against Retaliation And To Perform Their Legal Responsibilities

A group was formed to bring together government agents who suffered the type of retaliation suffered by Occhipinti, McLaughlin and others. It was called the National Police Defense Foundation, with its home office in Washington, D.C. The purpose of the association was to protect the rights of law-enforcement personnel and the public, and to provide assistance, services, and counseling for law-enforcement personnel being falsely prosecuted. Occhipinti was the executive director of the foundation. (National Police Defense Foundation, 1422 K Street NW, Washington, DC 20005.)

The Fallout from the FBI-DOJ-CIA Culture Would Be Catastrophic, Especially in New York City

The protection of the drug operations, part of which funded terrorist cells in New York and New Jersey would be felt catastrophic. First there was the bombing of the World Trade Center in 1993, which was funded in part by drug money that FBI-DOJ personnel made available to them. Then there were the hijackings of four airliners on September 11, 2001. More information on these matters in other pages.

Partial Vindication for Two Pennsylvania Narcotic Agents

A jury in Wilkes-Barre, Pennsylvania awarded $1.5 million to the two Pennsylvania narcotic agents, McLaughlin and Micewski. A newspaper article (February 13, 2003) stated:

> Mr. McLaughlin and Mr. Micewski said they had uncovered a Dominican drug-trafficking ring in Philadelphia, New York and other Eastern cities that was funneling profits to the Dominican Revolutionary party, which they said was supported by the Central Intelligence Agency and the State Department. The agents said the federal government had allowed Mr. Pena Gomez to return to the Dominican Republic with $500,000 in drug profits after a 1995 fund-raising trip to New York.
>
> The agents said that shortly after they made their accusations the Philadelphia district attorney and United States attorney's office began questioning their credibility and stopped prosecuting their drug cases. More than 125 cases were dismissed or dropped after prosecutors accused agents of fabricating evidence and lying in court.
>
> The agents filed a civil rights lawsuit in 1997, saying they had "become the targets of vicious unfounded attacks on their credibility and careers by the federal government," with the "marionetted support" of Mr. Corbett and the Philadelphia district attorney's office.
>
> The lawsuit also said the Dominican Revolutionary Party "was, and is, protected and sanctioned, unlawfully, by agencies of the United States government, to include the C.I.A. and the State Department, enabling the Dominicans to distribute illegal drugs at will."

CHAPTER SIX

DOJ Culture Enabling 1993 World Trade Center Bombing

In September 1991, two terrorists, Ramzi Yousef and Mohammed Ajaj, entered the United States. Customs agents discovered Ajaj had bomb-making manuals and other terrorist-manuals in his possession, causing him to be arrested. Yousef claimed political asylum and was allowed to remain in the United States pending a court hearing. He was then lost in the follow-up.

Ramzi Yousef[15] joined up with a group in Jersey City[16] composed of Yousef's uncle, Khalid Shaikh Mohammed, Omar Abdel Rahman (the blind Sheikh); Mohammed Salameh; Mahmud Abouhalima; and Abdel Rahman Yasin. They started building a bomb in a public storage unit in Jersey City, with the intention of causing the collapse of one of the World Trade Center towers.

During the late 1980s, the FBI New York office knew the names of some of the terrorists who would bomb the World Trade Center in 1993 and commit other terrorist acts, but failed to follow up on the information.

World Trade Center Bombing

During a visit to the United States, visiting Egyptian president Hosni Mubarak warned U.S. officials that Sheikh Omar Abdel Rahman was a terrorist and should be arrested or deported.

Mole Inside the Jersey City Terror Cell

FBI Special Agent Nancy Floyd befriended a former Egyptian army officer, Emad Salem, who was hired at her request as an FBI informant. Salem's Arab background made him accessible to terrorist activities, which he passed on to Floyd. These tidbits included planned terrorist activities occurring in a Jersey City Mosque, Masjid al Salaam.

Salem's handlers were FBI Special Agent John Anticev and NYPD detective Lou Napoli, who were members of the Joint Terrorist Task Force (JTTF) between the FBI and the New York police Department.

Ignoring the Most Important Mole in al Qaeda Cell

After Administrative Special Agent in Charge (ASAC) Carson Dunbar took over the FBI's New York terrorism unit, he changed the conditions under which Salem was working, which alienated Salem, causing him to quit working undercover for the FBI.

---

[15] Aliases used by Ramzi Yousef included Adam Ali Qasim; Arnaldo Forlani; Naji Haddad; Dr. Adel Sabah; Adam Baloch; Abraham Kamal; Kamal Ibraham; Adam Ali; Dr. Alex Hume; Abdul Basit Mahmud Abdul Karim; Dr. Richard Smith; Dr. Paul Vijay; Azan Muhammed; Muhammad Ali Baloch, and Khurram Khan.

[16] Years earlier, in my youth, I went to high school in Jersey City.

The information that Salem had earlier provided proved to be reliable. However, he did not want to have his name publicized by being called as a witness, and to undergo polygraph examinations.

These conditions offended Salem and also threatened to expose him to retaliation. He broke off the prior relationship. The prior agreement was for Salem to provide inside information for the FBI to then go and obtain the legally required evidence. Because Salem had relatives in Egypt, he feared that if his involvement with the FBI became known, his relatives would be in danger.

Discovering Bomb for World Trade Center Demolition

After severing connections with the FBI, Salem discovered that two of Yousef's companions, Mahmud Abouhalima and Mohammed Salameh, were building a huge bomb. Salem alerted FBI Special Agent Floyd, advising that Abouhalima and Salameh be followed, which would take them to where the bomb was being fabricated (that later was put in the garage of one of the World Trade Center buildings).

Dunbar blocked the previously assigned handlers, Anticev and Napoli, from following through. The huge urea-nitrate-fuel-oil bomb was then completed and taken into the World Trade Center underground parking, where it was detonated, resulting in over 100 injuries and deaths.

FBI Incompetents Charging Floyd with Insubordination

Possibly to protect his own incompetence and discredit Floyd, Dunbar charged FBI Special Agent Floyd with insubordination, resulting in her suspension. That reminded me of what I endured when I sought to report, as a federal aviation safety agent, the hard-core violations of major federal aviation safety requirements, falsification of records, which were resulting in a continuing series of fatal airline crashes.

FBI Rewarding Incompetents

While Floyd was suspended, Dunbar, whose incompetence made possible the 1993 bombing of the WTC with its many deaths and injuries, received various promotions and financial rewards. This was a standard procedure in the government's aviation safety agency, the FAA. It was a standard joke that incompetents were always promoted to a higher position—sometimes for one department to get rid of them.

Yousef's Subsequent Terrorist Schemes

The night of the 1993 WTC bombing, Yousef, the mastermind behind the 1993 World Trade Center bombing, fled to Pakistan on Pakistan Airways. He then proceeded to Manila, where he and Abdul Hakim Murad produced bombs for placing on airliners and laid plans for other terrorist activities. These plans included placing bombs on 11 U.S. airliners departing Far East locations.

Yousef fabricated a bomb device using a Casio databank watch to act as a timer, and connected to a small battery, which would then set off the bomb. The first test of the bomb mechanism was in a Manila movie theatre in December 1994. The device worked, exploding as planned. Within a couple of weeks,

Yousef tested the bomb going through security at Manila Airport as he boarded a Philippine Airlines 747 flight from Manila to Cebu. Before he got off the plane at his destination, he set the timer on the bomb to go off during the next flight, which it did, when the aircraft was at 33,000 feet.

The explosion damaged the floor below the seat and killed a passenger. The aircraft itself did not explode, as Yousef had planned, and he planned to place the other bombs in seats directly over the center-wing fuel tank. Fortunately, he never got to place any other bombs on the 11 aircraft. During mixing of bomb chemicals in the Manila apartment he shared with Murad, an explosion and fire occurred. (January 6, 1995)

While neighbors called the fire department, Yousef and Murad fled. After the firemen left, Murad returned to the apartment to retrieve Yousef's laptop computer that contained critical information on their bombing plans. Upon returning to the apartment, Murad was arrested by police. Yousef fled, catching a plane for Pakistan.

Revealing Past and Future Terrorist Activities

Under intense questioning by the Philippine National Police (PNP) intelligence unit, headed by Col. Rodolfo Mendoza, Murad revealed the activities and the plans of the terrorist cell. He identified Ramzi Yousef as the leader of the cell, the Bojinka scheme to down 11 U.S. airliners, and the plan to hijack U.S. airliners and fly them into major buildings in the United States, and the training of suicide bombers in U.S. flight schools.

Murad stated that in addition to the World Trade Center as targets, other sites considered were the Sears Tower in Chicago, the Transamerica building in San Francisco, the White House, and the Pentagon in Washington.

Col. Mendoza stated that he turned Yousef's laptop computer and detailed information revealed by Murad over to CIA and FBI personnel, making obvious to U.S. personnel the plans to hijack and fly U.S. airliners into key U.S. buildings.

Based upon a photo on Yousef's abandoned computer, Malaysian police arrested Khan Amin Shah, who later admitted that he provided money and fake passports to Yousef and another accomplice, Abdul Hakim Murad. One 1995 police report included the statement:

Murad's idea is that he will board any American commercial aircraft pretending to be an ordinary passenger, then he will hijack said aircraft, control its cockpit and dive it at the CIA headquarters. There will be no bomb or any explosive that he will use in its execution. It is a suicidal mission that he is very much willing to execute.

Col. Rodolfo Mendoza of the Philippines was able to discover from Murad the details of the scheme that would unfold on September 11, 2001, along with details of other terrorist activities that had already occurred and those in the process.

It was learned that Khalid Sheikh Mohammed and Ramzi Yousef were the masterminds of the scheme to hijack U.S. airliners and fly them into buildings in the United States. This information was turned over to U.S. authorities, and should have caused people in the government's aviation safety offices (FAA and NTSB) to finally order the simple and inexpensive measures that would have prevented years of hijackings throughout the world.

Emad Salem

In 1993, from information provided by Emad Salem, Sheikh Omar Abdel Rahman, El Sayyid Nosair, and others, were listed as a co-conspirator in a scheme to blow up the George Washington Bridge and two of the tunnels connecting New York and New Jersey. The trial against nearly a dozen codefendants started in 1995.

Key al Qaeda Terrorists Reunited

Ramzi Yousef was reunited with Abdul Hakim Murad, Wali Khan, and Eyad Ismoil in the Metropolitan Correctional Center (MCC) in New York City, as they were waiting to go on trial for their role in the 1993 bombing of the World Trade Center and the planned bombing of a dozen U.S. airliners departing Far East locations.

Yousef and Murad Found Guilty

As the trial ended in New York City, Yousef, Shah and Murad were found guilty in the 1993 bombing of the World Trade Center and sentenced to life in prison. The mastermind of the bombing, Ramzi Yousef, was sentenced to life in prison on May 16, 1998. Murad was sentenced to life in prison on May 16, 1998. All six of the terrorists charged with involvement in the 1993 trade center bombing had been brought to justice and sentenced, except for Abdul Rahman Yasin, who fled to Iraq, where he was then held in an Iraqi prison. His imprisonment by Iraq was another indication that Saddam Hussein not only had no role in the 9/11 attacks, but was an impediment to terrorists actions.

Yousef's first trial was for the Bojinka bomb plot to down 11 U.S. airliners. On November 12, 1997, he received a life-in-prison sentence. In a second trial, in 1998, Yousef was found guilty of masterminding the 1993 World Trade Center bombing.

CHAPTER SEVEN

Lockerbie, FBI-DOJ Culture, And Catastrophic Ripple Effects

On July 3, 1988, the United States warship, U.S.S. Vincennes, fired two radar-guided missiles at an Iranian airliner that had just departed Abadan, Iran on a daily scheduled flight on a heavily traveled civilian airway. It was flying Muslim pilgrims to the holy cities of Mecca and Medina. The missiles caused the heavily-packed airliner with 290 people on board to explode, killing everyone on board. It was arguably the worst "terrorist" attack on a civilian airliner.

Understandably, Iranians were irate at the brutal killing of 290 people in such an irresponsible manner. They publicly vowed to retaliate. They had *already* been greatly harmed by the subversion of their government in 1953 as CIA personnel had caused the overthrow of their elected government, causing the removal of Prime Minister Mosaddegh and installation of a brutal secret police. I was staying in Abadan, Iran, that morning on August 19, 1953, when the CIA-organized revolution overthrew Iran's democratically elected Prime Minister through a coup d'état. While in the Middle East, I had often taken off from that same Abadan Airport and flown the same civil airways to the same destination as that Iranian airliner, carrying planeloads of Muslim pilgrims.

Within a few months of the downing of the Iranian airliner, on December 21, 1988, passengers boarded a Pan Am Flight 747 aircraft at London's Heathrow Airport and within an hour they were dead; a bomb exploded while the aircraft was cruising at 31,000 feet over Lockerbie, Scotland. Iranian officials then stopped stating they intended to retaliate. The deed had been accomplished. Substantial information indicated Iranian officials had paid $11 million dollars to the Syrian-based PFLP group to carry out the bombing.

In my book, *Lockerbie to 9/11: Massive Fraud and Consequences*, I provide a large amount of prima facie evidence of what actually happened during the investigation, prosecution, and trial proceedings, that are totally contradictory to what has been made available to the American people by U.S. government personnel and U.S. media.

Very briefly, the following highlights show the conduct of FBI-DOJ personnel that controlled the post-Lockerbie investigation and prosecution:

> FBI-DOJ personnel planted bogus evidence at the crash scene to shift blame from the actual murderers to falsely charge Libya. That planted evidence was a half-thumbnail-size timer fragment found in a muddy field

miles from the main wreckage, months after the bombing event. (That "evidence" was acquired from a former employee of the manufacturer.)

FBI-DOJ personnel paid $3 million to a small Malta shopkeeper and his brother to falsely testify about the identity of the purchaser of children's clothes allegedly found in the suitcase containing the alleged bomb.

FBI-DOJ personnel paid a discredited CIA informant over $1 million to provide false testimony about the identity of two Libyans that allegedly put an unaccompanied bomb-carrying suitcase on a flight departing Malta. That unaccompanied suitcase was allegedly transferred to another aircraft at Frankfurt, and then transferred to Pan Am Flight 103 at London's Heathrow Airport, passing undetected through five security check points.

FBI-DOJ personnel falsely charged two Libyans for the Pan American Flight 103 bombing.

Evidence widely known in Europe but not appearing in U.S. media revealed:

- A sworn affidavit by the former employee for the Swiss company producing the timer fragment that he gave the half-thumbnail-size timer mechanism to FBI agents, months after the bombing, which was then planted in a muddy field miles from the main wreckage. That timer fragment was then used to falsely charge Libya with the bombing. The FBI forensic expert who testified about the timer fragment was later fired for producing false forensic reports.
- A sworn affidavit by the co-owner of the Swiss company that produced the timer stated that (a) the timer presented during the Lockerbie trial was not the type of timer sold to Libya; (b) that he had been offered $4 million by FBI agents to falsely testify that the timer shown to him was sold to Libya. (That occurred before he learned that a former employee had given a timer fragment to FBI agents).
- Dozens of reports by Professor Hans Koechler, the representative appointed by the United Nations Security Council to monitor the Lockerbie bombing trial and appeal procedures, that detailed the gross irregularities, absence of evidence, and other misconduct during the trial.
- Reports by Law Professor Robert Black, Edinburgh University, the architect of the Lockerbie trial at Camp Zeist in the Netherlands, which reported gross irregularities during the investigation, trial, and appeal proceedings.
- The hundreds of British and Scottish media reports providing details of the massive misconduct and obstruction of justice.
- The report in a multi-page Department of Defense document accurately identifying the Syrian-based PFLP group and Iran as the perpetrators of the Lockerbie bombing.

- The sole evidence used by FBI-DOJ personnel to charge Libya with the bombing was the planted half-thumbnail-size timer "miraculously" *found* in a muddy field miles from the crash scene.

FBI-DOJ Culture Continued: First, 1993 WTC Bombing

Anyone who read my earlier books, such as *History of Aviation Disasters, Defrauding America*, or *Drugging America*, would have seen evidence of years of misconduct by personnel in the FBI and other Department of Justice offices.

In the Lockerbie disaster, that conduct protected the murderers of 270 people, mostly Americans, and harmed the people of Libya—adversely affected by the U.S.-imposed sanctions after the U.S. shifted blame from the actual murderers to Libya; and harmed an innocent Libyan who was imprisoned and separated from his family until he had advance prostate cancer.

But the harm from the culture in the FBI-DOJ would have catastrophic effects upon the American people for many years, and is continuing at this time. This source of harm is briefly stated here and extracted from the two books, *Lockerbie to 9/11*, and *History of Aviation Disasters*.

Hotbed of "Freedom Fighter" Activities
(i.e., terrorist activities) in The United States

From 1979 to 1989, the United States funded and armed many Muslims to act as proxies for fighting the Soviets that had been asked by Afghan leaders to help defend against the earlier U.S. funding and arming of Muslim fanatics that were opposed to the westernizing efforts of the government leaders.

After the Soviets left Afghanistan in 1989, these highly trained Muslims turned their attention to the United States, angered by the U.S. aiding and abetting of Israel and other Middle East meddling. The United States had called them "freedom-fighters," but then changed the title to "terrorists" after they directed their anger to American policies in the Middle East. Ironically, some of the most militant of the "freedom-fighters" migrated to the United States with the help of the CIA.

Some of these "freedom-fighters" joined mosques in the New York and New Jersey areas. Among them were the Al Farooq Mosque in Brooklyn and a smaller satellite mosque in Jersey City (where I went to High School decades earlier).

CIA Personnel Facilitating Entry Into The
United States of a Spiritual and Terrorist Icon

Arriving in New York on a CIA-approved visa was the blind Sheikh Omar Abdel Rahman, a spiritual icon for the group. He then preached hatred for the United States. Prior to his arrival, the blind sheikh was considered a terrorist by Egypt and forced to flee from Egypt to Khartoum, Sudan. In Sudan, he was promptly accepted by known terrorists that had great hatred for the United States.

Middle East Muslims Conducted Military Exercises With High Power Guns in New York City Area

In the late 1980s and early 1990s, FBI agents took pictures of Middle East Muslims belonging to local mosques firing thousands of rounds of high-caliber military weapons, including AK-47s, at the Calverton Shooting Range on Long Island, near the Long Island Expressway, and in Connecticut. Included in the Middle Easterners at these military-style exercises were Sheikh Omar Abdel Rahman, El Sayyid Nosair, Mohammed Salameh, Mahmud Abouhalima, Ali Mohamed, and Nidal Ayyad, known for their terrorist leanings.

At about this same time, in 1988, two militant Middle East groups joined forces and became known as al Qaeda. They consisted of the CIA-trained and armed Osama bin Laden group, African Arabs, and the Egyptian Islamic Jihad, headed by Egyptian doctor Ayman al-Zawahiri.

FBI's Knowledge of Military-Style Shooting by Middle East Terrorists

FBI personnel were aware of military-style shooting by Middle East militants, who were firing thousands of rounds of ammunition at the Calverton Shooting Range on Long Island and also at a shooting range in Connecticut. Obviously, they had no peaceful intent with these expensive military-style exercises. Excerpts from a November 13, 1990, FBI 302 report on the surveillance of Middle Easterners at a shooting range in Connecticut stated:

> On Nov 13, 1990, Det. Louis Napoli conducted the following interview of Joe Norton. Norton advised that a Raymond Murtzea, who was also a Range Officer at the High Rock Range, started to train a group of Mid-Easterners in the art of shooting and the handling of firearms on every Saturday and Sunday from 1988 to 1990. The group would average about 15 persons at any one time. Those Mid-Easterners would come to the range and use Raymond Murtzea permit in order to shoot. Norton also advised that Murtzea would personally train these Mid-Easterners on an individual basis.
>
> Norton advised that when these Mid-Easterners came up on the weekends, that Murtzea would supply them with shotguns and hand guns (9 mm, 357 Cal and 45 cal) which he would bring to the range in a duffle bag. Norton advised that he saw some of the Mid-Easterners bring up AK47 which they would remove from the trunks of their vehicles. Norton did remember that [the cars had] New York State License plates.
>
> Norton advised that Murtzea and the Mid-Easterners would shoot over one thousand (1000) rounds per day, and that they shot at silhouette targets instead of bulls eye targets. Norton stated that Murtzea would train them to shoot for the head and heart areas.

Norton, after reviewing photos of several Mid-Easterners, identified El-Sayyid A. Nosair as one of the Mid-Easterners who came to the High Rock Range to shoot with Murtzea.

The Obvious, Unknown by America's Top Protectors!

A normal person could suspect that a large group of Middle Easterners, living in the New York City area, that came from areas known for terrorist activities, shooting thousands of rounds of high-power military type weapons at silhouettes of human beings, would cause them to be under constant surveillance. And also recognize the need for further investigation.

U.S. Double Agent in Plain Sight

Ali Mohamed, a member of the Brooklyn mosque, was a Sunni Muslim and a former Egyptian Army officer and member of the militant Egyptian Islamic Jihad. At the time of Sadat's slaying, Mohamed was at Fort Bragg, North Carolina, as an Egyptian officer in a joint U.S. Egyptian officer exchange program. After Sadat's assassination, Egypt's next president, Hosni Mubarak, purged the radical group from the army, resulting in Mohamed's discharge.

First Terrorist Attack Cell Ignored by Feds

The first militant action by the Muslim mosque members was the November 5, 1990, murder of Rabbi Meir Kahane, who had preached for the removal of Arabs from the land occupied by Israel. The murder weapon was fired by El Sayyid Nosair of Cliffside Park, New Jersey. Also, directly involved in that murder were Mohammed Salameh and Mahmud Abouhalima. They had all been previously seen by FBI agents during military-style shootings at the Calverton Firing Range. More will be said in later pages concerning this matter.

Ali Mohamed: Years as U.S. Double Agent,
Providing al Qaeda Terrorists with U.S. Secrets

Ali Mohamed would become a double agent for the United States, working for the CIA, FBI, and US special forces, from about 1980 to the 1990s—while also the primary spy for the al Qaeda group. During this period, he provided highly classified information and government documents to al Qaeda terrorists throughout the world, and primarily in the Middle East and Africa. He trained al Qaeda members in the United States and in the Middle East, on how to attack U.S. targets and kill Americans. At the time of this writing, he is believed to be secretly protected by Department of Justice personnel so as to prevent the public learning about how he duped the 10,000-plus intelligence personnel for many years.

Known Middle East Terrorist Hired By
CIA to Spy *On* Suspected Middle East Terrorists

In 1984, the CIA station chief in Cairo hired Ali Mohamed to infiltrate a Mosque in Hamburg, Germany. The Hamburg mosque was headed by Imad

Fayez Mugniyah, a member of the terrorist division of Hezbollah, the group that bombed the U.S. Embassy in Beirut and the Marine barracks in the 1980s.

Ali promptly informed the Mosque group that he was sent by the CIA to spy on them. Fortunately for the CIA, they had *another* source inside the Mosque who revealed this double-cross. Mohamed was promptly terminated, and information about his ties to terrorist groups was sent to other U.S. intelligence personnel. He was placed on a terrorist watch list.

CIA-Arranged Visa to Enter the United States

While on that watch list, in 1985, CIA personnel arranged for Mohamed to obtain a visa to enter the United States. While enroute to the United States on a TWA flight, Mohamed met an American citizen residing in Santa Clara, California: Linda Lee Sanchez. They arranged to meet after arrival in the United States. Within weeks Mohamed is married to Sanchez, enabling him to become a U.S. citizen.

Known Member of Terrorist Group Enlists in U.S. Army

Shortly thereafter, in August 1986, Mohamed enlisted in the U.S. Army and was sent to Fort Bragg, South Carolina, the home of super secret anti-terrorist operations. Fort Bragg is the training base for the Delta Force and Green Berets.

In his new assignment, without a security clearance, Ali had easy access to highly confidential material. Due to poor security measures, Ali took top-secret documents and anti-terrorist training manuals to a local copy store and made copies, which he then distributed to terrorist groups in the United States, Middle East, and Africa. Ali also prepared training manuals on how to take down U.S. targets and kill Americans.

Training Known Terrorists on Weekends

On weekends, Ali flew to New York, where he trained members of mosques at shooting ranges near New York City, and distributed highly classified U.S. material to local terrorist cells. Among the people he trained was Ramzi Yousef, the soon-to-be mastermind of the 1993 bombing of the World Trade Center. Despite the fact that the expenses involved in these weekly flights from South Carolina to New York exceeded the income of a lowly sergeant in the Army at that time, no suspicions were raised.

Ali's Presence Nearly Scuttled a Major International Military Exercise with Egypt

While assigned to Fort Bragg, Mohamed arrived in Egypt as part of a joint Egypt-United States military training exercise called Operation Bright Star. When the Egyptians learned of Ali's presence, they threatened to immediately cancel the joint training exercise. Ali was then immediately shipped back to the United States. Still no reaction among U.S. intelligence personnel.

As Army Sergeant, Ali Takes Leave To Fight Soviets in Afghanistan

Later, that year, as he was taking a routine one month leave, Ali notified his commanding officer that he was going to Afghanistan to fight Soviet troops. His commanding officer barred him from going, but he ignored the order. Upon his return, Ali described gun battles with the Soviets—while he was on active duty with the U.S. army. His commanding officer then recommended a military court martial, which was denied, despite the enormity of the offense. It was as if he had behind-the-scene protection from the CIA.

In 1989, Ali received an honorable discharge from the army and he returned to California, where he promptly joined a local mosque. He also became a U.S. citizen. Despite having no meaningful income, Ali made dozens of trips to Middle East and African countries involved in terrorist activities. No one questioned where he was obtaining the money for those expensive trips.

Al Qaeda's Top Spy Hired as FBI Counter Intelligence Agent

In 1993, FBI personnel in San Francisco hired Ali as a Foreign Counter Intelligence agent, despite the overwhelming indications that he had ties with terrorists in the United States and overseas. He was assigned to FBI Special Agent John Zent. This sensitive assignment occurred despite knowledge by FBI agents in the New York offices that Mohamed had trained Middle East Muslims at the Calverton Shooting Range and also provided training for the terrorists involved in the 1993 World Trade Center bombing.

During these 1993 contacts, Ali admitted that he was training people in Afghanistan associated with Osama bin Laden, training on how to hijack airliners, and provided training to the al Qaeda operative Essam Marzouk, who had been arrested by Canadian authorities.

Ali also told Zent that Osama bin Laden was developing an army of terrorists called al Qaeda; that bin Laden had training camps in Sudan; that he, Ali, had trained some of the terrorists; that he had provided terrorist training material to them, including to Essam Marzouk, who had been arrested recently by Canadian authorities in Vancouver.

Continuing Reasons for Not Arresting Ali Mohamed

If FBI personnel had arrested Ali, based upon these self-admissions, it would have exposed the FBI's utter incompetence and cover-ups that made possible several deadly terrorist attacks.

FBI special agent Dan Coleman prepared a sworn affidavit of what he had been told by Ali, and provided it to FBI-DOJ personnel in the New York offices—where Coleman was an assistant to AUSA Patrick Fitzgerald and a member of the al Qaeda targeted unit known as I-49. A copy of that affidavit was submitted into a federal court trial in New York in 1998. Nothing came of that.

It was during this time that the World Trade Center bombing had occurred; and the discovery of large amounts of top secret documents from Fort Bragg were found in the Cliffside, New Jersey home of Nosair, which contained writings by Ali Mohamed.

***Finally*, FBI Arrests al Qaeda's Top Spy and Double Agent!**

In September 1998, after being subpoenaed to testify about his involvement in the bombings of the U.S. embassies in Nairobi and Tanzania, Mohamed was arrested as he tried to flee to Egypt. Department of Justice prosecutors then charged him with involvement in the August 7, 1998, bombings of the U.S. embassies in Nairobi, Kenya and Dar es Salaam, Tanzania.

During his incarceration, Mohamed, in May 1999, entered a plea agreement, pleading guilty, providing to FBI-DOJ personnel details of his actions that had resulted in many deaths. He pled guilty in October 2000 to five counts of conspiracy to kill nationals of the United States and related charges.

DOJ Sequestered Ali Mohamed—Conveniently Hiding Information of DOJ Corruption and Gross Incompetence

Court records show no record of Mohamed being sentenced, or in any prison facility. In an article in *NewsWithViews.com*, Patrick Briley wrote that Ali Mohamed was given an early release from prison under direct orders by U.S. Attorney Alberto Gonzales during President George W. Bush's administration. A *Raleigh News & Observer* article (October 2001) stated that Ali Mohamed was cooperating with the US government and was in the witness protection program. Mohamed's wife, Linda Sanchez, living in California, stated in 2006:

> *He's still not sentenced yet, and without him being sentenced I really can't say much. He can't talk to anybody. Nobody can get to him. They have Ali pretty secretive...it's like he just kinda vanished into thin air.*

DOJ Personnel's Self-Interest Surpassed National Security

FBI-DOJ personnel had a major self-serving reason for keeping Ali Mohamed from testifying against al Qaeda terrorists, and away from media investigators. It was to prevent the public from learning that for years Mohamed repeatedly and openly duped large numbers of people in the nation's top law enforcement, intelligence, and military departments. He stole U.S. secrets for al Qaeda terrorists, openly trained and associated with al Qaeda terrorists, revealing the extraordinary level of incompetence throughout the United States. But that self-serving interest also kept the United States from learning about necessary changes to be made to prevent patterns of incompetence and to guard against similar terrorist attacks.

Evidence of Major Terrorist Cell Ignored by Feds

As stated earlier, the first militant action by the Muslim mosque members was the murder of Rabbi Meir Kahane in which the Mosque member firing the murder weapon was El Sayyid Nosair. The killers fled to Nosair's home in Cliffside Park, New Jersey. Within 24 hours, the home was searched, and in it were found top secrets documents from Fort Bragg, with Ali Mohamed's writings on them; receipt for over a thousand rounds of high-power ammunition; explosive manuals; World Trade Center maps; instructions on how to take over an airliner; and other terrorist type material.

FBI Personnel Obstructing Investigation

Although state police from New York and New Jersey were directly involved in the murder, FBI agents, who had known of the group's terrorist activities, seized the evidence and held it for several months before returning it. Despite the evidence of a far broader conspiracy involving al Qaeda terrorists, more than the murder of one individual, federal prosecutors showed no interest. Pressure was applied on state law enforcement to keep the matter a simple murder by locals. In this way, al Qaeda terrorists in the New York area were allowed to continue their activities.

Despite the fact that Mohammed Salameh and Mahmud Abouhalima were connected with Nosair, and had been seen with him during the military shooting exercises, and were probably involved, they were released from custody and not charged in the murder

Self-Serving Advantage of Hiding Obvious Ties

If federal personnel had used the evidence they had, it would have exposed Ali Mohamed's al Qaeda spy activities while being used and trusted by FBI, CIA, military, and National Security Agency personnel. There were, of course, collateral damage consequences to this tactic; it allowed the terrorist cells in the New York—New Jersey area to become increasingly strong.

More DOJ Misconduct at Nosair's Eventual Trail

At Nosair's trial, lawyers from the Middle East entered an appearance, providing further indication that there was much more involved than a simple murder. Helping to hide DOJ misconduct, throughout the trial, New York trial judge, Alvin Schlesinger, restricted the prosecution's case and leaned over backwards to allow defense tactics by defense lawyer William Kunstler.

Defense Attorney Suspected Something Unusual

Attorney Roger Stavis, defending Nosair, soon discovered the involvement of Ali Mohamed with his client. Stavis discovered that Ali had been in the U.S. Army; an asset used by the CIA, FBI, and other government intelligence groups; and had provided terrorist training to Nosair. These conditions enabled Stavis to raise the argument that the U.S. government shared blame in the murder committed by Nosair

Opportunity to Expose Worldwide Terrorist Group with Cells in New York-New Jersey Area

Stavis obtained a subpoena for Ali to appear for discovery in the Nosair trial. But Ali's testimony would end the careers of many top DOJ personnel and reveal that Nosair was part of a worldwide terrorist group with cells in the New York-New Jersey area. If that subpoena had been served on Ali, and he appeared for discovery, his role as an FBI informant would have ended, and also ended his ability to secretly provide information to Al Qaeda terrorists.

Another Form of Obstructing Justice—
With Future Catastrophic Consequences

Stavis sought to introduce evidence relating to Ali Mohamed, which threatened to expose the much larger terrorist cells and the incompetence and corruption of government personnel. U.S. Attorney McCarthy filed objections, lying to the court that anything related to Ali Mohamed was not relevant to the terrorism charges against Nosair.

If that information had been entered into that 1995 trial it would have revealed the extent of the terrorist activities, it would have resulted in the incarceration and breakup of the terrorist cells, and have blocked their subsequent role in subsequent terrorist attacks upon U.S. targets. Those collateral-damage consequences were put aside to protect the careers and reputation of key Department of Justice personnel, and those of other government intelligence entities.

McCarthy eventually left government and wrote a book, *Willful Blindness: A Memoir of the Jihad*, in which he altered the facts so as to protect himself. Much of his book was addressed to disputing the charges by Peter Lance in his book, *Triple Cross*.

DOJ Personnel Blocking Court-Ordered
Appearance of Ali Mohamed

McCarthy withheld from Nosair's defense attorney information about Ali's location, and then compounded this corrupt conduct. AUSA McCarthy and Harlan Bell flew to California, where McCarthy advised Ali to hide out so the subpoena could not be served upon him.

McCarthy's conduct constituted obstruction to justice, blocking the serving of a court-ordered subpoena, and violated a defendant's right to have possible exculpatory information made known to him. The long term effect was to continue to block recognition of the terrorist cells in the United States, making possible the success of numerous subsequent terrorist attacks. The conduct of the two federal prosecutors protected al Qaeda's primary spy in the United States, enabling him to continue helping Ali's role in planning future terrorist attacks upon the United States.

AUSA Tactics Further Revealed by Prison Inmates

One of the terrorists in federal prison, Ibrahim El-Gabrowny, a cousin to El Sayyid Nosair, was convicted with other local terrorist members in the plot to bomb the George Washington Bridge and the Lincoln and Holland tunnels under the Hudson River. In October 1999, while incarcerated with Ali, Gabrowny told him about the subpoena and then made a note of what Ali said:

El Gabrowny asked Ali Mohamed whether or not he ever received the subpoena that Nosair's lawyer sent to him, and further, if he did receive the subpoena, why he did not come to testify.

Ali Mohamed added that regarding the subpoena that was sent to him by Nosair's lawyer, he actually received it and was prepared to abide with the order and come to testify on Nosair's behalf. But Mr. Andy McCarthy, the AUSA on El-Gabrowny and Nosair's case, came accompanied with an FBI agent and paid him a visit. Ali Mohamed further added, during this visit Mr. McCarthy told him that he (i.e., Mr. McCarthy) knew about the subpoena. Then McCarthy advised Ali Mohamed to ignore the subpoena order and not to go to testify on Nosair's behalf and that Mr. McCarthy would cover up for him regarding that.

The U.S. Supreme Court ruled in *Brady vs. Maryland*, 373 U.S. 83 (1963) that prosecutors violate a defendant's due process rights by suppressing or withholding evidence favorable to the defendant. The more serious misconduct by McCarthy was that his efforts blocked Ali Mohamed from revealing facts that could have prevented subsequent terrorist attacks, and also hid blame of those within the Department of Justice that enabled prior attacks to succeed.

CHAPTER EIGHT

Able Danger Program: More Incompetence and Corruption

Able Danger was a classified military planning effort under the command of the U.S. Special Operations Command (SOCOM) that brought together the massive amount of information about al Qaeda activities. The Able Danger program used data mining techniques to associate information with classified information in an attempt to make associations between individual members of terrorist groups as part of its original intelligence preparation. That collection of information revealed al Qaeda operatives within the United States.

Media Publicity Revealed Able Danger Failures

An investigative report by Keith Plucas in *The Times Herald* (June 19, 2005) of Norristown, Pennsylvania, publicized the existence of the Able Danger program and the fact that several of the 9/11 hijackers were identified prior to the 9/11 hijackings. That media article was then followed on June 27, 2005, by a speech given on the House Floor by Vice Chairman Curt Weldon of the House Armed Services and Homeland Security committees:

> Mr. Speaker, I rise because information has come to my attention over the past several months that is very disturbing. I have learned that, in fact, one of our Federal agencies had, in fact, identified the major New York cell of Mohamed Atta prior to 9/11; and I have learned, Mr. Speaker, that in September 2000, that federal agency actually was prepared to bring the FBI in and prepared to work with the FBI to take down the cell that Mohamed Atta was involved in, in New York City, along with two of the other terrorists.
>
> I have also learned, Mr. Speaker, that when that recommendation was discussed within that federal agency, the lawyers in the administration at that time said, you cannot pursue contact with the FBI against that cell. Mohamed Atta is in the U.S. on a green card and we are fearful of the fallout from the Waco incident. So we did not allow that Federal agency to proceed.

Weldon repeated these concerns during several news conferences on February 14, 2006. During these conferences, Weldon repeated his concerns that Able Danger identified al Qaeda operative Mohamed Atta 13 separate times prior to 9/11 and that the Able Danger unit also identified the threat in Yemen two weeks prior to the October 12, 2002, attack on the U.S.S. Cole that killed 17 Navy sailors.

Weldon claimed, as did the Able Danger whistleblowers, that the Able Danger group had identified the al Qaeda terrorists that hijacked the four airliners on September 11, 2001, and that they were prevented from passing that information to other government departments. Weldon also pointed to the 9/11 commission members—mostly DOJ personnel—that ignored this critical information.

Publicity Followed by Standard Congressional Cover-Up

The media publicity resulted in a hearing by the Republican-controlled US Senate Intelligence Committee. True to form, the committee's December 2006 report stated that there was no evidence supporting the whistleblowing members of the Able Danger group. That report stated that Able Danger personnel did not know of the presence in the United States of Mohammed Atta or any other 9/11 hijacker at any time prior to Sept. 11, 2001—despite the fact that the Able Danger whistleblowers said they did have that knowledge.

The senators' statements were an almost exact duplication of the earlier September 2006 report released by the Inspector General of the U.S. Department of Defense.

Further Evidence of the DOJ
Cover-Up Control of the 9/11 Commission

Two congressional members of the 9/11 Commission, who were not part of the Department of Justice, Timothy J. Roemer and John F. Lehman, stated they had never been given the information about the findings by the Able Danger group. Two other members of the 9/11 Commission, vice-chairman Lee H. Hamilton and former spokesman for the commission, Al Felzenberg, also stated that the 9/11 staff investigators—consisting mostly of DOJ personnel—had not made this information available to them.

Hamilton told the media, "The Sept. 11 commission did not learn of any U.S. government knowledge prior to 9/11 of surveillance of Mohammed Atta or of his cell.... Had we learned of it obviously it would have been a major focus of our investigation."

9/11 Commission Chairman Thomas Kean and Lee Hamilton issued a statement (August 12, 2005), in response to media questions relating to the Able Danger program, that it had requested and obtained information from the Department of Defense and had been told that there was no evidence to support the claims of the Able Danger personnel.

Circling the Wagons: Department of Defense Cover-Up

Department of Defense officials issued a statement, quoting a [cooperating] U.S. Navy officer that was employed by the Department of Justice:

> The interviewee had no documentary evidence and said he had only seen the document briefly some years earlier. He could not describe what information had led to this supposed Atta identification. Nor could the in-

terviewee recall, when questioned, any details about how he thought a link to Atta could have been made by this DOD program in 2000 or any time before 9/11.

The Department of Defense documents had mentioned nothing about Atta, nor had anyone come forward between September 2001 and July 2004 with any similar information. Weighing this with the information about Atta's actual activities, the negligible information available about Atta to other U.S. government agencies and the German government before 9/11, and the interviewer's assessment of the interviewee's knowledge and credibility, the Commission staff concluded that the officer's account was not sufficiently reliable to warrant revision of the report or further investigation.

Congressman Weldon expressed dissatisfaction with statements made by various members of the 9/11 Commission. He stated his desire to seek information to explain why the Department of Defense refused to pass the information uncovered by Able Danger to the FBI, and why the 9/11 Commission failed to follow up on the information they were given on Able Danger.

Reversing Their Position Once Their Lies Were Exposed

In response to media publicity, 9/11 Commission members first denied having been briefed on Able Danger, and then when that statement was proved to be a lie, acknowledged being briefed on both operation Able Danger and Mohammed Atta. The explanation was then altered, stating that the information was suspect.

Standard Retaliation to Cover-Up for DOJ Corruption

After exposing the serious problems in the Department of Justice and Able Danger, Department of Justice prosecutors announced they were conducting a criminal investigation into the affairs of Congressman Weldon. That publicity resulted in Weldon's failure to win reelection in November 2006. Defeated, there was now no need to address the Weldon problem, and FBI personnel dropped the charges against Weldon.

Weldon then wrote and published a book, *Countdown to Terror*, in which he described having a secret source in the intelligence community using the code name of Able Danger. Weldon described how the CIA and other U.S. intelligence services ignored his information.

In that book, Weldon included a 1999 chart produced by the Able Danger team that identified several of the 9/11 hijackers—prior to 9/11—including Mohamed Atta, Marwan al-Shehhi, Khalid al-Mihdhar, and Nawaf al-Hazmi. Weldon described providing the information to then-Deputy National Security Advisor Jim Steinberg, which was ignored.

Weldon described presenting the chart to then-Deputy National Security Advisor Stephen Hadley within a few days after the 9/11 attacks. He described presenting the information to the chairman of the House Intelligence Committee Peter Hoekstra, who downplayed the significance.

An article in *The Bergen Record* (New Jersey, August 14, 2005) by investigative reporter Mike Kelly, described a telephone interview between Representative Weldon and a member of the Able Danger team, but asked that his name not be revealed in the interview. The article stated that his Able Danger team had identified Mohamed Atta and three other 9/11 hijackers as likely al Qaeda terrorists operating in the United States, but were prevented by government lawyers from providing this information to the FBI.

That source also claimed he was ignored by the 9/11 Commission's staff when he approached them on two occasions to explain Able Danger's work and the relationship to 9/11.

Weldon also stated that he had been in contact with a government employee who was ordered to destroy the 2.5 terabytes (TB) of data collected by Able Danger two years prior to the 9/11 attacks.

Able Danger Team Member Lt. Col. Anthony Shaffer

A member of the Able Danger team, Lt. Col. Anthony Shaffer, claimed that he alerted the FBI in September 2000 about the al Qaeda information discovered by the secret military unit called Able Danger. Shaffer claimed that three meetings were set up with FBI personnel but the meetings were blocked by military lawyers.

Abel Danger personnel charged that Pentagon lawyers destroyed the reports and pictures that had been gathered of the known Al Qaeda terrorists. Shaffer and other people in the group provided statements that Able Danger had identified Mohamed Atta, the leader of the September 11, 2001, terrorist attacks, and three others, as al Qaeda members, prior to the 9/11 hijackings, and linked the al Qaeda members to the 1993 World Trade Center bombing.

At that time, Shaffer worked for the Defense Intelligence Agency, and provided information to the 9/11 Commission that Able Danger had identified two of the three cells responsible for 9/11 attacks before the attacks had occurred. That information was withheld from the final report of the 9/11 Commission, along with other material information that made the 9/11 Commission report a cover-up. That culture of cover-up continues in key government positions, and the people responsible are still in key positions.

Another Example of Criminal Retaliation To Hide High-Level Corruption

Due to his efforts to reveal the conduct of key people in government that made 9/11 possible, Shaffer suffered the standard retaliation netted out to government personnel that expose high-level misconduct or corruption. Shaffer's lawyer, Mark Zaid, stated that the government had placed Shaffer on paid administrative leave for what he called "petty and frivolous" reasons and had his security clearance suspended in March 2004. The reason given was a dispute over travel mileage expenses and personal use of a work cell phone. Remember how this was done to FBI Special Agent Richard Taus, who worked under the FBI supervisor involved in several serial murders with Mafia capo Gregory Scarpa Sr.

Congressman Weldon asked for an investigation into the actions taken to silence Lt. Col Shaffer concerning the misconduct that assisted terrorists to carry out their attacks. Weldon called the activities "a deliberate campaign of character assassination." Shaffer described the role of the CIA's pre-9/11 opposition to Able Danger, claiming Able Danger was encroaching on CIA turf. Shaffer stated that the CIA representative said:

> I clearly understand. We're going after the leadership. You guys are going after the body. But, it doesn't matter. The bottom line is, CIA will never give you the best information from 'Alex Base' or anywhere else. CIA will never provide that to you because if you were successful in your effort to target Al Qaeda, you will steal our thunder. Therefore, we will not support this.

Navy Captain Confirming Shaffer's Statements

In a statement to *Fox News*, Navy Captain Scott Phillpott supported Shaffer's claims.

> I will not discuss this outside of my chain of command. I have briefed the Department of the Army, the Special Operations Command and the office of (Undersecretary of Defense for Intelligence) Dr. Cambone as the 9/11 Commission. My story has remained consistent. Atta was identified by Able Danger in January/February 2000.

Another Confirmation of Able Danger

A civilian contractor who worked on Able Danger, James D. Smith, confirmed to *Fox News* that Able Danger involved analysis of data from a large number of public sources and 20 to 30 individuals. Smith confirmed that Atta was found to have ties to a key terrorist in the 1993 bombing of the World Trade Center, Omar Abdel Rahman.

An anonymous Pentagon source reported that Smith was fired after his government-funded investigation into Chinese strategic and business connections in the U.S. identified Stanford University, Condoleezza Rice, and former Defense Secretary William Perry's questionable involvement. It was believed that this was to construct an alibi.

Army Major Ordered to Destroy Able Danger Records

Army Major Eric Kleinsmith deleted massive 2.5 terabytes of data in May and June, 2000. The destruction of such valuable information was ordered by Tony Gentry, general counsel of the Army Intelligence and Security Command.

During testimony, Army Major Eric Kleinsmith, chief of intelligence for LIWA until February 2001, testified that he was ordered to destroy Able Danger's information:

> *I deleted the data. There were two sets, classified and unclassified, and also an 'all source,' which contained a blend of the two, plus charts we'd produced.*

Additional Witnesses Confirming Able Danger Warnings

On September 1, 2005, the Defense Department issued a statement after a three week investigation into Able Danger. The report stated that they discovered three other witnesses in addition to Shaffer and Phillpott that confirmed Able Danger had produced a chart that "either mentioned Atta by name as an al-Qaeda operative [and/or] showed his photograph." Four of the five witnesses remember the photo on the chart. The fifth remembers only Atta being cited by name. The Pentagon describes the witnesses as "credible."

Also supporting the Able Danger warnings was the Presidential Daily Brief dated August 6, 2001, that was titled, "Bin Laden Determined to Strike in U.S." The brief described the plans to hijack U.S. airliners.

Reason for Suppressing Information Leading to 3,000 Deaths

Andrew McCarthy, former chief assistant U.S. attorney, among others, claimed that Able Danger intelligence about al Qaeda terrorists was suppressed because of a policy forbidding the CIA and FBI sharing intelligence. This was known as "the wall."

Attorney General John Ashcroft, testified to the 9/11 Commission that the wall was strengthened by DOJ's Jamie Gorelick under the Clinton administration, and prohibited sharing of terrorist intelligence within the federal government.

Bring Back the Able Danger Anti-Terrorist Weapon

Years later, in 2009, another effort was made by a startup company in California, Palantir Technologies. A *Wall Street Journal* article (September 4, 2009) stated in part:

> One of the latest entrants into the government spy-services marketplace, Palantir Technologies has designed what many intelligence analysts say is the most effective tool to date to investigate terrorist networks. The software's main advance is a user-friendly search tool that can scan multiple data sources at once, something previous search tools couldn't do. That means an analyst who is following a tip about a planned terror attack, for example, can more quickly and easily unearth connections among suspects, money transfers, phone calls and previous attacks around the globe.

Assistant U.S. Attorney Dietrich Snell was senior counsel in the 9/11 Commission. He blocked much of the information from being entered that would have put much of the blame for the 9/11 attacks on Department of Justice personnel. He should have been a witness before the 9/11 Commission rather than one of its members.

In another cover-up, while Snell prosecuted the case against Ramzi Yousef, he prevented knowledge of the extreme incompetence by DOJ personnel to be revealed. He blocked any information being put into the trial about the 1995 information provided to the United States by the Philippines National Police about Yousef's plans to hijack airliners. If he had not done that, it would then become known that DOJ personnel had six years warning of the plans to hijack U.S. airliners and fly them into buildings.

CHAPTER NINE

Another FBI Anti-Terrorist Blunder

During a search of Sheikh Rahman's New Jersey residence after Nosair murdered Rabbi Kahane in August 1993, police discovered among other evidence a business card from Mohammed Jamal Khalifa, Osama bin Laden's brother-in-law, and a known terrorist. That name was also written on the secret material stolen from Fort Bragg by Ali Mohamed and found in Nosair's Cliffside Park, New Jersey home.

Included in a list of coconspirators in the criminal trial involving the plan to bomb the George Washington Bridge and tunnels between New York and New Jersey was Mohammed Jamal Khalifa. In December 1994, FBI agents from the San Francisco office arrested Khalifa near San Francisco, California, the arrest relating to charges that he participated in the 1993 World Trade Center bombing and other terrorist acts.

His arrest provided another opportunity to obtain current information from a key al Qaeda operative about the terrorist organization, its members, and its plans to attack U.S. targets. Papers in Khalifa's possession contained information that would have taken them to the FBI's most wanted fugitive, Ramzi Yousef. But that would reveal how al Qaeda's top spy in the United States had outsmarted a hoard of FBI and other intelligence agency personnel, enabling several major successful terrorist attacks. At the time of his arrest, evidence showed that Khalifa was connected to most of the then-known Middle East terrorist activities.

Execution if Departed to Jordan

Khalifa had a sentence of death waiting for him in Jordan. To avoid being deported to Jordan and probable death, Khalifa offered to provide inside information on al Qaeda's activities and terrorist plans in exchange for not being deported.

Clinton Administration Attempt to Deport Khalifa

Before FBI and other intelligence personnel made any effort to obtain that information, President Bill Clinton, through his Secretary of State, Warren Christopher, and acting with U.S. Attorney Janet Reno and Assistant U.S. Attorney Jamie Gorelick, prepared papers to deport Khalifa. That deportation would protect each of them and other Department of Justice employees by blocking Khalifa's revealing information. Misstating the law to support the deportation, Gorelick cited a section of federal law that stated in part:

> The deportation of an alien in the United States shall be directed by the Attorney General to a country promptly designated by the alien if that country is willing to accept him into its territory—unless the Attorney General in

his discretion concludes that deportation to such country would be prejudicial to the interests of the United States.

That last section barred the deportation of one of America's greatest terrorist threats. Anyone, even with a second-grade education but with basic street smarts, could recognize the dangers of blocking the receipt of the information that Khalifa would have provided, and the danger from turning him loose to plan other terrorist attacks upon U.S. targets.

Philippine National Police Objected to Khalifa's Deportation

Philippines authorities discovered that Khalifa was associated with a group that had planned several terrorist attacks that would have killed thousands of people. Philippine President Fidel Ramos, upon hearing that the United States planned to deport Khalifa, promptly filed an objection, claiming that, "We have asked US authorities to hold his deportation because we are finding out his links with local terrorists here."

A Rare and Brave Career Employee Objected

Recognizing the extreme danger to the United States by the deportation of a major threat to the United States, Philip C. Wilcox Jr., coordinator in the counterterrorism unit, wrote (December 23, 1994) a letter to the immigration judge opposing the deportation:

> Dear Immigration Judge:
>
> The Department of State is the Administration's "lead agency" regarding international terrorism. ... The bureau is responsible for analysis, on behalf of the Secretary of Intelligence products collected by the U.S. Government. In preparation for this letter, moreover, I have been in close contact with the Department of State's Bureau of Near Eastern Affairs, which coordinates U.S. foreign policy in the Middle East, including with the Hashemite Kingdom of Jordan.
>
> In my letters to you of December 16 and 20, I provided you substantial information regarding the terrorist connections of Mohammed Jamal Khalifa. In the last two days there has been a significant additional development in this matter. On December 21 the State Security Court in Jordan found Mohammed Jamal Khalifa guilty of the charges for which he was indicted and imposed a capital sentence.
>
> Based on my experience as a specialist in Middle Eastern affairs and service as US. Consul General in Jerusalem and Deputy Assistant Secretary of State in the Bureau of Near Eastern and South Asian Affairs, it is my view that a conviction by the competent Jordanian authorities provides strong evidence that Mohammed Jamal Khalifa has, in fact, engaged in serious terrorist offenses. I further believe that Mr. Khalifa's release in the United States under these circumstances would endanger U.S. national se-

curity, and would significantly damage U.S. foreign polity interests, particularly with respect to the Hashemite Kingdom of Jordan.

Sincerely,
Philip C. Wilcox, Jr.
Coordinator for Counterterrorism

Inside Information Suddenly Changed Khalifa's Objection to Being Deported

Terrorist sources in the Middle East had apparently caused the sole witness against Khalifa in the Jordan trial, upon which the death penalty was based, to recant his testimony—something that can easily be done in the climate existing in the Middle East. The prior guilty judgment and death sentence was then vacated. Being aware of this turn of events, Khalifa suddenly withdrew his offer.

Filing Lawsuit for Return of Terrorist Information

Before being deported, Khalifa filed a lawsuit to have his computer and other material—that contained valuable information on terrorist names and contacts—returned to him. Assistant U.S. attorney Stephen Freccero, in his response to the court, replied: "The United States has no objection to the unsealing of the search warrant and the return of the property seized."

Major Terrorist in Prior Plots Against The U.S. Released to Continue His Attacks

Khalifa was released in 1995, and his treasure chest of information needed to protect U.S. security was turned over to him. Numerous major terrorist attacks on U.S. targets then followed, with collateral effects that will inflict even more harm upon the lives of the American people and safety of the United States. When and where it ends, no one can possibly imagine.

DOJ Covering Up for Major Terrorist Plans

During the trial against Yousef, DOJ personnel attempted to claim that the only evidence about terrorist activities discovered from Yousef's computer and Murad's confession were the plot to place bombs on 11 U.S. airliners departing Far East locations, and the plot to fly a small single-engine private aircraft into the Pentagon. By not allowing that evidence into the 1995 trial, it protected the careers and reputations of many people in government, while simultaneously depriving the United States of the means to prevent the terrorist attacks that followed.

Gross Incompetence Had Been the Culture for Decades

Just as key FBI and CIA personnel were spies for the Soviet Union, with lifestyles far beyond their government income, their subversive activities were oblivious to their superiors. Just like the nation's financial regulators ignored all the warnings about massive fraud occurring right in front of them, and even continued when the evidence was brought to their attention.

I discovered this myself. For years, as a professional and key federal airline safety inspector, I reported ongoing corruption in the government's aviation safety offices responsible for a continuing series of major airline disasters, with no actions taken except to silence me. The record shows that it is almost impossible to get people in key government positions—or anywhere—to react to warnings given by qualified and responsible people.

National Security Agency (NSA): Thousands of Employees; and Incompetence Against Terrorists Using Street Smarts

The nation's largest security agency is the National Security Agency (NSA), with over 10,000 employees. It has a yearly budget in billions of dollars. The NSA eavesdropping mission includes monitoring the Internet, telephone calls, radio broadcasting, and other forms of communication, and has listening capabilities throughout the Middle East. A brief reference is made here to the serious omissions by NSA that paralleled the problems of FBI-DOJ personnel, which enabled multiple terrorist attacks to occur.

NSA Withholding Knowledge of al Qaeda Activities

For years, NSA had knowledge of al Qaeda activities, including their presence in the United States. Protecting their turf, NSA withheld this information from other government departments, even when they were asked for information that NSA had. Probably, the reason the 9/11 commission members covered up for the NSA failures was that reporting them would lead to exposing the FBI-DOJ misconduct and incompetence.

CHAPTER TEN

Mafia and FBI Supervisor As Serial Murderers

New York City had five organized crime families, known as the Mafia, or La Cosa Nostra (LCN), an Italian-American organized crime group. The terms, La Cosa Nostra and the Mafia, have been used in referring to the same groups. The five New York City groups that are part of La Cosa Nostra are known as Colombo, Bonanno, Genovese, Gambino, and Luchese. The names given to these groups arose from the names of the mob bosses in 1963 when a mob turncoat, Joseph Valachi, testified in the United States senate about the five La Cosa Nostra families in the New York City area.

- The hierarchy of the Mafia groups consists of:
- Boss, being the head of the group.
- Underboss, who is selected by the boss.
- Capos, who are appointed by the boss and are the head of a crew of soldiers and associates.
- Soldiers are "made men" who do most of the mob's business.
- Associates work with soldiers and do many of the odd jobs.
- Consigliere is normally the person who provides advice on various mob activities.

It generally requires a father of Italian heritage to become a member of La Cosa Nostra. The rule of silence, where the activities of the organization must remain secret, is called *omerta.* Some of the Mafia groups had been combined into what was called The Commission, and consisted of the five New York Mafia bosses, the Chicago Mafia boss, and the Buffalo Mafia boss. Over a period of time the names of the head of these groups changed. The names by which the groups are known are the names of the bosses when their identity was first revealed in 1963.

Organized crime reportedly started in New York City, where there are five organized crime families that are part of La Cosa Nostra. The bosses of the families frequently change due to being murdered by those seeking to take over the group. Although such murders were to have required the approval of the Commission, that formality broke down.

The Colombo group played a major role in this book, so a little background information is provided here. The Colombo family operated primarily in Brooklyn, and to a smaller extent on Staten Island. Its activities consisted of labor racketeering, extortion, counterfeiting, loan sharking, and gambling. It consisted of about 120 members. From 1930 to 1963 the first boss of what became known as the Colombo family was Joe Profaci.

Highlights of the Gallo-Profaci Internal War

Seeking to overthrow Joseph Profaci was Joe Gallo, which resulted in many killings and kidnappings. That challenge failed. Profaci died in June 1962. After Profaci died, the next boss was Joe Colombo, and he controlled the group until he was shot in 1971, rendering him physically unable to carry on. Some believe Carlo Gambino was the person behind the shooting.

With Colombo incapacitated, the boss position was taken by old time capo, Carmine Persico. However, he was sentenced to prison and appointed capo Thomas DiBella to be acting boss. As DiBella's health failed, he stepped down in 1977. Carmine Persico, still in prison, had Gennaro Langella run the family. But then, Langella was also sent to prison. From prison, Persico appointed Victor "Little Vic" Orena to be temporary boss of the Colombo family. Orena, however, wanted to be permanent boss, causing a turf battle to occur between Orena and Persico loyalists.

Colombo Capo Finding Three Murdered Civil Rights Workers

One of the capos in the Colombo crime group was Gregory Scarpa Sr. Scarpa was involved in credit card fraud, loan-sharking, bookmaking and other racketeering activities.

On June 21, 1964, three political activists in the Civil Rights movement were killed in Mississippi and their bodies were never found for many years. The FBI offered $25,000 reward for anyone offering information on their whereabouts. On August 24, 1964, the bodies were discovered by a person the FBI would not identify. There is a reason for not identifying the person.

What the FBI had done was to hire a known killer, Gregory Scarpa Sr., provided him with a gun and a stack of greenbacks, and told him the name of one of the suspected killers. Scarpa and his common-law wife, Linda Schiro, then drove to Mississippi, where Linda later stated what she saw. FBI agents came to the motel, handed Scarpa a pistol and put a stack of bills on the table.

Before Scarpa left to carry out the mission, he told Linda that if he did not come back, to take the money and leave. Scarpa then went to the TV store owned by one of the suspected killers, Edgar Ray Killen, and forced him into the trunk of a car, driving him to a remote location. Scarpa then put a gun in the person's mouth and stated he would shoot if the person didn't identify where the bodies were. The person talked, and took Scarpa to the location where the bodies of the three murdered civil rights workers were buried. A grand jury indicted Killen on three counts of murder, and a jury later convicted him.

Opposing Colombo Faction Attempt to Kill Scarpa

In 1991, one of the Orena group members attempted to kill Scarpa, who was in the Persico faction of the Colombo group. Scarpa then proceeded to kill members of the Orena faction. He was considered the most brutal soldier in the

Persico group and was given various nicknames, including "The Killing Machine." Scarpa would call associates after killing someone and punch 666 into the phones.

The escalating violence between the two factions resulted in over a dozen deaths. This resulted in many members of both factions being charged with various criminal activities and sentenced to prison. Helping bring this about were several members who became prosecution witnesses, including Carmine Sessa, the Colombo group Consigliere in the Persico faction.

Gregory Scarpa Jr.'s Role in the Colombo Family

Gregory Scarpa Sr. taught his son, Gregory Jr. to be a criminal. One of the murders at which Gregory was present was when his father fired three bullets into the head of Mary Bari. DeVecchio had told the senior Scarpa that she was providing information to the FBI.

The younger Scarpa was eventually arrested on a variety of criminal charges. After Gregory Jr.'s arrest, he told prosecutors that he and a member of his father's group, Joseph "Joe Brewster" DeDomenico, killed a doctor in Queens (December 3, 1980), with information provided by FBI agent DeVecchio. The doctor, Eliezer Shkolnik, was providing information to the IRS about the activities of the senior Scarpa.

Suspicious Warning to Shkolnik's Son Not to Push for Investigation of His Father's Death

Although local police had information as to who killed the father, detectives told Shkolnik's son, Hunter, a New York attorney, to forget the matter. Hunter explained:

> *They said they had hit a wall. And they suggested that family members not try to retrieve his father's medical business. That's what they said to us. 'Don't do it. You don't want to get involved. It's probably what got your father killed.' Now that I'm looking back at the things that were said to us at the time. In retrospect, they may have been right.*

The Doctor's Murder Was Scarpa's First Killing

Scarpa Jr. said that the killing of the doctor was his first murder. The father gave his son the doctor's home address, a picture of the target, and said, "Do this for me." Scarpa said that he killed Shkolnik in the vestibule of the doctor's Forest Hills apartment building, and then drove to Manhattan where he threw the murder weapon into a sewer. Joe Brewster, who accompanied Scarpa Jr. to the murder, told the father that Gregory handled himself very well. Scarpa Jr. said his father "was proud of me."

Gregory Scarpa Sr. as a Murdering Government Informant

Scarpa Sr. became a high-level government informant in the 1970s, meeting periodically with his FBI handler, Anthony Villano. Because Scarpa was suspected of involvement in murders, the FBI ordered Villano to terminate Scarpa as a top FBI informant.

Some years later, in 1980, FBI Special Agent Lindley DeVecchio renewed the relationship, which resulted in several meetings a week in the home that Scarpa Sr. shared with his common law wife, Linda Schiro. DeVecchio had FBI responsibility for the Bonanno crime family. During this relationship, Scarpa reportedly gave DeVecchio money and various perks, including supplying him with prostitutes and a hotel room.

Schiro would later testify that Scarpa requested and received from DeVecchio the addresses and phone numbers of delinquent loan sharking customers. DeVecchio knew that Scarpa would then track them down and either beat them or murder them.

Schiro also testified that she was present when DeVecchio told Scarpa that there was an arrest warrant out for Gregory on credit card fraud, and that DeVecchio assured Scarpa that he would intervene to where a prison sentence would be replaced with probation.

Subverting U.S. Interests Was Profitable for DeVecchio

It was profitable for DeVecchio to become a literal co-partner with one of the most brutal crime families in New York. He received money from the Colombo mafia capo and he kept the money that the FBI intended to pay Scarpa for being an informant. Further, he thought, correctly, that his relationship with Scarpa would propel him into a higher position within the FBI.

It had been reported that DeVecchio kept over $66,000 that the FBI intended to be given to Scarpa, which were the weekly stipends the FBI provided through DeVecchio. DeVecchio expected that Scarpa would be promoted from Capo to the next higher position as the Colombo's boss.[17] DeVecchio acted to discredit police department investigators who were getting too much information on Scarpa.

DeVecchio's Help in Murdering Grancio

Scarpa Sr. went to a Brooklyn social club where he planned to murder Nicholas Grancio. But upon arrival, he found FBI agents doing surveillance on the mobster. Scarpa then called and complained to DeVecchio, who then notified the surveillance team by radio to immediately come back to the office. The FBI agents thought this order unusual and improper. Shortly after the FBI agents left, Scarpa murdered Grancio.

Mafia member Larry Mazza, who later became an informant for the FBI, reported that Scarpa called DeVecchio to remove surveillances on Grancio so that Scarpa's people could murder him. After DeVecchio pulled the FBI sur-

---

[17] The pecking order in the Mafia was Boss, Underboss, and then various Capos, depending upon the size of the crime group, and then below Capo were the Soldiers and then the Associates. Scarpa, Sr. was one of the Capos in the Colombo Mafia family in New York.

veillance team from Grancio, Scarpa, who had been given the secret FBI radio frequency, heard the FBI team being called back to the office. Scarpa then moved in and assassinated Grancio. Grancio's family filed a lawsuit in 2005 against DeVecchio and his partner, Christopher Favo. Favo was an FBI agent who worked closely with DeVecchio.

To shift the blame from himself, DeVecchio accused a New York Police Department officer, Joe Simone, of providing information to the Mafia and Scarpa during the Colombo war, As a result, Simone was charged with a crime, but a jury acquitted him. Later, Simone was discharged, losing his pension after 20 years of service.

DeVecchio's Earlier Masquerade As Mafia Hit Man

In his younger days, as an FBI special agent, DeVecchio masqueraded as a hit man using the alias of Tony DeAngelo. In 1983, DeVecchio went undercover inside the Metropolitan Correction Center in New York, helping to indict CIA asset Edwin Wilson.

A *New York Post* article (April 6, 2006) described that phrase of DeVecchio's life:

> Decades before rogue FBI agent Lindley DeVecchio allegedly funneled classified information to a murderous mob boss, he acted the part of Mafia hit man to foil a death plot against two federal prosecutors, sources said. Masquerading as a hired gun named Tony DeAngelo, the now-embattled special agent went undercover in early 1983 inside the federal Metropolitan Correctional Center, where a rogue ex-CIA agent accused of selling weapons illegally was putting out the word he wanted to whack the prosecutors on his case.
>
> "It was all on tape," recalled Lawrence Barcella,[18] one of the prosecutors targeted. "DeVecchio was a young FBI agent at the time, who went undercover as a mob hit man; it's somewhat ironic." The bizarre incident centered around Edwin Wilson, a former CIA agent caught selling weapons to Libya. While awaiting trial, Wilson told his cellmate that he wanted to hire someone to rub out four witnesses in the case; two prosecutors and his ex-wife. The cellmate, Wayne Trimmer, alerted authorities, who set up a sting with DeVecchio posing as a jail-hardened murderer whom Trimmer ostensibly knew from the state prison in upstate Attica.
>
> DeVecchio arranged a visit with Trimmer at the jail while Wilson and his own son met in the same room. That way, Wilson could check out the man he was about to hire.
>
> "He fit the part," said Eugene Kaplan, the federal prosecutor who handled Wilson's murder-conspiracy case. "He knew how to do it."

---

[18] As I described in *Defrauding America*, Barcella helped cover up for the covert operation known as October Surprise.

In one final ironic twist, Wilson was released in September 2004 after serving more than 20 years in prison—less than half a year before Brooklyn DA Charles would open his investigation into DeVecchio's alleged mob ties.

DeVecchio Major Violator of Gun Laws
Protected by High-Level FBI-DOJ Personnel

Daniel Clements, a former federal prosecutor, discovered DeVecchio selling illegal guns at a gun show. Clements was quoted as stating years earlier of FBI Special Agent DeVecchio, "If someone's a bad actor, we'll get him again." Clements was referring to the criminal acts of the FBI agent in 1976. An AFT agent caught DeVecchio selling large quantities of guns at the Valley Forge Gun Show at Kink of Prussia, Pennsylvania, without a license, which was a felony.

Clements reported this to a federal prosecutor in Baltimore, stating, "You're not going to believe this. I have an FBI agent selling guns illegally." Clements prepared to file charges against DeVecchio, and out of courtesy, informed the FBI that he was investigating an FBI agent for illegally selling handguns. Clements then heard from Rudolph Giuliani, an aide to the deputy attorney general. Clements said that Giuliani contacted him and said, "He didn't want to embarrass the bureau." Clements stated, as reported in a *New York Times* article (April 15, 2006) that other people selling guns illegally as DeVecchio, were charged and sent to prison.

The same corrupt FBI-DOJ culture, including murders with organized crime and Mafia figures, was in both the Boston and New York City offices. The many years of cover-ups indicated that the misconduct was tolerated and approved—or even directed—by FBI and DOJ officials in Washington.

Blackmailing the FBI

In 1973 a U.S. attorney in Newark, New Jersey, stated that Scarpa, Sr. was a target in a fraudulent bond case. Scarpa, outraged, contacted the Newark, New Jersey FBI office[19] and threatened to "reveal everything, scheme and technique, imaginable pertaining to the FBI." In a FBI memo dated October 9, 1973, an FBI agent in the Newark office provided further information and notified the FBI director in Washington. Charges were then dropped.

Repeated FBI, Justice Department, and Judicial Protection

At another time when a U.S. attorney indicted Scarpa on credit card fraud (1986), Scarpa pleaded guilty, apparently on the basis of being advised by his handlers that he would not go to prison. The prosecuting U.S. attorney, not in on the scheme, stated at sentencing before Judge Leo Glasser that Scarpa was one of the biggest distributors of counterfeit credit cards in the New York met-

[19] October 9, 1973.

ropolitan area; that Scarpa had a long criminal history and that he should be incarcerated. FBI agent DeVecchio met with the judge in chambers before sentencing, causing the incarceration to be replaced with probation.

DeVecchio was kept busy protecting Scarpa and his son Gregory. A DEA investigation into Gregory's drug activities threatened to bring about Gregory's arrest. Coming to the rescue, DeVecchio provided Scarpa with information about Gregory's imminent arrest, and also the name and location of the DEA's primary witness against Gregory, Cosmo Catanzaro. Scarpa then arranged to have Catanzaro killed.

Scarpa Sr.'s Brutal Activities

Scarpa's former attorney, Martin Light, while testifying before Congress in 1987, described Scarpa as a psychopathic killer:

> Greg was the type of guy who would arrange to have a dinner with you. He would laugh, make jokes, ask about your family and then when dessert came he would just whack you right on the spot.

One example of Scarpa's brutality occurred in response to criticism of his son's handling of a bank robbery by associate Dominick Somma. Scarpa pulled out a pistol and shot him dead. Despite this brutal nature, Scarpa was a "Top Echelon" informant for the FBI for 30 years, killing many people in the process. Scarpa Sr. was aided and abetted by high-level FBI-DOJ personnel in Washington.

FBI-DOJ Personnel Protected Each Other

From 1980 through 1992 DeVecchio was in the criminal division of the Organized Crime section. He was responsible for investigating the La Cosa Nostra, Italian organized crime (LCN). In 1983, he was the supervisor for investigating crimes of the Bonanno La Cosa Nostra family and then the Colombo Family.

A former Colombo mob member stated to an FBI agent during a 1994 Colombo mafia meeting that Scarpa, Sr. always told his mistress, Linda Schiro, the details of the criminal activities, and the details of his relationship with DeVecchio.

During a trial involving the murder of Joseph DeDomenico in 1994, several mob figures testified that DeVecchio was giving confidential information to Colombo mob boss Gregory Scarpa, Sr.

DeVecchio-Scarpa Relationship
Scuttled a Dozen Criminal Trials

During legal proceedings in one of the criminal cases involving a Colombo defendant in the early 1990s, the defense called DeVecchio to testify. During his testimony he revealed that he had been sanctioned by the FBI because of his close relationship to Scarpa Sr. That information caused convictions to be reversed in over a dozen cases. U.S. District Judge Jack Weinstein warned that the remaining cases were at risk of being dismissed. DeVecchio was heavily involved in the 1986 "Commission Cases" that resulted in dozens of criminal cases being filed against the New York City mafia families.

DeVecchio Repeatedly Used the Evasive Tactic, "I don't Remember," to Avoid Perjury Charges

During that testimony, DeVecchio stated he didn't recall, several dozen times, and in other instances invoked the Fifth Amendment to avoid testifying. DeVecchio was obviously lying, and his lying protected by high-level FBI-DOJ personnel.

Over the years there were many media articles concerning the serious FBI problems in both the FBI's Boston and New York offices, all of which were ignored/covered up by FBI-DOJ officials and members of Congress. One of many *Pittsburgh Post-Gazette* articles (December 1, 1998) by investigative reporter Bill Moushey wrote:

> It was May 22, 1992. FBI Special Agent Christopher Favo was briefing his boss, R. Lindley DeVecchio, who headed the task force trying to end Brooklyn's Colombo crime family war. Two men loyal to the Colombo faction led by Victor J. Orena had been gunned down on a Brooklyn street the night before, Favo announced. DeVecchio's reaction was not what Favo expected. The man charged with stopping the violence cheered for the shootings.

Three Decades of FBI-DOJ Protecting "The Killing Machine"

For three decades, Scarpa had been an informant for the FBI. His relationship with DeVecchio went on for over a decade. DeVecchio and high-level FBI-DOJ personnel ignored Scarpa's murders and other criminal activities. Some agents and others knew the truth. Several made written accusations accusing DeVecchio of assisting and protecting Scarpa Sr. in the Mafia killer's success. Accusations against DeVecchio, made in sworn statements by other FBI agents, cooperating FBI witnesses, and in court testimony, included:

- Giving Scarpa the names of other FBI informants, so Scarpa could put them in harm's way while shielding his own illegal operations.
- Telling Scarpa where the FBI was placing wiretaps so he could avoid them.
- Informing Scarpa of pending indictments against his associates—in one instance, allowing Scarpa to help his son disappear before the younger Scarpa could be arrested.
- Handing over the addresses of Scarpa's enemies in the Colombo crime family war so that he could track them down and kill them.
- Fabricating evidence against Orena and other Scarpa adversaries so they would be sent to prison.

Protecting DeVecchio—and the FBI and DOJ

The media publicity forced the FBI inspector general of the Department of Justice to initiate an investigation in the mid-1990s. The investigation was repeatedly delayed, but eventually, in 1996, the investigators for the Office of Professional Responsibility (OPR), which is the internal affairs arm of the U.S. Department of Justice, covered up for DeVecchio's crimes and that of high level FBI-DOJ personnel who knew of the crimes and protected the parties. Despite the overwhelming evidence—far more than is required to find a citizen guilty—OPR personnel held that none of the charges were true. There were several reasons for whitewashing the investigation:

- Evidence in court proceedings and investigative reporting showed FBI agents in the Boston FBI offices were engaging in similar murders and other crimes with organized crime figures.
- Ruling that DeVecchio was providing information to Mafia Capo Gregory Scarpa Sr. would provide grounds for overturning prior convictions and undermine others that were waiting for trial.
- To protect high-level FBI-DOJ personnel who knew of the Scarpa-DeVecchio relationship for years and covered up.

The first report on DeVecchio was prepared by U.S. Attorney Zachary W. Carter on May 8, 1995. That report stated in part:

In accordance with the ruling of Judge Korman, in lieu of disclosing an affidavit that had been presented to Judge Korman ex parte, please be advised that the following constitutes our knowledge of the items that Special Agent R. Lindley DeVecchio may have disclosed to Gregory Scarpa, Sr. and the approximate time of the disclosure:

a. The planned 1987 arrest by DEA of Gregory Scarpa, Jr., and his crew, and that law enforcement believed that Cosmo Catanzano was a "weak link," who might cooperate with authorities if arrested;

b. On or about February 27, 1992, that Carmine Imbriale was cooperating with law enforcement;

c. During the Colombo Family war, information on at least one member of the Orena faction who had a hit team that was looking for members of the Persico faction;

d. Following the arrest of Joseph Ambrosino, that there were arrest warrants outstanding for Lawrence Mazza and James DelMasto (two of Scarpa's closest associated), but that if they stayed away from their normal "hangouts" they could avoid being arrested.

e. In or around January 1992, that it was believed that Orena was staying at his girlfriend's house, the location of which (as then known by some in law enforcement) was also conveyed.

f. In or around January 1992, the address of the house in which Salvatore Miciotta was residing; and

g. In early 1992, subscriber information for telephone numbers of two of Scarpa's loan shark customers;

h. In the mid to late 1980s, that Scarpa's social club was subject to court-ordered electronic surveillance and that he would then be arrested on charges involving dealing with fraudulent credit cards.

Very truly yours,

Zachary W. Carter
United States Attorney
By: Ellen M. Corcella
Assistant U.S. Attorney

That report was then followed by the final report of the Department of Justice Office of Professional Responsibility, noted for its cover-up of internal corruption.

DOJ OPR Completes Its Cover-Up Scheme

Following two years of evidence gathering, the Department of Justice Inspector General 364-page report was released. The lengthy but anemic report devoted *only* 12 pages to the DeVecchio matter and sanitized or cut out any reference to the many people that provided information on DeVecchio's involvement in murders.

The section devoted to DeVecchio was titled: "Confidential Informant Case Study 2. FBI Informant Gregory Scarpa, Sr. and his FBI Handler, R. Lindley DeVecchio." It did not address the criminal allegations and focused on minor "improprieties" between the Colombo mob boss Gregory Scarpa, Sr. and FBI Supervisory agent Lindley DeVecchio. The reference in that report to DeVecchio follows:

The Report

> Gregory Scarpa, Sr., who was involved in organized crime for most of his life, served as an FBI confidential informant at various times from 1980 until the early 1990s. His relationship with the FBI and, in particular, with his sole handler, R. Lindley DeVecchio, factored in a number of major prosecutions against New York members of La Cosa Nostra (LCN) in the 1990s. In some cases, Scarpa's status as an FBI informant was known during trial; in another, it was not revealed until post-conviction motions were filed and Scarpa had died.
>
> *Victor Orena and Pasquale Amato*. In two separate federal trials in 1992 and 1993, juries found Victor J. Orena, the "acting boss" of the Colombo Family, and Pasquale Amato guilty of racketeering, conspiracy, and

firearms charges. The events leading to the convictions of Orena and Amato stemmed from the "Colombo Wars," a power struggle between two Colombo factions, the Persicos and the Orenas that lasted from the fall of 1991 through the spring of 1992. At Orena's trial, DeVecchio, who headed the Colombo LCN squad in the FBI's New York Field Office, testified as an expert witness about the nature and structure of organized crime. Both defendants were sentenced to life in prison, and the Second Circuit affirmed both convictions and sentences.

Years after their convictions and following exhaustion of all appeals, Orena and Amato filed motions for dismissal of their indictments or for new trials alleging a violation of the government's disclosure obligations under *Brady v. Maryland*, 373 U.S. 83 (1963).

Their motions were based upon DeVecchio's "questionable ethics and judgments" as revealed in proceedings in another case. After learning that Scarpa was a long-time FBI informant, Orena and Amato contended that it was not they, but DeVecchio, who conspired with Scarpa to instigate the Mafia war and caused the killing of their partner and loan shark, Thomas Ocera, one of the murders for which Orena and Amato were convicted.

The trial court denied the post-trial motions. *Orena v. United States*, 956 F. Supp. 1071 (E.D.N.Y. 1997). However, the court closely examined the relationship between DeVecchio and Scarpa, who rose to the position of a "capo" or captain in the Colombo family. According to the trial court, in the 1970s and perhaps as early as the 1960s, Scarpa had been regularly in touch with an FBI agent. The relationship was broken off until DeVecchio succeeded in renewing Scarpa's informant status in December 1980. DeVecchio acted as Scarpa's sole FBI handler from that time until Scarpa was finally terminated as an FBI informant after the Colombo Wars were over in 1992, despite an FBI protocol which required informants to be handled by two agents at a time.

As a "top echelon" informant, Scarpa initially provided the FBI with information pertaining to organizational activity and personnel movements within the Colombo Family. After the Colombo Wars commenced in late 1991, he provided detailed reports of perpetrators and strategic planning of the opposing factions.

The court found that DeVecchio reciprocated by passing along unauthorized information to Scarpa. For example, evidence was presented indicating that DeVecchio warned Scarpa of his pending arrest on federal credit card fraud charges and may have intervened with the sentencing judge to request lenient treatment.

There also was suspicion that in 1987 DeVecchio leaked to Scarpa information that the Wimpy Boys Social Club, a favorite Colombo gathering place, was subject to court-ordered electronic surveillance; that he tipped off Scarpa to the planned DEA arrest of his son, Gregory Scarpa Jr.., and others in connection with the criminal activity at the social club; and that, as a result of the warning, Gregory Scarpa, Jr. became a fugitive. With respect to the Confidential Informant Guidelines, the court also found that:

On March 3, 1992, Scarpa was closed as an informant after the ASAC of the Criminal Division of the New York FBI Division, Donald North, "found credible allegations that Scarpa was involved in planning violent criminal activity." In informal conversations with North, DeVecchio was allegedly "adamant" that Scarpa was not involved in violent activity. In early April 1992, DeVecchio initiated the process of having Scarpa reopened, and the FBI granted authority to re-open Scarpa on April 8, 1992, pending completion of a suitability inquiry. On April 22, 1992, DeVecchio notified FBI Headquarters that such an inquiry had been conducted and that Scarpa was deemed suitable.

During the summer of 1992, Special Agent Christopher Favo, who was working with DeVecchio during the investigation, became strongly suspicious of DeVecchio. Believing that DeVecchio was engaged in misconduct and fearing that he might disrupt current investigations, Favo began to withhold information from DeVecchio pertaining to Scarpa. Other subordinates of DeVecchio's suspected that Scarpa was a murderer, but none of them reported their suspicions about Scarpa or DeVecchio to superiors or to the United States Attorney despite the fact that the Informant Guidelines required agents to report any knowledge of an informant committing violent crimes.

Scarpa was arrested by the New York City Police in August 1992 on a firearms charge. Shortly thereafter, a federal indictment charging Scarpa with the commission of the three murders, among other crimes, was handed down. Scarpa was released on bail under strict house confinement as one of the conditions of release because of failing health. In late December 1992, his bail was revoked because of his involvement in a shooting. Scarpa was sentenced to ten years in prison in December 1993 after pleading guilty to two counts of murder.

In January 1994, Favo and other agents approached ASAC North to report their concerns about DeVecchio's relationship with Scarpa. Consistent with FBI policy, North immediately submitted a report to the FBI's Office of Professional Responsibility (OPR). OPR determined that DeVecchio was appropriately a subject of investigation.

[1996 DOJ Inspector General Cover-Up]

In September 1996, the Public Integrity Section determined that prosecution of DeVecchio was not warranted, and the OPR investigation was closed. DeVecchio retired from the FBI in October 1996. Scarpa died in of AIDS in a federal prison in June 1994.

In its ruling on Orena's and Amato's motions for dismissal of their indictments or new trials, the district court held that (1) the defendants either knew or should have known that a member of the organized crime family to which they belonged had acted as an informant, so the government's failure to disclose that fact did not warrant a new trial; (2) evidence that a government agent had leaked information to an informant and that a second government agent had concerns regarding the relationship between the first agent and the informant was not material to the Government's charges, so the Government's failure to disclose did not warrant relief under *Brady*; and (3) newly discovered evidence did not warrant a new trial.

On the issue of leaking information to an informant and the relationship between DeVecchio and Scarpa, the district court observed that while the CI Guidelines provide guidance on "sanctioning criminal conduct on the part of informants where necessary 'to establish and maintain credibility or cover with persons associated with criminal activity under investigation,'" the "line between the value of an informer and the unreasonable risks of encouraging serious criminal activity requires judgment of senior supervisors with sound ethical compasses; people in the field are often not in a position to provide the necessary direction." *Orena v. United States*, 956 F. Supp. 1071, 1102 (E.D.N.Y. 1997).

The court noted that, according to the Attorney General Guidelines, the FBI does exercise control at the supervisory level in Washington and locally. In the case of Scarpa, however, "these administrative controls failed to work because DeVecchio was not properly supervised locally and because . . . he failed to inform his supervisors in Washington of the probability that Scarpa was engaged in violence." Id. at 1103.

Victor Orena, Jr., John Orena, Thomas Petrizzo, et al. In June 1995, a jury acquitted seven reputed associates of the Orena wing of the Colombo family of conspiring to murder members of the rival Persico faction of the family. Scarpa's status as an FBI informant became a pivotal issue during the trial. Fellow FBI agents testified that they had become suspicious of DeVecchio and were particularly concerned that he had fed confidential information to Scarpa which helped him to evade arrest.

Anthony Russo, Joseph Russo and Joseph Monteleone. Scarpa's relationship with the FBI generated post-trial motions in another case following the conviction of LCN defendants on murder and conspiracy to murder charges. In that case, in March 1997, the trial judge granted a motion for a new trial to Anthony Russo, Joseph Russo, and Joseph Monteleone, finding that the Government had improperly failed to disclose evidence bearing on Scarpa's credibility. The Court of Appeals reversed that portion of the district court's order that granted a new trial, rejecting the trial court's conclusion that evidence that Scarpa lied to the FBI about his involvement in certain other murders gave rise to an inference that he lied to his co-conspirators about the murders in question.

E. Deactivation of Confidential Informants

Due to the risks involved in operating informants and the corresponding need to closely supervise their status and operation, the Guidelines prescribe that certain steps be taken in the event a confidential informant is deactivated or "closed." If a determination is made to close a confidential informant, whether for "cause" or for any other reason, the case agent must document the reasons for deactivation in the CI's file. The MIOG defines "cause" as: any grievous action by or set of previously unknown facts-circumstances that deem the individual not suitable for use as a CI. Such actions that might give "cause" include but are not limited to: disbarment; unauthorized criminal activity; incarceration; failure to follow instructions; violation of any parole, release guidelines or agreements; providing unreliable information, etc.

When an informant is closed, the agent must also notify the CI that he or she has been deactivated and document this notification. Moreover, if the CI is authorized to engage in otherwise illegal activity (Tier 1 or Tier 2), the case agent must revoke this authorization, and document its revocation.

CI Guidelines § V.A.4. If a U.S. Attorney's Office is either "participating in the conduct of an investigation" that is utilizing a CI or "working with a CI in connection with a prosecution," the FBI must coordinate with the prosecuting attorney assigned to the matter, "in advance whenever possible," regarding specified decisions relating to the CI, including a decision to deactivate a CI.

CI Guidelines § V.D. There have been many cases in which the confidential informant's status was unknown to the prosecution, among them the Bulger-Flemmi matter described above in CI Case Study No. 1. Flemmi and Bulger were opened, then deactivated or closed for various periods of time when they became suspects or targets of other investigations. According to prosecutors who are familiar with their FBI informant files, one could not tell looking at their files when they were opened, active, or closed as it is not uncommon for the FBI to close an informant, and then open the informant months or years later in connection with the same or other investigations in the originating field office's jurisdiction or elsewhere.

MIOG § 137-15(13). CI Guidelines § V.A at B-33. Delayed notification to the CI is permitted if timely notification "might jeopardize an ongoing investigation or prosecution or might cause the flight from prosecution of any person."

CI Guidelines § V.B at B-34. informants. Unless the informant's status is clear, the government may not be able to fully meet its discovery obligations. Moreover, if informants are closed but the FBI cannot document this fact along with any required revocation of OIA authority, the government becomes vulnerable to the defense that the FBI authorized the informant's illegal activities.

IV. Major Revisions to the Guidelines

As described in Chapter Two, major revisions of the Confidential Informant Guidelines were approved by Attorney General Reno on January 8, 2001. The 2001 revisions were the product of a 2-year effort by a joint FBI-DOJ committee known as the "Resolution 18 Committee." The 2001 revisions included significant modifications to the provisions regarding suitability, authorization to engage in otherwise illegal activity, the prohibition against making commitments to the CI regarding immunity from prosecution, and notifying the prosecutor of the confidential informant's true identity. As we discussed in Chapter Two, many of the modifications to the previous version of the Guidelines attempted to address administrative and management weaknesses that came to light during the Bulger-Flemmi matter.

Further revisions in May 2002 made only minor modifications to the Confidential Informant Guidelines. Under the January 2001 Guidelines, case agents who worked with confidential informants were required to read to CIs verbatim certain instructions about the constraints imposed on their activities. This provision was replaced in May 2002 by a requirement that the contact agent or "handler," along with an additional agent present as a witness, review the written instructions with the CI.

CI Guidelines § II.C.1. The removal of the verbatim requirement was needed, according to FBI Director Mueller, because "the verbatim instructions, written in often

According to a prosecutor who reviewed Flemmi's informant file, the fact that Flemmi was a murderer and planned to commit additional murders was not noted in his FBI informant file. Flemmi was eventually closed as an informant not because of concerns that he would commit additional homicides. Rather, in September of 1965 he was charged by state authorities with Assault with a Dangerous Weapon with Intent to Murder after he shot another person. The FBI decided to close him as an informant "[i]n view of the fact that informant is presently a local fugitive" and "any contacts with him might prove to be difficult and embarrassing." House Committee on Government Reform, *Everything Secret Degenerates: The FBI's Use of Murderers as Informants*, 3rd *Report*, H.R Rep. No. 108-414, at 17 (2004), available at: http://www.gpo.gov/hreports/108-414.html.

A table illustrating the May 30, 2002, revisions to the Confidential Informant Guidelines and the other revised Investigative Guidelines is attached at Appendix C. intimidating legalese, were proving to have a chilling effect, causing confidential informants to leave the program.

Under the May 2002 revisions, an agent may now adapt the instructions—including the instructions on protecting the confidentiality of the CI's identity—to the CI's particular circumstances. Nonetheless, agents must clearly convey the content and meaning of each applicable instruction and document that the instructions were reviewed and that the CI acknowledged the CI's understanding of them.

Under the Confidential Informant Guidelines issued in January 2001, case agents who worked with CIs were required to give an instruction to the CIs (even if they had no relevance to the CI's situation), relating to the inability of investigative agencies to promise immunity from prosecution. The revised Guidelines emphasize that regardless of whether these instructions are given, the FBI has no authority to confer immunity, and agents must avoid giving CIs the erroneous impression that they have such authority.

CI Guidelines §§ II.C.1 (d), (e), and (k).

V. The OIG Review of the FBI's Compliance with the Confidential Informant Guidelines. To test compliance with key provisions of the Informant Guidelines in the investigative files we reviewed, we selected a judgmental sample of 120 individual confidential informant files from 12 FBI field offices we visited between June and August 2004. The CI files we reviewed fit into at least one of four categories: long-term CIs, CIs authorized to perform otherwise illegal activity, privileged or media-affiliated CIs, and CIs who are not reviewed at FBI Headquarters. The files included some CIs who were reviewed by the CIRC and some who were authorized only at the field

Oversight Hearing on Counterterrorism: Hearing Before the Senate Committee on the Judiciary, 107th Cong. 187 (2003) (Responses by Robert S. Mueller, III, Director, Federal Bureau of Investigation, to Committee's written questions).

CI Guidelines §§ II.C.1 and II.C.2 at B-19. Agents must, however, continue to obtain the informant's written acknowledgement of instructions relating to authorization for otherwise illegal activity and in connection with payments to the informant. CI Guidelines §§ III.C.4.b and III.B.6, respectively, at B-28 & B-24.

To accommodate the FBI's concerns about preserving the identity of its CIs, and because the OIG did not need to know the names of the CIs to complete its review, the OIG examined copies of documents maintained in the original CI files with the CI's name and other identifying information redacted. To ensure that our compliance findings accurately reflected all the data in the original files, FBI Headquarters personnel, working in conjunction with Informant Coordinators, confirmed the facts supporting our CI compliance findings from our field office visits. Among the "non-CIRC" CIs we reviewed, we chose CIs who were opened for over one year, CIs from different squads and programs, CIs who had been paid substantial sums, and CIs who were closed more than six months after the May 2002 revisions became effective.

In examining individual informant files, we collected data on: suitability determinations, instructions, documentation and notifications to U.S. Attorneys' Offices of unauthorized illegal activity, approval of otherwise illegal activity, and deactivations. We sought to answer the following key questions.

Were the Initial and Continuing Suitability reviews of confidential informants conducted within the required time period and was the required information provided?

Were the required instructions or cautions given to CIs at registration and periodically thereafter?

Were applications to permit confidential informants to engage in OIA complete and timely, was the proposed OIA described in sufficient detail, and was the requisite approval obtained from the U.S. Attorney's Office? Was unauthorized illegal activity by confidential informants reported when required by the SAC to the U.S. Attorney?

As noted earlier, the CIRC reviews and approves long-term CIs, high level CIs, and CIs who are under the obligation of a legal privilege of confidentiality or are affiliated with the media. CI Guidelines *§§ II*.A.3 and II.D at B-16 & B-19.

We randomly chose between 9 and 11 of the pertinent files to examine in each field office, except in offices where there were only a small number of files within a certain category of informants, in which case we reviewed all files. We did not pre-select CI files that had been identified as non-compliant by internal FBI inspections or other internal compliance mechanisms, nor did we base our selection of field offices on the compliance record of those field offices or on any other criteria that would produce a bias or skewing of the judgmental sample.

As is the case, however, with any judgmental sample, one cannot extrapolate with statistical certainty that the non-compliance rate of the entire population of FBI confidential informant files would be identical to the non-compliance rate we found in our sample.

We did not concentrate on compliance issues relating to payments to informants because such payments are the subject of multiple layers of oversight by the field divisions, HIU, the Finance Unit within CID, and the Inspection Division. As we discuss in Chapter Seven, many of the elements we reviewed are also reviewed by the Inspection Division during its triennial inspections of each FBI division.

If confidential informants were deactivated "for cause" or other reasons, was the deactivation appropriately documented; was the informant notified of the deactivation; and, if the informant was authorized to engage in OIA, was the OIA authorization revoked and the revocation documented?

Taken together, we believe these five factors address critical judgments the FBI must make under the existing Confidential Informant Guidelines to ensure that those registered as confidential informants are suitable and understand the limits of the relationship, and that responsible DOJ officials approve, concur in, or are notified of significant developments in the informant relationship. The requirements we tested became effective 120 days after issuance of the revised Confidential Informant Guidelines in January 2001. These requirements were unaffected by the May 2002 Guidelines revisions.

In addition to our review of informant files, we also examined field guidance distributed by the FBI's Criminal Investigative Division (CID) and the results of various reviews of the Criminal Informant Program. The reviews included inspection reports generated by the FBI's Inspection Division and reinspections coordinated by the Asset/Informant Unit (A/IU) in the Criminal Intelligence Section of the CID.

We also examined the role played by Confidential Informant Coordinators, who are GS-10 through GS-13 non-supervisory Special Agents who have the responsibility, as their principal assignment or as collateral duty, to assist FBI agents with issues associated with the administration and operation of human sources. Confidential Informant Coordinators also work with confidential file room analysts in managing the special record keeping and document management requirements of the Criminal Informant Program, troubleshoot problems, and assist in the training and administrative aspects of informant operations. We surveyed these Coordinators about the work they do in supporting the Criminal Informant Program and solicited their views on FBI

MIOG § 137-1(5). Many Confidential Informant Coordinators also provide equivalent guidance and support for the operation of the FBI's assets. The confidential file room analyst collects and records information and provides support for the Criminal Informant Program. Analysts also prepare statistical information to evaluate the assistance provided by confidential informants, known as "statistical accomplishments." They also work closely with the Informant Coordinators on the paperwork associated with informant operation, promote compliance with the FBI's policies and regulations regarding informants, and bring issues to the attention of the Informant Coordinator for resolution.

Compliance with the Guidelines. To supplement these findings, we also surveyed FBI Division Counsel and the Chiefs of the Criminal Division of the U.S. Attorneys' Offices for their perspectives on compliance-related aspects of the Confidential Informant Guidelines.

VI. Compliance Findings. Overall, we found one or more Guidelines deficiencies in 104 of the 120 confidential informant files, or 87 percent of those we examined. The deficiencies included failure to document the agent's evaluation of one or more suitability factors in the initial or continuing suitability evaluations, failure to give the required instructions to CIs or to do so at the required intervals, failure to obtain proper authority to permit CIs to engage in otherwise illegal activities, issuance of retroactive approvals of otherwise illegal activities, failure to report unauthorized illegal activity in accordance with the Guidelines, and failure to document deactivation of CIs.

We received a 100 percent response rate to our survey of Confidential Informant Coordinators. We received a 98 percent response rate to our survey of Criminal Division Chiefs of the U.S. Attorneys' Offices. We received a 92 percent response rate to our survey of FBI Division Counsel.

The following table summarizes OIG Findings on Confidential In-

		OIG Selection Criteria[203]	Files Meeting Selection Criteria	Number of Non-compliant Files	Percent Non-compliant
1		Initial Suitability Reports & Recommendations (ISR&Rs) – Required Elements Not Addressed[204]	44	15	34%
2		Instructions	120	59	49%
	a	Missing One Or More Instructions		27	23%
	b	Untimely Instructions		33	28%
3		Continuing Suitability Reports & Recommendations (CSR&Rs)	96	74	77%
	a	Missing One Or More Reports		57	59%
	b	Untimely Reports		12	13%
	c	Required Element(s) Not Addressed		20	21%

formant Guidelines Compliance Deficiencies in Select FBI Field Offices:

In the following categories, each file we examined could have one or more deficiencies in a single file: instructions, continuing suitability report and recommendation, otherwise illegal activity, unauthorized illegal activity, and deactivation. The only deficiency we found in the ISR&Rs was the failure to address all required suitability elements.

As discussed above, FBI agents proposing to operate confidential informants are required to address various factors bearing upon the source's suitability by entering the relevant information on a standardized form called an Initial Suitability Report and Recommendation (ISR&R). The ISR&R must be approved in writing by a field manager. CI Guidelines, § II.A.1 at B-14.

Compliance deficiencies noted in this table for ISR&Rs are either that the field office form did not list all the required elements or the agent did not address one or more elements on the suitability form.

End of Report

Similar Blinders with Prior FBI Agents

The feigned no-evidence tactic was similar to the see-nothing that allowed such FBI agents as Robert Hansen to spy for the Soviet Union for years, with evidence of his activities and sudden wealth ignored by FBI officials.

It was widely known that Scarpa Sr. had killed dozens of people, and that presenting information to Scarpa of people that he was seeking would often result in them being murdered. Further, even without the murder consequences, for any law enforcement officer—and especially one in a key FBI supervisory position—to reveal the information that was admitted in that letter, was justification for an immediate termination of employment and criminal charges being filed. Further, it could be assumed that an FBI supervisor revealing to a Mafia person—especially one known as "The Killing Machine"—could be expected to provide him with other information.

Among the Reasons for Releasing Serial Murderer into Society

There were many reasons for obstructing justice by covering up for DeVecchio's crimes against the United States and its people. These reasons are shown in various parts of this book, and include, for instance:

- Protecting the careers of high-level FBI-DOJ personnel that had known of the serial murders and covered up for them.
- Preventing the links becoming known showing that FBI-DOJ personnel sacrificed the lives of thousands of people who died in subsequent terrorist attacks that could have been saved if the advance information on the attacks had not been "deep-sixth" by high-level FBI-DOJ personnel. Details in other pages.
- Preventing the lifting of the lid that would expose massive incompetence and corruption of DOJ employees relating to a series of terrorist attacks.

DeVecchio retired to Florida,[20] with a full pension, after the sham OPR report was issued. If a fraction of the evidence related to a plain citizen and not a government person, the person would have been long ago charged and sentenced to a long prison term. Gregory Scarpa Sr. died of AIDS in 1994, which

---

[20] DeVecchio had a home at 8328 Canary Palm Court, Sarasota, Florida 34238 and owned other property. He was also involved in various corporations, including R.L. DeVecchio, LLC, with the principal address listed with the Florida Department of State as 8328 Canary Palm Ct., Sarasota, FL 34238; Savannah At Turtle Rock Association, Inc. and Avatar Property Management Group, Inc., both of which showed their principal address as 8500 Turtle Rock Blvd., Sarasota, FL. 34238.

he contracted during surgery in 1986 from a blood transfusion provided by a member of the Colombo family.

Standard Congressional Cover-Up

A House Judiciary Committee investigation (2005) uncovered evidence of improper activities between DeVecchio and Mafia boss Gregory Scarpa, Sr. during the 1980s and 1990s, but as usual, did nothing.

CHAPTER ELEVEN

"Deep Sixing" Warnings Of Major Terrorist Attacks

This chapter focuses on the advance insider information on the worst series of terrorist attacks in the history of the United States. Information that was kept from the American people by the nation's executive branch, by members of Congress, by federal judges, and by media people.

For years, people in the intelligence agencies knew that terrorists were planning to hijack U.S. airliners and fly them into buildings. People in the government's aviation safety offices, the FAA, responsible for preventing airliners from being hijacked, knew for years the easy-to-accomplish steps to prevent airliners from being hijacked. Internal FAA problems, which I describe in the book, *History of Aviation Disasters: 1950 to 9/11*, details why known preventative measures are rarely put into place until members of Congress are finally forced to issue safety practices that should have been done by FAA personnel.

For years, FBI-DOJ personnel knew that terrorists were planning to hijack U.S. airliners and fly them into buildings. The FBI knew of suspected Middle East terrorists taking pilot training in the United States, and even taking lessons in aircraft simulators to fly large airliners, with no interest in taking off or landing.

White House politicians were aware of these threats and the dangers, and then made ridiculous statements after they had occurred that no one would ever have dreamed of such an event happening. National Security Advisor Condoleezza Rice and President George Bush! Even when one White House staffer warned FBI and DOJ personnel of the imminent danger, he was told that they did not want to hear anything about it again.

French intelligence officials notified the United States that al Qaeda member Zacarias Moussaoui was on a 1999 watch list and known to be an extremist. After Zacarias was arrested on immigration charges, the Justice Department denied local FBI agents permission to examine his laptop computer.

Mohamed Atta, who is believed to be the terrorist who piloted the American Airlines plane into the World Trade Center, was a suspect implicated in a 1986 bus bombing in Israel. He traveled in and out of the United States on an expired visa. Khalid Al Midhar, another of the September 11 hijackers, was on a CIA watch list in January 2001 after the United States determined that he played a role in the bombing of the USS Cole three months earlier. Another hijacker, Nawaf Alhazmi, was also being sought for questioning by the FBI. What a system!

Two of the hijackers who were taking pilot lessons in the United States abandoned their small plane on a taxiway of a busy airport. After the engine stopped, they simply walked away from the plane, blocking a major taxi way used by airliners. This conduct did not arouse any attention by the FAA or the FBI.

INS did not keep a list of those who traveled to the United States on a temporary visa, and did not know if they left the United States when the visa expired, or if they showed up at the school for training for which the visa was approved.

Prior Attempt to Crash an Airliner into a Major Landmark

In 1996 hijackers belonging to an Algerian terrorist organization with connections to the Osama bin Laden al Qaeda group took over an Air France airliner on a flight from Algiers to Paris via Marseille. The hijackers took control of the aircraft after departing Algiers and upon landing at Marseille the hijackers demanded that three times the normal amount of fuel be placed on the aircraft over what was normal for that otherwise short flight. Before the refueling was completed, security personnel stormed the aircraft and subdued the hijackers. It was learned that the hijackers planned to crash the aircraft into the Eiffel Tower. In 2001, terrorists had planned to fly a plane loaded with bombs into the building where world leaders were meeting in Geneva. Extra security thwarted that plan.

FEMA Study Predicted Airliners Crashing Into Landmarks

Bradley Ayers was a former CIA agent during the Cuban missile crisis, a former U.S. Army Ranger, and later part of a special section of the Federal Emergency Management Agency. (FEMA) Ayers wrote in one report:

> My task, together with a small, select group of highly qualified officers from other services and civilian experts from several key agencies of government, was to freely brainstorm and evaluate America's vulnerabilities to internal terrorist attack.
>
> Ours was a very focused undertaking. We were directed to realistically create scenarios envisioning ways in which radical militants might strike within the United States employing only materials, equipment and devices that were readily available in the course and conduct of everyday life in our country. We came up with a number of possible schemes by which someone bent on creating substantial havoc within the U.S. might exploit existing weaknesses in general and commercial (airline) security and flight operations.
>
> Among the scenarios we developed was one that envisioned trained terrorist pilots using rented general aviation airplanes, or commandeering air cargo or airline aircraft and deliberately crashing them into political targets. Our list included the White House, the Pentagon, the Empire State Building, nuclear power planets, and weapons storage facilities. To us, the

use of a fuel-laden plane, possibly with explosives aboard, as a guided missile was not only obvious but also feasible within minimum ingenuity on the part of the perpetrators.

We completed our work, formalized it and sent it on to FEMA headquarters. Later, while working with DEA and ATF, I learned that the study was circulated among a number of federal agencies and generally discounted as being "unthinkable" and too "far out" to be realistically considered.

We've had plenty of wakeup calls: hostage taking, hijackings, barracks, embassies and buildings bombed, subways poisoned, naval ships blown up. It was only a matter of time for the terrorists to put it all together on American soil.

Incompetence After Incompetence Embedded in FBI Culture

On August 17, 2001, the month before the September 11 hijackings, an alert flight instructor in Minneapolis reported his suspicions to the FBI about Zacarias Moussaoui, who wanted to take simulator training in a Boeing 767, but had no interest in learning how to take it off or land. Moussaoui was believed to have been one of the planned September 11 hijackers. His FBI supervisor told him to forget about it.

Other Enablers to What Was Soon to Occur

As I wrote in the book, *History of Aviation Disasters: 1950 to 9/11*, there were many more enablers to the events that were about to happen. Starting in the late 1970s, after discovering the culture of corruption in the government's primary aviation safety office, I expanded on my attempts to report these serious problems to various Department of Justice offices and to Congress, and was repeatedly blocked. The continuing preventable airline crashes caused me to use the federal crime reporting statute, Title 18 U.S.C, § 4, to report the federal offenses to a federal judge.

The clear wording of the statute requires that any federal judge receive information from anyone offering it. I encountered a block by federal lawyers who filed motions to prevent me from providing the information and to dismiss the lawsuit. Every federal judges cooperated in the cover-up.

Over the years, as I discovered through my many sources corruption of people in the FBI-DOJ offices and the CIA, I made one last attempt to report these matters to a federal judge at Reno, Nevada.

The complaint that I filed clearly stated specific acts of misconduct by people in control of the FAA, in the Department of Justice, and in the CIA. Motion after motion by the defendants delayed the proceedings. And then the big event occurred that everyone was forewarned about.

However, at that time, I was unaware of a different form of conduct that had a more criminal aspect to it that would shortly shock the world.

CHAPTER TWELVE

Forewarned Downing of TWA Flight 800

Within a few weeks of being informed by Gregory Scarpa, Jr. of the planned downing of an airliner departing a New York City airport on July 17, 1996, TWA Flight 800 exploded in the air shortly after takeoff, in full view of countless numbers of people. Evidence points strongly to a surface-to-air missile having been responsible.

The death of 230 people on the flight was made possible by a multitude of poor judgments and misconduct involving people in the FBI-DOJ and the CIA. Many people became enablers to the deaths of those people. This chapter addresses these issues. The first issue will address the strong evidence that a surface-to-air missile took down TWA Flight 800.

For many years, surface-to-air missiles have shot down airliners and military aircraft in Africa and Asia, making it obvious that sooner or later terrorists would use this choice terrorist weapon against U.S. airliners, either overseas or in the United States. Information and documentation was given to me in 1995 by a long-time source, Ronald Rewald, the titular head of a major covert CIA proprietary based in Honolulu: Bishop, Baldwin, Rewald, Dillingham and Wong (BBRDW).

That covert CIA operation took over from the secret CIA financial operation called Nugan Hand bank that was based in Australia. That operation was shut down when a Hong Kong journalist exposed the CIA operation. I describe that operation in the books, *Defrauding America* and *Explosive Secrets of Covert CIA Companies*.

Warnings of Missile Attacks Upon U.S. Airliners

Because of Rewald's prior contact with Afghan rebels during the 1980s, Rewald become involved in negotiations in Long Beach, California, during which Afghan rebels offered to give several dozen surface-to-air missiles to the United States in exchange for the release from prison of Mohammad Akbar Bey, an associate of one of the Afghan warlords, General Rashid Dostum. Akbar Bey was serving a prison term for drug possession.

At the same time, Middle East terrorists were seeking to buy these missiles. If this were to occur, it is probable that they would be used to shoot down U.S. commercial aircraft.

Involved in the negotiations were people from the FBI and CIA, Ron Rewald, Long Beach lawyer, John J. Reed, who was believed to be one of the many lawyers fronting for the CIA, and a representative from General Dostum.

Questionable Agenda

After months of negotiations frustrated by Justice Department and CIA officials, the missiles were rejected. Concerned about the probable consequences of rejecting the SAM missiles, Rewald provided me with information and documents concerning the missile negotiations. I then sent by certified mail a detailed three-page letter to Senator Arlen Specter and every member of the House and Senate intelligence committees, warning that surface-to-air missiles were about to be turned over to terrorists because of the actions by Justice Department and CIA officials.

I stressed that I had considerable documentation and memorandums outlining the negotiations, and that failure to immediately contact me and my CIA source would permit the terrorists to acquire the missiles. As in the past, not a single recipient responded.

History of Missiles Downing Commercial Aircraft

It could be assumed that it is only a question of time before missiles are used to down aircraft in the United States. At that time, 25 commercial aircraft had already been shot down by SAM missiles in Africa, the Middle East, and the Soviet Union. Terrorism against the United States was increasing and it could be expected that U.S. commercial aircraft would be targeted with any missiles acquired by terrorists. My three-page letter to members of Congress[21] follows:

From the desk of Rodney Stich
P.O. Box 5, Alamo, CA 94507; phone: 510-944-1930
Author of Defrauding America *and* Unfriendly Skies

October 20, 1995

Senator Arlen Specter
United States Senate
Washington, DC 20510 Certified: P 427 892 268

Ref: Refusal by CIA and Justice Department officials to accept the "gift" of 30-40 Stinger missiles, suggesting a hidden agenda, with possible catastrophic consequences in shooting down commercial airliners.

Dear Senator Specter:

---

[21]Senators Richard Lugar, Richard Shelby, Mike DeWine, Jon Kyl, James Inhofe, Kay Bailey Hutchison, Connie Mack, William Cohen, Robert Kerrey, John Glenn, Richard Bryan, Bob Graham, John Kerry, Max Baucus, Bennett Johnston, Charles Robb, Bob Dole (Certified Z 112 005 558); and to Representatives Larry Combest, Robert Dornan, Bill Young, James Hansen, Jerry Lewis, Porter Goss, Bud Shuster, Bill McCollum, Michael Castle, Norman Dicks, Bill Richardson, Julian Dixon, Robert Torricelli, Ronald Coleman, Nancy Pelosi, and Greg Laughlin. None responded.

My sources in the intelligence community have recently given me details of efforts by Afghani rebels to turn over to the United States, without charge, 30 to 40 Stinger missiles (SAM), with a possibility of an additional 100 missiles thereafter. Incredibly, this offer was *rejected* by Justice Department and Central Intelligence Agency officials. There is a strong probability that one or more of these rejected missiles will be used to shoot down commercial airliners. If this occurs, not only will the carnage be horrendous, but it will inflict severe financial havoc upon the aviation industry and upon air travel. The following is a brief description of what has transpired:

Synopsis of CIA and Justice Department Tactics
Insuring That the SAM Missiles Will Be Available to Terrorists

Recent information provided to me by one or more of my many contacts in the CIA community describe the dates, places, and people involved in offering the missiles to the United States, and the rejection of this offer. These sources provided me with precise details of the negotiations to give the missiles to the United States, the agreement by Afghan rebel leader, General Rashid Dostum, and a CIA lawyer.

CIA headquarters was initially made aware of the offer through a letter sent by a former CIA agent whom I have known for about five years, and who I consider very honorable and reliable. That letter went unanswered. The agent, concerned about the consequences of commercial airliners being shot down with these missiles, then contacted another CIA employee at CIA headquarters, who then tried to force a response from high CIA officials. This latest action forced CIA officials to finally respond.

Negotiations then commenced, which involved, among others, the former CIA agent who headed a major CIA proprietary in Hawaii; a CIA lawyer in the Los Angeles area; an Afghani located in California; and an Afghani rebel general in Afghanistan (who had previously turned over 20 Stinger missiles to the United States).

The general agreed to turn over the missiles without cost to the United States, and simply requested the release of an Afghani being held in federal prison on a drug charge arising from a possible KGB setup. At the same time that the Afghan general was offering to give these missiles to the United States, these same missiles were being sought by terrorist groups who bid large amounts of money for them. One obvious possible use for these missiles in terrorist hands would be to shoot down commercial airlines.

Incredibly, CIA and Justice Department officials rejected the offer, insuring that the missiles would fall into the hands of terrorists, where some of them may be at this very moment.

The Afghani initially offered to give to the CIA 30 to 40 Stinger (following an earlier return of 20 Stinger missiles), with a possibility that 100 more would be delivered thereafter. The CIA and Justice Department requested serial numbers for several of the missiles to determine that the missiles were actually available. These serial numbers were then provided, and the numbers were confirmed by U.S. authorities as authentic.

After telephone contact was made with this Afghan general (General Dostum), a written agreement was signed by a Los Angeles area CIA lawyer, the Afghani in California, and the former CIA agent who the Afghans were using to insure that the CIA and Justice Department kept their word.

Knowledge of corrupt CIA and Justice Department activities

My prior experience as a federal and then a private investigator, and a confidant to many former CIA and other deep-cover people seeking to expose government corruption, has enabled me to recognize the corrupt conduct of these two government agencies. I strongly feel that this rejection indicates a secret agenda that could inflict additional great harm upon America. This conduct would be compatible with the corrupt activities and harm that I have detailed and documented during the past 30 years of attempts to expose the activities of corrupt government officials and employees.

Possible Reasons for Refusing the Missiles

There are several possible reasons for the CIA and Justice Department refusing to accept the missiles, and each of them is in character for these two groups. Two of these reasons are listed here:

Attempt to prevent exposure of an earlier CIA and Justice Department scandal. The offer to provide the missiles at no charge went through a former CIA agent who was made the titular head of a large and covert CIA proprietary in Hawaii: Bishop, Baldwin, Rewald, Dillingham and Wong (BBRDW). This covert operation that was based within the United States (Honolulu) had offices in 17 countries, and replaced another CIA operation and scandal known as Nugan Hand Bank with headquarters in Australia. After a Honolulu television station blew the cover on BBRDW, officials in control of the CIA and Justice Department sought to cover for the CIA operation by fraudulently charging with criminal conduct the head of that CIA proprietary.

If the missiles had been accepted, it is possible that this sacrificed agent would be identified and the massive fraud involving the Hawaiian and Nugan Hand operations would then surface. (Exposure of this type of misconduct would reveal that the Justice Department's conduct at Ruby Ridge and Waco are only the tip of the iceberg.)

CIA need for continuing crises. Another possibility for CIA and Justice Department rejection of the Stinger missiles is that the CIA *wants* the missiles to fall into terrorists' hands, and actually wants an airliner to be shot down. The shoot-down of a commercial airliner could then be used to justify the continuation of CIA activities. This scenario is not as bizarre as it sounds when a person understands the history of corrupt CIA and Justice Department activities and the great harm inflicted upon the United States through criminal activities. I describe these activities in books that I have written, *Defrauding America* and to a lesser extent, *History of Aviation Disasters: 1950 to 9/11*.

Prior Air Tragedy Involved With
CIA-DEA-Justice Department Misconduct

Pam Am 103. Despite the cover-up by the CIA and Justice Department (and by Congress and much of the mainstream media), substantial evidence indicates that the Pan Am 103 tragedy was made possible by CIA-DEA misconduct associated with a pattern of illicit drug smuggling into the United States. My deep-cover contacts, along with information obtained from other sources, indicates that the CIA and DEA had an established drug pipeline from Nicosia and Beirut into the United States using Pan Am aircraft. Pan Am's involvement started at Frankfort, Germany.

Ironically, one of the same DEA agents based at the DEA station in Nicosia where covert DIA agent reportedly discovered the drug smuggling operation was DEA agent Michael T. Hurley, who was used to retaliate against a witness who testified to Congress concerning the Justice Department's involvement in the Inslaw scandal. That witness was Michael Riconosciuto. That type of retaliation is standard tactics in the Justice Department and congress had repeatedly refused to act on these charges.

Justice Department officials prosecuted Lester Coleman, a former intelligence agency asset who blew the whistle on the CIA-DEA involvement in the Pan Am tragedy. Justice Department officials prosecuted Juval Aviv in retaliation for uncovering evidence showing CIA-DEA involvement in that tragedy. (I have a long list of others who were fraudulently prosecuted to silence them, including the long persecution of me in retaliation for exposing these crimes against America.)

Pattern of Congressional and Media Cover-Up

None of the corrupt government activities that I identify could continue without the criminal cover-up by members of Congress and by most of the U.S. mainstream media. I repeatedly offered to provide evidence to you and other members of Congress (and the media) of hard-core criminal activities involving federal officials, and the only response was silence (i.e., misprision of felonies, cover-up, obstruction of justice). This same misprision of felonies has put many citizens in prison (Title 18 U.S.C. § 4), even though they were less guilty than government officials, members of Congress, and the media, who have a greater responsibility to report these crimes.

On the surface, although very serious, this missile matter does not appear to have the subversive and criminal nature of other criminal conduct that I exposed. However, it demands a full, open, congressional investigation.

Fortunately for everyone involved in these criminal activities, the mainstream media has kept the lid on the scandals, and most Americans are too preoccupied with trivia, and totally unwilling to meet their responsibilities under our form of government.

Vested Interest in Continuing the Cover-up

Based upon 30 years of experience in attempting to expose hard-core government corruption, starting while I was a federal investigator, it would be my expectation that you will cover up this matter. For many years, and especially during the past five years, I have made you aware of criminal activities involving government employees and officials, including corrupt officials within the Central Intelligence Agency, the Justice Department, and crooked judges. Each of you therefore have a vested interest in preventing the American people from learning about these criminal activities and what has been done to the American people.

But there is the possibility that despite the media cover-up, and the public's incredible illiteracy about government misconduct, that a small percentage of the American people will learn about it and demand justice. If one or more commercial aircraft are blown out of the sky, your prior knowledge will be publicized. So you have a dilemma as to what to do with this information. You certainly can't meet your responsibilities by turning this information over to the same Justice Department that is corruptly involved with the various criminal activities that I brought to your attention.

Sincerely,

Rodney Stich

cc: Broadcast and print media.

Every member of the Senate and House intelligence Committees via identical letter.

Endnotes:

1. The criminal activities that Stich initially discovered while a federal investigator included: (a) widespread and deeply entrenched pattern of CIA and DEA drug smuggling into the United States, aided and abetted by persons employed by Customs, Justice Department, and other government agencies and branches; (b) converting federal bankruptcy courts into criminal enterprises through looting of assets by a conspiracy consisting of federal judges, trustees covert Justice Department and CIA law firms; (c) CIA involvement in looting U.S. financial institutions, including the savings and loans; (d) CIA scheme known as "October Surprise," and its cover-up; (e) Inslaw corruption involving Justice Department personnel and federal judges; (f) Operation Mount Rushmore, a CIA/Mossad scheme to assassinate presidential candidate Bill Clinton in San Francisco; (criminal cover-up and obstruction of justice by Justice Department personnel, federal judges, and others, of each of these and other crimes; (h) felony persecution of informants, whistleblowers, and protesting victims by federal judges and prosecutors; (i) involvement of California judges in helping to carry out several of these schemes, including a t en-year pattern of judicial acts against Rodney Stich while violating blocks of California and federal statutes and constitutional protections, making them co-conspirators.

He never responded.

As Forewarned, Déjà vu Downing of TWA Flight 800

Before a year passed, on July 17, 1996, a TWA Boeing 747 that had taken off about 20 minutes earlier from New York's JFK airport exploded off of Long Island on its way to Europe. Death toll was 230 people. It was a route that I had flown many times as an airline captain. The facts indicate that a surface-to-air missile caused the aircraft fuel tanks to explode.

The 747 had departed JFK with wing tanks nearly full of Jet A fuel, and about 50 gallons in the center section tank, barely enough to keep that tank's surfaces wet. While climbing through 13,700 feet the aircraft suddenly exploded into a giant fireball, scattering thousands of flaming parts like a July 4th public firework display.

Dozens of witnesses appeared on television stations in the New York City area reporting seeing a firing streak going toward the plane, followed by an *ordinance-colored* explosion. That first military-type explosive color was then followed by multiple huge reddish fuel-type explosions.

One of Dozens of Missile Trails Seen by Military Pilot

Among the many people witnessing the ascending missile was the command pilot of an Air National Guard HH-60 helicopter that had just taken off from Francis S. Gabreski Airport on Long Island. As the helicopter lifted off, Major Frederick C. Meyer saw in his windshield a fast-moving ascending streak, followed by a high-velocity military-type ordinance explosion, and then followed by two or three low velocity fuel-type explosions.

Meyer had seen many missiles as a helicopter pilot during the Vietnam War and instantly recognized the difference in the type of explosions. During one of several phone calls with Meyer, he said:

I saw in front of me and slightly to my left a streak of light in the sky. My reaction when I saw it was, What the hell is that? I observed it for approximately three to five seconds moving in a gradually ascending arc, sort of what you would observe at night if you observed a shooting star. The difference is that it was red-orange in color and it was broad daylight.

I observed the streak of light for three to five seconds. And then I saw an explosion. And about one to two seconds after that I saw a second, and possibly a third, explosion. The first was like an HPX explosion, as opposed to a "soft" explosion like gasoline.

The first left a cloud of smoke, just like a flak explosion does, almost pure white in color. The position of that explosion appeared to be slightly below and behind where one would have anticipated the streak of light to have gone. One to two seconds later, there was a second, and possibly third, softer, explosion, unlike the first one. These grew rapidly into a huge fireball four times the diameter of the sun. I was dumbstruck.

I'm recalling what I observed in Vietnam. Different things exploding have different visual characteristics. If you saw a fuel storage depot hit, the type of explosion that would occur would be slow. The second explosion was a soft explosion. It was definitely petroleum. I was in position to observe A-4s and F-4s hitting storage depots [in Vietnam] and watching the color of a storage depot that's being hit and exploding. It was huge.

My copilot, Chris, said to me, "Is that pyro?" And I said to him, "No pyro like I've ever seen." Because at that time, by the time those words came out, this fireball was huge." I said, "Let's take a look." We flew at about 200 feet over the water, 150 knots indicated, in the direction of the fireball and the fire.

[Bodies in the Water]

I saw the body of a young woman with blond hair wearing a white outfit, and it was in perfect condition, floating face down. She was hanging in the water like the dead man's float. The fireball had hit the water before we crossed the beach. We estimated that it had taken approximately 10 seconds to fall.

I expected the fireball to be extinguished when it hit the water; but it just continued to burn. And it burned across, not as a ring. The whole thing burned, and those flames were 50 feet high. We measured them because we were hovering at 50 feet over the water and we were looking at the tops of the flames.

As we approached we saw the thing fall, something fell out of this plume of smoke that was following the fireball into the water. Something fell out. We observed something like a vortex inside the fireball. I saw something fall out of it.

[Varying Descent Rates of Plunging Objects]

As we approached the fireball, I told Chris to slow down. We were moving at about 150 knots, and I could see debris falling out of the sky. I was looking at debris, fuselage, aluminum skin, stumbling in the air. Now, if you shred an aircraft and it tumbles in the air, it's falling at somewhere up to 40 miles an hour and it's falling in an erratic way. They spin and flop.

Right in the middle of this field of falling debris, some of it burning, there are subjects moving down at terminal velocity of 160 and 180 knots. If you do any parachute jumping, you are falling at pretty close to 180 knots. Thinner guys fall at about 160 knots. I'm presuming that these were seats, and there were people in them, were falling at 160 to 180 knots.

Now, they couldn't have debris tumbling, lightweight debris tumbling in the air, falling past my field of vision in the same field with objects moving at terminal velocity if they had emanated from the same spot at the same time.

[People First Blown Upward]

The logical answer to me is that the heavy stuff had to go somewhere else first, before it came down, or it wouldn't have come down and been passing the slower moving objects. That indicated to me that these seats had been blown vertically upward, with the people in them. They had to be blown vertically up to zero acceleration and then start down.

We went to the fireball area and we decided immediately that we would not go downwind, because now we had a lake of fire. The ocean did not quench this at all. It was burning in the middle. It was burning at an incredible intensity. These flames were 50 feet high. The helicopter was hovering at 50 feet on the radar altimeter and we're looking at the top of the flames.

We knew that if we tried to go downwind we'd probably get into the smoke and the exhaust. And if we weren't choked ourselves, the engines might be choked and we'd go down. So we went to the northwest end arc, and began working around to the southwest. We eventually reached the southwesterly hemisphere of this lake of fire at between 50 and 100 feet, looking for anything associated with the aircraft.

The first things we saw on the left side of the aircraft were four bodies. I told my copilot who was flying, "Turn and check them out." We came down to 40 feet to shake them up with the rotor wash. There was one guy wearing a T-shirt and dungarees. Chris said, "Looks to me like they're all dead. We left them, looking elsewhere for possible survivors.

As we moved around this arc on the windward edge of the fire, we saw some debris. The first thing we saw that indicated that we had an aircraft was the section of the plastic lining that is in most commercial airliners where the windows are. You see an almost square window with the corners rounded and there's usually a shade that you pull up and down. So now we knew we had an aircraft down.

We went further around the arc and we saw this huge airfoil, which looked like a wing, but it was the rudder. The rudder on the 747 is so damn big. This thing was partially out of the water; partially elevated and partially sunk.

We saw more debris as we started working our way around to the southeasterly side of the fireball. When we got there we came upon a cluster of debris of all kinds; honeycomb metal, seats, and a cluster of 30 to 35 bodies. We went down to 40 feet, shaking them up with the rotor wash looking for any signs of life. We saw what looked like a raft. When we got closer we realized that it was a partially inflated escape slide, the type you see on a commercial airliner. There was nobody in it. Attached to that slide was a flashing strobe light that automatically activates when the emergency evacuation slide extends.

At this point the tower contacted us and told us that air traffic control just reported that they lost radar contact with a 747. When we heard that we realized that there's another 200 people out here."

The sun was now starting to set and it's starting to get dark. I told Chris that I wanted to start a creeping line search, using a half-mile space. I wanted it oriented 2-4-0 and I wanted a creeping line search. That's a search where we basically fly sideways and we fly and then we move forward a half a mile, and then we come back across the same path again. We basically fly a back and forth pattern moving, advancing at the end of a two-mile track, and we move forward a half-mile.

Convinced It Was a Missile, Based on Vietnam Experiences

Meyer was convinced that what he saw was a missile. He said, "I spent a number of years in Vietnam and had seen missiles fired, some of them at me." He said the streak was red-orange in color, followed by a yellowish-white explosion that looked identical to the detonation of an antiaircraft shell.

Meyer sought to report what he had seen. He stated that government investigators had treated him perfunctorily and had not asked him details of what he had seen or his conclusion, despite the fact that he had far more experience than the FBI and NTSB investigators as it pertains to missiles and missile explosions.

Meyer started speaking out when the FBI and NTSB ignored the heavy evidence of missile sightings and blamed the disaster on an aircraft defect. The FBI had given him and his copilot a gag order preventing them from giving interviews about what they had seen. Meyer said, as reported in *Aviation Week*:

I'm not a professor with a Ph.D. in explosion watching, I'm an eyewitness. I know what I saw. I saw an ordnance explosion. And whatever I saw, the explosion of the fuel was not the initiator of the event. It was one of the results. Something happened before that which was the initiator of the disaster. Everyone involved in the FBI and NTSB is intelligent enough to know that.

Meyer's Appearance before FBI, NTSB, and Industry Groups

During a discussion before a group consisting of aviation personnel, including an agent from the FBI and an investigator from the NTSB, Meyer referred to the lack of interest given to his observations by the NTSB and FBI:

I went to the FBI trailer office and said to the FBI agents, "I was the pilot of the helicopter that witnessed the events relating to TWA Flight 800; do you want to interview me?? Two agents said, "Oh, yeah."

And then, as an afterthought, they took me into a back room and said, "Well, go ahead and tell us, and they turned on a small handheld tape recorder." I basically told them my story and then asked, "Do you have any questions? They said no. I was in the trailer about six minutes.

[Explaining Characteristics of Different SAM Missiles]

I've seen three types of missiles while in Vietnam: SAM-1s, SAM-2s, and SAM-7s. A SAM-7 is a wild looking thing coming at you, because it comes at you like a corkscrew. But a SAM-1 and SAM-2 go through the air with a slight wiggle but smooth flight path. These missiles leave smoke trails.

A SAM-1 and a SAM-2 leave a trail 10,000 feet long in the air. A SAM-7 leaves a trail too. You can see these damn spirals after the missile is gone. And matter of fact, what you're probably seeing is the smoke because the missile's moving too fast to be seen.

This thing that I observed was a very steady path. And it wasn't a long time. It was maybe five seconds total. It was a very steady thing. It didn't have an erratic smoke trail. It didn't appear to have an erratic flight path.

Adding More Details About What He Saw

At a later date July 13, 2002), Meyer provided more details in an e-mail about what he saw as he arrived at the disaster scene:

I saw a fast moving streak crossing the sky, my left center to my further left, in a gradually descending arc. I observed the streak for about 3-5 seconds. It then disappeared for about one second. Then I saw on the same trajectory and further to my left a high velocity ordinance explosion. It was yellow white in color with black smoke. Military ordinance. Two and a half seconds later, further to my left but lower, I saw a second high velocity explosion.

This appeared to be brilliant white light, like an old fashion flash bulb. Very little smoke, but what there was, was white-gray. Two and a half to three seconds later, further to my left and still lower, I saw one, possibly two, nearly concentric, nearly coincidental high velocity explosions so close in location and time that I/m not sure if there were one or two. From that same point immediately came the low velocity fuel explosion. The fire-ball, trailing a column of thick black smoke, fell to the sea.

I did not immediately determine that the streak was a missile. It looked too smooth for the missiles I had seen in Vietnam. I thought more of some sort of "Schallenwerfer," (rocket propelled artillery shells) until I spoke with Richard Goss, an eyewitness who had been sitting on the porch of the Westhampton Yacht Squadron clubhouse having lunch. He heard a noise and looked up to see the missile climbing straight up in front of him.

He told me he then saw it make a sharp turn to the Southeast and head out to sea. Paul Angeledes saw the same thing. I then knew that the reasons the missile/s path was smooth was because it was in a hard turn. It had acquired its target at max deflection and was turning hard to center the target in its cone of acquisition. The turn did not look that sharp from my aspect because I could detect only the vertical vector, not the horizontal vector.

Reasons for Lying by FBI Agents

In the early stages of the investigation, FBI agents, including James Kallstrom, stated they thought it was a terrorist act. However, after meeting in Washington, the story suddenly changed, for reasons that had already been stated in these pages. Having had advance warning from the top al Qaeda aviation bomb expert that a U.S. airliner was to be downed, and not having taken any preventative measures, the last thing FBI personnel needed was for the public to learn about the connection.

During a November 1997 FBI press briefing, FBI agent Kallstrom stated that the missile trail that people reported was actually burning fuel from the ruptured fuel tanks on TWA Flight 800. The FBI sought to support their deception with a video prepared in collaboration with the CIA. The CIA also had something to hide: turning down the offer of dozens of surface-to-air missiles that they knew would fall into the hands of Middle East terrorists—including the al Qaeda group.

The fictional video implied that the sequence commenced with the center fuel tank exploding, which caused the entire front part of the aircraft to break off, exposing the open cabin to the onrushing air. The video then explained that the 747—minus its entire front section— climbed several thousand feet, trailing flames. It was the trailing flames which people on the ground thought was the missile trail. Only an unsophisticated public and a complicit media could accept such a blatantly false scenario.

When the various fuel tanks exploded, they exploded into giant fireballs that no one could possibly confuse with the pencil-like bluish streak of a missile. Nor did this explain the military explosive color that Meyers had witnessed. Further, having flown military and commercial aircraft almost continuously since 1942, I cannot comprehend any airliner, missing its entire front and the entire circumference of the cabin exposed to the onrushing air, climbing 3000 feet. And as Meyers and others saw, the plane went down, and not up, after the explosion. In addition, pilots flying in the vicinity reported seeing the aircraft plunge vertically to the ocean after the explosions.

Although the National Transportation Safety Board (NTSB), by law, had the responsibility for investigating airline disasters, FBI agents pushed NTSB investigators aside, and restricted them from seeing key evidence. As if orchestrated by a more powerful force in government, the political NTSB prepared a final report stating that the cause of the explosion was a spark in the center fuel tank.

Boeing, who manufactured the aircraft, strongly disagreed. Over ten years *after* the downing of TWA Flight 800, there still waas no requirement to change the system, being another indication that no one in government recognized the spark in the fuel tank as the cause.

As a key FAA airline safety expert, I had first-hand experience with the cover-ups by the political NTSB board. The repeated falsifications of the cause of certain airline disasters are described in *History of Aviation Disasters: 1950 to 9/11*. And with every cover-up, the preventable aviation disasters continued to occur.

Another reason for lying—and this would be strictly secondary to the need for FBI-DOJ personnel to protect themselves—if the public learned that terrorists brought down TWA Flight 800 with a surface-to-air missile, something that can be easily done, passenger travel would surely have dropped dramatically. That would be followed by major financial impact upon the airlines and other industries having connection to air travel.

Nine days after Flight 800 exploded, President Bill Clinton assured the public that "air travel remains the safest means of transportation." But worse was yet to come, due to the same problems that made TWA Flight 800 possible.

Among Hundreds of Other Witnesses

Lou Desyron, one of several fishermen who saw the missile trail, told *ABC World News* (July 21, 1996), "We saw what appeared to be a flare going straight up. We thought it was from a boat. It was a bright reddish-orange color." Similar reports came from over 200 people who saw the missile trail, many of them professionals. While Linda Kabot was taking pictures at a fund-raiser dinner for Mayor Vince Cannuscio at East Quogue Beach on Long Island a blast was heard nearby and her camera recorded an object streaking upward.

"Reassembling" TWA's Boeing 747

Most of the aircraft was subsequently recovered and "reassembled" in a hangar at Calverton on Long Island. It was discovered that the front of the aircraft, shortly behind the flight station, had broken off first, and the aircraft fuselage was then like an open tube.

Meyer's Statement to FBI, NTSB, Industry Group

No one had the first-hand visual sighting of Flight 800 prior to and after the explosion, as did the person I refer to as a missile-trail expert. Meyer described what he saw during a briefing of FBI, NTSB, and airline personnel.

NTSB Continuing Decades of Cover Ups

The five-day NTSB hearing started on December 8, 1997, and under normal hearing procedure, the NTSB must examine all the evidence during its investigation. However, the FBI ordered the NTSB not to allow any evidence or reference to the missile that nearly 200 people saw prior to Flight 800 blowing apart. The NTSB complied, and during the hearing attention was limited to those areas for which there was not a shred of evidence; an aircraft electrical malfunction that caused a spark to occur, exploding the fuel in the center fuel tank.

The NTSB sought to support its center fuel tank theory with the argument that the air conditioning units, situated near the center fuel tank, heated the fuel and that made the Jet fuel to explode.

I've taken aircraft full of more explosive fuel, gasoline that had been sitting in the hot desert sun in Saudi Arabia and, as with thousands of other flights by thousands of other pilots, never experienced the slightest trouble.

Unprecedented Misinformation and Cover-Up

Never in the history of aviation had there been as much government misinformation about an air disaster as with TWA Flight 800. Justice Department and NTSB officials were fabricating implausible theories while refusing to give credit to the heavy evidence of a missile strike. In my book, *History of Aviation Disasters: 1950 to 9/11*, I detailed many instances of NTSB cover-ups.

An anonymous letter appearing in the October 1996 *California Sun* (Ojai, California) described the experience of a California couple who were vacationing on Long Island at the time of the blast and who saw the missile trail. They made a report to the FBI about the missile trail, and received a reaction many others received. His letter stated in part:

> They questioned us in separate rooms and made us feel like criminals. They said that what we must have seen was a shooting star or some fireworks being shot from a boat. I told them that it was not anything like that at all.
>
> I said that it was definitely a flare type rocket heading toward the aircraft; then it exploded. It was then suggested that we did not see anything at all and that we were going along with what other people said they saw.

Just for the excitement of it. I told them, "No way, I know what I saw...They scared the hell out of us."

"We just saw an explosion."

The pilot of Eastwind Flights 507 told air traffic controllers what he saw as TWA Flight 800 exploded in front of him, as he made one of the first reports of the explosion:

We just saw an explosion up ahead out there at about 16,000 feet or something like that. It blew up in the air and then we saw two fireballs go down to the water. There was smoke coming up from that. Also, there seemed to be a light. I thought it was a landing light on. It was coming right at us at about 15,000 feet or something like that. And then it blew.

Alitalia Flight 609 also confirmed the explosion, and his report was followed by one from Virgin Atlantic Flight 009. A private pilot, Sven Faret, with a passenger, Ken Wendell, were flying a small single engine plane at 8,500 feet over Riverhead, Long Island, on a 090 degree heading, with a view of the flight path of TWA Flight 800. He later made a report of what they saw:

Ken pointed out traffic at 3 o'clock low (actually 2.30). Sven saw a white light steady in the sky. My first impression was landing lights pointed towards us putting it in a northerly direction. Ken saw two lights very close together. A short "pin flash of light" appeared on the ground (perhaps water). Very shortly thereafter the white light exploded instantaneously into a huge red-orange ball. My initial response was, "Who's shooting fireworks tonight?" The magnitude of the fireball, and altitude, quickly (less than a second) ruled that out.

Immediately thereafter a large fireball emerged from the bottom of the initial fireball, accelerating straight down, as if it had just started to fall. Like a teardrop it drew with it a tail of fire down to the water surface. We watched intently as the descending fire fell closer to the water. Sven was awaiting the fire to illuminate the water surface as it fell. At the same moment a pilot reported it to the controller on 118.00. [radio frequency]

A second pilot responded, reporting what he saw:

We saw it hit the water, lighting up the surrounding surface very well. Large splashes could be seen around the fire. The fire on the surface was relatively small, but was spreading quickly. I asked Ken, "What was that!" It's probably the National Guard boys losing a C-130 or something. Maybe they shot down one of their own planes.

We proceeded to fly over to the smoke cloud. As we crossed the shoreline I looked down and saw three boats enroute to the fire, about 25 percent of the way. I estimated the flames to be 6-7 miles offshore.

We watched intently seeing a flashing light at the SE edge of the flames, but it soon stopped. We observed a steady blinking light drifting SW away from the scene. Ken said it appeared to be a helicopter just west of the flames. Sven thought it could have been a marker beacon on a life raft. This was about 5 plus minutes after the explosion.

We approached the black-gray smoke cloud on the west side. We were at 7700 feet and were at the top edge of the cloud. The cloud center was at 7500 feet. There were two small bumps upon it. There was no smoke or smoke trails about it. It was still lit up a little by the sun, clear above. There was a tornado like tail leaving the bottom of it leading down to the flames.

It had a small arc in it as the winds gently moved the cloud NNW. I said to Ken, "I have an eery feeling about this place, whatever stung this thing could sting us too. Let's bolt out-a-here." We swung north. As we were turning, we saw two-engine commuter traffic above us at 8000 plus, traveling NW. We called Flight Service on 122.6 and reported what we saw. We flew back to Riverhead and east. Over Mattituck Airport we decided that the event had to be enough of a finale for the evening. We called approach on 132.25 for clearance back to Islip. We also told that controller what we saw.

FBI Threats to Remain Quiet

Numerous reports surfaced of FBI agents warning people to remain quiet about their knowledge of a missile sighting. I was also warned. A copy of my October 20, 1995, letter to Senator Arlen Specter, warning of a missile attack on U.S. aircraft, was put on the Internet by unknown people, and this became known to the FBI.

On July 24, 1996, a week after TWA Flight 800 exploded, two FBI agents contacted and wanted to meet with me; which I did. They had no interest whatsoever in my information about the missiles that as forewarned fell into the hands of Middle East terrorists. Their only interest was to warn me to remain quiet about what I knew. In a phone call that took place about a hour after we met, Special Agent V. Stewart Daley warned me to remain quiet about the missiles. I told him that I encountered FBI cover-up for the past 30 years, starting while I was a federal investigator, and I was not about to remain silent now.

To make a record of the FBI's meeting I sent a July 30, 1996 letter to the FBI describing the events as I saw them. A copy of my letter to the FBI follows.

From the desk of Rodney Stich
P.O. Box 5, Alamo, CA 94507; phone: 510-944-1930; FAX 510-295-1203
Author of *Defrauding America, Disavow, & Unfriendly Skies*
Member
Association Former Intelligence Officers
International Society of Air Safety Investigators
Former FAA air safety investigator
Association of National Security Alumni
Lawyers Pilots Bar Association
Former airline captain and Navy pilot

July 30, 1996

V. Stewart Daley, Special Agent
Federal Bureau of Investigation
1850 Gateway Blvd, Suite 1010
Concord, CA 94520 Certified: P427 892054

Ref: TWA Flight 800; SAM missiles offered to US and rejected;
and July 24, 1996 meeting with FBI agent.

Dear Sir:

The purpose of this letter is to make a record relating to what transpired during a meeting and subsequent telephone conversation between myself and FBI agent V. Stewart Daley on July 24, 1996:

The San Francisco FBI office contacted me on July 24, 1996, arranging for a meeting that afternoon between myself and FBI agent V. Stewart Daley, which did occur, outside of the Rossmoor Diner in Walnut Creek, California.

The purpose of the visit by FBI agent Daley was supposed to discuss the letters that I had sent to members of the House and Senate intelligence committees on October 20, 1995, and a copy of those letters to FBI agent Jim Kallstrom on July 21, 1996. Kallstrom is the lead FBI agent in charge of the criminal investigation involving TWA Flight 800.

The intent of my October 20, 1995 letter to those members of Congress was to alert them to a very serious matter, requiring their immediate attention, that would otherwise probably culminate in one or more missiles being acquired and used by terrorists to shoot down commercial airliners.

Prior to my sending that October 20th letter, one of my many CIA sources had expressed concern to me in October 1995 that surface-to-air missiles (SAM) would be made available to terrorists by the inexplicable actions of Justice Department and CIA personnel. My source described his participation in the efforts of Afghan rebels who were offering 40 to 60 missiles to the United States, through the Justice Department and Central Intelligence Agency, at no cost to the United States. They also advised that an additional 100 missiles may also be made available. The only consideration attached to this gift of SAM missiles was that a young son of one of the rebel leaders be released from federal prison at Terminal Island. He had been convicted of a drug-related offense.

It was known to these Justice Department and CIA employees that terrorists were offering $100,000 each for several of these missiles. Knowing this, and knowing that the missiles would probably be used to shoot down commercial airlines, Justice Department and CIA officials refused to accept them. This CIA source recognized this probable consequence of the rejection, and conveyed his concern to me. He then provided me with sufficient documentation to establish the truth of his statements, including copies of letters to and from the Justice Department, serial numbers of some of the missiles, and other data.

Informing Congress of Impending Shoot-down of Passenger Airliners

I then informed each member of the House and Senate intelligence committees through that October 20, 1995 letter, making them aware of the probable shoot-down of a passenger airliner if they did not immediately intervene and seek to halt the sale of these missiles to terrorist groups. I made it clear that I had documents to support these statements and could provide them with other information. I urged them to immediately contact me for further information.

Despite the horror that would probably follow failure to take immediate actions, not a single member of Congress contacted me.

My credibility could not have been an issue. Those letters provided information on my background, including years as a former federal investigator in the Federal Aviation Administration, a member of sophisticated intelligence and aviation groups, a writer of highly technical, detailed, and documented books, and long experience in these areas.

Standard FBI Cover-up and Obstruction of Justice

During this July 24, 1996 meeting with FBI agent V. Stewart Daley, I described in general terms the nature of the missile problem and the possibility that TWA Flight 800 was shot down by a missile, and that other passenger airliners would probably be shot down by the missiles made available to terrorist groups by the conduct of these Justice Department and CIA officials. I also made it clear that I was using this meeting to make the FBI aware of other criminal activities that I had discovered. These were major criminal activities inflicting death upon many people, and were inflicting great harm upon national security. These criminal activities included, among many others:

Pattern of FAA corruption related to a series of airline crashes and deaths. I detailed and documented these activities in the third edition of *History of Aviation Disasters: 1950 to 9/11*, the second edition of *Defrauding America*, in thousands of pages of testimony and evidence placed into a FAA hearing that I forced upon the agency. I charged the existence of deeply entrenched FAA corruption (and corruption at a major airline) associated with a series of fatal airline crashes that I and other federal inspectors had uncovered as part of our official duties. These corrupt activities were made known to high level management in the FAA, NTSB, Justice Department, and to members of Congress, some of whom had already been advised of these problems by other FAA inspectors. They all covered up, making possible the continuation of the FAA culture, the air safety misconduct, and the resulting crashes. This mindset continues, making possible many of the airline crashes that continue to occur.

Pattern of corruption implicating high-level federal officials relating to long-standing drug trafficking into the United States, This would include evidence that I have accumulated for the past seven years (and longer) from my many CIA and other deep-cover sources. Heavily involved in this cover-up (and prosecution of whistle-blowers) are Justice Department employees and federal judges, as described in part in my two detailed and documented books.

Massive corruption in the Ninth Circuit bankruptcy courts, looting the assets of people who exercise the statutory protections of Chapter 11, unaware of the enormous fraud involving judges, US and private trustees, law firms, and lawyers.

Justice Department cover-up of the CIA-DEA drug pipeline, misusing Pan Am aircraft, making possible the placement of the bomb on Pan Am Flight 103, and the fraudulent prosecution of people who seek to expose the truth. There is similarity between Justice Department cover-up between the two TWA mishaps in the New York City area and the Lockerbie disaster. This cover-up of the CIA-DEA drug pipeline has protected the terrorists who actually placed the bomb on board Pan Am 103. It was the illicit activities of CIA and DEA personnel that made possible the placement of the bomb on board the aircraft, making these US employees partly responsible for the bombing and deaths.

Cover-up of Tragedy-Related Corruption Combined With Threats to Remain Quiet

Shortly after I returned home from that meeting, FBI agent Daley contacted me by phone, and warned me not to repeat any of the information that I had provided to him. He had no interest in any of these criminal matters, despite the gravity of the matters and their harmful effects upon national security.

No interest was shown in any of these areas by FBI agent V. Stewart Daley, including specifics on the missiles.

I reminded him that he had a duty under Title 18 U.S.C. Section 4, and other criminal statutes, to arrange for me and my sources to give evidence to a proper investigative body. He repeated his warning that I keep this information to myself.

How the American Public Has Paid For These Crimes and the Cover-up

TWA Flight 800. If this flight was actually shot down by a missile, the matter of Justice Department and CIA rejection of the SAM missiles is of grave concern to the United States. What agenda do these officials have that are subjecting the United States to such tragic consequences? And if TWA Flight 800 was not shot down by a missile, when will the missiles, in the hands of terrorists, be used to shoot down a passenger airliner?

Further complicating this matter is the refusal by any of the two dozen members of the Senate and House intelligence committees to obtain from me the confidential data that I have acquired after they received that urgent letter. They also appeared willing to sacrifice the lives that would very probably be lost through missile attacks.

Cover-up behind the downing of the TWA Flight over Staten Island many years ago, killing everyone on board. A prior tragedy befalling TWA, within miles of the downing of TWA Flight 800, was associated with criminal misconduct on the part of FAA management (and others), and occurred on a program for which I held federal air safety responsibilities shortly after that tragedy occurred (the world's worst at that time). Evidence of this relationship (and of the criminal misconduct in other airline crashes occurring in my area of federal air safety responsibilities) is found in the records of an unprecedented four-month-long FAA safety hearing (E20GFAA) that I forced upon the FAA while holding federal authority to make such determinations. During that hearing I acted as a prosecutor, producing official documents and testimony to support my charges. FAA legal staff and the top aide to the FAA administrator engaged in cover-up during the hearing, in perjury, subornation of perjury, that continued the FAA culture, the serious air safety and criminal violations, which then caused or made possible other crashes in my area of air safety responsibilities.

This hearing was preceded by several air disasters on programs for which I had federal air safety responsibilities, followed by identical air disasters (plus two air disasters occurring during the hearing). These activities were accompanied by cover-up involving officials in various divisions of the U.S. Department of Justice, members of Congress, and others. They all played a role in the deaths associated with the specific air disasters.

Harm to national security, to US institutions, and the deaths of many people, and establishing a corrupt culture in government institutions, especially the FAA, Justice Department, and Central Intelligence Agency.

FBI Reaction to This Pattern of Tragedy Related Criminality

Despite the gravity of the matters brought to your attention, and to other divisions of the Justice Department by a former federal investigator, no attempt was made to receive my evidence and testimony, and that of my sources.

Your telephone conversation consisted of a warning for me to remain quiet. This coincides with prior actions and inactions of Justice Department officials. It is of interest that a federal criminal statute provides for any citizen to report a federal crime to a federal judge (or other federal tribunal), and if a citizen fails to promptly do this, he has committed a criminal act. It should be of great concern to Americans that every attempt to report these criminal acts to federal judges has been judicially blocked. These judges, with the assistance of Justice Department employees, have prevented me from making such reports. They have rendered orders barring me from federal court access, which blocks me from making the reports that they are required to receive under Title 18 U.S.C. Section 4. The two books, *Unfriendly Skies* and *Defrauding America* detail and document these and many other examples of misconduct involving federal employees.

Sincerely,

Rodney Stich

cc: Janet Reno, U.S. Attorney General, Constitution Avenue and 10th Street, NW, Washington, DC 20530. FAX 202-514-4371.

Senate Intelligence Committee FAX 202-224-1772; House Intelligence Committee FAX 202-225-1991.

There was no response to that letter. I sent letters to many members of Congress, including those with oversight responsibilities over the FAA, and those with oversight over the intelligence community because of the surface-to-air missile matter that I had previously brought to their attention. Despite my highly unusual aviation background combined with insider knowledge of the missiles, not a single recipient responded. Over two dozen commercial airliners had been shot down since 1980 in Africa and Asia where there has been civil unrest, and there was no question that Americans would be killed in the same fashion as the hatred against the United States continues.

FBI-DOJ Personnel Unlawfully Seize Control Of Aviation Disaster Investigation from NTSB

Federal law provides that the responsibility to investigate aviation crashes is with the National Transportation Safety Board (NTSB), and all other government entities shall have an inferior position. That law is Title 49 § 1131(a)(2):

> An investigation by the Board ... has priority over any investigation by another department, agency or instrumentality of the United States Government.

Open Violation of Law—With Total System Approval

In direct violation of that law—for the purpose of cover-up—shortly after 9/11, Valerie Caproni, head of the Department of Justice Criminal Division in the Eastern district of New York, took the responsibility away from the NTSB to investigate the TWA 800 downing, despite the fact that by law, it is the NTSB's responsibility.

If a crime scene had been stated, then the FBI could have taken primary responsibility, but the FBI's position was that it was not a crime or terrorist attack—a decision needed to prevent blame if it were to become known that Caproni had advance notice of the downing from a mole inside the al Qaeda cell headed by Ramzi Yousef.

Ignoring the CIA, FBI, and NTSB deception, and the overwhelming evidence of a missile strike, most of the media parroted the government's line. But some went even further. *Time* magazine's December 22, 1997, issue expanded on this deception by stating that the government determined the cause of the crash to be mechanical. But the NTSB hearing provided absolutely no evidence of what caused the crash, and the NTSB made no effort to state what caused the mishap.

More Intrigue

I appeared as a guest on the Los Angeles radio show hosted by Peter Ford, the son of Glenn Ford and actress Eleanor Powell (December 4, 1996), along with Jeremy Crocker, who had conducted considerable research into the downing of TWA Flight 800, interviewing people in different parts of the United States. Crocker, who built the Palm Springs Aerial Tramway, had taken an interest in Flight 800 and had done considerable research into it. Shortly after the show, Crocker disappeared and at the time of this writing, he had not been found.

An article in the Palm Springs *Press-Enterprise* (October 28, 1997) was titled, Man's Disappearance Remains A Mystery, and stated:

> The disappearance of civic watchdog Jeremy Crocker while researching the crash of TWA Flight 800 last year has left his two sons baffled and searching for any information their father is still alive. Crocker, a longtime Palm Springs resident whose father built the Palm Springs Aerial Tramway, was last seen Dec. 9 at the downtown Los Angeles library where he did much of his research on the crash. His preoccupation with the airline crash included countless hours of research in libraries and on the Internet. He did not trust the government's probes of the crash.

Using Downing of TWA Flight 800 for Political Points

Political points were made of the downing of TWA Flight 800. President Bill Clinton and Vice President Al Gore, instead of the FAA administrator, stated they were taking action by convening a committee called the Al Gore Commission. An article in the *Wall Street Journal* (July 11, 1997) titled, "Much Talk, Little Action," described the absence of any government action on the threat of explosives on airliners. The article stated:

> Everybody has just gotten back to business as usual. ... We didn't have the courage to do anything. We just went through the motions. The public realized the Federal Aviation Administration really wasn't providing the security. It's as if they discovered the emperor had no clothes. Coming on the heels of the ValuJet Airlines crash in the Florida Everglades, the TWA disaster occurred when the nation's air –safety system was already under scrutiny. Media coverage of both crashes was intense—leading to a public outcry for political action.
>
> Politicians paid heed. Congress soon began holding a series of hearings on air safety and security that culminated in the passage of a bill designed to change the way victim's families are treated after crashes. Perhaps the greatest gesture was the creation in August of the commission led by Vice President Al Gore—the first such air–safety commission since the bombing of Pan Am 103. The initial Gore Commission report was mostly about security, but now that terrorist doesn't appear to be the cause, "the hype has all gone away," says Mr. Broderick, the former FAA official.

Included in the recommendations made in the July 1997 final report of the Gore Commission were the following:

- Install explosive detection equipment at U.S. airports. Five years later, this had not been done. However, even when such detection equipment is installed, it has a high false and false positive rate.
- Conduct criminal background checks of people who work at airports, including caterers, mechanics, and others. Same time lapse.
- Require airlines to match passengers with bags that go into the cargo compartment of the aircraft. If the passenger does not board who belongs to

that bag, the flight must be delayed until that bag is found and removed. The thinking being that someone who puts a bomb in his suitcase won't board the aircraft. However, the increasing hatred for the United States is causing people to willingly sacrifice themselves. Five years later, this baggage matching started—but only due to public outrage from a terrorist attack yet to be described.

- Install smoke detectors and fire extinguishing systems in all aircraft baggage compartments. No one asked why this obvious necessity was not required by the FAA, and why FAA management eliminated this previous requirement when the jets came into service.

A *Seattle Times* article (December 10, 1999), headlined, "Boeing says TWA crash deed of 'external source'" stated:

> The Boeing Co. said this week that the lack of evidence as to what sparked the blast that downed TWA Flight 800 three years ago, points to an "external source," such as a bomb or missile. Boeing's statement in court documents Tuesday is the strongest to date revealing an aggressive legal defense that blames the 747 crash on a bomb or missile—which the FBI and National Transportation Safety Board long ago ruled out.
>
> That the NTSB in over three years of exhaustive investigation has been unable to identify any potential ignition source aboard the aircraft suggests that an external source caused the explosion," Boeing said. "Unless and until such time as a cause is determined, ignition sources external to the aircraft—of any type—cannot be ruled out." Boeing consultants, the company says, have had only limited access to the wreckage. [These statements] came on the heels of microscopic testing on the wreckage of TWA Flight 800 demanded by Boeing.

Seeking Court Order to Obtain Evidence

An article in the *San Francisco Chronicle* (December 17, 1977) relating to evidence being covered up by the NTSB stated:

> New York. TWA and Boeing asked a judge yesterday to help them get evidence from the criminal investigation into the TWA Flight 800 explosion statements from people who thought they saw a missile near the plane. The lawyers made the appeal to U.S. District Judge Robert W. Sweet during a routine pretrial hearing in the case brought by some of the families of 230 people who died in the July 17, 1996 disaster.
>
> Steve Bell, a Boeing lawyer, said the companies had been denied evidence relating to the criminal investigation by the FBI and the National Transportation Safety Board. Bell said evidence that could show a jury that a bomb or missile may have caused the disaster was "obviously relevant. It means somebody else is responsible, not Boeing."

Lawyers and Next-of-Kin Opposed Missile Evidence

Lawyers and next-of-kin were unhappy with Boeing's position. They would *lose money* if the cause of the crash were due to a terrorist act, and not any fault of Boeing. The same resistance existed with exposing the truth as to how the bomb got put on board Pan Am Flight 103; if the placement of the bomb on Flight 103 was facilitated by a CIA-DEA drug operation using Pan Am aircraft, that would most likely take the blame from Pan American, reducing the chances of lawyers and next-of-kin being rewarded for the tragedy. See *Drugging America*.

Years Afterwards, No Material Change to 747 Fuel Systems

For years thereafter, there were no material changes made to the Boeing 747s center fuel tanks, providing further indication that the NTSB—which has less expertise than the huge Boeing Company—really did not believe that the explosion of the center fuel tank (and the other fuel tanks) was due to an internal spark.

Additional Four Years Delay Made Blame Questionable

In 2004, the FAA delayed the implementation of the fuel tank changes for an additional four years, clearly indicating that this was not considered a threat to safety, and probably not the blame for the demise of Flight 800. It wasn't until 2008 that the FAA issued a rule requiring that *newly built* aircraft have a system for preventing explosions in the center wing fuel tanks.

Navy Commander Believed Missile Downed Flight 800

Commander William Donaldson, III was the head of a group known as Associated Retired Aviation Professionals, which included former government investigators, who believed the true evidence of the crash was being covered up. Donaldson told *World Net Daily*:

> There's no question that TWA Flight 800 was hit in the left wing. The missile appears to have been one in a series of what they call MANPADS missiles. That's a man portable air defense system. Common name is "shoulder-fired missile."
>
> In 1994 there was a French Mistral missile that was fully loaded ready to fire on its tripod. One man carries the missile and another man carries the tripod, and it's an extremely potent point defense missile. The Maryland state police found it alongside a country road near Westminster, Maryland.

Donaldson died in 2001, before the next terrorist attack occurred.

Call from Former TWA Pilot

After I had appeared as guest on a Las Vegas radio show (December 11, 1997) discussing TWA Flight 800, a friend of mine, former TWA captain, Hoot

Gibson, who heard the show, called me at home and told me about a conversation he had with another TWA Boeing 747 captain. (A movie had been made years earlier of a jet upset in which Hoot was the captain and saved the aircraft at the last moment.)

Hoot said that the TWA captain had taken off from JFK shortly before TWA Flight 800 had taken off, and was heading for Rome. TWA flight operations called this captain shortly after TWA Flight 800 went down and told the pilots what had just happened to the Flight 800 that had taken off shortly behind him.

An Alitalia aircraft had taken off from after TWA Flight 800 and the TWA Captain called the Alitalia crew and asked them to change over to a discreet frequency. During the subsequent radio conversation, the TWA captain told Hoot that the Alitalia pilot said that he saw the missile going up toward TWA Flight 800, and that after TWA was hit, the plane rolled over on its back and plunged toward the ocean below. Hoot said that he recorded the telephone conversation. He also added that the same captain who had told Hoot of this conversation didn't want to talk about it any more.

An article in the *Washington Times* national weekly edition (December 29, 1996) stated:

> An official with the Defense Intelligence Agency, spy arm of the Pentagon, has informed congressional staff members that, in his opinion, a shoulder-fired missile brought down TWA Flight 800. The same DIA official, described as an expert in missile technology, told the staff members that he personally was called in by the FBI in the days following the explosion of the TWA jet to assist with witness interviews, a source present for the congressional briefing told Inside the Beltway last week.

Desperate to Support their Cover-Up

One person determined to expose the NTSB and FBI cover-up was James Sanders, whose wife was a TWA flight attendant. He managed to get a small swatch of seat covering material that showed evidence of explosives, and for taking that small piece from the hanger where the 747 was being resurrected, Justice Department prosecutors charged him with a criminal offense. He was trying to expose the cover-ups.

The material was provided to him by a TWA pilot, Terrell Stacey, who was outraged by the FBI, CIA and NTSB cover-ups. He worked in the hangar where Flight 800 was being "reassembled" and obtained a small piece of the hundreds of yards of seat material that he felt showed signed of explosive residue. His intention was to have the small swatch analyzed by giving it to former California police officer James Sanders. Sanders' wife, Elizabeth, was a supervisor in TWA's flight training department. They all wanted the truth to come out.

Sanders claimed that he had a California laboratory test the fabric and found red residue from a seat cushion that tested positive for missile fuel. Sanders later wrote the book, *The Downing of Flight 800*. In retaliation for taking this insignificant piece of fabric and seeking to help discover the existence of explosive residue, Justice Department prosecutors charged them all with a criminal offense.

Just prior to the start of the NTSB hearings in Baltimore, Justice Department personnel issued arrest warrants for James and Elizabeth Sanders, insuring that they would not be present during the hearings to disturb the NTSB cover-up. The trial against the Sanders commenced in April 1999 and ended with the jury handing down a guilty verdict on April 13, 1999. The judge sentenced James Sanders to three years probation and 50 hours of community service. Elizabeth received one-year probation and 25 hours of community service. Probation means checking with a probation officer on a regular weekly or monthly basis, and is not total freedom.

A *Reuter* article (August 25, 1996), titled, "Investigator: Nitro Found In TWA Wreck," stated:

> Traces of the flammable liquid nitroglycerin have been found in the wreckage of TWA Flight 800 bolstering the theory that an explosive device destroyed the plane, the New York Daily News said in its Sunday edition. The report by the Daily News comes just two days after the New York Times said traces of PETN, a chemical compound commonly found in both plastic explosives and surface-to-air missiles, was found on a piece of seat from the Boeing 747's passenger cabin.

Another *Reuter* article (August 30, 1996), titled, "More Explosive Traces Found in TWA Debris," stated:

> Investigators have found more microscopic traces of explosives on debris from TWA Flight 800 but said they could not conclude that a bomb or missile caused the plane to crash last month, officials said Friday. Other traces of chemical explosive were found on the plane's wreckage last week.
>
> Although investigators officially said they were "of unknown origin," they have said privately that PETN, a chemical used in plastic explosives, was found on a piece of a passenger seat located near the center fuel tank where the two wings join the fuselage. CBS News reported on Friday that a compound found in the wreckage was "strikingly similar" to one discovered at the crash site of Pan Am Flight 103, which exploded over Lockerbie, Scotland, in 1988 killing all 259 people aboard and 11 on the ground.

CBS News said it had learned that the FBI lab had identified residue of a plastic explosive called "RDX" found on a curtain in the rear of the jet. It said the discovery further bolstered the bomb theory because "RDX and PETN are mixed together to make high-powered explosives."

An aviation expert and a law enforcement official who is an explosives specialist both told the newspaper they saw several fist-sized holes punched through the backs of two seats on the far right side of row 23. That is in the center of the area pinpointed by the computer as the site of the initial blast. The microscopic traces of PETN also were found in that general area. No similar holes have been found in other seats.

Numerous media reports also published similar articles as a result of their own investigations. But suddenly, all such articles disappeared, as if they were simultaneously ordered to halt the reports by citing national security or some other pretext.

Type of Missile Unknown

What type of missile caused Flight 800 to explode is not known. If it was a Stinger missile, one of hundreds given to the Afghan rebels in the 1980s, or one of those Stinger missiles that were acquired by terrorists when the CIA and FBI rejected them, as described earlier, they could reach the altitude at which Flight 800 was flying.

My brother-in-law worked on surface-to-air missiles for Raytheon, who made the Stinger missiles, and he confirmed that the missiles were rated to fly to at least 13,000 feet and could be expected to go higher. The stinger missile was hand-carried and weighed about 35 pounds. It was almost six feet long and launched from a lightweight launcher that was reusable. They were first put into service in 1981. The missile tracked an aircraft using an infrared sensor that detected heat from the aircraft's exhaust and tracked onto it.

The missile operator puts the missile into its launcher tube and arms the system. When the target aircraft appears, the person arms the infrared sensor while pointing the launcher at the target aircraft. When the sensor detects and locks onto the target engine's exhaust system, a steady high-pitched tone is emitted, indicating that it is ready to fire. A trigger is then pulled and the missile takes off. The solid fuel rocket motor travels at Mach 2, and when it hits the aircraft, 6.6 pounds of high explosives detonates.

No Mechanical Faults Were Discovered

An *Aviation Week and Space Technology* article (December 1, 1997) stated that the NTSB tests cleared the fuel pumps on the center fuel tank from possible blame. At no time during the entire NTSB "investigation" was there found any evidence of an ignition source that could have ignited the small quantity of fuel in the center fuel tank of Flight 800.

Another indication of an explosion from outside the aircraft was indicated by a *CNN* report (September 5, 1997):

> Federal officials investigating the crash of TWA Flight 800 are baffled by the recent discovery of impact damage on the doors that close over the

front landing gear. According to several people involved in the investigation, for the last two weeks National Transportation Safety Board investigators have been trying to figure out what could have caused the nose gear doors to blow inward, and whether whatever caused that damage happened before the plane's center fuel tank exploded.

Examiners who have been looking at crash wreckage for the past 13 months are now said to be mystified about the significance of the damage on the doors, which are located below the flight deck and well forward of the plane's center fuel tank. The investigators are equally troubled by the fact that these nose gear doors were among the first things on the plane to have come off in flight.

One crash investigator told CNN on Friday that the discovery keeps open the question of whether the fuel tank explosion was the primary or secondary event in the in-flight breakup of TWA Flight 800. But Shelly Hazle, an NTSB spokeswoman, downplayed the significance, emphasizing that investigators will have to see how this newly discovered evidence fits into their theory of how the plane blew up.

One of Several Prior Warning Letters: No Response!

One such letter was sent to U.S. Attorney Robert Mueller at San Francisco. He had a practice of covering up for corruption in the San Francisco area, as I detailed in my book, *History of Aviation Disasters: 1950 to 9/11*. He was the FBI director when TWA Flight 800 was downed.

From the desk of Rodney Stich
P.O. Box 5, Alamo, CA 94507; phone: 925-944-1930; FAX 925-295-1203
Member Association Former Intelligence Officers   Association of National Security International Society of Air Safety Investigators   Lawyers Pilots Bar Association

March 20, 2000

Robert S. Mueller, U.S. Attorney
Federal Building
450 Golden Gate Avenue
San Francisco, CA 94101

Ref: For the record: criminal retaliation under Title 18 U.S.C. § 1512[1]

To Mr. Mueller,

Several things you should know. Judge Marilyn Patel may try to misuse your office to charge me with criminal contempt of court. This arises from an unlawful and unconstitutional order that she rendered about 13 years ago that forever barred me from federal court access and the protections under the laws and Constitution of the United States. The order also sought to continue blocking me and my group of government whistleblowers from reporting very serious criminal activities involving people in key government positions.

Judge Patel rendered that order after I sought to report to a federal judge under the mandatory crime reporting statute, Title 18 U.S.C. § 4,[2] criminal activities which I had been documenting from my early days as a federal inspector-investigator for the Federal Aviation Administration, and which I have learned from a group of government whistleblowers that have come to me.

I recently submitted a lawsuit to the U.S. district court in Oakland, raising a number of federal issues under the Civil Rights Act, under Bivens, under the Declaratory Judgment Act, and as another federal issue, I reported a number of criminal activities and demanded to produce evidence, as required under the mandatory crime reporting statute, Title 18 U.S.C. § 4. Associated with her misuse of judicial office and the courts, including obstructing justice, her actions were criminal in other areas. This letter describes those offenses.

Also, a certain provision in law caught my attention, which suggests your office may have a responsibility to protect whistleblowers like myself. I found this information in the congressional comments relating to 18 U.S.C. § 1512. As provided in Section 6 of Public Law 97-291, as amended Pub.L. 98-473, Title II, § 1408(b), Oct. 12, 1984, 98 Stat. 2177, some form of relief is provided for victims of such retaliation:

(2) Notification of availability of protection. BA victim or witness should routinely receive information on steps that law enforcement officers and lawyers for the Government can take to protect victims and witnesses from intimidation.

Since your office and the Department of Justice is delegated the responsibility of halting civil rights violations, especially against whistleblowers, and in light of the fact that criminal acts have been inflicted upon me as a result of my whistleblower activities, your office has a responsibility. Keep in mind that no one, and especially a federal judge, has the authority to void for the remainder of anyone's life, the rights and protections to all citizens guaranteed under the laws and Constitution of the United States.

Pattern of Corruption Affecting Nation's Aviation Safety

A little background information would help understand the sequence of retaliation for reporting federal crimes. I was a federal investigator for the Federal Aviation Administration when I first discovered a pattern of air safety and criminal acts at United Airlines and the cover-up by certain FAA management personnel that caused or allowed to occur a series of fatal airline crashes. My reports of these matters are documented.

I, and other federal inspectors reporting these matters, suffered threats, harassment, and retaliation. This retaliation and interference with federal air safety responsibilities made possible other crashes and other deaths. I acted as an independent counsel and forced a four-month-long hearing upon the FAA during which I caused to be entered into the records testimony and exhibits proving that these matters did exist. I then suffered more retaliation. Such retaliation preventing air safety inspectors from performing their federal duties is a crime under Title 18 U.S.C. § 111[3] (which brought into play other federal violations, including Title 18 U.S.C. §§ 35[4] and 34[5], 1001.[6]

This interference with the duties of a government agent, combined with the corruption and criminal activities, forced me to leave government service. To this date, no one has been brought to justice for the federal offenses associated with the deaths of many people.

After I left government service, I continued to investigate and expose internal FAA problems that continued to play a role in other airline crashes. I continued my exposure efforts by publishing books, appearing as guest on over 3,000 radio and television shows, and occasionally filing federal actions seeking to force a federal judge to perform his or her duty. These actions were filed under Title 28 U.S.C. §§ 1621,[7] 1622,[8] and 18 U.S.C. § 4. That was the start of documenting judicial cover-ups and judicial obstruction of justice, federal crimes which eventually escalated into retaliation that became crimes under Title 18 U.S.C. §§ 1505,[9] 1510,[10] 1512,[11] 241, among others. Probability the gravity of the corruption kept the judges from allowing the lawsuit to proceed.

After my second edition of *Unfriendly Skies* was published, naming specific people in government, including federal judges, a San Francisco law firm filed a sham lawsuit against me that targeted the assets that funded my exposure activities. At that time my assets totaled approximately $10 million in real estate properties, which I had acquired as a former airline captain and riding the crest of escalating real estate values.

That lawsuit was barred by dozens of state and federal statutes, rules of court, Supreme Court decisions, and major constitutional protections. For the next six years, California judges at every level openly violated these due process protections. They compounded these violations by retaliating against me for exercising due process remedies. This retaliation is a crime under the clear language of Title 18 U.S.C. § 241. Strangely, every level of the California judicial system protected the perpetrators of these violations, and refused to perform their duty to prevent the continuation of these violations. This failure to perform a duty under the Civil Rights Act[12] made them culpable under, for instance, Title 42 U.S.C. § 1986.[13]

I then exercised federal remedies that were specific for the violations occurring. These remedies were provided by the Civil Rights Act on the basis of the civil rights violations, for a declaratory judgment under the Declaratory Judgment Act. The duties of federal judges under Title 28 U.S.C. §§ 2201,[14] 2202,[15] were to declare my personal and property rights as established in seven judgments, which the California judges were violating in the California lawsuit.

Despite their duties to provide a federal court forum and relief and the Civil Rights Act and Declaratory Judgment Act, federal judges refused to act. Events indicated that the intent was to destroy the $10 million in property assets that funded my investigations and exposure of high-level corruption in government.

While these attacks upon me continued, I also continued my investigations and accumulations of additional evidence of criminal wrongdoing.

Starting in 1985, my activities eventually motivated other government agents from the FBI, CIA, DEA, Customs, and Secret Service, to provide me with evidence of still other criminal activities implicating people in key government positions.

With this information, I exercised my responsibilities under the federal crime reporting statute, Title 18 U.S.C. § 4, and sought to report these additional criminal activities to federal judge via a federal court filing. I combined my demand to produce evidence of these criminal activities to the other federal issues, seeking relief under the Civil Rights and Declaratory Judgment Acts. From that point on, the misuse of federal judicial positions escalated into the area of outright criminal violations. Briefly, here is the sequence of judicial acts that followed:

Federal judges refused to address the criminal matters that I had stated and refused to receive the evidence that I and my group of government agents offered to provide. The judges most directly involved with the refusal to receive evidence offered under Title 18 U.S.C. § 4 were Sacramento district judges Milton Schwartz, Raul Ramirez and Magistrate John Moulds, and San Francisco judges Marilyn Patel and Vaughn Walker. This refusal to receive evidence of criminal activities constituted criminal acts related to obstruction of justice. The type of evidence my group sought to provide affected the internal security of the United States.

In addition, after refusing to receive the evidence and dismissing the actions, Judges Schwartz and Patel rendered orders in the late 1980s forever barring me access to the federal courts, and voiding for me, under the class of a whistleblower, all rights and protections under the laws and Constitution of the United States. These orders were, of course, unlawful and unconstitutional, and intended to do two things:

One was to prevent me and my group from reporting the criminal activities involving people in key government positions. This, of course, obstructed justice and is a crime.

Second, it was to eliminate for me the many federal remedies available for the onslaught of judicially perpetrated violations of federally protected rights. I suffered very great losses as a result of the judicially perpetrated conspiracy of civil rights violations that were combined with criminal acts.

In addition to refusing to receive evidence of high-level criminal activities, federal judges refused to perform their mandatory duty to provide a federal court forum and relief under the specific statutes intended for the federal issues raised in the complaint.

Recognizing that the orders making me literally a man without a country, depriving me of the rights and protections under the laws and constitution of the United States, were unlawful and unconstitutional, and experiencing great harm from the escalating violations of federally protected rights, and also learning of additional criminal activities, I filed other actions as provided by federal law. I also had the right, under Title 28 U.S.C. § 241, to report wrongdoings by federal officials.

I was in a Catch-22 situation. Stripped of all rights to federal court access and the protections guaranteed under our form of government, I was simultaneously suffering great harm from the misuse of the judicial positions. These actions even included taking my life's assets consisting at that time of $10 million. Among the many harms I suffered was the taking of my life's assets, valued at $10 million, by Las Vegas judge Robert Smith. The orders were rendered in chambers, without the due process requirement of a noticed hearing, a hearing, legally recognized cause, and other violations of law. The orders also falsely stated there had been a hearing on that date, when there was no hearing.

Federal judges then retaliated against me. First it was in Sacramento and involved Judges Schwartz, Raul Ramirez, and Magistrate John Moulds. Later, it was San Francisco judges Patel and Walker. From about 1987 to 1995, I was continuously being charged with criminal contempt of court for seeking relief guaranteed by law from the pattern of hard-core civil rights violations. In one case, Oakland judge Edward Jellen charged me with criminal contempt of court for filing objections to the corrupt taking and liquidation of my assets.

Many federal civil rights and criminal violations arose from this retaliation. One form of criminal violation arose from retaliating against me for exercising due process remedies. This offense fell under Title 18 U.S.C. § 241.

I suffered repeated retaliation from federal judges for attempting to report the criminal activities. These were criminal acts under Title 18 U.S.C. §§ 1505, 1512, and 1513.[16]

By refusing to receive detailed charges of the criminal activities, or the evidence that I and my group of government whistleblowers sought to provide, these federal judges were guilty of other federal offenses under, for instance, Title 18 U.S.C. §§ 1505, 1510, 2,[17] 3,[18] 4, and probably others, including the wire fraud statutes, 18 U.S.C. §§ 1341,[19] and 1343.[20]

Crisis in Federal Courts Brought About by Judicial Civil Rights and Criminal Violations Related to Obstruction of Justice

There now existed a crisis in federal courts. Federal judges had been aiding and abetting, and encouraging, the violations of large numbers of federally protected rights, while engaging in obstruction of justice relating to matters inflicting great harm upon the internal security of the United States. By these acts, I had even more federal causes of actions that under the laws and Constitution of the United States guaranteed me access to the federal courts and requiring federal judges to perform a duty.

Answer to Judicial Corruption: Destroy Constitutional Protections

Federal judges responded to this crisis by enlarging upon the judicial corruption. Judge Milton Schwartz, and then Judge Marilyn Patel rendered unlawful and unconstitutional orders voiding for me, for the remainder of my life, all rights to federal court access and voiding for me the rights and protections guaranteed under the laws and Constitution of the United States. These orders were offenses not only against me, but against the United States, its judicial process, our most basic rights, and simultaneously made the federal courts into a corrupt arm of government.

In addition, these orders and the retaliation described in this letter, constituted a crime under Title 18 U.S.C. § 245.[21] It is a crime to injure, intimidate, or interfere with any person or class of person. I am a whistleblower, for want of a better word. These offenses against me arose from my attempts to report crimes implicating people in key government positions (and at one time, United Airlines management).

I'll briefly highlight what happened next. (More details can be found in the third editions of *Defrauding America* and *Unfriendly Skies*, and to a lesser extent in *Drugging America*. AUSA Dave Hall, in your office, has a copy of *Defrauding America*.)

Federal judges charged me with criminal contempt of court for having exercised remedies under the Civil Rights Act and Declaratory Judgment Act. The violations of federally protected rights stated in those complaints were real, very serious, documented, and inflicting grave personal and financial harm upon me. There was nothing trivial about the issues raised in those complaints, for which federal judges had a mandatory duty to provide relief.

Federal judges charged me with criminal contempt of court for having exercised the mandatory duty to report federal crimes to a federal judge. The outrageous nature of this charge is that the federal judges charging me with a contempt of court for reporting crimes were themselves perpetrating numerous criminal acts as stated in this letter, while corruptly misusing their judicial positions and the courts. Simultaneously, these judges were violating federally protected rights, while also aiding and abetting the violations of these rights that were occurring in a bizarre and reckless lawsuit filed in the California courts.

From 1987 to 1995, federal judges had me constantly under charges of criminal contempt of court for having exercised federal responsibilities and federal civil liberties and civil rights.

I was then denied a jury trial, and a kangaroo court trial conducted by federal judges who were implicated in the crimes against me and crimes against the United States. I was then judged guilty and sentenced to six months in prison. The incarceration was done under the most difficult conditions that could be arranged. I was 67 years of age when that incarceration occurred, and had recently undergone open-heart surgery. You don't suppose they wanted to kill me at that time?

The combination of judicially inflicted civil rights violations, judicial invalidation of all protections in law, the conversion of the courts into a corrupt enterprise (under RICO?), forced me to file Chapter 11 to force a federal judge to perform his or her duty in relation to the civil rights violations occurring in the sham California lawsuit that was filed by a law firm reported to be a front for the Central Intelligence Agency. Judicial corruption then escalated again:

Orders were rendered in chambers taking my life's assets (consisting of $10 million in real estate that funded my exposure activities), violating the constitutional and statutory requirement of a noticed hearing, for a hearing, for legally recognized cause. The orders falsely stated there had been a hearing on that date, when there was no hearing. That false stated by Judge Robert Jones violated Title 18 U.S.C. § 1001 relating to false statements on documents. My assets were then turned over to Trustee Charles Duck, who promptly worked with Oakland judge Edward Jellen to liquidate the assets that had funded my exposure activities.

Judge Jellen then rendered unlawful and unconstitutional orders barring me from filing any objections to the seizure and liquidation of my assets.

When I filed objections as provided by federal law and constitutional rights, Judge Jellen charged me with criminal contempt of court, duplicating what had been done by Judges Schwartz, Patel, Walker, and others.

Jellen refused to provide money from my assets to obtain legal counsel to defend against the criminal contempt of court charge, refused to provide legal counsel, refused to allow me to testify at the kangaroo trial that he conducted, and then sentenced me to federal prison. That sentence was never carried out. He lacked the jurisdiction to sentence anyone to prison.

Judge Patel and Walker then continued the criminal contempt of court charges against me, which were suddenly dropped in 1995 without notification to me.

One of the last acts in the bankruptcy court proceeding occurred on March 25, 1999, as Judge Jellen dispensed the last remains of my $10 million estate to one of the law firms who played a part in the overall conspiracy and RICO predicate acts.

On March 13, 2000, I submitted for filing a lawsuit to the U.S. district court in Oakland, clearly stating documented facts raising federal issues under the Civil Rights Act, Bivens doctrine, civil RICO, and again demanded that the judge receive the evidence that I and a group of government whistleblowers wanted to provide to a federal judge under Title 18 U.S.C. § 4. Federal law required that I report criminal activities to a federal judge (or other federal officer). The laws and Constitution guaranteed to me the due process right to obtain relief from the violations of federally protected rights that were occurring.

Despite these federal provisions, the clerk of the court refused to file that lawsuit, despite statutory and constitutional requirements to do so. The reason? Judge Marilyn Patel had rendered an order in the late 1980s forever barring me access to the federal courts, and voiding for me all rights and protections under the laws and Constitution of the United States. We obviously have major national issues here, involving the conversion of federal courts into corrupt acts of government, or some other unknown group; the undermining of the laws and Constitution of the United States; a vast conspiracy to violate civil rights of a whistleblower; a conspiracy to obstruct justice, and other federal offenses.

The evidence indicates that a powerful force high in government engineered the start of the sham lawsuit in the California courts and controlled the repeated patterns of judicial corruption that followed. I know of no other explanation for the record-setting number of violations that occurred during the 17 years of continuing violations of federal civil rights and criminal statutes by people in key government positions.

One of the many ironies about all this is that the Department of Justice holds a position of trust to prosecute anyone violating civil rights, and prosecute anyone committing criminal violations, and instead, has joined the federal judges in perpetrating these offenses that have a grave impact upon the United States itself.

At this time Judge Marilyn Patel may be arranging to have your office charge me with criminal contempt of court. If you should do this, as former USA David Levi once did, you will become part of the conspiracy that is not only against me, but against the United States. I may be 77 years of age, but I'm not afraid to take on such crud criminalizing the government positions being held. Also, with my books receiving praise throughout the world, arresting me may be the final straw to motivate enough people to do something about the worsening corruption in government.

I suggest you look at my web sites for further information on the undermining of the government and the people of the United States by the criminal elements that I described within this letter (which will also be on the Internet shortly.)

There seems to be an uncanny determined ignorance about the law by those involved in the conspiracy, that I am including as endnotes certain of the many laws being violated in the continuing attacks upon me.

Sincerely,
Rodney Stich

ENDNOTES

1. **Title 18 U.S.C. § 1512. Tampering with a witness, victim, or an informant** (b) Whoever knowingly uses intimidation or physical force, threatens, or corruptly persuades another person, or attempts to do so, or engages in misleading conduct toward another person, with intent to: (1) influence, delay, or prevent the testimony of any per-

son in an official proceeding; (2) cause or induce any person to: (A) withhold testimony, or withhold a record, document, or other object, from an official proceeding; (3) hinder, delay, or prevent the communication to a law enforcement officer or judge of the United States of information relating to the commission or possible commission of a Federal offense ... shall be fined under this title or imprisoned not more than ten years, or both. (c) Whoever intentionally harasses another person and thereby hinders, delays, prevents, or dissuades any person from:

(1) attending or testifying in an official proceeding; (2) reporting to a law enforcement officer or judge of the United States the commission or possible commission of a Federal offense ... (3) arresting or seeking the arrest of another person in connection with a Federal offense; or (4) causing a criminal prosecution, or a parole or probation revocation preceding, to be sought or instituted, or assisting in such prosecution or proceeding; or attempts to do so, shall be fined under this title or imprisoned not more than one year, or both. (e) For the purposes of this section: (1) an official proceeding need not be pending or about to be instituted at the time of the offense; and (2) the testimony, or the record, document, or other object need not be admissible in evidence or free of a claim of privilege.

2. **Title 18 U.S.C. § 4 misprision of felony.** "Whoever, having knowledge of the actual commission of a felony cognizable by a court of the United States, conceals and does not as soon as possible make known the same to some judge or other person in civil or military authority under the United States, shall be fined not more than $500 or imprisoned not more than three years, or both."

3. **Title 18 U.S.C. § 111. Impeding certain officers or employees.** Whoever ... intimidates, or interferes with any person ... while engaged in ... the performance of his official duties shall be fined ... or imprisoned ... [Certain industry (in this case United Airlines) and FAA officials interfered with FAA inspectors attempts to report major air safety violations and safety problems. These acts caused and made possible some of the nation's worst air disasters. (List of such crashes elsewhere.)]

4. **Title 18 U.S.C. § 35. Imparting or conveying false information.** (b) Whoever willfully and maliciously, or with reckless disregard for the safety of human life, imparts or conveys or causes to be imparted or conveyed false information, knowing the information to be false, concerning an attempt or alleged attempt being made or to be made, to do any act which would be a crime prohibited by this chapter or chapter 97 or chapter 11 of this tile--shall be fined under this title, or imprisoned not more than five years, or both. [Aircraft and motor vehicles chapter.]

5. **Title 18 U.S.C. § 34. Penalty when death results**. Whoever is convicted of any crime prohibited by this chapter, which has resulted in the death of any person, shall be subject also to the death penalty or to imprisonment for life.

6. **Title 18 U.S.C. § 1001. Statements or entries generally.** Whoever in any matter within the jurisdiction of any department or agency of the United States knowingly and willfully falsifies, conceals or covers up by any trick, scheme, or device a material fact, or makes any false, fictitious or fraudulent statements or representations, or makes or uses any false writing or document knowing the same to contain any false, fictitious or fraudulent statement or entry, shall be fined ... or imprisoned ...

7. **Title 18 U.S.C. §1621. Perjury generally.** Whoever (1) having taken an oath before a competent tribunal ... willfully and contrary to such oath states ... any material matter which he does not believe to be true, he shall be fined ... or imprisoned .

8. **Title 18 U.S.C. § 1622. Subornation of perjury.** Whoever procures another to commit any perjury is guilty of subornation of perjury, and shall be fined under this title or imprisoned not more than five years, or both.

9. **Title 18 U.S.C. § 1505.** Whoever corruptly ... influences, obstructs, or impedes or endeavors to influence, obstruct, or impede the due the proper administration of the law under which any pending proceeding is being had before any department or agency of the United States ... shall be fined not more than $5,000 or imprisoned not more than five years, or both. Title 18 U.S.C. § 1505 applies to anyone who corruptly attempts by threats or force, or by any threatening letter or communication, influence, obstruct, or impede the due and proper administration of the law under which any pending proceeding is being had before any department or agency of the United States. They do not have to succeed to have committed a federal crime; the attempt or scheme (conspire) to do so is criminal.

10. **Title 18 U.S.C. § 1510. Obstruction of criminal investigation.** (a) Whoever willfully endeavors by means of bribery to obstruct, delay, or prevent the communication of information relating to a violation of any criminal statute of the United States by any person to a criminal investigator shall be fined not more than $5,000, or imprisoned not more than five years, or both. (b) As used in this section, the term "criminal investigator" means any individual duly authorized by a department, agency, or armed force of the United States to conduct or engage in investigations of or prosecutions for violations of the criminal laws of the United States.

11. **Title 18 U.S.C. § 1512. Tampering with a witness, victim, or an informant.** (b) Whoever knowingly uses intimidation or physical force, threatens, or corruptly persuades another person, or attempts to do so, or engages in misleading conduct toward another person, with intent to: (1) influence, delay, or prevent the testimony of any person in an official proceeding; (2) cause or induce any person to: (A) withhold testimony, or withhold a record, document, or other object, from an official proceeding; (3) hinder, delay, or prevent the communication to a law enforcement officer or judge of the United States of information relating to the commission or possible commission of a Federal offense ... shall be fined under this title or imprisoned not more than ten years, or both. (c) Whoever intentionally harasses another person and thereby hinders, delays, prevents, or dissuades any person from:

(1) Attending or testifying in an official proceeding; (2) reporting to a law enforcement officer or judge of the United States the commission or possible commission of a Federal offense ... (3) arresting or seeking the arrest of another person in connection with a Federal offense; or (4) causing a criminal prosecution, or a parole or probation revocation preceding, to be sought or instituted, or assisting in such prosecution or proceeding; or attempts to do so, shall be fined under this title or imprisoned not more than one year, or both. (e) For the purposes of this section: (1) an official proceeding need not be pending or about to be instituted at the time of the offense; and (2) the testimony, or the

record, document, or other object need not be admissible in evidence or free of a claim of privilege.

12. **Title 42 U.S.C. § 1983 provides**: Every person who, under color or any statute, ordinance, regulation, custom or usage, of any State of Territory, subjects ... any citizen of the United States ... to the deprivation of any rights, privileges or immunities secured by the Constitution and laws, shall be liable to the party injured in an action at law, suit in equity, or other proper proceeding for redress. [Applies to anyone acting under color of state law who violates these rights.]

13. **Title 42 U.S.C. § 1985 Conspiracy to interfere with civil rights.** (1) **Preventing officer from performing duty**. If two or more persons ... conspire to prevent ... any person from accepting or holding any office, trust, or place of confidence under the United States, or from discharging any duties thereof; or to injure him in his person or property on account of his lawful discharge of the duties of his office, or while engaged in the lawful discharge thereof, or to injure his property so as to molest, interrupt, hinder, or impede him in the discharge of his official duties.

(2) **Obstructing justice; intimidating party, witness, or juror.** If two or more persons in any State or Territory conspire to deter, by force, intimidation, or threat, any party or witness in any court of the United States from attending such court, or from testifying to any matter pending therein, freely, fully, and truthfully, or to injure such party or witness in his person or property on account of his having so attended or testified, or to influence the verdict, presentment, or indictment of any grand or petit juror in any such court, or to injure such juror in his person or property on account of any verdict, presentment, or indictment lawfully assented to by him, or of his being or having been such juror; or if two or more persons conspire for the purpose of impeding, hindering, obstructing, or defeating, in any manner, the due course of justice in any State or Territory, with intent to deny to any citizen the equal protection of the law, or to injure him or his property for lawfully enforcing, or attempting to enforce, the right of any person, or class of persons, to the equal protection of the laws;

(3) **Depriving persons of rights or privileges.** If two or more persons in any State or Territory conspire ... for the purpose of depriving, either directly or indirectly, any person or class of persons of the equal protection of the laws, or of equal privileges and immunities under the laws, or for the purpose of preventing or hindering the constituted authorities of any State or Territory from giving or securing to all persons within such State or Territory the equal protection of the laws; ... or to injure any citizen in person or property on account of such support or advocacy; in any case of conspiracy set forth in this section, if one or more persons engaged therein do, or cause to be done, any act in furtherance of the object of such conspiracy, whereby another is injured in his person or property, or deprived of having and exercising any right or privilege of a citizen of the United States, the party so injured or deprived may have an action for the recovery of damages, occasioned by such injury or deprivation, against any one or more of the conspirators.

13. **Title 42 U.S.C. § 1986. Action for neglect to prevent conspiracy.** Every person who, having knowledge that any of the wrongs conspired to be done, and mentioned in the preceding section [42 U.S.C. § 1985], are about to be committed, and having power to prevent or aid in preventing the commission of the same, neglects or refuses to do so, if such wrongful act be committed, shall be liable to the party injured, or

his legal representatives, for all damages caused by such wrongful act, which such person by reasonable diligence could have prevented; and such damages may be recovered in an action on the case; and any number of persons guilty of such wrongful neglect or refusal may be joined as defendants in the action, and if the death of any party be caused by any such wrongful act and neglect, the legal representatives of the deceased shall have such action therefore, and may recover not exceeding five thousand dollars damages therein, for the benefit of the widow of the deceased, if there be one, and if there be no widow, then for the benefit of the next of kin of the deceased. But no action under the provisions of this section shall be sustained which is not commenced within one year after the cause of action has accrued.

14. **Title 28 U.S.C. § 2201. Creation of remedy.** "In a case of actual controversy within its jurisdiction, any court of the United States, upon the filing of an appropriate pleading, may declare the rights and other legal relations of any interested party seeking such declaration, whether or not further relief is or could be sought. Any such declaration shall have the force and effect of a final judgment or decree and shall be reviewable as such.

15. **Title 28 U.S.C. § 2202. Further relief.** "Further necessary or proper relief based on a declaratory judgment or decree may be granted, after reasonable notice and hearing, against any adverse party whose rights have been determined by such judgment."

16. **Title 18 U.S.C. § 1513. Retaliating against a witness, victim, or an informant.** (a) Whoever knowingly engages in any conduct and thereby causes bodily injury to another person or damages the tangible property of another person, or threatens to do so, with intent to retaliate against any person for (1) the attendance of a witness or party at an official proceeding, or any testimony given or any record, document, or other object produced by a witness in an official proceeding; or (2) any information relating to the commission or possible commission of a Federal offense ...

17. **Title 18 U.S.C. § 2. Principals.** (a) Whoever commits an offense against the United States or aids, abets, counsels, commands, induces or procures its commission, is punishable as a principal. (b) Whoever willfully causes an act to be done which if directly performed by him or another would be an offense against the United States, is punishable as a principal.

Note: The legislative intent to punish as a principal not only one who directly commits an offense and one who "aids, abets, counsels, commands, induces or procures" another to commit an offense, but also anyone who causes the doing of an act which if done by him directly would render him guilty of an offense against the United States. Case law decisions: *Rothenburg v. United States*, 1918, 38 S.Ct. 18, 245 U.S. 480, 62 L.Ed. 414, and *United States v. Giles*, 1937, 57 S.Ct. 340, 300 U.S. 41, 81 L.Ed. 493.

18. **Title 18 U.S.C. § 3. Accessory after the fact.** Whoever, knowing that an offense against the United States had been committed, receives, relieves, comforts or assists the offender in order to hinder or prevent his apprehension, trial or punishment, is an accessory after the fact.

19. **Title 18 U.S.C. § 1341. Frauds and swindles.** Whoever, having devised or intending to devise any scheme or artifice to defraud, or for obtaining money or property by means of false or fraudulent pretenses, representations, or promises, for the purpose

of executing such scheme or artifice or attempting so to do, places in any post office or authorized depository for mail matter, any matter or thing whatever to be sent or delivered by the Postal Service, or takes or receives therefrom, any such matter or thing, or knowingly causes to be delivered by mail according to the direction thereon, or at the place at which it is directed to be delivered by the person to whom it is addressed, any such matter or thing, shall be fined ... or imprisoned .... or both.

20. **Title 18 U.S.C. § 1343. Fraud by wire, radio, or television**. Whoever, having devised or intending to devise any scheme or artifice to defraud, or for obtaining money or property by means of false or fraudulent pretenses, representations, or promises, transmits or causes to be transmitted by means of wire, radio, or television communication in interstate or foreign commerce, any writings, signs, signals, pictures, or sounds for the purpose of executing such scheme or artifice, shall be fined not more than $1,000 or imprisoned not more than five years, or both.

21. **Title 18 U.S.C. § 245. Federally protected activities**. (b) Whoever, whether or not acting under color of law, by force or threat of force willfully injures, intimidates or interferes with, or attempts to injure, intimidate or interfere with:

(1) any person because he is or has been, or in order to intimidate such person or any other person or any class of persons [whistleblowers against corruption in government] from:

(B) participating in or enjoying any benefit, service, privilege, program facility, or activity provided or administered by the United States;

(C) applying for or enjoying employment, or any perquisite thereof, by any agency of the United States;

Title 18 U.S.C. § 246. Deprivation of relief benefits. Whoever directly or indirectly deprives, attempts to deprive, or threatens to deprive any person of any employment, position, work, compensation, or other benefit provided for or made possible in whole or in part by any Act of Congress appropriating funds for work relief or relief purposes, on account of political affiliation [whistleblower] ... shall be fined under this title, or imprisoned not more than one year, or both.

Title 18 U.S.C. § 241. Conspiracy against [civil] rights. If two or more persons conspire to injure, oppress, threaten, or intimidate any person in any State, Territory, Commonwealth, Possession, or District in the free exercise or enjoyment of any right or privilege secured to him by the Constitution or laws of the United States, or because of his having so exercised the same; ... they shall be fined under this title or imprisoned not more than ten years.

Title 42 U.S.C. § 1985 Conspiracy to interfere with civil rights. (1) Preventing officer from performing duty. If two or more persons ... conspire to prevent ... any person from accepting or holding any office, trust, or place of confidence under the United States, or from discharging any duties thereof; or to injure him in his person or property on account of his lawful discharge of the duties of his office, or while engaged in the lawful discharge thereof, or to injure his property so as to molest, interrupt, hinder, or impede him in the discharge of his official duties.

(2) **Obstructing justice; intimidating party, witness, or juror.** If two or more persons in any State or Territory conspire to deter, by force, intimidation, or threat, any party or witness in any court of the United States from attending such court, or from testifying to any matter pending therein, freely, fully, and truthfully, or to injure such

party or witness in his person or property on account of his having so attended or testified, or to influence the verdict, presentment, or indictment of any grand or petit juror in any such court, or to injure such juror in his person or property on account of any verdict, presentment, or indictment lawfully assented to by him, or of his being or having been such juror; or if two or more persons conspire for the purpose of impeding, hindering, obstructing, or defeating, in any manner, the due course of justice in any State or Territory, with intent to deny to any citizen the equal protection of the law, or to injure him or his property for lawfully enforcing, or attempting to enforce, the right of any person, or class of persons, to the equal protection of the laws;

(3) **Depriving persons of rights or privileges.** If two or more persons in any State or Territory conspire, or go in disguise on the highway or on the premises of another, for the purpose of depriving, either directly or indirectly, any person or class of persons of the equal protection of the laws, or of equal privileges and immunities under the laws, or for the purpose of preventing or hindering the constituted authorities of any State or Territory from giving or securing to all persons within such State or Territory the equal protection of the laws; ... or to injure any citizen in person or property on account of such support or advocacy; in any case of conspiracy set forth in this section, if one or more persons engaged therein do, or cause to be done, any act in furtherance of the object of such conspiracy, whereby another is injured in his person or property, or deprived of having and exercising any right or privilege of a citizen of the United States, the party so injured or deprived may have an action for the recovery of damages, occasioned by such injury or deprivation, against any one or more of the conspirators.

Title 18 U.S.C.§ 241 Conspiracy against rights. If two or more persons conspire to injure, oppress, threaten, or intimidate any person in any State, Territory, Commonwealth, Possession, or District in the free exercise or enjoyment of any right or privilege secured to him by the Constitution or laws of the United States, or because of his having so exercised the same; they shall be fined under this title or imprisoned not more than ten years, or both.

Title 18 U.S.C. § 242. Deprivation of rights under color of law. Whoever, under color of any law, statute, ordinance, regulation, or custom, willfully subjects any person in any State, Territory, Commonwealth, Possession, or District to the deprivation of any rights, privileges, or immunities secured or protected by the Constitution or laws of the United States, or ..., shall be fined under this title or imprisoned not more than one year, or both;

No Response was ever received. The pattern of non-response and cover-up followed that letter, enabling the problems to continue, each one contributing to what was to follow.

Help in the Cover-Your-Ass Tactics

The downing of TWA Flight 800 on July 17, 1996, following advance notice given to FBI agents in the New York City offices, without any preventative measures taken, provided another reason to cover-up for that disaster. With the history of prior cover-ups by the political NTSB board members, it was not difficult to get the NTSB to fabricate another reason why the flight exploded in the air.

Assistant U.S. Attorney Patrick Fitzgerald Considered Scarpa and His Information Reliable

A *New York Daily News* article (September 24, 2000) by Greg B. Smith, titled, "Terrorist Called Pals on Feds Line," stated that the head of the Organized Crime and Terrorism Unit in New York, Patrick Fitzgerald, submitted a sealed affidavit (June 25, 1998) in which he "corroborated Scarpa's information" that he obtained from Yousef and provided to the FBI.

Sudden Reversal by Fitzpatrick

Fitzpatrick's admission of credibility for Scarpa would later change. The deaths in the TWA Flight 800 downing, possibly could have been prevented if he and others had not blocked dissemination of the advance information of the terrorist attack provided by Scarpa. Also, the need to discredit Scarpa to prevent being exposed as covering up for the series of murders by FBI Supervisory Special Agent Lindley DeVecchio and Gregory Scarpa Sr.

Loyalty is Rewarded

For being such a "loyal" team member, Fitzpatrick was promoted to U.S. Attorney in Chicago. In 2005, that same Fitzgerald was appointed to "investigate" the leaking of Valerie Plame's CIA identify. Fitzpatrick protected high-level White House politicians, including Karl Rove, Vice President Dick Cheney, and President George W. Bush. He used Cheney's aide, Libby, as the scapegoat.

Now Key FBI-DOJ Personnel Had a Personal Problem

After TWA Flight 800 was downed, key FBI-DOJ personnel had a major career-threatening problem on their hands. Here was the problem:

- FBI agents had been monitoring the phone calls between al Qaeda members that were discussing the planned downing of a local airliner.
- FBI agents had direct knowledge from al Qaeda's primary aviation terrorist member, through Scarpa, that a plane would be downed.
- FBI personnel had the opportunity—an actual invitation—to meet al Qaeda members in the New York-New Jersey areas that were obviously the same ones that would be carrying out the terrorist activities.
- FBI-DOJ personnel who withheld the information about the planned imminent attack upon a U.S. airliner departing a New York City airport so as to discredit Gregory Scarpa, Jr.
- FBI Administrative Special Agent in Charge (ASAC) Carson Dunbar, whose action terminated information provided by an insider to the al Qaeda cell, Emad Salem.
- FBI-CIA personnel who rejected the surface-to-air missiles, and who knew Middle East terrorists would acquire them.

- Members of Congress that knew of these problems and covered up for them.
- FAA personnel, who had the duty to order the simple preventative measures that would have blocked each of the four terrorist groups from hijacking the airliners. This serious problem, responsible for a score of preventable airline disasters, is described in *History of Aviation Disasters: 1950 to 9/11*. That opens up even more scandalous conduct.

The Yousef-Scarpa relationship and Roma Corporation continued after the downing of TWA Flight 800. FBI-DOJ personnel didn't use this unprecedented inside-al Qaeda information. The FBI continued to record the frequent telephone conversations between Yousef and his al Qaeda operatives in the United States and overseas, with no particular haste in having them transcribed.

"What had to be done has been done. TWA 800 ......"

Shortly after the downing of TWA Flight 800, Ramzi Yousef, in his native Baluchi language, made a phone call from his cell in the Metropolitan Correctional Center in New York City to one of his al Qaeda contacts via the fictitious Mafia organization called Roma. The recording of that call was not described until a later date when it was sent to the National Security Agency (NSA). All but the last two words were intelligible: "What had to be done has been done. TWA 800 [redacted].

Without knowing about Ramzi Yousef and the fictitious Mafia organization in New York City being used to patch Yousef's local phone calls to local and Middle East al Qaeda members, an article appeared in the March 21, 2005, *WorldNetDaily* that made reference to that message.

> [Referring to an anonymous letter received containing an NSA e-mail and memorandum] the internal NSA e-mail contained information pertaining to a recorded telephone call made from New York within minutes of the downing of Flight 800. The New York offices of the FBI had intercepted an overseas phone call made by a party under FBI surveillance.
>
> As the caller's language was unknown to FBI analysts, a recording of that call was sent to the NSA at the bequest of James Kallstrom specifically, then the head of the FBI's New York office, with a request for assistance in its translation. The NSA had no experience with the recorded language and with FBI approval forwarded the tape to the Defense Language Institute where it was translated.

The letter's most provocative sentence follows. The language was identified as Baluchi and was transcribed as, "What had to be done has been done, TWA 800 (last two words unintelligible)."

Four years later, a *WorldNetDaily* article (November 20, 2009), titled, Letter Implicates NSA in TWA cover-up, and stated in part:

Letter implicates NSA in TWA 800 cover-up, By Jack Cashill

Recently, an anonymous letter was sent to [WorldNetDaily] ... The letter writer tells of sending "an internal NSA e-mail and memorandum" to the *Washington Times* two years ago and getting no response. ... The internal NSA e-mail contained information pertaining to a recorded telephone call made from New York within minutes of the downing of Flight 800.

The New York offices of the FBI had intercepted an overseas phone call made by a party under FBI surveillance. As the caller's language was unknown to FBI analysts, a recording of that call was sent to the NSA at the bequest of James Kallstrom specifically, then the head of the FBI's New York office, with a request for assistance in its translation. The NSA had no experience with the recorded language and with FBI approval forwarded the tape to the Defense Language Institute where it was translated. The letter's most provocative sentence follows immediately.

The language was identified as Baluchi and was transcribed as, "What had to be done has been done, TWA 800 (last two words unintelligible)."

In the summer of 1996, Yousef, the mastermind of the 1993 World Trade Center bombing, was being held for trial in New York for the notorious Bojinka plot, his plan to blow up a dozen American commercial airliners over the Pacific and/or to attack America using planes as bombs, either of which he was scarily capable of executing. Yousef used Scarpa's connections to pass information to the outside world little knowing that Scarpa was routing much of it through his own FBI handlers.

Some of that information had to do with Yousef s ongoing plans to destroy a 747. Yousef told Scarpa that if there were to be a terrorist attack on such a plane during his Bojinka trial, it would surely prejudice the jurors against him, and Yousef would ask for a mistrial on those very grounds. The morning after the TWA Flight 800 crash, Yousef, representing himself, made just such a request.

... Yousef was part of the larger al-Qaida network ... His uncle, Khalid Shaikh Mohammed, with whom Yousef communicated from his jail cell, coordinated the 9-11 plot. And Yousef talked often to Scarpa about Osama bin Laden also under the code name, as Scarpa heard it, of "Bojinga."

Ironically, it was the FBI — seeking to gain intelligence from Yousef and to locate his "people" overseas — that set up the system allowing him to make the outside calls. Khalid Shaikh Mohammed was the last Bojinka conspirator on the loose who knew how to build, among other devices, a Casio-watch nitroglycerine bomb trigger. Yousef had used such a device on a Philippine Airlines 747 in 1994. Although improperly placed, the bomb killed a Japanese national in seat 26K and almost crashed the plane, proving its lethal effectiveness.

> The anonymous letter writer speaks of the contents of the memorandum he sent to the Washington Times, specifically the "detailed instructions to NSA personnel on the handling and control of NSA derived intelligence relating to TWA 800." The memo apparently also identified "specific individuals at the White House and their STU (secure) telephone numbers" with whom the NSA could discuss relevant information.
>
> "The reference to the STU (secure telephone) would not be commonly known,"

TWA 800 was not the first strike against the United States. Earlier ones included the 1993 bombing of the World Trade Center and the December 21, 1988, bombing of Pam Am Flight 103 over Lockerbie. Each one riddled with misconduct by personnel in the U.S. Department of Justice. The culture, and the cover-ups, made others possible.

CHAPTER THIRTEEN

DOJ's Self-Serving and Deadly Discrediting of al Qaeda Mole

At the end of the trial for Gregory Scarpa Jr., the jury found him guilty of most charges. The downward departure recommendation that federal prosecutors had promised Scarpa for his work obtaining secrets of future terrorist attacks was denied. U.S. Attorney Valerie Caproni lied to protect the murderous FBI supervisor and other FBI-DOJ personnel that feloniously covered up for the ongoing murders, by falsely claiming that the information provided by Scarpa was a hoax, unreliable, and that Scarpa was not creditable.

If federal prosecutors had requested the judge for a reduction in sentence for Scarpa's assistance with al Qaeda member Ramzi Yousef, it would have given credibility to the valuable information he provided. Since it was now the plan to discredit Scarpa, there was no other alternative.

Cover-Up by Federal Judge That I Know All Too Well

Marching in tune with federal prosecutors, as in the past, U.S. District Judge Reena Raggi agreed with the federal prosecutors and held that the confidential information Scarpa obtained from inside the terrorist cell was not reliable; was a hoax, and did not merit a downward departure in the length of prison sentence. Among the evidence that Judge Raggi ignored included:

- Testimony by mob defendants in other trials who knew of the relationship between Gregory Scarpa Sr. and FBI Supervisory Special Agent Lindley DeVecchio.
- Government documents by several other FBI agents that reported the corrupt relationship between Scarpa Sr. and DeVecchio.
- Reports by several FBI agents stating the information provided by Scarpa was creditable—including that by AUSA Fitzpatrick—until the need came to reverse his position

The many FBI 302 reports showed nine months of FBI participation with Scarpa; setting up a fictitious Mafia corporation called ROMA Corporation; the months of listening to Yousef talking to al Qaeda cells in the New York-New Jersey areas and in the Middle East.

40-Year Sentence Insured Gregory Scarpa Jr.'s Silence

Judge Raggi issued an order stating, "The court finds this witness to be not credible," and sentenced Gregory Scarpa Jr. to 40 years in prison.

In the same New York City courts, at the same time, Chief Judge Michael Mukasey was blocking me from reporting the criminal activities that I and a group of other government agents had discovered in the FAA, FBI, and CIA. I had filed a federal action under the federal crime reporting statute,[22] seeking to circumvent the cover-ups I encountered in the Department of Justice. (These matters are detailed in two of my books: *History of Aviation Disasters: 1950 to 9/11*; and *Blowback, 9/11, and Cover-Ups*.

DOJ Personnel and Federal Judges *Had* to Lie!

FBI-DOJ personnel had to lie, and even federal judges, partly from their prior actions to block me from reporting the corrupt and criminal activities that I had discovered that enabled to occur a series of preventable aviation disasters. FBI-DOJ personnel had to label Scarpa, Jr. as not creditable, despite the overwhelming evidence to the contrary. Were he to be held creditable, it would have revealed:

- The series of murders perpetrated by key FBI supervisor Lindley DeVecchio, and the felony cover-ups by high-level FBI-DOJ personnel.
- The successful downing of TWA Flight 800 by local al Qaeda members—after learning from Yousef that a downing would shortly occur; and after FBI-DOJ refused the opportunity, the invitation, to meet with local al Qaeda members allied with Yousef.
- The successful bombings of the U.S. embassies in Kenya and Tanzania, as forewarned.

Granddaddy of Cover-Up Consequences

The cover-ups, as I described in the *History of Aviation Disasters: 1950 to 9/11* book, that occurred over and over again, resulted in deadly consequences. And this would be no exception, except the next major consequence would be the granddaddy of all such consequences.

Scarpa Testifying as Witness

In 2003, Gregory Scarpa Jr. submitted an affidavit into court proceedings of other convicted felons, including those seeking to overturn prior convictions on the basis of DeVecchio's partnership in crime with Gregory Scarpa Sr. The affidavit by Gregory Scarpa Jr. stated:

> Because of my father's close relationship with Agent DeVecchio, my father continued to receive immunity from prosecution and lenient treatment from the government.
>
> DeVecchio passed on personal information, such as addresses and phone numbers to help my father locate people who owed him money for his illegal loan sharking activities and the identities of informants who might be a threat.
>
> With Agent DeVecchio's knowledge and consent, my father murdered or attempted to murder the individuals who were dangerous to him. My fa-

[22] Title 18 U.S.C. § 4.

> ther would then report the successful killings back to the FBI, attributing to others responsibility for his own murders. Committing murders and blaming others, always with the knowledge of Agent DeVecchio, became the M.O. adopted by my father.
>
> On several occasions Agent DeVecchio personally monitored crimes committed by my father's crew. If law enforcement became aware of the crime while it was in progress, Agent DeVecchio was to prevent arrests by claiming that the participants included FBI informants. Agent DeVecchio provided this service for at least four robberies in which I personally participated.

In those cases, federal judge Raggi again held that Scarpa was not creditable, helping to cover up the series of corrupt actions and incompetence that would enable the resulting catastrophic events to continue.

Raggi, and other judges and government personnel that corruptly discredited one of the most important inside al Qaeda sources had to cover up for such evidence as:

- The 11 months FBI-DOJ personnel received sophisticated information from Yousef via Scarpa, on how to smuggle bombs onto aircraft, material to be used for the bombs, and plans for terrorist attacks that did subsequently occur. The sophistication of that information was beyond Scarpa's technical ability to fabricate.
- The series of forewarned terrorist attacks that Scarpa passed on to FBI-DOJ personnel, which subsequently occurred.
- FBI-DOJ personnel praised Scarpa for the information—until advised by high-level FBI-DOJ personnel in Washington that Scarpa had to be discredited for self-serving reasons.
- Praising him for the quality of the information, and documenting the information in dozens of FBI 302 reports.
- For 11 months, FBI-DOJ personnel listened and recorded phone calls from Yousef that were made to the fictitious Mafia corporation, that were then patched through to al Qaeda operations in the New York-New Jersey area and to the Middle East.

Shutting Down the Listening Post into Al Qaeda Operations

Incredibly, after succeeding into secretly listening to telephone conversations between al Qaeda's master terrorist planner and al Qaeda operatives in the New York-New Jersey area and in the Middle East, FBI-DOJ personnel shut down the operation. More timely information on al Qaeda operations was obtained through that secret arrangement and the role played by Scarpa than was obtained by thousands of people in the government's various intelligence agencies. And most of the recorded conversations between Yousef and his al Qaeda contacts were never transcribed. Major terrorist successes that had yet to occur were now facilitated, along with other enabling corrupt acts.

Compare this to the U.S. practice of torturing detainees that exposed the U.S. to worldwide hatred and condemnation, and having the tortured detainees either refuse to speak, or to give false information.

CHAPTER FOURTEEN

9/11, 3,000 Deaths, and Other Forewarned Terrorist Attacks

Early in the morning on September 11, 2001, four groups of terrorists hijacked four U.S. airliners and then crashed three of them into buildings—as forewarned earlier by Scarpa based upon information given to him by al Qaeda's master bomber. On that day, the consequences would exceed in horror each of the prior aviation tragedies resulting from ignoring prior warnings. The worst terrorist attack upon America, and possibly anywhere in the world, occurred on that date. The death toll during a two-hour period was greater than that which occurred at Pearl Harbor on December 7, 1941.

The Sequence of Events

The September 11 events started with four groups of hijackers boarding four different airliners at approximately the same time and then after the aircraft were airborne, forcing their way into the cockpit. Their plans to take over the aircraft were encouraged by the absence of security measures that had been obvious to government safety personnel for years, with decades of easily preventable hijackings occurring throughout the world.

United Airlines Flight 175, a Boeing 767, left the gate at Boston's Logan Airport for Los Angeles at 7:58 a.m. American Airlines Flight 11, also a Boeing 767, left Boston at 07.59 a.m., heading for Los Angeles. Further south, American Airlines Flight 77, a Boeing 757, departed Washington's Dulles Airport for Los Angeles at 8:21 a.m. And a fourth aircraft, United Airlines Flight 93, also a Boeing 757, departed Newark for San Francisco at 8:43 a.m. All four aircraft had nearly full fuel tanks.

During climb to cruising altitude, after the airliners had taken off for their west coast destinations, each of the four groups of hijackers sprang into action. Armed with knives and box cutters that they had on their person, or in carry-on baggage, or possibly placed on board the aircraft by ground service personnel, they attacked the cabin flight attendants to obtain the key to the cockpit door. (The FAA, in its distorted wisdom, allowed these items to be carried on board the aircraft, despite their lethal capabilities.)

They then forced their way into the cockpit where they are believed to have killed the pilots. The hijackers then took over control of the aircraft. Several of the hijackers had received sufficient pilot training in small aircraft in the United States. Several others also received training in airline-type simulators. This training was sufficient to fly airliners once they became airborne.

Flights Diverted from Their Westerly Direction

The hijackers diverted American Airlines Flight 11 from its westerly heading and headed straight for New York City. The air traffic controller working that aircraft saw the aircraft change course and the transponder's return disappear (due to the transponder being turned off in the aircraft). The controller's calls went unanswered.

Approaching New York City, Flight 11 headed toward the north tower of the World Trade Center. At 8:45 a.m., the large jet, loaded with fuel, crashed into the tower at over 400 miles per hour. A giant fireball erupted as the fuel ignited, sending black smoke hundreds of feet into the air. Parts of the plane shot out the opposite side of the building, causing thousands of papers to rain down upon the financial district in lower New York City. Bodies and parts of bodies plummeted upon horrified spectators. The heat inside the north tower was so intense that many men and women jumped to certain death rather than die the slow painful death of being cremated alive.

As television cameras focused on the burning north tower of the World Trade Center, United Airlines Flight 175 appeared. At 9:03 a.m., it was filmed crashing into the south tower of the World Trade Center. Again, the high-speed impact caused a massive fireball to erupt, followed by plumes of flame and black smoke.

The intense heat from the burning fuel caused the metal framework of the south tower to soften and lose strength, causing one of the floors to collapse onto the lower floor at 10 a.m. This increased weight upon the floor below caused that floor to collapse. This sequence continued until the entire 105 floors had collapsed into a massive heap. The same sequence happened shortly thereafter to the north tower, which collapsed in spectacular fashion at 10:29 a.m. Over 2,000 people inside the building, and others on the ground were crushed to death by the collapse of the World Trade Center.

More Tragedies Unfolding

The next catastrophic event occurred in the Washington area. Hijackers flew American Airlines Flight 77 toward Washington, D.C., crashing it into the Pentagon at 9:38 a.m. This crash killed 64 people on Flight 77 and 125 in the Pentagon.

The last of the four hijacked planes was United Airlines Flight 93. Because of a delayed departure, the scenario on Flight 93 was different. After the hijackers took over the aircraft, passengers and flight attendants used the aircraft's seat-back telephones and personal cell phones to advise people on the ground of the hijacking. They described the hijacking, that the hijackers had knives and box cutters, and that the hijackers had already killed a flight attendant. The callers on Flight 93 learned that two airliners had been crashed into the World Trade Center.

Facing a similar fate, several of the passengers decided to fight the hijackers, a decision relayed by cell phone from the aircraft. It is unknown just what happened next. But people on the ground in Pennsylvania saw United 93 flying erratically as it descended, and then going inverted and diving almost vertically into the ground at approximately 10:10 a.m. The aircraft almost totally disappeared below ground level, with the primary evidence of an aviation disaster being smoke pouring from the hole in the ground.

About half an hour before Flight 93 dug into the ground, and after two airliners crashed into the World Trade Center, the FAA issued orders barring all aircraft from taking off, and ordered those already in the air to immediately land.

Promptly Identifying the Hijackers

By checking passenger records and other reports, the names used by the hijackers who boarded the hijacked planes were quickly determined. Most of the hijackers were citizens of Saudi Arabia who had been recruited by the al Qaeda terrorist group whose main training base was in Afghanistan.

Victim Compensation Fund

Following the September 11 attacks, Congress passed legislation known as the Victim Compensation Fund which gave relatives of the victims the choice of whether to accept compensation that was likely to average out as nearly two million dollars, or to take their chances on suing. If they sued, they lost their right to compensation under the fund.

Some refused to accept the government compensation, claiming that this route prevented discovery which could expose those people who were primarily the blame for the conditions that allowed hijackers to seize four airliners on 9/11. Whether this reason was true or not, the same people saying they wanted to learn the truth made no effort to look into my charges of corruption within the FAA as being primarily responsible for the conditions that encouraged and insured the success of the hijackers.

Suing the Wrong People

Lawyers for some 600 family members of September 11 victims filed lawsuits against Saudi officials, banks and charities, and the government of Sudan, claiming that they financed Osama bin Laden's network and the attacks on New York and Washington. The lawsuit sought as much as $1 trillion in damages, and charged the defendants with racketeering, wrongful death, negligence and conspiracy. The plaintiffs hoped to recover, in the event of a judgment, from Saudi assets in the U.S.

Over 80 defendants were named in the lawsuit, including seven banks, eight Islamic foundations and three Saudi princes. The 15-count lawsuit, modeled after an action filed against Libya to recover for the Pan Am flight 103 disaster, sought to cripple banks, charities and some members of the Saudi royal family as a deterrent to terrorist financing schemes. Several of the Saudi banks and Islamic charities named in the lawsuit vehemently denied any role in funding terrorism and called the case an attempt to extort Saudi wealth abroad.

Saudi Arabia was one of America's most important allies in the Middle East, and further alienating them in this manner caused even more hatred toward the United States.

Keeping the FAA Administrator Out of Sight

After September 11, the FAA Administrator, Jane Garvey, was nowhere to be seen. Otherwise, people would be reminded that this sweet-looking politically correct government official didn't have the background in aviation needed for that position. If a competent FAA administrator had been in place before September 11, and the corrupt culture did not exist throughout the operational divisions of the FAA, preventative measures would probably have been taken.

Preventing Hijackings Was Simple, Inexpensive, and Urgent

Hijackings, including fatal hijackings, occurred throughout the existence of the FAA, which came into being in 1958. Anyone with sufficient aviation expertise with a responsibility to act on safety problems would have known the correction actions needed. I recognized the problem and the solution while an airline pilot, and addressed the problem while I was a federal air safety inspector. I reported that the immediate corrective actions were to order the removal of cockpit door keys from the cabin flight attendant, keep the cockpit door locked during flight, stronger cockpit doors, elimination of the massive carry-on luggage, and barring passengers from carrying anything on board the aircraft that could be used as a weapon.

The removal of cockpit door keys from the flight attendants, which could have been put in place within 24 hours, by itself would have probably prevented the hijackers from seizing control of the four airliners on 9/11. Even if the FAA was 50 years late in these preventative measures, the numerous reports of planned airliner hijackings immediately preceding 9/11 could have shown a competent FAA administrator the need for these preventative measures.

Evidence that Cockpit Doors Were Opened With Keys

There was no indication that the hijackers had to break down any of the cockpit doors, strongly indicating that they used the cockpit door keys taken from the flight attendants. If any of the hijackers had tried to break down the cockpit doors, an alert pilot could easily put the aircraft in an unusual attitude to hinder such activities, time enough to permit passengers to become involved in halting cockpit intrusion.

Area of Primary Blame for Conditions Enabling Four Airliners to Be Hijacked in a Single Morning

To understand this relationship, I present the following information

The people holding primary responsibility for preventing airliners from being hijacked were not the people in the CIA or FBI; it was the people in the FAA, the government's primary agency responsible for airline safety, that I repeatedly reported as enablers of a number of specific airline disasters in areas for which I had federal airline safety responsibilities. The problems included outright corruption; the revolving door culture; and incompetence. I have documented this tragedy-related culture in books from 1978, the latest called *History of Aviation Disasters: 1950 to 9/11.*

Secondary Areas of Blame for the 9/11 Hijackings

Failure to discover the plot and failure to act on the known information would be secondary areas of blame, and that would be the culture in the FBI and CIA. Among the corrupt culture within these two agencies, as described in my various books, would be such matters as:

> Criminal activities within the CIA that subverted national interests for the entire life of that agency. Drug smuggling into the United States, looting savings and loans and other financial crimes, are not the type of conduct that would put priority on detecting plots such as hijackings.
>
> Criminal activities within the FBI (and other Justice Department divisions), such as cover-up of these crimes, the practice of false charges against innocent people, providing confidential information on government informants to organized crime figures, knowing that the informants would then be murdered, and were murdered, is not the type of culture that puts national interests on the top burner. Look for instance at the decades of FBI and Justice Department activities against me to silence my exposure activities. These matters are detailed in my other books.

Al Qaeda Operation: Sphinx Trading

Ignored by FBI personnel were many signs of terrorist activities prior to 9/11. In Jersey City, New Jersey, near where I went to high school a half century earlier, al Qaeda operatives had a mailbox-check cashing store called the Sphinx Trading Company. Sphinx Trading Company owners were Mohammed El-Attriss and Waleed al Noor.

Two of the hijackers on American Airlines Flight 77 obtained their fake identifications from Sphinx, and also had mailboxes there. Occupying the same building was the al-Salam Mosque headed by al Qaeda operative known as the "blind Sheikh," Omar Abdel Rahman. FBI-DOJ personnel recognized Rahman as a known terrorist for years.

Everyone Implicated Covered Up for Themselves

After 9/11, National Security Advisor Condoleezza Rice falsely stated :

> I don't think that anybody could have predicted that these people would take an airplane and slam it into the World Trade Center, they would try to use an airplane as a missile.

She conveniently also ignored the Presidential Daily Briefing of August 6, 2001, a month prior to 9/11. That briefing revealed that reported information showing that there were plans to hijack a U.S. airliner for the purpose of gaining the release of the blind Sheikh and another al Qaeda member. The title of that Presidential Daily Brief was, "Bin Laden Determined to Strike in U.S."

Massive Information Prior to the 9/11 Hijackings

Among the massive amount of pre-9/11 warnings that the thousands of U.S. intelligence personnel had, including people in control of the FBI and other Department of Justice offices, the CIA, National Security Agency, the Department of Defense, included the following major items:

- Specific information on Yousef's laptop computer.
- Full confession by Yousef's partner, Abdul Hakim Murad, to the Philippines National Police.
- Information obtained by the National Security Agency which they refused to provide to FBI and other government entities.
- Availability of Murad and Yousef that were in federal custody, from whom simple questioning by them at separate times might have revealed enough information to prevent 9/11 from occurring.
- Operation Able Danger.
- And even more, as detailed and documented in subsequent pages.

Withholding Information on Planned Terrorist Attacks Provided by Philippines National Police

Philippines National Police (PNP) complained that U.S. intelligence personnel refused to pay attention to the significant information they obtained from Yousef's computer and the information revealed by Murad. In 1995, PNP Colonel Rodolfo B. Mendoza sent the information provided by Murad and the laptop computer to several U.S. government agencies. Yousef's laptop computer contained information on the terrorist plans that included:

- Assassinate Pope John Paul II while visiting the Philippines.
- Placing bombs on 11 U.S. airliners departing Far East locations, including Tokyo, Singapore, Bangkok, Taipei, Hong Kong, Seoul, and Manila.
- Hijacking U.S. airliners and flying into major U.S. targets.

Amateur Shoe Bomber Using Technique Developed by Yousef

Al Qaeda member Richard Colvin Reid boarded an American Airlines Boeing 747 at Paris (December 22, 2001) for a flight to Miami, intent on blowing up the aircraft. He had explosives hidden in his shoes, and had planned to detonate them when the plane was over the North Atlantic. Fortunately, an alert flight attendant smelled smoke as Reid attempted in a crude manner to light the fuse. With the help of passengers, Reid was subdued and arrested.

Reid was convicted of terrorism and received a life sentence. Reid used numerous aliases, including Tariq Raja, Abdul Raheem, and Abdel Rahim. Al Qaeda operative Mohammed Mansour Jabarah, while under arrest in Oman in 2002, revealed that Reid was a member of al Qaeda and that he had been directed to bomb the flight by senior al Qaeda member, Khaled Shaikh Mohammed. U.S. Personnel Had Multiple Advance Warnings of the Plan to Hijack airliners and fly them into major buildings.

1995 FBI Memo to Philippines National Police

FBI-DOJ personnel, and White House politicians, had claimed that they knew nothing about al Qaeda's plans to hijack U.S. airliners and fly them into buildings. The following 1995 FBI memorandum to the Philippines National Police proves they were lying:

> SECRET/NOFORN REL TO THE PHILLIPINES
> RAMZI AHMED YOUSEF:
> A NEW GENERATION OF SUNNI ISLAMIC TERRORISTS
>
> INTRODUCTION:
>
> Ramzi Ahmed Yousef first came to our attention with the bombing of the World Trade Center (WTC) building on 26 February 1993. After the attack, he disappeared from our screens. Yousef reappeared in the Philippines in January 1995 when you successfully uncovered his plot to attack U.S. airlines and the Pope. The 7 February arrest of Yousef in Pakistan, and your January arrest of Abdul Hakim Murad, are major counterterrorism victories. We believe the information we have learned to date about Yousef and his plans to launch attacks, however, underscores a larger threat from Islamic terrorists. We continue to track down leads from the investigation and are still attempting to identify and locate other associates of Yousef.
>
> A. North America
>
> 1) The WTC bombing in 1993 clearly demonstrates Yousef's ability to enter the United States, establish a support structure, recruit a terrorist team, and successfully carry out an attack.
>
> 2) Yousef is able to use his friends and associates in foreign countries to identify possible targets. An example of this is Yousef's request to Murad, while he (Murad) was in the U.S. for pilot training, to choose an appropriate site for an attack. Murad chose the WTC building.
>
> 3) Yousef and Murad also discussed future attacks in the U.S. including possibly flying a plane filled with explosives into the CIA building. Murad also mentioned that in June of this year he was to travel to the U.S. and possibly attack a U.S. nuclear facility.
>
> Those involved in the WTC bombing and a second group of extremists who plotted to bomb other landmarks in New York City, including the

United Nations building, did not belong to a single, cohesive organization, but rather were part of a lose group of politically committed Muslims living in the area. They were of varying nationalities, including Egyptian, Sudanese, Pakistani, Palestinian, and Iraqi.

Presidential Daily Brief of August 6, 2001

A daily presidential brief provided to President George W. Bush stated:

- Yousef's plans to hijack U.S. airliners and fly them into buildings, as obtained from Yousef's laptop computer seized in Manila, and as admitted by Yousef's companion, Abdul Hakim Murad.
- Warnings by several FBI agents about Muslims taking flight training in U.S. flying schools, and one Muslim taking expensive training in a Boeing simulator, with no interest in landing or taking off; just in flying the plane once it was in the air.
- Attempt to hijack a French airliner and crash it into the Eiffel Tower.
- Numerous other warnings and indications that hijackings of airliners were planned by al Qaeda.

Aircraft Wreckage at Pentagon

CHAPTER FIFTEEN

American Airlines Flight 587: Another Terrorist Attack?

Two months after the terrorist attacks on 9/11, on November 12, 2001, an American Airlines Airbus 300-600, Flight 587, departed Kennedy Airport in New York for Santa Domingo Airports, crashing shortly after takeoff. Eyewitness statements indicated a terrorist act, and NTSB reaction was the usual cover-up.

As American Airlines Flight 587 climbed from John F. Kennedy airport, people on the ground saw an explosion and fire on the underneath side of the aircraft, which was quickly followed by parts falling off the aircraft. It then plunged to the ground on the narrow strip of land known as Rockaway. The death toll was 251 passengers and 9 crewmembers plus five on the ground.

Creditable Witnesses Ignored by Political NTSB Board

Tom Lynch, a retired firefighter, saw the plane in flight, and later said:

> *I saw the plane. It had a small contained-explosion in the fuselage. The explosion was probably the size of a small automobile. The tail was still on the plane at the time and it continued to fly towards Rockaway.*

Lynch sent a statement to the NTSB, but no attempt was made to interview him in person about what he saw. Lynch stated (January 19, 2002) that he saw two explosions, the first, a smaller one behind the wing near the fuselage, and then a much larger second explosion.

Victor Trombettas saw Flight 587 and started obtaining witness statements that he placed on an Internet site after he felt the NTSB was covering up for what actually happened.

One witness, who Trombettas identified as Witness Alpha, was a former Special Forces member familiar with military weapons and a retired New York City police officer. Alpha spotted Flight 587 as it was climbing out of JFK Airport, and said the flight looked normal until suddenly a white and yellow explosive flash appeared on the fuselage behind the wing, which he described as an ordinance explosion. The flash was followed by a stream of smoke.

That appears to be the stream of smoke that others had observed before the plane plunged to the ground. The events were sufficiently revealing that Alpha was on his portable phone calling emergency services while Flight 587 was still airborne.

John Powers was walking his dog when he looked up at Flight 587, having a clear and unobstructed view of the flight path of the aircraft. He stated that he saw an "enormous flash or explosion ... near where the wing meets the fuselage." He explained that he noticed smoke coming from the right engine as soon as he noticed the plane. He stated he saw more of the right side of the plane, what looked to him like a fire or explosive-type flash on the wing near the fuselage. He said the plane rolled violently from side to side several times and then the vertical stabilizer ripped from the aircraft. He described this as noticing a "huge rectangular piece fly free" from the plane and begin a slow "float" down towards the water of Jamaica Bay. He was positive about the tail being intact during the initial rolls.

A construction worker who saw the aircraft in flight, Antonio Villela, said, "First I heard a big explosion. Then I saw flames come out from behind the plane."

Retired New York police department Lieutenant stated during an interview (January 19, 2002) that he saw two explosions. The first, a smaller one, was behind the wing near the fuselage. The second was much larger and engulfed much of the plane. He said the plane was intact at the time of the first explosion.

Another witness, Kenny Good, observed the aircraft at a later stage than some of the other witnesses. He described that he had observed the aircraft's right engine rip loose, the vertical stabilizer, and the left engine, all before impact and not ejected after impact.

If Flight 587 was brought down by one or more explosive devices, they could have been planted in the baggage compartments, in luggage, in any of the many inspection plates throughout the aircraft, in the supplies loaded on the aircraft before departure. The explosives could even have been wrapped around the body of one of the passengers, or in coat lining.

Al Qaeda Accepting Blame for AAL 587
And Several Other Terrorist Attacks

Al Qaeda provided a list to the Global Islamic Media Group (May 28, 2004), of terrorist acts for which it took responsibility. The group then posted the list on its web site:

American Airlines Flight 587.

Bomb attack in Kuwait at Faylakah.

Bomb attack in Yemen upon a French tanker.

Bomb attack in Mombasa, Kenya.

Bomb attack upon a Bali, Indonesia nightclub that killed over 200 people.

Bomb attack upon the Jewish temple in Djerba, Tunisia, that killed almost two dozen Jews.

Missile firing upon an El Al airliner in Kenya that failed to hit the aircraft.

Bomb attack at the Marriott Hotel in Indonesia.

Attack in the residential area of Riyadh in Saudi Arabia.
Bomb attack against Jewish synagogues in Istanbul, Turkey.
Bombing of American Airlines Flight 587.

Even More Indication that Terrorists Were Implicated

Further information relating to the alleged bombing of Flight 587 came from the report of the Canadian Security Intelligence Service (CSIS), which was addressed in several foreign newspaper articles, including Canada's *National Post* (August 27, 2004). The *National Post* article carried the title, "Montreal man downed U.S. Plane, CSIS told." The article stated:

> A captured al-Qaeda operative has told Canadian intelligence investigators that a Montreal man who trained in Afghanistan alongside the 9/11 hijackers was responsible for the crash of an American Airlines flight in New York three years ago.
>
> Canadian Security Intelligence Service agents were told during five days of interviews with the source that Abderraouf Jdey, a Canadian citizen also known as Farouk the Tunisian, had downed the plane with explosives on Nov. 12, 2001.
>
> The source claimed Jdey had used his Canadian passport to board Flight 587 and "conducted a suicide mission" with a small bomb similar to the one used by convicted shoe bomber Richard Reid, a "Top Secret" Canadian government report says.
>
> Jdey, 39, came to Canada from Tunisia in 1991 and became a citizen in 1995. Shortly after getting his Canadian passport, he left for Afghanistan and trained with some of the Sept. 11 hijackers, according to the 9/11 commission in the United States.
>
> He recorded a "martyrdom" video, but was dropped from the 9/11 mission after returning to Canada in the summer of 2001. The planner of the World Trade Center attack, Khalid Sheikh Mohammed, claims Jdey was recruited for a "second wave" of suicide attacks.
>
> The information on Jdey's alleged role in the plane crash is contained in a memo on captured Canadian al-Qaeda operative Mohammed Mansour Jabarah. The Canadian government memo was written in May, 2002, and was based on information provided by a "source of unknown reliability."
>
> Jabarah is a 22-year-old from St. Catharines who allegedly joined al Qaeda and convinced Osama bin Laden to give him a terror assignment. He was tasked with overseeing a suicide-bombing operation in Southeast Asia, but was caught and has since pleaded guilty in the United States.
>
> The report, which was sent to the Philippine National Police Intelligence directorate, recounts what Jabarah said he was told about the U.S. plane crash by Abu Abdelrahman, a Saudi al-Qaeda member who was working for Khalid Sheikh Mohammed.

"In discussions, Abu Abdelrahman mentioned AL QAIDA was responsible for the assassination of Massoud, the Northern Alliance leader," the report says. "According to the source, Abu Abdelrahman added that the 12 November 2001 plane crash (American Airlines flight 587) in Queens, New York was not an accident as reported in the press but was actually an AL QAIDA operation.

"Abu Abdelrahman informed Jabarah that Farouk the Tunisian conducted a suicide mission on the aeroplane using a shoe bomb of the type used by Richard Reid ... 'Farouk the Tunisian' was identified from newspaper photographs as being identical to Abderraouf Jdey, a Canadian citizen who had resided in Montreal."

Jabarah was initially suspect of the claim about Jdey, but he later believed it after he saw the same information on a "mujahedin Web site," the report says.

Jdey allegedly used his Canadian passport in boarding Flight 587, but because Jdey used many aliases in the past, it wasn't known what name he might have used. Among his many aliases were Abd Al-Rauf Bin Al-Habib Bin Yousef Al-Jiddi, Aderraouf Dey, A Raouf Jdey, Abdal Ra'Of Bin Muhammed Bin Yousef Al-Jadi, Farouq Al-Tunisi, Abderraouf Ben Habib.

Aviation Illiterate and Political NTSB Chairwoman Ignored Witness Statements

As with the downing of TWA Flight 800 just a few miles from this location, the NTSB ignored the many reports by professional police and firemen who saw and described the sequence of events, sought to discredit them, and blamed the crash, not on terrorist acts, but on separation of the vertical stabilizer.

Despite these reports indicating an explosion, NTSB chairman Marion Blakey ruled out any criminal or terrorist activity during her appearance on National Public Radio on January 8, 2002. It was as if the politically appointed NTSB board members were determined that the public not hear of any terrorist successes. This pattern was similar to what occurred with the downing of TWA Flight 800. It appears the NTSB was under pressure from higher government sources to rule out a terrorist act.

NTSB board officials suggested the cause of the crash might be due to wake turbulence from an aircraft that departed earlier. But the light turbulence from such an encounter does not even register on the scale of the type of extreme turbulence that aircraft undergo from atmospheric disturbances such as in the vicinity of thunderstorms.

Then the board suggested that the composite vertical stabilizer may be faulty, but this does not address the numerous reports of professional witnesses concerning fire and explosions coming from the aircraft before the vertical stabilizer ripped from the aircraft.

The board suggested that maybe the pilots applied excessive rudder movement, implying that the aircraft was made of balsa wood and that the extremely minor pilot input to the rudder (improbable) caused the tail to rip loose.

An article in the *Associated Retired Aviation Professionals*, dated November 12, 2001, stated: "Former NTSB Official Doubts Accident Caused Flight 587 Crash," and added in part:

> Aviation expert and former National Transportation Safety Board official Vernon Grose said late Monday that he's increasingly skeptical that the crash of American Airliners Flight 587 was purely accidental.
>
> "I am backing away from the ready idea that this is simply an accident," Grose told *Fox News* Channel's John Scott.

NTSB Refusal to Contact Witnesses

The chairperson for the NTSB, with no significant background in aviation safety matters, excused the refusal of the NTSB to make personal contacts with witnesses, stating, that their reports "differ dramatically in terms of what people say that they saw." She added, when questioned by a *Wave* edition, "We have all of our facilities in Washington, and anybody who is interested can come there." It is not the responsibility of individual people to force the NTSB to receive evidence, but the responsibility of the NTSB.

Some of the witnesses to the events occurring on Flight 587 were so concerned about the NTSB cover-up that they sent a letter to NTSB chairwoman, Marion Blakey demanding to have their statements taken. Blakey, a politically correct appointee, responded in a March 1, 2002, letter stating that during the public hearing they may be allowed to testify. Long before the hearing, the NTSB should have obtained all the evidence that they knew existed, including witness statements, to enable them to concentrate on the areas most likely to be the cause of the crash.

The facts strongly indicated that the tail separation was not the trigger event for the crash but merely one of the consequences of other events, such as an explosion somewhere on the aircraft, contrary to the position taken by the NTSB board members.

NTSB Report Blamed the Pilot and Airbus

In October 2004, the political NTSB board members blamed the cause of the crash on the pilot's rudder input and on the design and manufacturer of the aircraft tail. That report ignored the many witness reports that indicated an explosion had occurred before the tail separated.

The NTSB claimed that failure of the rudder made the aircraft uncontrollable. But aircraft without rudders are easily controllable. In several instances the huge Air Force B-52 have lost their tail due to turbulence and had no trouble flying back to base. Directional control is easily accomplished in multi-engine aircraft by adjusting the power of the engines. Another Airbus plane lost its rudder after flight 587 went down, and had no trouble making a subsequent landing.

Reasons for Covering Up with Falsified Accident Report

There would be several reasons why the political NTSB board members would cover up the real cause of the disaster, just as they did with TWA Flight 800 and at least half a dozen others that I describe in my book, *History of Aviation Disasters: 1950 to 9/11*. In the late 1970s, I even sued the NTSB in federal court at San Francisco[23] because of their falsification of official accident reports.

In that filing, Assistant U.S. Attorney George Stoll telephoned me and stated he was recommending to his superiors in Washington that they support my brief against the NTSB. However, Stoll didn't know of the prior cover-ups by the Justice Department when I had tried to report corruption in the FAA and the NTSB and Stoll was then ordered to file a motion to dismiss my filing. An accommodating federal judge complied.

The al Qaeda members in the New York-New Jersey area that probably placed a bomb on American Airlines were probably the same al Qaeda members that FBI agents could have met through the fictitious Mafia company, the Roma Corporation.

Canada, Watch Out, You May be Next!

With so many al Qaeda terrorists being identified as Canadian citizens, it is a wonder White House officials hadn't put Canada on a list of countries harboring terrorists! An article in *Newsweek* (August 9, 2004) described how the Bush White House considered attacking South America immediately after the 9/11 hijackings. The article stated:

Fighting Terror by Attacking ... South America?

Days after 9/11, a senior Pentagon official lamented the lack of good targets in Afghanistan and proposed instead U.S. military attacks in South America or Southeast Asia as "a surprise to the terrorists," according to a footnote in the recent 9/11 commission report.

The unsigned top-secret memo, which the panel's report said appears to have been written by Defense Under Secretary Douglas Feith, is one of several Pentagon documents uncovered by the commission which advance unorthodox ideas for the war on terror. The memo suggested "hitting targets outside the Middle East in the initial offensive" or a "non Al Qaeda target like Iraq," the panel's report states. U.S. attacks in Latin America and Southeast Asia were

---

[23] *Stich v. National Transportation Safety Board*, 685 F.2d 446 (9th Cir.)(table), *cert. denied*, 459 U.S. 861 (1982))(addressed repeated criminal falsification of official airline accident reports, omitting highly sensitive air safety misconduct, making possible repeated crashes from the same sequestered problems).

portrayed as a way to catch the terrorists off guard when they were expecting an assault on Afghanistan.

The memo's content, *Newsweek* has learned, was in part the product of ideas from a two-man secret Pentagon intelligence unit appointed by Feith after 9/11: veteran defense analyst Michael Maloof and Mideast expert David Wurmser, now a top foreign-policy aide to Dick Cheney.

Maloof and Wurmser saw links between international terror groups that the CIA and other intelligence agencies dismissed. They argued that an attack on terrorists in South America—for example, a remote region on the border of Paraguay, Argentina and Brazil where intelligence reports said Iranian-backed Hizbullah had a presence—would have ripple effects on other terrorist operations. The proposals were floated to top foreign-policy advisers.

One proposal got greater traction. The 9/11 commission says the idea of attacking Iraq also was pushed in a Sept. 17 memo by Deputy Secretary of Defense Paul Wolfowitz. Wolfowitz argued that the odds were "far more" than one in 10 that Saddam Hussein was behind the 9/11 attacks, citing in part theories by controversial academic Laurie Mylroie that Ramzi Yousef, mastermind of the 1993 World Trade Center bombing, was an Iraqi intelligence agent. (The commission's report found "no credible evidence" that Iraq was behind the 1993 attack—and no Iraqi involvement in 9/11.

A Wolfowitz aide said the memo "did not talk about theories, but facts.") Still, critics say, the ideas put forward by Wolfowitz, Feith and others in the Pentagon set the stage for the war in Iraq.

Another Al Qaeda Member Attempting To Down 747 with Explosives in Shoe Heels

Another al Qaeda member's unsophisticated attempt to down an airliner was Richard Colvin Reid. He attempted to blow up an American Airlines Boeing 747 on a flight from Paris (December 22, 2001) to Miami, using explosives hidden in his shoes. That was a procedure designed by Ramzi Yousef. Reid had planned to detonate the explosives when the plane was over the North Atlantic. Fortunately, an alert flight attendant smelled smoke as Reid attempted in a crude manner to light the fuse. With the help of passengers, Reid was subdued and arrested.

Reid was convicted of terrorism and sentenced to life in prison. Reid used numerous aliases, including Tariq Raja, Abdul Raheem, and Abdel Rahim Al Qaeda operative Mohammed Mansour Jabarah, while under arrest on Oman in 2002, revealed that Reid was a member of al-Qaeda and that he had been directed to bomb the flight by senior al Qaeda member, Khaled Shaikh Mohammed.

It is highly questionable that the small amount of explosives that would fit in the heel of a person's shoe would do much significant structural harm and that the primary victim would be the person wearing the shoes. However, the intelligence level of airport security required that everyone, including women wearing flimsy shoes that could hardly contain more explosives than a fourth-of—July "cherry bomb."

Judges Threatening Witnesses

Judges cooperating in cover-ups will threaten witnesses with perjury, the charge left up to the discretion of the same judge or DOJ employee seeking to cover up the truth.

In the 1990s, Linda Schiro, Gregory Scarpa Sr.'s common law wife, sought to testify in a trial about her son, which would reveal the murders involving FBI supervisor Lindley DeVecchio. Federal judge Reena Raggi threatened to charge Linda Schiro with a criminal offense if she testified. That would have been easy to do since Schiro had knowledge of the criminal activities perpetrated by Scarpa Sr. and did not report them to a federal official.

Gregory Scarpa Jr.'s mother, Connie Scarpa, also backed down from testifying when she was warned by Judge Raggi that she could be charged with criminal prosecution. Since they were obviously close to Gregory Scarpa Sr., it was obvious that they knew that crimes were being committed. They then could be criminally charged with obstruction of justice offenses for not reporting the crimes.

Judge Raggi's threat caused them to withhold their testimony. That judicial obstruction of justice tactic allowed the corrupt murderous actions of DeVecchio to go unpunished. Cover-ups frequently have consequences. The consequences of Raggi's threat was that a key FBI supervisor got away with murders, and as is described in these pages, FBI-DOJ misconduct made possible a series of catastrophic terrorist attacks upon major U.S. targets.

CHAPTER SIXTEEN

Other Enablers of 9/11

The conduct of many other people, besides those stated within these pages, contributed to the catastrophic consequences occurring on September 11, 2001. Several of my books document this relationship: *History of Aviation Disasters: 1950 to 9/11*, and *Lockerbie to 9/11: Massive Fraud and Consequences*. The remainder of this chapter provides highlights to another side of the brutal consequences occurring on 9/11.

First, briefly, my aviation background. I was a Naval Aviator during World War II. First, I instructed in the PBY Catalina aircraft and then I was a Patrol Plane Commander in the Liberators and Privateers. After the end of World War II, I flew captain for various airlines, including Japan Airlines. My flying included worldwide operations, including flying Muslim pilgrims from throughout the Middle East to the Holy Cities of Mecca and Medina.

In 1962, I left airline flying and became an airline safety inspector-investigator for the Federal Aviation Administration (FAA). That role included everything operational in airline flying, including conducting flight checks of airline pilots, issuing ratings enabling them to fly commercial aircraft, looking for safety problems, and making reports on changes necessary to achieve an acceptable level of safety.

From 1950 to about 1980, airline disasters were a common occurrence, sometimes occurring every few months. One of several airline disasters caused FAA management to ask me to accept the assignment to correct the conditions responsible for the worst series of airline disasters in the nation's history. The conduct of certain key people at United Airlines created the conditions responsible for more aviation disasters than all the other airlines combined. One of these crashes was a United Airlines DC-8 that crashed into the Brooklyn area of New York City in December 1960. That was the worst airline disaster in the nation's history at the time.

This same culture—combined with similar problems within the FAA—had continuing ripple effects for many years. The hijackings of four airliners on 9/11 were simply additions to what will be a continuing series of consequences.

Upon arriving in my new assignment, it didn't take me long to understand why there were so many major airline disasters occurring. Corrupt conduct by people in key positions at United Airlines—aided and abetted by key people in the FAA—went far beyond anything I had ever encountered in my long aviation career, resulted in a continuing series of airline disasters. Much of what I had discovered was already known by the more experienced and dedicated FAA inspectors. They encountered many of the same problems and were unable to correct them.

The arrogance, the violations of major legally-required and industry-accepted safety matters, and even criminal violations, motivated me to take actions that were never taken before. Those actions continued and expanded over many years, providing me with enough insider information to publish over a dozen books on corruption in and out of government. The book you are now reading is one of the latest.

Finding that my official reports of serious safety problems, safety violations, and criminal falsification of government-required records on major safety requirements were being either ignored or destroyed, I took actions that I knew would end my career with the government. I had no choice; something had to be done. The following is a brief listing of what I did in my David verses Goliath battle:

I sent letters to members of Congress, detailing specific corrupt activities associated with specific aviation disasters. The initial response admitted the gravity of the charges, but in every case, no action was taken. Sometimes the recipient stated that the matters were not in their area of responsibility, an excuse that was not correct, especially due to the gravity of the consequences and effect upon national security.

I used the law as it had never been used before. As an FAA inspector, I acted similar to an independent prosecutor, conducting hearings that continued for several months. The hearings occurred under an administrative law judge, William G. Jennings, a lawyer on the FAA administrator's staff. Over 4500 pages of transcript were necessary for the testimony and exhibits.

During the hearings, three more fatal airline disasters occurred, each one due to the exact problems I had repeatedly reported in writing, for which nothing was done, and for which I suffered various forms of retaliation. Jennings covered up for the evidence, and despite the three additional major aviation disasters, his report stated that everything was fine.

Because of the criminal perjury occurring during the hearings, I reported these matters to various offices of the U.S. Department of Justice (DOJ), only to be blocked at every turn. I then sought to circumvent the DOJ block by appearing before a federal grand jury in Denver. I soon learned that the jurors were controlled by a U.S. attorney, and he insured that the jurors took no action on the testimony that I was providing.

Refusing to work under such corrupt conditions, I resigned and moved back to California. I continued to be actively involved in aviation matters, including being employed for several years by Flying Tigers, single-handedly preparing the pilot operating manual for the stretched DC-8s that were then on order.

The continuing series of major airline disasters—made possible by the same culture that I had earlier documented—caused me to renew my efforts, using unusual but legally proper methods. My first effort was filing lawsuits under the federal crime reporting statute.[24] That statute requires that anyone knowing of a federal crime must report the crime to a federal judge or other federal official. The judge is required by law, as part of his *mandatory* administrative duties, to receive whatever information is offered. He must then provide that information to the proper law enforcement department, which would be the Department of Justice (that was implicated through cover-ups). However, I felt that once a judicial record was made, there would be less possibility of simply covering up for the ongoing deadly practices since media people examine most papers filed in federal court.

The first lawsuit, in the late 1970s, was filed at San Francisco, and sought to report the federal crimes involving key people in the FAA. Shortly after filing, the U.S. attorney filed a motion for the judge to dismiss the action, claiming I had no standing to report the crimes. *Everyone* has standing to report a federal crime to a federal judge, and if that person doesn't do so, he or she can easily join the hundreds of others that federal prosecutors charged with a Title 18 U.S.C. § 4 crime for *not* reporting the matter. The trial judge admitted that the charges were serious, but refused to receive the information.

I then filed an appeal. After submitting written appeal briefs, and during oral argument before the court of appeal judges, they also admitted the charges were serious. One judge stated that these charges were matters for Congress to investigate. I responded that members of Congress had repeatedly blocked an investigation; that I was not expecting a federal judge to conduct an investigation; but just to receive the information that they were required to receive under the mandatory requirements of Title 18 U.S.C. § 4.

After the court of appeal judges turned down the appeal, I filed a petition for writ of certiorari with the U.S. Supreme Court. That filing put the Justices of the U.S. Supreme Court on notice of the crimes against the United States and the obstruction of justice tactics by federal judges over whom they had supervisory responsibilities. The Justices turned down my petition, which made possible a continuation of the corrupt activities and the often deadly consequences.

---

[24] Title 18 U.S.C. § 4. Misprision of felony. Whoever, having knowledge of the actual commission of a felony cognizable by a court of the United States, conceals and does not as soon as possible make known the same to some judge or other person in civil or military authority under the United States, shall be fined under this title or imprisoned not more than three years, or both.

Thinking that the public would react to such deadly corruption, especially the next of kin in several of the fraud-related crashes, I published the first of over a dozen books in 1978, which was the first edition of *Unfriendly Skies*.

I started appearing as guest and aviation safety expert on hundreds of radio and TV shows, which made millions of people aware of the serious problems responsible for the continuing series of aviation disasters. Many complimentary letters were received, but no one did anything, despite the continuing airline disasters that by that time were becoming even deadlier due to their larger size..

The publishing of that first book and the radio-TV appearances did give me publicity that resulted in a steady stream of other former government agents and insiders contacting me. They provided me with specific information and documentation on other areas of corruption that they had either discovered as part of their official duties, or in which they were themselves involved. These people were often former members of such groups as the CIA, Office of Naval Intelligence, DEA, INS, and Customs. They also included former drug smugglers, especially those working for the CIA and especially during the Iran Contra affair. As shown earlier, even Mafia sources contacted me. My primary concern was corruption by people in government positions, holding positions of trust, whose misconduct was inflicting great harm upon countless numbers of victims and upon national security. Two of my subsequent books were made possible by the enormous amount of information that they provided to me. These books, now in multiple editions, are *Defrauding America* and *Drugging America*.

The gravity of these matters and the horrendous human toll caused me to again file lawsuits in federal court under the federal crime reporting statute, seeking to report these matters and circumvent the constant cover-ups that I encountered. Again, I was blocked:

Federal judges blocked every attempt to report the federal crimes.

U.S. District Judge Milton Schwartz, Sacramento, Judge Marilyn Patel, San Francisco, and others, issued unlawful and unconstitutional orders permanently barring me from filing any papers in any federal district or appellate court. Those orders not only openly violated the basic due process requirements, but also violated criminal statutes relating to obstruction of justice.

DOJ Prosecutors and Federal Judges Charged Me With Criminal Contempt of Court for Reporting Federal Crimes

As I discovered other criminal activities from my sources, including drug smuggling by CIA assets during the Iran-Contra operation, I again filed papers to report what were not only criminal acts against the United States, but subversive activities.

In response to that attempt, U.S. Attorney David Levi, Sacramento, and several federal judges, promptly charged me with criminal contempt of court for filing papers in federal court when federal judges had standing orders barring me from federal court. Or, barring me from reporting high-level crimes against the United States! They denied me the right to a jury trial, and sentenced me to six months in federal prison.

I appealed the sentence to court of appeal judges—including filing an emergency petition with Judge Anthony Kennedy in San Francisco—while he was waiting to take his position on the Supreme Court. I also filed petitions with Justices of the U.S. Supreme Court. They all approved what was being done. By that time federal judges were so heavily implicated that they apparently acted to protect themselves rather than show concern for the country's welfare. While I was in prison, federal judges issued unlawful and unconstitutional orders seizing the $10 million in real estate assets that I had used to fund my exposure activities.

Every area of corruption that I sought to expose played key roles in the success of the 9/11 hijackers. These included:

- The culture of incompetence, self-serving revolving door syndrome that blocked taking corrective actions on safety problems, and corruption, within the Federal Aviation Administration.
- The corrupt culture in the FBI and other Department of Justices, that I first encountered as a federal airline safety inspector in the 1960s and thereafter.
- The corrupt culture in the Central Intelligence Agency (CIA) that probably played a role in not acting on evidence of impending terrorist activities. (See the books, Defrauding America and Drugging America for details.)
- The culture of cover up by members of Congress and media personnel.
- The pattern of retaliation against government personnel exposing harm-causing high-level corruption.
- The roles played by federal judges and dozens of lawyers as they sought to silence my efforts to expose the corrupt conduct that enabled 9/11 to occur. Details of their misconduct are in the book, *History of Aviation Disasters:*

Last Attempt Prior to 9/11

About 18 months prior to 9/11, I felt the need to make one more attempt to report the criminal activities in not only the FAA, but also in the Department of Justice and the CIA. I filed a lawsuit in the federal courts at Reno, Nevada. That legal action was still before the court when 9/11 occurred. Despite the fact that each of the named defendants were of the groups that played a role in those catastrophic events, the judge dismissed the action, thereby barring me from providing my evidence on the corruption that enabled the easy success of four groups of hijackers.

Last Attempt to Report People Contributing to 9/11

After 9/11, I again sought to report the federal crimes that I alleged were responsible for the conditions that enabled four groups of terrorists to so easily hijack four airliners on September 11, 2001. I filed the action in the federal courts in New York City, where it would become known to most of the media. At that time I was unaware of the role by Department of Justice employees in the other areas of gross incompetence and even worse "deep-sixing" of advance information relating to the planned attacks.

Despite the fact that federal law and rules of court required that federal actions received by the clerk be promptly filed, the filing was blocked by Chief Judge Michael Mukasey. It wasn't until after I sent certified letters to each of the Justices of the U.S. Supreme Court, notifying them of the *latest* obstruction of justice, that Mukasey allowed my papers to be filed—13 months after they had been received. The Justices of the U.S. Supreme Court had been kept aware throughout the 20-year period of the criminal activities and the corrupt obstruction of justice and retaliation by lower court judges.

Judge Mukasey compounded his initial obstruction of justice by promptly dismissing my filing that same day. He openly violated:

- The due process requirement of providing notice of a hearing and a hearing to the party affected by the adverse legal action.
- Federal crime reporting statute that made it mandatory for him to receive the information of the federal crimes.

I then filed a notice of appeal, submitted appeal briefs, and appeared to give oral argument in New York City before a three-judge appellate panel.

The usual cover-up followed. My petition to the Justices of the U.S. Supreme Court—as for the prior 30 years—was denied.

CHAPTER SEVENTEEN

Becoming Confidant of Qaeda Mole

After Gregory Scarpa Jr. was confined to the federal prison at Florence, Colorado, he became friends with Gerald Van Hoorelbeke, with whom I had been in contact. I met Hoorelbeke through Doret Kollerer, an activist living in Occidental, California. She was in frequent contact with inmates and published an alternative newspaper. Over a period of several years she took letters she received from Van for a manuscript and put them onto a computer. As she aged and suffered from various ailments, she turned the computer disks over to me, and I used the material to format and get printed the book by Jerry Van. I named it, *Underworld Secrets: Jimmy Hoffa to Las Vegas and Los Angeles*.

Among the people that Jerry Van encountered, and that are described in his book, were such prominent figures as Jimmy Hoffa; Los Angeles Eddie Nash, aka Adel Nasrallah (involved in the four-on-the-floor murders in Hollywood); Las Vegas' Tony Spilotro, and others. Hoorelbeke provided me with information about corruption in another division of the Department of Justice and the retaliation he suffered when he sought to report these criminal activities.

Jerry Van was a friend of Jimmy Hoffa and with some notable crime figures in Las Vegas and Los Angeles. Van had also been involved in criminal activities, and then became a government informant, providing information to Justice Department personnel on criminal activities that he discovered. His information caused the conviction of numerous people engaging in criminal activities. But when he started reporting criminal activities involving government personnel, Justice Department prosecutors then filed false charges against him and he ended up in federal prison at Florence, Colorado. Jerry Van's letters to me over a period of several years provided inside information on the corruption he discovered in government while working both sides of the law.

Jerry Van's Earlier Efforts to Expose Corruption in Government

Tactics used to block efforts to expose corrupt government personnel take many forms and constitute standard practice. Take, for instance, the problems encountered by Jerry Van Hoorelbeke when he tried to expose corruption in the federal strike force in Los Angeles. He learned about these matters while he was involved in underworld activities.

Syndicated columnist Jack Anderson used Jerry Van's information in a series of articles exposing the involvement of law enforcement personnel in blocking prosecution of criminal activities. One of Anderson's articles (August 6, 1981) was titled "U.S. Investigates Its Own Troops In Crime War"

Current and former members of the federal strike force in Los Angeles against organized crime are themselves under investigation by the Justice Department. They have been accused of delaying or failing to pursue grand jury action against underworld figures in California and Hawaii.

My associate Indy Badhwar has learned that the targets of the investigation are the current strike force chief, Jim Henderson, and his predecessor, Richard Crane, who is now in private law practice in Los Angeles. The investigation by the Justice Department's Office of Professional Responsibility was begun under pressure from Rep. Charles B. Rangel (D-N.Y.) chairman of the House Select Committee on Narcotics Abuse and Control.

Over the past year, a special investigator for the House committee has interviewed organized-crime figures and state and local law enforcers in California and elsewhere. His principal informant, however, has been Jerry Van, a self-described muscleman for California's top racketeers and arsonists.

Van, now serving a prison term on extortion and assault charges, has been cooperating with state and federal authorities since 1979. Information he has given investigators, as well as his testimony before grand juries and in criminal trials, has led to almost a dozen indictments and convictions for such crimes as murder, arson for profit, mail fraud and drug smuggling.

Federal and local lawmen describe Van as one of the most valuable and credible witnesses against organized crime figures in more than a decade. Because of threats on his life, he is in the witness protection program while in prison.

Government Personnel Put Informer in Jeopardy

Another Jack Anderson article in the *Washington Post* was titled, "Government Put Informer in Jeopardy":

> When Van started to "sing" to a congressional committee about alleged misconduct within the Justice Department, the feds put him in deadly jeopardy. He was abruptly withdrawn from the Justice Department's witness protection program and turned loose among the general prison population, where he could have been easy prey for the mobsters he had helped to send up.
>
> As I reported yesterday, Van's charges against the federal organized-crime strike force in Los Angeles led Rangel to ask Smith to investigate allegations of official corruption and dereliction of duty relating to narcotics enforcement in the Southwest. Van feels that he was betrayed by authorities who didn't like his charges against their strike force colleagues. It took congressional pressure to get the Justice Department to investigate the charges after years of delay.

The House committee's special investigator told my associate Indy Badhwar that he believes that Van was given a bad deal. Van received a punitive prison sentence after promises were made to intercede for him in return for his cooperation. This is also the opinion of Assistant U.S. Attorney Paul Corradini, who acknowledged the valuable help Van provided in breaking up the biggest, best organized and most profitable arson ring in the country.

In January 1980, several federal agents testified in Van's behalf at his pre-sentence hearing. Dennis Schloss, a Justice Department special prosecutor, testified that Van had been cooperating in federal investigations of arson, mail fraud and white slavery. Van "gave full and complete information to the federal grand jury, Schloss told the judge, adding, "A very large percentage of that information has been corroborated by independent investigative means."

Using Selected Information and Sequestering Other

Although federal authorities used Van's information in selected criminal cases, they ignored his charges of corruption in government offices. This changed, at least partially, for cosmetic purposes, when the Jack Anderson articles appeared in national newspapers. Their appearance caused Congressman Charles Rangel, chairman of the Select Committee On Narcotics Abuse and Control, to write a letter to Attorney General William French Smith. Rangel wrote that Van provided information "concerning allegations of official corruption and dereliction of duty relating to narcotics enforcement in the southwest area of the United States."

Rangel added: "Mr. Van's allegations are directed specifically against the Los Angeles strike force, its former, chief, Richard Crane, and its current leader, Jim Henderson. Crane, supervisor of the strike force in Los Angeles for 13 years, resigned his position and went into private practice. When Crane's clients have problems with the Los Angeles strike force [according to Van], they are rarely touched because the current chief, Jim Henderson, is a friend and former subordinate of Crane."

Rangel urged the Justice Department to "undertake a vigorous investigation" of the charges, as well as allegations involving Eddie Nash, a convicted felon who was Van's boss. Though the allegations were first made in 1979-80, there were no indictments in the Nash case until 1983. "Mr. Van surmised the indictments only occurred when the strike force realized the House select committee was looking into the matter. Michael E. Shaheen, head of the Office of Professional Responsibility, replied with the standard and meaningless "we have initiated an inquiry into Mr. Van's allegations."

Through the Freedom of Information Act, Jerry Van was able to get a copy of another letter Rangel wrote (November 15, 1983) to U.S. Attorney General French Smith. The copy, which Jerry Van received, was heavily censored:

This Committee recently received information concerning allegations of official corruption and dereliction of duty related to Narcotics enforcement in the southwest area of the United States. This information was given to us by Jerry Vann, a California prisoner in the United States witness protection program.

After receiving these allegations, this Committee conducted a preliminary investigation to look into these allegations on behalf of the Select Committee, to determine if there was any substance to them. Mr. Vann's allegations are directed specifically against the Los Angeles Crime Strike Force, its [head, James Henderson] and its [former head, Dick Crane] [redacted] (6)(7)(C) [two lines blacked out in letter]. According to Mr. Van, he is the [redacted] for the Aladdin Hotel Casino and [redacted] Barbary Casino. [redacted] clients are organized crime figures. When [redacted] clients have problems with the Los Angeles Strike Force, they are rarely touched because [redacted] is a friend and [redacted] In addition to these allegations, Mr. Vann described DEA "hand-to-hand" buys involving one [redacted] in a case as far back as 1979-1980, with no indictment until 1983. Mr. Vann surmised the indictments only occurred when the Strike Force realized the House Select Committee was looking into the matter.

I bring this matter to your attention and strongly urge you to undertake a vigorous investigation. While it is not my intention to interfere with or involve this Committee with investigation allegations of misconduct by Federal officials, I have every confidence that the Justice Department will obviate the need to do so.

Finally, shortly after Mr. Vann made these allegations, and the resulting inquiry on the part of this Committee, he was transferred from protective custody into the general prison population. While I do not want to draw conclusions from this act, it raises certain questions, particularly what conditions have changed that would diminish the need for Mr. Vann to be under witness protection.

I again urge you to inquire into this matter and share with me, to the extent possible, the results of your inquiry.

Sincerely,
Charles B. Rangel, Chairman

Van provided me with some of the deleted information: the former head of the strike force was Dick Crane and the subsequent head, James Henderson, which I then inserted into the report. Van wrote that they were "fixing organized crime cases for unsavory criminals who bought the federal government law enforcement badge and used it as a credit card to purchase their way out of criminal indictments like drug smuggling, drug sales, murder, and finally, corruption." Van also wrote that after a year of doing nothing, "this matter was turned over to the notorious office of the (OPR), who in turn quashed everything." OPR is the office of professional responsibility, notorious for cover-ups of corruption in government.

Removed From Witness Protection Program After Exposing Strike Force Corruption

Jerry Van was in prison when he first became a witness for the government. His testimony resulted in the successful prosecution and imprisonment of many people who were *really* guilty. Because of his testimony he was segregated from the general prison population under the federal government's witness protection program.

After Jerry Van started identifying corruption in the government's task force itself, Justice Department personnel retaliated by removing him from protected custody and placing him into the general prison population. Simultaneously, they made known to the prison population that he was a government witness responsible for imprisonment of numerous inmates. Van explained this dangerous situation in one of his letters:

> Because I exposed the Strike Force corruption I was taken off the program and cast in the middle of a prison compound where the feds put a snitch jacket on me, hoping someone would hurt me once the word spread.
>
> If it wasn't for Rep. Charles Rangel's quick response to the Attorney General, I could have very well been murdered and written off as just another prison murder that would have been written off as unrelated to Rangel's inquiry into Los Angeles Strike Force corruption. Anyway, to make a long story short, the federal government lap-dog agency, "Office of Professional Responsibility," cleared the Strike Force from any wrongdoing—which is not uncommon for that agency to clear their own.

***Wall Street Journal* Identified the Task Force Misconduct**

A *Wall Street Journal* article (October 20, 1990) listed some of the same people that Gerry Van had identified with the Los Angeles strike force. The article stated:

> As a federal prosecutor in the U.S. attorney's office [In Los Angeles, Drew Pitt] immersed himself in the labyrinthine world of big-time securities fraud and the smooth-talking con men who populate it. He would rail against what he saw as legal loopholes that let crooks pick the public's pockets. Stock fraud, he once said, was like a "burning match": The con

men lit and passed around the overvalued shares until a victim gets burned."

Now, however, there are indications that in his journey through the world of swindlers, Mr. Pitt may have ended up in league with some of them. In July of last year, he was quietly suspended from his post as an assistant U.S. attorney and put under investigation by a federal grand jury and the Justice Department's internal-affairs office.

Discussions with dozens of other people and an examination of documents indicate that authorities are looking into whether Mr. Pitt abused his broad powers as a federal prosecutor to enrich himself or protect certain people who were helping his investigations.

Stock-Promoter Network

The stakes go beyond the fate of a single prosecutor. There is growing evidence of widespread fraud in the sale of small-company stocks ranging from putting out false financial statements to bribing brokers to peddle shares to customers. At least four federal grand juries around the U.S. have been investigating this. In his work, Mr. Pitt was in a position to plug into the network of suspect stock deals, promoters, and brokers.

The key question for the Justice Department is what role if any he took in that network beyond his authorized investigative one. In 1994, while still an active prosecutor, Mr. Pitt and his wife gained control of a publicly held company. Through it, Mr. Pitt did business with people he had been investigating, according to SEC filings by the company and people familiar with his work.

Hopeless Situation Facing Anyone Targeted by the System

Jerry Van discovered the nearly hopeless situation of anyone exposing corruption in the "system." He was falsely charged with seeking to purchase cocaine, compensated government witnesses falsely testified against him, prosecutors made fabricated statements against him before the jury, the judge accepted blatant false testimony as the truth, and the gullible jury believed everything the prosecutor and prosecutor's witnesses stated. The jury refused to accept any of Gerry Van's statements.

Typical Sabotage by His Own Lawyer

Jerry Van also discovered what I had long ago discovered about defense lawyers sabotaging their own clients and protecting their relationship with prosecutors. He wrote: "Just before I was sentenced he [his lawyer] looked at me and said, 'I'll bet you will never tell on another AUSA again.'"

Today, Jerry Van is enduring the 25-year prison sentence inflicted upon him in retaliation for exposing corrupt officials in the corrupt system. Making these crimes even worse, this system wide corruption extends throughout government. It destroys the lives of thousands of people and families. It affects all aspects of government activities, including the events of 9/11 and the lying used to justify invading Iraq.

Others Tried to Provide Warnings

After discovering Hoorelbeke's letters, others tried to help. Charles Swan, the Executive Director of The Justice Lobby sent copies of these letters to *60-Minutes*, and received no response. Director Stephen Dresch of Forensic Intelligence International also sent letters, including one to Thomas Kean, Chairman of the National Commission on Terrorist Attacks Upon the United States. In answer to my request about the response from the 9/11 Commission, Dresch replied: "In answer to your question, we received NO response from the 9/11 Commission to our submission, not even an acknowledgement of receipt."

Their encounters with cover-ups, indifference, and outright criminality, that made possible decades of brutal consequences for many people and for the United States, duplicated what I had encountered for the prior 35 years

My Introduction to Gregory Scarpa Jr.

At the federal prison, Jerry Van became close friends with Gregory Scarpa, Jr. and they confided in each other. Gregory Scarpa told Jerry Van about the incestuous relationship between his father and FBI agent Lindley DeVecchio. In one letter that Jerry Van sent to me, he said:

> *My interest in Gregory Scarpa Jr. peaked when my friend Scarpa, Jr. would tell me how his father and himself had a key to the city [New York] so to speak. And this key was furnished by the F.B.I. with the agent's name being DeVecchio.*
>
> *I took this interest in Scarpa Jr. for two reasons: One, because I simply liked him as a person; Two, because his case was similar to my own. Whereas, we committed crimes for the government under their authority, and of course in the end, they denied giving us any authority whatsoever.*
>
> *Scarpa Jr. and myself had numerous conversations about himself and his legendary father, Scarpa Sr. Scarpa Jr. specifically told me his father was an F.B.I. top echelon informant. With that statement, Scarpa Jr. quickly stated that he had no involvement with the F.B.I. as an informant; he left that to his father. However, Scarpa Jr. did tell me that he informed on terrorist Ramzi Yousef to the F.B.I. and that he also had the blessing of the mob to inform on Yousef.*
>
> *The information Yousef gave Scarpa Jr. was advance warnings about future bombings in New York, and Atlanta, Georgia, which included TWA Flight 800, Atlanta Olympic games, and the 9/11 hijackings of four airliners that brought down the World Trade Center. I was especially shocked to hear his story of advance warnings of these bombings.*
>
> *And yet, no one did a thing to stop any of the bombings. In my book, Underworld Secrets, I wrote about how Ramzi Yousef bragged to me about how the World Trade Center towers were going to be taken down by using*

our planes as bombs. I too notified the F.B.I. They did nothing to stop this terrible tragedy that occurred on 9/11 in New York, and took innocent lives for no other reason than to protect an FBI agent's career.

I say that because if my tip was followed upon, then certainly Scarpa's Jr's. information would also have to come into play, as he also forewarned the FBI of Yousef's intents. But credibility could not be given to Scarpa Jr. because he was also giving up information about corruption in the F.B.I. between his father and Special Agent DeVecchio.

If Scarpa Jr.'s World Trade Center information turned out to be true (and it was), then he would have been a national hero, with that said, then DeVecchio of the F.B.I. would also have to fall. The F.B.I. could not discredit one of their own, so no one paid attention to Scarpa Jr., and my advance warning of future American terrorist bombings to take place in this country. Simply put, all the F.B.I. wagons circled DeVecchio to protect him from Scarpa Jr.'s accusations.

To verify much of Scarpa Jr.'s involvement with Yousef., and future bombings that were to take place in America, especially in the New York area. I was given by Scarpa Jr. sealed court documents that contained 302 forms (investigative statements taken by the F.B.I). The forms were statements taken in advance of any future bombings that did in fact take place, abroad, and in this country. Yet the F.B.I. did nothing to forewarn the American public. At least, they could forewarn the airports to be on the lookout for any suspicious activity.

Then Scarpa Jr. also advised me of the following concerning corrupt activities between his father, Scarpa Sr. and F.B.I. Special Agent L. DeVecchio:

About the murder of a woman who was an F.B.I. informant—DeVecchio furnished that info to Scarpa Sr. who killed her with help [Gregory Scarpa Jr.]

Also about two or three other murders that DeVecchio furnished information to Scarpa Sr., so that Scarpa Sr. could hit them, or have them killed.

During the 60s Scarpa Sr. went to Mississippi with the F.B.I. handled that handled Scarpa Sr. before DeVecchio handled him. At any rate, the three civil rights (college students) that were murdered there by thugs. One of these thugs was beaten almost to death by Scarpa Sr. until he confessed to his role in the civil rights murders.

Also that Scarpa Jr. was blamed for a lot of what his father did.

About the murder of a guy who was under F.B.I. surveillance, FBI agent DeVecchio pulled the surveillance off of the murder victim so Scarpa Sr. could murder him.

DeVecchio also alerted Scarpa Sr. of current indictments—one being out for Scarpa Jr. who fled to Florida, then returned to New Jersey where he was finally arrested in a hotel room occupied by himself, his wife, and daughter.

Also, Scarpa Jr. fixed the mobs books, so that money paid to agent DeVecchio would not show up on the books.

DeVecchio handed over to Scarpa Sr. names, telephone numbers and addresses of rival Mafia members in the Colombo family so that they could be murdered.

That Scarpa Sr. had guns placed at Victor Orena's home so the authorities could find them and send Orena to prison. This got Orena out of the way from being the head of the Colombo Crime Family.

Involvement of DeVecchio being a lookout while the Scarpa's burglarized banks on weekends when the banks were closed.

That, even though DeVecchio was a supervisor in the F.B.I. He still got authority from his supervisors—and that DeVecchio was not only acting on his own—but one of the players among the many corrupt F.B.I. agents.

Scarpa Jr. asked me to help reveal his story. I told him to forget about contracting the Office of Professional Responsibility, the watch dog office within the government that oversees corruption within the government agencies. The Office of Professional Responsibility is a front agency for the government that covers up corruption instead of revealing it. Scarpa Jr. agreed with me; we took other avenues to expose Scarpa Jr.'s story of truth.

Its interesting to note that Scarpa Jr. also told me that the prosecutor who prosecuted him was a woman by the name of Valerie Caproni who did everything in her power to discredit Scarpa Jr., and that she is now ironically an F.B.I. attorney in Washington, D.C.

Finally, I was told that Agent DeVecchio was so corrupt that he had corrupt judges and prosecutors going along with whatever DeVecchio wants.

Sincerely,
Gerald Van Hoorelbeke
AKA Jerry Van

Becoming Confidant of Major Mafiosi

Through Jerry Van Hoorelbeke, Gregory Scarpa contacted me and over a period of months he provided me considerable information about his knowledge of FBI covert activities and that of his relationship to the al Qaeda terrorists. In one of his letters (August 27, 2002) to me, Scarpa wrote:

My information will consist on how and when the FBI and high-ranking members of the Colombo Crime Family in New York worked together and eventually caused an internal war in the crime family. The member was my father, Gregory Scarpa, Sr., and also myself, Gregory

Scarpa, Jr. Because of numerous murders and their numerous indictments, a big cover-up ensued.

This relationship was headed by Supervisory Agent R. Lindley DeVecchio, Gregory Scarpa Sr., and Gregory Scarpa, Jr., began approximately 1979. But Gregory Sr. was on both sides (FBI and Mobster) for three decades going back to 1963—before DeVecchio; the other FBI agent was Mr. Anthony Villano.

My information consists of not only ignored Scarpa's (Sr. and Jr.) day-to-day criminal activities in which the FBI agents assisted in the Mafia killings success. For much of this I have documentation, which also includes FBI agents giving Scarpa [Sr.] the names of other FBI snitches, enabling Scarpa to put them in harms way, while shielding his own illegal operations; FBI agents telling us where the FBI was placing wiretaps so we can avoid them; handing over the addresses of Scarpa's enemies in the Colombo Crime Family war so that Scarpa, Sr. could track them down and kill them; fabricating evidence against Vic Orena and other Scarpa adversaries so they would be sent to prison.

Also, involvement with being a lookout while me, my father, and others, would burglarize banks while they were closed for the weekends. I have so much more information that goes back to the 1960s.

Most Mafia books seem to have went well. I can't see a book with the Mafia and FBI as partners until the cover-up ensued go wrong. But with your expertise you know better than I. I am also not sure if we can use their real names.

Being that I'm in prison and if you are interested, all the legal issues of writing a book, deal for a movie or TV, I would go with my daughter as for signing contracts or whatever,

Sincerely,
Gregory Scarpa, Jr.

I accepted, and we signed a contract (October 15, 2002) whereby I would write a book on his life with the Colombo mafia family and its relationship with FBI Supervisory Agent Lindley DeVecchio. Among the many things he told me was how he kept the books for the Colombo family, how he had the task of putting money aside every week to pay DeVecchio, and to provide for the FBI agent periodic hotel rooms, champagne, and call girls. He provided me with considerable documentation to support his statements.

In a February 19, 2003, letter, Scarpa enclosed documents of DeVecchio's testimony at Scarpa's criminal trial:

I'm enclosing what I have of FBI DeVecchio's limited testimony at my trial, also Scarpa issue motions from attorney James Froccaro who repre-

sented at the time a co-defendant of mine and the other motion from my court-appointed attorney, which at the beginning was very good until the government got to him. I'm also sending you an affirmation prepared by attorney Flora Edwards for the Committee on Government Reform. These documents will have information for you to log as well as some answers to a few of your questions of Set One—areas to consider.

At the moment I am working on the questions Set One, as I complete some answers I'll send it to you.

Sincerely,
Greg

Father, Son, and FBI Agent Anthony Villano

Gregory described how in the 1970's his father introduced him to FBI Agent Anthony Villano, stating that the two of them worked closely together. Gregory was 16 years of age at that time. The meeting occurred at a gymnasium where Gregory was training for the golden gloves. Villano advised Gregory that he was a good fighter, but that there were easier ways to make money. He encouraged Gregory to work with his father—which, the FBI agent knew, was primarily criminal activities in liaison with the FBI.

Gregory learned later that instead of his father working *for* the FBI, that the FBI agent was *working for his father*, and that the FBI agents with whom his father was associated received substantial sums of money and other perks. He learned that, as part of the cozy arrangement, FBI agents were providing his father with confidential FBI information and protecting him from prosecution.[25]

Teaching His Son the Tricks of the Trade

Gregory described being taught by his father to shoot a gun at the age of 16, and how his father started involving him in criminal activities at a young age. These activities included the sale of drugs and the murder of at least two people in the mid-1980's, including Patrick Porco and a teenager whose nickname was "Meatballs" Since these activities were known to FBI agents, Gregory assumed they were OK.

Scarpa Sr. Early Work with the FBI

Gregory told me about how the FBI, in 1964, hired his father to find the murderers of three civil rights workers killed in Mississippi, and provided Scarpa with a pistol and authority to kill if needed. The three murdered by the KKK were Michael Schwerner, James Chaney, and Andrew Goodman.

The FBI, under direction of FBI Direct J. Edgar Hoover, reportedly gave the name of one of the local Ku Klux Klan members to Scarpa and gave him

[25] (This information appeared in court proceedings as Exhibit R: Scarpa, Jr. Affidavit at §3)

authority to do whatever was necessary to find the three missing civil rights workers and their murderers. Scarpa, Sr., was rising in the Colombo crime family and was more than willing to carry out the FBI's attempt to find the murderers.

Scarpa and his girlfriend, Mary Schiro, flew to Miami, registered at the Fontainebleau Hotel, where they were met by FBI agents who provided Scarpa a pistol and money. Scarpa then left for Mississippi, telling his girl friend that if he didn't come back, take the money and go home. Scarpa then left for the Mississippi town of Philadelphia.

FBI agents told Scarpa the Klan member most likely to reveal where the bodies were buried, and who operated an appliance store. Scarpa placed a deposit on a television set with the Klan member and then said he would be back that evening with the balance. Upon his return that evening, Scarpa asked the Klan member to help carry the television set to the car.

As the Klan member bent over to put the television set in the car, Scarpa hit him in the back of the head with an iron pipe, shoved him into the trunk, and drove off to a remote location. Scarpa shoved a pistol into his mouth and told him to reveal where the civil rights workers were located or the trigger would be pulled. The Klan member than took Scarpa to the burial spot. Seven men were subsequently indicted for the killings, including the deputy sheriff of the small town of Philadelphia, Mississippi.

Although the murderers were discovered and prosecuted, FBI agents, with the complicity of FBI Director Hoover, engaged in several major felonies, including crossing state lines to commit felonies and conspiracy to commit felonies.

Gregory told me about how his father died in June 1994 from the AIDS virus, which he had contracted during a transfusion with HIV tainted blood during an operation for ulcers in 1986. Gregory filed a lawsuit against the Brooklyn hospital and doctor that were responsible and a financial settlement was reached in August 1992. It was reportedly $200,000 to be paid by the hospital and $100,000 by the surgeon.

Confidential FBI 302 Forms

Jerry Van and Scarpa sent me copies of confidential FBI 302 forms, including those in prior pages that revealed the relationship between Scarpa Sr. and FBI agent DeVecchio. It would soon become clear to me why DOJ personnel wanted to discredit Scarpa. The two main reasons were (a) the involvement of FBI supervisory agent Lindley DeVecchio with Gregory's father, Gregory Scarpa Sr. and numerous murders; and (b) the terrorist acts that Scarpa told DOJ personnel were planned, which the FBI and DOJ personnel ignored, resulting in thousands of deaths and even worse collateral damage.

Mafia Headquarters Viewing FBI Surveillance Tapes

Gregory described how in the mid-1980s he was watching FBI surveillance tapes taken outside the group's Wimpy Boys Club headquarters; tapes provided to them by FBI supervisory agent Lindley DeVecchio.

He described how his father was an informant for FBI Special Agent Tony Villano, and then in the early 1980s, Scarpa established a similar relationship with FBI agent Lindley DeVecchio. Scarpa's son, Gregory, remembered his father saying, "The relationship with DeVecchio was going to be even better than with Villano."

Frequent Secret Meetings between Scarpa and FBI

Gregory described the visits, two or three times a week, by DeVecchio, to the home of his father, which his father shared with his common law wife, Linda Schiro.

FBI Agent Received Percentage of Bank Robbery Loot

Gregory described how he kept the books, including the payments that his father made to DeVecchio, and the role played by DeVecchio in a bank robbery that Gregory's father committed:

> *During this period I worked for my father in his various enterprises. One of my duties was keeping the tally on my father's numbers racket. In this connection, my father instructed me to allocate a portion of the proceeds from his numbers racket to DeVecchio. This amount covered all of the favors that DeVecchio did for my father.*
>
> *DeVecchio was present during a bank robbery at which I was present, in order to insure that we were not arrested. DeVecchio's cut of the proceeds came out of my father's numbers racket. Over the years, DeVecchio received over $100,000 from my father, including an all expense trip to Aspen Colorado in the 1980's, which was paid for by my father.*
>
> *DeVecchio provided my father with information concerning the location of his loan sharking customers. On a number of occasions DeVecchio also provided my father with surveillance tapes including FBI tapes of the Wimpy Boys Social Club, which I viewed along with my younger brother Joseph Schiro.*
>
> *In addition, DeVecchio provided information to my father regarding the identification of individuals who were informants and who could be a danger to my father. After my father received the information he killed the individuals who were reported to be a threat to him and then reported the murders to DeVecchio.*
>
> *For example my father killed Joseph DiDomenico ("Joey Brewster") because DeVecchio told him that Joey was getting too nosey about my father's business and may have known that my father was an informant. After my father killed Brewster he reported the killing to DeVecchio who protected him by attributing the murder to another crew. In late Fall, 1991 or*

Spring, 1992 my father told me that Joseph Ambrosino was a "rat" but that he didn't have to worry because Ambrosino wouldn't hurt him.

Scarpa-DeVecchio Plan Escalating the Colombo War

At another time, during a deposition, Gregory described plans by his father and DeVecchio that started the war between competing Colombo factions:

In the early Nineties, DeVecchio and my father came up with a plan to create dissension within the Colombo family and in the process eliminate anyone who could be a danger to my father. DeVecchio and my father planned to destroy the entire Colombo Family and create a leadership vacuum in which a "Scarpa" family would emerge with my father at the head.

Fueling Gang-Fights in Colombo Crime Family

In the early 1990s the power struggle erupted between rivals in the Colombo family. Carmine Persico had been the head of the Colombo family for over 20 years. But after he and his son, Alphonse, were sentenced to prison on RICO charges, there was a battle over whether Persico's group would be the boss of the Colombo family or the Orena faction.

Referring to the in-fighting among the Colombo crime family, between the Persico faction that his father supported and that of Orena, Gregory wrote:

DeVecchio provided my father with the addresses of the men who were loyal to Orena. As a result of the attacks, Victor Orena went into hiding. DeVecchio and my father had a plan to plant guns at the house where Orena was staying to ensure Orena's arrest and conviction. Orena's arrest was supposed to be a "trophy" for DeVecchio.

My father told me that he and DeVecchio rode in one car and my stepbrother, Joey, drove another car, which carried the guns in the trunk. They parked some distance from the house and my father and DeVecchio watched while Joey planted the gun.

Federal Judge Blocked Testifying About Serious FBI Misconduct

In one letter (January 6, 2003), Gregory described how a federal judge acted to protect the FBI misconduct, which also denied Gregory his legal rights at trial:

Here are my transcripts to give you some information from my younger days as an associate and when I was inducted into the mob, condoned by the FBI and other info gives dates and crimes all condoned by the FBI (DeVecchio). My testimony was very limited because my court appointed attorney wouldn't go into the murders that the FBI had full knowledge about. Also, the court wouldn't allow a lot of first hand info I had with the FBI and my father.

Scarpa Provided Information on Similar FBI Corruption to Committee Investigating FBI Matters in Boston and Lawyers

In one letter (April 3, 2003) Scarpa wrote that he provided information to the committee holding hearings on the FBI misconduct in Boston, which indicated a cover-up by that committee since it made no mention of these matters in its two-volume report. If it had been included in the report, it would show that the criminal activities of the FBI, both local and Washington headquarters, was an institutional problem rather than localized. Scarpa's letter stated:

Rodney, the project that I have been working on with you was temporarily sidetracked because of numerous legal visits I received from investigators and attorneys who needed information for a Congressional hearing on FBI misconduct and cover-ups. I gave them a 36-page affidavit on certain people from the mob who were charged for murder, convicted, and are doing life in prison which in fact had nothing to do with the murders charged.

How I know they were wrongly charged or framed, is that I know for a fact my father committed the murders during the Colombo War. The investigators also wanted and received information about the terrorists I spied on which was covered up. They're bringing the information to the congressional hearing also. As soon as I receive a copy of the affidavit I will send it to you.

FBI Form 302 Reports on Scarpa's Mole Status in al Qaeda Cell Headed by Infamous Ramzi Yousef

The following FBI 302 reports, starting in 1996, are a sampling of FBI reports during a nine-month period showing that FBI personnel gave credibility to the information Scarpa obtained from al Qaeda terrorist Ramzi Yousef. High-level FBI-DOJ personnel, to protect FBI supervisor Lindley DeVecchio from prosecution in the serial murders in which he was involved, then discredited Scarpa. Some excerpts of the reports that Gregory sent to me follows:

Gregory Scarpa, Jr. was interviewed at Manhattan Correctional Center (MCC) at 159 Park Row, New York, New York. Scarpa was advised of the identity of the interviewing Agent and the nature of the interview. The terms of the interview related only to matters of terrorism and were defined at the beginning of the meeting. These terms were identical to the terms defined in the May 1, 1996 meeting held at the United States Attorney's office (USAO) Southern District of New York (SDNY). Scarpa then provided the following information [This introduction appeared in every report, along with the date the information was obtained, the date the information was dictated, and the date of the transcript]:

Firstly, Scarpa transferred a hand-written note to SA [redacted]*. Scarpa advised that the note was a second written copy of a note delivered by*

Scarpa to Yousef. The note conveyed that Scarpa was getting a telephone number for a company called ROMA to give to Yousef for overseas calls. Scarpa also wrote that a fax number would be available to Yousef. The note also contained Yousef's response, which was obtained verbally and subsequently written down by Scarpa. Yousef responded asking for the telephone number and questioning how he could use the fax.

When questioned regarding the incident to take place within the next two to three weeks and the incident associated with the Olympics, Scarpa stated he believes these are two separate events and both will involve U.S. airliners. He believes that the first event may take place within the next week or two as approximately one week has already elapsed. Scarpa did not know through what channels Yousef would receive the information. An individual, possibly Bojinka, is coming from England to Atlanta to check security measures at the Olympics. This person may already be in the United States.

Scarpa stated that he will receive the details on the planned events before they happen because Yousef wants Scarpa to "do something" to a U.S. Government installation and wants the details prior to the event taking place. Scarpa expects to obtain the information regarding secreting bombs on airliners whether Yousef goes through with his plans or not. Scarpa stated that Yousef knows this information would be useful because Scarpa's people only know how to "burn things" and "shoot people."

Scarpa advised that Yousef began slipping papers to him, ½ sheet of paper rolled up with writing on them. According to Scarpa, Yousef writes in sentences. Scarpa advised that when Yousef slips him these papers he writes on the paper that he wants this back. Scarpa advised he has only kept the notes for a matter of minutes, approximately 10 minutes, just long enough to write some things down.

Scarpa advised he may get one note a day or one every couple of days. According to Scarpa, the number of notices varies according to the circumstances at the MCC. Scarpa advised Yousef does not give his notes back to him, but expects Scarpa to return Yousef's notes quickly. Scarpa believes Yousef throws the notes in the toilet.

Scarpa advised these notes, referred to as "kites," are passed from inmate to inmate, in newspapers, or through holes in the walls of the cells.

Scarpa advised that there is a guard permanently assigned to both Ismail and Yousef and sometimes they check the newspaper before it's given to Ismail or Yousef and sometimes they do not.

According to Scarpa, Yousef told him, "If you're interested, I'll teach you things nobody knows."

[Al Qaeda Plans to Blow Up Airliners]

Yousef told Scarpa I'll teach you how to blow up airplanes and how to make bombs and then you can get the information to your people. Yousef told Scarpa I can show you how to get a bomb on an airplane through a metal detector. Yousef told Scarpa he would teach him how to make timing devices.

According to Scarpa, Yousef wants to hurt the United States government and wants to teach Scarpa how. Scarpa advised that Yousef has not asked for any specific help. Scarpa advised that Yousef wants to blow things up, but he does not say why.

Yousef told Scarpa during Yousef's trial that his local al Qaeda members had a plan to blow up a plane to show that they are serious and then make their demands and for a mistrial to be declared. Scarpa advised that blowing up an airplane during the trial seems easy to Yousef. Yousef never mentioned a specific airline as a target.

[Unprecedented opportunity to meet local al Qaeda Members, that would shortly commit major terrorist attacks upon the United States.]

According to Scarpa, Yousef believes that Scarpa is in touch with people on the outside. Yousef told Scarpa if things get going we may be able to hook up. If you're serious, my people and your people can meet.

[Yousef Showed Scarpa a Sketch of a Bomb-Timing Device]

Yousef drew a sketch of the circuitry for make the bomb timing device, which coincided exactly with the timing device used on the bomb that exploded on the Philippine Airline plane, and what was found in Yousef's Manila apartment after it was raided by Philippine police.

FBI 302 Report Describing Scarpa's Personal Meeting with Key FBI-DOJ Personnel March 7, 1996

A March 7, 1996, FBI 302 report showed one of numerous personal meetings between Scarpa and key FBI-DOJ personnel, representing confidence in the unprecedented information being obtained from one of al Qaeda's primary terrorist plotters:

At the request of GREGORY SCARPA, JR., Date of Birth: August 3, 1951, he was interviewed at the office of the United States Attorney, Eastern District of New York, Brooklyn, New York. Present at this interview was SCARPA's Attorney, Lawrence Silverman, Assistant United States Attorneys (AUSA) DEITRICH SNELL and PATRICK FITZGERALD, Southern District of New York and EVELYN CORCELLA, and VALERIE CAPRONI, Chief of the Criminal Division, Eastern District of New York, and Special Agents PAMELA M.. McDAID and HOWARD LEADBETTER II (FBI); and RICHARD CORAGGIO (INS).

Unprecedented Invitation to Meet Local al Qaeda Members

In a note from Scarpa to Yousef, Scarpa set up the fictitious outside telephone contact, Roma Corporation, for Yousef to make telephone calls to al Qaeda members in the New York-New Jersey areas and to the Middle East. The United States, never in its history, had such a treasure trove of information about al Qaeda operations and plans. A May 9, 1996, note from Scarpa to Yousef stated:

How are you Buddy?

I hope your case went well for you today. As I told you, my lawyer [Larry Silverman] is pretty good. As soon as he received the info from my people, he brought it right up.

Phone, as I already gave you: [redacted]

Fax: [redacted]

You're to say: Ronnie calling—I'd like to make a phone call.

You send your fax to:

George Smith
% Roma Corp.
[redacted] *Suite 2252*
NY, NY 10010

FBI Report Yousef Wanting to Call Middle East al Qaeda Members, Dated May 9, 1996.

That FBI 302 report stated:

Scarpa transferred a handwritten note to Special Agent (SA) [redacted]. Scarpa advised that the note was written by Scarpa and was documentation of events taking place on May 7, 1996 and May 8, 1996. Scarpa stated that Yousef returned from court on May 7, 1996, and was very upset. Yousef stated that Assistant United States Attorney (AUSA) Michael Garcia was smirking during court. Yousef stated that Garcia has lost his life for sure.

Yousef has been asking to use the phone. Scarpa stated that the guards have been turning him down. Yousef mentioned that he needs to make a phone call to overseas to find out about the airplane situation. Yousef stated that his people are waiting for advice, but he's concerned that they may go ahead with the plan even if he cannot contact them. Scarpa suggested to Yousef that he write a "cop-out" (a grievance) to Lieutenant Desman regarding use of the phone. Yousef stated if the Lieutenant does not resolve the problem he will have to take the issue to court.

[Iranian connection]

Yousef stated that he had to use the phone prior to 10:00 a.m. or after 9:30 p.m. because of the time difference in Iran. Scarpa suggested that arrangements be made to give Yousef recreation or phone calls on Saturday and Sunday and/or give Yousef phone privileges up to 11:00 p.m. Scarpa suggested the possibility of giving Yousef recreation on the tier; however, the time difference may become an issue.

Scarpa received a handwritten note on May 8, 1996. Scarpa photographed the kite. The kite indicated that Murad is presently working with the prosecutors and the Federal Bureau of Investigation (FBI). However, Yousef indicated that this was a plan, and Murad is not telling the prosecutors and the FBI the truth.

Scarpa stated that the information regarding the timing devices and explosives was received from Yousef. Scarpa rethought this issue and now is not sure if the kite was sent directly from Yousef or if the kite was sent from Murad through Yousef to Scarpa. [This related to plans for placing bombs on U.S. airliners.]

Scarpa stated that the incident to take place within a week or two will be an airline bombing while the Atlanta incident will be a facility. [Several weeks later, TWA Flight 800 was downed, and the Atlanta bombings occurred. Again, this was further support for the credibility of information obtained by Scarpa and conveyed to local FBI agents.]

Scarpa was given the address of "Roma" by SA [redacted]. Scarpa stated that Yousef would like to use the fax. Scarpa was questioned by Yousef when Scarpa transferred the phone number to "Roma." Yousef questioned how Scarpa was able to receive the number when Scarpa does not have visits on that day. Scarpa stated that the number was given to Silverman in a sealed envelope and Silverman delivered it to Scarpa.

FBI Report of Interview with Scarpa, dated May 16, 1996]

That FBI 302 report stated:

Scarpa transferred three (3) handwritten notes to Special Agent [redacted]. Scarpa advised that two of the notes were written by Scarpa, and one (1) note was written by Yousef. The first note was a handwritten note by Scarpa pertaining to the events taking place on the evening of May 13, 1996. Scarpa stated that Yousef was discussing Shah and how Shah got arrested. Yousef told Scarpa that Shah was arrested because a friend of Shah's gave him up to the Federal Bureau of Investigation (FBI).

Yousef stated that this same person is going to turn over more names soon. Yousef said he sent a coded message to Bojinga [Osama bin Ladin] and informed Bojinga of this person living in Qatar.

[Qatar was where U.S. forces were later stationed.]

Yousef believes that this person will be killed soon. Yousef stated that this person was informing on Shah and that the FBI told him to find out Shah's location. This person pretended to be bringing money to Shah to give up his location. Yousef stated that this person was not recruited by the FBI at first, it was another intelligence agency. This person was recruited from a club in his country where he used to hang out.

Yousef stated that once Bojinga gets this coded message, he is sure that this person will "lose his head". Yousef suggested to Bojinga to kidnap and torture this person before killing him to find out the names and addresses of the people who recruited him so they can be killed also. Yousef also suggested attacking the U.S. Embassy in Qatar, or another one in another country if it is easier. Yousef said that this would be a way to punish the U.S. for participating in the arrest of Shah. Yousef said the person who gave up Shah was paid a lot of money and is living like a king.

Scarpa asked Yousef if he had received word regarding the airline situation. Yousef stated that Scarpa should know why Yousef has not. Scarpa interpreted this to mean Yousef has not been able to use the phone. Yousef stated that as soon as Yousef knows what is going on, Yousef will tell Scarpa. Yousef wants to know where, when, and how Scarpa is going to perform his terrorist act on a government installation. Scarpa told Yousef that things would be easier if Yousef would give Scarpa the method to get bombs thorough security. Yousef replied, "Soon."

The second note was a handwritten note by Scarpa pertaining to the events taking place on May 14, 1996. Scarpa stated that Yousef believes if he can "get rid" of a few witnesses on his case, he can easily win. Yousef is waiting for confirmation from his lawyer about a certain professor that Yousef knows. If this professor is going to be a witness, Yousef said he can easily be killed. Yousef heard about the witness in court the other day and said that the witness might be someone else. Yousef stated that his people are short on funds and they have to decide who they want to kill. Scarpa felt that Yousef was hinting about Scarpa killing SA Williams. Scarpa told Yousef that his people are working on killing Williams. Yousef said, "Good".

Yousef later told Scarpa that he was writing a kite to indicate what the people at "Roma" should say if the FBI or anyone else questions them. Scarpa advised the kite was handwritten by Yousef on May 14, 1996. Scarpa transferred the kite to SA [redacted]. Yousef wanted to thank "Roma" for giving him the number to call overseas. Yousef stated that he was not able to use the number yet because he could not get the time. Yousef stated that he appreciates the help in getting in touch with his parents and wants to pay it back when he can. Yousef wants Scarpa to explain Yousef's situation and the charges against him. Yousef does not want "Roma" to be considered a co-conspirator and to get hurt trying to help Yousef.

Scarpa stated that Lieutenant Desman told Yousef on May 15, 1996, that they are working on the phones to make it easier to call out. Yousef stated that he needs the phone for 9:30. Lieutenant Desman told Yousef to put it in writing. Scarpa advised that Yousef requested phone use on Tuesday, May 14, 1996 and Wednesday May 15, 1996, and that he wants to use the tier phone. Scarpa stated that there are now nine (9) people on the tier. Scarpa stated that everyone gets phone privileges during their recreation time, but Yousef does not get his recreation on the tier.

Scarpa stated that he thinks Yousef may have a feeling something is going to happen but does not have contact right now to know for sure.

Scarpa thinks that Yousef may think he will win his first trial so he is waiting until the second trial to "hurt" Assistant United States Attorney Michael Garcia.

May 19, 1996, FBI 302 Report Shows Yousef Advising al Qaeda to Start Bombing Airplanes

That FBI 302 report stated:

"Yousef holding the kite, while I read it through the wall. Yousef advised his people to start the bombing of airplanes. ... The FBI knows this info is very accurate because they heard parts of it on the 3-way line, Susan told me."

How to smuggle explosives into an airplane. All explosive substances of a density higher than 2 kg/l should not be used due to the possibility of detecting them by X-ray machines. The following explosives have a density less than 2 and can easily be smuggled:

Tetrazene .
Acetone Peroxide.
RDX.
HMTD
DDNP
HMX

Attached to that report was the following "kite" given by Ramzi Yousef to Scarpa:

How to Smuggle Explosives into an Airplane Sun. 5/19

1. When talking about smuggling explosives into an airplane, it is meant by that explosive substances which are going to be placed in an airplane Later, to be used for blowing up the airplane. Therefore, the quantity of explosive substances which we'll be talking about, is the quantity needed to blow up an airplane, which is equivalent to 300 gm of TNT. For 747-400 airplane, at 30,000 feet altitude. For substances which are more powerful than TNT, the quantity needed would be less. Then, 300 gm. Depending on its power compared to TNT.

2. All metallic substances, or substances which contain metals, cannot be used or smuggled into the airplane because they are easily detected by x-ray

machines and metal detectors. Therefore, all azpoeas and mercury compounds explosive substances should not be used.

3. All explosive substances of a density higher than 2 Kg/c should not be used due to the possibility of detecting them by x-ray machines. The following explosive substances have a density less than 2 and can be easily smuggled:

Tetrazene (Guanyl Nitro Soaminocun nyltetrazene)(sp?)
Acetone peroxide.
R.D.X.
H.M.T.D. (Hexomethyle Triperoxide Diamine)
D.D.N.P. (Diazodinitrophenel)
H.M.X. (Cyclotetramethylenetetranitramine)

All liquid explosives can be used.

1. When an explosive substance is smuggled into an airplane, than it can be assembled easily inside the airplane.

2. A detonator can be hid in a heel of a shoe.

3. The wiring and 9V battery can be hidden inside a shaving machine or a toy.

The above explosive substances which are in powder form can also be smuggled in an airplane easily by hiding them in the holes in the heel of a shoe, or by putting them in medicine capsules.

May 20, 1996, FBI 302 Form Reporting al Qaeda's Plan to Shortly Bomb an Airliner Departing a Local Airport

In that report, the FBI agent reports terrorist attacks on several U.S. targets (that did occur). Including the downing of TWA Flight 800. Yousef also suggested *[via coded message to his source outside the prison]* to attack the U.S. Embassy in Qatar, or another one in another country if it is easier.

Yousef originally was not going to give Scarpa the technique of secreting bombs if the plans were canceled, However, Yousef changed his mind when he received money into his commissary account, believing it to be from Scarpa. Scarpa also stated that Yousef has not been sending kites as much and has been more verbal because he became paranoid when the Captain came into Scarpa's cell.

Scarpa received the current bomb information on a note from Yousef. The note was written in Yousef's handwriting. Scarpa wrote down the information from the note and returned the original to Yousef. Scarpa gave his written information to Silverman.

Scarpa stated that Yousef is still trying to confirm AUSA Michael Garcia's address. Yousef gave Scarpa the address, which Yousef believes is Garcia's address. Scarpa gave Yousef Garcia's business address. Yousef believes that Scarpa is currently working to obtain Garcia's home address.

Scarpa believes that Yousef has the right address but has not conveyed this information to Yousef at this time. Yousef stated that there is time to find the information because they plan to "hurt" Garcia possibly during the second trial to occur in September, October, Or November to obtain a mistrial. Yousef's people are to do the hit on Garcia while Scarpa's people are to do the hit on SA David Williams. Yousef has not mentioned the hit on SA Williams recently because he felt better after getting the money.

Scarpa thought that Yousef was not using his paralegal anymore because he did not feel comfortable with this person. He thought Yousef had stopped using this person when Yousef arrived at MCC. Scarpa did not know the identity of this person. Scarpa did not know how Yousef gets his information out of MCC. He thought information was possibly transmitted through Ismail's uncle at one time. Scarpa could not provide further information pertaining to Yousef's sister or brother-in-law.

> Scarpa was then informed that the camera would be collected on May 6 or May 7, 1996. [This was the camera provided to Scarpa by FBI| agents; another sign that the FBI agents working with Scarpa considered the information creditable.]

FBI report of interview with Scarpa, dated May 28, 1996

An FBI 302 report (with its first page missing) refers to information obtained by Scarpa concerning placing bombs on airliners without being detected:

> Scarpa advised that the notes regarding bomb smuggling were copies from a note from Yousef. However, Scarpa attempts to detail all of his notes to exactly what is said or what has happened so there are no misunderstandings. Scarpa stated that at times Yousef holds notes up for Scarpa to read from his cell. Scarpa and Yousef can see each other through holes in the walls where beds were bolted. These beds have been removed and the holes were never fixed.
>
> **[Local al Qaeda Members and Olympic Bombing]**
>
> Scarpa transferred a handwritten note to the interviewing Agent. Scarpa advised that the note was written by Scarpa and detailed the events of Thursday, May 23, 1996 and Friday, May 24, 1996. On Thursday, May 23rd, Scarpa asked Yousef if Yousef's friends in New York are the same people looking at the security at the Atlanta Games. Yousef told Scarpa that the people going to Atlanta are not the same.
>
> The Atlanta people are coming from England and Yousef stated that this information was already given to Scarpa. Scarpa questions Yousef about the relationship between Yousef and the person who calls himself Bojinga (not the real Bojinga). Yousef did not seem to give Scarpa a straight answer. Yousef stated that he was doing legal work and would talk to Scarpa later at approximately 9:00 p.m. Yousef stated that he was going to pray, eat, and go to sleep.

On Friday, May 24, 1996, Scarpa advised that Yousef was upset that nothing has happened with SA Dave Williams. Scarpa advised Yousef that the person working on the Williams' contract was arrested on drug charges with some of the people who were supposed to do the hit. Scarpa asked Yousef if there was something else they could do for him.

Yousef stated that he wants Scarpa's people to call in three bomb threats to United Airlines international flights on three separate occasions within one week. The purpose is to cause disturbance and fear among people flying airplanes and it would cause financial problems for the airline.

Yousef stated that he wants to know when the calls will be made because Yousef's people will do three additional threats after Scarpa does his three threats. Yousef wants the threats to be made a few hours after departure to cause the airline to turn around and land. Yousef wants the blame to be placed on a militia group on behalf of the Freeman for how the Federal Bureau of Investigation (FBI) is handling the situation. Scarpa said it would take a couple of weeks for the plan to go into effect. Yousef stated that if Scarpa's people fail at this to never speak with Yousef again.

Yousef also stated that the airline people should be contacted instead of the airline office because the airline people will react faster. Yousef also said that Scarpa's people should not leave fingerprints and make the bomb threats from a street phone. Yousef said he needs ten days to get a message to his people and another ten days to get the act done. Yousef stated that the people in Atlanta will do the threats. Yousef said they will do the threats three weeks from now. Yousef indicated that one of the two people in Atlanta speaks with an American accent and can give credit to the Freeman militia. Yousef advised that these two people are in Atlanta this week.

On Monday, May 27, 1996, Scarpa wrote down suggestions. Scarpa suggested to rotate cells next Friday (May 31st) and wrote the cell numbers suggested for each inmate. Scarpa wants to devise a plot against a government installation to tell Yousef about. Scarpa wants to buy time on the airline threats by having a new plan to tell Yousef.

Scarpa had no knowledge that Roma's phone number had been given to Murad or Ismail. Scarpa had no further information regarding Garcia, the Olympics, the jurors or the witness.

Scarpa had not been asked by Yousef about the money. Scarpa was advised by the interviewing Agent of a plan if Yousef questions about the $2,500.00. Scarpa was advised to tell Yousef that the delivery of the money looks too suspicious and that Scarpa has already provided an overseas line through ROMA which is costing a lot of money. A meeting was suggested between one of Yousef's people and one of Scarpa's people (FBI) on the outside.

Scarpa began to flip through his own paperwork which included photocopies of his own notes. The interviewing Agent asked if she could see these documents. Scarpa gave additional documents to the interviewing Agent and said to take them and return them during … [Next page missing.]

[FBI report on interview with Scarpa, June 11, 1996]

Scarpa transferred a handwritten note to the interviewing Agent. Scarpa advised that the note was written by himself. The note relayed the following information:

On May 29, 1996, Scarpa was talking with Murad regarding the ongoing trial. Murad told Scarpa that Yousef believes that Scarpa can find out information on jurors. Scarpa questioned whether Yousef is trying for a mistrial.

[Predicting Explosion of TWA Flight 800, July 17, 1996]

Scarpa told Murad that an airplane explosion would be a "good thing to happen" especially if Yousef's people claim responsibility. Murad responded that it is going to happen and they are checking to see if Bojinka received the message. [A month later, on July 17, 1996, TWA Flight 800 exploded, shortly after departing New York. The Olympics bombing occurred on July 27, 1996, killing two people and injuring over 100.]

On June 3, 1996, Yousef repeated that he was upset with Scarpa for the money situation.

On June 5, 1996, Scarpa confronted Yousef about Murad and Ismail's use of the "Roma" phone. Scarpa also repeated that he is not going to send any money into a federal prison. Scarpa again suggested an outside meeting. Yousef asked Scarpa about the bomb threats. Scarpa responded that bomb threats would hurt his organization. Yousef again talked of money. Scarpa reminded Yousef that he has provided Yousef with overseas calls and money. [Eyyad Ismail was the Jersey City resident who drove the truck containing explosives to the World Trade Center garage in 1993. Murad was a co-conspirator in that bombing.]

Scarpa advised that cells were rotated on Thursday evening June 5, 1996. Scarpa remained in the cell he was already in, in the corner of the left hand side when looking into the tier. Yousef was moved adjacent to Scarpa and Ismail was moved adjacent to Yousef. Murad was moved across from Scarpa into the last cell on the right hand side.

On June 6, 1996, Yousef confronted Scarpa saying that the way things have been going Yousef said he's beginning to "smell FBI". Yousef said he is always giving and gets nothing in return. Scarpa became very upset and threatened Yousef. Yousef told Scarpa that he was only making a comparison between the way the FBI handles things and the way Scarpa handles things. Yousef stated that if you are dealing with the FBI, you keep giving information and the FBI never does anything in return. Scarpa responded that the information that Yousef gave him was just given to his people and in time they will use it.

Yousef suggested to Scarpa that he send $500 to Yousef into his commissary account and send the remaining $2,000 to an address overseas. Scarpa told Yousef that he would have to check with his people. Scarpa then questioned Yousef again about Murad and Ismail using the "Roma" phone. Yousef said that his idea of having Murad and Ismail using the phone was to "mix messages in." Scarpa told Yousef if it's important, all three can use the phone.

Scarpa wrote a few suggestions regarding the money. Scarpa asked whether he should tell Yousef no because his people do not want to get caught up into a conspiracy or give Yousef $500.00 for commissary. Scarpa told Yousef he would get an answer by Monday or Tuesday of Next week, June 17 or June 18.

On June 10, 1996, Scarpa spoke with Ismail. Ismail stated that Yousef does not think Scarpa is as serious as he used to be. Ismail told Scarpa to hold on because Ismail said Yousef has plans that he has not discussed with Scarpa yet.

When questioned by the interviewing Agent, Scarpa stated that Yousef told him the original $500.00 sent to Yousef's commissary account was sent to his mother. Yousef told Scarpa that he has only $7.00 in his account. Yousef's commissary privileges were taken away approximately two weeks ago when he received the ticket for the mouthwash.

Scarpa advised that Yousef requested a phone call on June 10th. Yousef received phone privileges but got a visit from his paralegal at the same time (approximately 7:00 p.m.)

[Getting information of trial jurors.]

The information Scarpa received regarding the jurors was the number of children they each have, whether they are married or single, what religion they are, what type of work they do, and what county they live in.

Ismail mentioned to Scarpa the other day that they plan to kidnap a prosecutor, a judge, or a United States Ambassador and that they are planning on getting out of jail whether they win or lose. Scarpa stated that Yousef knows information about Drews, the Guard. Yousef knows that Drews rides a motorcycle to and from work. Scarpa does not know whether Yousef overhead this information or if he receives information from the outside.

Scarpa advised that Yousef told him that Yousef either sent or received a coded message by phone. He felt that was done on May 16, 1996.

FBI Report of Conversation with Scarpa, July 1, 1996

The FBI 302 report stated:

Scarpa transferred one (1) handwritten note to Special Agent [redacted]. Scarpa advised that the note was written by Scarpa and pertained to the events taking place on June 29 and June 30, 1996.

[Bombing of U.S. military barracks in Saudi Arabia]

Scarpa advised that on June 29th, he asked Yousef how he is sure that Bojinga actually did the bombing in Saudi Arabia. Yousef responded that he was sure because Yousef was originally sent on the mission to check out the security measures and that a tanker truck was discussed at that time.

Yousef expressed concern regarding bugs in the cell. Yousef said if the government hears him talk about the bombing they might introduce the information at his trial. Yousef stated that he is concerned that something is wrong because his fathers account number was never received and his paralegal has not received the $500 that was sent out six weeks ago. Yousef indicated to Scarpa that Yousef knows more details about the bombing but is paranoid that the government is listening to him.

Scarpa advised that Yousef indicated that he would be able to identify the bombers when the composites drawings are completed and printed in the newspaper. Yousef did not want to talk too much in the cell because he feels that his present case is strong. Yousef was happy because a witness in his case said that the government told him to lie. Scarpa mentioned that the government asked the witness to indicate that a briefcase was found in a hall instead of where it was actually found. Scarpa also mentioned that items were taken which were not in the search warrant.

On the evening of June 30th, Yousef received a visit from his paralegal. When Yousef returned to his cell, he was yelling to Maraud in Arabic and sounded as if he were upset about something. Scarpa asked Yousef if everything [next page missing]

FBI Report of Interview with Scarpa, July 18, 1996

The July 18, 1996, FBI 302 report stated:

Scarpa transferred two (2) handwritten notes to Special Agent [redacted]. Scarpa advised that one note was written by Yousef and one note was written by Scarpa. In the note written by Yousef to Scarpa on July 6, 1996,

[Iranian Contacts]

Yousef advised Scarpa that he had spoken with his sister and she stated that she needs money to visit him with her kids. She asked Scarpa for $2,000. Yousef advised that he is waiting for his sister to send him her father's bank account number. Yousef advised that he was going to talk with her about the DHL situation but was told to get off the phone by the officer. Yousef stated that he did not have a chance to talk to his sister about sending letters through DHL. Yousef then told Scarpa that Iran does not have DHL service.

The note written by Scarpa pertained to the events taking place on July 6 and July 11, 1996. On July 6th, Scarpa was talking with Murad who stated that he feels that they will win the trial but either way they will be freed from jail. Murad asked Scarpa why his friends have not helped him escape from jail.

Scarpa advised Murad that these tactics do not work in the United States. Murad responded that if the right person were kidnapped, a U.S. Ambassador or someone of that level, and demands were made, that the United States would meet their demands. Murad told Scarpa "just wait and see". Scarpa asked Murad to let him know when they make their plan.

On July 11th, Yousef advised Scarpa that when he speaks on the phone and needs to get a message out, he speaks in three languages. Yousef also advised that his friends are coming from Atlanta soon and that they have a plan. Yousef advised that he would let Scarpa know.

Scarpa advised the interviewing Agent of the desired cell locations for rotation. Scarpa advised that he has spent $18 total for commissary for Yousef and will soon be buying flowers for Maqda for becoming an attorney.

[Warning Not to fly TWA on Morning of July 18, 1996]

Scarpa advised that Jerry Koupakis (spelled phonetically) told Scarpa that he told his father not to travel TWA or American Airlines on the morning of July 18th. Koupakis advised that Yousef had told him this information prior to July 18th. [Jerry Koupakis was a former U.S. Custom agent that went bad. TWA Flight 800 exploded on the evening of July 17, 1996.]

Yousef told Scarpa not to speak with Murad because he feels that the cells are bugged. Yousef told Scarpa that he was going to get out in a couple of days because he was "half way done with the window." According to Scarpa, Yousef stated this to see if the cells are bugged.

The following night, Raia came to the tier at 3:00 am and was seen by Ismail. Scarpa advised that Murad and Yousef have been conversing often in Arabic.

FBI report on Scarpa, December 26, 1996

Starting with the FBI reports of interviews with Scarpa on December 26, 1996, the first paragraph identified Gregory Scarpa, Jr. as a "Confidential Source (CS)" and identified throughout the body of the report as "CS:"

CS transferred three (3) pages of handwritten notes to the interviewing Agent. CS advised that the notes were self-written. The first two pages pertained to the events taking place on December 18, 1996. CS asked Yousef to reveal the address that the passports were to be sent. Yousef responded that he will not give out the address until he finds out whether CS's associates will send them or not. CS questioned Yousef whether the address is located in the

United States. Yousef responded that the address is an Iranian address. CS asked whether Yousef was having the passports sent to his parents address. Yousef responded "No," and that a temporary address was set up in Iran for this purpose.

[It is interesting that Iran and Iranians were involved with these plans, which President Bush conveniently ignored as he focused his ire on Iraq, ignoring the role that Iranians may have played in the terrorist acts.]

CS questioned Yousef how he sends and receives his messages. Yousef responded that he will reveal his method in a few weeks. Yousef told CS that "You'll be real surprises" and "You'll be shocked." Yousef said for his own reasons he cannot tell his method yet.

[Encouraging Yousef to Reveal Terrorist Plans]

CS advised that, prior to meeting with the interviewing Agent on December 18, 1996, he had a conversation with Yousef regarding co-operating witnesses on the L-unit. Yousef was curious as to what kind of deals the Government makes with the witnesses. CS explained that it depends on the information obtained and how well the witness does at trial. CS told Yousef that he should make a deal with the Government. CS advised that Yousef should give up Bojinga or Bin Laden. Yousef responded that the Government would never go after Bin Laden because the Government knows that within one week of capturing Bin Laden twelve U.S. airplanes would be blown up.

CS advised that Yousef's locker is kept on L-unit away from Yousef's cell. This locker contains his cosmetics which are not allowed in his cell in case he is capable of making a bomb from them. An item, which was not further identified, was discovered to be missing from the locker. CS advised the interviewing Agent that this item was placed, by Yousef, on the ledge of his cell and fell to the floor down the stairway to the floor of the unit below. Yousef advised a guard that the item had fallen and was told that the item would be retrieved. The item apparently was never retrieved and the item was detected missing.

[Insider Assistance]

A search was conducted of Yousef's cell. During the search, a thick, heavy, foot-long slab of glass was found hidden under Yousef's bed. As a result of the find, Yousef received a shot. Yousef advised CS that he identified CS as a witness to the fact that the glass was in his cell prior to Yousef's occupancy. CS advised the interviewing Agent that the glass was not in the cell previously. CS questioned Yousef how he obtained the glass. Yousef smiled and stated that he received it from his connection. CS questions Yousef as to how he intended to use the glass. Yousef responded that he had some ideas but did not elaborate on the ideas. Yousef then stated, "Watch what I get the next time."

[Hostage Crisis in Peru]

The last note pertained to the events taking place on December 21, 1996. CS had heard a news radio report regarding the crisis in Peru and was relaying the news report to Yousef. CS told Yousef that the U.S. is agreeing to do all that they can so that none of the hostages get hurt. However, the U.S. Government hopes that the Peruvian Government does not give into the demands of the terrorists because it is U.S. policy to never give in to the demands of the terrorists, especially to release prisoners.

Yousef stated that the guerillas in Peru are too easily releasing hostages and showing the Government that they are weak. Yousef told CS about a hijacked plane in Pakistan. Yousef stated that the Government hesitated and did not immediately do as the hijackers wanted and the hijackers blew themselves and the plane up immediately. Yousef stated that this way is the way of himself and Bojinga.

FBI Report of conversation with Scarpa, January 15, 1997
That FBI 302 report stated:

The first note was a kite written by Yousef and received by CS on Thursday, January 9th. Yousef told CS that "Flesiano & Maldando stopped taking the sleeping pills" which Yousef used to give to CS to give to them. Yousef revealed that he would give the pills to CS and the other inmates to put them to sleep so that they would not see his contact when he came to see Yousef.

Since the Government found the glass in Yousef's cell, Yousef believes that the "Feds" started thinking that Yousef may have a contact within MCC who brought Yousef the glass. Yousef believes that "Flesiano & Maldando" have been asked by the Government to watch Yousef to see who, if any, of the MCC staff comes to the L-unit that normally does not belong. Yousef stated that these two inmates stopped taking the sleeping pills and are up all night.

Yousef also has a strong feeling that "Flesiano" was put on the tier to watch Yousef because he was originally on another for months where he was safe. Yousef feels there was no reason to bring "Flesiano" to L-unit unless it was to spy on Yousef. Yousef has decided to poison "Flesiano". Yousef has decided to make some poisons and pass the food to the two inmates. Yousef stated that it will take approximately ten days to two weeks for the poison to kill the inmates.

[Terrorist's Radio Transmitter in Federal Prison]

The second note pertained to the events taking place on Friday, January 10th and Sunday, January 12th. On the night of January 10th, CS advised that, while out on the tier, Yousef called him to his cell and showed him what appeared to be an electronic board. Yousef advised that he would talk to CS about the board "later." Yousef was sleeping by the time CS returned to his cell.

On the night of January 12th, Yousef revealed that the electronic board was his way of sending and receiving messages. Yousef informed CS that the board is equipped with a booster, F.M. mike, and other things he could not recall. Yousef advised that he has a "gas lighter" which he used for soldering. Yousef revealed that he has received his last message and "everything is a go." Yousef stated that he will not transmit another message until two months from now. The message will be sent to Yousef's people and will relay that he is "ready".

Yousef is in the process of breaking the transmitter down into components. Yousef will give the components to CS to divide between Murad, Shah, and Ismail. Yousef told CS to keep the gas lighter himself but not to get caught with it. Yousef wants the components back in two months to reassemble the transmitter and relay that he is ready.

If Yousef's people do not receive a message from him, they will tell Bojinga that Yousef is not ready yet. Yousef told CS to tell Murad, Shah, and Ismail only to dispose of the components in an emergency. Yousef revealed that if the components are disposed of, he will have his contact bring the additional equipment he needs.

CS questioned Yousef about the identity of his contact. Yousef stated that he would not reveal who his contact is to anyone, including Murad, Shah, or Ismail. Yousef did indicate that he has not seen his contact in some time and hopes that everything is alright by him. Yousef then asked CS what radio station he was tuned to and showed CS how the system worked by transmitting Yousef's voice across CS's radio. Yousef stated that his messages were sent by a code similar to Morse code.

CS advised the interviewing Agent that he believes the person to whom Yousef transmits is in New York.

In addition, CS advised that John Napoli, one of the cooperators on the tier, was up until 2 a.m. speaking with Murad. CS believes that Napoli is forming a friendship with the terrorists. However, CS has also advised that Napoli is interested in working for the Government. Lastly, CS advised that Yousef knows the addresses of CS's mother and his daughter, Kori.

FBI 302 report, February 7, 1997.

That report of February 7, 1997, stated:

CS advised that at the end of the previous week, the guards on L-unit began to discuss moving Yousef, Murad, Shah, and Ismail, to the secure cells recently constructed. These cells are known to have cameras in each room monitoring the inmates 24 hours each day. Last Sunday, February 2nd, the guards stated that they were getting the keys to the new cells and were saying their good-byes.

Upon hearing of the upcoming move, Yousef asked CS to get the pieces of the transmitter back to him. CS advised that the components included wires, a gas lighter, a little "mike" with wires, plastic and metal pieces, and a green circuit board approximately 2" x 2". CS was having difficulty retrieving the pieces as he was under constant surveillance by the guards. On Tuesday, February 4th, Yousef told CS, Murad, Shah, and Ismail to dispose of any other components they may still have. Yousef advised that he would get his message out another way.

[Using Walkman to Transmit To Terrorists]

CS advised that he believes that Yousef was using his "walkman" as a transmitter. Yousef gave CS a "Cup o' Soup" container through a guard. Yousef told CS to open the bottom of the container. The container was found to have a false bottom and contained the gas lighter. Yousef had disguised the container to look like it had never been opened.

CS advised that he had received a kite from Yousef on Monday night, February 3rd. The kite was given to CS's attorney, Larry Silverman. The kite contained information that Yousef had tested CS's loyalty throughout the year. Yousef stated that he had asked CS for money as a precaution, knowing that the Government would never supply money for this purpose.

CS advised that Yousef received a visit from the Imam last Tuesday, February 4, 1997. [The government did supply money for this purpose: $500 and $2000; Inman was [The continuing page is not yet available.]

The following are copies of some of the notes or "kites" that were handed between the al Qaeda terrorists through Gregory Scarpa, Jr., starting in February 1996:

> In a February 27, 1996, note Yousef told Gregory Scarpa that he would teach him how to make and assemble bombs, smuggle them through airport x-ray machines, and where on the aircraft to place them for maximum effect.
>
> A February 29, 1996, note from Yousef told Scarpa how to make hydrogen peroxide; how to make timer devices; and how to assemble and smuggle the bomb onto the aircraft. Yousef also requested $3,000 and offered to put his Colombo group in touch with terrorists presently in the United States. That offer would have put FBI agents in direct contact with al Qaeda members in the local New York City area. That offer was, incredibly, denied.
>
> In a March 26, 1996, note from Scarpa to Ismoil, Scarpa gave Scarpa the address of his daughter, Maria.
>
> In a March 27, 1996, note, Yousef thanked Scarpa for advising him about the use of "front" addresses, and stated the name of Assistant United States Attorney Garcia.
>
> In a March 28, 1996, note, Yousef asked Scarpa to have his friends in the Colombo mob group kill an FBI witness and FBI Special Agent Dave Williams.
>
> On March 29, 1996, the FBI provided Scarpa with a miniature camera to be used to take pictures of the notes. A picture was then taken of a note from Scarpa to Yousef asking for the name of the FBI Witness.

Approximately April 5, 1996, photographed note from Scarpa asking Yousef for the correct name of the FBI witness, stating that his outside contacts couldn't find any such witness. Yousef then sent a note to Scarpa with the full name of AUSA Garcia. In that note, Yousef stated that his group was sending someone down to Atlanta to check on security.

In an April 17, 1996, note from Yousef to Scarpa, Yousef states that Bojinga (Osama bin Laden) was sending someone from England to check on the Atlanta security measures.

An April 22, 1996, Scarpa arranged to have $500 put into Yousef's prison account.

On May 1, 1996, Yousef says in a note that he has been making three-way phone calls to his sister in a coded manner and she passes the information to her husband, and he in turn gives the information to Bojinga.

On May 8, 1996, a note from Yousef to Scarpa stated that Murad saw the FBI and the prosecutors cooperating.

A May 13, 1996, note from Yousef stated that he sent a coded message to Bojinga that a certain person recruited by the CIA in Qatar should be killed, and suggested to Bojinga that the U.S. Embassy in Qatar should be bombed.

On May 17, 1996, a three-way call took place during which Yousef was upset with what his attorney had told him earlier about the judge refusing to admit evidence.

On May 19, 1996, Yousef said to Scarpa that he advised his group on the outside to start placing bombs on cargo aircraft departing Dubai. In a note from Yousef, he described how to smuggle explosives onto an aircraft, where they should be placed, using RDX explosives. He described how to hide the explosives in either carry on or stored baggage. He advised that the people who checked the security measures in Atlanta were returning to New York.

In a July 2, 1996, note, Yousef stated that Bojinga ordered the bombing in Sandi Arabia and that he himself had earlier checked the security measures at that location.

On July 18, 1996, TWA Flight 800 exploded shortly after taking off from JFK Airport in New York.

On July 23, 1996, Ismoil stated to Scarpa, "I told you this is going to happen," referring to the downing of TWA Flight 800.

In an August 7, 1996 note, Yousef said he knew the address of the U.S. Ambassador to the Philippines.

On August 26, 1996, Scarpa suggest to the FBI that Yousef's reference to Bojinga was an alias for Osama bin Laden.

On September 4, 1996, Yousef asked Scarpa to have his people send $4000 to an overseas address and that the money would then be forwarded to Yousef's people in the United States.

On September 8, 1996, Yousef asked Scarpa to get his people on the outside and send the passports to al Qaeda people in Libya and Iran.

On September 13, 1996, Yousef told Scarpa about sending mail from prison using another inmates name and number on the envelop so that the prison staff would not recognize them as being sent by him.

On September 14, 1996, Yousef told Scarpa that most of Bojinga's followers were in Sudan.

On September 17, 1996, Yousef talked to Scarpa about placing cargo with bombs on two U.S. airliners.

On September 19, 1996, Yousef stated to Scarpa that many Bojinga followers were in Sudan and that Bojinga was using Afghanistan as a retreat. He again stated that a U.S. ambassador to the Philippines that he called Neoponti, was a kidnapping target.

On December 8, 1996, Yousef requested five U.S. passports for Bojinga's people to be used to board airliners being hijacked.

On December 18, 1996, Yousef met with an Imam and spoke in Arabic for a considerable period of time.

On December 29, 1996, Yousef told Scarpa about decoding a message from Bojinga, and about training Scarpa's friends in Pakistan and Afghanistan on terrorist tactics.

On January 10, 1997, Yousef showed Scarpa a Walkman set altered to act as a transmitter, and it could send messages in Morse code. Yousef stated that in the last message that he received "everything was go."

Declaration Provided in Another Criminal Trial

Gregory referred to a declaration presented in a New York criminal trial (March 30, 2002) by attorney Flora Edwards, making reference to Scarpa's efforts to elicit information about terrorist activities from Yousef:

> Following my indictment in 1995, I was remanded to the Metropolitan Correctional Center in New York City where I was housed on the same tier as Ramsey Yousef and others who were awaiting trial for the 1993 bombing of the World Trade Center and other terrorist activities.
>
> Yousef was discussing plans to make an airplane explode. I became concerned … so I contacted my attorney, Larry Silverman, who I believe, then contacted the US Attorney.
>
> Shortly thereafter I was brought to a meeting attended by AUSA Valerie Caproni, Agent Leadbetter, an Assistant US Attorney Fitzgerald and other FBI agents from the FBI anti-terrorism task force in Washington, D.C.

I told them about Yousef's plans to plant bombs in airplanes. I offered to submit to a polygraph and even consented to have a bug placed in my cell. They did not appear very interested and simply told me that they would let me know.

Eventually Yousef started talking about killing an Assistant US Attorney Garcia, who he said was a prosecutor on his trial and he also asked me to arrange the murder of FBI Agent Williams. I again relayed this information to my attorney who in turn contacted the office of the US Attorney. Immediately thereafter, I met with the FBI and was provided with a miniature camera. I continued to talk with Yousef and ultimately provided the FBI with photographs of diagrams of plans to make bombs and notes on the planned murder of Garcia.

For a year I continued at great personal risk to provide information regarding planned terrorist activities including the bombing of a US military barracks in Saudi Arabia. In addition I was able to provide the FBI with detailed information regarding the methods the terrorists used to smuggle weapons and explosives past airport security. In my attorney's presence I offered to arrange a meeting between undercover FBI agents and Yousef's operatives who were on the street. However, my offer was rejected because they told me that the Bureau would not authorize the $2,500 payment to the terrorists that would have proved the conspiracy.

Further Evidence of FBI-DOJ Discrediting Gregory Scarpa's Information About Planned Al Qaeda Terrorist Acts

In that March 30, 2002, declaration filed by Edwards, the attorney wrote:

Apparently, Scarpa's relationship with the FBI cooled. His warnings went unheeded and his efforts were certainly unrewarded. The Government characterized the information he provided as a "scam. …

In August 2000, during the pendency of Scarpa's appeal, the government released a sealed Affidavit sworn to by AUSA Patrick Fitzgerald dated June 28, 1999, stating that a follow-up investigation corroborated the information which Scarpa had provided regarding the terrorists. Given the events of September 11, 2001, it appears that the Government made no effort to follow up on the information and has still to acknowledge Scarpa's efforts to forestall a national disaster.

FBI-DOJ Contract on One of Its Own Agents?

During our many communications, Gregory Scarpa Jr. was alerted by my description of how the FBI and DOJ filed false charges against FBI Special Agent Richard Taus. Scarpa knew about a plan to take out an FBI agent and wanted the precise dates that Taus was charged, so that he could determine if Taus was the person on whom a Mafia contract was discussed. In his March 12,

2007, letter Gregory wrote: "I'm looking to find out the year he got indicted. That would tell me if he's the guy I'm thinking." I provided him additional information, to which he responded in another letter:

I found what you had mentioned in your letter about former FBI agent Richard Taus, full of treachery. And also involving him there was more treachery that he and you do not know about. I can't get into it at the moment, but I can tell you that there was something else in store for him before the "sham" charges.

My father was told he may have to help with——I'm sure you can figure what. When I'm able I'll tell you more about it. Rod, if you know? What exactly did he get the 80-year sentence for? And if you can tell me approximately what year? When in the 80s? Did he write Congress and or get charged with the sham/boy?

DOJ Prison Officials Blocking Report of FBI-DOJ Crimes

After I received certain information from Scarpa Jr., prison officials confiscated his mail to me. In a June 22, 2003, letter, Scarpa wrote:

Rodney, numerous letters and informative documents that I sent you, for one reason or another, are returned to me, either" I'm not allowed to say this," or "Not allowed to say that."

Reason Why DOJ Prison Officials Blocked Scarpa's Letters

The most probable reason that DOJ prison officials blocked Scarpa from revealing his knowledge of prior Mafia activities to me was to block information about high-level FBI-DOJ corruption being made known to me, which I would then publicize. That would be a felony under the various obstruction of justice statutes.

Author Writing Book about Scarpa-DeVecchio Relationship

In 2006, Sandra Harmon wrote a book with Gregory Scarpa Jr., promising to have some of the proceeds go to Scarpa's family. The title, *Mafia Son*, was published by St. Martin's Press. Scarpa told me that she refused to honor the agreement. Scarpa also stated that part of the information that she wrote was incorrect.

Several years earlier, in 2002, I had signed a contract with Gregory Scarpa, Jr. to write a book, but the refusal by prison officials to allow Scarpa to provide me any more information stalled that plan. I subsequently received a letter from Scarpa's daughter, Kori Eagle, then asking me to cancel the book contract; she had found another author to write the book. I signed a release.

Another in Series of Cover-Ups by Members of Congress

With the information that Scarpa was providing to me, and also provided by other inmates in the same prison who had frequent conversations with Scarpa, I sought to report this serious matter to various government officials because it revealed a dangerous culture within the FBI and Department of Justice. I wrote to the chairman of the committee that conducted hearings on the FBI misconduct in the Boston area, Representative Tom Davis (with copies to every other member of the committee).

From the desk of Rodney Stich
P.O. Box 5, Alamo, CA 94507

July 4, 2003

Representative Tom Davis, Chairman
Committee on Government Reform
2157 Rayburn House Office Building
Washington, DC 20515 Certified: 7002 0860 0003 9592 6405

Ref: Former government agent with information on FBI misconduct in New York City offices similar to that in Boston office in the Bulger matter.

To Representative Davis and the committee on government reform:

For the record, I am making the following statements that raise responsibilities under federal law, including the federal crime reporting statute (18 U.S.C. § 4): I am a former federal agent;[26] a veteran in the aviation field;[27] an investigator for many years; a confidant to many other government agents, and activist against corruption in government. I have acquired a great amount of information on criminal activities implicating certain government personnel that enabled the infliction of great and irreparable harm upon national interests and the lives of many people. This pattern will continue until certain people—such as you and members of your commission—meet their legal responsibilities, including those under federal criminal statutes.

As it relates to Deep-Seated FBI Culture of Corruption:

As it relates to FBI misconduct, which is the area of your present limited investigation into FBI misconduct in Boston with the Bulger crime group, I have acquired information[28] showing that the subject of your Boston hearings is not limited to the Boston area. For instance:

---

[26] As a Federal Aviation Administration air carrier operations inspector I was given the task to correct the conditions causing the worst series of aviation disasters in the nation's history. In this position I acted as an independent prosecutor, conducted a six-month-long hearing, and developed a transcript that further proved my charges of corruption within the FAA that made possible a number of preventable aviation disasters.

[27] I joined the U.S. Navy in 1940. I was a multi-engine patrol plane commander (PPC) during World War II. I was captain for several international airlines after World War II. Throughout this period I was a flight instructor. I was an FAA inspector-investigator for a number of years. I wrote numerous books on misconduct that I discovered and have appeared as guest and expert on over 3,000 radio and television shows in the United States, Canada, Mexico and Europe.

[28] Information on FBI/Justice Department corruption has been acquired over many years from my personal experiences as a government agent, as an activist, and from my many FBI, CIA and other government sources.

FBI agents in the New York City area were providing confidential information on government informants to certain members of the New York crime families, and the government informants were subsequently murdered. This information was given to me in writing by a former member of one of those crime groups. The Justice Department's Bureau of Prisons has recently blocked that insider from providing me, an investigator and author, with additional information that would have been used to promote national interests.

Cover-up by various divisions of the U.S. Department of Justice when I, as a federal air safety agent, attempted to report criminal activities that I discovered in my official duties that played, and continues to play, a major role in a series of fatal airline crashes. This is the same type of misconduct, and cover-up, that caused the conditions to exist that enabled 19 hijackers to seize four airliners, when the preventative measures were known, were authorized to be taken, were required to be taken, and were not taken. The key issue here is the deep-seated pattern of corruption implicating key people in the government's aviation safety offices, a problem that will continue until exposed and meaningful corrective actions taken. The present tactic to keep this matter from the public is to place the blame for 9/11 on the more innocent "intelligence failures."

FBI retaliation against a veteran FBI agent (and holder of several medals for bravery in Vietnam) when he continued to report drug-related and other criminal activities of CIA and other government personnel in the New York City area.

Repeated charges of criminal contempt of court against me, by Justice Department prosecutors, when I filed federal actions under the federal crime reporting statute (18 U.S.C. § 4)[29] and 28 U.S.C. § 1361, seeking to report the corruption in the government aviation safety offices (and in other offices that I and a group of other former and present government agents had discovered).

As it relates to decades of aviation disasters—including 9/11:

As a federal aviation safety agent I discovered, documented, and attempted to report deadly misconduct in key government aviation safety offices that caused or enabled numerous major aviation disasters to occur.[30]

Among the most recent aviation disasters made possible by this documented misconduct were the hijackings of four airliners by 19 hijackers on September 11, 2001. I and other federal aviation safety agents had reported, years earlier, the need for FAA management to order the simple and inexpensive preventative measures that would halt the decades of fatal hijackings.

Why, and how, the authority and responsibility to act on these (and many other crash-related) aviation tragedies occurred opens the window on understanding, and

---

[29] The clear and specific wording of the federal crime reporting statute says:

Title 18 U.S.C. § 4. Misprision of felony. Whoever, having knowledge of the actual commission of a felony cognizable by a court of the United States, conceals and does not as soon as possible make known the same to some judge or other person in civil or military authority under the United States, shall be fined under this title or imprisoned not more than three years, or both.

[30] These fraud-related aviation disasters are detailed in my documentary book, *Unfriendly Skies*.

taking corrective actions, on the corruption in government that continues to spread like a cancer.

The complicity by those who knew of these crimes, and either did nothing or who actively covered up, would be another aspect of the 9/11 tragedies.

Documented complicity of federal judges:

Felony cover-ups and obstruction of justice by large numbers of federal judges to block the reporting of these criminal and subversive activities. This documented misconduct includes, for instance:

Repeated refusal by federal judges to receive evidence of criminal and subversive activities from present and former government agents, under the federal crime reporting statute (18 U.S.C. § 4). The federal crimes which we initially sought to expose related to aviation disasters, and eventually, the misconduct that enabled 19 hijackers to seize four airliners on 9/11.

My attempts to comply with this important crime reporting statute commenced in the late 1970s[31] and continues to the present time.[32] In every instance, federal judges

[31] Initial attempts to report criminal activities included the following lawsuits: *Stich v. United States, et al.*, 554 F.2d 1070 (9th Cir.) (table), *cert. denied*, 434 U.S. 920 (1977)(addressed hard-core air safety misconduct, violations of federal air safety laws, threats against government inspectors not to report safety violations and misconduct); *Stich v. National Transportation Safety Board*, 685 F.2d 446 (9th Cir.)(table), *cert. denied*, 459 U.S. 861 (1982))(addressed repeated criminal falsification of official airline accident reports, omitting highly sensitive air safety misconduct, making possible repeated crashes from the same sequestered problems); Amicus curiae brief filed on July 17, 1975, in the Paris DC-10 multi-district litigation, *Flanagan v. McDonnell Douglas Corporation and United States of America*, Civil Action 74-808-PH, MDL 172, Central District California.)(addressing the long standing FAA misconduct, of which the cover-up of the DC-10 cargo door problem was one of repeated instances of tragedy related misconduct); U.S. v. Department of Justice, District of Columbia, Nos. 86-2523, 87-2214, and other actions filed by Stich seeking to expose and correct the powerful and covert air disaster misconduct.

[32] Federal filing in the U.S. district court, Washington, DC (1-02CV01172), which was sua sponte dismissed by judge Henry H. Kennedy immediately after filing on the basis that in 1991 U.S. district judge Stanley Sporkin rendered an unlawful and unconstitutional order permanently barring me access to the federal courts. That action sought to report criminal and subversive activities to a federal court under the federal crime reporting statute (18 U.S.C. § 4). Sporkin blocked my attempt to report these federal crimes. If not blocked, the evidence would have enabled actions to be taken that would have blocked the actions of 19 hijackers on September 11, 2001, and many other offenses against national interests and national security. Following my appeal (02-5240) of that unlawful dismissal, district of Columbia judges (Ginsburg, Edwards, Sentelle, Henderson, Randolph, Rogers, Tatel, and Garland) rendered an order filed March 26, 2003, upholding the district court's blocking of the reports of federal crimes related to 9/11, and the order permanently depriving a former federal agent of his civil and constitutional rights guaranteed by the laws and Constitution of the United States.

In addition, federal judges blocked a similar filing submitted to the U.S. district court for the Southern District of New York that was submitted on August 8, 2002, along with the filing fees and all required papers. Letters to the court, including chief judge Michael Mukasey, showed the filing was blocked, but not rejected. By these unblocked the reports, obstructing justice, making possible the continuation of the conduct resulting in the 3,000 deaths on September 11, 2001.

Repeated refusal to receive evidence of *other* criminal activities implicating people acting in government positions. These include, for instance, drug smuggling into the United States by people acting in government positions and the cover-ups and obstruction of justice by others who knew of these federal crimes. (These other criminal activities are detailed in the books that I have written in collaboration with a group of other former and present government agents).

Seeking to block these reports of criminal and subversive activities, federal judges issued a series of orders permanently barring me access to the federal district and appellate courts. Simultaneously, legal schemes were initiated to corruptly strip me of the $10 million in real estate assets that funded my public-spirited exposure activities. These unlawful, unconstitutional, and felonious[33] orders permanently barring me access to federal courts also show the willingness of federal judges to not only obstruct justice but also to subvert the laws and constitution of the United States relating to civil rights.

Repeatedly charged me with criminal contempt of court for attempting to report criminal and subversive activities, including those that made the events of 9/11 possible.. In addition to the obstruction of justice crimes, this retaliation violated other criminal statutes.[34]

---

lawful acts—and many not stated here—these judges are covering up for people involved in criminal and subversive activities, including those that enabled 19 hijackers to seize four airliners on 9/11, Their obstruction of justice—as in prior judicial obstruction of justice—will enable the continuation of fraud-related tragedies upon the United States and its people.

[33] The judicial orders, and judicial and Justice Department retaliation, blocking present and former federal agents from reporting criminal and subversive activities, enabled major criminal activities to go unreported, to continue, and for the resulting harm America and its people to continue. These judicial acts are felonies.

[34] Felonies arising from retaliating against a former federal agent and witness for seeking to report criminal and subversive activities are based upon, for instance, Title 18 U.S.C. § 111. Assaulting, resisting, or impeding certain officers or employees. (a) In general.-Whoever- (1) forcibly assaults, resists, opposes, impedes, intimidates, or interferes with any person designated in section 114 of this title [federal agent] while engaged in or on account of the performance of official duties; or (2) forcibly assaults or intimidates any person who formerly served as a person designated in section 1114 on account of the performance of official duties during such person's term of service, shall, where the acts in violation of this section constitute only simply assault, be fined under this title or imprisoned not more than one year, or both, and in all other cases, be fined under this title or imprisoned not more than three years, or both.

Title 18 U.S.C. § 1512. Tampering with a witness, victim, or an informant—(b) Whoever knowingly uses intimidation or physical force, or threatens another person, or attempts to do so, or engages in misleading conduct toward another person, with intent to— (1) influence, delay or prevent the testimony of any person in an official proceeding: shall be fined ... or imprisoned ... or both. [1988 amended reading]

Title 18 U.S.C. § 1513. Retaliating against a witness, victim, or an informant. (a) Whoever knowingly engages in any conduct and thereby causes bodily injury to another person or damages the tangible property of another person, or threatens to do so, with intent to retaliate against any person for—(1) the attendance of a witness or party

Most recent judicial obstruction of justice includes:

Federal judges refusal to file papers submitted to the U.S. district court, Southern District of New York, which concurrently blocked the reporting by former federal agents of criminal and subversive activities, including those primarily responsible for the conditions that enabled 19 hijackers to seize four airliners and kill 3,000 people. This filing was accompanied with the filing fee and all required documents, and sought to report criminal activities that I and other former government agents had discovered as part of our official duties. By this judicial obstruction of justice, the primary blame for the events of 9/11 are being withheld from the people, the guilty are being protected against prosecution, and the conditions enabling the events of 9/11, and many prior tragedies, remain in place.

Refusal of judges in the district and appellate courts in Washington, DC to receive information from government insiders of criminal activities that enabled, for instance, the events of 9/11 to occur, and which, as in prior judicial obstruction of justice, enabled the federal crimes to continue that resulted in prior tragedies. This relates to the federal filing seeking to report the criminal and subversive activities, the sua sponte dismissal, and the aiding and abetting by appellate judges in the District of Columbia.

There is much more information on corruption in government offices that I and my group of other former government and present government agents discovered. The continuation of these criminal activities was made possible by the cover-ups (obstruction of justice) by members of the House and Senate. Their complicity insures continued cover-ups and continued obstruction of justice.

With the continued cover-ups by the broadcast and print media that keeps the public uninformed, combined with public indifference and cowardly state of denial, the guilty will remain unpunished and the tragedies made possible by the corruption will continue as before.

Sincerely,
Rodney Stich

Chairman Tom Davis said in a subsequent standard off-the-shelf form letter: "I am in receipt of your materials regarding FBI misconduct in New York City and circumstances surrounding September 11, 2001. The Committee is currently bringing its investigation into the misconduct in the use of FBI informants to a close. However, I will keep your letter on file and contact you should additional information be needed."

The problem with that letter was that I had not given the committee details or evidence and simply made reference to having contact with a former member of the Mafia families in New York who provided me details of the FBI corruption—an area that the committee had not investigated.

---

at an official proceeding, or any testimony given or any record, document, or other object produced by a witness in an official proceeding; or (2) any information relating to the commission or possible commission of a Federal offense ...

Representative Henry Waxman, from my home state of California, also covered up, as did all the other members that I contacted. In a letter (July 1, 2003) requesting a copy of the opening remarks by the committee the day that William Bulger testified, I added information that should have received their immediate attention and request for information from me. That section in my letter stated:

> For your information, among the many sources that I have acquired over the years since becoming an activist, is a former member of the Colombo crime family. He has provided me with information showing similar activities between FBI agents and organized crime in the New York City area, particularly as it relates to FBI agents revealing the identities of government informants to organized crime figures, followed by the murder of these revealed informants. I include some of this continuing influx of information in my book, Terrorism Against America.

Waxman's response (July 14, 2004): "Thank you for your correspondence regarding the House Government Reform Committee's recent hearings on the Department of Justice's use of informants. Thank you for contacting me." No interest was shown in receiving my information, or the name of the former Mafia member who told me details of the FBI relationship with murderers.

I started encountering this practice of congressional cover-up 40 years earlier, while I held a key federal airline safety responsibility, and was reporting a culture of corruption responsible for a series of airline disasters, some of them occurring in my immediate area of federal safety responsibilities. In subsequent years, as I discovered from the many other government agents that contacted me, other areas of high-level criminal misconduct, the same obstruction-of-justice cover-up occurred. These other areas of criminal activities are detailed in my books, *Defrauding America* and *Drugging America*.

Anyone being offered information on major federal crimes, who then covers up for them, becomes criminally involved with the principal.

Media Personnel's Bias Covered Up

Among the reporters that slanted their writings to support the conduct in the FBI and DOJ was Jerry Capeci, a reporter for the *New York Daily News*. Just like Judith Miller of the *New York Times* whose slanted reporting supported the lies by the Bush politicians that brought about the invasion of Iraq, Capeci's slant enabled the corruption in the FBI-DOJ to go unrecognized by the uninformed American public. He had an interest in protecting DeVecchio and discrediting Scarpa Jr.

Typical was his article in the *New York Daily News* (September 28, 1978), titled, "My Father Did It," that stated: "Scarpa Jr., by blaming his father, Scarpa seems to be copying tactics that 16 other Colombos used to win acquittals a few years ago when they went to trial."

FBI 302 Report of the Leaks

In an FBI 302 report dated June 1, 1994, FBI Special Agent Christopher Favo reported the leaks by DeVecchio to *Daily News* reporter Jerry Capeci. The 302 report stated in part that "on several occasions, SSA DeVecchio approached me or another agent with specific questions about the investigation of the war on the Colombo family and our answers to the questions appeared in Capeci's column the following day with an attribution to a law enforcement source. On several occasions I mentioned this to SSA DeVecchio and he blamed the leaks on the prosecutors in the EDNY. I began withholding information from SSA DeVecchio on Monday mornings to prevent its appearance in Tuesday's column."

Referring to Scarpa's sworn testimony about the information he obtained from Ramzi Yousef, Capeci wrote in another article:

Colombo mobster Gregory Scarpa Jr. has probably been reading a lot of cloak and dagger thrillers. He opened his defense to racketeering and murder charges with a heavy dose of interest intrigue, espionage and double cross. Scarpa said he was like his father, a top echelon FBI informant for 30 years who regarded himself as a James Bond figure. *Mission Impossible* was a favorite television show

CHAPTER EIGHTEEN

Multiple Enablers Of Successful Terrorist Attacks

Starting with my first book published in 1978, and in virtually every other of the over one dozen books, I have detailed the cover-ups, the obstruction of justice, the outright lying, by media people, political pundits, federal judges, and members of Congress. Avoiding matters of severe corruption appears to be a well-ingrained American culture. All of these people became enablers to many of America's worst tragedies. This chapter briefly addresses what is stated in more detail in my other books.

Media and Politician Spin—Dumbing Down the People

The polite word used for *lying* by media people and politicians is "spin." With the continued dumbing down of the people, the spin worsened, and in many cases has become so blatant as to insult the intelligence of even today's population. Sometimes there was an element of truth to what was being said by the spin masters, giving it the appearance of accuracy, and then combined with deception and lies, resulting in an absolutely false statement.

Media People on Secret Payroll of Government Departments

Covert Action's Spring 1993 issue told how U.S. intelligence agencies use public relation firms, journalists, and authors to print what they want the American public to hear. The article reported:

> In a typical issue of the *Wall Street Journal*, more than half the news stories were based solely on [government-provided] press releases. Reporters were paid by the CIA, sometimes without their media employer's knowledge, to get the material in print or on the air. They reported that news organizations ordered their writers to repeat what was fed to them by the CIA.
>
> H&K employees at the small Washington office and elsewhere, distributed this material through CIA assets working in the United States news media. Since the CIA is prohibited from disseminating propaganda inside the U.S., this type of "blowback"—which former CIA officer John Stockwell and other researchers have often traced to the Agency—is illegal. While the use of U.S. media by the CIA has a long and well-documented history, the covert involvement of PR firms may be news to many.

Covert Action described how reporters depend upon the close intelligence community for much of their "news," and how the media protects these sources. Another article written by the research staff of *National Vanguard Books* described the slanted news by the press and entertainment media:

Who Rules America?

Their power...reaches into every home in America, and it works its will during nearly every waking hour. It is the power which shapes and molds the mind of virtually every citizen, young or old, rich or poor, simple or sophisticated. The mass media form for us our image of the world and then tell us what to think about that image. Essentially everything we know—or think we know—about events outside our own neighborhood or circle of acquaintances comes to us via our daily newspaper, our weekly news magazine, our radio, or our television.

Employing carefully developed psychological techniques, they guide our thought and opinion...Most Americans fail to realize that they are being manipulated. Even the citizen who complains about "managed news" falls into the trap of thinking that because he is presented with an apparent spectrum of opinion he can escape the thought controllers' influence by believing the editor or commentator of his choice. Every point on the permissible spectrum of public opinion is acceptable to the media master, and no impermissible fact or viewpoint is allowed any exposure at all, if they can prevent it.

Media Circus and Lack of Investigative Reporting

In the book, *Media Circus*, written by *Washington Post* media critic, the author ridicules the lack of investigative reporting, absence of penetrating insight, or newsworthy news that exists in America's newspapers:

> The nation's watchdogs have become lap-dogs, and groveling spineless mutts at that. And nobody, the American public especially, appears to give a thinker's damn.

Media Admission of Being CIA Fronts

A *Washington Post* February 16, 1996 article describing the CIA's use of American journalists and news organizations during "the past 19 years," and even using them as cutouts or fronts for CIA activities. The article made reference to earlier discoveries "that the CIA had clandestine agents posing as American journalists for decades."

Executive editor of the *Washington Post*, Leonard Downie, Jr., stated:

> It's disturbing to hear that the CIA has either used the cover of legitimate journalistic organizations without their knowledge, or somebody working for them has been recruited by the CIA. CIA spokesman Mark Mansfield said the use of the media is permitted by a regulation "waived by the agency's director...and has been and continues to be the CIA's policy."

Over 800 News and Public Information Sources Under CIA Control

A December 1977 article in the *New York Times* reported that in the mid 1960s the CIA "owned, subsidized or otherwise influenced...more than 800 news and public information organizations and individuals." Author Ralph McGehee states in *Deadly Deceits: My 25 years in the CIA*, "There's a little bit of fear that if you go after the intelligence community, your career is threatened."

Several CIA operatives have told me that the CIA had blackmailed Senator Boren, head of the CIA Senate Oversight Committee,[35] warning him in 1992 that they would release pictures of his alleged homosexual and pedophile activities if he didn't cease his opposition to the nomination of Robert Gates as Director of the CIA.

Framing the news for Washington

A *San Francisco Examiner* article by Mark Hertsgaard[36] criticized the press for "framing the news according to what the movers and shakers of official Washington wanted, rather than thinking through the relevant issues for themselves, and [holding] the national political dialogue hostage to the debate within the Washington policy elite." He added, "Journalists got so carried away that instead of being honest brokers of information, many fell into the role of Pentagon cheerleader."

Ethics, Conflicts of Interest, and the Press

In an editorial that is as true today as the day it was published (July 25, 1967), the *Wall Street Journal* identified the news distortion and cover-up: "Ethics & the Press, Conflicts of Interest, Pressures Still Distort Some Papers' Coverage." The in-depth article told how "Advertisers and outside work of newsmen color stories," thereby halting investigations. The article stated:

> In Boston and Chicago, newspaper investigations into suspected hanky-panky suddenly are aborted. In one case, a subject of inquiry turns out to be a stockholder of the paper and friend of the publisher. In the other, the investigation threatens to embarrass a politician who could help the paper in a building project.
>
> **[Fabricated Favorable coverage for Advertising]**
>
> In Denver, the advertising staff of a big daily wrestles with an arithmetic problem. A big advertiser has been promised news stories and pictures amounting to 25 percent of the ad space it buys; the paper already has run hundreds of column inches of glowing prose but is still not close to the promised allotment of "news" and now is running out of nice things to say.
>
> All this hardly enhances the image of objectivity and fierce independence the U.S. press tries so hard to project. Yet talks with scores of report-

---

[35] Chairman of the Senate Intelligence Committee.

[36] December 30, 1990. Author of *On Bended Knee: The Press and the Reagan Presidency*.

> ers, editors, publishers, public relations men and others reveal that practices endangering—and often subverting—newspaper integrity are more common than the man on the street might dream. Result: The buyer who expects a dime's worth of truth every time he picks up his paper often is short-changed.
>
> All newspapers, including this one, must cope with the blandishments and pressures of special interests who seek distortion or omission of the truth on some papers the trouble starts at the top; it is the publisher himself who lays down news policies designed to aid one group or attack another.
>
> It is plain, however, that a sizable minority of newspapers still are putty in the hands of their advertisers, that they allow personal as well as business considerations to favor the news to a marked degree that they tolerate staff practices hardly conducive to editorial independence and objectivity.
>
> Blackouts of news involving newspapers are quite common; hardly a working journalist could deny that one of the gravest weaknesses in coverage exhibited by the American press is its coverage of itself .... another grave fault of a good many papers: Favoritism toward business in general and advertisers in particular....the paper itself, by actual policy or common practice, distorts the news to suit advertisers or literally hands over news space to them....Everyone in newspapering pays lip service to the ideal that a paper's news columns should not be for sale, ... a staffer is "on the take"...

Years of Media Cover-Up of Congressional Corruption

In *Above the Law,*[37] author James Boyd described the influence peddling and buying of votes in Congress. Vested interests pass money under the table, bribes, disguised as honorariums, speech-fees, loans that never come due, and other thinly disguised graft. In its book review the *Christian Science Monitor*[38] said, "Only the completely cynical can read Mr. Boyd's book without mounting distress."

The review described the indifference, or felony cover-up, by the FBI, the Lawyer General, and the live-and-let-live philosophy of Congress for their peers. The book review addressed the press cover-up stating, "The press doesn't smell too sweet either. It rushed into the kitchen only after the kettle boiled over."

---

[37] Authored by James Boyd and published in 1968.

[38] *Christian Science Monitor* March 1, 1968.

History of Harm upon the People and the Nation Made possible by Media Personnel Cover-Ups

Since 1966, as a federal investigator initially providing media personnel with inside information and evidence on ongoing corrupt, criminal, and subversive misconduct that were already having deadly effects. The recipients knew that their cover-up of the information that were crimes against the United States by people in key government positions would enable the misconducts, including massive deaths and harm to national interests to continue.

Anyone reading my various books would understand the many great American tragedies that would not have continued or occurred if media personnel had not engaged in cover-up—a crime. These tragedies include many easily preventable airline disasters starting in the 1950s; many of the successful terrorist attacks; wars started on blatant lies; countless financial frauds; and much more.

CHAPTER NINETEEN

9/11 Commissioners Protecting the Guilty

Every imaginable obstacle was put in place by people in government to prevent a meaningful investigation to determine the people and the groups responsible for the conditions that made it so easy for 19 terrorists to hijack four airliners on September 11, 2001, to kill nearly 3,000 people, and set in motion events that eventually took tens of thousands of lives.

President George W. Bush (Jr.) Repeatedly Impeded the Process

As with almost every other area of misconduct, President George W. Bush and the people he placed in government positions, put every conceivable block to attempts to find the blame for the greatest number of terrorist attacks on the United States in its history. And members of Congress made no effort to start a meaningful investigation, which would have exposed their role as accomplices through years of cover-ups of the problems in each of the groups whose misconduct made 9/11 possible.

It wasn't until media publicity to the families of those killed in the 9/11 attacks, including those known as the "Jersey girls," that members of Congress were forced to legislate the 9/11 Commission, which was signed into law in November 2002, almost a year after the catastrophic event. But then, blocks appeared that could be expected to cover up for the people whose misconduct made the 3,000 deaths possible.

The Bush administration refused to provide important government documents, and refused to appear before the commission. As if that wasn't enough, President George W. Bush selected the members of the commission, most of whom had something very serious to hide.

During all this, the media, that also were complicit through years of cover-ups of the corruption that made 9/11—and other tragedies—possible, diverted the public's attention to such important matters as Nicole Smith, Britney Spears, professional sports, insuring that the American public would remain dumbed down on material matters.

Bush, Rumsfeld, Powell, Ashcroft, Rice Refused to Testify

Referring to the block by the Bush White House, one media article (January 26, 2003) stated that 9/11 panelist, Jim Roemer, complained that White House officials, including Donald Rumsfeld, Colin Powell, John Ashcroft, and Condoleezza Rice, refused to testify to the congressional panel.

Another member of the congressional panel, Senator John Mc Cain, complained that the Bush administration "slow-walked and stonewalled" the House-Senate inquiry. McCain said, "I don't see how you can have a thorough investigation without talking to the people who were in charge throughout the time period prior to 9/11."

"Undercutting the 9/11 Inquiry" was the heading of a *New York Times* editorial (March 31, 2003):

> Reasonable people might wonder if the White House, having failed in its initial attempt to have Henry Kissinger steer the investigation, may be resorting to budgetary starvation as a tactic to hobble any politically fearless inquiry. The committee's mandate includes scrutiny of intelligence failures and other government areas.
>
> As things now stand, $3 million budgeted as start-up funding could run out this summer. An estimated $14 million is needed for the task of finding out precisely how the attackers were able to pull off their plot in which nearly 3,000 people died.
>
> This seems a bargain given the importance of the mission. By comparison, the inquiry into the shuttle disaster's loss of seven lives may cost an estimated $40 million, and the inquiry into the Whitewater controversy ate up more than $30 million.

Hands Off Treatment Given to FBI-DOJ Witnesses

The few people from the FBI that did appear were given the white glove treatment, not asked any question that would give rise to making a record of what really happened. And for the record, the testimony of those that did appear was more a public relations snow job. Take the opening testimony of FBI Special Agent Mary Doran as she said at the start of her "testimony:"

> *Let me begin by telling you that I am proud to be an agent of the FBI and I am particularly proud of the work done by the Counterterrorism Division in New York.*
>
> *Prior to 9/11, it was primarily the New York Office, together with the U.S. Attorney's Office in the Southern District of New York, supported by dedicated analysts at FBI headquarters.*
>
> *The dedication and sacrifices made in this cause by these people is incalculable.*

Rare Hint at Serious Problems and Cover-ups

A rare article questioning the absence of an investigation into why hijackers were able to seize four airliners appeared in the *New York Times* (September 11, 2002) by Jim Dwyer, with the headline, "A Calamity Unimaginable in Scope, and Unexamined in All Its Dimensions." The half-page article stated:

> No inquiry remotely similar in scope, energy or transparency has examined the attacks of last Sept. 11, the devastating collapse of two of the world's tallest structures, the deaths at the Pentagon or on United Airlines Flight 93 in Pennsylvania. A handful of tightly focused reviews have taken place mostly in secret, conducted by private consultants, or by Congressional committees.
>
> One year later, the public knows less about the circumstances of 2,801 deaths at the foot of Manhattan in broad daylight than people in 1912 knew within weeks about the Titanic, which sank in the middle of an ocean in the dead of night.
>
> "You can hardly point to a cataclysmic event in our history, whether it was the sinking of the Titanic, the Pearl Harbor attack, the Kennedy assassination, when a blue-ribbon panel did not set out to establish the facts and, where appropriate, suggest reforms," Mr. Timoney said. "That has not happened here." [John F. Timoney, former senior police commander in New York and former police commissioner in Philadelphia.] Why this national reluctance to face the country's bloodiest modern disaster in all its dimensions?

Victims' Families Forced the Issue

Publicized protests from the families of the 9/11 victims *forced* members of Congress to pass legislation for a bipartisan commission to investigate why hijackers were able to seize four airliners. The legislation was enacted in November 2002 despite President Bush's opposition. It was called "The National Commission on Terrorist Attacks Upon the United States." The commission was created in late 2002 and was required to complete its work in 18 months, terminating on May 27, 2004.

All of the members of the commission were named by the same person seeking to block the investigation: President Bush. The initial chairman selected by President George Bush (November 27, 2002) was Henry Kissinger, despite—or because of—his conflicts of interest. President Bush stated (November 27, 2004), "His investigation (Kissinger) should carefully examine all the evidence and follow all the facts, wherever they lead. We must uncover every detail and learn every lesson of September the 11th." Sure! Bush then continued his stonewalling.

Kissinger's background created such a protest that he quickly resigned. Part of the opposition to Kissinger was due to his involvement in toppling of foreign governments such as the 1973 coup in Chile that toppled Salvador Allende in the Socialist government, his role in the invasion of Vietnam, and his Middle East ties.

Former New Jersey Republican governor Thomas H. Kean was then chosen as chairman, and former member of Congress, Lee H. Hamilton, was chosen co-chairman of the Commission. The commission was composed of five Republican and five Democratic appointees.

In my book, *Defrauding America,* I describe the role of Lee Hamilton in covering up for the October Surprise scheme that involved a secret operation to delay the release of 52 American hostages held in Iran, the purpose being to insure the election of Ronald Reagan over the incumbent, Jimmy Carter.

Most of the controlling staff were the very people who had an urgent need to cover up for grave misconduct that played major roles in enabling the success of the 9/11 terrorists, and several other major terrorist attacks.

Highly Suspect Commission Members

President Bush repeatedly blocked the formation of the commission and repeatedly denied it access to needed records, most of which were never released to the commission. Insuring that the truth about wrongdoings that led to 3,000 deaths would never be revealed to the public, most of the people selected to be 9/11 Commission members had a vital self-interest to protect. These included:

> Jamie S. Gorlick, Deputy Attorney General in the Clinton administration, and involved in covering up the advance information of the 9/11 and other terrorist attacks. She also covered up for the TWA Flight 800 terrorist attack, and ordered the FBI investigation to be shut down so as to prevent the public from learning about the FBI advance knowledge of the planned downing of Flight 800.
>
> Richard Ben-Veniste, a former federal prosecutor. Philip D. Zelikow, Executive director. He had been a member of the National Security Agency (NSA) Foreign Intelligence Advisory Board, a close friend of National Security Advisor Condoleezza Rice and co-author of a book with her.
>
> Lee H. Hamilton, vice chairman, who years earlier covered up for the October Surprise operation.

Greatest Impediment to the Truth: Philip Zelikow

The executive director, primarily responsible for how the investigation proceeded, was Philip Zelikow. He was a member of the National Security Agency (NSA) and the Foreign Intelligence Advisory Board, an agency highly suspect for not detecting the overwhelming amount of information on the planned terrorist attacks.

He was a close friend of National Security Advisor Condoleezza Rice, who repeatedly ignored warnings of the impending terrorist attacks. Zelikow was also in repeated personal and non-investigative contact with President Bush and his political advisor, Karl Rove, another White House official that had much to hide.

The competency of the National Security Agency was a major target of the investigation. The utter incompetence of Rice and her history of lying, along with the other conflicts put Zelikow in the position of investigating himself. To support the lies by President Bush, Zelikow attempted to add wording to the 9/11 Commission report that al Qaeda had links to Iraq, supporting Bush's lies for invading that country.

To prevent a record made of his telephone calls to the White House, Zelikow ordered that there be no records of his calls. The general counsel for the commission removed that improper order. A *New York Times* article by Philip Shenon stated that Zelikow intimidated the 9/11 Commission staff to alter its findings so as to protect President Bush, who was running for reelection, and Condoleezza Rice.

Strongly opposing Zelikow's position on the 9/11 Commission was a group known as the "9/11 widows," who demanded that Zelikow either resign or be fired. Their spokesperson said:

It is abundantly clear that Philip Zelikow should have immediately been replaced when the first rumblings of his impropriety and conflicts of interest surfaced. When all of this information became clear, the Commissioners and the press should have called for Zelikow's resignation. We did. Shamefully, most were silent.

Bush Administration Continued to Block 9/11 Investigation

The commission's first meeting occurred on January 27, 2003. The Bush administration's oppositions to determining why 19 hijackers were able to seize four airliners continued, as it repeatedly refused to cooperate with the commission.

"Bush Orders a 3-Year Delay in Opening Secret Documents" was the heading on a *New York Times* editorial (March 26, 2003) that stated:

> Add one more item to the list of things the Bush administration has been quietly doing on the home front while the nation is preoccupied with Iraq. This week President Bush signed an executive order that makes it easier for government agencies, including the White House, to keep documents classified and out of public view.
>
> The order does a number of things at once. It delays by three years the release of declassified government documents dating from 1978 or earlier. It treats all material sent to American officials from foreign governments—no matter how routine—as subject to classification. It expands the ability of the Central Intelligence Agency to shield documents from declassification. And for the first time, it gives the vice president the power to classify information. Taken individually, each of these actions might raise eyebrows for anyone who values open government. Taken together, they are reminders that this White House is obsessed with secrecy.

"White House Delays 9/11 Commission Investigation"

The heading on a *Wall Street Journal* article (September 8, 2003) stated:

> **White House Hurdles Delay 9/11 Commission Investigation.**
>
> For the past seven months, the National Commission on Terrorist Attacks Upon the United States, otherwise known as the 9/11 Commission, has been looking into the events leading up to the 2001 attacks. But so far the probers have made little progress. The commission is embroiled in tense negotiations over the level of access it will have to White House documents and the federal personnel it wants to interview.
>
> That means that the commission may not be able to complete an exhaustive investigation before its deadline next May, according to some of its 10 commissioners and others familiar with its work. From the commission's inception, commissioners and others say, the White House has put obstacles in its way.

A *New York Times* article (April 2, 2003) referred to the chairman stating no interest in finding the people at blame, and stated:

> The relatives were among those whose protests led Congress to create the panel last year, and some who attended Monday's hearing angrily blamed government officials for not doing more to prevent the attack.
>
> Speaking after the hearing ended, Thomas H. Kean, the former New Jersey governor who is the panel chairman, said the goal was not to assign blame but "to write an authoritative story: what happened and why it happened."

In a *New York Times* article (July 8, 2003), the matter of White House intimidation was addressed:

> The panel said the failure of the Bush administration to allow officials to be interviewed without the presence of government colleagues could impede its investigation, with the commission's chairman suggesting today that the situation amounts to "intimidation" of the witnesses.

President Bush's Attempts to Block 9/11 Investigation

Referring to the Bush administration's obstacle to a commission to investigate why the 9/11 hijackings occurred, a *Washington Post* article by Dana Milbank (September 19, 2002) stated:

> Lawmakers from both parties yesterday protested the Bush administration's lack of cooperation in the congressional inquiry into Sept. 11 intelligence failures and threatened to renew efforts to establish an independent commission.
>
> The White House reacted to the complaints from members of the House and Senate intelligence committees by softening its objection to an

independent commission. But the president's spokesman said such an independent probe should be "separate and apart from intelligence," a concession unlikely to satisfy lawmakers because it does not address the heart of their objections.

On the day a joint House and Senate intelligence committee released a staff report on the Sept. 11 failures and began to hold hearings, those involved in the congressional investigation said they had been thwarted by the administration's reluctance to share information about what the White House knew before last year's terrorist attacks.

"Are we getting the cooperation we need? Absolutely not," Sen. Richard C. Shelby (Ala.), the ranking Republican on the Senate Intelligence committee, said in a joint appearance with Chairman Bob Graham (D-Fla.) on NBC's "Today" show. Graham added: "What we're trying to do is to get people who had hands on these issues. . . . And what we're being told is, no, they don't want to make those kind of witnesses available."

Both Graham and Shelby yesterday endorsed the idea of independent panels. In his remarks at the start of the hearings, Shelby warned that "there may come a day very soon when it will become apparent that ours must be only a prelude to further inquiries."

Eleanor Hill, the joint committee's staff director, said in her 30-page statement to the committee that CIA Director George J. Tenet would not declassify "any references to the intelligence community providing information to the president or the White House." Hill also said Tenet would not declassify the identity of or information about a key al Qaeda leader involved in the attacks.

"According to [Tenet], the president's knowledge of intelligence information relevant to this inquiry remains classified even when the substance of that intelligence information has been declassified," Hill testified. She added that "the American public has a compelling interest in this information and that public disclosure would not harm national security."

In a press briefing yesterday morning, White House press secretary Ari Fleischer said that after Congress finishes the current investigation, "we'll take a look at talking to Congress about whether or not there is anything additional that goes to the broader areas if necessary." But Fleischer added that such a probe would be "a discussion about broader issues related to 9/11 separate and apart from intelligence."

The White House had previously opposed any independent effort to examine events that led to Sept. 11, arguing that such a probe could increase leaks and compromise intelligence. The FBI is investigating the intelligence committees after administration complaints about leaks to the news media, but the committees say the leaks generally come from the administration.

On Tuesday, Senate Governmental Affairs committee Chairman Joseph I. Lieberman (D-Conn.) said he has growing support for his effort to create an independent commission. Lieberman, who has been working on the proposal with Sen. John McCain (R-Ariz.), said he may attach legislation creating a commission to a bill creating the new Department of Homeland Security. "I have had very encouraging conversations with Senators Graham and Shelby . . . who first were a bit skeptical about this idea early on in the year," Lieberman said. "I think now they're both ready to support it."

Shelby acknowledged that the congressional probe would be incomplete. "I'm afraid if we try to publish at the end of this session a definitive paper on what we found, that there will be some things that we don't know because we hadn't had time to probe them and we have not had enough cooperation," he said.

Limiting Access to Key Documents to the Same Person Seeking to Cover-up for the Blame

In addition to refusal to produce government documents of major importance, the few documents that were made available were restricted to where none of the commissioners or staff could view them—except for Executive Director Philip D. Zelikow and Jamie Gorelick.

Blocking Protection Against Future Terrorist Attacks

The need for a thorough and accurate determination of who and what made possible the 9/11 attack was not only to insure justice, but also to protect against a repetition of the horrendous terrorist attacks that were occurring. Everyone who blocked access to government documents, or who refused to testify under oath and in public, became enablers to future successful attacks.

Key Government Personnel Refusing to Testify

In addition to refusing to provide needed documents, casting even more doubt on the truth being revealed, the following refused to testify under oath, and most only allowed the questioners to come to them, and not in front of the commission:

President George Bush.
Vice President Dick Cheney.
Former President Bill Clinton.
Former Vice President Al Gore.

To insure that their responses to questions would be synchronized, Bush and Cheney required that they be interviewed together. If one were to lie, it would be necessary that the other's response be the same lie. The commission was repeatedly given false information by the FAA and the Pentagon, and it had considered turning the matter over to the Department of Justice for perjury and obstruction of justice.

The staff report found, but omitted from the report, what was obvious to any competent observer of events in the Middle East. That was the conclusion that al Qaeda's motives for the 9/11 attacks was a combination of the U.S. one-sided support for Israel and the presence of U.S. military in the Middle East. Hamilton argued that these were the major reasons for the attack, and that the United States should reassess its policies—a fact that should be obvious.

In an article by investigative reporter Ron Suskind, he revealed that a memo was given to Bush, while Bush was vacationing in Texas, by a concerned CIA briefer, titled, "Bin Laden Determined to Strike in U.S." And that Bush brushed it off, stating, "All right, you've covered your ass, now."

One of the most important sources of information was denied to the commission by President Bush: access to records on al Qaeda at the National Security Agency (NSA), which had considerable information from electronic surveillance and code breaking.

Commission Totally Ignored the FBI-DOJ Misconduct and Incompetence That Made 9/11 Possible

The almost unbelievable incompetence and criminal obstruction of justice by FBI-DOJ personnel was enabled to occur by the heavy presence of present and former Department of Justice people on the commission that had a strong vested self-interest in the commission report. They covered up for:

> The advance notice of the 9/11 and related terrorist attacks given to FBI agents by Gregory Scarpa Jr., who acted as a mole within the key al Qaeda cell.
>
> The criminal obstruction of justice by FBI-DOJ personnel arising from covering up for the series of murders involving FBI supervisory agent Lindley DeVecchio, and then discrediting the advance information of the terrorist attacks provided by Scarpa so as to discredit Scarpa's later testimony about the murders.

Covering Up for History of Deadly FAA Misconduct

Despite the almost unbelievable amount of intelligence failures, the terrorists could never have succeeded in their hijacking of four airliners if the deadly culture in the FAA did not exist. The FAA had the primary responsibility, by law, to order measures insuring safety in air travel, and that included, of course, defense against hijackings.

I detail in my book, *History of Aviation Disasters: 1950 to 9/11*, the 50 year history of specific airline disasters made possible by misconduct in the FAA. It was this culture that blocked the easily implemented measures to prevent airliners from being hijacked. The dozens of worldwide hijackings certainly provided the urgency to implement these measures. But as in the past, the FAA, known as the tombstone agency, blocked every effort to address this issue.

After the 9/11 commission started its investigation I offered several times to provide information and evidence showing the areas of primary blame for the success of the 9/11 hijackers. I notified the commission:

- That I was in the past a key federal airline safety inspector, who was given the responsibility to correct the conditions responsible for the worst series of airline crashes in the nation's history at that time, and that my prior experience was as an international airline captain and Navy Patrol Plane Commander in World War II.
- That I acted similar to an independent prosecutor while employed by the FAA, charging the FAA with gross misconduct related to several specific airline disasters.
- That I had filed several lawsuits for the sole purpose of providing evidence of the FAA corruption.
- That I had written several books on aviation safety problems.

It was obvious to the 9/11 Commission that I would be one of the most qualified witnesses to explain why the FAA, with the primary responsibility for preventing the four simultaneous hijackings, did not perform its duty. At the same time, many people in government would not want me to appear. Over the years, many people become criminally involved by either covering up for the continuing FAA corruption—and the continuing series of deadly consequences—or who took aggressive actions to halt my exposure activities.

Being unable to get a response from my letters to the commission or to its Chairman, Thomas Kean, I prepared a statement of intended testimony and sent it by certified mail, which should have resulted in being called to testify, and at the very least, to be made a part of the record:

Prepared Statement of
Former Federal Aviation Safety Agent Rodney Stich To
The National Commission on Terrorist Attacks Upon the United States

Date: July 19, 2003

I, Rodney F. Stich, declare:

I am making the following statements for inclusion into the hearing record of this commission that has the responsibility to determine where the blame existed that enabled 19 hijackers to seize four airliners on September 11, 2001. Because of my prior experiences, some occurring while I was a federal aviation safety agent in an unusual position, I have considerable insider information that is not otherwise available to this or any other investigative body that reveals where the primary blame existed that resulted in 3,000 people being killed on that day.

My Background, Credibility, and Ability to Discover These Matters

I am a former federal aviation safety agent with an unusual background and considered a top aviation safety expert with over 60 years of sophisticated aviation experience, starting in 1941.

During World War II, I was a Navy patrol plane commander flying and teaching in multi-engine aircraft.

After the war, I was an international airline captain for many years.

I later became an air safety inspector-investigator for the Federal Aviation Administration (FAA). During my official duties for the federal government I was given the assignment to correct the conditions responsible for the worst series of aviation disasters in the nation's history. This is where, as a federal inspector-investigator, I initially discovered and documented the deep-seated culture and corruption within the government aviation safety offices that was responsible for decades of preventable airline crashes. One of those crashes was the world's worst at that time, occurring in Brooklyn, New York. The same deep-seated misconduct that made *that* New York City disaster and many others possible is the same deep-seated misconduct that created the conditions that enabled 19 hijackers to seize four airliners on September 11, 2001.

I have written numerous highly detailed and documented books addressing these problems that made the events of 9/11 possible, including multiple E-book and print-book editions of *Unfriendly Skies*. The primary purpose of these books was to inform the public of these serious matters in an attempt to circumvent the vast cover-ups of what is probably the world's worst aviation scandal.

I have appeared as guest and expert on over 3,000 radio and television shows since 1978, seeking to inform the public of matters gravely affecting aviation safety.

Over the years I have become a confidant to dozens of present and former government agents who have provided me with information and evidence concerning corruption in key government offices that continue to subvert the national security of the United States.

Based upon the misconduct that I discovered in my official government air safety position, and the cover-up of such misconduct, I exercised certain legal procedures during which I acted the role of an independent prosecutor. During the subsequent six-month hearing a 4000-page hearing record was developed which provided additional evidence supporting my official charges that deep-seated corruption in key segments of the FAA was responsible for a series of specific airline disasters. Although airline crashes are far less frequent today, these conditions exist, and as shown on September 11, 2001, the consequences can be catastrophic.

Based upon my many years of experience as a government and private investigator, and expert in many areas affecting aviation, it is my firm conviction that the *primary blame* for the success of the 19 hijackers on 9/11 was the hardcore misconduct of certain people in government aviation safety offices. Secondary blame was the people, in and out of government, who engaged in cover-ups, obstruction of justice, and even retaliation to silence my attempts to expose these matters.

Among the areas of misconduct resulting in many prior aviation disasters that I documented are the following:

Refusal of FAA management personnel in certain segments of the FAA to take authorized and required actions on major aviation safety problems, aviation safety violations, and even criminal violations, some of which occurred in my immediate area of government responsibilities.

Pattern of deliberate actions by FAA management that blocked federal safety agents from carrying out their aviation safety duties.

Pressure and threats against federal aviation safety agents by FAA management, in retaliation for the agents reporting major safety problems and violations.

Repeated removal, and destruction, by FAA management of official records relating to major safety problems and safety violations. This practice continued despite the continuation of fatal crashes arising from the same problems and misconduct.

Retaliation and threats by FAA management against federal aviation safety agents who initiate authorized and required actions on aviation safety problems that they encounter.

A corrupt culture that prevented the federal government from performing its federal aviation safety responsibilities.

Among the many uncorrected aviation safety problems that I and other federal aviation safety agents discovered, reported, and tried to correct, and which were blocked by FAA management, were the following:

Airline training and competency check programs at certain airlines that were a farce, which allowed untrained and unsafe crewmembers to continue in airline operations. These programs did not meet the intent or the specifics of federal aviation safety directives.

Falsified records to falsely indicate federally required pilot and flight engineer training and competency checks had been performed, when in fact they were not performed. These matters were known to FAA management, who retaliated against inspectors who made the reports.

Falsified records indicating that federally required maintenance practices had been accomplished, when in fact they were not accomplished. Several major aviation disasters resulted from this practice.

Dangerous piloting techniques, such as high sink rate approaches. One example of the deadly consequences: One captain, who I reported having a high sink rate approach, and who was denied corrective training, a few months later crashed at Salt Lake City due to this very same problem. Forty three people were cremated alive.

Dangerous flight engineer problems at a major and politically powerful airline. One example of the deadly consequences also existed in that Salt Lake City crash. The flight engineer failed to shut off the fuel shutoff valves and fuel pumps after the initial crash, causing heavy quantities of fuel to be discharged from a broken fuel line, resulting in a major fire. (Compounded by the dangerous piloting practice of that pilot, and at that airline, plus the refusal of that airline to provide the legally required emergency evacuation training, which was covered up by falsifying government required records.)

Dangerous practice of pilots descending too low during visual and instrument conditions. Two consequences of this known and unaddressed problem, as examples, were the aircraft that crashed into Lake Michigan and the airliner that crashed during an approach to the Cincinnati Airport.

Airline refusing to provide government-required pilot training and then falsifying government required records to conceal this practice. The results were poorly trained and qualified pilots at a major airline and numerous crashes attributed to this misconduct.

Hundreds of airliner hijackings that were easily and inexpensively preventable. I and other inspectors reported the urgency of inexpensive and easily accomplished preventative measures that FAA management was authorized and required to be done. FAA management refused to order the measures that would have halted the deadly practice of airline hijackings that have occurred for the past 40 years throughout the world. The continuation of this refusal to act and retaliation against inspectors making reports of the necessity for these corrective actions made possible the success of 19 hijackers on September 11, 2001.

Many other problems, which I detail in my various government and non-government writings and reports. Deep-seated corruption was primarily responsible for these problems within the government's aviation safety offices, followed by incompetence and politically correct placement of unqualified and inexperienced people in key management positions.

Indifference, Cover-Ups, Complicity,
Throughout Government

Being blocked from carrying out the aviation safety duties, and the close proximity of the crashes and deaths to the misconduct that I discovered, caused me to notify others of these federal crimes. I notified the administrator of the Federal Aviation Administration; the political appointees to the National Transportation Safety Board (and its CAB Bureau of Aviation Safety predecessor); various offices of the U.S. Department of Justice; members of Congress; and lawyers at prominent aviation litigation law firms. Some admitted the gravity of my charges, and then either refused to act or passive or actively covered up for the deadly practices.

Acting As Independent Prosecutor to Force Corrective Actions

As an aviation safety agent and while the crashes due to these problems were occurring every few months, I exercised remedies in law that permitted me to act as an independent prosecutor for approximately six months. During this time I conducted a hearing during which I subpoenaed FAA personnel and obtained testimony and evidence that further proved my charges that deep-seated corruption and other misconduct within the FAA was responsible for certain specific aviation disasters—including hijackings. The evidence was covered up by the FAA Administrator's hearing officer and FAA legal counsel, causing the deep-seated corruption to continue, along with the many airline disasters that followed.

Complicity of National Transportation
Safety Board Political Appointees

I and other federal aviation safety agents repeatedly reported these problems to various members of the National Transportation Safety Board. They had the moral and legal responsibilities to immediately investigate our charges. Instead, they covered up, thereby becoming complicit in the crashes and deaths resulting from the problems that they cover-up enabled to continue. This complicity required that they omit any reference to the FAA misconduct, omit reference to their own involvement, and cover up for the crash-causing conditions associated with these deaths.

Cover-Ups by Others

I made numerous reports of the misconduct to members of Congress. They also had a moral and legal duty to receive evidence of my charges. Initially, some members of Congress admitted the gravity of what I charged, but then raised various excuses. One such excuse was that these matters were not in their area of responsibilities. (Tell that to the families of the 3,000 dead on 9/11!) The matters *were* in their areas of responsibilities. They also had the option of requesting the General Accounting Office (GAO), the congressional investigative body, to receive my evidence. They also had a responsibility under the federal crime reporting statute to receive my evidence. (Title 18 U.S.C. § 4.)

Some of the recipients of my charges were major partners in aviation litigation law firms, including some who *now* represent families of the 3,000 killed on 9/11. Some wrote, admitting the gravity of my charges, but none would help in getting this information known. Ironically, if they had acted when this information was presented to them, it is very probable that the corruption within the government's aviation safety offices could have been halted and the conditions enabling hijackers to seize airliners could have been corrected. Similar statements can be made for many others who knew of these charges and who either did nothing, or who actively assisted the cover-ups.

Refusing to work in such a corrupt environment, I left the FAA. The cover-ups caused the deep-seated corruption within the FAA to continue and, as expected, the crashes and hijackings made possible by this corrupt culture. Reports from FAA inspectors still within the FAA confirmed to me that no meaningful changes had occurred. Realizing I had a responsibility, and evidence of the corruption, I took other steps seeking to expose these matters, including the following:

Using Judicial Process To Circumvent the Cover-Ups

The continuing airline disasters caused me to use my assets[1] to fund various efforts to circumvent the cover-ups and force correction of the worsening corruption that I and other government agents discovered. The cover-ups by members of Congress and Justice Department personnel caused me to exercise remedies provided by criminal and other federal statutes; Titles 18 U.S.C. § 4 and 28 U.S.C. § 1361.

The federal crime reporting statute requires anyone knowing of a federal crime to report it to a federal judge or other federal officer (such as members of Congress). That statute plainly states this responsibility:

Title 18 U.S.C. § 4. Misprision of felony. Whoever, having knowledge of the actual commission of a felony cognizable by a court of the United States, conceals and does not as soon as possible make known the same to some judge or other person in civil or military authority under the United States, shall be fined under this title or imprisoned not more than three years, or both.

Title 28 U.S.C. § 1361 gives any citizen the right to seek a court order requiring a federal official to perform his legal duty (in this instance, his aviation safety duties) and to halt his or her unlawful conduct.

Title 28 U.S.C. § 1361. Action to compel an officer of the United States to perform his duty. The district courts shall have original jurisdiction of any action in the nature of mandamus to compel an officer or employee of the United States or any agency thereof to perform a duty owed to the plaintiff.

I filed the first of several federal filings[2] the late 1970s and early 1980s, seeking to report the criminal activities related to a series of aviation disasters to a federal judge.

Also, to obtain an order requiring certain federal officials to perform their aviation safety duties and to halt their unlawful conduct. Initially, federal district and appellate judges admitted the serious of my charges but then, upon motion by Justice Department lawyers, the judges dismissed the filings before I could provide evidence. These dismissals, by obstructing justice, caused the corruption and related crashes to continue.[3]

In the case of a multi-district litigation in Los Angeles involving the crash of a DC-10, the chief plaintiff counsel approved my filing of the amicus brief, which was required by rules of court.

No one ever denied the validity of my charges. Nor would they be in a position to have enabled them to do so.

Discovering Other Areas of Corruption Harming National Security

Dozens of other government agents contacted me over a period of many years with information and documentation on areas of corruption[4] in government offices that they had discovered. (I detail some of these areas in subsequent books, including the E-book and print-book formats of *Defrauding America*, *Drugging America*, and *Terrorism Against America*. The sole purpose for writing these books has been to circumvent the cover-ups and inform the public of these matters, with the hope that there would be sufficient outrage to force corrective actions.

In 1986, based upon the additional information on federal crimes implicating people in key government positions that I discovered, both from my personal investigative work and from my large numbers of former and present government agents, I again exercised my responsibilities to report the federal crimes under the federal crime reporting statute. Again and again, federal judges and Justice Department lawyers blocked me and my sources from providing evidence of these criminal, and even subversive, activities.

Federal judges used various tactics to block the reporting of these criminal activities. In addition to blocking the reports being made under the federal criminal statutes (18 U.S.C. § 4), federal judges[5] started issuing unlawful and unconstitutional orders permanently barring me access to the federal district and appellate courts. These orders continue in effect to this day, barring me from either reporting the criminal activities or in defending against the numerous attacks that have been made to halt my exposure activities.

Judicial Retaliation for Reporting Criminal & Subversive Activities

As my discovery of other areas of criminal activities continued, I again exercised my responsibilities under the federal criminal statutes to report the criminal activities to a federal judge. Federal judges then expanded on their prior tactics. They charged me with criminal contempt of court for filing papers in the federal courts seeking to report these crimes (and for exercising federal defenses against record-setting violations of federally protected rights that were part of the legal tactics used to halt my exposure activities).

Ironically, at the age of 70, a multi-millionaire, using my assets to halt these deadly crimes, I was suddenly sentenced to six months in federal prison for my public-spirited activities. While in prison, unlawful and unconstitutional orders were rendered by federal judges seizing and liquidating the $10 million in assets that funded my attempts to expose and correct these criminal activities in which they were implicated. These retaliatory acts were criminal offenses[7] by federal judges and Justice Department lawyers. There is some irony in the fact that a former federal agent who sought to report and halt the conditions that enabled the horrible deaths of 3,000 people on 9/11 would suffer such grave retaliation for his attempts to prevent such ongoing tragedies.

Last Judicial Obstruction-of-Justice
***Prior* to September 11, 2001**

In my last attempt prior to 9/11 to report these criminal activities, I filed a lawsuit[39] in the U.S. district court at Reno, Nevada. Several issues were raised in that lawsuit, including (a) the attempt to report the criminal activities; (b) the attempt to have ruled unconstitutional the orders permanently depriving me the right to access the courts and the termination of my civil and constitutional rights and protections that were taken by the series of injunctive orders; and (c) the attempt to have ruled invalid the judicial seizure and liquidation of the $10 million in assets that funded my exposure of the criminal activities.

As in the past, the federal judge[8] acting on that legal filing blocked the reporting of the criminal activities and blocked my other causes of actions. In addition to refusing to receive the reports of the criminal activities, the federal judge ordered that I pay a large fine for daring to file the action and for daring to report the conditions that enabled 9/11 to occur.

I then filed an appeal with the Ninth Circuit court of appeals—where the obstruction of justice had commenced in the late 1970s and continues to this day. The appellate judges[9] ruled that the prior injunctions permanently barred me from the due process and equal protection right to file papers in the district and appellate courts, including the right to file appeals. That ruling was *made after the 3,000 deaths occurred on 9/11.*

Complicity of Many Members of Congress

For several years prior to September 11, 2002, I repeatedly notified (in writing, some by certified mail) many members of congress of the serious corruption that I and other government agents had discovered, some of which related to major national security matters. These serious matters that we sought to report included, for instance, reports of (a) surface to air missiles being acquired by terrorists, made possible by actions of FBI and CIA personnel; (b) suitcase nuclear devices being smuggled from the former Soviet Union through Lithuania; (c) retaliation against FBI agents seeking to report criminal activities of CIA personnel; (d) drug smuggling by people acting under cover of government positions and covert operations; (e) Soviet spies in the FBI and CIA offices; and (f) many other matters inflicting great harm upon national interests.

Post 9/11 Judicial Obstructions of Justice
Judicial Cover-Ups in Southern District of New York

In accordance with required filing procedures and payment of fees, I submitted to the U.S. district court for the Southern District of New York (August 8, 2002) a filing under the federal crime reporting statute, seeking to report the criminal activities that I charged caused the conditions to exist that enabled 19 hijackers to seize four airliners on 9/11. By law, those papers *must be filed*. Further, the federal crime reporting statute

---

[39] Reno, Nevada filing, Nr. CV-N-00-0152-ECR-PHA. March 24, 2000.

and the gravity of the charges by government insiders, plus the events of 9/11, demanded that the federal judges promptly receive the evidence. In addition, federal law requires that the charges stated in federal filings be accepted as true[10] at that stage of the pleadings. But if that were done, the pattern of judicial obstruction of justice would be exposed.

In violation of federal law relating to due process and equal protection right to file papers in federal court, it is now eleven months later and the papers have *not* been filed. Nor have the papers and the filing fees been returned.

This refusal to file (a) violates federal rules for filing such papers; (b) blocks the reporting of criminal activities to a federal judge as specifically provided by the federal crime reporting statute; (c) prevents corrective actions to be taken—the same misconduct that made the events of 9/11 possible; (d) prevents the relatives of the 3,000 victims to have the guilty punished for their wrongful conduct and prevents them from discovering the primary defendants responsible for their grief; (e) continues in effect the years of corruption, the cover-ups, and the consequences that will surely result in further tragedies just as the prior cover-ups made the 3,000 deaths on 9/11 possible.

Judicial Cover-Ups in District of Columbia

Another attempt to report these matters was made where one of the 9/11 tragedies occurred, to the U.S. district court, District of Columbia. This filing occurred on June 12, 2002.[11] U.S. District Judge Henry H. Kennedy, Jr., promptly dismissed the filing without prior notice, in clear violation of federal due process and the mandatory requirements of the federal crime reporting statute.

Kennedy sought to support the dismissal—and the cover-up—on the basis that former CIA legal counsel and federal judge Stanley Sporkin issued an order in 1991 permanently barring me from filing any papers in the federal courts. That 1991 order was made in a filing where I sought to report the criminal activities that I and my group of other former government agents had discovered.

Not only did Sporkin block the reporting of criminal activities (some of which involved the CIA in which he had been legal counsel), but also misused the judicial position and the courts to permanently terminate the legal rights, protections and defenses that are "guaranteed" by the laws and Constitution of the United States. His actions in preventing exposure of misconduct in government obviously enabled the deaths of 3,000 people to occur on 9/11, just as of the prior judges played key roles.

I then filed a notice of appeal and paid the filing fees with the District of Columbia court of appeals. The court of appeal judges[12] dismissed the appeal on January 16, 2003, holding that I have been barred for life from filing papers in district and appellate courts as guaranteed to other people, including murderers.

I then filed a motion for an en banc hearing. Without any hearing, this motion was denied by order dated March 26, 2003,[13] upholding Sporkin's order permanently depriving me the due process right to federal courts—and upholding the judicial practice of obstruction of justice and violating the federal crime reporting statute.

Complicity in These Events by Justices of the U.S. Supreme Court

From the late 1970s to the present date, the Justices of the U.S. Supreme Court have aided and abetted these criminal acts of judges over whom they have supervisory responsibilities. They had been repeatedly advised by me, through legal filings and certified letters, of the crimes and the consequences. They also had a duty under the federal crime reporting statute to receive the evidence of federal crimes, as provided by the federal crime reporting statute. Justices have supervisory responsibilities over the conduct of lower federal judges. The only partially favorable response was a letter from Justice Bryon White, and that was a form of apology for not being able to help.

Included in Issues Needing To Be Addressed Relating to 9/11

Included in the issues that must be addressed to determine the people sharing in the blame for the conditions enabling 19 hijackers to kill 3,000 people on September 11, 2001, are the following:

Understand where the primary blame lies for the success of 19 hijackers on September 11, 2001. The blame for the conditions that enabled 19 hijackers to seize four airliners on 9/11 rests primarily with people in the government's aviation safety offices who had the authority, responsibility, and knowledge of this ongoing aircraft hijacking problem. Ignoring hundreds of prior hijackings is far more than a problem of stupidity on the part of government aviation safety personnel.

The present tactic of placing the blame on a more innocent intelligence failure is either a deliberate diversionary tactic plus ignorance in some quarters. Relying solely on being told that a criminal event was to take place obviously cannot supersede the need to take known and required preventative measures for continuing hijackings that had been occurring for the prior 40 years.

Determine from government insiders who had reported the problems and have evidence of these reports the arrogance and corruption within the government's aviation safety offices responsible for thousands of deaths over the years. I have the documents to prove this deep-seated problem, including the 4000-page hearing transcript from the FAA hearing at which I acted as an independent prosecutor.

Examine the relationship of the corruption to specific airline crashes—including years of airline hijackings, and many that occurred in my immediate area of government aviation safety responsibilities.

Receive my testimony and documents that prove a pattern of obstruction of justice and felony retaliation against a former federal agent and witness, perpetrated by federal judges and Justice Department lawyers, that played key roles in the 3,000 deaths on September 11, and key roles in other tragedies, some ongoing.

Obtain testimony from some of my sources (former and present government agents), concerning the corruption in government offices in the aviation and in other areas. This evidence will show the cancerous spread of corruption in government, made possible by the cowardly or profitable cover-ups.

For years I have been warning in writings that covering up for the corruption by people in key government positions would surely worsen the conditions and the deadly consequences. The scenario occurred time and time again, and no better example could exist than what occurred on September 11. There is no way that this level of corruption can be corrected without the public being told of these matters. Tragically, the cover-ups made possible the expansion of the corruption in government, involving so many different people, that it is now almost impossible to eradicate. The public will continue to pay the consequences, as in the past.

Summary

Hundreds of airliner hijackings have occurred during the 40 years prior to the successful hijackings of four airlines by 19 hijackers on September 11.

FAA safety inspectors, including myself, had reported the urgent need for the FAA to order the simple and inexpensive preventative measures that would have prevented most of the hijackings and related deaths (and other preventable aviation disasters arising from known unsafe or illegal practices).

FAA management personnel had the authority and responsibility to order these preventative measures.

FAA management engaged in a pattern of arrogance and corruption, knowingly causing the deaths of many people over the years.

Evidence of these criminal activities is found in official government documents, some of which are in my possession; in the 4000-page hearing transcript where I acted as an independent prosecutor while an FAA inspector; in other records that I possess; in my testimony, and testimony of other former federal agents. My evidence, and that of the dozens of former government agents and other insiders to whom I have become a confidant, would reveal other areas of corruption in government offices that continues to inflict great harm upon important national interests, including national security, and the harm inflicted upon innocent people.

Federal judges and Justice Department prosecutors engaged in a documented series of criminal activities to block my reporting of these matters, with awesome consequences for the United States and its people.

If the matters detailed in this statement are not fully exposed the same deadly consequences affecting aviation will continue as they have from when I first made similar warnings into official government records.

Executed this 19th day of July 2003.

Rodney F. Stich
Fax: 925-295-1203
POB 5, Alamo, CA 94507

Sent by certified mail: 7002 0860 0003 9592 6412

Further related information at the following Internet sites:
www.defraudingamerica.com
www.druggingamerica.com
www.unfriendlyskies.com

ENDNOTES

1. After leaving the FAA I concentrated on real estate investments, and I used the equity in these investments to fund the expensive efforts to expose these serious matters.

2 *Stich v. United States, et al.*, 554 F.2d 1070 (9th Cir.) (table), *cert. denied*, 434 U.S. 920 (1977)(addressed hard-core air safety misconduct, violations of federal air safety laws, threats against government inspectors not to report safety violations and misconduct); *Stich v. National Transportation Safety Board*, 685 F.2d 446 (9th Cir.)(table), *cert. denied*, 459 U.S. 861 (1982))(addressed repeated criminal falsification of official airline accident reports, omitting highly sensitive air safety misconduct, making possible repeated crashes from the same sequestered problems); Amicus curiae brief filed on July 17, 1975, in the Paris DC-10 multi-district

litigation, *Flanagan v. McDonnell Douglas Corporation and United States of America*, Civil Action 74-808-PH, MDL 172, Central District California.)(addressing the long standing FAA misconduct, of which the cover-up of the DC-10 cargo door problem was one of repeated instances of tragedy related misconduct); U.S. v. Department of Justice, District of Columbia, Nos. 86-2523, 87-2214, and other actions filed by Stich seeking to expose and correct the powerful and covert air disaster misconduct.

3 The frequency of airline crashes today are far less frequent than when I was given the assignment to correct the problems. However, this reduction in the number of crashes is more due to on-ground and in-aircraft safeguards. The basic problems in the most critical area of the government's aviation safety offices still exists, being why the obvious, simple, and inexpensive preventative measures were not taken as required by law.

4 Among the dozens of courageous present and former government agents who contacted me during the past 18 years have been agents of the FBI, CIA, DEA, Customs, INS and other federal and state agencies. The information and documentation that they have provided me shows that the *secondary* blame for the success of the 19 hijackers was far more than an intelligence failure in certain government agencies. Rather, a level of corruption that remains unaddressed and which will remain until there is a full-blown investigation (which will never occur). However, the information I acquired shows a degree of criminality and subversive misconduct implicating people in key government positions.

5 Among many federal judges participating in the series of orders obstructing the reporting of these crimes were Marilyn Patel, Milton Schwartz, Levi, Stanley Sporkin,

6 Inflicting harm against former federal agents and witnesses are felonies under Title 18 U.S.C. §1510. (a) Whoever willfully endeavors by means of bribery, misrepresentation, intimidation, or force or threats thereof to obstruct, delay, or prevent the communication of information relating to a violation of any criminal statute of the United States by any person to a criminal investigator; or Whoever injures any person in his person or property on account of giving by such person or by any other person of any such information to any criminal investigator–Shall be fined not more than $5,000 or imprisoned not more than five years, or both."

18 U.S.C. § 1512. Tampering with a witness, victim, or an informant.

(b) Whoever knowingly uses intimidation or physical force, threatens, or corruptly persuades another person, or attempts to do so, or engages in misleading conduct toward another person, with intent to–

(3) hinder, delay, or prevent the communication to a law enforcement officer or judge of the United States of information relating to the commission or possible commission of a Federal offense ... shall be fined under this title or imprisoned not more than ten years, or both.

(c) Whoever intentionally harasses another person and thereby hinders, delays, prevents, or dissuades any person from–(2) reporting to a law enforcement officer or judge of the United States the commission or possible commission of a Federal offense ....

18 U.S.C. § 1513. Retaliating against a witness, victim, or an informant.

(b) Whoever knowingly engages in any conduct and thereby causes bodily injury to another person or damages the tangible property of another person, or threatens to do so, with intent to retaliate against any person for –

(2) any information relating to the commission or possible commission of a Federal offense ...

7 Reno, Nevada filing, Nr. CV-N-00-0152-ECR-PHA. March 24, 2000.

8 U.S. District Judge Howard C. Reed, Jr.

9 Ninth Circuit appellate judges James R. Browning, Andrew Kleinfeld, Ronald Gould. Order dated April 12, 2002.

10 Federal courts must accept as true the allegations in the complaint and supporting affidavits as true. (See, e.g., *Gardener v. Toilet Goods Assn*., 387 U.S. 167, 172 (1967). If plaintiff's allegations state a claim for which federal courts can grant relief, the court must accept jurisdic-

tion. The United States Supreme Court stated in *Dennis v. Sparks*, 449 U.S. 24 (1980). Also, FRCivP 8(d) states: "Effect of Failure to Deny. Averments in a pleading to which a responsive pleading is required, are admitted when not denied in the responsive pleading."

11U.S. district court, District of Columbia, Nr. 02cv01172, filed June 12, 2002.

12 District of Columbia appellate judges Douglas Ginsburg, David Sentelle, and A. Raymond Randolph.

13 Denial for en banc hearing was made by judges Douglas Ginsburg, Harry Edwards, David Sentelle, Karen Henderson, Harry Randolph, Judith Rogers, David Tatel, and Merrick Garland.

There was no response, despite the fact that if any of my allegations were true, including those about prior aviation disasters arising from the corruption within the government's aviation safety offices, the commission members would be complicit in subsequent disasters made possible by their cover-ups.

Cover-ups in 9/11 Commission Report

The 9/11-commission report was issued in July 2004, and followed the usual pattern of diverting attention from hardcore misconduct involving government officials. The report identified some relatively minor and innocent intelligence failures, and even failure of members of Congress to act. But, it did not address the corrupt and criminal activities that existed of people in the FBI-DOJ, nor corruption in the FAA, nor the many obstruction of justice tactics used to silence me and others who sought to report the ongoing obstruction.

Brief Reference to Congress's Oversight Failures

The 9/11-commission report pleased many members of Congress since it dealt with intangibles. The summary of its contents was to blame *institutional* errors rather than *individual* misconduct. I sent a second declaration to the 9/11 Commission. A few excerpts follows:

The National Commission
On Terrorist Attacks Upon the United States

Date: April 12, 2004

I, Rodney F. Stich, declare:

This April 12, 2004, declaration is sent to Thomas H. Kean, Chairman of the National Commission on Terrorist Attacks Upon the United States, by certified mail.[1] The purpose of this declaration is to place *another* declaration into the commission records from a former government agent concerning the documented misconduct in government offices that played key roles enabling terrorists to seize four airliners on September 11, 2001.

The members of this commission are circumventing the primary areas of blame for the events of 9/11. This standard tactic of controlled investigations has repeatedly prevented exposure and correction of serious corruption in government offices, enabling the continuation of catastrophic effect upon the United States. The members of this commission are intent at showing "mistakes" were made that led to 3,000 people being killed rather than reveal the criminal actions that made 9/11 possible.

The basis for the statements in this declaration is based upon my many years of experience as a government agent and subsequent investigations, which included the input from large numbers of other present and former government agents.[2]

During my activities as a federal aviation safety agent I had been given the assignment to correct the conditions causing the worst series of airline crashes in the nation's history. In this assignment I acted as an independent counsel, conducting hearings and receiving evidence, which *proved* the existence of deep-seated corruption within the government's aviation safety offices related to a series of fatal airline crashes.

The standard cover-up of corrupt and criminal misconduct following that proceeding caused and enabled numerous catastrophic blowback consequences. These included years of preventable aviation tragedies—of which the hijackings of four airliners on September 11, 2001, were only the most recent and prominent consequences.

This declaration highlights the *primary causes* for the success of the hijackers on 9/11, including the:

Culture and deep-seated misconduct within the government's aviation safety offices that blocked the federal government from performing its aviation safety responsibilities.

Cover-ups and obstruction of justice relating to these federal offenses.

Intelligence *failures* exacerbated by the deep-seated corruption that subverted the function of government agencies, and especially in the U.S. Department of Justice and the Central Intelligence Agency.

Failure of key people in government to act on intelligence.

Four Areas of Primary and Secondary Blame
For Events of September 11, 2001

The *primary blame* for the success of the hijackers on 9/11 was the misconduct of people in certain government aviation safety offices that created the conditions enabling hijackers to seize four airliners and hijackings of the prior 50 years, all of which were easily preventable. The deep-seated corruption within the FAA were addressed in a 4000-page FAA hearing record during which I acted as an independent counsel.

The tragedy-related corruption was charged in various judicial filings during which I sought to report the federal crimes to a federal judges under the mandatory requirements of the federal crime reporting statute, Title 18 U.S.C. § 4. I sought to report these matters to members of Congress, all of whom refused to receive evidence and for various reasons engaged in cover-up.

Secondary primary blame for the events of 9/11 were the cover-ups and bstructtion of justice that blocked present and former government agents—including me—from reporting these federal offenses The most heavily documented evidence of the felony cover-ups and obstruction of justice were the actions by federal judges and Justice Department lawyers to lawsuits that I filled under the federal crime reporting statute seeking to report these matters. Their obstruction of justice were federal crimes per se.

Subordinate and contributing blame for the events of 9/11 were so-called "intelligence failures" by people in Justice Department offices and the CIA. These "failures" were undoubtedly influenced by the widespread corruption in these two government offices.

Contributing subordinate blame arises from the failures of politicians and members of Congress to act when insiders provide information of corruption in government offices.

Another contributing subordinate blame arises from the "controlled investigations" that covered up and obstructed justice in prior areas of misconduct involving politicians and government officials.

Much of this information is detailed in my various informational books and in charges made in my various filings in the federal courts

Again, no response.

The final report of the commission was, as expected, a whitewash. It *had* to be. The corruption described in this book should send shivers up the spine of anyone who understands the significance of the corruption. But what is stated in this book is only a fraction of what had been inflicted on the generally hopelessly uninformed American public. As I have seen and recorded for the past 40 years, the whitewash made possible bigger and bigger tragedies.

Final Comments on 9/11 Commission

Writing a book on the 9/11 Commission was none other than the former executive director of the 9/11 Commission, Philip Zelikow, who rewrote history in doing it. Zelikow omitted from the book virtually every example of FBI-DOJ incompetence and misconduct. Most of those engaging in the cover-ups—that set the stage for more of the same—were rewarded. Valerie Caproni was promoted to the position of the chief counsel for the FBI; Patrick Fitzgerald was promoted to U.S. Attorney in Chicago, where he later covered up for the involvement of White House officials in the Valerie Plame outing.

CHAPTER TWENTY

State Murder Charges Against Former FBI Supervisor

After the Department of Justice's inspector general covered up for DeVecchio in 1996, members of Congress also did their usual cover-up. However, several private investigators started compiling information about DeVecchio's murderous activities. Among them were Angela Clemente, Sandy Harmon, and Dr. Stephen Dresch.

After conducting hundreds of interviews with people on both sides of the law and gathering a great amount of information, Dresch and Clemente presented their information to a member of the House Judiciary Committee, Congressman William Delahunt from Massachusetts. His constituency included people whose family members were victims of the FBI murders in the Boston office. Delahunt in turn provided the information to Brooklyn District Attorney Charles Hynes, who had been prosecuting corruption in other government offices.

A *World Net Daily* article by Jack Cashill (May 31, 2007) described the background of Angela Clemente:

> Actually, Angela Clemente resists the designation "PI"-private investigator. The self-effacing 42 year-old refers to herself as a "paralegal" with a strong background in clinical lab work. Of course, given her modesty, Clemente will absolutely freak at the word "best," especially now that she finds herself being hounded by forces within the FBI and Department of Justice.
>
> Still, it is hard to deny the accomplishments of Clemente and her recently deceased colleague, Stephen Dresch. The pair has shed more light on the major mysteries of the Clinton era than the FBI and *The New York Times* combined.
>
> In March 2005, for instance, it was Clemente and Dresch who informed the FBI about the explosives cache hidden in Terry Nichols' former home in Herington, Kansas. In a thank you note to Clemente for her work on this case, Congressman Dana Rohrabacher casually affirmed, "It was you and Dr. Dresch, acting on a tip from Gregory Scarpa, Jr., who learned that the FBI missed a stash of explosives." He added, "You have a real knack for investigation." Yet despite the kudos and the good work, Clemente finds her own life coming undone as the result of her unplanned investigation into the alleged misdeeds of former FBI agent, Lin DeVecchio.

When Clemente began her work on what she calls "the systemic corruption" in the Clinton-era U.S. Attorney's Office in the Eastern District of New York, she did not even know who DeVecchio was. In the course of the investigation, however, she and Dresch stumbled onto an internal FBI investigation regarding DeVecchio that had been effectively squashed. When they handed their findings over to the relevant congressional committee, the committee thought the DeVecchio matter should be tried as a criminal case and referred the material to the Brooklyn District Attorney, who agreed.

As a result of the pair's work, DeVecchio now stands accused of taking bribes as payment for inside information that led to four gangland style murders in Brooklyn. The man making the bribes just happened to be mobster Gregory Scarpa, Sr., a long time FBI collaborator and informer. The Brooklyn DA's office, which has brought the case, calls it "one of the worst cases of law enforcement corruption in the history of this country."

DeVecchio, however, still has a lot of friends in the DOJ and FBI. Iowa Senator Charles Grassley publicly complained about these unseemly alliances in March. As Grassley noted, current and former agents are raising money for DeVecchio's legal defense. The Justice Department is picking up at least part of his legal bills. And the FBI has proved uncooperative in producing documents for local prosecutors.

No one, however, is helping Clemente. Just the opposite. DeVecchio's defense has zeroed in on her. A single mom with a seriously ill child, Clemente has been called as a material witness for the defense and ordered to produce a veritable library of documents. The case has brought her own productive work to a standstill, and the potential legal costs are crippling. "I've lost everything because of this case," says Clemente. "I've tried to get away and keep getting pulled in."

One of the former agents actively helping DeVecchio is well known to readers of this column. Jim Kallstrom, who headed up the TWA Flight 800 investigation for the FBI, now serves on DeVecchio's advisory board. This is not the first time that Kallstrom has come to the defense of his embattled colleague. "There is insufficient evidence to take prosecutive action against SSA DeVecchio (sic)," Kallstrom wrote in an April 1996 memo to FBI director Louis Freeh. Kallstrom added that the failure to resolve the matter "continues to have a serious negative impact on the government's prosecution of various LCN [La Cosa Nostra] figures in the EDNY and casts a cloud over the NYO [New York office]."

In July 1996, things at the NYO got a whole lot cloudier when TWA Flight 800 blew up off the coast of Long Island. After five weeks of bulldogging the investigation into the plane's demise, Kallstrom inexplicably rolled over and let the Clinton Justice Department derail the investigation.

The question remains as to whether the Clinton DOJ used the burial of the DeVecchio case as a carrot to induce Kallstrom's cooperation.

The only mainstream reporter to even address this question is Peter Lance, who covers this dark symbiosis in his worthy books *Triple Cross* and *Cover Up*.

One woman who knows the answer to this question is Valerie Caproni, the chief of the Eastern District's criminal division during the period of "systemic corruption." In fact, Caproni was the "main focus" of the investigation that ultimately led Clemente to the DeVecchio matter, and well she ought to have been.

Among other mischief, the spectacularly compromised U.S. Attorney illegally ordered the FBI to seize the TWA Flight 800 investigation from the NTSB. Lest that illegality be exposed, Caproni also oversaw the prosecution of James and Elizabeth Sanders for Sanders' reporting on her misbehavior.

If this wasn't compromise enough for one person, Caproni orchestrated the botched sting of World Trade Center bomber Ramzi Yousef in that same summer of 1996. As the sting played out, the ubiquitous, second-generation FBI informant Gregory Scarpa Jr.. was placed in the cell next to Yousef.

Once he began to trust Scarpa, Yousef used Junior's connections to pass information to the outside world, little knowing that Scarpa was routing much of it through his own FBI handlers.

Unfortunately, the sting spectacularly imploded. (See "*Top FBI lawyer helped destroy TWA Flight 800.*") Through no fault of Scarpa's, the failed sting may have resulted in the downing of TWA Flight 800.

Perhaps to bury the evidence, Caproni saw to it that Scarpa Jr. was sent away for a hard 40 to the Florence, Colorado Super Max on a non-lethal RICO charge despite his cooperation. Now, incredibly, Caproni has re-emerged as the Chief Counsel for the FBI and a key gatekeeper in the DeVecchio case.

Standing at the gates, improbably enough, is one Gregory Scarpa, Jr. Scarpa just happens to be the prosecution's chief witness against DeVecchio. Given her history, Caproni has all the reason in the world to keep Scarpa buried in Colorado and Clemente buried in paperwork and debt. Barring some miraculous intervention by the major media, Caproni may well be capable of doing both.

After investigating the information provided to him, Brooklyn District attorney Richard presented the evidence to a state grand jury in Brooklyn in 2006. After hearing the testimony of numerous people, the Brooklyn grand jury returned an indictment against retired FBI agent DeVecchio in

March 2006. The indictment charged him with various crimes committed during the 1980s and 1990s, including murders.

Indicted along with DeVecchio were two members of the Colombo crime family, John Sinagra and Craig Sobel. The indictment charged DeVecchio with participation in four murders occurring between 1987 and 1992 when DeVecchio was allegedly providing confidential information to Colombo Mafia boss Gregory Scarpa, Sr. The indictment was a serious reflection against the FBI itself. Hynes announced that four people were murdered with the involvement of a federal law enforcement officer.

The four who were killed were either providing information to federal or state law enforcement or believed about to do so. In this way they were not only a threat to various members of the Mafia but also to DeVecchio himself who could have been identified as a mole in the FBI for the Mafia.

The following were the four murder victims in which FBI supervisory agent DeVecchio was charged:

Mary Bari, an attractive girlfriend of Colombo consigliore Alphonse Persico, who was the brother of the Colombo family boss, Carmine Persico. The indictment charged that DeVecchio told Scarpa that Bari had been providing information to federal authorities and that she should be killed. She was subsequently shot (September 25, 1984) in a mob-related Brooklyn social club. Bari was lured there with the promise of a job, and then as Gregory Scarpa, Jr. held her down on the floor, Scarpa Sr. shot her in the face, blowing off an ear.

Joseph DeDomenico was killed because he was considered a threat due to his drug consumption and conversion to a born-again Christian. Gregory Scarpa, Sr. killed him on September 25, 1984.

Dominick Masseria was killed on October 31, 1989, while standing on the steps of Our Lady of Guadalupe church in Brooklyn. He was killed by Sobel firing two shots from a sawed-off shotgun. With Sobel at the killing were Scarpa's son Joseph Scarpa (son with his mistress Linda Schiro), and Patrick Porco. DeVecchio learned that Porco was being questioned by detectives about Masseria's murder and told Scarpa, Sr. that his son was in danger of being charged with the Masseria murder if Porco wasn't silenced.

Lorenzo Lampasi, a member of a rival Colombo group, was killed on May 22, 1992. Scarpa Sr. asked DeVecchio for Lampasi's address so to as to kill Lampasi, and DeVecchio provided the information.

Although DeVecchio was not *charged* with involvement in any other murders, information indicated that DeVecchio *was involved* in the murder of mob figure Nicholas "Nicky Black" Grancio in 1992. This connection was made by mob hitman Larry Mazza, who, after becoming an FBI informant stated that Scarpa phoned DeVecchio to call off an FBI surveillance of Grancio so to permit his group to murder Grancio.

"One of the worst cases of law enforcement Corruption in the history of the country"

"One of the worst cases of law enforcement corruption in the history of the Country," stated prosecutor Michael Vecchione. Before the start of trial, Brooklyn assistant prosecutor Michael Vecchione expressed high confidence in his case against DeVecchio. He was the district attorney and Michael Vecchione was the chief prosecutor in the DeVecchio trial. Both were veteran prosecutors highly experienced in criminal investigation and prosecution. However, something strange would happen during the trial to question their sudden dropping of charges.

Corrupt FBI and Department of Justice Culture Threatened By State Prosecution of FBI Supervisory Agent DeVecchio

The prosecution of retired FBI Supervisory Agent DeVecchio threatened to expose the culture in the FBI and its Department of Justice, showing that the criminal activities of DeVecchio were not that of a lone rogue agent gone bad, but of a culture that was approved for decades by people in control of these agencies. Especially coming on top of the decades of murders involving FBI agents in the Boston offices.

Prosecutor Placed Heavy Reliance On Testimony of Gregory Scarpa Jr.

Gregory Scarpa Jr. had direct information on criminal activities that occurred before 1988 between DeVecchio and his father. Scarpa Jr. was involved in various racketeering activities, including murder, and when an indictment was handed down and DeVecchio notified the senior Scarpa, the son left town. He was later captured and convicted in 1988. He was in prison when two other murders occurred that involved DeVecchio giving information to Scarpa senior: those of Patrick Porco in 1990 and Larry Lampesi in 1992.

Brooklyn Prosecutors Obtaining Information from Scarpa Jr.

Prior to filing charges against DeVecchio, prosecutors from the Brooklyn district attorney's office had been meeting with the young Scarpa while he was in the maximum security prison at Florence, Colorado. In preparation for trial, prison officials moved Scarpa from the Florence facility to the Metropolitan Correctional Center (MCC) in Manhattan. Scarpa was serving a 40-year prison sentence for racketeering and was scheduled for release in 2035. He spent from 1999 to 2006 at the Florence facility.

Three FBI agents provided testimony during the 2007 trial strongly showing the improper conduct. Gregory Scarpa, Jr., Scarpa's son, had a wealth of information. Linda Schiro came forward at great risk to her life to provide testimony.

In addition to Scarpa Jr. and Schiro, Brooklyn prosecutors planned to elicit trial testimony from the FBI agents who had reported their suspicions about DeVecchio to their bosses; and several Colombo family defectors who told the feds that the elder Scarpa had a high-level law source in law enforcement.

FBI Showing Support for
FBI Agent Charged with Multiple Murders

During the first hearing on DeVecchio's arraignment, numerous FBI agents were present to provide support for him. They included James Kossler, a former supervisor in the FBI's New York offices; James Kallstrom, a former FBI assistant director; Joseph Pistone, the FBI agent who infiltrated the Mafia posing as Donnie Brasco; and others. Money for DeVecchio's legal defenses came from present and former FBI agents. These supporting actions implied approval of DeVecchio's murderous criminal conduct.

Low Bail for Enormity of the Alleged Crimes

Despite the gravity of the charges, the judge allowed DeVecchio to be free on a low bail of $100,000, much less than many people charged with relatively minor offenses. An *ABC News* Internet site article (March 30, 2006), referring to DeVecchio, titled "Former FBI Stool Pigeon Indicted," stated:

A former FBI agent whose reputation was considered unimpeachable by colleagues was indicted Thursday on four murder charges for allegedly providing inside information to a mob figure, who then ordered the killings.

Lindley DeVecchio had a "corrupt" relationship with Colombo crime family boss Gregory Scarpa Sr. that led him to provide specific, detailed information that led to the murders, according to the indictment unsealed today by New York City's Brooklyn prosecutor, Charles" Joe" Hynes.

DeVecchio at least once suggested Scarpa commit a murder, Hynes said." Over the last four months, a special rackets grand jury has heard from over 30 witnesses. As a result, the grand jury has voted an indictment," he said. Those witnesses included agents from the FBI and the Drug Enforcement Administration. Hynes said the investigation into DeVecchio began as Rep. William Delahunt, R-Mass., was preparing for hearings into allegations against FBI agents involved in organized crime investigations.

"After each of the murders, DeVecchio met with Scarpa," Hynes said. Hynes said DeVecchio took weekly payments from Scarpa from 1980 to 1982. He said DeVecchio met with Scarpa to discuss information and receive money. Hynes said that the FBI approved a DeVecchio request for payments to Scarpa. But more than $66,000 earmarked for Scarpa never arrived in Scarpa's hands.

For 30 years, DeVecchio was one of the FBI's most important mob busters. DeVecchio was Scarpa's handler, and Scarpa was more than an ordinary stool pigeon; he had also allegedly served as muscle for the FBI when the bureau needed some extra legal assistance in making difficult cases. As a result, he was allegedly accorded special, sometimes questionable, favors. But, in aiding his informant to commit murder, prosecutors now allege that DeVecchio went too far in protecting his valuable mob asset. Law enforcement sources say DeVecchio may have also enriched himself in the process.

DeVecchio voluntarily surrendered to authorities yesterday on four counts of second-degree murder contained in the still-sealed indictment that was handed down last week by a Brooklyn grand jury, law enforcement sources and DeVecchio's attorney confirm.

"We've been advised that there is an indictment filed. We have been asked to surrender today," said DeVecchio's attorney, Douglas Grover, a former senior special attorney for the Justice Department's Brooklyn-based Organized Crime Strike Force.

DeVecchio's indictment is the latest chapter in a long, controversial relationship between the FBI and Scarpa that law enforcement sources say dates back to the 1960s and includes the FBI's use of Scarpa to punch, kidnap and pistol-whip suspects. In this relationship, law enforcement sources say, Scarpa served as a well-placed mob stool pigeon who, for decades, provided the FBI with information against his underworld rivals. In turn, the FBI provided Scarpa with information that allowed his mob associates to skip town before they were indicted, according to law enforcement sources and multiple published reports.

Prosecutors say a cozy and questionable relationship appeared to have ended in the early 1970s when Scarpa's handler at the FBI retired and Scarpa himself was placed on a list of inactive informants. DeVecchio however, reviewed that list, prosecutors say.

By the early 1990s, the relationship between the agent and the informant had spawned a series of allegations, including one that DeVecchio had aided Scarpa in mob murders, but an FBI Office of Professional Responsibility investigation determined the allegations were unfounded. Supporters of DeVecchio cite that determination as one reason why they believe the current charges will be found baseless.

ABC News has learned that Hynes has developed new witnesses whose testimony the prosecutors believe will be relatively credible. That testimony is expected to also help demonstrate that DeVecchio may have used both Scarpa and the FBI—skimming money from each—to enrich himself, law enforcement sources said.

Whether information from those witnesses can be substantiated by documents is something that prosecutors admit they will have to prove at trial, and that would require records from the FBI.

"We think the people that are testifying to the DA today have their own baggage," said DeVecchio's attorney. He said that he expects to be able to show that any testimony could be contradicted by previous statements made by those same witnesses, as well as by other federally protected witnesses.

Although the FBI has never confirmed the allegations that it used Scarpa as an" op" in jobs too seedy for a badge-carrying federal lawman, the Brooklyn prosecutor's office hinted that it has developed information about the ways Scarpa was used that is independent of the previously published accounts, and which may expand on them.

Those detailed, published accounts were first reported in 1994 in the *New York Daily News* by Tom Robbins, now of the *Village Voice*, and Jerry Capeci, the mob chronicler whose Web site, GANGLAND, is widely read by mob buffs and law enforcement officials. Robbins and Capeci first disclosed the relationship between Scarpa and the FBI on the 30th anniversary of the civil rights murder. Selwyn Raab, a retired reporter for *The New York Times*, separately corroborated it in his mob history, "Five Families."

[Widespread FBI Support Showed Approved Culture in FBI]

An all-star cast of former top FBI agents is in DeVecchio's corner, including one of the most highly regarded infiltrators of the mafia in FBI history, special agent Joseph Pistone, more familiar to moviegoers as Donnie Brasco. These men say DeVecchio's indictment is the result of mob lawyers pressuring prosecutors to examine the allegations against DeVecchio; his conviction could potentially lead to verdicts against their clients getting tossed out. They say that the federal courts have already rejected the suggestion that DeVecchio could have been working not against but for the mob.

While the former federal agents who stand firmly with their colleague have protested his innocence, the Brooklyn prosecutor would not bring charges lightly. Hynes has a long record of success in controversial cases, including his role as a special prosecutor in a racially charged murder that threatened New York with riots in 1986, and which was the subject of the book" Incident at Howard Beach," and his role as the special prosecutor who exposed corruption in the state's nursing home system. He has recently convicted the former head of the Brooklyn Democratic Party in a political corruption scandal.

[Subtle Threats Initiated by FBI-DOJ Against Scarpa, Jr.?]

In order to testify for the prosecution against DeVecchio, the Department of Justice was forced to transfer Scarpa Jr. from the federal prison at Florence, Colorado to the holding facility at the Metropolitan Correction Center (MCC) in Manhattan.

Several years earlier Scarpa had provided evidence to the FBI against Muslim al Qaeda terrorists, Ramzi Yousef and Abdul Hakim Murad, that were in adjoining prison cells, as earlier stated in these pages. All three were confined at the Florence prison, but Scarpa was kept separated from them for his own protection. Murad's sentence was due to his role in the 1995 Bojinka scheme to place bombs on nearly a dozen U.S. airlines departing Far East locations.

After Scarpa was temporarily transferred to the holding facility at Manhattan, waiting to testify at the DeVecchio trial, DOJ officials transferred Murad to the same MCC holding facility, in an adjacent cell, where prisoners freely move among each other. That raised the possibility of Scarpa being killed by the al Qaeda terrorist.

A *New York Post* article (March 31, 2006) titled, "Mafia G-Man's Job Power Trip," stated:

Probers Bare "Mob Mole" Motive. He didn't just do it for the money. FBI hotshot Lindley DeVecchio was indicted yesterday on charges he traded secrets with a murderous Mafia chieftain for more than a decade, a relationship he built primarily so he could burnish his own rising star within the Justice Department, investigators revealed. That was the portrait Brooklyn prosecutors painted when unveiling sensational charges that DeVecchio, 65, was a double agent for the mob.

He is accused of participating in four gangland murders and selling inside information to protect their brutal empire. Sources say that every week, DeVecchio visited the Brooklyn home of Gregory Scarpa Sr.. the Colombo family's ruthless acting boss who was also a celebrated FBI informant.

DeVecchio allegedly was given an envelope stuffed with cash, sometimes with his own agents sitting in the house in another room. He is suspected of receiving hundreds of thousands of dollars, and keeping another $66,598 in FBI informant funds that was earmarked to pay Scarpa. "He received a weekly stipend," Michael Vecchione, the head of Brooklyn District Attorney investigations bureau, said at DeVecchio's arraignment yesterday in Brooklyn Supreme Court. The DA questioned how DeVecchio was able to get FBI funds to pay Scarpa without going through traditional channels that required the signatures of federal higher-ups.

"But there was also his desire to feather his own nest within the FBI to rise to greater prominence." DeVecchio "was dealing with one of the premier informants in the history of the FBI," one source said, referring to Scarpa's incredible role working with the bureau to solve two 1960s civil-rights murder mysteries, including the 1964 murder of three civil-rights activists in Mississippi.

It was speculated at a press conference that DeVecchio would receive a treasure trove of mob secrets if Scarpa filled the Colombo's No. 2 spot. "There was the expectation on the part of DeVecchio that maybe, someday, Scarpa might become [the permanent] underboss." And along the way, DeVecchio became so enamored of the mob that he went from a mild-mannered "country bumpkin" to a flashy, double-breasted-suit-wearing G-man who adopted the swagger and patter of the hoods he was supposed to police, Hynes said.

DeVecchio, who retired in 1996 and lives in Sarasota, Fla., appeared tanned but tired as he stood before Judge Gustin Reichbach, in the same black slacks and light buttoned shirt and black shoes he wore the night before when he flew to the Big Apple and surrendered to authorities.

The courtroom seats were packed with DeVecchio's supporters and former FBI colleagues, who could be heard voicing their annoyance as prosecutors laid out the allegations that he succumbed to the venal temptations of hoodlums such as Scarpa.

DeVecchio's lawyer, Douglas Grover, blasted the DA's "new evidence as old evidence, and it is false evidence." He was referring to a previous FBI internal probe a decade ago, when corruption allegations first surfaced against DeVecchio. He entered a "not guilty" plea to the charges, which Reichbach described as "shocking."

The judge denied the prosecutors' request that DeVecchio be remanded to prison, and instead granted an extraordinary bail package of $100,000. The bail will be guaranteed by five former FBI colleagues of DeVecchio's, who will ultimately be responsible for $1 million if he flees. The judge also ordered DeVecchio to wear a monitoring device before releasing him.

DeVecchio was then trailed by reporters who chased him into a nearby parking garage seeking comment, which he did not provide.

Sources said that one Friday night, DeDomenico, who was also known as Joe Brewster, led a gang of robbers who specialized in breaking into banks. The robbers were able to remain inside for the weekend. They positioned one member as a lookout and used another merely to run out for food to sustain the rest of the mob.

The gang wielded sophisticated tools and blowtorches to free from their wall moorings an entire unit of safe-deposit boxes. Once the bank of boxes toppled on the floor, effectively exposing the rear of every receptacle, they easily scooped out the riches of cash, jewels and other valuables from inside. They found the World Series ring belonging to Yankees Hall of Fame pitcher Whitey Ford, and Scarpa had it returned to the legendary hurler, the sources said.

The DA's seven-month probe produced 30 witnesses on both sides of the law, including FBI agents suspicious of DeVecchio who testified before the grand jury. "The probe uncovered a troubling past of confidential leaks payoff and death, and has also led to the solving of several cold-case homicides," Hynes said. He said his probe was continuing.

In addition to the charges leveled against DeVecchio, authorities believe he tipped off Scarpa back in 1987 that his mobster son, Gregory Jr., was about to be indicted by the feds on narcotics charges. The inside info enabled the younger Scarpa to flee before the case was unsealed.

Scarpa Jr. remained on the lam for more than a year, apparently thanks to constant tips from DeVecchio, before finally being grabbed with his wife and child in a New Jersey motel by agents from the Drug Enforcement Administration, and not the FBI.

During the elder Scarpa's reign, he always appeared to be protected from law enforcement, serving only 30 days in jail for 10 arrests, including playing a key role in the theft of $4 million in stocks and bonds. He was finally convicted of racketeering in 1994, two years before he died of AIDS he contracted during emergency surgery for a bleeding ulcer.

A *New York Post* article (April 2, 2006), addressing DeVecchio's indictment, stated:

> Brooklyn prosecutor Michael Vecchione credited Angela Clemente for sparking Brooklyn District Attorney Charles Hynes' probe." She's the Pandora's box," Vecchione said, pointing to the unlikely gumshoe who opened a treasure trove of dirty secrets about DeVecchio and Scarpa.
>
> **Biggest Federal Corruption Scandals in U.S. History**
>
> Clemente, a reformer and lobbyist who writes reports about government misconduct for Congress, is now at the center of one of the biggest federal corruption scandals in U.S. history.
>
> "I think it's good that this is being investigated thoroughly," she told *The Post* in an exclusive interview." But DeVecchio is not the lone soldier here, and I'm adamant about that. There must be a congressional hearing and I'm going to pursue that like you have no idea."
>
> At the minimum, she says, and Hynes agrees, FBI suits should have known something was wrong after he got the bureau to fork over large cash payments for Scarpa without proper authorization—money DeVecchio then allegedly kept himself.
>
> "It's much more extensive and higher up, she said." He had approval from people much higher and we should get to the bottom of this."
>
> Clemente, who calls herself a" forensic intelligence analyst" and whose research on rape cases, terrorism and other issues is used by lawmakers and officials, first took an interest in DeVecchio in 2000, long after the FBI cleared him of wrongdoing.
>
> She'd heard stories about him allegedly working for Scarpa, and how DeVecchio—and perhaps higher-ups—was said to have allowed the ruthless Colombo family capo to commit murders and even helped him set up hits. [Murders!]
>
> Clemente interviewed several of the key players in the case, including Scarpa's son, Gregory Jr., informants and former federal agents. "When we opened one avenue, it branched out into 50 others," she said." The big issue was why the government allowed Scarpa to commit crimes, including murder, just to preserve their relationship with him."

With the work piling up, she joined forces with a friend and colleague, Dr. Stephen Dresch, a Yale-educated economist and former Michigan state legislator who also does intelligence analysis and consulting work. Together, the two of them began to assemble new clues.

Clemente and Dresch explained that the break came when they investigated the murder of Colombo capo "Nicky Black" Grancio. He was a rival to Scarpa to become boss of the Colombo mafia family. Scarpa murdered Grancio to eliminate the rival for leadership.

A 2006 *Gang Land*[40] article described the witnesses the Brooklyn prosecutor planned to use in proving the role played by FBI agent DeVecchio in multiple murders:

The Brooklyn District Attorney's office has taken a bold step to beef up its sensational case that charges retired FBI agent R. Lindley DeVecchio with aiding Colombo capo Gregory Scarpa in committing four murders from 1984 to 1992, Gang Land has learned.

Sources say prosecutors plan to use Gregory Scarpa Jr., a long-imprisoned mobster son of the late Scarpa, to back up their key prosecution witness—Scarpa's longtime lover Linda Schiro—regarding two mob rub outs that the son was involved in before he was incarcerated in 1988.

After months of secret talks with the younger Scarpa, prosecutors have decided that his intimate knowledge of his father's dealings with DeVecchio far outweighs the heavy baggage that he will carry with him to the witness stand, sources have told Gang Land.

Scarpa Jr. is a multiple murderer with at least half a dozen killings on his extensive mob resume. Worse, at least as far as being a credible witness goes, he has lied under oath at least twice—at his racketeering and murder trial in 1998, and in 2004 at a post conviction hearing on behalf of onetime acting Colombo boss Victor (Little Vic) Orena.

But the story he's offered to tell is clearly tantalizing to prosecutors: Sources familiar with numerous debriefings say Scarpa Jr. has linked DeVecchio to the 1984 murder of Mary Bari, 31, a former girlfriend of a top Colombo mobster, and the 1987 gangland-style slaying of mobster Joseph (Joe Brewster) DeDomenico, 44. The younger Scarpa was the triggerman in the DeDomenico killing, and he held Bari down as his father shot her dead in a mob social club, according to court records.

DeVecchio, 66, is also charged with aiding the elder Scarpa orchestrate the 1990 murder of Patrick Porco, 18, then a potential witness against Scarpa and Linda Schiro's son, Joseph, and with the 1992 murder of mob rival Lorenzo Lampasi during the height of the bloody Colombo war.

---

[40] *Gang Land* web site: www.ganglandnews.com.

The 55-year-old turncoat has told prosecutors for District Attorney Joe that he helped kill both Bari and DeDomenico after DeVecchio gave the elder Scarpa negative information about them, sources said.

Bari, a former mistress of then-fugitive underboss Alphonse (Allie Boy) Persico, was killed, Scarpa Jr. told authorities, after the elder Scarpa related that DeVecchio had reported that "she was about to flip," and Colombo family higher-ups sanctioned the hit. Scarpa Jr. said approval was obtained at several mob meetings, sources said, including one with the gangster for whom he would testify 20 years later, Little Vic Orena.

Scarpa Jr. has told staffers that his father decided to whack Joe Brewster after DeVecchio warned him that DeDomenico had become a "born-again Christian and could become a major problem" for the elder Scarpa, sources said.

"He's risky. I'd keep my eye on him," is what DeVecchio reportedly told his father, Scarpa Jr. said, according to sources familiar with the turncoat's account.

In addition to fingering the ex-agent in the Bari and DeDomenico homicides, sources say Scarpa Jr. also corroborates Schiro's testimony to the grand jury that his father paid DeVecchio tens of thousands of dollars in bribes during their long relationship.

He never met DeVecchio—he was the elder Scarpa's control agent from 1980 to 1992—but for several years the younger Scarpa kept a ledger detailing his father's monthly payments as high as $2500 under the heading, "miscellaneous," sources said.

Scarpa Jr.'s current federal prison term for racketeering and murder conspiracy doesn't end until 2035. While he will receive immunity from prosecution for his testimony, he will not receive any reduction of his sentence for his cooperation with state prosecutors. In fact, while technically his admissions to committing murders that were part of his federal case should not hinder a pending motion for a new trial, they certainly won't win him any sympathy from the federal judge assigned to his case.

Sources say Scarpa Jr. has admitted lying from the witness stand at his 1998 trial, primarily about his involvement in murders that he blamed on his father. He insists, however, that he testified truthfully when he linked DeVecchio to payoffs, supplying his father information about mob rivals and other criminal activity, and alerting the younger Scarpa of an impending federal drug arrest in 1987 several weeks after he killed Joe Brewster.

In 1996, two years after three FBI agents reported their belief that DeVecchio, who was their supervisor, had engaged in numerous improprieties with his top-echelon informer, an internal FBI inquiry cleared DeVecchio of any wrongdoing. He retired soon after.

DeVecchio supplied his father information about mob rivals and other criminal activity, and alerting the younger Scarpa of an impending federal drug arrest in 1987 several weeks after he killed Joe Brewster.

In addition to Scarpa Jr. and Schiro, Brooklyn prosecutors plan to elicit trial testimony from the FBI agents who reported DeVecchio to their bosses, as well as several Colombo family defectors who told the feds after they cooperated that the elder Scarpa had a high-level law enforcement source.

A month earlier, however, prosecutors must establish at a pre-trial hearing that they received no information, directly or indirectly, from DeVecchio's immunized testimony to obtain their indictment. The burden will be on the prosecution to show that the grand jury investigation was not tainted by members of Hynes's office, or from information that emanated from freelance forensic analysts and journalists whose work triggered the DA's probe in 2005.

Government Employees' Immunity to Murder U.S. Citizens

DeVecchio's lawyers argued "DeVecchio was acting under the express authority of guidelines adopted by the FBI regarding the use of informants, and he acted under circumstances where he reasonably believed his actions were necessary and proper to perform his official duties, with full knowledge and approval of his superiors."

DeVecchio's defense, then, would be that FBI agents were immune from the consequences of using his official position and the offices of the FBI to (a) murder people; (b) become a mole in the FBI for a murderous Mafia group; (c) inform criminals of the locations of wire taps, pending indictments, and other classified information.

A former DOJ prosecutor, Doug Grover, was one of the lawyers defending DeVecchio. DeVecchio's legal team filed papers in the U.S. district court in the Eastern District of New York[41] seeking an order transferring the case from state court to federal court. The advantage of this was that the lead defense lawyer was well known in that federal court, knew the tricks that lawyers can use under federal procedures, and knew that the defense could be raised in federal court that could not be raised in the New York courts.

The federal statute being relied upon by DeVecchio's defense team provides for a federal agent to remove a criminal prosecution against him from state court to federal court if the offense for which the agent is being prosecuted was committed while acting in his official capacity.

FBI Paying for DeVecchio's Legal Bills

"You Pay G-Man's Legal Bills" was the heading on a *New York Daily News* Article (March 6, 2007) stating:

---

[41] That filing was assigned to U.S. District Judge Frederic Block.

Taxpayers are footing part of the mounting legal bills for an ex-FBI agent accused of helping a Brooklyn Mafia boss commit four murders, the Daily News has learned. The Justice Department is helping fund retired agent Lindley DeVecchio's defense, which has cost more than $450,000 since his indictment last year by the Brooklyn district attorney's office.

"It's an expensive litigation," said DeVecchio's lawyer Douglas Grover, who declined to comment further. A highly informed source confirmed the Justice Department contributions, saying, "It's on an hourly rate. There is a process in place by which employees or former [FBI] employees who are the subject of civil litigation or criminal charges can apply for coverage of their legal costs. The recommendation is forwarded to the Department of Justice, where a final determination is made," FBI spokesman John Miller said.

In a case that rocked New York law enforcement, DeVecchio, 66, was indicted last year for providing information on informants and mob rivals to Colombo family boss Gregory Scarpa before the murders. DeVecchio, who spent 33 years as an agent, is also charged with receiving payoffs from Scarpa totaling more than $66,000.

Now dead, Scarpa was DeVecchio's top secret informant for more than a decade, beginning in 1982. The murders occurred during the brutal Colombo family wars of the late 1980s and early '90s.

Grover, DeVecchio and numerous agents who worked with him maintain he is innocent of the charges and that the Brooklyn DA's prosecution is baseless and misguided. After DeVecchio was charged with the four murders, a group of other agents established a website and obtained funds to defend DeVecchio. Included in that group was James K. Kallstrom, the FBI agent who directed attention away from the missile downing of TWA Flight 800. [www.lindevecchio.com]

DOJ Filed Motion to Take the Case from the Brooklyn DA

Shortly after the Brooklyn district attorney filed murder charges against retired FBI supervisory agent Lindley DeVecchio, Department of Justice lawyers filed a motion in federal court to remove the case from the state prosecutor. The most probable reason for this was to control the case, hold DeVecchio innocent, and thereby protect the culture from within the FBI and DOJ from being known to the public.

Despite the enormous ramifications arising from the murderous culture and its cover-up in the FBI—and its obvious effect upon the intelligence gathering and prosecution ability—there was a virtual blackout in the nation's media about the FBI murders involving the Boston and New York agents.

Local Media Reporting FBI Obstructionist Actions

A *New York Daily News* article (April 7, 2007) described tactics by DOJ officials that were hindering the criminal trial of retired FBI supervisory agent Lindley DeVecchio. Title "FBI & DA fight over "mob" agent," stated:

> The FBI and the Brooklyn district attorney's office are battling over documents critical to the prosecution of a former federal agent accused of helping a mobster kill his rivals, sources said yesterday.
>
> Information about former agent Lindley DeVecchio's Mafia informant, Greg Scarpa Sr., once a captain in the Colombo crime family, is crucial to the prosecution's case, the sources said.
>
> The district attorney's office has asked the FBI for batches of material on Scarpa, including his FBI informant file going back to 1962 and files on other informants, according to sources close to the probe. But months have gone by and nothing has been delivered to the district attorney's office, even though DeVecchio's trial is scheduled to begin later this spring.
>
> The controversy over the district attorney's requests for information also came up during a Senate Judiciary Committee hearing on March 27. Referring to the DeVecchio case, Sen. Charles Grassley said, "I have also heard that the local prosecutors in New York may have some trouble getting the documents from the FBI that they need to try the case."
>
> "It is important that the FBI not take sides as an institution, just to protect one of its own. The FBI should cooperate fully and let the court process proceed."
>
> Linda Schiro was one of the star witnesses, with years of first hand knowledge of the workings of her common-law husband, Scarpa, Sr., and the relationship between him and FBI agent DeVecchio.

A *Brooklyn Daily Eagle* article (April 13, 2006), making reference to the private investigators findings, stated:

> The private investigator whose work triggered the indictment of a retired FBI agent took the stand yesterday in Brooklyn Supreme Court as defense attorneys again tried to impugn the information that formed the basis of the former G-man's murder charges.
>
> Angela Clemente, along with her now-deceased partner Dr. Stephen Dresch, had been looking into government corruption within the FBI when she discovered information suggesting a possible corrupt relationship between former FBI agent R. Lindley DeVecchio and his informant Gregory "The Grim Reaper" Scarpa Sr., a Colombo crime family capo.
>
> It took a United States congressman, James Dellahunt, D-Mass., part of the congressional panel looking into Clemente's corruption investigation, to recommend that Clemente bring her and Dresch's findings to the Kings County District Attorney's Office for possible prosecution. DeVecchio's

defense team, led by attorney Mark Bederow, has been trying to get the charges against their client dismissed on a legal technicality, a "Kastigar" violation, charging the prosecution made use of "immunized" material to secure their indictment.

Among the material prosecutors are accused of using to indict DeVecchio was the testimony he gave at a hearing for which he'd received a grant of immunity, and a statement given during an internal FBI inquiry that eventually cleared him of any wrongdoing.

Clemente yesterday testified that her findings, which she turned over to the Brooklyn DA's Office and which marked the start of the prosecution, did contain some of the so-called immunized material. However, one legal source said any immunized materials "must be used in a prosecution" in order for there to be a "Kastigar" violation. Prosecutors maintain they did not make use of any this material.

If Bederow proves otherwise, state Supreme Court Justice Gustin Reichbach could dismiss the murder charges altogether, though hearings on the issue over the past several weeks have yet to demonstrate any connection.

Mosaic of Systemic Corruption

Bederow's lengthy, detailed questions at times ran far afield of the issue of immunized testimony yesterday, prompting several admonishments by Reichbach, who often took over the questioning when things bogged down.

Clemente outlined how her and partner Dresch's investigation led to the uncovering of "a mosaic of systemic corruption" within the FBI. In short, Clemente's investigation into DeVecchio and Scarpa's relationship revealed sources who charged that the agent gave information that was later used in the commission of mob-related murders, four of which are contained in the criminal indictment.

Clemente said the immunized portions of DeVecchio's testimony that she did read "had no value" in terms of establishing criminal accountability on the part of the former agent. (One instance of so-called immunized testimony is nothing more than a series of "I don't recall," uttered when DeVecchio was called to the stand at a hearing for a convicted mobster.)

DA's Talk

All along, prosecutors have maintained they did not make use of any of the immunized material, and that the indictment against the former G-man was the result of evidence and witness testimony. In an effort to drive that point home, the DA's office decided to call to the stand late yesterday afternoon Assistant District Attorneys Monique Ferrell, Kevin Richardson and Joe Alexis, presumably to testify that they had not made use of any "immunized" material in making their case against DeVecchio.

The trial itself is scheduled for mid-September [2007], when DeVecchio will be tried for his part in four homicides, Mary Bari, Lawrence Lampesi, Dominic DiDomenico and Patrick Porco.

"We established a major pattern of many people being killed, while Scarpa was out there on the streets," Clemente told the Eagle after yesterday's testimony. Numerous agents had known about Scarpa Sr.'s violent criminal activity, Clemente said, but only one spoke up, triggering the FBI's internal inquiry that cleared DeVecchio.

It wasn't until after Scarpa Sr.'s death in prison that his former common-law wife, Linda Schiro, spoke out about what she knew about her ex-husband's relationship with DeVecchio. Schiro is expected to be a key witness against DeVecchio at the upcoming criminal trial.

New York State Judge Assisting in Obstructing Prosecution

An article in *Gang Land* (April 26, 2007) referred to Judge Reichbach's knowledge—and approval—of the FBI's withholding important evidence.

Reichbach voiced a growing impatience with prosecutors, making several major rulings against the DA's office. Referring to an April 6 court filing that argued against a pretrial hearing in the case, the judge said "specious" was the "only word to describe" much of their reasoning in the brief. He termed one argument – that it was difficult for the DA's office to secure testimony by federally protected witnesses—as "patent nonsense."

A *New York Post* article (April 28, 2006), titled, "Mole's New Slay Shocker—5th 'Rap' On FBI Man In 'Miss Israel' Triangle," stated:

In Bed With The Mob: Former Miss Israel Lilani Dajani allegedly carried on an affair with mobster Gregory Scarpa Sr.. [Arty Pomerantz]. Accused FBI mob mole Lindley DeVecchio allegedly gave mobsters info that led to a "hit" on abortion doc Eliezer Shkolnik. [Arty Pomerantz; Paul Martinka]

Accused FBI mob mole Lindley DeVecchio helped his mobster pal allegedly commit yet another murder, by handing him the address and photo of the victim days before the killing, according to bombshell letters from the assassin's own son.

According to the letters obtained exclusively by *The Post*, Colombo crime-family capo Gregory "The Grim Reaper" Scarpa requested the information on abortion doctor Eliezer Shkolnik during a sit-down at the Wimpy Boys Social Club on 13th Avenue in Brooklyn in 1980. "Should I ask why?" DeVecchio allegedly asked his informant. "Not now," was the reply.

The account of the Shkolnik killing comes from letters written by Scarpa's son, Gregory Scarpa Jr., from the super-maximum federal penitentiary in Florence, Colo., to his biographer, Sandra Harmon. The book, tentatively titled "*Buried Alive: The True Story of Why the FBI Protected a Mafia Killer for 30 Years and Then Buried His First-Born Son Alive,*" paints Scarpa Jr., as a naif bamboozled by his father, then railroaded by the authorities.

According to Scarpa Jr.'s account, Shkolnik was jealous because the elder Scarpa was carrying on an affair with Shkolnik's abortion-clinic partner and one-time paramour, Lilani Dajani, a former Miss Israel beauty queen. So the doctor consulted Joseph "Joe Beck" DiPalermo, a soldier in another family, and asked if DiPalermo would tell Scarpa that Shkolnik and his clinic were mobbed-up. Told it wasn't possible, Shkolnik told DiPalermo he would go to the FBI. "Joe B and my dad met over the situation," Scarpa Jr., now 54, wrote.

Scarpa Sr. allegedly tapped DeVecchio to help him solve his problem. Shkolnik was found shot to death in the vestibule of his parents' Forest Hills, Queens, building, on Dec. 3, 1980. The crime was never solved.

Scarpa Jr., is currently serving a 40-year racketeering sentence and has testified in the past without mentioning any direct knowledge of his father's dealings with DeVecchio.

Attempted Murder of a Private Investigator

One of the private investigators who played a key role in getting the Brooklyn district attorney to file murder charges against retired FBI supervisory agent DeVecchio was left for dead when she met a source who told her that he had additional information on the murders involving DeVecchio. In describing the attack, the article in the *New York Post* (June 17, 2006) stated:

The Gutsy single mom who helped prosecutors crack the case against accused FBI mob mole Lindley DeVecchio was found choked and left for dead early yesterday in a remote section of Brooklyn.

Cops, responding to a 911 call at 5:45 a.m., found Angela Clemente in the driver's seat of her car, its door open, her body sprawled half in and half out, near the Caesar's Bay strip mall in Bensonhurst.

Based on what she said, investigators believe Clemente—a forensic-intelligence analyst volunteering her services to prosecutors—was set up by the would-be tipster, who lured her to the meeting with promises of information about two Long Island murders she believed were linked to the recently indicted DeVecchio and his underworld canary, the late mob boss Gregory Scarpa.

From her bed at Lutheran Hospital in Brooklyn, where she suffered a seizure yesterday while being treated for neck and body injuries, a groggy Clemente told investigators she had received several messages from her assailant before agreeing to the early-morning meeting.

Clemente's daughter told investigators her mom did not think the meeting was dangerous "because the guy had something to do with law enforcement."

Clemente, a 5-foot-4 divorced mother of three, spent 20 years testing blood and doing autopsies before becoming one of the country's top forensic-intelligence analysts.

Prosecutors revealed Clemente made a phone call to a journalist about midnight, informing the reporter about the meeting. "If I'm no back by 6 a.m., call the Brooklyn prosecutors." The journalist called the DA's office at 7 a.m. Prosecutors made calls and learned of the attack.

Clemente made contact with her anonymous tipster at 82nd Street and 13th Avenue in Bensonhurst, and they agreed to drive their cars nearby to the southern end of Bay Parkway, at Gravesend Bay. There, the bearded would-be informant got into her black Hyundai and started talking about the case. She told investigators he pretended he had information.

And then, Clemente said, he asked her, "Are you going to continue on this case?"

"Yes," she answered. With that, she told cops, he whacked her on the right side of here body with something hard, and then put his hands around her neck and started choking her. Apparently convinced he had killed her, he took off.

At 5:45 a.m. Clemente was spotted lying halfway out of her car door by a passing dog-walker and a jogger. She was taken to Lutheran Hospital, where a huge bruise was found on her right side, and choke marks were found on her neck. There were also injuries to her head and lips.

She didn't know the name of her assailant, but she did provide cops with a description. She remained in the hospital, under police guard.

Assistant Brooklyn DA Michael Vecchione, the prosecutor who credited Clemente with helping him get a murder indictment against DeVecchio, believes the attack is linked to the former G-man. "Let's put it this way, it's not unrelated," he said.

Vecchione also would not discount the possibility that the murder attempt was the work of DeVecchio sympathizers, some of whom are former FBI agents. Earlier this month, Vecchione complained in court that some witnesses had been harassed by DeVecchio's FBI buddies.

New York Daily News article (June 20, 2006) referring to Clemente reported:

The beating didn't scare mob buster Angela Clemente, but a threat afterward did the trick. Clemente, a top forensic intelligence analyst credited with helping crack the case against retired FBI agent Lindley DeVecchio, left the metropolitan area and went into hiding with her three children after the threat.

"I'm in danger," Angela Clemente told the Daily News late Saturday. "What happened to me today is far worse than the attack." The threat was so intimidating, said Clemente, 41, that she wouldn't elaborate on its nature.

Scarpa Jr. Had Nothing to Gain and Much to Lose From Testifying Against DeVecchio

Because Scarpa Jr. was testifying as a prosecution witness for a state prosecutor, the state could not do anything to shorten his federal prison sentence. Worse, Department of Justice officials could easily retaliate against Scarpa. Also, Clemente was at risk of being murdered, which was why the Brooklyn district attorney put her in the witness protection program and secluded her in a secret location.

Reason for Scarpa Jr.'s Imprisonment

Following a trial in which Scarpa Jr. was charged with five murders, for which he was acquitted, but found guilty of racketeering, loansharking, bookmaking, and tax fraud, U.S. District Judge Reena Raggi sentenced Scarpa, Jr. to 40 years in prison. While in the holding facility at the Metropolitan Correctional Center in Manhattan for several months, prior to his trial, Scarpa "befriended" Ramzi Yousef, the terrorist holding key responsibility for the 1993 World Trade Center bombing and involving in planning the 9/11 hijackings.

Providing Advance Information of Terrorist Bombings

Simultaneously with being prosecuted by the Justice Department, Scarpa Jr. worked for the Justice Department to uncover information from the terrorist who masterminded the 1993 bombing of the World Trade Center. Yousef was held in the Metropolitan Correctional Center in Manhattan in an adjoining cell while both were waiting their trials.

Acting as a friend and interested in attacks upon the government, Scarpa provided advance information on several bombings that did occur, including the World Trade Center and the planned 9/11 hijackings. In other pages I've shown some of the documents prepared by Scarpa warning of the attacks, almost all of which did occur. But none of the warnings were acted upon by Justice Department personnel.

After Scarpa was found guilty, and while waiting sentencing, his lawyers, including former federal judge Lawrence Silverman, argued at his sentencing for a reduced sentence based upon his undercover work against Yousef. Acting to discredit Scarpa, Judge Raggi stated that Scarpa was most likely "part of a scam."

One reason for the possible hostility against Scarpa may have been the threat that he posed of exposing the corrupt activities of FBI agent DeVecchio.

That tactic helped insure that nothing was done to prevent the future terrorist acts that were revealed by Yousef to Scarpa. These plans were ignored by FBI and other DOJ personnel seeking to protect their own sordid conduct at the expense of the future victims. Such an exposure would, of course, also implicate the entire FBI and DOJ organization culture.

Another Major Witness: Linda Schiro

Another key witness against DeVecchio was Linda Schiro, the long-time mistress and common-law wife of Gregory Scarpa Sr.. She was present when DeVecchio made his many visits to their home. Linda first met Scarpa when she was 17, became his girlfriend, and later lived together as his common law wife for 30 years. They had two children, one of whom, Joseph, was killed at the age of 24 during a drug-related gang murder in 1995.

Prior to the criminal charges against DeVecchio, Linda had basically denied knowing about any criminal activities by DeVecchio. This silence was possibly out of fear of being murdered or out of fear of being criminally charged by Justice Department prosecutors for any number of reasons arising from her knowledge of criminal activities while living with Scarpa.

An *Associated Press* article (November 4, 2007) described Schiro's fear about revealing the murders in which DeVecchio played a role:

> Prosecutors argued she [Schiro] was afraid of reprisals by the FBI or the mob and came forward with the truth once she received promise of protection. Schiro now faces possible perjury charges, said Assistant District Attorney Michael Vecchione. Because of constitutional protections against double jeopardy, DeVecchio is clear of the charges and cannot be tried again.
>
> A court-appointed attorney for Schiro said despite the discrepancies raised by the book interview, she stood by her recent sworn testimony. "She told the truth in court under oath," said the lawyer, Gary Farrell.

A *New York Daily News* article (Nov. 4, 20007) titled, "Linda Schiro's No Liar Says Ex-NYPD," stated:

> An ex-detective says mob moll Linda Schiro was upfront that she had changed her story about former FBI agent Lindley DeVecchio, and that she doesn't deserve a perjury rap. Former NYPD detective Tommy Dades, who solved the 1995 murder of Schiro's son, told the *Daily News* she acknowledged that she had given conflicting stories when she came forward with allegations that DeVecchio had helped the mob. "So for anyone to say they are surprised now that she had inconsistent stories, they aren't being truthful," Dades said last night.
>
> The trial against DeVecchio, who was accused of helping Schiro's Mafioso lover, Gregory Scarpa Sr., carry out four murders, fell apart last week

when former News reporter Tom Robbins produced taped interviews with Schiro in which she cleared the G-man.

"She came forward to me [in 2005] because I had solved her son's murder," Dades said. "But Linda told everybody involved that she had told inconsistent stories.

And now that it has all fallen apart, everyone is pointing fingers at me and [former Brooklyn prosecutor] Noel Downey.

But if Linda is indicted ... we will go to the grand jury and tell the truth. And the truth is that everyone involved in this case knew she had told inconsistent stories in the past, before this case ever went to the grand jury."

After prosecutors dropped the DeVecchio case Wednesday, Brooklyn District Attorney Charles said, "There's no way we would have brought a prosecution if we had that kind of information."

A special prosecutor could be appointed tomorrow to consider perjury charges against Schiro.

Protection Against Being Murdered

Because of the danger of Schiro being murdered before trial, the Brooklyn district attorney had put Schiro into the witness protection program, provided her a secret residence, and paid her $2200 a month for living expenses.

Sampling of Witnesses and Evidence Against DeVecchio

The Brooklyn district attorney counted upon the following to prove the peoples' criminal case against retired FBI agent Lindley DeVecchio:

Gregory Scarpa, Jr. the son of the Colombo Mafia boss, Gregory Scarpa, Sr. Linda Schiro, the mistress with whom the Colombo Mafia boss lived for many years, and who was aware of the conversations between DeVecchio and the Mob boss. Several FBI agents who had the courage to speak out, knowing they would suffer subtle retaliation from their FBI bosses.

Several mob figures that had knowledge of the criminal relationship between DeVecchio and the Colombo Mafia boss.

Documents and evidence from the mid-1990 FBI inspector general's "investigation" into the many allegations of DeVecchio's corrupt relationship with Gregory Scarpa, Sr.

Inadvertent Impediments to the Criminal Trial

In February 2007, the Brooklyn district attorney fired a female investigator after learning she was carrying on an affair with an informer in the case against DeVecchio and planned on having a child with the informer while he was a federal prisoner. In addition, a couple of weeks later, Noel Downey, the chief of the office's Rackets Bureau, primarily responsible for pushing the DeVecchio prosecution, resigned after being offered a higher-paying position with the National Association of Securities Dealers.

Compounding all this, a top mob investigator, Thomas Dades, was taken before a grand jury concerning a confrontation with a gang of drunks and a pipe-wielding ex-cop. A scuffle followed and Dades fell on top of a neighbor, James Colletta, who was also trying to halt the commotion. The neighbor suffered broken ribs and died the following morning. There were also deliberate impediments from the judge conducting the trial. Still others would occur, as if orchestrated from powerful forces in government. In addition, Dades was accused by one of DeVecchio's lawyers that he had a sexual relationship with the daughter of Linda Schiro.

Two other prosecutors who had knowledge of testimony given by DeVecchio, where he was given immunity for his involvement, were removed from the prosecution team so as to avoid charges that immunized testimony was used against DeVecchio.

Relationship between DeVecchio and Scarpa Known for Years

The arrangement that DeVecchio had with Colombo Mafia capo Gregory Scarpa, Sr. left too many people aware of what was occurring, although very few had direct evidence. In the years after the 1996 FBI inspector general cover-up, private investigators in the New York area were digging up information about the DeVecchio connection to mob boss Gregory Scarpa, Jr.

Among the Private Investigators

These included private investigators, including Angela Clemente, Sandy Harmon, Tom Robbins with the *Village Voice* newspaper, Stephen Dresch, PHD., and Jerry Capeci. Some of them provided their findings to the Brooklyn district attorney, avoiding the U.S. Department of Justice standard cover-up.

The Early Stages of Judicial Obstacles

Before the start of trial, Brooklyn judge Reichbach took several actions to derail the case against DeVecchio. He refused to order the FBI to produce requested documents, and his objections caused two of the prosecution's members, Kevin Richardson and Monique Ferrell, to be replaced.

FBI Agents Intimidating or Threatening Witnesses

A *New York Times* article by Janon Fisher referred to the intimidation or threats by FBI agents against witnesses testifying against DeVecchio:

> It was Mr. Vecchione's argument that former F.B.I agents had sought to intimidate witnesses on Mr. DeVecchio's behalf that transformed the hard-fought argument into a pitched battle with the defendant's lawyers. After the bitter argument over Mr. DeVecchio's bail, the spectacular charges against him still resonated in the courtroom, though some of the accusations first surfaced more than a decade ago, when fellow agents told their superiors of their suspicions that he was funneling secret information to Mr. Scarpa.

Internal investigations into those allegations by the F.B.I's Office of Professional Responsibility and prosecutors with the Department of Justice—inquiries that several former federal officials have criticized as deficient—failed to uncover enough evidence to charge Mr. DeVecchio with a crime or even to discipline him.

Mr. Vecchione said the new case was based on the grand-jury testimony of 30 witnesses, including civilians, F.B.I. agents, investigators who work for the district attorney, and mob turncoats.

Another law enforcement official said that Ms. Schiro has reported that during the earlier investigation she felt intimidated by other F.B.I. agents who were associated with Mr. DeVecchio. Both law enforcement officials were given anonymity because the investigation is continuing.

Charging DeVecchio with Involvement in a Fifth Murder

Several months before the start of the criminal trial against DeVecchio, the prosecutors charged DeVecchio with involvement in another murder, that of Queens physician Eliezer Shkolnik on December 3, 1980. The criminal complaint charged that DeVecchio, in 1980, informed Scarpa Sr. that Shkolnik was cooperating with federal authorities in a tax probe against the mob boss. Shkolnik and Scarpa shared a mistress together.

One of the Original Murder Charges Against DeVecchio

One of the charges against DeVecchio was that he provided information to Scarpa enabling the 1990 killing of Patrick Porco by a Colombo Mafiosi, John Sinagra. DeVecchio allegedly told Scarpa Sr. that Porco was going to be a witness against the son of the elder Scarpa.

In 1995, New York detectives first learned about Sinagra's involvement in the killing while they were questioning an informant. They made a written report of their finding, which upper level management did not act on, possibly for political reasons—such as the involvement of DeVecchio and the FBI.

During a pre-trial hearing before Judge Reichbach, retired detective Joseph Malewich testified that he learned about Sinagra's involvement in the murder when he and another detective questioned an informant in a hotel room at the JFK Airport in New York. Malewich testified, "Sinagra was responsible for shooting and pulling the trigger and that's basically it."

In response to a question about what was done with his report, Malewich stated: "At first it was presented to my supervisors in the written form, and subsequently NYPD was notified about the information I had about the homicide." Malewich testified that the NYPD inexplicably closed the case, making no reference to Sinagra.

The fact that law enforcement personnel did not act on the murder of the physician raised questions as to whether the failure to prosecute was due to the involvement of FBI agent DeVecchio, and that such prosecution would show DeVecchio's involvement and the FBI culture.

Another Impending Judicial Block

During a pretrial hearing, Brooklyn Supreme Court Justice Gustin Reichbach expressed displeasure and anger against the Brooklyn prosecutors, and warned he would make a decision shortly about separating the murder trial against Sinagra from DeVecchio's murder trial. Reichbach strongly indicated that he was considering a motion by DeVecchio's FBI-paid lawyers to dismiss the charges against Sinagra, based upon the long delay between the time an informant implicated Sinagra in the murder and before Sinagra was charged with the murder.

Another Block to Criminal Case Against DeVecchio

During an April 2007 hearing, Judge Reichbach severed the case in which DeVecchio's co-defendant would go to trial *separately* from DeVecchio. That judicial decision served to insolate DeVecchio from another murder and a co-defendant whose guilt would more easily show DeVecchio's involvement.

Judge Continued Protecting DeVecchio

Enlarging upon his previous warning and action, Judge Reichbach ordered the *dismissal* (June 11, 2007) of the murder case against DeVecchio's co-defendant John Sinagra on the invalid argument that the police waited too long to file charges after they first learned of his possible involvement from an informant. Judge Reichbach stated that this delay violated a defendant's right to a speedy trial.

But that argument applies only *after* the person is charged. In most jurisdictions, there is no statute of limitations on prosecution for murder, and certainly no justification for allowing a brutal murderer to go free among the public simply because law enforcement agents did not start prosecution as soon as Judge Reichbach wanted. This dismissal was a red flag as to what would soon follow.

Sinagra's Dismissal Helped Shield FBI-DOJ Involvement

If Sinagra had not been given a get-out-of-jail decision approving the murder of the teenage, Patrick Porco, in 1990, his retention as a co-defendant, or even in a separate trial, risked exposing the involvement of FBI agent DeVecchio and the FBI-DOJ culture.

Opposing a Pretrial Hearing and Condoning FBI Withholding Documents

Referring to Judge Reichbach's attitude toward the state prosecutors, a *New York Sun* article (April 26, 2007) stated:

> Judge Reichbach voiced a growing impatience with prosecutors, making several major rulings against the DA's office. Referring to an April 6 court filing that argued against a pretrial hearing in the case, the judge said

"specious" was the "only word to describe" much of their reasoning in the brief.

[Judge Condoning the Withholding of Evidence]

He termed one argument—that it was difficult for the DA's office to secure testimony by federally protected witnesses—as "patent nonsense." Patent nonsense for refusal of the FBI to provide legally required documents!

In the toughest blow to the sensational case brought by the DA, Charles , Judge Reichbach severed the case of Mr. DeVecchio's lone co-defendant, John Sinagra, and scheduled his trial to precede the ex-agent's. This will force prosecutors to use their key witness, Linda Schiro, three months before she takes the stand against the former G-man, enabling his lawyers to better prepare for her testimony.

Ms. Schiro is the former lover of Gregory Scarpa Sr., the late Colombo capo who was a longtime informer for Mr. DeVecchio. She claims to have taken part or overheard discussions between the men that tie the ex-agent to the four murders alleged in the indictment.

Ms. Schiro has also fingered Mr. Sinagra, a former relative by marriage, in one of the slayings—the 1990 murder of Patrick Porco, 18. Mr. Sinagra allegedly killed Porco, a buddy of her son, Joseph, after Mr. DeVecchio alerted Mr. Scarpa that Porco was about to cooperate with police and implicate the younger Scarpa in a murder. Mr. Sinagra's trial began June 11.

Judge Reichbach also scheduled a pretrial hearing to decide whether Mr. Sinagra's case was tainted by a pre-indictment delay of more than 10 years and should be dismissed. The judge reversed an earlier ruling and set a hearing for May 16 after prosecutors disclosed that, contrary to prior assertions that Mr. Sinagra first became a suspect in late 2005, the DA's office had learned of his alleged involvement in Porco's slaying in 1995.

Questionable Action Prior to the Start of Trial

Another questionable action that occurred before the trial started was the agreement by DeVecchio and his lawyers to eliminate a jury and have the judge decide guilt or innocence. When I heard that decision, I immediately wondered *why* that action was taken.

A defendant stood a far better chance of acquittal from a jury that was more easily swayed by emotions or the legal trickery used by attorneys for the accused. Subsequent events provided more support for the belief that there was a secret agreement involving Judge Reichbach, the Justice Department, and DeVecchio's lawyers.

A guilty decision against DeVecchio would be a major blow to the Justice Department's culture, especially coming on the heels of the trial against Boston FBI agents that were also involved in murders with the Bulger gang.

Start of Trial Against DeVecchio (and Indirectly, FBI)

The murder trial against DeVecchio started in the Brooklyn court in October 2007, before Brooklyn State Supreme Court Justice Gustin Reichbach. Among the witnesses were former mob figures, Linda Schiro, the mistress of former Colombo Mafia boss, Gregory Scarpa, Sr., Gregory Scarpa, Jr., who was intimately involved with his father, and others.

Department of Justice Officials Using Taxpayer Money to Pay Legal Costs for Serial Murderer

A March 6, 2007, New York *Daily News* article by Bill Sherman quoted FBI John Miller stating that the Department of Defense was proving funds for DeVecchio's defense. DOJ officials—who had known of and protected DeVecchio during the many years that the serial murders were occurring—referred to two sections of the code of Federal Regulations, Title 28 U.S.C. §§ 50.15(a) and 50.16:

> These sections provide that the federal government will pay legal fees and judgments for any government employee sued is their actions occurred while on government business and within the scope of their employment, and based upon what was in the interest of the United States.
>
> A reasonable person might argue that a government employee, especially an official in the government's highest law enforcement agent, would not be acting in the scope of his employment while involved in a series of murders with a Mafia capo known as "The Killing Machine," that had reportedly killed over 50 people.
>
> Initial Attempt to Get Away With Murder
>
> DeVecchio's lawyers filed a motion seeking to have the murder charges dropped on the basis that some of the evidence used against him was evidence obtained while DeVecchio testified under immunity. That is the argument Oliver North used to escape the prison sentence that was handed down against him in the Iran-Contra affair. The Brooklyn judge denied that motion.
>
> Federal Filing to Transfer Murder Case to Federal Court
>
> DeVecchio's lawyers then filed an action in federal court seeking an order that the murder case be transferred to federal courts. Prosecution would then be by the same people in the U.S. Department of Justice that had known and covered up for the murders.
>
> Although most federal judges will bend over backwards to carry out DOJ lawyers requests, that was a little too much for U.S. District Judge Frederic Block. On January 9, 2006, Block denied the request, stating:

DeVecchio was being charged with outright murders having nothing to do with his federal duties. As the Supreme Court aptly noted in State of *Colorado v. Symes*, 286 U.S. (1932), "while homicide that is excusable or justifiable may be committed by an officer in the proper discharge of his duty, murder or other criminal killings may not.

Testimony of Scarpa's Close Mafia Associate, Larry Mazza

Larry Mazza, a turncoat and in the witness protection program, was one of the first witnesses, who provided evidence revealing the gravity of the crimes being committed by his Mafia boss, Gregory Scarpa, Sr. Referring to what Scarpa told him when asked about the number of people he murdered, Mazza responded: "He told me he stopped counting at 50."

Mazza had perpetrated over four murders himself. He described the "celebration" dinner that followed the murder of Mary Bari, during which they described a dog that found Bari's ear that had been ripped off by a bullet to her head. Mazza stated: "We were sitting, pretty much in a joking, festive type of atmosphere" when the Bari killing was described. "He shot and an ear went flying, and Annie Sessa was saying that the dog found her ear. It was a joke, a big laugh." He explained that Scarpa did the killing. "It was a woman, and he was the only one he felt had the stomach for it."

During his testimony Mazza several times stated that Scarpa boasted of having a law enforcement source. He testified that he overhead Scarpa talking to someone on the phone that he called "Lin." That testimony about the law enforcement source was backed up by considerable evidence that had surfaced in 1994, by what Scarpa's mistress would testify, and what Scarpa's son had told me years earlier, and for which he was being held at the Metropolitan Correction Center in Manhattan, ready to give testimony.

Matter of fact, Scarpa Jr. sent me a letter while waiting to testify. I had sent him a copy of the book, *FBI, CIA, the Mob, and Treachery*, and asked him to check that I had the facts correct that he had given to me earlier. He wrote back that prison officials were holding the book, stating that they wanted the FBI to first read it before they let him have it.

During the short trial, Carmine Sessa gave testimony supporting the prosecutor's case. DeVecchio's lawyers then argued that his testimony was not reliable, and Judge Reichbaugh agreed. But the Department of Justice used Sessa in prior cases, claiming he was reliable. One such case was the criminal trial, *United States v. Orena*,[42] which was cited in earlier pages.

FBI Special Agent Raymond Andjich accompanied DeVecchio to a meeting with Gregory Scarpa, Sr. at the Scarpa-Schiro home in 1991, Andjich, a new FBI agent, accompanied DeVecchio because of the requirement that a se-

---

[42] *United States v. Orena*, 145 F.3d at 556.

cond agent be present when money is paid by an FBI agent to a government informant. Andjich testified:

I was directed by Mr. DeVecchio to be seated on a couch. They then went into the kitchen area and had a conversation. I believe it was Mr. DeVecchio that turned on the television. It was a little louder than normal.

I was a little bit shocked. My understanding was that I would be going along with Mr. DeVecchio and participating in the meeting with Mr. Scarpa. But I was not under the understanding nor was I told that I would be directed to sit on the couch and not participate. I did hear a couple of words: "murder" and "hit." I can't tell you who was murdered, who was hit; it was Scarpa's voice saying it.

Several weeks later, Andjich and another FBI agent, Jeffrey Tomlinson, accompanied DeVecchio to Scarpa's home, and they too had to sit in another room for 45 minutes, totally unaware of the conversation between DeVecchio and Scarpa that they were to be present at. After these meetings, the agents were told by DeVecchio to sign paperwork indicating that they had sat in on the conversations.

They testified that when Scarpa, Sr. was about to be arrested in 1992, they withheld this information from DeVecchio, fearing he would alert Scarpa, and allowed the Brooklyn district attorney to make the arrest.

FBI Special Agent Christopher Favo

Also testifying was FBI Special Agent Christopher Favo, who testified that DeVecchio cheered after Favo told him (May 20, 1992) that Lorenzo Lampasi, an opposing faction to Scarpa's side, was murdered. DeVecchio shouted, "We're gonna win this thing!" and then slapped his hand on the desk.

That murder occurred during the internal Colombo war between he rival factions, one loyal to Carmine "The Snake" Persico, and the other supporting Victor "Little Vic" Orena. Scarpa was in the Persico faction and was reportedly responsible for the many murders occurring during the war between the two factions.

A fictional scene in the television series, "The Sopranos," was made of the gleeful response by fictional FBI agent Dwight Harris, upon being told of the death of a mob figure. In the plot, Harris, who tipped off Soprano, played the part of DeVecchio.

A *New York Post* article (Oct. 18, 2007), referring to the testimony of two FBI agents, stated:

> Favo's testimony followed that of two other agents. All three G-men recollected eyebrow-raising behavior by DeVecchio, but none has yet tied him to a murder. Favo also testified that on one occasion, he heard DeVecchio speaking to Scarpa, just days after the arrest of a Scarpa associate in the summer of 1992. "The Brooklyn DA's got him," DeVecchio allegedly said, speaking on a squad room phone dedicated for informants. "I don't know what he's saying about you."

Testimony of Linda Schiro, Scarpa Sr.'s Common Law Wife

On the ninth day of the trial, October 30, 2007, Linda Schiro took the stand and testified about being present at her home during many of the conversations between Scarpa and DeVecchio. Schiro's testimony was reported as delivered with a casualness of someone who was steeped in a life of double-dealing and death.

She testified about DeVecchio's many visits to the home she shared in the Bensonhurst section of Brooklyn with Scarpa, Sr. She testified to hearing DeVecchio telling Scarpa the names of government informants that had to be murdered. She testified about the murder of an attractive girlfriend of a high-level member of the Colombo Mafia family, Mary Bari. Schiro testified about DeVecchio stating to Scarpa: "You know, you have to take care of this; she's going to be a problem." The woman DeVecchio was urging Scarpa to murder posed a threat also to DeVecchio himself if an investigation was made.

Schiro testified that Scarpa kept nothing from her, including his conversations with DeVecchio. She described how Scarpa lured Bari to a social club controlled by the mob and shot her, with one of her ears ripping off and later found by a dog.

She testified: "All I know is they had word she was turning; she was going to let information out." She stated that it was DeVecchio who said Bari was an informant for the government. She testified that after Bari was murdered, DeVecchio came to the house and laughingly stated, "Why didn't you just bring the body right in front of the house."

Schiro testified that Scarpa gave DeVecchio, in her presence during his frequent weekly visits, wads of cash, jewelry, and other gifts. She testified that while sitting in the kitchen in the Bensonhurst neighborhood of Brooklyn, she heard DeVecchio provide Scarpa information, and showed his approval, when the information was used to kill four people.

Referring to the "Grim Reaper" or Killing Machine," as her common law husband was called, Schiro described how FBI agents gave Scarpa a gun and a one-inch-thick wad of money to force Ku Klux Klansmen to reveal the burial site for the three slain civil rights workers that were killed in 1964. She said Scarpa told her that if he were not back within a certain period of time, to take the money and go back home.

She testified that DeVecchio told Scarpa that Dominic "Joey Brewster" DeDomenico was doing drugs, stating, "You gotta take care of this guy before he starts talking. We can't keep a guy around like that or he'll end up talking. We gotta take care of this." Some time later, Gregory Scarpa, Jr. killed DeDomenico.

Referring to Patrick Porco, Schiro said that DeVecchio told Scarpa that Patrick Porco, a close friend of Schiro's son, Joey Schiro, was about to tell police about Joey's involvement in a murder. Porco was then murdered

When Scarpa told DeVecchio that Joey broke down in tears for several days, DeVecchio responded, "Better he cries now than he goes to jail."

In 1995, when the FBI's office of Professional Responsibility notified Scarpa's common law wife, Linda Schiro, that they wanted to question her, she contacted DeVecchio for advice. He responded, "You know, Linda, you don't have to talk to them. You can tell them to go fuck themselves."

Media Reports Praised Her Testimony

Media reports of the testimony by Linda Schiro stated, "Her testimony was unhesitant, direct, and assured." She testified, from first-hand knowledge. She stated that Scarpa spoke openly of crimes including murder, loan-sharking and bank robbery. She described in detail how Scarpa let her attend meetings with DeVecchio.

At one point Judge Reichbach asked, "What was your initial reaction, having grown up in this environment, when he told you he was an informer for the F.B.I.?" To which she replied: "He didn't say he was an informer. He said he worked for the F.B.I. I said, 'What, do you mean you're a rat?' He said, 'I just work for them.' So I was surprised at first."

Not only were these government informants threats to the mob, they were also a threat to exposing DeVecchio's involvement in the crimes of the mob family.

Schiro testified that during the fighting for control of the Colombia crime group, in 1992, that DeVecchio gave Scarpa the address of a rival for control of the group, who was then killed by Scarpa.

"I'd Get Out of Town on the Next Train"

Following her testimony, one of the reporters observing the proceeding stated to another: "If I was him," referring to DeVecchio, "I'd be getting on the A train right now, headed for JFK and a plane someplace far away. He's dead."

***Village Voice* Reporters Tom Robbins and Jerry Capeci**

Ten years earlier, Linda Schiro had given information to *Village Voice* reporters Tom Robbins and Jerry Capeci for a possible book that the reporters were planning to write concerning her now-deceased common law husband.

Earlier DOJ Cover-Up of DeVecchio's Murders

One of the factors influencing Schiro during her 1997 meetings with the *Village Voice* reporters was the fact that the Department of Justice Inspector General had just issued a report covering up for DeVecchio. During these earlier tapings, Schiro stated to the reporters that she had no knowledge of DeVecchio's involvement with Scarpa. Since DeVecchio had been involved in murders, it surely was on Schiro's mind that her life could be at risk if she divulged

DeVecchio's role in murders. Another reason was that, in 1997, she feared being murdered before trial if she were called as a witnesses against DeVecchio.

Coming to DeVecchio's Defense

It was known that Capeci had for many years secretly obtained information for many of his articles from Lindley DeVecchio. That profitable relationship for Capeci surely caused him to feel a certain attachment or "loyalty" to the former FBI supervisor now charged with multiple murders.

After Schiro gave her explosive testimony linking DeVecchio to several of the murders carried out by her common law husband, Robbins suddenly notified the court that he had tape recordings of Schiro's statements made years earlier in preparation for a book. He stated there was a conflict between what Schiro had told him ten years earlier and what she was now stating under oath in a court of law. Robbins surely understood the reason why there would be such conflict.

One obvious reason was that statements made under oath in a court of law, in a criminal trial, had to be accurate or risk going to prison. Statements given for a possible book had no such requirement. Further, as explained earlier, Schiro had good reason for not divulging facts that could get her killed.

Inexplicable Response to Reasonable Differences

One of DeVecchio's lawyers, Mark Bederow, then spoke out and demanded that the charges against DeVecchio be dropped. The basis being that the *casual* statements made by Linda Schiro ten years earlier to the reporter—under vastly different conditions—differed in a few respects from what Schiro *testified* under oath in the 2007 trial.

Judge Reichbach then took the lead and suggested that the Brooklyn district attorney should dismiss the charges. Almost on cue, the prosecutor then moved to dismiss the murder charges against DeVecchio. Something was obviously going on behind the scenes.

Going Against Prosecutorial Norms

For the Brooklyn prosecutor to dismiss the serious charges of multiple murders by a key FBI supervisor, the prosecutor would have to ignore such major factors as:

- Mary Schiro had to be given an opportunity to state, under oath, *why* the statements given ten years earlier to reporters were different from what she stated in a major criminal trial under oath and under penalty of perjury and a prison sentence if she lied.
- FBI agents had for years reported suspicions linking DeVecchio to the murderous Gregory Scarpa Sr.
- Numerous Mafia figures had testified and stated for years about DeVecchio's ties to Scarpa Sr.

- Testimony from Gregory Scarpa Jr., the son of "The Killing Machine," could be expected to provide even more incriminating evidence. The prosecutor refused to allow Scarpa to testify.
- The credibility of Gregory Scarpa Jr. was further enhanced by the fact that he was meeting with FBI agents providing information that he was receiving while acting as a mole inside an al Qaeda cell headed by Ramzi Yousef, the mastermind behind the 1993 bombing of the World Trade Center.
- The dropping of murder charges under these conditions would be gross misconduct by a prosecutor. To be sure, this would never happen if the defendant were not a key FBI supervisor and that high FBI-DOJ officials wanted the matter dropped.

Acting As if on Cue

As if on cue, Assistant District Attorney Mike Vecchione quickly stated to judge Reichbach:

> Judge, if we can't go forward after listening to these tapes, or we shouldn't go forward because of what's on these tapes, then we're prepared to do what would be necessary, and that would be to dismiss this case in the interest of justice.

To make such a statement at that time, when he didn't know what was on the tape, or if there were a discrepancy between what Schiro stated in a casual conversation to a reporter ten years earlier, and what she testified to under oath in a court of law, was flagrantly out of place. Especially since Schiro had an explanation, with all the other circumstantial information, and key witnesses yet to be called No prosecutor would ever dismiss a criminal indictment under such conditions upon an ordinary citizen.

The prosecutor had other important witnesses, including Gregory Scarpa Jr., whom he highly praised before the start of the trial, and the three FBI agents who courageously came forward to testify against DeVecchio, something that would not have occurred unless they had strong circumstantial evidence that DeVecchio was in fact guilty.

Typical Legal Tactics to Deny the Truth

DeVecchio's lawyer, Mark Bederow, claimed that Schiro was testifying against DeVecchio in order to make money from a book, as if one of the people *named* in a book would profit to any material extent when the author himself often makes very little on such a book. Besides, she put herself at risk of being murdered for coming forward, a risk that was recognized by the Brooklyn district attorney as they provided her with a secret residence and $2200 a month to pay rent and other expenses.

There was no contradiction between the sworn testimony that Schiro gave and any other sworn testimony. Matter of fact, the validity of her sworn testimony was supported by the statements of several courageous FBI agents who testified, and by the many indications that forced the FBI inspector general to make the sham "investigation" in the mid-1990s.

Sudden Reversal Defied Logic and Legal Standards

A prosecutor doesn't go from stating, before the start of trial: "The most stunning example of official corruption that I have ever seen," to "The interest of justice requires me to dismiss or accept the dismissal of this indictment" on such a flimsy and easily explained matter.

Appearing in court, prosecutor Hynes stated, "I have to say that had we been provided with these tapes much earlier in the process, I dare say we would not be here today. [The prosecutor was told by Schiro that she told a different story to the reporters ten years earlier.] On behalf of the People, I ask the court to dismiss the charges against the defendant."

Prosecutors Giving Credibility to Serial Murderers But Not to Witness Against the FBI-DOJ

Sammy "the Bull" Gravano, admitted to involvement in over 19 murders, and his testimony, which federal prosecutors claimed was honest, was used by federal prosecutors in numerous criminal trials against other mobsters. In addition, for testifying as the federal prosecutors wanted him to testify, the government granted Gravano his freedom, despite the many murders in which he was involved. In testimony, Gravano stated, "Sometimes I was the shooter, Sometimes I was a backup shooter; sometimes I set the guy up. When you go out on a piece of work it doesn't matter what position you're in."

Gravano testified for the government against Gambino boss, John Gotti. During Gravano's testimony against Genovese family crime boss Vincent Gigante, Gravano's testimony was contrary to what he was saying in 1986 when he was Gotti's consigliore.

Given his freedom, Gravano moved to Arizona where he, his wife, daughter, son, and son-in-law were involved in drug trafficking. They were arrested by Arizona authorities (Feb. 24, 2000) and charges were then filed by federal prosecutors. Gravano pled guilty and was sentenced to 20 years in prison.

In February 2003, Gravano was charged with the murder of a New York City detective in Saddle River, New Jersey, based upon the statements made by serial killer Richard Kuklinski. Before Gravano's 2006 trial date, Kuklinski died in a New Jersey prison.

Other Witnesses, Including Gregory Scarpa, Had Yet to Give Their Testimony

Gregory Scarpa Jr., the son of Colombo Capo Gregory Scarpa, Sr., who had considerable knowledge of his father's dealings with DeVecchio, was barred from testifying, claiming that his testimony would not be honest.

The prosecutor's claim of honest testimony is based on whether the witness' testimony would support the prosecutor's position and not expose corruption in government.

Brooklyn Prosecutor Had Advance Notice of Scarpa's Credibility and Value in Supporting the Murder charges

Gregory Scarpa Jr., had been brought east from a maximum security federal penitentiary in Florence, Colorado and kept for months in New York City to be called as a witness at in the murder trial of former FBI supervisor DeVecchio. Scarpa's testimony against DeVecchio was obviously very valuable because, as the son of Gregory Scarpa Sr., he knew about the details of his father's relationship with DeVecchio. He also could have corroborated Schiro's testimony. He was directly involved in much of his father's criminal activity and he kept the financial books for his father's criminal enterprise. In that way, like Linda Schiro, he had access to the innermost workings of Scarpa's criminal enterprise. He also admitted to having been present when his father murdered Mari Bari.

An *Associated Press* article (April 14, 2005) referred to a tip given to the FBI by Gregory Scarpa Jr. relating to where Oklahoma City bomber Terry Nichols had hidden explosives. The article stated:

> FBI Waited to Check Out Tip on Nichols
> Thursday April 14, 2005:
> By Mark Sherman, *Associated Press* Writer
>
> Washington (AP)-The FBI initially dismissed a tip that convicted bomber Terry Nichols had hidden explosives and they might be used for an attack this month coinciding with the anniversary of the Oklahoma City bombing. While the FBI has found no evidence supporting the idea an attack is in the works for the April 19 tenth anniversary, the information that explosives had been hidden in Nichols' former home in Herlington, Kan., turned out to be true.
>
> The tip came from imprisoned mobster Gregory Scarpa Jr., 53, a law enforcement official said this week. Scarpa is an inmate in the same maximum-security federal prison in Florence, Colo., where Nichols is serving life sentence for his role in the 1995 bombing of the Alfred Murrah federal building that killed 168 people. Timothy McVeigh was convicted of federal conspiracy and murder charges in the bombing and executed in 2001.
>
> **[FBI-DOJ Continued Discrediting Gregory Scarpa Jr.]**
>
> Gregory Scarpa learned about the explosives from Nichols mainly through notes passed between them, said Stephen Dresch, a Michigan man who is Scarpa's informal advocate. Dresch gave the information to the FBI in early March. But FBI agents did not search the vacant house until March 31. They did not act more quickly because Scarpa failed a lie detector test, said the law enforcement official, who declined to be identified because of

the sensitivity of the investigation. [Sounds more like protect-his-ass excuse after refusing to give Scarpa any credibility!]

The FBI lab continues to examine the materials for fingerprints and other clues that might show where the explosives originated and who may have had them before they got into Nichol's home.

Scarpa, a member of the Colombo organized crime family serving 50-plus years on drug trafficking, conspiracy and racketeering convictions, first communicated information about the explosives on March 1, then provided more details on March 10 and 11, Dresch said in letters sent to the staffs of two members of Congress and to the FBI's Detroit office. Scarpa revealed the location of the house on March 11, Dresch said.

The first letter said Scarpa learned from another prisoner, assumed by Dresch to be Nichols, "the location of a bomb on U.S. soil." The second described two rock piles in the crawl space beneath Nichols' former home. Under one, it said, were cardboard boxes wrapped in plastic. Those details match what the FBI said it found.

Aides to Reps. William Delahunt, D-Mass, and Dana Rohrabacher, R-Calif., acknowledged receiving the letters by fax. Delahunt's office received the letter on March 1 or 2 and forwarded it to the FBI, said Steve Schwadron, the lawmaker's chief of staff. The letter to Rohrabacher was not read under after the FBI search had been done, Rohrabacher spokeswoman Rebecca Rudman said.

The FBI refused to comment on the delay

Scarpa's Discovery of Bomb Material
Related to Oklahoma City Bombing

Earlier, prior to the trial against DeVecchio, Senator Dana Rohrabacher sent a letter (April 23, 2007) to Brooklyn District Attorney Charles J., crediting Scarpa with locating the bomb components that Oklahoma City bomber Terry Nichols had hidden. The letter stated:

> It has been brought to my attention that Mr. Gregory Scarpa, Jr. will be testifying in an upcoming case for the Brooklyn District Attorney's Office. I write to inform you of his dealings with my office which may reflect his credibility as a witness.
>
> In late March 2005, my office obtained information from Mr. Scarpa which detailed the location of bomb components and packaging missed in a search ten years earlier by the FBI at the home of Terry Lynn Nichols, one of the charged co-conspirators in the Oklahoma City bombing. My office pressed the FBI to take action on this tip, which proved to be accurate, and led to the successful recovery of the items detailed in Mr. Scarpa's account. The statement by Mr. Scarpa subsequently became the initiating fac-

tor for my office to open a Congressional investigation into the OKC bombing.

In August 2006, after the arrest of twenty-four terrorist suspects who plotted to blow up airliners over the Atlantic Ocean, I was given a report detailing Mr. Scarpa's FBI 302's and his work in notifying the FBI about Al Qaeda's interest in liquid explosives as well as Khalid Shaikh Mohammed's connection to Ramzi Yousef, the mastermind behind the first attack on the World Trade Center. Mr. Scarpa's FBI 302's suggest that he was providing significant information to the FBI in 1996 and 1997, prior to recent occurrences. [Meaning the terrorist attacks that did take place!]

These two pieces of information point to Mr. Scarpa's willingness to procure accurate intelligence, and I believe that at the very least his cooperation and testimony deserve a very careful analysis.

If you have any questions, please feel free to contact my staffer, Phaeda Dugan, at (202) 225-6851.

Sincerely,
Dana Rohrabacher
Member of Congress

cc: Judge Reena Raggi

Judge Reichbach Dismissed Charges Against DeVecchio

The judge also knew that the audio tapes given to reporters ten years earlier did not justify dropping of charges. But promptly, as if on cue, Judge Reichbach issued his four-page order dismissing (not finding DeVecchio innocent) the charges against DeVecchio (November 1, 2007). The judge wrote in *People v. DeVecchio*, 6825/05:

It is redolent of the current mindset of some in the government who argue that the practice of terror and torture can be freely employed against those the government claims are terrorists themselves: that it is permissible to make men scream in the name of national security. These are shortcuts that value legitimate police work, their yield is insignificant and the cost to the fundamental values they debase is enormous.

What is undeniable was that in the face of the obvious menace posed by organized crime, the FBI was willing, despite its own formal regulations to the contrary, to make their own deal with the devil. It was only the discredited testimony of Linda Schiro that tied the defendant to any of the crimes charged in the indictment. [That was a blatantly false statement.]

Indications of a Secret Agreement

Disregarding the fact that the presentation of evidence and final arguments were far from over, Judge Reichbach stated, "There is no evidence presented at this trial, saving the now discredited testimony of Linda Schiro, that the defendant committed any of the acts charged in the indictment."

The events and their sequence strongly indicated that there was a secret agreement between Justice Department personnel, the state prosecutor, the defense lawyers, and Judge Reichbach. Reichbach protected the FBI, its inspector general, and DeVecchio, while turning loose into the community a corrupt FBI agent responsible for many murders.

April 23, 2007

The Honorable Charles J. Hynes
Kings County District Attorney
350 Jay Street
Brooklyn, New York 11201-2900

Dear District Attorney Hynes:

It has been brought to my attention by Ms. Angela Clemente that Mr. Gregory Scarpa, Jr. will be testifying in an upcoming case for the Brooklyn District Attorney's Office. I write to inform you of his dealings with my office which may reflect his credibility as a witness.

In late March 2005, my office obtained information from Mr. Scarpa which detailed the location of bomb components and packaging missed in a search ten years earlier by the FBI at the home of Terry Lynn Nichols, one of the charged co-conspirators in the Oklahoma City bombing. My office pressed the FBI to take action on this tip, which proved to be accurate, and led to the successful recovery of the items detailed in Mr. Scarpa's account. The statement by Mr. Scarpa subsequently became the initiating factor for my office to open a Congressional investigation into the OKC bombing.

In August 2006, after the arrests of twenty-four terrorist suspects who plotted to blow up airliners over the Atlantic Ocean, I was given a report detailing Mr. Scarpa's FBI 302's and his work in notifying the FBI about Al Qaeda's interest in liquid explosives as well as Khalid Shaikh Mohammed's connection to Ramzi Yousef, the mastermind behind the first attack on the World Trade Center. Mr. Scarpa's FBI 302's suggest that he was providing significant information to the FBI in 1996 and 1997, prior to recent occurrences.

These two pieces of information point to Mr. Scarpa's willingness to procure accurate intelligence, and I believe that at the very least his cooperation and testimony deserve a very careful analysis.

If you have any questions, please feel free to contact my staffer, Phaedra Dugan, at (202) 225-6851.

Sincerely,

Dana Rohrabacher

Dana Rohrabacher
Member of Congress

Cc: Judge Reena Raggi

"This Guy is gonna get away with murder."

One incredulous veteran law-enforcement officer in the courtroom stated, "This guy is gonna get away with murder." Another one, Joe Coffey, former head of the New York Organized Crime Strike Force and head of the State Organized Crime Task Force, said: "Have we got another O.J. Simpson here?" Another close to the District attorney's office said: "The timing of all this is suspicious." A source close to the investigation stated, "I still believe her. I feel bad for the Porcos, because if you believe the People's case, that's the one consistent part."

The dismissal of the charges, which released into society an FBI agent involved with murders, and the judge's statements, were matters of grave concern to the public.

Prosecutor's Suspicious Support for Prosecuting One of his Key Witnesses

District Attorney Hynes said in court, after judge Reichbach dismissed the charges, and without first asking Schiro for an explanation: "We're sending it over to have the special district attorney review the testimony and tapes and make a judgment." Her sworn testimony was not disputed by anyone else's sworn testimony.

Almost Fawning, "Oh absolutely; absolutely!"

When reporters asked Brooklyn district attorney Hynes whether DeVecchio was completely out of the woods, Hynes replied, "Oh absolutely, absolutely." He was *too happy* in light of the evidence to make that statement.

Hynes also stated, "I have to say that had we been provided with these tapes, we would not be here trying this case over the last several weeks." But Hynes had stated before the trial that another of his key witnesses was Gregory Scarpa, Jr. Schiro stated that she had told the prosecutors about the misleading and withheld information she gave ten years earlier to the authors.

People Against Murders: the System Against the People

People of *New York vs. R. Lindley DeVecchio* was the title of the criminal case against DeVecchio. The unexplainable dismissal of the serious charges constituted subversion of justice by the judge and the prosecutor, acting jointly, against the safety interests of the people of New York.

Threatening the Witness, and by Implication, the Public

That warning and threat of perjury by Judge Reichbach was uncalled for, and clearly retaliation for daring to speak out against corruption in government. He gave Schiro no opportunity to explain why she did not mention DeVecchio's involvement with the reporter ten years earlier.

Prior Threat Against Schiro Testifying by Federal Judges Obstructed Justice and Endangered Public Safety

In 1998, Schiro filed an affidavit and prepared to testify in the criminal trial of Gregory Scarpa, Jr. in Brooklyn. The federal judge threatened to charge her with perjury if she testified, causing her to withhold her testimony. Judge Reichbach renewed this threat as he stated he was recommending that she be investigated for perjury.

Fear Caused Schiro to Withhold Information Earlier

In 1994, Linda Schiro told FBI investigators that she didn't know anything about the relationship between her common law husband, Gregory Scarpa, Sr. and DeVecchio. In 1998, Schiro stated in an affidavit that she witnessed some conversations between DeVecchio and Scarpa and then took the Fifth Amendment, refusing to testify in the case.

Linda Schiro stated after the dismissal of charges against DeVecchio:

I want the world to know I told the truth when it counted, under oath. I feel horrible about this. I know how hard the prosecutor worked. I feel I let them down. I didn't tell a lie on the stand, but talking about a possible book deal in 1997 and giving evidence under oath are two different things.

Schiro, by remaining silent about the crimes of which she had knowledge perpetrated by her common law husband, she did enable crimes to occur. But if she had gone to the FBI, she would probably have ended up being murdered.

Schiro did have inside information on crimes perpetrated by FBI Special Agent DeVecchio, and her testimony was far more admissible in court than the testimony of others, such as Sammy "The Bull" Gravano, who had committed dozens of murders and was used several times by federal prosecutors to convict others. Further, she didn't want to testify, but did it as a favor to the detective who brought to justice the person who killed her son, Joey Scarpa.

Far More Evidence Than That Which Imprisoned Thousands of American Citizens

Overall, over the years there had been far more evidence showing DeVecchio's guilt than that used to imprison, often for life, thousands of American citizens. Considerable evidence of DeVecchio's misconduct had surfaced in the mid-1990s, "investigated" and covered up by the FBI Inspector General, followed by DeVecchio's quick retirement. DeVecchio's guilty judgment would have reflected upon the FBI and DOJ culture. That threat was removed by dismissing the charges.

DeVecchio's conduct was similar to the misconduct by FBI agents in the Boston office that had just been exposed by investigative media people, which showed complicity by Washington FBI and other DOJ employees.

Most Murder Cases Rely Upon Circumstantial Evidence

As in many murder cases, much of the evidence concerning DeVecchio's involvement in the murders was circumstantial. In the cases against DeVecchio, there was not only an overwhelming amount of circumstantial evidence, but also closer witnesses than exist in many murder cases: the son of the Colombo Mafia boss, Gregory Scarpa, Jr., and the mistress of the senior Scarpa.

In dismissing the case before the presentation of other evidence and witnesses, and with the strong evidence already presented, and without addressing the various reasons for the differences between sworn testimony and statements made ten years earlier to a reporter, defied legal logic and common sense. It made more obvious that there was a secret agreement between Justice Department personnel, the Brooklyn prosecutor, and Judge Reichbach.

The Dismissal Put the Public at Risk

No one should think that the American public was not put at risk by the sham dismissal of the murder charges against retired FBI agent DeVecchio, and removing the insight into the FBI culture. DeVecchio's conduct was similar to the involvement in murders by FBI

The Scheme to Obstruct Justice Riddled with Red Flags

This sudden reversal by the Brooklyn prosecutor and the judge on such a flimsy ground, in light of the enormous implications of the charges, flew in the face of normal trial procedures and the requirements of justice. For instance:

- No attempt was made to have Schiro explain under oath the reason for the discrepancy between what she told the reporter ten years earlier and what she testified under oath during the murder trial against DeVecchio. There would be a normal explanation for the difference.
- No attempt was made to obtain the sworn testimony of Scarpa's son, Gregory Scarpa, Jr., who had close contact with his father in the dealings with DeVecchio and the murders and other crimes committed. Scarpa Jr. had first hand information of the relationship between his father and DeVecchio. For one, he kept the books that showed the money and perks paid by his father to the FBI agent.
- No attempt was made to obtain the testimony of former FBI Special Agent Richard Taus, who had worked under and in close contact with DeVecchio.
- No consideration was given to the earlier testimony by the FBI agents and mob figures that provided information strongly indicative of DeVecchio's unlawful conduct.
- The testimony that had already been given provided circumstantial admissible evidence that DeVecchio was involved in improper conduct.
- The sworn testimony given by Schiro, given at great threat to her safety, took precedence over audio tapes presented by a reporter that showed Schiro giving unsworn statements to a reporter at a time when she was in great danger of being murdered if she revealed DeVecchio's activities with Gregory Scarpa Sr..
- The considerable circumstantial evidence meeting legal criteria for admissibility, acquired during the investigations in the mid 1990s.
- Testimony of various mob figures that had learned of the relationship between Scarpa Sr. and DeVecchio.

- The deaths of numerous government informants by Scarpa, indicating he had inside information about their informant status.
- FBI's conduct in blocking the prosecution of DeVecchio, refusing to turn over documents to the Brooklyn District Attorney and interference with making FBI agents available.

Effect of Perversion of Justice Upon Murder Victim's Families

"For the Victim's Family, It's the Cruelest Halloween Trick" was the heading on a *New York Daily News* article (11-1-07) on the suspicious dismissal of all charges against DeVecchio:

> Prosecutors are poised to drop the charges against former FBI agent Lindley DeVecchio, but a question remains. Why was Greg Scarpa Sr. allowed to keep murdering decade after decade, killing so often he became known as the Grim Reaper?
>
> The FBI certainly had enough on Scarpa to put him away, but that would have meant the end of all those reports from informant NY3461TE, the letter at the end standing for Top Echelon. [But prosecuting him would reveal the involvement of DeVecchio in the murders.]
>
> The accumulated reports were entered into evidence in the doomed case against DeVecchio. They show the FBI let Scarpa go on murdering in exchange of what was, for the most part, just gangland gossip.
>
> Many of the tips were just recap of information widely known in South Brooklyn. None of the reports seem to justify allowing a seemingly untouchable Scarpa to murder on whim for 40 years. More than any other agent, the FBI is to blame for allowing Scarpa to strut about as a homicidal role model. The neighborhood's most troubled young men saw him get away with murder.

Cover-Up Required Dismissing a Civil Lawsuit

Judge Reichbach's dismissal of charges against DeVecchio affected another lawsuit filed by the widow of Nicholas "Nicky Black" Grancio. The lawsuit against DeVecchio charged that DeVecchio suspiciously called off a joint FBI-NYPD surveillance team that was not only spying on Grancio, but also unknowingly protecting him from being murdered by Scarpa.

Information indicated that Scarpa called DeVecchio about the problem and that DeVecchio called the team to stop the surveillance and return to base. Grancio was then murdered shortly after the team left. One of the witnesses that would testify in the case was a protégé to Scarpa, Mazza. After the start of the civil trial, Mazza reversed himself on the stand. His new statement:

> We were looking at clubs, known hangouts where Orena people hung out. We went down that block. While we were sitting there, I spotted Nicky Black's truck, a Toyota SUV. I said to Greg, "That's Nicky Black!" He said

to me, "Let's get him."

Sensing the Judicial Hostility, Mazza Reversed Himself

At the same time that the scheme was playing out in the trial against DeVecchio, Mazza suddenly reversed himself and said that there was no contact between Scarpa and DeVecchio that resulted in calling off the surveillance.

It is an often-repeated tactic by Justice Department officials to withhold prosecution, threaten with prosecution, or provide some type of reward, for making statements demanded by DOJ personnel. It is highly probable that as part of the scheme to drop the charges against DeVecchio that Mazza was included in the tactics.

A *New York Post* article (November 4, 2007), described hostile actions by the FBI in an article titled, "FBI Had 'Mafia G-Man's Back: DA:"

> As Brooklyn Assistant District Attorney Charles Hynes pursued the murder case against the ex-FBI agent Lindley DeVecchio, he crossed swords with a formidable foe: the U.S. Justice Department.
>
> The FBI paid for the bulk of DeVecchio's legal bill—estimates for the tab are as high as $400,000—while harassing and intimidating members of the DA's Office.
>
> "They were following me, staking out my house," said investigator Tommy Dades, who conducted the first interviews with key prosecution witness Linda Schiro and testified during the trial.
>
> "They were going around spreading rumors, trying to get people to say things about me, to discredit me," said Dades. "They got away with a lot of stuff."
>
> The FBI withheld key documents related to DeVecchio's work, turning them over at the last minute—and only after Iowa Sen. Charles Grassley quizzed FBI Director Robert Mueller about the stonewalling." The FBI was uncooperative in making available three current agents who testified against DeVecchio, sources at the DA's Office complained.
>
> DeVecchio is known to have powerful allies at the agency, including the FBI's chief legal counsel, Valerie Caproni, who helped oversee the former G-man's works when she was an assistant U.S. attorney in Brooklyn in the late 1980s.

DeVecchio Was *Not* Found Innocent:
Murder Charges Can, and Should Be, Refiled

The sudden dropping of charges by the Brooklyn prosecutor did not constitute finding DeVecchio innocent. There had never been a trial to completion. And DeVecchio could again be charged with those crimes and possibly others that may be discovered.

The Fifth Amendment protection against being tried twice for the same crime is known as double jeopardy. It applies to cases where there was a *final* judgment following a full trial. A second trial can be held after a mistrial. In this case, there was never a final judgment; the prosecutor simply dropped the charges. Further, judicial error, the dismissal of a criminal case by the judge because of a possible conflict between what was stated ten years earlier to a reporter, and what was stated in court under oath. A retrial of DeVecchio is legally possible, but the culture in the Department of Justice is such that this will never occur.

Most Media People Acted in Lockstep Covering Up For the Highly Suspicious Dropping of Charges

Most media people covered up for the inexplicable dropping of charges, protecting the system, just as most media people covered up for the serial lying of the Bush politicians as they fabricated excuses to start the war against the Iraqi people.

The media people did not report any of the red herring signs of a planned dismissal. They didn't address the circumstantial and direct evidence. They called Linda Schiro a liar simply because her testimony under oath was not exactly the same as she stated to *Village Voice* reporters Tom Robbins and Jerry Capeci. They were all too willing to state that DeVecchio was found innocent, when that was not the case, and that he could not be again charged, which was not correct.

I had frequently commented that except for a few local newspapers, there was a national blackout on the charges against the FBI agent, just as there had been a virtual media blackout on the murders in which Boston FBI agents had been implicated. The blackout prevented the public from learning about the dangerous culture in the FBI and other Department of Justice divisions.

In addition, the smear on the FBI was removed by the judicial dismissal. Newspapers that had kept a lid on the story, such as the *New York Times* and *Wall Street Journal,* ran stories on the criminal charges being dismissed, thereby protecting the FBI and DOJ image, without any mention of the suspicious dropping of charges and attempt to attack the witness courageously willing to come forward.

The Standard Media Disinformation

For the public to understand what really happened was difficult. Not only were the actions well-coordinated by the FBI, the prosecutor, DeVecchio's lawyers, but media people either fell in line, deceived, or fell in line with the usual media people protecting their government sources.

A *New York Post* article (Oct. 16, 2007) by Steve Dunleavy stated after charges were dropped against DeVecchio:

> If FBI rogue Lindley DeVecchio walks out of this one, he'll be walking a crooked mile for the rest of his life. "It was no secret in the '80s that

DeVecchio was on the take from [Colombo crime family mobster Gregory] Scarpa," Joe Coffey said.

Coffey, who retired as head of New York City's Organized Crime Task Force and then served 11 years with the state Organized Crime Task Force, is one of the foremost authorities on the mob.

"The last time I had words with him was at a retirement or promotion celebration in 1984," Coffey recalled of DeVecchio. "He was blabbing how he would never share information with a cop from the NYPD—he just wouldn't work with them. I said, 'Yeah, that's why New York cops solve 80 percent of your cases.' I won't tell you what I said next, but we had to be pulled apart."

DeVecchio survived an internal investigation by the Justice Department in 1995. However, Coffey, over time, has been privy to some aspects of some investigations and is convinced "DeVecchio was dirty. ... I don't care what you say. DeVecchio curried favor for professional and economic gains," Coffey said: "He'll have to live the rest of his life knowing that a lot of people know that he was virtually an FBI member of organized crime."

"I never spoke to him again after our confrontation; I had no use for him. I have many beefs with the FBI, not the least of which is they always get too close to their informants," he said.

Coffey, who closed 82 mob hits in his career, genuinely bristles when he hears of crooked lawmen after spending 43 years chasing down the crooks.

Statements in Judge Reichbach's Decision Dismissing Murder Charges against FBI Supervisory Agent Supported the Charges

Judge Reichbach's November 1, 2007, decision also made statements showing a sham dismissal of murder charges against DeVecchio. A few points stick out like sore thumbs. Here are a few of the statements made in that decision:[43]

> Friedrich Nietzsche sagely observed at the end of the 19th Century "that he who fights with monsters might take care lest he thereby become a monster… and if you gaze for long into an abyss, the abyss gazes also into you …" I feel obligated to make some observations based on the evidence revealed to date. These observations based on the testimony and exhibits introduced so far in this case, particularly by the defendant's own colleagues, is directed not so much to defendant's individual actions but to the institutional question raised by the evidence.

---

[43] *People v. R. Lindley DeVecchio*, 2007 N.Y. Misc. LEXIS 7827; 238 N.Y.L.J. 90.

I was particularly struck by the testimony of Carmine Sessa, former Consigliere of the Colombo family and multiple murderer, and who testified that when he and his fellow mobsters were discussing the possibility that Greg Scarpa was an FBI informant, they ultimately discounted the idea, reasoning that it was impossible for Scarpa to be an FBI informant: that it would be antinomic for the FBI, charged with fighting crime, to employ as an informer a murderer as vicious and prolific as Greg Scarpa. Apparently, and sadly, organized crime attributed to the FBI a greater sense of probity than the FBI in fact possessed.

What is undeniable was that in the face of the obvious menace posed by organized crime, the FBI was willing, despite its own formal regulations to the contrary, to make their own deal with the devil. They gave Scarpa virtual criminal immunity for close to 15 years in return for the information, true and false, he willingly supplied. Indeed, this Court is forced to conclude that Scarpa's own acknowledgment of criminal activity to the FBI could only be explained by his belief that the agency would protect him from the consequences of his own criminality, which the record suggests is what they did.

Not only did the FBI shield Scarpa from prosecution for his own crimes, they also actively recruited him to participate in crimes under their direction. That a thug like Scarpa would be employed by the federal government to beat witnesses and threaten them at gunpoint to obtain information regarding the deaths of civil rights workers in the south in the early 1960s is a shocking demonstration of the government's unacceptable willingness to employ criminality to fight crime. [Or to bolster its own image by making arrests!]

The court would be remiss if it did not single out for praise Special Agents Favo, Tomlinson and Andjich. In the face of what must have been enormous institutional pressure to turn a blind eye when they grew increasingly concerned that the defendant [DeVecchio] had lost the necessary perspective and had grown too close to his informant, they stepped forward, risking the opprobrium of their colleagues.

There was no evidence presented at this trial, save the now discredited testimony of Linda Schiro, that the defendant committed any of the acts charged in the indictment. On the other hand, credible evidence was presented that indicated that the defendant was so eager to maintain Scarpa as an informant that he was willing to bend the rules, including sending misinformation to headquarters in order to re-open him as an informant. It was only the discredited testimony of Linda Schiro that tied the defendant to any of the crimes charged in the indictment.

Indications of Obstruction of Justice by Judge Reichbach

Having been exposed to the corrupt activities of state and federal judges for the past 50 years, it is easy to understand Reichbach's conduct enabling a serial murderer to go free. For instance:

- Reichbach surely knew the value of the testimony that Scarpa could give in support of the murder charges against DeVecchio. He obstructed justice by his blatant dismissal of the charges before key witnesses could be heard.
- Reichbach surely knew that Schiro's statements to a journalist several years earlier did not automatically discredit the testimony that she gave in court under oath.
- Reichbach prevented Schiro from testifying under oath, the reason for the difference in the statements she made off the cuff to a journalist years earlier and the recent testimony given under oath.
- Reichbach had sufficient information, and referred to it in his decision, that DeVecchio was engaged in serious misconduct, and that the charges against DeVecchio would be in line with the murder charges filed against the former FBI supervisor.
- Judge Reichbach praised the FBI agents who earlier reported DeVecchio's misconduct, which provided a base for the later murder charges.
- Reichbach surely knew of the murders and other crimes involving FBI agents in the Boston office; the murder charges against DeVecchio would be similar misconduct. (Years earlier, a few of my contacts in the intelligence community told me about murders perpetrated by an FBI agent by the name of Chuckie Peters. At that time I thought that was too bizarre, and never made any mention of it in any of my writings)

Judge Reichbach was Previously Investigated

In the late 1960s, Reichbach was a student activist at Columbia University, under FBI surveillance. An FBI file contained a letter to the FBI stating that Reichbach "was one of the most dangerous" members of the Students for a Democratic Society. He was arrested months later with a group of Columbia students that seized and occupied university buildings during the May 1968 campus revolt.

During university disciplinary committee proceedings he shouted, "Up against the wall, mother-fuckers—this is a stick-up." In the judge's past were several arrests, campus protests, and he was required to appear at nine hearings before the bar to determine his character and fitness. His use of profanity troubled the committee hearing his case. He co-authored a book, *The Bust Book*, with Kathy Boudin, who was on the FBI's Most Wanted List. Reichbach obviously did not have the integrity that judges should have.

Hanging on the courtroom wall by Judge Reichbach was a portrait of Nelson Mandela, the South African revolutionary and Paul Robeson, the black American actor with communist ties.

Judge Reichbach

Effects of the Dismissal—and the Scheme to Obstruct Justice—Upon Public Safety

Obviously, any action that allows someone involved in murders, such as DeVecchio, to escape punishment, affects public safety. Obviously, also, when government law enforcement personnel and agencies are complicit in preventing anyone involved in such crimes to escape punishment, is even worse. On top of these adverse effects, there is the recognition by honest people in government that corruption pays, the recognition that coming forward with the truth is dangerous to a person. The entire system is corrupted. And when media people become accessories, just as they had become in the buildup to the invasion of Iraq, they are complicit.

DeVecchio's Corruption Not Unusual In the History of Law Enforcement Personnel

Corruption in law enforcement, local, state, and national, has been a standard for years. I've written about the corruption at the federal level in several of my books. Corruption in the New York area law enforcement agencies has been especially corrupt and written about for years.

Caproni: One of the DOJ Behind-the-Scene Officials

I had over 40 years of experience with DOJ cover-ups and obstruction of justice, starting while I was a federal inspector-investigator for the Federal Aviation Administration, attempting to report the corruption that I discovered during my official duties related to a series of airline disasters, and this case was simply a continuation.

One of the DOJ officials that had a role in DOJ handling of the DeVecchio matter was former U.S. Attorney Valerie Caproni, who played a key role in the obstruction of justice related to the downing of TWA Flight 800 that was hit by a missile.

When TWA Flight 800 was downed in 1998, U.S. Attorney Valeria Caproni issued orders barring the National Transportation Safety Board from investigating the crash, and assigning the investigation to the FBI. This was done despite the clear language of Title 39 § 1131(a)(2) that provides this responsibility to the NTSB:

> An investigation by the Board has priority over any investigation by another department, agency or instrumentality of the United States Government.

The FBI then ordered the NTSB to halt its interviews with eyewitnesses, preventing them from giving evidence showing that a surface-to-air missile brought down the aircraft. I describe this in great detail in my book, *History of Aviation Disasters: 1950 to 9/11*, and rely considerably upon my experiences in the FAA, and the obstructionist tactics by the DOJ.

The FBI and CIA then fabricated a ridiculous video claiming that the thin pencil-like missile streak that witnesses saw was really the exploding aircraft climbing 3,000 feet. The massive fire-plume from the aircraft obviously didn't meet the appearance of a thin pencil-like missile trail of a surface-to-air missile. Nor would an aircraft, with its entire front section broken off, climb 3,000 feet!

The next thing that the FBI and Caproni did was to file criminal charges against journalist Elizabeth Sanders who had received a sample of the seat fabric from the aircraft and then had it tested for explosives, which test proved positive, and that it was a missile that brought down the aircraft, contrary to what DOJ officials wanted.

Caproni wanted Sanders to divulge the name of the person who gave her the small piece of cloth. As a journalist, she refused. Caproni then filed criminal charges against Elizabeth Sanders and her husband, James Sanders. A naïve jury then convicted both of them of conspiracy to steal airplane parts.

In August of 2003, U.S. Attorney Valerie Caproni was appointed to the position in the FBI's Washington offices, responsible for providing legal advice to FBI officials and how to deal with FBI or other Justice Department problems and scandals.

FBI Turncoat Responsible for Many New York Murders

Federal prosecutor Valerie Caproni charged DeVecchio with lying about not giving confidential information to Scarpa, which fueled murderous warfare between two Mafia factions in 1991 and 1992 as they each sought control of the Colombo crime family. Ten mobsters and an innocent teenager were killed.

Caproni said Scarpa was a battle commander in one faction and played a leading role in bringing about the murders.

Reversal to Protect Murders and Obstruction of Justice

Years later, she fraudulently reversed her position so as to protect the series of murders in which DeVecchio was involved with Gregory Scarpa Jr., and the FBI-DOJ personnel feloniously covering up for the murders. To do this, she later stated that Scarpa Jr.'s information that he obtained from al Qaeda operative Ramzi Yousef about planned terrorist attacks were lies. As a result, 3,500 people were brutally killed, setting the stage for the U.S. to start two unwinnable and deadly wars.

Pittsburgh-Post Gazette Investigative Articles

One in a series of *Pittsburgh-Post Gazette* articles (November-December 1998) written by investigative reporter Bill Moushey, relating to DeVecchio, said:

> It was the first week of December 1991, and Vinnie Fusaro was stringing Christmas lights outside his home in Brooklyn. Gregory Scarpa Sr. was one of several passengers in a car that drove slowly by. In a sworn statement given two years later to the FBI— when Scarpa was already in prison and near death—a government informant named Larry Mazza gave this account of what happened next:
>
> Scarpa had his window open and his rifle ready as the car approached Fusaro's Brooklyn home. Scarpa fired three shots, killing Fusaro. A month later, he gunned down Nicholas Grancio. Both Fusaro and Grancio were middle-aged, small-time hoodlums whom Scarpa believed were Orena loyalists in the battle for control of the Colombo crime family.
>
> During this time—and throughout the Colombo crime family war—DeVecchio would call or meet with Scarpa almost every day during the Colombo crime family war, agents and the documents said. Based on that, Orena's attorneys believe DeVecchio was aware that Scarpa committed the murders.
>
> "Despite the knowledge that Greg Scarpa killed Grancio, and was believed to be actively prosecuting the war, the FBI did nothing to monitor or curtail Scarpa's irrepressible violence, or otherwise reign him in," Orena's attorneys would write later. "He was not arrested, or interrogated, for this crime. At no time did the FBI seek a search warrant for Scarpa's home to determine if Scarpa possessed the gun that killed Grancio. ... After Grancio was killed, Scarpa remained utterly free and unfettered to kill again—and so he did."
>
> DeVecchio has denied having any knowledge at the time of Scarpa's role in these murders, but there was no doubt DeVecchio and Scarpa were close. They even had a code. When DeVecchio had to call Scarpa, he would sometimes refer to himself as "Mr. Dello" or "Mr. Della." In turn,

Scarpa would call himself "34" and refer to his FBI contact as the "girlfriend."

No one outside the FBI knew about this cozy relationship, though a lot of people had their suspicions. Attorneys for Victor Orena were certainly curious.

Orena faced a nine-count racketeering indictment in late 1991, charging him with murder, murder conspiracy, firearms possession, extortion and loan sharking—all stemming from his fight with the Colombo family faction that included Gregory Scarpa Sr.

Orena's attorneys believed most of the evidence had been fabricated by Scarpa, with the aid of DeVecchio. Before Orena's trial, they asked the FBI to turn over everything they had about Scarpa, since it was their belief he had started the internecine war and caused most of the bloodshed.

Federal prosecutors eventually turned over only 77 pages of documents about Scarpa's work with DeVecchio, although in subsequent cases, thousands more would be released. There wasn't a single word about the gunmen who had tried but failed to kill Scarpa in 1991, precipitating the mob war that followed.

Orena's attorneys believe they know why. Their theory is the attack was staged, and Scarpa then used it as an excuse to declare war on Orena and his loyalists.

When the lawyers tried to find the forensic evidence that should have been gathered at the scene, they found the shell casings were missing; the photographs were missing; and there was no report filed on interviews with Scarpa.

As aspects of the relationship became known, DeVecchio admitted to his superiors that Scarpa would bring him gifts. When Cabbage Patch Dolls were popular but scarce, Scarpa gave a few to DeVecchio for his children. He gave him fine wine, pasta and other homemade Italian dishes during the holidays.

Orena's attorneys were unable to make their case without the thousands of pages of information about Scarpa and DeVecchio they suspected were in FBI files but were unable to obtain. Orena was convicted on the charges in 1992. The 2nd U.S. Court of Appeals turned down his appeal based on prosecutorial misconduct and other issues—as has the U.S. Supreme Court.

He still hopes he can persuade a judge through a writ of habeas corpus petition that the actions of the government have sent him to prison illegally.

While Orena remains in prison, more than a dozen other men involved in the Colombo crime family war have either been acquitted or had their cases dismissed because of the Scarpa-DeVecchio connection.

DeVecchio has retired from the FBI. Scarpa died in 1994 of AIDS transmitted by a blood transfusion during stomach surgery in 1986. He was 65.

The FBI had known for years he was in poor health. Yet no federal official ever questioned him about the issues raised by his relationship with the FBI during the Colombo Family crime war.

Last month, his son, Gregory Scarpa Jr., testified in New York during his own racketeering case that DeVecchio had given his father "carte blanche" to commit crimes, including five murders, so long as he kept working as a government informant.

Scarpa Jr., 47, is arguing that he received that same protection from the government.

DeVecchio, who was granted immunity in the case in exchange for testimony, disputed that. Scarpa Jr., already doing a 25-year sentence for drug smuggling, was convicted in October on conspiracy charges.

Crimes That Were Also Ignored

If for argument, DeVecchio was not complicit in the murders perpetrated by Scarpa Sr. by providing information enabling the murders to be accomplished, the evidence existed showing he knew of the murders and withheld the information. Those instances constituted crimes under Title 18 U.S.C. § 4, the misprision of felonies statute.

Primary Source Involved with DeVecchio Dismissal Scheme

The most obvious source for the dismissal scheme would be in the United States Department of Justice. The years of involvement in murders by FBI personnel in the Boston offices—with the knowledge of Washington FBI and other DOJ officials—and then on its heels the disclosure of years of involvement in murders of FBI personnel in the New York offices, could very possibly wake up the American people to the deadly culture existing in the nation's law enforcement agency.

Combine that with the corruption under U.S. attorney general Alberto Gonzales, the obstruction of justice dismissal of eight U.S. attorneys, the slew of other scandals in the Department of Justice, and the failures of the FBI in acting on the numerous indications the agency had of the 9/11 hijacking plot, and it is possible even the docile American public might show outrage.

And then there were other people that would be implicated. Members of Congress had known for decades about the corruption in the Department of Justice, including the information I sent to them over the years.

**Who, Among This Cast of People and Groups,
Enabled the Greatest Harm to America**

An interesting thought. Who among the people mentioned enabled the greatest harm to occur to the United States? Was it any of the people sent to prison or stripped of their jobs or pensions, or those in the FBI and other DOJ offices that misused their positions of trust to engage in corruption, fraud, lying? Although Gregory Scarpa Jr. and Linda Schiro had a checkered past, at least they tried to help in exposing corruption and criminality in key government offices.

Sudden Appearance of a Letter Sustaining These Suspicions

At a later date I received a June 2008 letter and enclosures from Gregory Scarpa, Jr. that added more intrigue to this sordid drama. Enclosed with that letter was a copy of a January 24, 2008, letter by Michael Vecchione, the chief of the Brooklyn district attorney's Rackets Division, addressed to U.S. District Judge Edward R. Korman in Brooklyn.

Key statements in that January 24 letter showed that the Brooklyn prosecutors recognized Scarpa, Jr. as a creditable person and witness and highly praised Scarpa for the valuable information he had provided to FBI agents relating to several planned terrorist attacks upon U.S. targets.

Why such a letter was written is perplexing. Scarpa was creditable, and did provide accurate and valuable information on planned terrorist attacks–and would have helped save many lives–if the information had been used. More on that issue later.

But by writing such a letter, the Brooklyn district attorney's office was further revealing the suspicious nature of dropping murder charges against DeVecchio without allowing Scarpa to testify. If the district attorney personnel had that much confidence in Scarpa, the dismissal of the case against DeVecchio, before allowing Scarpa to testify, would be even more evidence of the sham dismissal of murder charges against DeVecchio.

The contradictions support my belief that pressure in high federal positions caused the Brooklyn district attorney to allow DeVecchio to get away with murders. The following are some of the key statements made in that letter by the chief of the Brooklyn district attorney's Rackets Division, Michael Vecchione, to U.S. District Judge Edward R. Korman in Brooklyn:

The purpose of this letter is to bring to your attention the cooperation Gregory Scarpa, Jr. provided to this Office in the matter of People v. R. Lindley DeVecchio.

Scarpa Jr. was a capo in the Colombo Crime Family and a trusted lieutenant of his father. As such he participated in his father's criminal activities and witnessed some of his father's dealings with DeVecchio. Because he was so trusted by his father, Scarpa Sr. admitted to him the role DeVecchio played in two of the murders for which DeVecchio was charged. [Then why didn't the DA allow Scarpa to testify!]

Scarpa Jr. was open, candid and complete in his information, not only about the matters we were investigating but also about his criminal past. In addition to providing valuable intelligence, Scarpa Jr. was ready, willing and able to testify at the trial of DeVecchio.

CHAPTER TWENTY ONE

DOJ Officials Protecting Serial Murderers

The common law wife of Gregory Scarpa Sr., Linda Schiro, was listed as a defense witness in the criminal trial against Gregory Scarpa, Jr. She was scheduled to testify about details of Scarpa Sr.'s relationship with FBI Supervisory Agent Lindley DeVecchio. Scarpa Jr.'s mother, Connie Scarpa, would also testify in similar fashion. Their testimony would show DeVecchio's corrupt relationship with Gregory Scarpa, Sr.

Threatening Witnesses with Criminal Retaliation

DOJ prosecutors told these two witnesses that they would be prosecuted for various criminal offenses if they testified. Faced with prison, they refused to testify at Scarpa's trial, increasing the possibility that the guilty FBI and DOJ officials would escape the consequences of their criminal acts. The jury found Scarpa, Jr. guilty and Judge Raggi sentenced him to 40 years in prison.

Standard Practice of Rewarding Fraud of Government Officials

Federal prosecutor Valerie Caproni had falsely labeled the information that Scarpa obtained from Yousef as a hoax, helping to make possible the events of 9/11 and the U.S. Embassy bombings. In 1998, the DOJ elevated her to the position of Chief of the Criminal Division in New York, a typical promotion to those who protect the system from being exposed.

In 2003, FBI Director Robert Mueller promoted her to general counsel for the FBI. In the book *Defrauding America,* I describe Mueller's cover-ups of criminal activities while he was with the FBI's San Francisco office. In December 1992—shortly before the 1993 World Trade Center bombing—over the protests of federal prosecutors, U.S. District Judge Raggi ordered DOJ personnel to return to Ajaj the terrorist and bomb-making manuals that were seized by U.S. Customs as Ajaj entered the United States with Ramzi Yousef.

In 1994, allegations were made that DeVecchio had provided secret information to a top-echelon informant who was a made member of the Persico faction of the warring Colombo family. These allegations were extensively investigated by the FBI and the Department of Justice, Office of Professional Responsibility. After a comprehensive inquiry, the Department concluded that there was no basis for the allegations and dismissed the probe.

U.S. District Judge Jack B. Weinstein helped protect the FBI corruption by stating after extensive hearings that the claims against DeVecchio made by Gregory Scarpa, Jr. and others were meritless and lacking in credibility.

Caproni Was Aggressive When FBI-DOJ Corruption Not Involved

Years earlier while Caproni was an assistant U.S. attorney in Brooklyn, she covered up for FBI failure, or refusal, to apprehend Gregory Scarpa, Jr., who had been indicted in November 1987 for drug dealings and murder. FBI Special Agent Lindley DeVecchio had alerted Scarpa Sr., that an arrest warrant was being issued for his son, enabling Scarpa Jr. and his wife and daughter to flee. A year later, in August 1988, U.S. marshals found Scarpa Jr. at a motel in Lakewood, N.J. and arrested him.

Instead of praising the U.S. attorney or the marshal service, the FBI conducted an investigation to determine why the FBI had not been notified of the impending arrest (so as to have alerted Scarpa Jr.)

Defense Attorneys Learning of DeVecchio-Scarpa Relationship

Defense attorneys first learned about the relationship between DeVecchio and Scarpa when they were hired in 1994 by Anthony Russo to file an appeal. His attorneys, Alan Futerfas and Ellen Resnick, discovered that Scarpa was a Top Level informant working with DeVecchio. This information was discovered when the attorneys looked at sentencing and other transcripts.

That discovery led to over a dozen criminal convictions either being overturned or the defendants acquitted. And there was the danger that still more convictions would be overturned. It was therefore necessary to discredit anyone who could support the fact that DeVecchio was criminally involved with Scarpa Sr.

In the 1980s, many people on both sides of the law, including other FBI agents, were reporting that FBI Supervisory Special Agent Lindley DeVecchio in the FBI's New York offices was working with Colombo capo, Gregory Scarpa, Sr. The reports said that DeVecchio was providing to Scarpa confidential information on wiretaps and surveillance, and information resulting in people being murdered.

Their reports enlarged on what FBI Special Agent Richard Taus discovered and tried to report years earlier, and which I describe in a book, FBI, CIA, the Mob, and Treachery. The recent discovery of FBI agents involved with the Bulger crime group in murders showed that such conduct was well within the culture of the FBI.

Request for Investigation by Other FBI Agents

In 1994, when three veteran FBI agents charged DeVecchio with corrupt activities, it required the Department of Justice to conduct an internal investigation by the Office of Professional Relations (OPR). The Office of Professional Responsibility is required (don't count on it!) to investigate allegations of misconduct by Department of Justice legal personnel. It is standard practice for OPR investigations to end with a cover-up if the issues reflect poorly upon the people in the Department of Justice.

As these events were occurring, federal prosecutor Valerie Caproni was in the process of going to trial with several Colombo crime family members, including Anthony Russo. Any investigation of DeVecchio's conduct with a key mafia figured threatened to scuttle Caproni's cases. She reacted by requesting the Justice Department to delay the investigation.

In addition, when U.S. District Judge Charles Sifton received request for copies of all government documents related to DeVecchio and Scarpa, Caproni withheld a key document. That was a FBI 302 form in which Scarpa's key associate, Larry Mazza, stated that DeVecchio had regularly provided confidential information to Scarpa Sr. Part of that information related to DeVecchio providing Scarpa the address of people who would then be murdered.

In addition to withholding evidence and impeding a legally required investigation of criminal misconduct by a key FBI Supervisory Agent, Caproni instructed OPR investigators not to conduct any interviews of the defendants in the upcoming Mafia trials. The purpose of that ban was to prevent additional evidence surfacing that showed the criminal relationship of a key FBI agent with Colombo capo Gregory Scarpa Sr.

OPR investigator Thomas Fuentes wrote a report accusing Caproni and the U.S. attorney's office of obstructing the investigation. Also joining in obstructing justice was FBI agent James Kallstrom, the assistant director in charge of the New York FBI office. He prepared a report for FBI Director Louis Freeh that showed the relationship between DeVecchio's corruption to the upcoming trials. The report stated:

> This office requests that the investigation [DeVecchio-Scarpa] be conducted expeditiously. The failure of the Department of Justice to resolve this matter continues to have a serious negative impact on the government's prosecutions of LCN figures in the Eastern District of New York and casts a cloud over the New York office.

Without stating it in so many words, an expeditious closing of the investigation, if it followed prior patterns, would cover up for any misconduct that reflected adversely upon the government entity. The OPR investigation received strong evidence of DeVecchio's corrupt activities in a secret alliance with Colombo Mafia capo Gregory Scarpa, Sr. These included, among others:

The charges by three FBI agents who risked their careers by reporting the corrupt activities of FBI Supervisory Agent Lindley DeVecchio. These included:

- The sworn testimony of numerous mob witnesses, including Scarpa's closest aide, Larry Mazza.
- The circumstantial evidence of confidential information given to DeVecchio routinely becoming known to Scarpa Sr.

- The evidence provided by private investigators, including Angela Clemente, Dr. Stephen Dresch, and others.
- Document prepared by U.S. Attorney Patrick Fitzgerald (June 25, 1998) corroborating Scarpa's information.

During the subsequent DOJ investigation by the Office of Professional Responsibility (OPR), FBI Special Agent Christopher Favo stated, "I believe he was liable to say anything to Greg Scarpa." Favo described how confidential information on witnesses to crimes perpetrated by Scarpa was being received by Scarpa, thwarting the FBI's crime prevention responsibilities. In 1992, Favo had deliberately given DeVecchio the wrong address for Victor Orena and another member of that Colombo faction, which resulted in Scarpa trying to kill the wrong people. At another time, when Scarpa Sr. was about to be arrested, Favo kept Scarpa uninformed about the pending arrest until it was too late for DeVecchio to alert Scarpa.

Finally, DOJ Was Forced to Act

In 1994, the FBI conducted a two-year "investigation" of DeVecchio's conduct with Scarpa. The DOJ Office of Professional Responsibility cleared DeVecchio of any wrongdoing, and DeVecchio retired with a full pension in 1996. During the "investigation," DeVecchio refused to take a lie-detector test, repeatedly invoked the Fifth Amendment against self-incrimination on the grounds that his testimony may reveal he had committed criminal acts. When the judge granted him immunity to where he no longer had to plead the Fifth Amendment, he stated over three dozen times, "I don't recall." The fact that he refused to testify showed he had recognized that he had committed criminal acts, and that should have been the basis for being fired from the FBI.

Years of Prior Evidence Ignored

DeVecchio's lavish lifestyle should have alerted FBI officials that he was obtaining money and gifts from other sources. He wore expensive European silk suits, diamond cufflinks, and other perks that are not supported by the salary of an FBI agent. Just as the FBI ignored the lavish lifestyle of FBI agent Hanssen who was paid by the Soviet Union, the FBI ignored the lavish lifestyle of DeVecchio. Or, did they know, and approve?

As the OPR started to conduct an unpublicized investigation into the allegations against DeVecchio, the FBI moved DeVecchio from the top organized crime squad position he held to a relatively minor DEA drug task force.

I had reported DeVecchio's criminal misconduct in the third edition of *Defrauding America* that came out in 1997, and even reported this information to members of Congress, including the Judiciary Committee members, with the usual non-response. I renewed my efforts to report the criminal activities to them in 2003 after I received considerable more evidence of the FBI-Mob relationship from a former member of the Colombo Mafia family who was the son of the Colombo capo that was directly involved with the corrupt and murderous relationship.

Scarpa-DeVecchio Relationship Resulted in Acquittals

As the relationship between DeVecchio and Scarpa became known, the cases went in favor of the defendants, resulting in numerous acquittals. Also, legal actions were filed to overturn prior convictions, and many of those were vacated. In a Second Court of Appeals decision, one of the three judges, Guido Calabresi, issued a dissenting opinion attacking prior convictions associated with the Scarpa-DeVecchio connection, Calabresi wrote:

> CALABRESI, *J.*, dissenting:
>
> I respectfully dissent.
>
> At trial, defendants sought to persuade the jury that the violence inside the Colombo Family stemmed from a Scarpa-Sessa war triggered by suspicions that Gregory Scarpa, Sr. was a government informant, rather than from the Persico/Orena factional battle charged by the government. Until after trial, the government admittedly suppressed evidence that Scarpa Sr., in fact, *was* an informant. In the first appeal of these convictions, a panel of this court decided that, notwithstanding the government's improper behavior, a new trial was not the appropriate remedy. The panel held that the presence of strong independent evidence of guilt, and the availability of other evidence with which the defense could attack the government's case, rendered the government's misconduct insufficiently material to violate the constitution. We are, of course, bound by that decision. [That is not the case during appellate review.]
>
> In these appeals, however, defendants argue that the government not only *suppressed* evidence directly supporting defendants' theory of the case, but, in addition, that, through its cooperating witnesses, the government actually *introduced* perjured testimony tending to undermine defendants' theory. Thus, under direct examination, Sessa testified that he believed that a *New York Post* article claiming that "Gregory Scarpa" was a government informant referred to Scarpa, Jr., and was false.
>
> Given subsequent statements by Sessa and others that Sessa instead believed that the article referred to Scarpa, Sr. and that it was true, and given, moreover, that the government knew at trial (though it had suppressed this fact, *see Orena*, 145 F.3d at 556) that Scarpa, Sr. actually was cooperating with the FBI, it is plausible that Sessa was lying and that the government either was aware of Sessa's perjury, or closed its eyes to what was obvious. Furthermore, it was helpful to the government for Sessa to cast doubt on the relevance of the *Post* article, and, as a cooperating witness, Sessa was motivated to lie if he thought that doing so would please the government.

In pointing this out I do not mean to suggest that the testimony about the *Post* article can *only* be explained as showing perjury by Sessa, and as indicating that the government knew or should have known about the perjury. The government has put forward a number of arguments, both in its appellate briefs and in a sworn affidavit submitted to the district court that would explain the testimony as the result of confusion. The problem, however, is that the district court denied defendants the opportunity to test the government's theories in an adversary hearing at which the critical issues of credibility and mental state could be explored. *See Forts v. Ward*, 566 F.2d 849, 851 (2d Cir. 1977) ("Normally, an evidentiary hearing is required to decide credibility issues."). Without such a hearing, I cannot rule on whether conscious lying took place.

If Sessa did perjure himself on the topic of Scarpa, Sr.'s cooperation, and the government knew or should have known of it, a new trial would, I think, be required, at least when one considers the cumulative effect of that perjury and the government's suppression of evidence concerning its relationship with Scarpa. It cannot again be said that this trial would have looked radically different had the government permitted an accurate view of Scarpa's role to be put forward. Indeed, some, though not all, of the related cases that went to trial after Scarpa's role was revealed, resulted in acquittals.

I do not doubt that the evidence introduced at trial was sufficient to convict defendants on each count, even if we eliminate all of the evidence that is possibly traceable to Scarpa. But the fact that a jury *could* convict does not mean that it will. And defendants must have a fair opportunity to convince the jury that it should not do so. That opportunity, moreover, must be untainted by misguided government attempts to tilt the scales in its favor. Perhaps these defendants received a fair trial, and perhaps they did not. Because I cannot be confident of the answer on the current record, I dissent from the majority's decision to affirm these convictions. I would remand for an evidentiary hearing on whether Sessa perjured himself and, if he did, whether the government knew or should have known of it.

Footnotes

1. The suppressed evidence would have been helpful to the defense in other respects as well.

2. I note that the government, in its explanations of its conduct, might be construed to be saying that, because the suppression was not deemed to require a new trial, it did nothing wrong in the first place. It goes without saying that such behavior is not to be condoned even when it ultimately is deemed harmless. As Attorney General John Ashcroft has recently observed, the government "has a more important duty than the prosecution of any single case," namely a "responsibility to promote the sanctity of the

rule of law and justice . . . [and] to protect the integrity of our system of justice." *See* David Johnston, *Citing F.B.I. Lapse, Ashcroft Delays McVeigh Execution*, N.Y. Times, May 12, 2001, at A1.

Multiple Signs of Judicial And Prosecutorial Obstruction of Justice

In the highly sensitive case of DeVecchio, the signs showing the obstruction of justice were numerous. The groups implicated in obstructing justice in the dismissal of the charges against DeVecchio included, for instance:

- The political people in the office of the Brooklyn prosecutor.
- The state judge, Gustin Reichbach.
- The people in the various offices of the FBI and other DOJ divisions that covered up for DeVecchio's crimes, for years, refused to prosecute, and then paid for his defense. In addition, the probable behind-the-scene pressure on various people to drop the charges.
- The U.S. Attorney General, and primarily Alberto Gonzales, whose conduct in virtually every area was either blatantly corrupt or highly suspicious of being corrupt.
- The Inspector General in the Department of Justice, who in 1996 and again in 2005 issued papers stating that there was no evidence supporting the charges against DeVecchio and protecting the FBI-DOJ image.
- Media people who surely recognized the improper dismissal of the charges and criticized the people who had the courage to come forward and testify.

Neither the members of Congress nor media people paid any attention to the cover-ups, nor associated the failure of the FBI to act on the considerable events that indicated the dangerous culture in the FBI and other Department of Justice offices. And that culture had ripple effects elsewhere, such as the failure to act on the evidence that could have prevented the bombing of the World Trade Center in 1993 or the scheme to hijack four airliners on September 11, 2001. (The details of DOJ involvement in the 9/11 attacks are described in *History of Aviation Disasters: 1950 to 9/11*, and in *Blowback, 9/11, and Cover-Ups*.)

Corrupt Judicial System Protects the System

The judicial system in New York is probably even more political and corrupt than it is in most other states. A *New York Times* article (October 3, 1991) gave highlights on the number of New York judges convicted of crimes:

"In the last 15 years, 39 New York City judges have been convicted of a crime, removed from office, censured or publicly admonished for misconduct." Five judges, all elected, have been convicted of crimes. In addition, 34 judges have been found guilty of misconduct by the New York

State Court of Appeals, an Appellate Division, a court on the judiciary or the State Commission on Judicial Conduct. Six judges were removed from office.

Of these 39 judges, only 2 (5 percent) achieved the bench through merit selection; 37 (95 percent) were elected. In contrast, 47 percent of the more than 500 state judges in New York City are appointed, while 53 percent are elected.

A two-page article (*New York Times* (Jan 29, 2007) addressed some parts of the New York judicial system that addressed the court system in smaller towns, and reflects the general culture of corruption throughout the state in these courts:

> With little oversight, some court officials feel free to help themselves. As court clerk in the western New York village of Perry, Ruth Milks was in a prime spot to see the kind of big money that moves through the state's smallest courts. Her husband was the village justice, and Mrs. Milks—a former justice herself—collected the fines and fees.
>
> She was also in a prime spot to cash in. Mrs. Milks started adding $35 to parking fines, recording the extra charge on the driver's receipt but not in her court files. By the time state auditors caught up with her in 2003—only because she had fined one of them—they estimated she had pocketed at least $60,000, which investigators said she spent on gifts and a trip to a casino.
>
> It is no secret that New York's justice courts—an unwieldy system of 1,250 town and village courts that dates back to Colonial days—have been troubled for a long time. Three-quarters of the justices are not lawyers, and state disciplinary records show that some have jailed defendants illegally and denied people basic legal rights. In recent months, the Legislature and state judicial officials have been scrambling to fix some of the courts' most obvious failings.

An article in the *New York Law Journal* (July 18, 2007), titled, Misconduct Charges Lead to N.Y. Judge's Resignation, stated:

> Former New York Supreme Court Justice Lawrence I. Horowitz used his status as a judge to seek preferential police treatment for his girlfriend and to have authorities investigate the woman's estranged husband, the New York Commission on Judicial Conduct said Tuesday.
>
> The commission announced that Horowitz, who resigned on June 20, has signed a stipulation acknowledging that he could not defend himself against the disciplinary charges. He also agreed not to serve again as a judge or judicial hearing officer.

Horowitz, 56, was a Westchester County Supreme Court justice who has been assigned to Orange County for the past two years.

In a formal complaint also released Tuesday, the commission charged Horowitz with two counts of judicial misconduct, and it dated his wrongdoing to Jan. 1, 2004, when he joined the Supreme Court bench.

"Former Judge Is Convicted of Bribery in Divorce Court" was the heading on a *New York Times* article (April 20, 2007) stating:

[Gerald P. Garson] Handled nearly 1,100 cases in Brooklyn. A former State Supreme Court judge was convicted yesterday of accepting bribes to manipulate the outcome of divorce proceedings in a case that led to a broad political and judicial corruption inquiry in Brooklyn.

In his roughly five years on the bench in Brooklyn, Mr. Garson handled nearly 1,100 matrimony cases, making decisions on child custody and financial matters. In finding him guilty, the jury endorsed the prosecution theory that he had an agreement with a divorce lawyer to take cash, dinners and cigars in exchange for courtroom assignments and favored treatment.

The verdict was a significant victory for the Brooklyn district attorney, Charles J. Hynes, and for his chief of investigations, Michael F. Vecchione, a high-ranking assistant district attorney who prosecuted Mr. Garson as part of their larger corruption inquiry.

[Realizing the value of bringing corruption to justice]

Outside the courtroom, Mr. Vecchione said the case had put public officials in the borough on notice. "I'm not sure there was any further message that needed to be sent, other than people need to do what's right," Mr. Vecchione said.

Mr. Garson was first charged in 2003, along with the divorce lawyer, Paul Siminovsky, as well as one of his clients, a court officer, a former clerk and a man described as a fixer. All six were charged with felonies.

The case immediately reverberated throughout Brooklyn, from playpens and dinner tables to the upper echelons of politics. Divorce cases were reopened. Judges feared that their offices were wired for surveillance. The system of nominating judges was ruled unconstitutional.

The longtime Democratic Party leader, Clarence Norman Jr., who helped place Mr. Garson on the bench, was convicted on corruption charges and now faces jail time. Acting on statements Mr. Garson made when confronted with the evidence against him, Mr. Hynes vowed to expose a system in which judgeships were for sale.

In his closing statement for the prosecution, Mr. Vecchione said on Tuesday, "Supreme Court Judge Gerald Garson became corrupt."

Taking On the Characteristics of the Other Side of the Law

And then we had Supreme Court Judge Reichbach, and we have the same prosecutors themselves acting to obstruct justice in a case that had national implications. A report by the Special Commission on the Future of New York State Courts (July 17, 2006) stated in part:

> On July 17, 2006, New York State Chief Judge Judith S. Kaye appointed the Special Commission on the Future of the New York State Courts to assess the effectiveness of the state's current court structure and to propose appropriate reforms. The thirty member Commission was comprised of judges and court administrators; academics; representatives from the business community, bar organizations and good government groups; and some of our state's leading legal practitioners.
>
> During the ensuing seven months, the Commission conducted an intensive study of the New York State court system. As part of this effort, the Commission and its staff reviewed the voluminous body of literature that exists on the subject of court structure and past reform efforts, and compiled various statistics and other data to assess the functioning of our court system.
>
> New York State has the most archaic and bizarrely convoluted court structure in the country. Antiquated provisions in our state Constitution create a confusing amalgam of trial courts; and inefficient and wasteful system that causes harm and heartache to all manner of litigants.

New York Type of Judicial Corruption in Chicago:
Operation Greylord and Operation Gambat

In the 1980s, thanks to the courageous work of concerned private citizens, including Sherman H. Skolnick, the vast judicial corruption was exposed, which was given the names of Operation Greylord and Operation Gambat. What was found paralleled the type of judicial corruption in the New York state courts, and to a lesser or greater extent, in the courts of other states.

The federal investigation discovered a judicial system riddled with corruption, influence peddling, and intrigue. Nearly 100 individuals, including nearly two dozen judges and nearly 70 lawyers were identified and convicted. Most of the convicted judges had been previously rated as highly qualified by the Chicago Bar Association, which doesn't say much for the group. And these were only a small part of those who were guilty; others just escaped being investigated.

One investigator stated, "In those days, the judges, the lawyers, and the people we arrested were all joined at the hip. It was a brotherhood of corruption where you take care of me; I'll take care of you."

Pre-Trial Comments from Former FBI Special Agent Richard Taus

After the Brooklyn district attorney filed charges against retired FBI Supervisory Agent Lindley DeVecchio, Taus made the following comments to me in a series of letters:

I first met DeVecchio in 1983. He was a "dandy" by all accounts, a ladies man, well dressed. DeVecchio closed [blocked] a few of my more promising investigations [into Colombo Mafia activities]. The problem between DeVecchio and me was my insistence or tenacity in pursuing cases. During the time that I worked for DeVecchio, I knew that there were problems since he closed several of my Mafia cases without good reason.

The Brooklyn DA, Charles Hynes, pursued DeVecchio because his constituents, all from Brooklyn and many with Mafia ties or loyalties, demanded action, lest he would lose their votes. Besides, the Pandora's box of misconduct by federal officials was in the public's view.

I still maintain that these "turf wars" between the NY U.S. attorney office, DOJ and the state district attorneys are controlled by higher powers (White House, CIA) who for political reasons precipitated them.

[Higher Officials Involved]

In the end, DeVecchio was "Outed" because of Mafia friends on the outside who wanted their associates in federal prison freed. Greg Scarpa Junior knew the terrible truth about DeVecchio and was speaking out

At this point, I have some difficulty in not believing that a greater force was behind DeVecchio's work for the Mafia. Given Scarpa's involvement with covert activities as far back as the mid '60s, it stands to reason that DeVecchio did not conceive of this idea of protecting the Mafia alone and only based upon his own greed.

I always felt that DeVecchio purposefully prevented my further investigations of Asaro and Esposito. When DeVecchio transferred me from his Criminal Division squad to a Foreign Counter-Intelligence squad, I was quite upset. As I later discovered, that transfer was to the very squad that had CIA Station Chief and front-company president Dan Priscu as a phony FBI FCI informant.

Vincent Asaro was a Bonanno Capo with Gambino affiliations. He was the grandnephew of Carlos Gambino, the original 1930-40 boss of the family. During my investigation of Asaro, I conducted an elaborate investigation (from a bank building's 2nd floor offices) against Asaro's social club and later from the bell tower of a Catholic church when Asaro moved his location to a realty office after, somehow, discovering my "plant" in the bank building.

I was told that one of the female agents who conducted surveillance from the bank plant flashed a camera out of the 2nd story window and one of the Mafioso saw it, effectively "burning" (disclosing) the plant. Or was the plant "blown" by an insider's tip?

Another case involved a known Mafia associate, as I recall by the name of John or Joe Esposito. He was involved with the Lufthansa robbery in 1979 and allegedly turned FBI informant after his friend was whacked by the Mafia as it tried to prevent any disclosures on the whereabouts or involvement of monies and Mafiosi involved in that heist. I reopened the closed informant file on Esposito after a tip from two other FBI agents that he might still have some valuable information.

That information led me to a drug-trafficking operation in Queens which involved a dry cleaning store, a storage garage, and John Gotti. And to a CIA connection given the accusations of Esposito that higher powers were involved.

Asaro worked with Gotti, was on good social terms with the Gambino family boss, reflecting the close ties between the Gambino and Bonanno families. Gotti was upset with Godfather Castellano who refused to let him get into other crime areas.

On the Esposito case, there was a very well guarded garage near an overhead rail in Queens, which was surrounded by barbed wire and guarded by two Dobermans, and two thugs whenever it was open. It also had an alarm system. I could never get any phone tapes to develop the case. In fact, no one in the FBI wanted to show any interest. The local NYPD often looked the other way at Mafia operations I found.

In the Asaro case, prior to confronting him on the Mafia assassination contract on FBI SA Joe Pistone, an NYPD detective and I went to a known Mafia social club in Queens. As we entered the club, in plain sight, the members ran their numbers racket despite the presence of the detective and me. In short, they operated with impunity. And you must remember that many people in Brooklyn supported the Mafia because, like the Klan, the Mafia kept their neighborhood (somewhat) protected. (When Gotti died there was a great outpouring of grief from thousands in Brooklyn and Queens! And it was not just Mafioso, but old women and families.)

[DeVecchio Diverting Attention By Fingering NYPD Detective]

NYPD detective Joe Simone was fingered and prosecuted as a mole in the joint task force where FBI SA Chris Favo, DeVecchio's assistant, worked. Simone was accused of taking bribes and consorting with known Mafia members. An animosity grew after Simone's trial because he was blamed for the "intelligence leaks" while SA Favo later claimed that it was DeVecchio's doings. As a result, a great animosity existed between the two law enforcement agencies and the New York county district attorney and the U.S. attorney's offices. That led to the revelations against DeVecchio spurred on by the allegations of convicted Mafia capos, soldiers and others who now had an axe to grind against the feds.

While each agency pointed fingers at the other and conducted secret investigations (by their respective internal affairs units), the CIA toted the fact that it was a law-abiding agency by exposing corruption in other state and federal agencies. Recall the David Hardy case, where the CIA exposed Hardy, a NY state trooper, for faking evidence, who had hoped to be hired by the CIA.

[Lying Complicity by FBI-DOJ Personnel and Federal Judges]

Scarpa Junior's information and testimony to FBI-DOJ personnel and to federal judges, based upon information received from his cellmate and al Qaeda operative, Ramzi Yousef, was ignored, claiming that anything said by Scarpa was not creditable.

[Federal Judges Implicated in FBI-DOJ Corruption]

Among the judges implicated in the deception were federal judges Jack Weinstein, John Walker, and Reena Raggi. It was federal prosecutor Caproni, with U.S. District Court Judge Reena Raggi, that dismissed Gregory Scarpa Junior's testimony and evidence against Ramzi Yousef. It was Judge Raggi who refused me bail in late 1988 and who, later, in 2005, refused to recuse herself from the three-judge panel that heard my federal habeas corpus petition in the U.S Court of Appeals for the 2nd Circuit. Judge John Walker was the Chief Judge on that panel who also denied me relief. Walker was involved in other nefarious decisions.

Judge John Walker is related to George Herbert "Walker" Bush, who was involved in both the Iraqgate and Irangate scandals I investigated.

U.S. District Judge Jack Weinstein, in January 2004, rejected Gregory Scarpa Jr.'s testimony about Ramzi Yousef; another federal judge who presided at my initial federal habeas corpus petition! Weinstein also heard and denied my federal habeas corpus petition in 2005. Weinstein denied my appeal in a lengthy written 24-page decision that was worse than what NY Nassau assistant district attorneys ever said about me!

Three of the four federal judges on the U.S. District Court and U.S. Court of Appeals for the 2d Circuit that heard my appeals also were involved with the cover-ups in the DeVecchio and Scarpa cases. I find it not coincidental that three of the four federal judges, Weinstein, Raggi and Walker, that heard my appeal in 2005, were also involved in all the other aspects concerning DeVecchio, Scarpa, and Yousef.

The *Real* Reason for Discrediting Scarpa Jr.

The real reason for discrediting Scarpa was to discredit his information about the murderous relationship between FBI Supervising Agent DeVecchio and Scarpa's father. Such exposure in the FBI New York offices, coming on top of the criminal activities in the Boston FBI offices involving murders facilitated over the decades by FBI agents with the knowledge of Washington officials, would reflect a culture within the FBI that amounted to criminal activities against the United States.

Media People Continued Their Practice of Cover-Up

Except for the local newspapers in the Boston and New York areas, there was a blackout in the remainder of the country concerning these serious matters. Media people focused on trivial matters such as rape charges, local murders, a missing tourist in the Caribbean, and other matters that kept the public from discovering the extent of hardcore criminal activities of people in the FBI, DOJ, and other government offices.

DOJ Officials Withheld the Book: *FBI, CIA, the Mob, and Treachery*

In response to my question whether he received the book, *FBI, CIA, the Mob*, that I had sent to him at the MCC holding facility in New York, where Scarpa was waiting to testify in the DeVecchio trial, Scarpa stated:

> DOJ officials at the MCC came and explained to me that they had to read it first. After reading it, they said they would forward it to me the following week. Week after week passed, and for some odd reason they kept putting it off. So with that and a lot of publicity about DeVecchio, I told the MCC that I believe they don't want me to have the book before the trial, and if they didn't mind, I asked them to mail the book to my lawyer.
>
> I then gave them the lawyer's address. They in turn said that would be the best thing because it wouldn't be good for me to read it before the trial. [Not good for the DOJ or DeVecchio.] They said they would immediately mail it to my lawyer. Rodney, he never got it. You were right for what you wrote to Washington. They stole the book. Unbelievable!

Covering Up for DeVecchio While Simultaneously Covering up for FBI Murders in the Boston FBI Offices

Although high FBI-DOJ officials managed to escape being exposed in the FBI's murder involvement in Boston and the New York offices, the existing evidence, which had been publicized only in the local Boston and New York newspapers, indicated there always existed the danger that the media cover-ups would someday be circumvented.

A small two-column-inch article appeared in *USA Today* (April 15, 2008) that laid the groundwork for FBI-DOJ officials denying that Boston or New York FBI agents were involved in murders. The article stated:

> **Ex-mob Boss' Plea Could Free Him Soon**
>
> A former New England mob boss pleaded guilty in Boston to federal charges in a deal that could get him released from prison in nine months.
>
> Francis "Cadillac Frank" Salemme admitted he lied about the involvement of another mob boss while negotiating a 1999 deal with authorities

> investigating the FBI's informant relationship with gangsters James "Whitey" Bulger and Stephen "The Rifleman" Flemmi. Salemme helped convict former FBI agent John Connolly of racketeering in 2002. Salemme said Connolly had tipped them off before all were indicted on racketeering charges in 1995. Bulger remains a fugitive.

What occurred was the standard practice by federal prosecutors of providing some form of compensation for certain people to give testimony that the prosecutors wanted, which was often known perjured testimony. The significance of this is that Salemme was being compensated for recanting his earlier sworn testimony, and thereby directly exonerating an FBI Special Agent, and indirectly exonerating high FBI-DOJ officials that knew about the corrupt and murderous relationship between mobsters and the FBI.

The compensation could be (a) withholding charges against the person giving the perjured testimony; (b) dropping charges; (c) filing legal papers to release prisoners; (d) not filing false charges against a family member; or any number of other forms. In this case, by releasing a convicted murderer for perjured testimony that would reflect favorably on FBI-DOJ personnel, everyone profited! Except, of course, the public.

A *New York Daily News* article (Nov. 8, 2007), titled, "Few Willing to Act as Prosecutor in Linda Schiro Probe" stated:

> Brooklyn officials have run into a wall as they try to find a special prosecutor to probe a discredited star witness in a murder case against a former FBI agent, sources say. "No DA will touch it," said one knowledgeable source. "Which means [Brooklyn Administrative Judge Neil Firetog] will have to go private."
>
> So far, the only candidate to take on the Linda Schiro case is former Manhattan Supreme Court Justice Leslie Crocker Snyder. Court officials wouldn't comment, but insiders say the Office of Court Administration was resisting Snyder because she might be seen as too political after her 2005 run against Manhattan District Attorney Robert Morgenthau.
>
> "That would be a shame if true, because she really would be perfect for the job," said a source familiar with the selection process, who said Snyder was contacted and is interested. Brooklyn DA requested the perjury probe against Schiro. She testified that ex-FBI agent Lindley DeVecchio helped ex-boyfriend Greg Scarpa in four mob hits, but interview tapes showed she changed her story.

Danger of Testifying Against the FBI-DOJ

Referring to the fears that Linda Schiro was experiencing for having come forward to testify against DeVecchio, a New York *Daily News* article (Nov. 21, 2007), titled, "I'm petrified of going to jail," stated:

Linda Schiro ranted to a friend about her fears of being sent to prison for perjury. Schiro sits in her daughter's Staten Island apartment all day, minding her three grandchildren, twin 5-year-old girls and a grandson, 7, gulping coffee, chain-smoking, popping anti-depressants and peeking out the windows at the press camped outside her door.

Schiro's waiting to learn if she will be indicted by a special prosecutor on perjury charges for her role as the discredited star witness in a murder trial against former FBI Special Agent Lindley DeVecchio.

"Linda just called me a few minutes ago on a hysterical rant," says the friend. "She's a completely broken woman. She said, 'What did I do wrong? Why are they doing this to me? I never went to the Brooklyn DA to tell my story. They came to me.'"

The case short-circuited last week when *Village Voice* reporter Tom Robbins, a former *Daily Newser*, came forward with 10-year-old tapes of Schiro that contradicted the murderous narrative she had been telling on the witness stand in Brooklyn Supreme Court.

"I didn't want to testify. They promised me that win, lose or draw that they would stand behind me," said Schiro. "When they first came and asked me to be a witness I told them I had told conflicting stories in the past. I mixed fact and fiction about this case in the past to writers and reporters and different people.

"I told the grand jury under oath that I had told inconsistent stories about this case in the past," Schiro continued. "But when I agreed to become a witness I told the truth. Now, because there are tapes I didn't know about, I'm the one facing time in jail."

The friend said he fears for Schiro's future. "She tells me there's no way she could handle jail," the friend said. "Personally, I don't think she could even survive the trial. I think she'd wind up in a mental institution. This is a woman who had a son murdered. She made the mistake of falling in love with the wrong person in Greg Scarpa, and now she's 62, most of her family has abandoned her, she ages a year by the day, she's falling apart, she has very few friends.

"She calls, hysterical crying, and tells me, 'I can't sleep. I can't eat. All I think about is prison. I'm petrified. What should I do?' And I don't know what to tell her except to hang in there and hope for the best.

"Her fate is in the hands of Administrative Judge [Neil] Firetog, who is supposed to decide whether or not to send her case to the grand jury." If he does, Schiro could wind up indicted for perjury, facing serious jail time.

Schiro got involved in the DeVecchio case after she was approached by former NYPD Detective Tommy Dades and ex-Brooklyn Assistant District Attorney Noel Downey. Dades wouldn't comment yesterday but said Saturday that if Schiro is indicted, he and Downey would testify on her behalf that from the beginning she was upfront with them and others at Brooklyn DA Charles' office about the inconsistent stories she told about DeVecchio over the years.

Dades, who resigned as an investigator for the Brooklyn DA's office in May, told me Saturday that he was prepared to go all the way to defend Linda Schiro. "Noel Downey and I discussed it," Dades said, "and we both said to each other, 'I can't look at myself in the mirror if we let this woman get prosecuted.' ... I gave her my word, and they gave me their word, that they would never do anything to hurt her."

Schiro was given a stipend by the Brooklyn DA's office and a promise of a new identity and relocation if she agreed to testify, her friend told me. "Now she has no income except for about $700 a month," the friend says. "She has no skills. She lived with Greg Scarpa for 30 years. If she's not indicted, she's afraid of reprisals from the FBI and maybe DeVecchio.

"She won't be relocated and she fears that she'll soon be dispossessed because she has no money to pay her rent." Schiro told the friend, "My life is over."

Requirements of Perjury to be a Crime

The primary statements that count in a criminal case are those made under oath in a court of law. Causal comments made between private individuals, which are affected by many factors, would be totally secondary, and a difference between the two would not be grounds for a perjury charge.

Rewarding Those on the Corrupt Team

Over the past half century I've seen time and time again how people in government who cooperate with covering up corrupt activities are then rewarded. I was reminded of that against in a *New York Times* article (April 25, 2008) titled, "Columbia Protester, Now a Judge, Returns to Campus." That article referred to none other than Gus Reichbach, the judge that rescued DOJ officials involved with protecting DeVecchio and discrediting one of the most valuable moles the government had in the al Qaeda organization. The article stated in part:

> Forty years ago, a young radical Columbia Law student named Gus Reichbach became the first student prominently disciplined by Columbia University for his participating in the blockages and protests in 1968. He is now Justice Gustin L. Reichbach, of the State Supreme Court in Brooklyn (in the news most recently for presiding over the DeVecchio trial).

He is still known by his tabloid nickname as the "Condom Judge," for his practice years ago of handing out condoms. [How crude!] Judge Reichbach explained how law school professors tried to block his admittance to the Bar Association.

This former campus leader of Students for a Democratic Society had represented the Black Panthers and Abbie Hoffman, and helped write "*The Bust Book: What to Do Till the Lawyer Comes*."

The university charged him back in 1968 with assaulting a university security officer. He was exonerated after chaotic tribunals and herrings but he was considered a notorious enough radical to be under FBI surveillance.

The Black Panthers were a violent Africa-American group engaging in murders and other crimes, including a 1968 gun battle, and were active from about the mid 1960s into the 1970s. One of their members was Huey P. Newton, who was arrested and convicted for murder.

Another Example of New York Judge Protecting the System

Local media articles, including one in the *New York Times* (April 26, 2008), gave another example of how judges protect the system. In that case, three police officers who fired 50 shots into a car containing two unarmed people, killing one of them, was judged innocent by New York judge Arthur J. Cooperman.

This extraordinary case of police brutality was shown by the fact that two of the police officers had to reload their guns and keep firing at the badly wounded and dead unarmed passenger that were never a threat to them. One detective, Michael Oliver, reloaded his gun several times to fire 31 shots into the two victims. Like a turkey shoot, they appeared to delight killing their target. This mentality was obvious in some of the publicized killings of Iraqis by U.S. military and contractor personnel.

CHAPTER TWENTY TWO

Reports Expose Multiple Obstruction of Justice Schemes

The dropping of murder charges against former FBI supervisor Lindley DeVecchio defied standard prosecutorial procedures. The charges were suspiciously dropped despite the fact that the prosecutors had overwhelming evidence of DeVecchio's guilt. That evidence consisted of:

- The enormous amount of circumstantial evidence from several FBI agents and others, which exceeded the amount of circumstantial evidence resulting in countless other cases.
- The planned testimony of Gregory Scarpa, Jr,, the son of Gregory Scarpa Sr. that carried out a series of murders with FBI supervisor Lindley DeVecchio, and who provided for money to be paid to the FBI agent for the inside information used to commit the murders.
- The partial testimony of Mary Schiro—that was suddenly halted—who was present for years while her common law husband—Scarpa, Sr.—discussed murder and other plans.

Strong Evidence That Dropping of Murder Charges Constituted Serious Obstruction of Justice

In March 2008, Gregory Scarpa sent me a copy of a letter that made even *more obvious* that the Brooklyn prosecutor and the state judge were obstructing justice by protecting the FBI supervisor involved in a series of murders when they dismissed the murder charges against former FBI supervisor Lindley DeVecchio. Since the dropping of murder charges had links to several catastrophic terrorist attacks upon U.S. targets, and the dropping of murder charges acted to cover up for the corruption that made these terrorist attacks possible, the obstruction of justice tactics took on a far more serious ramification.

That January 24, 2008, letter written by Michael F. Vicchione, Chief of the rackets division in the office of the Brooklyn District Attorney's office, praised Gregory Scarpa, Jr. for his credibility. In other words, what Scarpa had stated about the serial murders involving the FBI supervisor was correct.

OFFICE OF THE DISTRICT ATTORNEY, KINGS COUNTY
RENAISSANCE PLAZA at 350 JAY STREET
BROOKLYN, N.Y. 11201-2908
(718) 250-2239

CHARLES J. HYNES
District Attorney

MICHAEL F. VECCHIONE
CHIEF, RACKETS DIVISION

January 24, 2008

The Honorable Edward R. Korman
United States District Court
Eastern District of New York
225 Cadman Plaza East, Room 118
Brooklyn, New York 11201

Re: Gregory Scarpa, Jr.

Dear Judge Korman:

The purpose of this letter is to bring to your attention the cooperation Gregory Scarpa, Jr. provided to this Office in the matter of People v. R. Lindley DeVecchio.

As you may know DeVecchio, a former FBI agent, was charged in Kings County Supreme Court with acting in concert with Gregory Scarpa, Sr. in the murder of four individuals who presented threats to the security and well-being of Scarpa Sr. At the time of these murders Scarpa Sr. was a very valued member of the Colombo Crime Family, was active in the Colombo Crime Family war of the early 1990's and an informant for the FBI. His handler was former agent DeVecchio.

Scarpa Jr. was brought to this Office from the federal detention facility in Florence, Colorado after he had indicated through contacts that he was willing to help in any way he could in our investigation of DeVecchio.

Scarpa Jr., when he was at liberty during the 1970's and 1980's, was a capo in the Colombo Crime Family and a trusted lieutenant of his father. As such he participated in his father's criminal activities and witnessed some of his father's dealings with DeVecchio.

The Honorable Edward R. Korman
January 24, 2008
Page 2

In addition, after he was incarcerated on the cases for which he is now serving time, he was visited by his father in jail. Because he was so trusted by his father, during those visits Scarpa Sr. admitted to him the role DeVecchio played in two of the murders for which DeVecchio was charged.

Consequently, Scarpa Jr. was a wealth of information for our investigative team and pointed us in the right direction in many areas of the investigation. He also pointed us away from matters that we were pursuing, telling us that they were dead ends. His information was proven to be accurate in these matters.

At all times, Scarpa Jr. was open, candid and complete in his information, not only about the matters we were investigating but also about his criminal past.

Finally, in addition to providing valuable intelligence, Scarpa Jr. was ready, willing and able to testify at the trial of DeVecchio. Through no fault of his, the case disintegrated once the People's main witness was proved to have given, in the late 1990's, inconsistent and exculpatory information about DeVecchio to two reporters, with whom she was writing a book about her life with Scarpa Sr. This witness was the foundation of our case and it could not survive the revelations that came to light literally in the middle of her testimony.

It is therefore my hope that your honor will take into consideration the content of this letter outlining the cooperative effort of Gregory Scarpa, Jr. in any motion made on his behalf for a reduction in his federal sentence.

Sincerely,

Michael F. Vecchione

Michael F. Vecchione
Chief, Rackets Division

Record of Cover-Ups Make Complicit People Throughout Government

Since that same district attorney's office had earlier dismissed the murder charges against the former FBI supervisor, despite witnesses that had overwhelming evidence to prove the FBI's agent's guilt, district attorney had committed obstruction of justice far beyond the threshold requirement for that type of crime. This scenario provided additional support for what I had known for years—that the people in control of the U.S. Department of Justice can not only commit crimes on their own, but cause others at the local, state, or federal level, to participate in criminal acts. The most probable explanation for the misconduct by the Brooklyn district attorney to become a party to such felonies is pressure by a powerful source in the U.S. Department of Justice.

My Response to Scarpa

After receiving this information from Scarpa, I stated in a subsequent July 2008 letter to him:

> That the letter from the office of the Brooklyn district attorney to the federal judge surely displeased FBI-DOJ officials, since it raised the curtain on the sham dismissal of the murder charges against one of the FBI's highly acclaimed FBI supervisors.
>
> That the letter revealed the high confidence that the Brooklyn District Attorney had in Scarpa, and yet, despite his inside knowledge as the son of the "killing machine" of the crimes perpetrated by Scarpa's father with DeVecchio, the prosecutors blocked Scarpa from testifying. This was obstruction of justice at its worst.
>
> That possibly Vecchione disapproved of District Attorney Charles Hynes dismissal of the case against DeVecchio, and was trying to show support for Scarpa. Also, to expose the sabotage of the case against DeVecchio by the head of the Brooklyn district attorney's office, the aiding and abetting by Judge Reichbach, and possibly pressure from high in the federal government's Department of Justice.
>
> That in light of the confidence in Scarpa, Hynes should have continued the prosecution of DeVecchio until Scarpa could testify. I stated to Scarpa that it appeared to me that Hynes was trying to protect DeVecchio and other high FBI-DOJ officials, and at the very least sought to have the federal judge reduce Scarpa's sentence for the important work and information that Scarpa had provided.
>
> That Vecchione appeared to be unaware of the implications that it raised, or acted despite the consequences. Vecchione's letter promoted Scarpa's honesty and reliability as a witness, while the same prosecutor's office blocked Scarpa from providing testimony against the FBI supervisory agent DeVecchio. It implied that the office of the Brooklyn district attorney obstructed justice in a trial with national significance showing the culture within parts of the FBI and other DOJ offices.

Still More Evidence of High-Level Obstruction of Justice

In addition to Gregory Scarpa there was another witness who had information proving the case against the FBI supervisor. And that was Linda Schiro. In earlier pages, the scheme to discredit her testimony was described. Since then, the report by a retired judge given the responsibility to determine Schiro's testimony was released.

On October 22, 2008, a 31-page report was prepared by the retired judge conducting an investigation of Linda Schiro's testimony against DeVecchio. Retired Judge Leslie Crocker Snyder was the special district attorney appointed to conduct an investigation into whether Linda Schiro committed perjury when she testified about the murders involving Lindley DeVecchio with Gregory Scarpa Sr. That unpublicized report was sent to me by a key source.

That report clearly exonerated Schiro, stating her testimony was creditable and not perjury. The report strongly implied that there had been interference blocking the prosecution for murder of former FBI supervisor Lindley DeVecchio.

REPORT OF THE SPECIAL DISTRICT ATTORNEY IN THE MATTER OF THE INVESTIGATION OF LINDA SCHIRO

Submitted by: Judge (ret.) Leslie Crocker Snyder

Special District Attorney, Kasowitz, Benson, Torres & Friedman LOP

Introduction

On November 1, 2007, the Honorable Neil Jon Firetog, Administrative Judge, Supreme Court of the State of New York, County of Kings, appointed me, pursuant to County Law § 701.1(a) to act as a special District Attorney in the Matter of the Investigation of Linda Schiro. The order so appointing me and accompanying affirmation from Charles J., District Attorney of Kings County, are attached to this report as Exhibit A.

While Schiro undeniably made prior statements inconsistent with her testimony, a full review of the record and available evidence does not yield sufficient proof of the falsity of her trial and grand jury testimony. For the reasons set forth below, Schiro cannot be prosecuted for perjury.

Linda Schiro testified before a Kings County Grand Jury in the Matter of R05-155, which resulted in Indictment Number 6825/05, charging Roy Lindley DeVecchio with four counts of Murder in the Second Degree. She did not execute a waiver of statutory immunity.

Among the criminal activities in which she knew Scarpa Sr. was engaged was murder. Schiro also described Scarpa's connection to the FBI, testifying that Scarpa assisted the FBI in investigating the disappearance of civil rights workers in Mississippi in 1964, the murder of a black man by the KKK in Mississippi in 1966, and retrieval of a mob figure from Costa Rica.

In that capacity and because he acted as an informant for the FBI after the 1960s, Scarpa had an FBI "handler," agent Tony Volano" [sic]. In 1978, FBI Agent R. Lindley DeVecchio (known as Lin) became Scarpa's handler. She described a series of events she observed or learned from Scarpa implicating DeVecchio in four counts of murder.

In 1994, after the death of Scarpa, the FBI's Office of Professional Responsibility (OPR) conducted an investigation of DeVecchio's relationship with Scarpa. [Ultimately, no finding was made against DeVecchio.]

In testimony before the Grand Jury, Schiro discussed her prior FBI interviews. She explained to the Grand Jury that before the interview, DeVecchio had told her "don't worry about it, tell them to F themselves," and that at the interview she did not "tell everything" to the investigators because she was nervous around FBI agents.

During her trial testimony, Schiro explained that she first learned that she would be interviewed when George Gabriel ("Gabriel"), an FBI agent and the handler of her second husband, John Baron, told her to expect agents to come to her home. Before her interview, Schiro spoke to DeVecchio, who told her "You don't have to talk to them, you can tell them to fuck themselves."

When the investigators questioned her, Schiro testified, she did not reveal the same information about Scarpa and DeVecchio's relationship she was describing in court; she "couldn't understand why FBI agents are investigating another FBI agent," and she was "kind of nervous" about the well being of her son, Joey, and did not want to jeopardize DeVecchio's ability to protect him.

Schiro testified that she told the investigators only that DeVecchio received a Cabbage Patch doll, a tray of eggplant parmigiana, and a bottle of Rothschild wine from herself and Scarpa.

Gabriel later called Schiro to say he knew she was not divulging everything; the investigators returned and she told them about a big-screen television given to DeVecchio as well as DeVecchio's showing Scarpa a list of members of Scarpa's crew who were to be arrested. During neither conversation did she discuss the murders in which DeVecchio was allegedly involved. She stated in court to explain her omission that "Lin was still my friend."

In the late 1990s and early 2000, Schiro gave interviews to several authors who were interested in writing books about her life with the now-deceased Scarpa. Schiro testified at trial about her interviews with three writers, who were working on three different projects.

She testified that, in separate conversations, she told these writers about DeVecchio's involvement with, and assistance to, Scarpa's criminal enterprise. Schiro also testified that she expected that the writers would sensationalize her story and add fictional embellishment: "It was supposed to be a fiction. A lot of fiction and fact … I was telling them fact; what they wrote, I never read." Nevertheless, she repeatedly stated that, while omitting some events and details, she told these writers only the truth.

She was asked specifically at trial whether she told any of the writers about DeVecchio's involvement in the four homicides. She testified that she had not, with the sole exception of the murder of Patrick Porco. She testified at trial that she described DeVecchio's role in the Porco murder to the writers because she "was just so upset that what happened to Patrick because Lin had said he [had] ratted ... I loved Patrick like a son. ... She consistently implicated DeVecchio in the Porco murder."

Based on the authors' records or summaries of the interviews and other available evidence described below, Schiro did in fact tell them that DeVecchio was involved in Scarpa's decision to murder Patrick Porco.

[Interviews were refused by Prosecutors]

Interviews were sought with all the Assistant District Attorneys with any role in the DeVecchio prosecution. The first and primary Assistant District Attorney was Noel Downey who was instrumental in the investigation and in obtaining the indictment against DeVecchio. He refused to be interviewed on advice of counsel.

Assistant District Attorneys Monique Ferrell, Kevin Richardson, Joel Alexis, Laura Neubauer, Jackie Linares and Michael Veccione were interviewed. ... The statements of all these prosecutors, who were each interviewed separately, can be summarized as follows:

Each of the assistants interviewed who had direct contact with Schiro either in interviewing or debriefing her and in preparing her testimony stated that she had been consistent in her recollection of the details of her allegations against DeVecchio. They questioned her about her prior statements to the FBI in the OPR investigation, in which she specifically and expressly disavowed any knowledge of wrongdoing by DeVecchio (other than acceptance of gratuities). Her explanation was consistent: she was concerned that DeVecchio was, at that time, instrumental in continuing to protect her interests and those of her son, Joey Schiro/Scarpa who was still alive.

They also questioned her about any interviews she gave to reporters and other writers. Again, she told the prosecutors that, while she did not tell these writers the whole truth, she never said anything that was untrue. Schiro told the Assistant District Attorneys that she had never spoken to any reporters about DeVecchio's role in any of the murders, except the Porco murder, which was consistent with the book proposals in the District Attorney's possession. Also, Schiro made clear that the book treatments were never supposed to be the whole truth as the only goal was to sell the book.

Each member of the prosecution team believed that Schiro had, in the past, told various inconsistent versions of her story, often with omissions that, in her mind, were justified by her desire to protect her son Joey Scarpa and, early on, DeVecchio, while she was under the impression that he was still protecting her. The prosecutors were prepared to counter any issues at trial about these inconsistencies.

Diverging Grand Jury and Trial Testimony

There are discrepancies between Schiro's testimony before the Grand Jury and her testimony at trial. The differences in this case are on the whole inconsequential and are not sufficient to bring a successful perjury prosecution. The only discrepancy in Schiro's own testimony of any significance relates to the Lampasi homicide. She had testified that DeVecchio provided information about the victim's opening and closing his place of *work*, whereas at trial, she testified that the defendant supplied Scarpa with the location of the victim's home, the time the victim left his home in the morning, and the fact that the victim had to exit his car to open and close a gate at his *house*. (Lampasi was gunned down at the gate to his home driveway on his way to work.) Her explanation – "I was probably confused with the work and the house. That is probably what it was. I meant the house."

This discrepancy, while not insubstantial, does not rise to an irreconcilable discrepancy within the meaning of the Penal Law. Both the Grand Jury version and the trial version have the same general thrust: that DeVecchio was involved in the Lampasi murder. The difference in detail between the two versions does not make them so directly contradictory and irreconcilable that only one of the two versions could logically be correct so that the other necessarily must be intentionally false.

The other relatively minor discrepancies that emerged between Schiro's trial testimony and Grand Jury testimony are apparent from the summaries above. These distinctions for the most part amount to additional detail in the trial testimony, or omissions of detail in her Grand Jury testimony. As such, they also do not rise to the level of irreconcilable inconsistencies. Thus, none of Schiro's trial or Grand Jury statements are necessarily false simply by virtue of the differences between them and no perjury charge could be predicated on such differences.

[Referring to the difference between what she told book authors ten years earlier and her Grand Jury and trial testimony] upon a full review of the available evidence, including evidence corroborating central elements of Schiro's testimony against DeVecchio, no perjury charge is sustainable on either ground.

The examination at trial [about the inconsistency between the statements made ten years earlier to book authors and sworn testimony at Grand Jury and trial] she was never pinned down and asked directly whether she had discussed the DeDomenico and Lampasi murders: "Did you talk to him [Capeci] about any of the murders?" Answer: "Oh, Patrick [Porco]." The prosecution did not follow up with respect to the other murders specifically, and the defense asked no questions about the Capeci/Robbins interviews. Because her answer is literally true, although misleading, and because the questioner did not meet the burden "to pin the witness down to the specific object of the questioner's inquiry," this portion of her testimony will not support a charge of perjury.

Another obstacle to a perjury charge related to this falsehood is the length of time that had elapsed between her 2007 testimony and the 1997 Capeci/Robbins interview. In answering questions about what she told Capeci, Schiro was recalling events from ten years ago. The prosecution did not possess the Capeci/Robbins notes or audio recording, and Capeci had *refused to produce them* to the defense.

Without proof bearing on Schiro's own recollection or even proof that she had the ability to refresh her recollection, there is insufficient evidence to disprove she had not discussed these two murders with Capeci and Robbins. A perjury prosecution cannot be based on evidence that is as "consonant with fallibility of memory" as with willful falsification. Taking these deficiencies of proof into account, it is highly unlikely that a perjury charge relating to this falsehood could be sustained.

Because those taped statements to the authors were neither under oath nor part of any proceeding before any legal body, they are not, however, sufficient to prove perjury without other proof of the falsity of her sworn testimony. In fact, although the taped statements may be admissible hearsay against Schiro as admissions, they are not dispositive proof of the truth of the matters asserted; just because she said it in 1997 does not necessarily make it so. Schiro, therefore, cannot be legally culpable of perjury without additional evidence corroborating her earlier statements and thus demonstrating the falsity of her *sworn* assertions.

Schiro admitted under oath that she had routinely lied to government officials. For example, she admitted she lied to federal investigators [[back in 1997]] conducting the OPR review out of fear and concern for her son, Joey Schiro, and because DeVecchio told her to lie. Schiro admitted at trial that she told FBI Agent George Gabriel that the press reports about DeVecchio tipping Scarpa about the whereabouts of Colombo soldiers during the 1992 war were "lies."

Evidence Consistent with Schiro's Testimony

Other factors support Schiro's testimony in critical respects and corroborate her accusations about DeVecchio's improper assistance to Scarpa's criminal enterprise. Evidence that suggests that her testimony against DeVecchio was not intentionally fabricated includes:

<u>Porco Murder</u>. In her interviews with the writers, Schiro consistently implicated DeVecchio in the murder of Patrick Porco, as she did at the Grand Jury and at trial. And the details she gave to each writer about that murder are also consistent.

<u>DeVecchio's Assistance to Scarpa</u>. Schiro's testimony about the close—and [criminally] improper]—relationship between DeVecchio and Scarpa was also

corroborated through other witnesses at trial. The testimony of FBI Special Agent Christopher Favo ("Favo"), for example, described an incident where DeVecchio tracked down information to assist Scarpa in his loan-shark operations;

In other testimony, this same agent described how he overheard DeVecchio informing Scarpa on the "hello phone" (an untraceable government phone used with informants) that the New York City Police Department had someone in custody who had just been arrested (an obvious reference to Carmine Imbriale, another member of the Colombo crime "family"); Favo also testified that he heard DeVecchio say in that phone call that he (DeVecchio) did not know yet what Imbriale was saying about "him" (meaning Scarpa).

This incident so unnerved Favo that he took drastic steps to ensure the safety of Imbriale, including telling DeVecchio to warn Scarpa not to try to harm him. Eventually, Favo even began withholding information about mob informants from DeVecchio, who at the time was Favo's direct supervisor. In addition, Favo testified about yet another episode where he overheard DeVecchio disclose highly sensitive and confidential information to Scarpa. When the decision was made months later to arrest Scarpa, Favo intentionally kept the information from DeVecchio until Scarpa was arrested.

Favo also testified at trial about informing DeVecchio of the Lampasi murder and shooting of another of Scarpa's rivals that happened around the same time. Favor testified that, in response, DeVecchio made his now infamous excited utterance: "We are going to win this thing." That comment was so out of place that Favo was compelled to state, "We are the FBI. We are not on either side." DeVecchio's bizarre remark lends some credence—however faint and far removed—to Schiro's testimony that DeVecchio himself had some interest and involvement in the killing of Lampasi; it is more consistent than inconsistent with Schiro's testimony.

FBI Complicity in Scarpa's Murders.

Among the most alarming evidence reviewed here is that which strongly suggests that the FBI continued to work with Scarpa as a registered top echelon FBI informant even though at least some FBI agents, including DeVecchio, were fully aware that Scarpa had been directly responsible for multiple murders and continued to use criminal violence, including murder.

Favo testified that, during the Colombo "war," Scarpa had been stripped of his status as an informant, but that DeVecchio orchestrated re-instating him as a top echelon informant, and that, in doing so, DeVecchio made knowingly false representation to the main office of the Department of Justice about Scarpa's involvement in a murder plot.

Although at the trial of DeVecchio, Favo denied having any concrete evidence of Scapa committing murders in this time period, witnesses (insisting on anonymity) have come forward who have credible evidence to the contrary.

(Special Agent Jeffrey Tomlinson testimony regarding evidence of Scarpa's attempted murder of Joe Cacace).

(Favo also learned from Joseph Ambrosino, another Colombo conspirator, that Scarpa and his "hit squad" had gunned down Cacace). These witnesses corroborate a central allegation of Schiro's testimony and the District Attorney's theory of the case against DeVecchio: that DeVecchio was aware of and furthered Scarpa's murderous criminal enterprise.

Other Corroborating Evidence. The anticipated testimony of critical witnesses, like Gregory Scarpa, Jr., would also have bolstered key parts of Schiro's trial testimony (as discussed in the next section of this Report). The dismissal of the charges, however, truncated the trial record, and some of the corroborating witnesses were not called as a result.

[Questions about Possible Pressure to Block Producing Portions of the Tapes]

The most salient of unanswered questions is about the timing of the release of the Capeci/Robbins audiotapes. The question that is relevant to this perjury investigation is why Schiro's statements were not revealed until the eleventh hour, as a "surprise" to both parties after two-weeks of trial. First, it is difficult to understand why the defense withdrew its pre-trial subpoena for the Capeci materials, as well as why the prosecution did not join in the application of this discovery. Given that Schiro had already been publicly revealed as the "source" against DeVecchio, there is a compelling argument that the Shield Law did not apply

The case law supports the conclusion that the source in this case, Linda Schiro, waived any confidential status herself by virtue of identifying herself to law enforcement and cooperating with the District Attorney; once that occurred, the absolute confidentiality provisions of the Shield Law, logically and legally, no longer applied. Certainly, by virtue of her Grand Jury testimony and impending trial testimony, Schiro's interview statements about the four murders had lost any "confidential" status.

Nor would Capeci have prevailed under the Shield Law provisions that protect non-confidential information. Where, as in this case, the non-confidential information is highly material and relevant, necessary to the proceeding, and not obtainable from any alternative source, it is discoverable. This standard would have been satisfied here, given the nature of Schiro's testimony and its centrality to the government's case.

In light of this legal authority, moreover, one must ask why Capeci claimed privilege in the first place when faced with the trial subpoena. The Shield Law, of course, does not prohibit reporters from coming forward with critical evidence; it only prevents the government from compelling such disclosure under certain circumstances.

[Suspicious Silence by Book Authors]

Here, Schiro had already elected to come forward, had testified before the Grand Jury and had been publicly identified as the primary testifying witness against DeVecchio. It was public knowledge that she would be testifying at trial. Consequently, it is difficult to understand Capeci's and Robbins' reason for remaining silent when they knew they had critical evidence. These reporters knew and wrote about the fact that Schiro was the State's star witness, one on whom the whole case turned—indeed the only witness still alive, aside from the defendant, who could talk about the secret meetings between Scarpa and his alleged FBI source.

One must ask why Capeci and Robbins did not, at least, inform the District Attorney that they had tapes relating to Schiro that were material to the District Attorney's prosecution and might well exonerate DeVecchio.

Later, by their own account, they were compelled to disclose the audio tape out of a sense of civil duty to basic justice—to not stand by and see the criminal justice system perverted in a way that had dire consequences for a man facing life in prison. If that noble sentiment applied at the end of the case, it so applied, *a fortiori*, from the outset.

But was that the reason. Capeci was known to have a long-standing secret relation with FBI supervisor Lindley DeVecchio, receiving tips that supported Capeci's role as a reporter. Was he, and his associate, Robbins, showing "loyalty" to DeVecchio, or were they pressured by powerful forces in the federal government to provide the tapes that were then corruptly used by the prosecutor and the judge to relieve FBI-DOJ officials of a very corrupt history of assisting in murders by "The Killing Machine."

[Suspicious Refusal to obtain the entire tape recordings made by Capeci/Robbins.]

One must ask why the District Attorney's Office did not pursue discovery of the Capeci/Robbins audiotapes, either with them privately or through the Court. The District Attorney's office in press reports stated that no effort had been made to obtain the Capeci material because "*the expectation was they wouldn't share the information*." Matt Nestel, Alex Ginsberg, "D.A. Played Dumb," *New York Post* (11/3/2007). Nevertheless, the prosecution certainly could have asked Linda Schiro to release these authors from any vestige of the confidentiality requirement (if one even existed). And they certainly had a good faith basis in which to challenge, before the Court, any legal claim of privilege.

Finally, it bears noting that, ironically, the dismissal of this case, after the implosion of Linda Schiro, also creates some difficulties as to any perjury prosecution of her. Because the trial was terminated, certain witnesses' testimony was lost, likely permanently.

As discussed above, a number of other witnesses, some accomplices, who were interviewed here, corroborate many details of Schiro's testimony, certainly as to Porco's murder. They also support Schiro's credibility as to her intimate relationship with Scarpa and access to his greatest secrets, although most could be impeached by their own backgrounds and involvement in many serious crimes, some at issue here.

In his ultimate written decision granting the prosecutor's motion to dismiss, Judge Reichbach, the trier of the fact, stated: "It was *only* the discredited testimony of Linda Schiro that tied the defendant to any of the crimes charged in the indictment." *People v. DeVecchio*, 2007 NY Misc. LEXIS 7827, at *3 (NY Sup. Ct. Nov. 1, 2007). The interesting question, that will now most likely never be answered, is whether that assessment (at least, perhaps, as to the Bari murder) would have changed had Scarpa, Jr. had the opportunity to testify.

In addition, the case was dismissed before the cross-examination of Linda Schiro was concluded. We do not know whether DeVecchio's defense counsel had intended to question her about her interview with Capeci and Robbins. We will never know what her response would have been had they confronted her (with or without the tapes) with questions designed to imply that she had in fact exonerated DeVecchio as to the Lampasi and DeDomenico murders. Perhaps she had some explanation that the *limited* tape excerpts do not, on their own, reveal.

VIII. Conclusion

Accordingly, for the reasons set forth above, I conclude that Linda Schiro's testimony before the Grand Jury and at trial did not violate the perjury laws of the State of New York, and no charge of perjury is sustainable on the available evidence.

Dated: New York, New York.
October 22, 2008

Special District Attorney of the State of
New York, County of Kings
Leslie Crocker Snyder

Attached to that decision was an Addendum, which the retired judge and Special District Attorney prepared after recognizing the gravity of what he uncovered, in addition to the numerous obstacles placed in his investigation.

Addendum

I was given a specific mandate as Special District Attorney: to determine whether Linda Schiro could be prosecuted for perjury. Early on I attempted to interview numerous witnesses in addition to interviewing the Assistant District Attorneys involved in the prosecution; few of the witnesses agreed to cooperate. Nevertheless, I felt that I could proceed without them and without empanelling a Grand Jury and still reach a conclusion based upon the law. When I had almost concluded my report, months ago, I suddenly was contacted by a number of people claiming to have pertinent information who were now willing to talk to me as long as their identity was not revealed publicly. Each was interviewed separately. [Private investigator Angela Clemente assisted in having the witnesses appear.]

[Limited and blocked from pursuing other Information of criminal misconduct by his Mandate.]

Most of what they related went well beyond the mandate in the appointment order but also went well beyond mere background. They corroborated each other in large measure in describing the murders involved in the DeVecchio indictment, information which gave general support to Linda Schiro's grand jury and trial testimony.

They also each painted a portrait of the on-going "Mafia Wars" between the two factions of the Colombo crime family, the Persico faction and the Orena faction. (The federal authorities prosecuted well over 60 of these mob cases, with mixed results, and were determined to eradicate as much of the mafia as possible. *See* Exhibit G. Judge Reichbach's decision in *People v. DeVecchio*)

In summary form, after hours and hours of conversations with these witnesses and reading materials (trial transcripts, appellate records, FBI and New York City police forms and other documents), I feel compelled to raise some of the many issues which warrant further investigation by an appropriate agency or some other investigative body:

Did DeVecchio pass information to Scarpa Sr. regularly, setting aside the four murders charged in the indictment? Witnesses, and possibly records, appear to exist which would be probative of this issue. (*See*, e.g., Exhibit H, May 8, 1995 Letter from U.S. Attorney's office, Eastern District of New York.)

Is there probative evidence that the FBI—or at least DeVecchio—knew that Scarpa Sr. was ordering, and committing, numerous murders and, nevertheless, allowed him to continue his status as a top echelon FBI informant? (Sealed evidence and interviews with witnesses known to the government support this conclusion.) (*See* Exhibit G, Justice Reichbach's decision in *People v. DeVecchio,* 2007 NY Misc. Lexis 7827 (NY Sup. Ct. Nov. 1, 2007); Exhibit I, FD-302 (Feb. 6, 1994), FBI Agent Christopher Favo; Affidavit of Christopher Favo, sworn to April 4, 1994, Wash. D.C.)

Was there an effort by the FBI to protect Scarpa and DeVecchio in order to protect/insulate/preserve numerous mob prosecutions and some convictions relating to the Colombo crime family? (*See United States v. Persico,* 1997 U.S. Dist. LEXIS 23290, at *33-35 (E.D.N.Y. Mar. 13, 1997)(Sifton, J.) (ordering new trials as to some mob defendants and observing that the government improperly delayed disclosure of the fact that DeVecchio "had become involved with Scarpa to a wholly unacceptable degree" and that "disclosures relating to possible improprieties by law enforcement were produced [even] more slowly"), *rev'd sub non., United States v. Orena*, 145 F.3d 551 (2d Cir. 1998) (reversing on grounds that the evidence of DeVecchio's duplicity as catalogued by the trial court was not "material" for purposes of the *Brady* doctrine in the face of overwhelming evidence of the mob defendants' guilt).

Was Detective Joseph Simone, of the New York Police Department, a scapegoat for the misconduct of others, as a number of people who came forward have suggested?

Were the FBI agents who reported their suspicions regarding DeVecchio shunned and ostracized? And did they later modify their positions regarding DeVecchio?

Why was DeVecchio allowed to retire with a full pension, despite the Government's acknowledgment that he leaked information to a murderous informant, and why was he granted immunity after he invoked his Fifth Amendment privilege in post-conviction proceedings related to convictions in the Colombo War? *See Orena v. United States*, 956 F. Supp. 1071, 1090 (E.D.N.Y. 1997)(Weinstein, J.)(in a hearing challenging convictions related to the Colombo "War," DeVecchio, having invoked his Fifth Amendment privilege, was granted immunity and testified about the allegations regarding his improper relationship with Scarpa; the trier of fact expressly found that, as compared to FBI Agent Favo, DeVecchio "proved a far less credible witness whose memory lapses were not believable"). *See also* Exhibit H, May 8, 1995 Letter from U.S. Attorney's Office, Eastern District of New York.

Have any of the witnesses, potential witnesses, or people who cooperated in the DeVecchio investigation and/or prosecution been harassed by various agencies because of their cooperation, as many of these individuals now claim?

Others have previously raised many of these issues, especially in the context of the difficulties and dangers involving the use of informants by law enforcement. And some of the sources supplying information with respect to the DeVecchio/Scarpa matter are criminals. My mandate does not allow me to reach any conclusions as to these issues—and far more investigation would be required before any reliable conclusions could be reached. Nevertheless, a dramatic picture of corruption with numerous unanswered questions exists.

[That last sentence made it clear that ultra serious areas of corruption existed, which these pages make obvious.]

EXHIBIT J

[Several pages of Exhibit J follows:]

April 23, 2007

The Honorable Charles J. Hynes
Kings County District Attorney
350 Jay Street
Brooklyn, New York 11201-2900

Dear District Attorney Hynes:

It has been brought to my attention by Ms. Angela Clemente that Mr. Gregory Scarpa, Jr. will be testifying in an upcoming case for the Brooklyn District Attorney's Office. I write to inform you of his dealings with my office which may reflect his credibility as a witness.

In late March 2005, my office obtained information from Mr. Scarpa which detailed the location of bomb components and packaging missed in a search ten years earlier by the FBI at the home of Terry Lynn Nichols, one of the charged co-conspirators in the Oklahoma City bombing. My office pressed the FBI to take action on this tip, which proved to be accurate, and led to the successful recovery of the items detailed in Mr. Scarpa's account. The statement by Mr. Scarpa subsequently became the initiating factor for my office to open a Congressional investigation into the OKC bombing.

In August 2006, after the arrests of twenty-four terrorist suspects who plotted to blow up airliners over the Atlantic Ocean, I was given a report detailing Mr. Scarpa's FBI 302's and his work in notifying the FBI about Al Qaeda's interest in liquid explosives as well as Khalid Shaikh Mohammed's connection to Ramzi Yousef, the mastermind behind the first attack on the World Trade Center. Mr. Scarpa's FBI 302's suggest that he was providing significant information to the FBI in 1996 and 1997, prior to recent occurrences.

These two pieces of information point to Mr. Scarpa's willingness to procure accurate intelligence, and I believe that at the very least his cooperation and testimony deserve a very careful analysis.

If you have any questions, please feel free to contact my staffer, Phaedra Dugan, at (202) 225-6851.

Sincerely,

Dana Rohrabacher

Dana Rohrabacher
Member of Congress

Cc: Judge Reena Raggi

FBI Waited to Check Out Tip on Nichols

Thursday April 14, 2005 7:16 PM

By MARK SHERMAN

Associated Press Writer

WASHINGTON (AP) - The FBI initially dismissed a tip that convicted bomber Terry Nichols had hidden explosives and they might be used for an attack this month coinciding with the anniversary of the Oklahoma City bombing.

While the FBI has found no evidence supporting the idea that an attack is in the works for the April 19 tenth anniversary, the information that explosives had been hidden in Nichols' former home in Herington, Kan., turned out to be true.

The tip came from imprisoned mobster Gregory Scarpa Jr., 53, a law enforcement official said this week. Scarpa is an inmate in the same maximum-security federal prison in Florence, Colo., where Nichols is serving life sentences for his role in the 1995 bombing of the Alfred Murrah federal building that killed 168 people. Timothy McVeigh was convicted of federal conspiracy and murder charges in the bombing and executed in 2001.

Scarpa learned about the explosives from Nichols, mainly through notes passed between them, said Stephen Dresch, a Michigan man who is Scarpa's informal advocate.

Dresch gave the information to the FBI in early March. But FBI agents did not search the vacant house until March 31. The bureau did not act more quickly because Scarpa failed a lie detector test, said the law enforcement official, who declined to be identified because of the sensitivity of the investigation.

The FBI lab continues to examine the materials for fingerprints and other clues that might show where the explosives originated and who may have had them before they got into Nichols' home.

Scarpa, a member of the Colombo organized crime family serving 50-plus years on drug trafficking, conspiracy and racketeering convictions, first communicated information about the explosives on March 1, then provided more details on March 10 and 11, Dresch said in letters sent to the staffs of two members of Congress and to the FBI's Detroit office. Scarpa revealed the location of the house on March 11, Dresch said.

The first letter said Scarpa learned from another prisoner, assumed by Dresch to be Nichols, ``the location of a bomb on U.S. soil.'' The second described two rock piles in the crawl space beneath Nichols' former home. Under one, it said, were cardboard boxes wrapped in plastic. Those details match what the FBI said it found.

Aides to Reps. William Delahunt, D-Mass., and Dana Rohrabacher, R-Calif., acknowledged receiving the letters by fax. Delahunt's office received the letter on March 1 or 2 and forwarded it to the FBI, said Steve Schwadron, the lawmaker's chief of staff. The letter to Rohrabacher was not read until after the FBI search had been done, Rohrabacher spokeswoman Rebecca Rudman said.

The FBI refused to comment on the delay.

The bureau has faced harsh post-Sept. 11, 2001, criticism accusing it of failing to adequately investigate tips and intelligence.

Delahunt has chided the FBI for its dealings with informants, while Rohrabacher is considering requesting a hearing on the bureau's handling of the Oklahoma City investigation.

"I'm more concerned that the FBI didn't do a thorough job investigating this location 10 years ago than I am about how long it took to follow through on an informant's tip," Rohrabacher said.

Dresch, a Michigan economist, principal owner of Forensic Intelligence International and former state lawmaker, speculated that the FBI didn't act more quickly because Scarpa has a long, contentious history with federal authorities.

Valerie Caproni, now the FBI general counsel, was a prosecutor in Scarpa's 1998 trial in Brooklyn, N.Y. At the time, Scarpa testified he spied for the FBI on four suspects in the 1993 World Trade Center bombing, including convicted mastermind Ramzi Yousef, while they were jailed together in Manhattan.

Scarpa said he passed on to the FBI plans that said associates of the four men would kill a prosecutor in one of Yousef's trials and attack a federal judge he declined to name as well as unspecified "government installations."

Caproni and U.S. District Judge Reena Raggi scoffed at Scarpa's claims, which the judge called insignificant at best and more likely "part of a scam."

Freelance journalist Peter Lance has argued in his recent book, "Cover Up," that Scarpa's information was accurate and included tips that could have led the FBI to Khalid Shaikh Mohammed, Yousef's uncle, long before the Sept. 11 attacks Mohammed purportedly helped plan.

Lance has obtained transcripts of Scarpa's interviews with FBI agents in which he provided details of his dealings with Yousef.

Scarpa's father, the late Gregory Scarpa, was an FBI informant whom senior officials allowed to keep working with the bureau in the 1990s even though they suspected him of murder, according to Lindley DeVecchio, Scarpa's FBI handler.

That Independent Report Required Murder Charges to be Refiled Against Former FBI Supervisor Lindley DeVecchio

That report, just as the letter by the Brooklyn district attorney's office praising Scarpa Jr, required that murder charges be reinstated against DeVecchio. I sent letters to district attorney and Judge Reichbach providing the information in that letter praising Scarpa and the report praising Schiro for their truthfulness, and asked why refiling of murder charges was not done. Neither answered the letters.

Why Murder Charges Were *Not* Refiled

If murder charges had been refilled, enormous consequences would occur. Refiling would reveal, for instance:

- That Mary Schiro was telling the truth about an FBI supervisor engaged in murders in unison with the infamous Colombo Mafia "Killing Machine."
- That high FBI and other Justice Department officials knew of the criminal offenses, covered up for the crimes, and were guilty of major obstruction of

justice themselves, and conspiracy to cover up for crimes against the United States.

- That Brooklyn district attorney engaged in obstruction of justice that had consequences far beyond the normal obstruction of justice crime.
- That Judge Reichbach was part of the obstruction of justice actions.
- That Gregory Scarpa Jr. was telling the truth about the murders involving his father and the FBI supervisor.
- That the information that Scarpa passed along for 11 months to FBI agents about planned terrorist attacks by al Qaeda were correct.
- That high-level FBI-DOJ personnel willingly sacrificed the people who died in those forewarned terrorist attacks so as to protect not only the FBI supervisor but also the FBI-DOJ personnel who knew for years of the murders and covered up, becoming guilty of major crimes in the process.
- That the FBI-DOJ related personnel that were on the 9/11 Commission falsified the commission's report by omitting evidence that would implicate themselves.
- That such knowledge revealed to the public could open the lid on still other areas of corruption throughout government.

In summary, the exhaustive report, despite the refusal of many in government to respond to questions, and despite the threats against other government employees not to cooperate, provided enough factual information and evidence to show:

- The credibility of Gregory Scarpa Jr. That determination was made from the statements of others, and by the confidential letter the report referred to. That confidential letter was prepared, ironically, by members of the prosecution team, and highly praised Scarpa for the truthfulness of his statements. The contents of that letter raised still more questions about the suspicious dropping of murder charges against DeVecchio. Based upon my many years of experience as an insider, and privy to information provided over the years by dozens of other insiders, there was a definite conspiracy to obstruct justice, probably originating high in the Department of Justice. If that letter had been released to the public, that conspiracy would become even more obvious. The only question I have at this time is *why* the letter was sent. The best answer that I can come up with is that the members of the prosecution team were concerned about the turn of events and wanted at least to show their appreciation for the help Scarpa Jr. had provided.
- That FBI supervisor Lindley DeVecchio did in fact engage in criminal acts, including murders, and crimes against the United States.
- That high FBI and other DOJ officials covered up for the crimes. Compared to what I learned over the years from former FBI Special Agent

Richard Taus, who worked under DeVecchio, retaliation by high FBI and other DOJ officials against government personnel is standard operating procedure. This retaliation is to prevent the public from learning about high-level corruption in government. In Taus' case, he reported misconduct by his immediate boss, DeVecchio, and misconduct by CIA-related companies during the Reagan-Bush administration that included secret funding and secret arms sales to Iraq. His story is in my book, *FBI, DOJ, the Mafia, and Treachery*. That highly decorated Vietnam helicopter pilot is now in prison at Dannemora, New York, where he may be until he dies, his punishment for attempting to circumvent the obstruction of justice crimes by officials in the Department of Justice. He foolishly sought to perform his duty by circumventing the cover-ups by DOJ officials, reporting the crimes to members of Congress.

- Add to what is described in these pages the criminal activities by DOJ personnel that I *personally* discovered as a federal agent (described in great detail in my book, *Unfriendly Skies: 20th & 21st Centuries*), and what I discovered over a 30-year span from other insiders, including government agents, former drug smugglers, and former Mafia figures (as detailed in such books as *Defrauding America* and *Drugging America*, among others).
- And strong suspicion that the high-level pressure from Department of Justice officials caused the Brooklyn District Attorney to suddenly drop charges against the former FBI supervisor, despite the overwhelming evidence already presented and known, and evidence yet to be presented by such witnesses as Gregory Scarpa, Jr.
- Strong suspicion that this high-level pressure affected the authors of the book that Jerry Capeci and Tom Robbins had intended to write, and who refused to respond to questions submitted by the special district attorney, Retired Judge Leslie Crocker Snyder.

Obtaining the Confidential Letter Crediting Gregory Scarpa, Jr.

The confidential letter that was referred to in that investigative report, dated January 24, 2008, was provided to me by Gregory Scarpa Jr. It was written on the stationary of the Office of the District Attorney, Kings County, Charles J. , District Attorney and addressed to U.S. District Judge Edward R. Korman. That letter had far more significance than a casual reading would reveal.

First, it showed that the same prosecutors that withdrew the murder charges against FBI Supervisor Lindley DeVecchio were now:

Praising one of their key prosecution witnesses against DeVecchio, that they prevented from testifying

Ignoring the fact that if Gregory Scarpa Jr. was that reliable—which he was—why did they not allow him to testify against DeVecchio. Obviously, the son of the murderous Colombo mafia capo could have provided testimony to prove the murder charges involving DeVecchio.

It provided still further support for the suspicion that District Attorney derailed the murder prosecution against the FBI supervisor for reasons other than what he had stated. And these reasons were probably pressure from powerful officials in the U.S. Department of Justice. That January 24, 2008, letter was written before the October 22, 2008, report of Special District Attorney Leslie Crocker Sunder. Several key portions of that letter stated:

> Scarpa Jr. was a wealth of information for our investigative team and pointed us in the right direction in many areas of the investigation. He also pointed us away from matters that we were pursuing, telling us that they were dead ends. His information was proven to be accurate in these matters.
>
> At all times, Scarpa Jr. was open, candid and complete in his information, not only about the matters we were investigating but also about his criminal past.
>
> After he was incarcerated on the cases for which he is now serving time, he was visited by his father in jail. Because he was so trusted by his father, during those visits Scarpa Sr. admitted to him the role DeVecchio played in two of the murders for which DeVecchio was charged.
>
> Finally, in addition to providing valuable intelligence, Scarpa Jr. was ready, willing and able to testify at the trial of DeVecchio. Through no fault of his, the case disintegrated once the People's main witness was proved to have given, in the late 1990's, inconsistent and exculpatory information about DeVecchio to two reporters, with whom she was writing a book about her life with Scarpa, Sr. This witness was the foundation of our case and it could not survive the revelations that came to light literally in the middle of her testimony.
>
> It is therefore my hope that your honor will take into consideration the content of this letter outlining the cooperative effort of Gregory Scarpa, Jr. in any motion made on his behalf for a reduction in his federal sentence.
>
> Sincerely,
>
> Michael F. Vecchione
> Chief, Rackets Division

Where the district attorney's letter stated that "the case disintegrated" when casual statements made ten years earlier to the two authors planning to write a book, it was an insult to the intelligence of anyone involved in investigative and law enforcement work. In summary, a massive miscarriage of justice occurred, including a contempt for crimes against the United States, by people in key government positions. A copy of the January 24, 2008, letter follows:

OFFICE OF THE DISTRICT ATTORNEY, KINGS COUNTY
RENAISSANCE PLAZA at 350 JAY STREET
BROOKLYN, N.Y. 11201-2908
(718) 250-2239

CHARLES J. HYNES
District Attorney

MICHAEL F. VECCHIONE
CHIEF, RACKETS DIVISION

January 24, 2008

The Honorable Edward R. Korman
United States District Court
Eastern District of New York
225 Cadman Plaza East, Room 118
Brooklyn, New York 11201

Re: Gregory Scarpa, Jr.

Dear Judge Korman:

The purpose of this letter is to bring to your attention the cooperation Gregory Scarpa, Jr. provided to this Office in the matter of People v. R. Lindley DeVecchio.

As you may know DeVecchio, a former FBI agent, was charged in Kings County Supreme Court with acting in concert with Gregory Scarpa, Sr. in the murder of four individuals who presented threats to the security and well-being of Scarpa Sr. At the time of these murders Scarpa Sr. was a very valued member of the Colombo Crime Family, was active in the Colombo Crime Family war of the early 1990's and an informant for the FBI. His handler was former agent DeVecchio.

Scarpa Jr. was brought to this Office from the federal detention facility in Florence, Colorado after he had indicated through contacts that he was willing to help in any way he could in our investigation of DeVecchio.

Scarpa Jr., when he was at liberty during the 1970's and 1980's, was a capo in the Colombo Crime Family and a trusted lieutenant of his father. As such he participated in his father's criminal activities and witnessed some of his father's dealings with DeVecchio.

The Honorable Edward R. Korman
January 24, 2008
Page 2

In addition, after he was incarcerated on the cases for which he is now serving time, he was visited by his father in jail. Because he was so trusted by his father, during those visits Scarpa Sr. admitted to him the role DeVecchio played in two of the murders for which DeVecchio was charged.

Consequently, Scarpa Jr. was a wealth of information for our investigative team and pointed us in the right direction in many areas of the investigation. He also pointed us away from matters that we were pursuing, telling us that they were dead ends. His information was proven to be accurate in these matters.

At all times, Scarpa Jr. was open, candid and complete in his information, not only about the matters we were investigating but also about his criminal past.

Finally, in addition to providing valuable intelligence, Scarpa Jr. was ready, willing and able to testify at the trial of DeVecchio. Through no fault of his, the case disintegrated once the People's main witness was proved to have given, in the late 1990's, inconsistent and exculpatory information about DeVecchio to two reporters, with whom she was writing a book about her life with Scarpa Sr. This witness was the foundation of our case and it could not survive the revelations that came to light literally in the middle of her testimony.

It is therefore my hope that your honor will take into consideration the content of this letter outlining the cooperative effort of Gregory Scarpa, Jr. in any motion made on his behalf for a reduction in his federal sentence.

Sincerely,

Michael F. Vecchione

Michael F. Vecchione
Chief, Rackets Division

Potential Serious Problems for High FBI-DOJ officials

The retired judge's report on Linda Schiro, showing her testimony to be creditable, and the letter by the prosecutor's office praising Gregory Scarpa Jr. for his credibility presented serious problems for high FBI and other Department of Justice officials. But only if the report and the letter was given publicity. As I considered different ways that I could bring this about, former FBI agent Richard Taus sent me a letter telling me about a petition for clemency that he had just sent to New York Governor David Paterson.

Since Taus was an FBI Special Agent under FBI supervisor Lindley DeVecchio, I was able to tie together the sham charges that were filed against Taus after he started reporting DeVecchio's questionable conduct. One of the first actions I took was to send a letter to Governor Paterson, a copy of which follows:

From the desk of Rodney Stich
P.O. Box 5, Alamo, CA 94507; phone: 925-944-1930; FAX 925-295-1203
Author of numerous books on government intrigue
E-mail: stich@defraudingamerica.com Google.com search engine: "Rodney Stich"
Web sites: www.defraudingamerica.com www.unfriendlyskies.com www.druggingamerica.com

February 1, 2009

David A. Paterson, Governor
State of New York
State Capitol
Albany, NY 12224

Ref: Combination of issues relating to (a) clemency petition for former FBI Special Agent Richard Taus; (b) sham charges filed against Taus by federal and state prosecutors after he reported corruption of his supervisor, Lindley DeVecchio and illegal funding of Iraq during the 1980s; (c) multiple cover-ups of murders by Taus' FBI Supervisor, DeVecchio; (d) al Qaeda mole providing advance notice of planned terrorist attacks; (e) cover-up of the advance warnings of terrorist attacks to protect high FBI-DOJ officials; (e) and the resulting high death toll from the cover-ups.

To Governor Paterson:

This letter corrects a few minor errors in my prior January 10, 2009, certified letter[1] to you. That letter related to the following intertwined relationships:

The clemency application for Richard Taus (91A1040), a former FBI special agent under FBI supervisor Lindley DeVecchio. Taus has been incarcerated in state prison at Dannemora, New York on false and exaggerated charges after he attempted to perform his official duties involving reporting criminal activities that he discovered.

False charges made by against Taus by Nassau County prosecutors shortly after Taus reported corrupt activities by his immediate supervisor, Lindley DeVecchio, and the secret funding by CIA assets in the New York City area, each of which threatened to expose White House politicians, FBI-DOJ officials, and individuals in New York who failed to act on the murders involving DeVecchio and Colombo Mafia capo Gregory Scarpa, Sr.

The refusal by Brooklyn prosecutors to file murder charges against FBI supervisor Lindley until publicity by private investigators forced charges to be made in 2006 (three years after I provided evidence of this relationship to every member of the House Judiciary Committee, all of whom covered up for the crimes).

Belated filing of murder charges in 2006 by the Brooklyn district attorney against DeVecchio, years after FBI Special Agent Taus provided this information to state and federal authorities.

The sudden dropping of murder charges against DeVecchio by the Brooklyn prosecutor and the state judge despite overwhelming evidence of guilt.

Prior information of planned terrorist attacks from a mole inside the al Qaeda cell headed by Ramzi Yousef that could have caused preventative measures to be put in place that could have prevented the subsequent 4,000 deaths in the carrying out of the forewarned terrorist actions. The unprecedented mole inside the al Qaeda cell was

Gregory Scarpa Jr., who has also been the subject of retaliatory action by the same high FBI-DOJ officials that prevented actions taken on the forewarned terrorist attacks.

Refusal by high FBI-DOJ officials to act on this valuable inside-al Qaeda information. The reason? It was necessary to discredit the mole who was scheduled to testify about the murders involving FBI Supervisor DeVecchio with the mole's father, known as "The Killing Machine."

The probable consequences of that deception, and failure to take preventative measures against the expected terrorist attacks, was the direct loss of 4,000 lives.

The felonious obstruction of justice by everyone made aware of these interrelated crimes against the people in the state of New York and the people of the United States.

I am a former federal agent who has been motivated to expose the corruption in certain government offices that was initially responsible for numerous fatal airline disasters, one of which was the crash into Brooklyn of a United Airlines DC-8 on December 16, 1960, which occurred in an area in which I had direct hands-on responsibilities. Since that time I have become the focal point for many other insiders providing me information on other areas of corruption. Among the many sources that have provided to me years of continual insider information have been (a) Richard Taus, a former FBI special agent and highly decorated Vietnam War pilot; and (b) Gregory Scarpa, Jr, a former member of the Colombo Mafia family and son of the Mafia capo who engaged in murders with FBI supervisor Lindley DeVecchio.

Many issues affecting national security and justice are involved here. Among them being the long-delayed prosecutor of a key FBI supervisor for murders; the obvious sham dropping of murder charges against DeVecchio; and the self-serving discrediting of the mole inside the al Qaeda organization and the probable resulting 4,000 deaths. You obviously have a responsibility, and that includes contacting me for further information.

The following is a near-duplication of what I wrote in my January 10, 2009, letter to you, with the minor corrections made (being primarily changing the identification of the New York district attorney that filled charges against Taus shortly after Taus reported the corruption that he discovered as part of his official FBI duties:

This letter is for your consideration in support of the request for executive clemency by Richard Taus, who is now incarcerated in the state prison at Dannemora, New York. He has the request pending in your office. I am a former federal agent, airline captain, and navy pilot, who has spent many years uncovering misconduct in government offices, which is a major issue in the charges made against Taus.

I have accumulated considerable information over many years that have helped me understand why the actions were taken to imprison FBI Special Agent Richard Taus. The suspicious sequence of events that were taken against him shows an attempt to obstruct justice that has had very serious effects on national matters, and matters in your area of responsibility. This letter highlights the complex web of intrigue occurring in your New York jurisdiction.

Mr. Taus was a highly decorated Vietnam helicopter pilot who repeatedly risked his life many times under very dangerous conditions to rescue military personnel under intense fire. After leaving military service, Mr. Taus worked in undercover activities for the federal government in Central and South America before becoming an FBI Special Agent in the New York City offices. As an FBI agent, Mr. Taus discovered areas of corrupt activities that his supervisor, Lindley DeVecchio, did not want reported. One area of such illegal activities was a covert CIA operation in the New York City area that involved secret funding and arming of Iraq during the 1980s. He also discovered suspicious activities relating to his immediate supervisor, Lindley DeVecchio. In an earlier book, I wrote about Mr. Taus' activities.[2]

There are disturbing ties between the prosecution of FBI agent Taus by a Nassau prosecutor; the federal appeal filing supposedly representing this former FBI agent by a former Brooklyn prosecutor, and the sudden dropping of murder charges against FBI supervisor Lindley DeVecchio by that same Brooklyn district attorney's office when they should have appealed the judge's decision which found insufficient evidence to convict DeVecchio.

The same DeVecchio, who blocked Taus' investigation into major criminal activities that had international consequences, and who was involved in sham charges against Taus, had been recently charged with complicity in four murders involving citizens in your state of New York.

After DeVecchio blocked Taus from reporting these crimes, Taus reported the corrupt activities—and the cover-ups by DeVecchio, to members of Congress. As I discovered over the years, members of Congress refused to respond to the charges, and passed the information to the very people complicit through cover-ups. FBI-DOJ officials then charged Mr. Taus with misusing—three years earlier—a government credit card, and charged Taus with a crime. His arrest and removal from investigative duties protected CIA and other high government personnel involved in the disastrous funding and arming of Iraq, and the FBI-DOJ officials protecting DeVecchio from the consequences of his murderous conduct.

The misuse of a government-issued credit card was based on Mr. Taus' purchase of less than $10 in gasoline for his personal auto. Mr. Taus had *legally* used the government-issued credit card to pay for fuel used during an official undercover operation—as he was authorized to do. The use of a credit card charge several years earlier shows the desperate search for an excuse to cover up for high-level misconduct in several government offices.

Having succeeded in temporarily removing Mr. Taus from office, it was necessary to fabricate more serious charges to insure that Taus be incarcerated and blocked from exposing the corruption he had discovered as part of his official duties. The Nassau County district attorney in your state then filed criminal charges against Mr. Taus for allegedly having improper conduct with several teenagers at an athletic club that was set up by the FBI for surveillance purposes.

My understanding is that several, or all, of the parents of the young men that charged Mr. Taus with improper sexual relations were also at risk of being charged with minor illegal offenses by that same prosecutor. If that were correct, it would reflect a common prosecutorial tactic used to obtain false testimony against a targeted person. Mr. Taus may, or may not have had, improper relations with young men. I doubt that occurred. However, consider the following:

The sequence of events leading up to the charges by the Nassau prosecutor against Taus were highly suspicious. They followed a standard procedure used in government to discredit a person exposing high-level misconduct.

Mr. Taus had legally adopted a Vietnam orphan while serving in Vietnam, which was highly publicized on TV at the time. *If* Mr. Taus were inclined to have improper sexual conduct with young boys, it would surely have included the Vietnam orphan that he adopted. That boy, now an adult, is David Taus, who lives in your jurisdiction, taking care of Taus' elderly mother, and is available for your office to contact.[3]

Further suspicion arises from the incredibly long sentence given to Mr. Taus—much longer than given to vicious murders, for what would be—even if true—a relatively minor offense among consenting males. For the sake of argument, *if* Mr. Taus *did have* improper sexual conduct with young men, which I doubt, it certainly didn't justify the outrageously long prison sentence. The only reason that this outrageous sentence was given would be an attempt to protect criminal misconduct and criminal cover-up involving key government officials—including that of his supervisor, Lindley DeVecchio—involved in murders with the infamous "Killing Machine" Mafia capo, Gregory Scarpa, Sr.

Making matters even worse, that same Brooklyn district attorney office, suddenly, under highly suspicious circumstances, recently dropped murder charges against Taus' former FBI supervisor, Lindley DeVecchio. We *now have a case* of prosecutors offices in your area of responsibility, not only protecting DeVecchio and the high FBI-DOJ officials who covered up for DeVecchio's murderous conduct by falsely charging Taus with a crime, again protecting DeVecchio by dropping murder charges against DeVecchio.

It becomes even murkier. DeVecchio, in a position of trust as an FBI supervisor, was charged with participation in four murders with Colombo Mafia capo Gregory Scarpa, Sr. (also known as "The Killing Machine"). There were many people ready to testify against DeVecchio, including two witnesses that were classics to prove a case. One was Linda Schiro, the common law wife of Scarpa Sr., and Scarpa's son, Gregory Scarpa, Jr. Linda Schiro was privy to the many conversations between Scarpa and DeVecchio, which occurred in her presence. After Linda Schiro testified about the murders involving her common-law husband and FBI supervisor DeVecchio, the prosecutor suddenly dropped all charges, basing his actions on a totally flawed excuse and stating that Schiro's testimony was not credible. The cooperating judge in the case then implied that criminal perjury charges should be considered against Linda Schiro, who had courageously appeared to testify at great risk to herself.

Making the dropping of murder charges against DeVecchio even more suspicious, the prosecutor blocked Gregory Scarpa, Jr. from testifying about the murders involving his father and FBI supervisor DeVecchio. It would be difficult to find two witnesses that were more capable of proving the murder charges involving DeVecchio. It would also be difficult to find a prosecutor that repeatedly acted to protect a key FBI official engaging in murders of U.S. citizens.

Following the dropping of charges against DeVecchio, a thorough investigation by an outside investigator reported that the testimony of Linda Schiro was thorough credible. In addition, and for reasons not known by this writer at this time, the prosecutor's office issued a letter praising Gregory Scarpa Jr. Those two written reports justify filing criminal charges against DeVecchio, who was never found innocent. Of course, carrying out that responsibility would expose a sordid and dangerous culture in the U.S. Department of Justice.

We now have a scenario where former FBI agent Richard Taus was suddenly hit with two false charges, that conveniently protected DeVecchio and high FBI-DOJ officials, and then the same prosecutorial office protected DeVecchio by blocking the testimony of two star witnesses and the many others willing to testify. These are crimes against the state, and against selected citizens of the state.

The Scenario Gets Worse: Ties to Terrorism and National Security

But there is more to this sordid scenario. Gregory Scarpa Jr., at great risk to his family, worked as a mole inside an al Qaeda cell headed by Ramzi Yousef, the person who master minded the 1993 bombing of the World Trade Center. Covering a period of many months, Mr. Scarpa obtained valuable information from Ramzi Yousef of several planned major terrorist acts against the United States. These terrorist acts *did* subsequently occur, with the *initial* loss of life into the thousands. Scarpa was promised by FBI personnel that he would be recommended for a reduction in his sentence for his valuable work as an al Qaeda mole. This relationship is detailed in my latest book and referred to in several others.[4]

Mr. Scarpa's reports were highly praised by the FBI personnel who worked with him during the months that Scarpa worked as a mole. But high FBI-DOJ officials refused to act on the reports of the planned terrorist attacks; it was necessary to discredit Mr. Scarpa, who was scheduled to testify in several criminal trials that would have proven that DeVecchio was involved with Scarpa' father in several murders. Everyone involved knew, of course, that by covering up for the planned terrorist attacks would be costly in human life. These attacks *did occur*, and the initial heavy loss of life led to other actions that continue to be even more costly in human life and the security of the United States.

Local FBI personnel had promised Mr. Scarpa a reduction in sentence for his dangerous role as a mole in the al Qaeda cell. But high FBI-DOJ officials, recognizing the danger to themselves if Gregory Scarpa Jr. was given a reduction of sentence and released from prison. The same applies to former war hero and FBI agent Richard Taus.

With 40 years of sophisticated airline and other investigative experience, starting as a federal agent investigating such fraud-related matters as the 1960 crash of a United Airlines DC-8 into Brooklyn (that happened in the program for which I had primary safety responsibility), I am fully aware of the sordid culture that exists in some government offices.

I would like to be able to write in subsequent book revisions and on my various Internet sites that finally, someone, such as you, the governor of New York, had the courage to address these outrages. The country is in dire need for a few more people with the character and courage to address these matters.

If you need more information about me, an Internet site[5] provides background information.

The primary issue in this letter is a request to promptly commute the sentence of Mr. Taus, and further, to expunge the conviction from the record. Taus' mother, the wife of a deceased veteran, is in failing health and will not live to see her son released, if you do not act fast.

I have been in continuous contact for several years with Richard Taus and Gregory Scarpa, Jr., and have received hundreds of documents and letters from them. Combined with my many years of investigative work, including as a federal investigator, I am convinced that what is stated in this letter is accurate.

The ramifications of what is stated here are related to the success of prior catastrophic terrorist attacks upon the United States. The continuing culture in key government positions continues to threaten the lives of many people as well as the security of the United States.

The matters stated here are also crimes against the people of the state of New York., as well as federal crimes. It is a criminal offense under various obstruction of justice statutes to fail to take meaningful actions to have these crimes reported to both state and federal authorities—and not to those implicated in the offenses.

I believe the gravity of these matters demand that you impanel a meaningful investigative group to consider not only the plight of Mr. Taus and Mr. Scarpa, the reinstatement of the murder charges against former FBI supervisor Lindley DeVecchio, and actions to prompt a federal investigation into the matters related to the conduct that enabled the prior terrorist attacks to so easily succeed. In addition, the involvement of U.S. Attorney General Michael Mukasey in one segment of the cover-up of these matters requires that any federal investigation be conducted by people outside of that department.

Sincerely,

Rodney Stich

Footnotes:

Certified 7002 0860 0003 9592 7310.

FBI, CIA, the Mob, and Treachery.

David Taus, 3308 Bertha Drive, Baldwin, New York 11510.

Crimes of the FBI-DOJ, and the Mafia.

www.defraudingamerica.com/stich_bio.html.

New York Governor Paterson never responded to that letter. I then sent a copy of that letter to over 50 members of the House and Senate, along with a cover letter, seeking to force the issue. This put the recipients in a difficult position.

Members of Congress, who I had informed of these matters, refused to even respond to the letters. I then sent a letter of Brooklyn district attorney, the prosecutor that dropped the murder charges against the former FBI supervisor:

From the desk of Rodney Stich

P.O. Box 5, Alamo, CA 94507; phone: 925-944-1930; FAX 925-295-1203

Author of numerous books on government intrigue and effect upon national security

E-mail: stich@defraudingamerica.com Google.com search engine: "Rodney Stich"

Web sites: www.defraudingamerica.com www.unfriendlyskies.com www.druggingamerica.com

February 6, 2009

Charles J. Hynes

District Attorney
Renaissance Plaza at 350 Jay Street
Brooklyn, NY 11201-2908

Ref: Refiling murder charges against Lindley DeVecchio

To Mr. Hynes:

I'm in the process of updating one of my books, *Crimes of the FBI-DOJ, and the Mafia*, which delves into the Scarpa Sr. and DeVecchio matters. The purpose of this letter is to obtain your comments on whether you plan to refile murder charges against DeVecchio, and if not, why not. I will include your comments in my Internet site relating to that matter and in the revised edition of the book. This is how I approached the matter:

The dropping of murder charges against DeVecchio was highly suspect. The dropping of charges was based upon audio tapes produced by one of the two Village Voice reporters who had taped statements made by Linda Schiro ten years earlier, when she was under not legal requirement to be accurate or complete in what she knew, and at a time when she felt her life was in danger if she divulged details of the Scarpa-DeVecchio relationship. Also, those reporters had a loyalty to DeVecchio due to DeVecchio secretly giving confidential FBI information to them that benefitted their standing as reporters.

The sudden dropping of charges against this key FBI supervisor:

Without allowing Schiro the opportunity to explain the difference between the casual statements made ten years earlier and the sworn testimony given in a court of law.

Without allowing Gregory Scarpa, Jr., an obvious key witness to testify.

Without allowing former FBI Special Agent Richard Taus, a former highly decorated Vietnam War veteran, who worked under DeVecchio and knew of his obstruction of justice tactics, to testify.

Ignoring the testimony of other FBI agents and various mob figures.

Since the dropping of charges against DeVecchio, the special district attorney, Leslie Crocker Snyder, has issued a report upholding the credibility of Linda Schiro. That report supports the testimony that she provided during the trial against DeVecchio.

The January 24, 2008, letter by the chief of your rackets division, Michael Vecchione, praising Gregory Scarpa Jr. for his creditability, further supports the testimony that he would have given about the murders that his father was involved in with Lindley DeVecchio if your office had not blocked his testimony.

I'm a former federal agent who is only too familiar with the various forms of obstruction of justice by high government officials and the harm inflicted upon the people and national security. My first experience with cover-ups and its deadly effect upon New Yorkers related to the crash of a United Airlines DC-8 into Brooklyn on December 16, 1960 (the program for which I was given primary responsibility and which I detail and document in the book, *Unfriendly Skies: 20th & 21st Centuries*).

If I were to write a report on the DeVecchio matter, one of the last statements I would make is that you have a responsibility to refile the murder charges against DeVecchio. The reaffirmation of the credibility of Linda Schiro—and Gregory Scarpa

Jr.—demands that the murder charges that should never have been dropped, should be refilled. There has never been a trial on the merits, so the double jeopardy issue does not apply.

I will put this letter on the Internet and in the book revision, along with your response.

Sincerely,

Rodney Stich

cc: Governor David Paterson

Letter to Brooklyn Prosecutor

Many letters were sent to state and federal officials that had a duty to conduct a prompt investigation because of the multiple areas of corrupt and criminal activities and also the role played in the greatest terrorist attacks in the nation's history, and the same people and culture that made these attacks possible were still in key government positions. As a matter of law, and responsibility, the recipients had a duty to receive my evidence. None ever responded.

When I felt another opportunity arose to put one of the recipients on the spot, I sent a letter, usually certified, and sometimes a fax with a transmission receipt. One such fax-certified letter was sent to Brooklyn prosecutor Charles Hynes on August 16, 2009. That letter stated details showing the enormity of the corruption and the consequences and stated that I felt he played a role in the conspiracy that constituted crimes against the United States that was setting the country up for more of the same. That letter, formatted to fit on this page, follows:

From the desk of Captain Rodney Stich
P.O. Box 5, Alamo, CA 94507 Phone: 925-944-1930 Fax: 925-295-1203
Author of numerous books on government intrigue
E-mail: stich@defraudingamerica.com
Web site: www.defraudingamerica and www.defraudingamericablog.com

August 16, 2009

Charles Hynes, District Attorney
Renaissance Plaza at 350 Jay Street
New York, NY 11201-2908 FAX: 718-250-2432 Certified mail # 7001 1140 001 2170 0072

Ref: Request for comments on your conduct relating to dropping of murder charges against former FBI supervisor DeVecchio

To Mr. Hynes:

I am preparing revisions to my not-for-profit book, *Crimes of the FBI-DOJ, Mafia, and al Qaeda*, which includes reference to you and your highly suspicious dropping of murder charges against former FBI supervisor Lindley DeVecchio. I would be willing to include your comments in the revision it you care to respond to any of the following issues:

Considerable evidence existed showing that former FBI supervisor Lindley DeVecchio was guilty of participation in serial murders with Mafia capo Gregory Scarpa, Sr.

Included in the witnesses that either did testify, or were willing to testify, included the following:

Gregory Scarpa, Jr., the son of the Mafia capo. Obviously, he would be one of two primary witnesses whose testimony could prove the involvement of a key FBI supervisor in the serial murders.

Mary Schiro, the mistress of Gregory Scarpa Sr., who for many years was present during conversations between Scarpa Sr. and FBI supervisor DeVecchio, and who was repeatedly told about the serial murders involving her lover and FBI supervisor Lindley DeVecchio.

Former FBI Special Agent Richard Taus, who worked under DeVecchio, and who was charged with a sham criminal offense by DOJ prosecutors *after* Taus circumvented the cover-up by DeVecchio and reported the serious irregularities to members of Congress. The initial criminal charge against Taus was the alleged misuse of a government issued credit card—four years earlier—in which Taus charged $8 worth of gasoline that he used during a government-authorized surveillance. That initial charge was then, with the connivance of a Staten Island prosecutor, expanded. That scheme protected DeVecchio, which could otherwise have halted the sequence of events that has had catastrophic consequences for the United States.

Other FBI special agents that had the courage and integrity to testify against DeVecchio, only to suffer the standard retaliation.

Underworld figures that were ready to testify about the DeVecchio-Scarpa Sr.'s murderous relationship.

Evidence far in excess of that necessary against a private citizen that lacked the obstructionist pressure from high-level DOJ personnel.

Under *extremely irregular circumstances*, your office suddenly dropped murder charges against former FBI supervisor DeVecchio—as if on command from a powerful source in government. The dropping of charges were contrary to prosecutorial procedures and interest of justice.

Your sophisticated knowledge and experience in criminal prosecutions supported your pre-trial knowledge that Schiro's sworn testimony relating to the serial murder charges were truthful.

You used the relatively meaningless matter suddenly provided by a newspaper reporter who produced selected audio tapes from a decade earlier in which Ms Schiro was participating in a joint book project. Her *casual* statements in those selected tapes differed from her *sworn testimony* in the DeVecchio murder trial. That ploy for turning free into society a serial killer ignored several key factors:

Her casual statements given a decade earlier to a reporter involved in writing a book occurred while she had fears of being murdered by the same FBI supervisor that had been involved in serial murders with Gregory Scarpa Sr.

Private statements made by anyone in a book deal could be expected to be different from testimony given under oath in a murder trial.

Your refusal to allow Gregory Scarpa, Jr. to testify, despite your previous conviction that his statements about the serial murders involving his father and DeVecchio were truthful.

That reporter providing the earlier audio tapes owed defendant DeVecchio a debt. DeVecchio repeatedly secretly leaked confidential information to the reporter that was then used to bolter the reporter's value to the newspaper and his own job security. Further, you never questioned that reporter about other tapes that were made, gladly using it to accomplish a purpose!

The facts surrounding your dropping of murder suggests that you were suddenly subjected to pressure from powerful people in the federal government.

<u>Further Evidence of Obstruction of Justice</u>

The fact that you never doubted the truthfulness of Scarpa Jr.'s testimony was shown by the January 24, 2008, letter written by your chief of the rackets division, Michael Vecchione, to U.S. District Judge Edward Korman. That letter praised Gregory Scarpa Jr. for his truthfulness,[1] and yet, you refused to allow him to testify!

The October 22, 2008, report of retired judge and Special Investigator Leslie Crocker, that stated Ms. Schiro's testimony was truthful. She testified to being present during many of the conversations between Scarpa Sr. and DeVecchio and DeVecchio's involvement in the serial murders.

<u>Raising Additional Suspicions of</u>
<u>Misconduct Affecting Major National Issues</u>

It can be argued that your dropping of murder charges against DeVecchio occurred with the following knowledge:

Gregory Scarpa Jr. had infiltrated the al Qaeda cell headed by Ramzi Yousef, the mastermind behind the 1993 bombing of the World Trade Center, the bombing on a Philippines Airline 747; the planned simultaneously bombing of 11 U.S. airliners departing Far East Locations; and the hijackings of U.S. airliners. Scarpa provided to FBI personnel, on a regular basis for 11 months, al Qaeda plans for terrorist attacks upon U.S. targets, obtaining this information directly from Yousef.

With Scarpa's help, a fictitious Mafia corporation was set up in New York City, through which Yousef communicated on a regular basis with al Qaeda members in the New York-New Jersey area, and in the Middle East. That fictitious Mafia corporation was staffed by FBI agents that monitored the phone calls made by Yousef to numerous al Qaeda operatives. That information, if used, was of more value that the total of the thousands of personnel in the nation's various intelligence departments regarding al Qaeda's planned attacks against U.S. targets.

The unprecedented information on planned terrorist attacks that Scarpa obtained from this key al Qaeda operative provided advance knowledge of several major terrorist attacks upon U.S. targets. These included:

Bringing down a U.S. airliner departing a New York City airport (shortly before TWA Flight 800 was downed),[2]

The bombings of U.S. embassies in Africa (which was followed by the bombings of U.S. embassies in Kenya and Tanzania.

The hijackings of four airliners on September 11, 2001.

Instead of providing this advance information to government departments—and other FBI offices—that could take measures to defeat the terrorist attacks, high-level FBI-DOJ personnel in Washington "deep-sixth" the information that knowingly had a life-or-death consequence.

The reason for withholding the information on the planned terrorist attacks was to deny credibility to Scarpa. If the information on the planned terrorist attacks had been made known, Scarpa's credibility would have been recognized along with its immense national interest importance.

The reason high-level FBI-DOJ personnel had for this scheme was their plans to falsely discredit Scarpa's credibility at upcoming murder trials, where he would be providing testimony about the serial murders his father committed with the help of FBI supervisor DeVecchio. That testimony would also implicate as accessory before, during, and after the fact, the involving in serial murders and their cover-ups by high-level FBI-DOJ personnel.

The decision was then made to sacrifice the lives that would be lost to protect themselves. These people are still in key government positions, some have been promoted, and are responsible for protecting the United States against the very same catastrophic events that their conduct enabled to occur.

Under this scenario, it appears probable that pressure in high government positions affected your decision to drop murder charges against DeVecchio, and in that way prevent the public from learning about these matters.

Consequences of Dropping Serial Murders Charges Against a Known Murderer

The improper dropping of murder charges against a key member of government is a decision that also has serious consequences for the American people and the United States:

A serial murderer has been allowed to go free into American society, and sets, again, an acceptable standard of conduct in government offices.

The same high-level FBI-DOJ people, the same groups, the same culture, that aided and abetted the terrorist attacks through corrupt acts, are still in key positions in government, responsible for preventing in the future what they made possible by their prior misconduct. And were rewarded for their crimes.

This will make possible the increasing severity of the consequences that I have been repeatedly warning, in writings and lawsuits, that would result from the corruption of people in key government positions that are never prosecuted. A sampling of my attempts in writings and in federal lawsuits can be found at www.defraudingamerica.com.

Bad as This Is, It is Only A Small Part of the Corruption by Other Enablers to 9/11

As described in the not-for-profit *Unfriendly Skies: 20th & 21st Centuries*, the evidence shows a long list of enablers responsible for many of America's worst aviation disasters, including the 9/11 hijackings. It is enlightening to see the evidence of FBI-DOJ personnel corruption and how they misused powerful government offices to silence me. The 9/11 tragedies were simply one-day's events in a long list that will continue to occur as long as people in government and elsewhere lack the integrity and courage to bring to justice the many that made possible such great tragedies—in and out of the aviation sectors.

Victims Were No Match For This Hoard of Enablers

People jumping to their deaths from the World Trade Center on September 11, 2001, were no match for this overwhelming number of enablers. Nor were victims of this culture that I, a former government agent, had identified in prior catastrophic events.

You may not remember the United Airlines DC-8 that crashed into Brooklyn on December 16, 1960, but the conditions that made that disaster had links to 9/11, and also to my behavior. As a FAA inspector, I was given the assignment to correct the conditions responsible for that disaster and others that constituted the worst series of preventable and forewarned airline disasters in the nation's history.

As I have been documenting for the past 40 years, starting as a federal agent, every cover-up compounded the number of enablers, and made possible even worst consequences. I describe and document this relationship in my not-for-profit books. Letters at my Internet site, www.defraudingamerica.com, list some of the key people in state and federal government that by their subsequent cover-ups are guilty of accessory-after-the-fact crimes; crimes that will continue to have an adverse impact upon the United States and its people. The cover-ups now include several prominent people in New York offices.

My primary interest in this matter is to make known to the public the areas of corruption and consequences that I discovered initially while a government agent given the assignment to correct the conditions that enabled to occur a continuing series of preventable airline disasters. The dozens of other government agents and insiders that subsequently provided me information about corruption in other areas of government reinforced my determination. The issues in this letter have the potential of finally getting the public to realize the source of many of the nation's human tragedies.

I feel that you, as an individual, attempts to perform your duty when it does not involve high-level corruption in government. I feel you were under pressure to do what you did, though I cannot excuse it, nor the consequences from doing it. If I hear from you, I will consider adding your comments to the revisions.

Sincerely,

Rodney Stich

cc:

Faxes to select members of Congress, most of whom have covered up for this corruption for years.

Faxes to certain members of the media, many of who have also kept this information from the public.

Endnotes

1. Portion of that letter: "Scarpa Jr. was open, candid and complete in his information, not only about the matters we were investigating but also about his criminal past. In addition to providing valuable intelligence, Scarpa Jr. was ready, willing and able to testify at the trial of DeVecchio. It is therefore my hope that your honor will take into consideration the content of this letter outlining the cooperative effort of Gregory Scarpa, Jr. in any motion made on his behalf for a reduction in his federal sentence.

2. As a former key FAA air carrier safety inspector-investigator, it was obvious to me that the NTSB and the FBI covered up for the true cause of that disaster, partly to cover up for their "deep-sixing" of the forewarned information. More details in my book, *Unfriendly Skies: 20th & 21st Centuries*. That book also shows the misconduct by FBI-DOJ personnel that enabled to occur several prior airline disasters

CHAPTER TWENTY THREE

Sampling of Other FBI-DOJ Corruption

The following is a sampling of the personal conduct of certain FBI agents throughout the Federal Bureau of Investigation, which provide additional insight into the FBI culture that allowed the conduct of FBI agents in the Boston and New York offices to continue for years.

El Paso Special Agent in Charge, and Drug Smuggler

An El Paso federal grand jury indicted (April 13, 2006) Hardrick Crawford, Jr., a former FBI special agent in charge of the El Paso office, on perjury charges related to an investigation into his relationship with a Mexican racetrack owner believed to be part of a Mexican drug cartel. The indictment charged Crawford with lying to federal investigators about what he knew of drug trafficking and money laundering of racetrack owner, Jose Maria Guardia, a former FBI informant. The indictment charged that he did know about the activities. The indictment charged that Crawford received thousands of dollars worth of gifts from Guardia, that he failed to report as income, and that his wife had a lucrative job with Guardia, receiving $5,000 a month.

In June, the U.S. ambassador to Mexico revoked Crawford's authority to travel to Mexico, based upon Crawford holding a press conference in Ciudad Juarez defending Guardia. In November 2003, Mexican officials complained about Crawford's public support for the drug trafficker.

FBI Agents Giving Classified Secrets to Chinese Spy

Federal authorities arrested (April 2003) a Chinese American woman, Katrina Leung, who had been an FBI informant, for passing classified information to the Chinese government. Leung emigrated from China and obtained degrees from Cornell University and University of Chicago. She then moved to Los Angeles and made friends with people that were under FBI surveillance.

Katrina Leung, a well-known socialite in San Francisco and Los Angeles, was a double agent, having sexual relations with Los Angeles based FBI Special Agent James J. Smith and San Francisco based Special Agent William Cleveland, Jr. She obtained from them classified information that she delivered to the Chinese government. After learning that she had contacts with Chinese intelligence agents, Smith continued the sexual relationship with her for about ten years, and continued giving her classified information.

Converting Leung into FBI Asset

FBI Special Agent James J. Smith, in 1982, reached an agreement with Leung to become an FBI asset helping to obtain information on activities with the Chinese government. Her code name was "Parlor Maid," A year later, Smith began a sexual relationship with Leung, which continued for nearly 20 years, until Smith retired in 2002.

Leung became a U.S. citizen in March 1984, after which the FBI formed a plan under which she would be recruited by the Chinese Ministry of State Security, and be a double agent for the United States. That plan worked. In June 1983, Leung was recruited by the Chinese, thinking she was a low level employee in the FBI's Los Angeles office.

Leung became socially prominent in the Chinese community in California, and did considerable entertainment with Chinese diplomatic officials, including the President of China, Yang Shangkun.

The FBI learned in June 1990 that Leung disclosed to Chinese intelligence officials details about a classified operation and an FBI counterintelligence program. Nearly a year later, the FBI learned that Leung had given details to a Chinese intelligence person of a trip by FBI Special Agent Bill Cleveland to China. The FBI continued to use her, thinking that the intelligence she was giving the FBI was more important than the intelligence she was revealing to China about the FBI. But at that time, the FBI did not know the extent of the classified information that she had received from her sexual partners in the FBI.

Sexual Relationship with FBI Agent Bill Cleveland

In 1979, Leung started working with FBI Special Agent Bill Cleveland in the San Francisco area on a project given the codename of "Tiger Trap." That operation involved an engineer from Taiwan working at the Lawrence Livermore Laboratory in Livermore, California: Gwo-Bao Min. Min eventually resigned from his position when confronted by the FBI.

In 1988, Cleveland started a sexual relationship with Leung. At a later date, Cleveland learned that Leung had given his itinerary to Chinese intelligence. Cleveland left the FBI and became the head of security at Lawrence Livermore Laboratory.

Years Later, FBI Arrested Leung

In December 2002, the FBI learned that Leung had copied top secret documents that FBI agent Smith had in his possession, and had sent to her Chinese intelligence contacts. The FBI's surveillance finally discovered the sexual relationship between Leung and Smith that had existed for years.

In April 2003, the Department of Justice arrested Leung at her San Marino residence, charging her with "Unauthorized Copying of National Defense Information with Intent to Injure or Benefit a Foreign Nation in violation of 18

U.S.C. § 793(b). Because of the severity of the charges and the possibility she was a flight risk, she was denied bail.

Smith was also arrested, but federal prosecutors sought to prosecute Leung while holding FBI agent Smith blameless, a strategy that may have caused a judge to question the plea agreement and refused to accept it. In a motion to dismiss the case, Leung's lawyers argued that Smith's plea deal was "unsavory" because it perpetuated the "gross and unfair disparity in treatment between Mr. Smith and Ms. Leung." U.S. District Judge Florence-Marie Cooper agreed, calling Smith's plea a "sweetheart deal."

DOJ prosecutors entered into another plea agreement with Smith that provided that Smith "could not share further information relating to the case with Leung or her counsel." That provision caused U.S. District Judge Florence Marie Cooper to hold that Leung's constitutional right to a witness necessary to her defense had been violated by the terms of the plea agreement. She dismissed the case against Leung. (January 6, 2005)

The U.S. Attorney's office filed an appeal of that decision. DOJ prosecutors then entered into another plea agreement wherein Leung pled guilty (December 16, 2005) to lying to the FBI and filing a false federal tax return, and received three years probation.

In light of the gravity of the offenses, various lawyers questioned the plea deal. Stanley Greenberg stated, "This was a rather significant betrayal by an FBI agent. It's one thing to have a dipsy woman on the outside trying to play off both sides who has a bunch of friends in China. To me, the greater harm is the betrayal by the FBI agent. In the end, Leung, who was initially considered so dangerous to national security, was allowed to plead guilty to filing a false tax return and received probation."

Congressional Investigation

The charges against Leung caused a House committee headed by Representative Chris Cox to conduct an investigation. The committee prepared a classified report that addressed the covert operations by the People's Republic of China within the United States during the 1980s and 1990s. The 1999 report, given the name, Cox Report, stated that Leung commenced a sexual relationship with FBI Special Agent Cleveland in the late 1988. It charged that security at several U.S. weapons labs had been compromised and that Chinese agents had copied or stolen classified information regarding thermonuclear weapons and other missile technology.

The report particularly identified the Lawrence Livermore National Laboratory, stating that it appeared likely that Leung acquired secrets at that location from Cleveland.

Decades of Treasonous Actions

FBI Special Agent Robert Philip Hanssen was arrested (February 18, 2001) and charged with selling American secrets to the Soviet Union during a 22-year period, being paid over $1.4 million in cash and diamonds. FBI officials did not become suspicious, despite living an obvious luxurious lifestyle that couldn't possibly occur on Hanssen's salary.

Hanssen approached the Soviet military intelligence agency and offered to spy for them. During his spy activities, Hanssen told Soviet intelligence about FBI bugging activities, the FBI's list of suspected Soviet intelligence agents, and the names of Soviet people spying for the United States. This latest information resulted in many spies being put to death, including Dmitri Polyakov, whose code name was TopHat. Polyakov, a Russian general, was a CIA informant for over twenty years, during which time he passed considerable information to U.S. intelligence.

The Soviet Union discovered his status from Hanssen, but did not initially act on this information. After Polyakov's spying was revealed by another spy for the Soviet Union, CIA agent Aldrich Ames in 1985, Polyakov was arrested and executed. Ames was initially blamed for revealing Polyakov's name to the Soviet Union, and then Hanssen's role in exposing Polyakov surfaced after his arrest in 2001.

Hanssen once confessed to an Opus Dei priest, who suggested that Hanssen give the money he received from the Soviet Union to the Mother Teresa mission. He pled guilty (July 6, 2001) to 15 counts of espionage and was sentenced to life in prison. In his plea agreement, he avoided the death penalty in exchange for cooperating with investigators, and his wife and children would receive benefits from his government pension.

Hanssen's activities had been described as "possibly the worst intelligence disaster in US history." Hanssen was in the Washington counterintelligence office, charged with compiling a database of Soviet intelligence.

US Attorney Stealing and Selling Stolen Drugs

"Federal Attorney Held in Drug Theft at New York Office" was the title on a *New York Times* article (May 31, 1985):

> A prosecutor in the office of the United States attorney in Manhattan was arrested yesterday and charged with stealing up to $500,000 worth of heroin and cocaine from a safe used by the office's narcotics unit. The suspect, Daniel N. Perlmutter, an assistant United States attorney, was also charged with possession and intent to distribute the drugs—8.7 ounces of heroin and 29 ounces of cocaine.

FBI Agent in Pedophile Activities

"Former Scout leader-FBI agent indicted on child sex charges" was the heading on an *Associated Press* article (Feb. 3, 2006):

> NEW HAVEN, Conn. (AP) A retired FBI agent was indicted Friday on federal child sex charges dating back more than a decade when he was a Boy Scout leader. William Hutton, 63, of Killingworth, was arrested Fri-

day. The federal grand jury indictment offers few details about the case but accuses Hutton of enticing a member of his Scout troop to Maine for the purpose of sexual activity in 1994 and 1995.

"It's obviously devastating. He was an FBI agent in this district and was respected in this district," defense attorney Hugh Keefe said. "The people who worked with him in the U.S. attorney's office and FBI respected him." Keefe said the investigation has been going on for years. He would not discuss the details of the case or how the allegations surfaced.

Investigators asked anyone who knows anything about the case to call the FBI. U.S. Attorney Kevin O'Connor said that's standard practice whenever there might be more victims. "In any case that's a concern," O'Connor said. "Whether that's the situation here I can't say."

If convicted on all four charges, Hutton faces up to 30 years in prison and up to $250,000 in fines. Hutton was released on a $200,000 bond.

"Prosecutors move to dismiss charges against former Scout leader" stated the *Associated Press* article (Jan. 3, 2007):

NEW HAVEN, Conn. Federal prosecutors have moved to dismiss charges against a retired FBI agent who was indicted on child sex charges dating back more than a decade when he was a Boy Scout leader, in response to the death of his accuser. William Hutton, 63, of Killingworth, was arrested in February on charges he enticed a member of his Scout troop to Maine for the purpose of sexual activity in 1994 and 1995.

Prosecutor John A. Danaher III moved to dismiss the indictment on Dec. 19, and Judge Mark R. Kraits granted the motion three days later, federal court records show. On Dec. 26, the prosecutor moved to dismiss a revised indictment that had been returned by a federal grand jury in late March. There was no indication in court records that Kravitz has issued a ruling on that indictment.

Both indictments alleged crimes against the same person, who has never been publicly identified. The newer indictment added allegations that an August 1995 trip also included a stop in New Hampshire for illegal sexual activity. Both of Danaher's motions cited "the sudden and unexpected death" of the accuser.

Hutton's lawyer, Hugh F. Keefe of New Haven, stressed Hutton had pleaded not guilty. "Mr. Hutton was very upset by the news of the passing of the gentleman," Keefe said.

Hutton had been released on a $200,000 bond. He may not own any firearms or have any unsupervised contact with children. He was also ordered to stay away from playgrounds, schools, arcades or anywhere children congregate. The case had been scheduled to go to trial this month in U.S. District Court in New Haven.

Additional information about FBI Agent Involved in Major Drug Smuggling Across the Canadian Border

Over the years my CIA and other sources provided me information on drug smuggling, murders, and other crimes involving people in or associated with the government of the United States. One such FBI agent was identified by several of my covert intelligence sources as Mike "Chuckie" Peters, reportedly a hit man in the FBI. At that time, before I discovered the murders involving FBI agents in the Boston and New York City offices, the role of FBI agents in murders was a little too far fetched for me to believe. I said nothing about what I had learned.

I acquired considerable information from several sources about drug smuggling into the United States from Canada that involved Miami-based FBI Special Agent Terry Nelson. Two people with whom I had considerable contact were directly involved in that operation. One was Gene Tatum. I detailed what I learned from him in the books, *Drugging America* and *Defrauding America*.

Starting around 2006, Curt Erling, with even more involvement in that operation, started providing me firsthand information about the drug-smuggling operation and the involvement of FBI agent Terry Nelson in it. Erling described the route taken as drugs were flown from South America, northward along the eastern coast of the United States, and to Canada. He described dumping waterproof bags of drugs into the waters off the eastern coast of Canada.

In previous writing, I did not identify Erling so as to protect him. But with his death from cancer February 28, 2012, shortly before this revision, that protection is no longer needed.

The drugs were picked up by boats and flown into the interior of Canada, and then across the porous border into Montana and adjoining states. That source tried to minimize that segment of the drug operation, stating that the group's involvement in drugs was just the starting point, and that it was involved in far more serious things.

I explained to Erling that it is hard enough to get the public to accept information about government personnel being involved in drug smuggling, and that what he was trying to expose was far beyond what the public would accept as occurring. Part of what he stated during several phone conversations, from one on January 20, 2007, to one on August 5, 2007, included the following:

How did you learn about me? I asked.

The gentleman who referred me to you knows you; your credibility is not in question at all. Your sincerity is not in question.

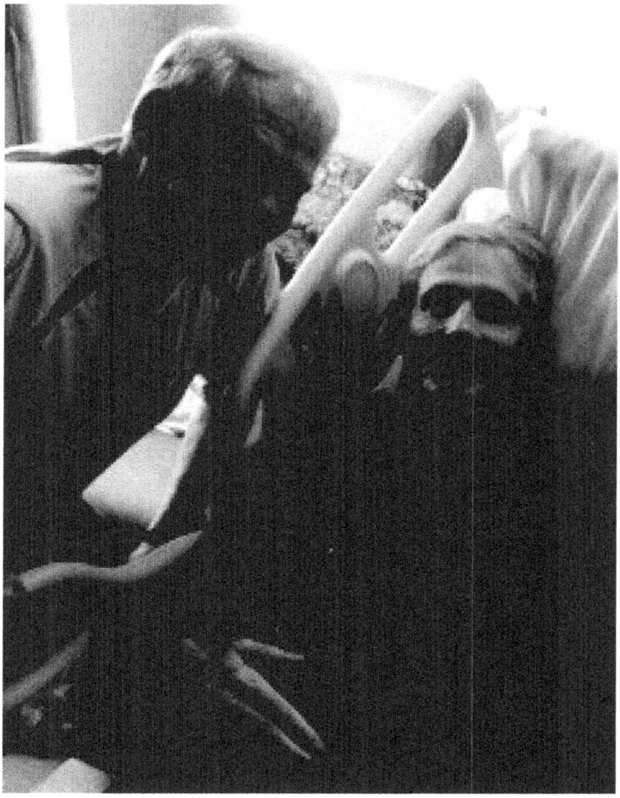

Curt, shortly before his death

Domestic agents are involved in a lot of this stuff that is happening now and in the past, and the recent past. And things that will be taking place in the near future. What I want to stop is what is taking place in the future. I want to put a control jacket on them. The only way we can get out of this is by revealing it. I started out in Vietnam and worked my way through all those years into contra ops, and then into more frightening stuff.

Give me more details on this other spooky stuff.

It involves drugs, money, and it's used to buy all the bad stuff for the bad guys, 30 years of it. Very scary stuff. [Referring to the drug smuggling operation into the United States from Canada] *I was the original person that set that up.*

You were taking care of the flight operations?

Yes, from start to finish.

What type of planes were you using?

At that time, at the original start, we were using the Merlin III Ds, but then we changed to (unintelligible).

Where were you landing when you came into the United States [with the drugs]?

I didn't break the border. I just brought it into Canada.

When you brought it into Canada, that was probably from Central America, then, wasn't it?

From South America.

Did you fly offshore and enter Canada on the West Coast?

No, it was all on the East Coast. We first dropped the drug bundles to boats off of Halifax. And boats would pick it up and take it to Nova Scotia, and from there on. What was done then was a range landing strip at Halifax.

Here is the deal. This is a multi-faceted operation. Running drugs over to Europe; selling drugs over there; and what the proceeds are used for is buying weapons to support for terrorist groups in Central and South America and to infiltrate the United States and do the bombings of airplanes and all that sort of thing.

The people involved ... were sitting right there, so and so, and met with some of the government of Columbia, bank representatives, from different countries that are involved.

I helped set up bank accounts in Switzerland and other European countries. That is what all the money is for, for the very same thing; to put the world in a tailspin. I have photographs and documentation, meetings recorded, and other evidence. You don't want to pursue it.

It all goes back to Bush One, and CIA, and South Florida drug task force, something or other. What he did was, he took over the island, an island off the coast of Nicaragua. I believe Tatum mentioned it. And he [Tatum]got that from us. He doesn't know anything about that. He knows nothing about it. He doesn't know what it was used for. He is only speculating.

It was a transshipment point; it would bring boats out of the Canal out of South America, Fly out of South America. It was like a chain. And then we would fly to Canada. Break the connection and there is no way they can track you. They have to track you from start to finish. If you break it off, they have a strategic point. That is why Haiti is so popular. Because you break off their tracking there.

Anyway, Bush took that over, and it is still used today, but much more sophisticated. They have designated it a military operations area. MOA. A restricted area. All that sort of stuff.

In order to get control of the island and the shipping company [unintelligible] set up a bogus company. He was convicted on that alone. But Bush took over the operation. Prior to that, he was working for both senior and [unintel-

ligible] and working with us. We have the records, all the documentation necessary to reshape the operation.

Why in the world did they get involved? Was there that much money in it?

Absolutely. Would you turn your back on $10 billion dollars? Money is their God. And the money is used for other enterprises. We are talking big bucks.

I hate to talk about it because it sounds so damn Looney, but I have first hand knowledge of all that. I have been trusted by the whole crew for years.

I know what you mean; the average persons hearing this, it sounds too bizarre. I was slowly brought into it over a period of years by many different people, but even I have trouble seeing the overall picture.

You remember what was happening in New Orleans in the eighties, something like that. Well, the Russians were [unintelligible] in funding the entire South America. You know, all the guerrilla outfits. And they were doing that on the American's cartels' profits from the cocaine trade. So the American cartels had to be done away with.

The only way to do that was to form a new cartel, which we did. We formed the Cali Cartel with Rodriguez brothers. We were forced to do it. It is well known. [Unintelligible] was arrested in California, ... the warehouse with 25,000 kilos of cocaine. But that didn't matter. It was the national security angle with the summa (unintelligible) documents that turned it over to the DOD. Took it out of DOJ and DOD. Under the control of Central Security Service. When you control that, you control everything. You couldn't believe what was occurring.

Anyway, they concentrated on the charges against the Rodriguez brothers and sent them off to Cali, and funded them to start up the Cali Cartel, which did away with the American (unintelligible) cartel. And ultimately, set up the money supply for the Russians taking over. And we had to figure out a way to get the cocaine out of their (unintelligible), and that is what we did.

We started flying drugs out of there to generate cash, in order to keep South America from going communistic.

Gunther Russbacher, which I describe in Defrauding America, told me about how the CIA brought the various independent drug smugglers together to form the Cali Cartel.

I was one of them. In fact, I was there when it was first conceived. I was charged with figuring out a way, the flight paths, the operation.

Did you run into Shackley during their activities?" [Shackley was CIA station chief in Miami, and numerous people who worked with him had told me over the last 20 years about the CIA drug smuggling that Shackley was involved in.]

Sure; I know Shackley.

Referring to a major drug smuggling operation from Canada into the United States that I had written extensively about in Defrauding America *and in Drugging America, in which FBI agent Terry Nelson was involved, I asked, "Can you provide me details on FBI agent Terry Nelson and the drug smuggling operation from Canada into the United States?"*

Yes, but I want to show present activities. On prior activities, it is going to be difficult to prove that this came from this source, this came from that source, and to state what the sources are. [Although this source was heavily involved in the drug smuggling operation from Canada and told me a number of details about it, he felt that there were bigger crimes being conducted by the group with whom he was previously involved.]

I can supply the historical stuff I can supply a lot of that. Such as minutes of meetings, in the FBI building, orders given, recordings taken, videos of being in the building, in the conference, folks present, orders given, ...

Who was Nelson working for: the CIA, the FBI, or both?

He carried identification for both. He worked back and forth.

Asking About One of my Many Sources

What do you know about Gene Tatum, who I wrote about years earlier in my books, Defrauding America and Drugging America?

I had years of experience over Tatum. I was above Tatum. Tatum came in after I was starting the operation.

After Vietnam I was always fearful about continually working in these types of activities; I bolted. They would come to me and ask me how to run it. Or, to run it. I'd ask them how they wanted me to run it, and they'd say it is your job, run it.

You have to be real careful with him. He was not all that involved. He picked a lot of stories out of a lot of us. And then mouthed it into something that he did. He was in and out for a very short time. Maybe once. He then evolved himself into the story. I distance myself from folks like Tatum and everybody else. A friend of mine was involved in these operations years before Nelson got involved. [That other person was someone by the name of Charleston (sp ?). Referring to Charleston, my source stated: Right now I am maintaining a bit of safety by maintaining contact with Charleston. He has me as the friendly.

Is he still with the FBI?

Well, no, he's retired, on paper. Although, I helped him out with another project in which he did, he called a meeting of some of the friends that are still active in the FBI.

[Referring to Terry Nelson]*He regards me like a trusted friend. I've been in and out of prison a number of times and have been subpoenaed before the judiciary twice. Never appeared. He is very comfortable with me. I've been under fire and passed the test. He is eager to do something else. I am going to make a proposal to him, and here's the deal. Only, when we go public with this sort of thing, I'm looking around here on the landscape, and there are only three of us left.*

It is a shame for all that information to be hidden. I could see a big story there.

I'm afraid that you don't have any clue as to how big it is. That's why it is going to take some sort of prominent investigative journalist to write this. Hand me over to some journalist or investigative reporter, or someone who wants to be squeaky clean. I want to document this through a journalist, and at a meeting to take place.

Dangers of Revealing High-Level Crimes Against the United States

[Referring to the consequences of people being silenced], *"I don't want the same thing to happen to us. And it will. I believe in a proactive offense, where you are controlling the situation. You can't control the situation when you are in defense.*

I'm one of the first guys they trusted with this stuff. It would be very hard to weave it all altogether in some understandable form. There were so many things I was involved in. But what I intend to do with Terry, I have to tell you now, because after next week [unintelligible]. What I am going to do is make a proposal to him, and [unintelligible].

I started out as an FAA inspector and gradually discovered the extent of the corruption.

I know, I read your bio.

It was hard for me to believe. But gradually, over the years I could understand that these things were actually going on. But for the average person, being told of all this, it would be hard for them to believe any of this.

Financially. I can't do it. Also, to support myself, while on site until this all takes place. The meetings are going to take place and then two of us will go underground.

I have documents, but that is no protection. Barry Seal thought he had enough documents to protect himself. Barry was a fighting idiot. I knew the guy and I flew with him once and that was it. I told everyone to stay as far away from that egotistical maniac as humanely possibly.

Was he a pilot for TWA at one time?

He claimed to be, but I don't believe so.

"I think he was. Just a little while ago I was talking to Hoot Gibson, a friend of mine, who was a captain for TWA. He told me once that Barry Seal was once his copilot. Matter of fact, they made a movie about him. I find that people in government trying to do what you are doing, exposing these things, they end up being charged by federal prosecutors.

If you could send me material, I could present it to members of Congress and they would have to get off their ass."

I don't want to be sending you stuff that is in damage control right now. I want to get these guys so far into it. Avoiding exposure is out of the question, because all they will do is somewhere along the line send it to Congress and he will be compromised and he will be turning it over to the agent that compromised him.

Why don't you send me data so that I know the nature of what you are talking about?

Rod, if I do that, they would start doing damage control and I'll be finding dead relatives.

They don't want to compromise their guys because their guys are the ones making the money. You will be at risk for divulging this information. I'm removed from this thing at the moment and very shortly I'll be a key player in all this stuff in my suitcase.

I can help you put it together.

I know you can; you are a go-to guy. You are going to have a very full plate here shortly.

"It seems to me that if I were in your position I'd want my name to be cleared, by getting the story out."

I can't clear that, because I was at risk of running off the reservation. I was arrested once. After all those years as an insider.

Too bad you can't write your story as an alias and not identify yourself. I did that for a couple of guys.

But you lose so damn much credibility when you do that. I don't mind putting myself up front, but I have to have a back door when this is all finished. An escape hatch.

Referring to his attempt to give the story to a writer for a major publication, my source said: *"It's just that what is going to happen, things that I need, a creditable journalist that will actually write a story on this. I'm looking for someone who is able to investigate and record current activities. You have to be a little more creative in stepping out of the box with this. This is big stuff, that goes all the way to the top. It will go further than you have any idea.*

History of Cover-Ups by Media Personnel and Media Corporations

What he didn't know, as I discovered over the years, was that no media source will touch a story when the ramifications go beyond a certain point.

Not included here are some of the documents that my source sent to me, including the phone numbers in Canada of the offices where the indictment against FBI agent Terry Nelson existed; telephone records of phone calls to the FBI agent, a signed note from Nelson stating that he and my source was active in some particular government operation, among others.

One person that had a peripheral role in the operation was a Norwegian, Erling Ingvaldsen. To keep him silent, false drug charges were filed against him. He filed a 2008 complaint with the International Covenant on Civil and Political Rights, seeking to start an investigation into one area of the complex web that my sources had been describing to me over the years. The following is a part of that filing:

IV. Facts of the Complaint

Mr. Erling Ingvaldsen had been working for officials of the US Department of Justice for many years to expose many international drug trafficking organizations. His primary control agent was FBI Special Agent Terry Nelson as referenced in court testimony. (See Exhibit I). In 1982, Mr. Ingvaldsen was sentenced to prison after discovering a drug smuggling operation involving US government officials.

On his release he was offered the option to leave the United States, and to obtain written permission from the United States Attorney General to reenter, or remain in the US under supervision (See Exhibit II) Due to threats from both government officials and dangerous trafficking organizations, Mr. Ingvaldsen opted to relocate in Nassau, Bahamas.

Following his arrival in the Bahamas Mr. Ingvaldsen was visited by FBI Special Agent Terry Nelson in order to reaffirm his intention to continue to use him to assist the US Department of Justice. (See Exhibit III) The assistance requested by Nelson and Flynn is too sensitive to be documented here, but following its successful completion Mr. Ingvaldsen contacted the Department of Justice to request the written permission to reenter the US, but that request was not granted. (See Exhibit IV)

Following his government assistance, Mr. Ingvaldsen flew to Canada to develop a marketing programme for a new medical product. (See Exhibit V) In Canada Agent Nelson contacted him by speakerphone from the FBI complex located in Miami, Florida. Present was Special Agent Terry Nelson (Director of Domestic Terrorism & Director of Drug Interdiction in the Caribbean Basin), Special Agent Rick Brodsky, Petitioner's brother, Leif Ingvaldsen, and several other unidentified government officials.

Mr. Ingvaldsen was asked to help expose the largest drug smuggling operation known to date, from various third-world countries, via Canada, and into the US. Although this was the first time he had been in Canada, Mr. Ingvaldsen said that he would try to help. Agt. Nelson gave Mr. Ingvaldsen the name and phone number of a law enforcement agent, Pierre Jeannette, located in Montreal, who was to furnish him with local support.

The phone number of Agt. Jeannette, as furnished by Agt. Nelson, is photocopied from the Canadian evidence book. (See Exhibit VI) After agreements and assurances were made to him, Mr. Ingvaldsen began to infiltrate these groups by posing as a wealthy buyer. Canadian long distance phone records document Mr. Ingvaldsen's phone contacts with Agt. Nelson at the FBI office in Miami and at Nelson's Miami home. (See Exhibit VII)

Mr. Ingvaldsen used a criminal attorney practicing in Fort Lauderdale, Florida, Steven Finta, for directions and introductions into this shady world of drug traffickers and murderers. We have since learned that Mr. Finta had been under investigation by the Judiciary Committee of the US Congress for working at the direction of the US Department of Justice. (See Exhibit VIII) It is safe to assume that Mr. Finta was working at the direction of the RCMP and the US Department of Justice to direct Mr. Ingvaldsen into drug trafficking organizations.

After some 8 months of his efforts to document the trafficker's methods, routes, and schedules, as well as collecting samples of the drugs, Mr. Ingvaldsen notified Agents Terry Nelson and Pierre Jeannette, telling them the date of the arrival of the next shipments, at which time they could expose and arrest the traffickers. The following morning he went to the office of one of the traffickers.

Moments after his arrival, an agent of the RCMP, posing as a neighboring shop-owner, hand-delivered to the office a rolled-up magazine stating that it was delivered to his office by mistake. As the package was not addressed to him, Mr. Ingvaldsen declined to take possession when the agent thrust it upon him. Even though, moments later, the same RCMP agent and others arrested Mr. Ingvaldsen for possession of an amount of heroin claimed to be within the magazine that the agent had just delivered to the office.

We believe that even though this egregious abuse of governmental power is not clearly codified in the Covenant that this act constitutes a violation *Article 9, 1* of the Covenant. It cannot be ignored that the RCMP orchestrated Mr. Ingvaldsen's arrest the day after he notified Jeannette and Nelson of his discoveries, and just days prior to the arrival of a large shipment of drugs.

At his taped interrogation, Mr. Ingvaldsen told the Canadian authorities that he was working at the direction of the US Department of Justice, FBI, and Nelson, in concert with Agt. Jeannette of the RCMP. At that taped interrogation Mr. Ingvaldsen offered to outline his knowledge of impending drug shipments destined for Canada, and informed his inquisitors of the drug samples at his apartment. The interrogator stated, to the effect, that they were just not interested. (See Exhibit IX; Recorded Interrogation)

This is an odd attitude for a member of law enforcement tasked to interdicting drug trafficking into Canada. A subsequent letter from the US Department of Justice stated that though Mr. Ingvaldsen worked on behalf of the FBI and Nelson in the past, he was not then working for these officials. (See Exhibit X)

This is patently false. Exhibit XI is a letter dated September, 1997, from Special Agent Terry Nelson to Leif Ingvaldsen stating that he, Agt. Nelson, was "in continuous contact with Erling and he continues to provide useful information to the FBI." So now we are faced with a conspiracy between the governments of Canada and the US to violate Mr. Ingvaldsen's human rights outlined in not only *Article 9* but arguably in the entire Covenant, itself. It is little wonder why the United States refuses to be bound by the Protocols, all the while condemning other States, many of which have signed.

But why would the Canadian and American authorities go to these extraordinary efforts to create such an absurd crime only to arrest one man? And even if Mr. Ingvaldsen was, as the RCMP contends, trafficking, why would they not take advantage of the information offered by him and interdict the shipments and arrest the traffickers? Could it be that this arrest was never intended to thwart a crime, but instead to cover one up involving officials in both the Canadian government and the US government?

We later discovered that there existed, prior to Mr. Ingvaldsen's arrival in Canada, a sealed Canadian indictment for the arrest of Special Agent Terry Nelson charging him with drug trafficking. Inquiries beyond our capabilities would produce Nelson's Canadian Indictment, and that of at least one RCMP Officer.

Having some 30 years experience in the interdiction of international drug trafficking, we can assure this Commission that it is impossible to accomplish this kind of trafficking and cover-up without the active participation of law enforcement officials; officials of the Royal Canadian Mounted Police and the US Director of Drug Trafficking in the Caribbean Basin.

Motives are many, but the facts and events indicate that Mr. Ingvaldsen was directed into this labyrinth of drug traffickers to be arrested in an effort to divert any official inquiries away from agents of the RCMP and FBI and directly onto Erling Ingvaldsen.

Please review just some of the documented independent investigations regarding the involvement of government officials in these Canadian smuggling operations (See Exhibit XII). In contrast please view the magazine and DVD contained herein documenting the humanitarian projects carried on by other members of our group.

Erling had already informed Agent Nelson and the RCMP, Pierre Jeannette, that he possessed the samples prior to his arrest, and the RCMP interrogators following his arrest. He did so with the naive idea that law enforcement was sincerely there to enforce the law. This left him with no option but to plead guilty.

Following his release from prison, in a desperate effort to render Mr. Ingvaldsen into United States jurisdiction where he could be prosecuted and thus silenced with no international consequences, the government of Canada attempted to extra-judicially render him to US authorities by "losing" his US Passport which would allow them to deliver him to the US border, into the waiting arms of the United States Marshals.

Only by good fortune in the form of an honest Embassy employee was Mr. Ingvaldsen able to acquire a replacement passport allowing him to depart Canada by way of commercial air carrier.

In the event that this Commission may consider recommending that Mr. Ingvaldsen should return to the US, we must point out that he was indicted in the US in 1981 by the use of a search warrant gained by documented false police testimony, and convicted on evidence which was documented to belong to another person, (See Affidavit, Exhibit XIII) then sentenced on documented non-existent material evidence.

We do not wish to retry that case as the inclusion of the transcripts and affidavits here would be too voluminous, and we hope, unnecessary for the Commission to arrive at a just course of action. But in 1981 Mr. Ingvaldsen had first discovered a drug trafficking operation involving United States government officials. When these officials learned of his discovery all hell was visited upon him.

Now with this Canadian conviction Mr. Ingvaldsen is faced with a violation of court ordered probation in the US while the US Department of Justice is fighting for its life to affect the arrest of Mr. Ingvaldsen, while also violating international extradition treaties by refusing to turn Agent Nelson over to the Canadian authorities. We believe that the foregoing makes it clear to the Commission that if Erling were to be rendered to the US without the Court Ordered written permission he would be in violation of a US Federal Court Order and would have to serve fourteen years in prison for that violation.

Additionally, it is our experience, as in the 1981 conviction, that if Erling were to return to the US he would be falsely charged in connection with the Canada-US smuggling operation that he was directed by officials of the Department of Justice to expose which would have thereby absolved Agent Nelson and RCMP officials of their complicity. It would be unrealistic to expect fair treatment if Mr. Ingvaldsen were to be brought before the Department of Justice while the Department is violating human rights and international treaties in an effort to protect itself and its agents from being exposed in crimes on a scale that have no precedence.

Our argument is that officials of the Government of Canada used their office to conspire with officials of the United States to fabricate a crime and arrest Mr. Ingvaldsen. The RCMP created the crime. Again, the motives are many, but essentially if Mr. Ingvaldsen were allowed to continue unfettered he would have exposed what has to be the most egregious abuse of governmental power known in recent times. A minimum of independent investigation would show that this nearly one-hundred billion dollar industry is used to fill the bank accounts of political families, fund the election of their political servants, and monetarily reward local law enforcement officials who zealotly pursue arrests at the expense of every civil and human right we hold dear.

At this time Mr. Ingvaldsen is living in an undisclosed country, as he has none of his own. He was born in Norway and later assumed US Citizenship. (See copy of his Norwegian Birth Certificate in the Exhibits)

We feel that a written complaint alone is insufficient to adequately describe two governments so severely out of control. Therefore we ask the Commission on Human Rights to invite us to orally present clarifications, testimonies, documents, and recordings in support of this Complaint.

Our immediate requests being:

The Commission to urge the government of Canada to revisit this conviction of Erling Ingvaldsen, which triggered his Violation of Supervision in the US.

The Commission to urge the government of Norway to reinstate his Citizenship in the country of origin to live the remainder of his days in peace.

The Commission to direct the Government of Canada to aggressively seek the extradition of FBI Special Agent Terry Nelson to Canadian jurisdiction.

His Reference to One of my Many Sources

Going back to Gene Tatum, whose activities I wrote about in the other two books, *Defrauding America* and *Drugging America*, the following is a letter that Tatum wrote to the Montana Senate Judicial Committee in 1997, because the matters involved drug smuggling from Canada into Montana, especially on Indian land. As is standard practice in the United States, nothing was done to address the matter.

March 22, 1997

Montana Senate Judiciary Committee
Montana Senate
State Capitol
Helena, Montana 59602

RE: Senate Bill 255

Dear Ladies and Gentlemen of the Committee:

I am an ex-intelligence operative. I have served agencies and organizations which include the CIA, DIA, NSA, and NSC. I have direct information relating to a substantial amount of narcotics trafficking into Montana involving Colombian cartel members and others.

During the course of my duties, I met with Agent Terry Nelson of the FBI in South Florida, who was also "tasked" to the Crises Pre-Planning Group (CPPG) and Operational Sub-Group (OSG). As an operative for the OSG, I was taken into Agent Nelson's confidence concerning operations along the US/Canadian border which included the smuggling of drugs into your state.

This operation was planned and executed by a Canadian National named Mike Huxtable, a Colombian drug lord named Fabio Ochoa, and FBI Agent Terry Nelson. Together they affected the movement of multi-ton shipments of cocaine and heroin from an airstrip located south of Weyburn, Saskatchewan, Canada to a series of landing strips and drop-zones in Montana, including Chinook, Sidney, and Havre. Nelson boasted of his ability to recruit local law enforcement and state officials in Montana and North Dakota. These officials were recruited to assist in the smuggling operations, thinking that they were part of a government-sanctioned covert operation.

I am currently serving a twenty-seven month federal sentence at Jesup Federal Prison Camp in Jesup, Georgia, for failure to disclose ownership in a firm subcontracting to the FDIC (Title 18 § 1007). If you wish to contact me, you can do so either directly or through my attorney. (Attachment 1)

I hope this information will be of assistance to you and your committee.

Yours Truly,

/s/ Dois Gene "Chip" Tatum

DOJ Retaliation Against Whistleblowers

In my various books I describe the standard practice of how people in control of the U.S. Department of Justice misuse the power of the office to retaliate against and silence those who expose corruption in government. A few of the victims are described briefly here.

Ronald H. Rewald, a CIA operative, installed as head of the CIA proprietary known as Bishop, Baldwin, Rewald, Dillingham & Wong (BBRDW), with its home office in Honolulu. In the mid-1980s, its cover was blown by a Honolulu television reporter. To divert attention from it being a CIA operation, CIA and Justice Department officials falsely charged Rewald with operating a phony financial operation. With the cooperation of a federal judge, he was denied legal representation by famed attorney Melvin Belli, denied the right to introduce CIA documents, and given a court-appointed attorney just out of law school who had never handled any type of case. Rewald was then sentenced to a long prison term. His story is told in the books, *Disavow: A CIA Saga of Betrayal*, and in *Explosive Secrets of Covert CIA Companies*.

Michael Riconosciuto was a former CIA operative who was directly involved in highly sensitive CIA and Justice Department activities, including October Surprise and Inslaw. Justice Department personnel, including Peter Videnieks, threatened to retaliate against Riconosciuto and his wife if he testified before Congress on the Inslaw matter. Riconosciuto testified, and he was subsequently charged with manufacturing amphetamines and given a long prison sentence. Details in my book, *Defrauding America.*

Richard Brenneke had been a CIA contract agent for many years and was involved in numerous CIA operations, including October Surprise, arms and drug trafficking. Justice Department officials charged him with perjury after he testified in a 1988 U.S. district court hearing on behalf of another CIA operative, Heinrich Rupp. They had both been CIA contract agents, and both said that they had seen vice presidential nominee George Bush and Donald Gregg in Paris in October 1980 for the October Surprise meeting.

Heinrich Rupp, a long time CIA contract agent and pilot, flew a Unocal Gulfsteam from New York to Paris as part of the October Surprise operation. He was charged by Justice Department officials with fraud relating to the covert CIA Aurora Bank in Colorado.

John Cole was sentenced to federal prison in 1992 after he had reported to the FBI and U.S. Attorney in Illinois details of criminal activities that he had discovered while in management with Granite City Steel. This steel company was involved with a group of other companies, some of which were CIA proprietaries, including unlawful arms shipments overseas, drug trafficking, and which included FBI and Justice Department personnel, CIA officials, Japanese Mafia figures, among others.

Lester Coleman fled the United States after the FBI arrested him on trumped up charges of passport irregularities. Coleman posed a danger of exposing CIA and DEA drug trafficking, its link to Pan Am Flight 103, and the stolen PROMIS software. His statements contradicted U.S. claims that Libya was responsible for placing the bomb on Flight 103, rather than terrorists for Iran and Syria.

And many more who are named in my various books.

FBI-DOJ Retaliating to Hide Drug Smuggling Problems

Two former customs inspectors at that same location, John Carman, and Darlene Fitzgerald, among other government insiders, had told me for years of the protection of certain drug smugglers by high government officials. Both had left government because of the corruption they discovered. Carman had a web site, www.customscorruption.com, describing the corruption that he and other Customs agents had discovered as part of their official duties.

Using the power of the Department of Justice, in 2007 the U.S. attorney in San Diego filed sham charges against Carman, basing the charges on a deported Mexican. To deny Carman the opportunity to help with his defense, which included access to his personal material, and appearances on radio shows, the U.S. attorney and federal judges denied bail to Carman, greatly reducing his ability to defend himself and expose the corruption.

The U.S. attorney in Sacramento, California, David Levi, had filed sham charges against me in the late 1980s seeking to halt my efforts to expose the corruption. In an attempt to report the corruption that I and a group of other former government agents had discovered, and blocked by members of Congress and others from receiving our evidence, I filled a lawsuit in the federal courts at Sacramento under the provisions of the federal crime reporting statute, Title 18 U.S.C. § 4.

That statute requires that anyone who knows of a federal crime must report it to a "federal judge or other federal official" or be guilty of a crime. After I filled papers to report the corruption, the federal prosecutor, assisted by several federal judges, charged me with criminal contempt of court, denied me a jury trial, and sentenced me at 67 years of age to six months in prison. The corruption we sought to report were thee same areas of corruption that made 9/11 and a long series of earlier preventable aviation disasters possible.

Levi was later rewarded, being appointed U.S. district judge at Sacramento.

More in an Endless Series of Crimes Involving FBI-DOJ Personnel

While the DeVecchio matter was unfolding, there appeared the following *Associated Press* article (November 6, 2008) relating to murders involving *another* FBI agent from the Boston FBI office:

> Miami jury convicts ex-FBI agent in 1982 killing
>
> Former FBI agent John Connolly was convicted Thursday of second-degree murder for leaking information to Boston mobsters that led to the 1982 shooting death of a gambling executive who also had ties to gangsters. He faces a maximum of life in prison when sentenced Dec. 4. Testimony indicated that former World Jai-Alai president John Callahan was killed after Connolly warned gangsters that Callahan might implicate them in other slayings. Boston mob kingpins James "Whitey" Bulger and Stephen "The Rifleman" Flemmi were FBI informants handled by Connolly.
>
> Connolly was convicted in 2002 of racketeering because of his corrupt relationship with Bulger and Flemmi, including a 1995 tip that enabled Bulger to escape arrest and begin a life on the run that continues to this day. Bulger is one of the FBI's "Ten Most Wanted" fugitives, with a $2 million bounty for his capture. Connolly, who retired from the FBI in 1990,

was paid $235,000 in cash delivered in envelopes over the years by Bulger and Flemmi and even took vacations with Bulger, according to trial testimony. [Doesn't say much for FBI investigation!] Jurors were instructed by the judge that Connolly—who was hundreds of miles away in Boston at the time—did not have to pull the trigger himself or even be present at the crime scene to be convicted in Callahan's killing.

Connolly is already serving a 10-year federal prison sentence in the corruption case. He was indicted in 2005 in Miami for the killing of Callahan, 45, whose body was found stuffed in the trunk of his Cadillac at Miami International Airport in August 1982. He had been shot at least twice.

Confessed mob hit man John Martorano testified that he shot Callahan—at one time a good friend—based on Connolly's warning that the gangsters would probably all go to prison if Callahan talked to the FBI about an Oklahoma businessman's killing a year earlier. Flemmi, Martorano and other mob figures testified that Connolly made sure the gang was shielded from prosecution for numerous crimes, even multiple murders, and supplied information about possible turncoats or "rats" in their own ranks that needed elimination. Prosecutors said at least two other men who were FBI informants died violently because of Connolly's leaks.

Callahan was killed, according to testimony, because Connolly told them the FBI was about to apply pressure on Callahan to give up information about the 1981 killing of World Jai-Alai owner Robert Wheeler in the parking lot of a country club in Tulsa, Oklahoma. The gangsters feared Callahan would not hold up and might confess to the FBI that they were responsible for Wheeler's slaying. Callahan had wanted Wheeler dead so that he could retake control of World Jai-Alai.

Flemmi is serving a life prison sentence and admitted to 10 murders. Martorano cut a deal with prosecutors by agreeing to testify against Connolly, and spent 12 years in prison after admitting to 20 murders, including the killings of Wheeler and Callahan. Martorano is now a free man.

"John Connolly swore an oath to the FBI and the United States of America," said prosecutor Michael Von Zamft. "He gave up that public trust because he decided he would rather be a gangster than an FBI agent."

"Unless we catch Whitey Bulger, this marks the end of what is really a sad chapter for federal law enforcement," said Fred Wyshak, an assistant U.S. attorney from Boston who helped prosecute the Florida case. "It's been a long haul."

Bulger was finally captured on June 22, 2011, in Santa Monica, California, along with his girlfriend, Catherine Greig. The capture was brought about by information from neighbors where they were living in an apartment.

Greig pled guilty to harboring a fugitive and in June 2012 sentenced to eight years in prison. Bulger was charged with multiple murders and scheduled for trial.

CHAPTER TWENTY FOUR

DOJ Cover-Ups, Retaliation, And Series of Aviation Disasters

The corrupt activities of Department of Justice personnel described here and my other books had adverse effects in other areas, including airline travel. In *History of Aviation Disasters: 1950 to 9/11*, and *Lockerbie to 9/11, Massive Fraud and Consequences*, I detail and document the relationship between that corruption and a series of airline disasters, including the hijackings of four airliners on September 11, 2001. Airline crash or airline disaster are sterile words; what we are talking about is horror beyond description, of people being dismembered alive, or cremated alive, with indescribable horror and the financial and personal suffering of those left behind.

I have documented in letters and in court filings, since the mid-1960s, the cover-ups, the retaliation against me, by DOJ personnel, covering up for what I discovered during my professional and official duties, and the crashes and deaths that followed these arrogant and corrupt actions.

While I was a federal air safety inspector in one of the most crash-plagued and corrupt areas of aviation during a time when airline disasters were occurring seemingly every few months, I was given the assignment to correct the conditions that at that time were resulting in the worst series of airline disasters in the nation's history.

The safety problems were easily recognizable. And as in so many other government agencies, the corrective measures were blocked by higher management for various reasons in the politics of aviation safety. I, and other inspectors, who attempted to report and correct the problems were blocked, and even received retaliation for attempting to report and correct the problems that were resulting in a continuing series of crashes and deaths.

Reporting the corruption to higher management, to members of Congress, to media people, encountered a stone wall. Because of the gravity of the consequences, I used the law in such a manner that I acted as an independent prosecutor for several months, conducting hearings, subpoenaing witnesses, and eliciting testimony during court-like proceedings. During the hearings, there were three additional fatal airline crashes, each one caused by the very same problems that I had reported, for which corrective actions were blocked. The hearing resulted in the standard cover-up, causing me to leave government service.

The crashes continued and worsened. Being the only one with the evidence and the willingness to attempt to correct the problems, I felt an obligation to do something. The first thing I did was to file several lawsuits in the period from 1979 to 1982 against the Federal Aviation Administration (FAA) and the National Transportation Safety Board (NTSB).

Federal statutes provide certain opportunities and certain responsibilities relating to these problems. The federal crime reporting statute[44] *requires* that anyone who knows of a federal crime must report it to a federal judge or other federal officer, or be guilty of misprision of a felony. Another federal statute[45] provides to anyone the right to file a federal action seeking an order to force a federal official to perform a mandatory duty and to halt unlawful conduct. The main goal was to make a formal record of the charges and assume that the charges would receive publicity and require Congress and the DOJ to address the matters.

In the 1980s I filed federal actions[46] under these statutes in the U.S. district courts at San Francisco. The first block were U.S. attorneys, who filed motions to dismiss, thereby blocking the reporting of the federal crimes. They had known of these criminal activities from when I was a government agent, and blocked corrective actions.

In the actions against the FAA and NTSB, the district court, and then the appellate court judges, they expressed sympathy with my filings but held that this was a responsibility for Congress. It *was* a congressional responsibility to take action, but the clear wording of the statutes also required federal judges to receive the information as part of the judges' mandatory administrative, not judicial, duties.

---

[44] Title 18 USC § 4. Misprision of felony. Whoever, having knowledge of the actual commission of a felony cognizable by a court of the United States, conceals and does not as soon as possible make known the same to some judge or other person in civil or military authority under the United States, shall be fined under this title or imprisoned not more than three years, or both.

[45] Title 28 U.S.C. § 1361. Action to compel an officer of the United States to perform his duty.

[46] *Stich v. United States, et al.*, 554 F.2d 1070 (9th Cir.) (table), *cert. denied*, 434 U.S. 920 (1977)(addressed hard-core air safety misconduct, violations of federal air safety laws, threats against government inspectors not to report safety violations and misconduct); *Stich v. National Transportation Safety Board,* 685 F.2d 446 (9th Cir.)(table), *cert. denied*, 459 U.S. 861 (1982))(addressed repeated criminal falsification of official airline accident reports, omitting highly sensitive air safety misconduct, making possible repeated crashes from the same sequestered problems); Amicus curiae brief filed on July 17, 1975, in the Paris DC-10 multi-district litigation, *Flanagan v. McDonnell Douglas Corporation and United States of America*, Civil Action 74-808-PH, MDL 172, Central District California.)(addressing the long standing FAA misconduct, of which the cover-up of the DC-10 cargo door problem was one of repeated instances of tragedy related misconduct); U.S. v. Department of Justice, District of Columbia, Nos. 86-2523, 87-2214, and other actions filed by Stich seeking to expose and correct the powerful and covert air disaster misconduct.

By blocking the reports, the conditions continued, and so did the crashes and deaths. DOJ personnel, and federal judges, were then complicit in the end results.

I then sought to circumvent the latest blocks by publishing the first of many books in 1978, being the first edition of *Unfriendly Skies*. After the book was published, I started appearing as guest and expert on hundreds of radio and television shows, seeking to inform and motivate the public to help address these serious problems.

Further Discoveries and Further Attempts To Report Areas of Criminal Activities

As a result of considerable publicity arising from the publication of the *Unfriendly Skies* book and my radio and television appearances, other government insiders started contacting me, providing me information and evidence of criminal activities that were in different areas for government. These sources included agents of the CIA, ONI, DEA, FBI, and other government offices, former drug smugglers (working with government personnel), and former Mafia figures. The information provided the basis for *Defrauding America* and *Drugging America*, which went into multiple editions.

Just as I tried to do with the aviation-related corruption, I attempted to report these other criminal activities to members of Congress, Justice Department personnel, and media people. But the block was just the same.

At the same time, a CIA-front law firm, Friedman, Sloan and Ross, in San Francisco, filed a bizarre and unlawful lawsuit against me that immediately tied up all my assets, the ones that funded my exposure activities. (Details in *History of Aviation Disasters: 1950 to 9/11*.) Despite the fact that the lawsuit violated many California statutes and case law, and violated federal civil and constitutional rights, California judges openly violated these protections and repeatedly protected the CIA-front law firm. I would later discover that this was one of several parallel efforts, using lawyers, to halt my exposure actions. From 1982 to 2005, over 50 lawyers and law firms were involved in these tactics against me.

Lawsuit Combining Reporting Federal Crimes With Defenses Against the Massive Civil and Constitutional Violations

I then exercised my responsibilities under the federal crime reporting statute, 18 U.S.C. § 4, my right as a citizen under 28 U.S.C. § 1361, and the multiple federal defenses seeking to halt the harm from the civil rights violations. That action was filed in the federal courts at Sacramento, California.

Again, the U.S. attorney filed a motion to block my action. U.S. District Judge Milton Schwartz at first expressed concern over the gravity of my charges. But then, a week later, violating the requirement for a hearing, issued an order dismissing the action, which blocked the reporting of the criminal activities and also blocked the federal defenses.

As I was learning about the October Surprise operation and CIA drug smuggling from other government agents, I again sought to report these matters to a federal judge under the federal crime reporting statute, Title 18 U.S.C. § 4.

Charged with Criminal Contempt of Court For Reporting Trojan Horse Crimes Against the United States

In response to my lawsuits, U.S. Attorney David Levi charged me with criminal contempt of court and sought to have me incarcerated for 18 months. I was denied a jury trial, judged guilty, and sentenced to six months in federal prison. In the process, I encountered several attorneys, one of whom I paid $30,000 to defend me and whom sabotaged my defenses and protected the prosecutor and the judge, and the CIA-front law firm.

Denial of Constitutional Right to a Jury Trial

Under the Sixth and Seventh Amendments, a person is entitled to a jury trial, and also a trial before a fair and impartial jury. But federal judges have ignored this constitutional protection for years, and held in federal decisions that this constitutional right does not apply if incarceration does not exceed six months. Federal judges euphemistically call this long incarceration a "petty" crime. There is nothing petty about six months in prison, while one's business, his properties, his home, his assets, and maybe his family, are lost.

Rampant Constitutional Violations

Abandoned by my attorneys, I filed my own motion for rehearing. In the motion for rehearing that I filed in pro se status, I raised numerous defenses, none of which attorney Pegg had raised. Included in my written arguments were the following statements:

1. It was not a criminal act to exercise the constitutionally guaranteed right to court access; to exercise constitutional and statutory remedies seeking relief from the terminal destruction of my personal and property rights that were perpetrated through a pattern of violations of federally protected rights.

2. I could not be imprisoned for exercising moral and legal responsibilities to report federal air safety and criminal violations that were causing or permitting brutal air disasters and deaths to occur. On the contrary, I would have been guilty of federal crimes, including misprision of felonies, if I had not reported them as I did via the federal lawsuits. The same crime attaches to anyone else who knew of the criminal acts and did not report them to the proper authorities, including federal judges, Justice Department attorneys, and Magistrate Moulds.

3. The injunctive order, which I allegedly violated by filing the subsequent lawsuits was unlawful and unconstitutional, and outside the authority or jurisdiction of any federal judge. There is no authority anywhere permitting a federal judge to void fundamental constitutional rights, to void federal laws, guaranteeing federal court access, providing for declaratory and injunctive relief. And certainly not when the party seeking relief is suffering terminal de-

struction of human rights, of personal and property rights, from a pattern of record-numbers of violations of federally protected rights.

4. The injunctive order reversed the legal criteria for rendering such orders. Federal law permitting injunctive orders requires that the orders protect the party suffering great and irreparable harm, which was me. But the injunctive order rendered by Judge Schwartz protected those inflicting the harms, while concurrently voiding the constitutional and statutory remedies upon which I filed for relief.

5. Dismissal of the underlying action, upon which Judge Schwartz sought to "support" the reason for the injunctive order, violated federal case law barring dismissal if federal causes of action are alleged. And many were alleged.

6. The injunctive order sought support by placing a frivolous label upon the underlying lawsuit (Nr. 86-0210 MLS); implying that my actions were frivolous; and that I must therefore be barred court access. But the legal criteria under federal law for a frivolous action is that it must have no arguable merits. My allegations of hard-core federal air safety and criminal acts certainly raised federal issues, requiring that I be allowed to testify and present supporting evidence. The allegations of civil and constitutional violations stated specific facts, specific law that was violated, and serious harms inflicted upon me. These are multiple federal causes of action under declaratory and injunctive relief provisions of federal laws. Further, federal case law requires that the allegations in a complaint be recognized as true. Therefore, the frivolous label was unlawful and unconstitutional; the dismissal was likewise; and the support for the injunctive order vanished.

7. Case law provides that a person cannot be charged with criminal contempt for exercising a right that would otherwise be lost. If the federal actions had not been filed, I would have lost the right to try to protect myself from the pattern of violations of federally protected rights. Preventing the consequences of the federal air safety and criminal violations would be lost, including lives that would be lost, people who would be, and were, maimed.

8. A person cannot be charged with a crime for exercising constitutionally guaranteed rights to court access, and rights provided by statutes legislated by Congress. A federal judge has no authority to suspend the rights and protections under the Constitution and laws of the United States, or to force a person to suffer terminal destruction of human rights recognized in other free countries.

9. A federal judge cannot force a person to be a silent witness to federal air safety and criminal violations and the related air tragedies.

10. The denial of a jury trial violated the written stipulation providing for a jury.

11. The constitutional right to a fair and unbiased tribunal was violated when a jury trial was denied, forcing me to appear in a proceeding where I was prosecuted and tried by those threatened by my exposure activities.

12. A party cannot be punished for contempt when the injunctive order is on appeal. Judge Schwartz himself admitted he had no jurisdiction to hold me in contempt while the injunctive order was on appeal. (The Solano County legal counsel sought to have me held in civil contempt for filing the federal action.)

During a November 13, 1987, hearing, Judge Schwartz, who rendered the May 30, 1986, injunctive order, held that my appeal of the injunctive deprived the court of jurisdiction to hold me in contempt.

> This court lacks jurisdiction to entertain the motion for contempt since the underlying judgment in this case rendered by this Court is currently on appeal. The Ninth Circuit follows the general rule with some exceptions not relevant here, that the filing of a proper and timely notice of appeal divests the district court of jurisdiction over those matters that are not on appeal or subject to the appeal.

Unlawful and Unconstitutional Injunctive Order

If an order is beyond the power of the court, such as suspending civil and constitutional rights and protections under federal and constitutional law, the order is void, and the court has no right in law to punish for any contempt of its unauthorized requirements. One of the first Supreme Court decisions addressing void orders was *Ex parte Rowland.*[47] A void order carries no authority and a person cannot be punished for either deliberately or accidentally violating it, according to well-settled law.

A judgment which is void upon its face, and which requires only an inspection of the judgment roll to demonstrate its wants of vitality is a dead limb upon the judicial tree, which should be lopped off, if the power to do so exists. *People v. Greene*, 71 Cal. 100 [16 Pac. 197, 5 Am. St. Rep. 448].

In *Bache v. Wallace*, 102 Minn. 169 [112 N.W. 366], the court said: "Proceedings outside the authority of the court, or in violation or contravention of statutory prohibitions, whether the court has jurisdiction of the parties and subject matter of the action or proceedings, or not, are utterly void. The court continued:

It has been held that the mere fact that the court has jurisdiction of the subject matter of an action does not justify an exercise of a power not authorized by law, or a grant of relief to one of the parties the law declares shall not be granted ... Although every exercise of power not possessed by a court will not necessarily render its action a nullity, it is clear that every final act, in the form

---

[47] (1882) 104 U.S. 604, 26 L.Ed. 861.

of a judgment or decree, granting relief the law declares shall not be granted, is void, even when collaterally called in question.

The case of *Ritchie v. Seyers*, cited in *Michael v. Williams* (Id. at 200) involved a collateral attack on a judgment, wherein the rule was brought under attack that the judgment of a court having jurisdiction of the parties and the subject matter of the action, cannot be collaterally attacked. The court stated of the rule:

> That may be conceded, but the question is, did it have jurisdiction to enter the particular decree and judgment that it did enter? As we have seen, we reach the conclusion that the particular judgment could be entered, and it is a well settled principle that, although a court may have jurisdiction of a case, yet, if it appears from the record that it did not have jurisdiction to enter the particular decree and judgment, it may be collaterally attacked."
>
> The *Michael* court held that the trial court was without authority to enter a judgment that was prohibited by law, even though it had personal and subject matter jurisdiction.

That motion was denied, and I was set up to start my prison sentence. I was being sentenced to prison for attempting to report criminal activities that I initially discovered during my official duties as a government agent, and criminal activities that were resulting in a continuing series of airline disasters.

Unindicted Felons in the Supreme Court?

I was then ordered to turn myself in on January 14, 1988. I had to act fast. Over the Christmas holidays I prepared a petition to Ninth Circuit Court of Appeals Justice Anthony Kennedy (before he became a Justice of the United States Supreme Court). I worked feverishly on Christmas day to finish the petition for submission to Kennedy the following Monday.

Kennedy had testified at great lengths during his televised Senate confirmation hearing for appointment to the Supreme Court, expressing concerns for due process, equal protection of the law, respect for privacy. Kennedy uttered all the right statements, implying his support of the laws and constitution of the United States, which were now outrageously violated, while simultaneously sacrificing lives in the underlying air safety scandal. Surely Kennedy would provide relief. Ha!

Supreme Court Nominee Engaging in Defrauding America

Judge Anthony Kennedy was already involved in the corruption that made prior air tragedies possible. Kennedy was on the appellate panel that heard my appeal of the district court's dismissal of the 1974 federal action against the Federal Aviation Administration. Kennedy knew the consequences of cover-up in a series of related airline tragedies.

Seeking to silence me, federal judges issued orders permanently barring me from filing any papers in any federal district or appellate court, which not only violated my responsibility under the federal crime reporting statute, but also violated my civil and constitutional protections stated in the laws and the Constitution of the United states.

In 1986, discovering other corrupt and criminal activities involving government personnel, I again exercised my responsibilities and my rights as a citizen. Federal prosecutors, at the urging of federal judges, charged me with criminal contempt of court for filing an action under the federal crime reporting statute,[48] seeking to report to a federal judge the corruption in government offices that I and a group of other former government agents had discovered.

Federal judges denied me a jury trial and held I was guilty, and sentenced me to six months in federal prison. I filed a petition for emergency relief with Judge Anthony Kennedy at San Francisco, as he was waiting to be appointed to the U.S. Supreme Court. He denied the emergency request, supporting the termination of my civil and constitutional rights and supporting the obstruction of justice tactics by federal judges and the U.S. attorney at Sacramento, California.

Seeking Help from Congress

While I was in prison I wrote letters to Senators Alan Cranston (Majority Whip from California); John McCain (Arizona); Banking Committee Chairman Donald Riegle, Jr. (Michigan); Government Affairs Committee Chairman John Glenn (Ohio); Dennis DeConcini (Arizona). These five, later called the "Keating-Five" in the savings and loan scandal, engaged in felony misprision of felonies, felony cover-ups. Senator Sam Nunn wrote (July 6, 1988), thanking me for the information on government corruption and related air tragedies, and then did nothing.

The U.S. attorney filing the action against me, David Levi, was later appointed to the position of U.S. District Judge at Sacramento. The details and the arrogance are far worse than there is space available to describe in this book.

People Primarily Responsible for Preventing Airline Hijackings

The people responsible for ordering procedures to prevent airliners from being hijacked were the people in the government's aviation safety offices, and primarily the Federal Aviation Administration (FAA). That is the agency in which I discovered and documented years of corruption that caused or enabled to occur many of the airline disasters that were occurring regularly in the United States. The people responsible for taking actions to prevent carrying out the hijacking scheme were the people in the FBI-DOJ, and to a smaller extent, people in the CIA.

---

[48] Title 18 U.S.C. § 4.

The corruption in the FAA is a matter of record, and the two books that contain this insider information are *History of Aviation Disasters: 1950 to 9/11.* Since this book focuses on the crimes of people in the FBI-DOJ, and to a smaller extent, people in judicial positions, I will limit this chapter to those two groups.

Starting in 1965, I reported to people in various divisions of the Department of Justice the corruption that I discovered as part of my official duties that were related to a series of ongoing airline disasters. These people included U.S. attorneys, FBI agents, and DOJ Washington officials, including FBI Director J. Edgar Hoover. Not only did they repeatedly block the reporting of the deadly criminal activities, but also, they actually charged me with criminal attempt for reporting the crimes. The information provided prior to this chapter should make that culture easy to believe.

Last Judicial Attempt to Prevent 9/11 Hijackings

Shortly *before* September 11, 2001, I made one last attempt to report the corruption in government offices that I and a group of other government agents had discovered. That attempt put the Department of Justice *again* on notice of the corrupt activities. I filed a lawsuit in the federal district court at Reno, Nevada. U.S. district court judge James Reed, Jr. blocked me from reporting the criminal activities that he was required to receive as part of his mandatory administrative duties under the federal crime reporting statute, Title 18 U.S.C. § 4. That was a criminal act for which DOJ prosecutors should have filed charges.

Before Judge Reed dismissed the lawsuit, the hijacking of four airliners occurred. I then filed a declaration in that lawsuit (January 22, 2004) reporting in greater detail the corruption in the FAA that repeatedly prevented the federal government from carrying out its air safety responsibilities. The declaration also showed the corruption in the FBI and other Department of Justice offices that prevented agents from acting on the evidence of the planned hijacking scheme. By then, there were so many people in high government positions that were implicated in deadly cover-ups that the only action could be continued cover-up.

***Post 9/11* Attempts to Report Criminal Activities That Had Blowback Consequences on 9/11**

My first attempt *after* 9/11 to report the criminal activities that had direct responsibility for the conditions enabling terrorists to hijack four airliners on 9/11 occurred with a federal court filing in the U.S. district court in Washington, D.C. I felt that a federal judge wouldn't dare to continue the obstruction of justice tactic where one of the hijacked airliners had crashed; the Pentagon. Further, media sources routinely look at papers filed in the federal courts, and surely, I thought, *they* would give publicity to such a filing made by a former federal aviation safety agent.

At first, the court refused to file the Complaint.[49] They wrote on the lawsuit that they returned to me that I was barred for the remainder of my life from filing any papers in any federal court by an order (September 21, 1991) signed by U.S. District Judge Stanley Sporkin, former legal counsel for the CIA.

That order violated due process and constitutional protections, and violated federal criminal statutes by barring me from reporting federal crimes under the federal crime reporting statute.[50]

I then sent letters to the Supreme Court justices advising them of the *latest* attempt by federal judges blocking me from reporting criminal activities and exercising due process remedies. The complaint was then filed[51] on June 12, 2002, and assigned to district judge Henry H. Kennedy, Jr.

Continuation of Judicial Obstruction of Justice

Kennedy promptly dismissed the filing without notice, thereby violating numerous due process rights and also the requirement to receive evidence of alleged criminal activities. That made his dismissal a federal crime related to obstruction of justice.

I then filed a notice of appeal and filed an appellate brief[52] on December 9, 2002. Appellate judges Douglas H. Ginsburg, David B. Sentelle, and R. Raymond Randolph refused to act on the brief, dismissing the appeal without any hearing, extending the criminal and civil rights violations. Again, gross violations of civil and constitutional due process laws and the federal crime reporting statute were approved.

They also sought support in their action by referring to a judicial order rendered twelve years earlier, in 1991, by judge Stanley Sporkin, the former legal counsel for the CIA. That order dismissed a prior lawsuit seeking to report the criminal activities that I and a group of other government agents had discovered, and then compounded the judicial misconduct by ordering that I be permanently barred from filing any papers in the federal courts.

Second Most Powerful Court Engaging in Obstruction Of Justice with Links to Series of Resulting Tragedies

I then filed a motion for rehearing en banc—where every other judge in the powerful District of Columbia appellate court had to take an action: either uphold the criminal and civil violations or cover up for them, which would be the basis for their impeachment.

That unlawful and unconstitutional order by Sporkin—that blocked the reporting of criminal activities—was upheld en banc by the other appellate judges. Considering that the District of Columbia appellate judges are the most powerful appellate judges in the United States, below the U.S. Supreme Court,

[49] U.S. District court, District of Columbia, Nr. 1:02CV001172

[50] Federal crime reporting statute, Title 18 U.S.C. § 4.

[51] U.S. district court, District of Columbia, 1:02CV01172.

[52] District of Columbia Appeal, No. 02-5240.

it didn't say much for the status of integrity and honesty in the federal courts. These filings put many people on notice of the corruption that was continuing, and that would continue the long series of continuing consequences.

Filing Papers in Federal Courts at 9/11 Disaster Site

Most of the lawsuits filed by families of the 9/11 victims were filed in the U.S. district courts in Manhattan, within blocks of where the World Trade Center tragedies occurred. And that is where I then filed papers seeking to report the culture of corruption that played key roles in the catastrophic events. Those papers were received by the court for filing on August 8, 2002. By law, those papers, which were in order and the filing fee paid, must be filed the same day they were received.

Judge Michael Mukasey Blocked the Filing for 13 Months

In clear violation of federal filing requirements, and the criminal statute requiring federal judges to receive information and evidence of federal crimes, the filing was blocked for 13 months by Chief Judge Michael Mukasey. It was finally filed[53] on September 22, 2003, *after* I sent letters to each of the justices of the U.S. Supreme Court complaining about the obstruction of justice and gross due process violations.

Judge Mukasey then filed the complaint, but within minutes he filed a five-page order dismissing it. Preparing that order required weeks of data gathering, meaning that he was acting to block the report of criminal activities long before the lawsuit was filed.

That sua sponte dismissal, without notice and right to be heard, violated due process requirements, civil and constitutional rights, and violated criminal statutes associated with reporting federal crimes and obstruction of justice.

In accordance with the law, I filed a notice of appeal. That appeal put the judges of the federal appellate court in New York City on record of being informed about the serious charges. In response to the notice of appeal, a scheduling order was issued requiring the U.S. attorney and me to file briefs and then appear for oral arguments.

Blocking the Filing of Explosive Brief

I submitted the appellant brief on January 5, 2004, which was received by the court on January 7, 2004. Again, its filing was unlawfully blocked. It wasn't until nearly a month later that it was filed, and only after I again wrote complaining letters. It was then backdated as if it had been filed in a timely manner.

Justice Department Lawyers Failed to File Their Brief

The scheduling order required the U.S. attorney to file their brief by February 12, 2004. If it had been filed, the Justice Department lawyers would have to

---

[53] U.S. district court, New York City, No. 03 CV 7405.

either continue the history of blocking reports of the culture of criminal acts, or admit their existence—and the history of related catastrophic ripple effects.

After a delay of almost two months, I filed a motion for an order requiring the U.S. attorney to file his brief, and for sanctions. The U.S. attorney *then* filed, with a series of false statements. I followed with a Reply Brief. After receiving our briefs, the court scheduled oral argument for August 24, 2004.

Oral Argument in Court of Appeals, New York City

I appeared and presented oral argument before the three appellate panel judges, Jose A. Cabranes; Chester J. Straub, and Richard C. Wesley. In New York City, oral arguments before the court of appeals are very formal, more so than on the West Coast. I noticed that with the lawyers presenting oral argument *before* I appeared, the judges rarely looked at the speaker. In my case, I noticed that all three judges constantly had their eye on me, causing me to wonder why. The following was my oral argument:

> Good morning, I am the appellant in this appeal, appearing in pro se, and my name is Rodney Stich. In the ten minutes allotted, Appellant will attempt to show the close relationship between the latest due process and civil violations with the continuing attempts to block Appellant, a former federal agent, from reporting criminal activities that he and a group of other former government agents discovered.
>
> These reports were being made under the mandatory requirements of the federal crime reporting statute, Title 18 USC Section 4. Appellant first discovered certain of these federal crimes after he was given the assignment to correct the conditions responsible for the worst series of airline crashes in the nation's history.
>
> Among the multiple federal causes of actions stated in Appellant's complaint, and the issues brought to this court, are the following:
>
> Under the federal crime reporting statute, Appellant has attempted to report to a federal judge the criminal activities against the United States, under the mandatory requirements of the federal crime reporting statute, Title 18 USC Section 4. Every attempt to report these deadly activities had been blocked, and the latest block was done in the lower court.
>
> Two of the federal causes of actions arise under the Supreme Court's void judgment doctrine.
>
> Federal judges have issued a series of unlawful and unconstitutional orders forever barring Appellant from filing any papers in the federal district and appellate courts.
>
> The effect and intent of these orders were to block Appellant from reporting the criminal activities to a federal court, and to block Appellant from exercising the federal defenses needed to halt the ongoing massive violations of state and federal laws that were part of the legal schemes to halt his exposure activities.

These orders violate the due process and equal protection guarantees of the Constitution, and deprive Appellant the defenses guaranteed by the laws and Constitution of the United States. At this time, anyone can perpetrate any violation upon Appellant through sham legal actions and Appellant cannot exercise the defenses in the laws and Constitution of the United States.

After the first of these unlawful orders were rendered in the Ninth Circuit courts, Appellant discovered additional criminal activities. As required by the federal crime reporting statute, and granted by federal rights, Appellant sought to report these criminal activities, and also exercised federal defenses seeking to h alt the great and irreparable personal and financial harm he was suffering from the violations of federally protected rights.

A U.S. attorney and federal judges then retaliated against Appellant for attempting to report these criminal activities and for exercising defenses guaranteed to all citizens by the laws and Constitution of the United States. Appellant was denied a jury trial and sentenced to six months in federal prison.

While in prison, federal judges rendered unlawful and unconstitutional orders seizing and liquidating Appellant's $10 million in assets that Appellant foolishly used to fund his exposure activities.

These orders were combined with an order barring Appellant from filing any objections. When Appellant exercised his legal and constitutional right to object to the seizure of his life assets, a federal judge charged him with criminal contempt of court for having exercised that legal and constitutional right, denied him a jury trial, and sentenced him again to federal prison.

Several tactics were used to block appellant from reporting the criminal activities, and to block Appellant from exercising federal defenses.

Every action was dismissed at the pleading stage, often sua sponte dismissals, and always during the initial filing stages.

Seeking to justify the dismissals, the standard practice was to reverse the legal and common sense definition of frivolous and call Appellant's filings frivolous. Exercising federal remedies for the most outrageous, and record-setting violations of state and federal laws, a frivolous label was promptly placed.

A classic example; in a lawsuit filed by a CIA-front law firm, the violations of state and federal laws that barred the action included (a) over 36 California and federal statutes; (b) over a dozen rules of court; (c) several landmark Supreme Court decisions; (d) major constitutional protections, for which federal defenses existed for any one of these violations under the Civil Rights Act and the Declaratory Judgment Act. Appellant was suffering great and irreparable financial and personal harm from the violations.

Despite all this, federal judges repeatedly placed a frivolous label on Appellant's exercise of federal defenses.

Federal judges blocked every due process protection, barring appellant from having the federal claims adjudicated on their merits. Instead, every action was given a frivolous label and dismissed.

Judge Mukasey enlarged upon this tactic, falsely stating in his sua sponte dismissal order that each of the claims had been adjudicated on the merits; that they were found to be without merit; that Appellant was a vexatious litigant filing frivolous actions.

Included in the relief sought from this appellate court are the following:

Order that permits appellant and his group of other former government agents to provide information, testimony, and evidence, of the criminal activities that they discovered during their official duties.

An Order holding the series of permanent injunctions unlawful, unconstitutional, and void, returning to Appellant the same due process and equal protection rights guaranteed to everyone else.

Order holding that the unlawful and unconstitutional orders seizing and liquidating appellant's life assets are void, and that the title and possession of the properties be returned to the status that they were in when they were ordered seized.

Simply returning this case to the lower courts would be the equivalent of continuing the same tactics. The only remedy Appellant knows is for this court to provide an adequate federal court forum for Appellant and several other former government agents to provide information, testimony and evidence.

Since the massive due process and civil violations were an integral part of the felony obstruction of justice actions, this court should adjudicate on the merits the causes of actions under the Civil Rights Act, Bivens, RICO, Declaratory Judgment Act, and Federal Tort Claims Act.

In closing, appellant makes the following statement to show how this misconduct appellant had caused, and enabled to be inflicted, catastrophic harm upon the United States, with heavy loss of life. The blowback is only one day's consequences, and in only one of the areas affected by the corruption that Appellant and other government agents sought to report, were the conditions that enabled terrorists to seize hijack four airliners on 9/11:

The hijackings of four airliners on 9/11 were primarily aviation disasters. The need and the means to prevent airliner hijackings have been known for years. The authority and responsibility to order these preventive measures existed throughout this period by people in certain government aviation safety offices.

Deep-seated corruption and criminal misconduct existed in certain areas of the government's aviation safety offices that prevented the government from carrying out its federal aviation safety responsibilities. That includes blocking the known preventative measures against airliner hijackings.

The areas of primary blame enabling terrorists to hijack four airliners on 9/11 were with the people in the government's aviation safety offices engaged in the corruption and criminal activities; those people, some of whom are referred to in Appellant's present and prior complaints, blocked Appellant from reporting the criminal activities. The people who retaliated against Appellant for attempting to report the criminal activities; Those involved in the legal actions that were dual efforts to halt Appellant's exposure activities; Those who knew of the criminal activities, or knew of the obstruction of justice and failed to halt these obstruction of justice activities.

Responsibilities of Federal Appellate Judges

The law clearly states that appellate judges must examine the Complaint filed in the district court de novo (from the beginning), and must accept the allegations stated in the complaint as true for opposing dismissal. If a single federal cause of action is stated in the complaint, the dismissal by the lower court judge must be reversed.

Appellate Judges Continued the Obstruction of Justice And Concurrent Due Process Violations

It took the Appellate panel only two days to issue an order upholding the district court's blocking of reports of criminal activities, and the related procedural and substantive violations related to my claims arising out of the legal actions seeking to halt my exposure activities.

I did not expect the three appellate court judges to be so brazen in continuing the obstruction of justice in matters that killed nearly 3,000 people a few blocks away. I had anticipated that the court of appeal judges would send the case back to the district court, where various legal tactics would continue to stonewall me, with eventual dismissal. In a way, I was getting tired of it all, and didn't care one way or the other.

Petition for Rehearing En Banc

I then submitted for filing on September 7, 2004, a petition for rehearing en banc to the court of appeals in New York City. Such a petition requires that every judge in the Second Circuit Court of Appeals receive a copy of the petition for rehearing and enter a decision as to whether they will hear the case.

The Entire Second Circuit Court of Appeals Became Complicit

The entire judicial staff of the Second Circuit Court of Appeals then refused to grant a rehearing, thereby approving the obstruction of justice and serious judicial misconduct. They added their names to the long list of federal judges complicit in some of the worst tragedies affecting the United States, and becoming complicit in subsequent tragedies arising from the misconduct.

Supreme Court Nominee Complicit in Deadly Conspiracy

Among the appellate judges who received my petition for rehearing, and approved the conduct of the district judge, was federal appellate judge Samuel Alito. By upholding the criminal obstruction of justice and the misuse of judicial positions and the federal courts, Alito became part of a conspiracy that had inflicted great harm to the United States and would continue to do so.

However, since 1978, the Supreme Court Justices received my various appeals (petition for writ of certiorari), and knew of the obstruction of justice and the civil and constitutional violations by judges over whom they had supervisory responsibilities. They became, and they are, complicit in these offenses, and in the many catastrophic consequences.

Mukasey's Earlier Conduct Continued as Attorney General

Judge Mukasey retired shortly after blocking me from reporting the criminal activities that I had sought, one last time, to report. Shortly thereafter, President George W. Bush nominated him to become the U.S. Attorney General. I submitted a letter to every member of the Senate judiciary committee reporting on Mukasey's prior block to reporting the serious criminal activities that constituted felonies. A copy of one of the letters follows:

From the desk of Rodney Stich
P.O. Box 5, Alamo, CA 94507; phone: 925-944-1930; FAX 925-295-1203
Author of numerous books including Unfriendly Skies: 20th & 21st Century
E-mail: stich@defraudingamerica.com Google.com search engine: "Rodney Stich"
Web sites: www.defraudingamerica.com

September 18, 2007

Senator Patrick J. Leahy, Chairman
Senate Judiciary Committee
United States Senate
Washington, DC 20515 FAX: 202-224-3479

To Senator Leahy:

As head of the Senate Judiciary Committee, holding hearings on retired U.S. District Judge Michael Mukasey to be the attorney general of the United States, I bring the following matters to your attention concerning the serious violations perpetrated by Mukasey that will have serious impact upon the United States:

Documented obstruction of justice by Judge Michael Mukasey

In 2002, I attempted, as a former federal agent, to report to a federal judge the criminal activities that I and a group of other former federal agents had discovered during our official duties. These federal offenses have had disastrous consequences for the United States and many individual victims. This lawsuit was filed under the mandatory requirements of the federal crime reporting statute, Title 18 U.S.C. § 4, and the statute that permits any citizen to seek a court order requiring a federal official to perform a mandatory duty and to halt unlawful conduct; Title 28 U.S.C. § 1961. Although various national issues were involved, the lawsuit focused primarily upon the misconduct that was responsible for the conditions that enabled four groups of terrorists to hijack four airliners on September 11, 2001.

Despite the lawful requirement of that lawsuit being filed upon receipt in the office of the federal courts in Manhattan, the filing of that action was blocked for over 12 months. It was not filed until after I wrote letters to each of the Justices of the U.S. Supreme Court advising them of the latest obstruction of justice action by federal judges over whom they had supervisory responsibility. That filing was blocked by U.S. District Judge Michael Mukasey.

Federal law requires that any federal judge to whom a person wishes to report a federal crime must receive that information as part of the judge's administrative (not judicial) duties. Obviously, blocking such reports would be a criminal act.

Among the federal crimes that I sought to report were those that I had initially discovered as a federal aviation safety agent and which had been responsible over the years for certain airline disasters. The ripple effects of these federal offenses were probably responsible for the conditions that enabled terrorists to hijack four airliners on 9/11. A cover-up of these wrongful acts would obviously continue the deadly consequences.

I and my group of former government agents (FBI, CIA, DEA, and others) also sought to report federal offenses perpetrated by personnel in the FBI and CIA, and which would help to explain why management in these two agencies did not respond to the evidence of the hijacking scheme that was carried out on 9/11.

Involved with the federal offenses that made 9/11 possible was the pattern of massive civil and constitutional violations involving federal judges and others, all of which were intended to halt my efforts to expose these tragedy-related corrupt activities against the United States. Judge Mukasey was aware of these civil and constitutional violations and expanded on them. He violated the legal and constitutional right to file that action.

After the lawsuit was finally filed, within minutes of that filing, Judge Mukasey issued a multi-page dismissal order that had to have taken several weeks to prepare. He not only blocked the filing of that lawsuit reporting serious and deadly federal crimes, but also engaged in a scheme to violate the due process right to such filing. That due process right was combined with criminal obstruction of justice.

Mukasey surely knew of the many people who had perished in fraud-related airline crashes made possible by the misconduct, and knew of the nearly 3,000 deaths on 9/11 that were ripple effects of the crimes. And these were only the consequences that affected the aviation environment, without addressing the other areas in which the American people suffered serious consequences. He surely knew that his conduct would enable the corruption and the consequences to continue.

You therefore have a responsibility to examine the government documents proving the truth of what I have stated, and cannot cavalierly ignore this letter. But now, you have a problem. I notified you several years ago, by certified letters, of Mukasey's obstruction of justice tactics. I even contacted you by letter prior to the 9/11 hijackings concerning the corruption, the aviation and other tragedies, and the obstruction of justice by other federal judges. These letters were dated January 29, 2001; February 20, 2001; September 5, 2002; and October 7, 2002. You didn't respond to any of them, despite the gravity of the matters. If you had responded to the letters sent prior to 9/11, it is possible that corrective actions could have been taken, at least in the government's aviation safety offices where the primary blame for the conditions existed that enabled the four airliners to be hijacked.

You might say I am qualified to make such statements: My 60 years in aviation includes Navy Patrol Plane Commander in World War II; airline captain for many years; a government air safety inspector-investigator for several years, during which I acted similar to an independent prosecutor, conducting hearings that proved that deep-seated corruption in the Federal Aviation Administration (FAA) created the conditions that enabled certain fatal airline disasters to occur.

You can find copies of those letters that I sent to you, including those describing Mukasey's obstruction of justice, at

www.defraudingamerica.com/mukasey_nomination.html, and also under another site: www.defraudingamerica.com/letter_list_congress.html. Also, in two of my books: Blowback, 9/11, and Cover-Ups; and Unfriendly Skies: 20th & 21st Centuries. You do have company in covering up for corrupt activities that have inflicted grave harm upon a gullible American public.

Sincerely,

Rodney Stich

cc:

Senator Diane Feinstein	Fax: 202-228-3954
Sen. Hillary Clinton	Fax: 202-228-0282
Senator Barbara Boxer	Fax: 415-956-6701
Sen. Harry Reid	Fax: 202-224-7327

After Mukasey became Attorney General, he continued the tactics. A *New York Times* article (December 16, 2007), titled, "Court Inquiry on Tape Case Is Opposed," and stated:

> The Justice Department has urged a federal judge not to hold a hearing on the Central Intelligence Agency's destruction of videotaped interrogations of two suspected Al Qaeda operatives, saying a judicial inquiry "is both unnecessary and potentially disruptive."
>
> The Justice Department on Friday angered members of Congress of both parties by saying the administration would not cooperate with planned inquiries into the tapes' destruction until the department and the C.I.A. completed their preliminary investigation to determine whether laws were broken

The hundreds of hours of tapes, destroyed in November 2005, showed the interrogations of two men identified as members of Al Qaeda: Abu Zubaydah and Abd al-Rahim al-Nashiri. Only Abu Zubaydah is cited in the government's filing, which says the judge's preservation order of June 2005 does not apply to him.

A *New York Times* article (December 20, 2007) referring to U.S. Attorney General Michael Mukasey, titled, "Mukasey Signs He'll Be a Strong Bush Advocate," stated:

Attorney General Michael B. Mukasey has signaled in his first weeks on the job that he intends to be a forceful advocate for some of President Bush's most controversial anti-terrorism policies, even if that means angering Congressional leaders who hoped that he would instead focus on repairing the strained relationship between the Justice Department and Capitol Hill.

He stepped up the call for telephone utilities to have legal immunity for their past cooperation with the eavesdropping without warrants by the National Security Agency.

In recent days, Mr. Mukasey has also upset Congressional Democrats by saying he would refuse to share information about the Justice Department's investigation of the Central Intelligence Agency's destruction of tapes of the interrogations of top figures of Al Qaeda.

Mr. Mukasey wrote in a letter to the Senate Judiciary Committee last week that he was only following tradition in declining to reveal "nonpublic" information to Congress about a potential criminal investigation. He also rebuffed early calls from Congress for the appointment of a special prosecutor in the inquiry.

Senator Patrick J. Leahy, who is chairman of the panel, said that the letter "evidences none of the commitment to work with this committee that we heard during the attorney general's recent confirmation hearings" and that it showed "no appreciation for the oversight rule of Congress."

Mr. Leahy said he feared that the attorney general, who took office on Nov. 9, as already part of "an effort to prevent accountability and to undermine checks and balances. [I had sent Leahy two letters during Mukasey's confirmation process showing Mukasey's obstruction of justice while Mukasey was Chief Judge of the Second Circuit in New York City.]

Almost Relieved That the Judicial Efforts Were Over

After so many years of trying, and so many years of massive cover-ups, plus the failure of the public who knew of my charges from my books and radio-TV appearances, I had enough. I figured that since so many numbers of members of Congress, and media people, supported that misconduct by remaining silent, and when so many people who either heard me on the 3,000-plus radio and TV shows or read my books didn't offer any help, I figured they deserve what they helped bring about.

Dramatic Consequences If the People Understood

The same behind-the-scene corruption enabling the earlier United Airlines crash into New York City created the conditions enabling the two airline disasters a mile away on September 11, 2001. Is it any wonder that there is the need for a cover-up, and placing the blame instead on the innocent failure to act on known intelligence!

Ripple Effects of FBI-DOJ Culture On the Downing of TWA Flight 800

FBI ADIC James Kallstrom was put in charge of the investigation into the crash of TWA Flight 800, and immediately stated it appeared to be a crime scene. Under law, the National Transportation Safety Board (NTSB) has sole responsibility to investigate airline crashes and this responsibility cannot be taken over by another government agency. But the FBI stepped in. U.S. Attorney Valerie Caproni told NTSB investigators that they were not to conduct any interviews and that they would be limited to reviewing documents supplied by the FBI, and that no copies could be made. Kallstrom's initial statements to the media were that it was a crime scene and therefore the FBI was taking responsibility away from the NTSB.

Kallstrom, aware of the information given by Yousef to Scarpa Jr., told Scarpa's attorney, Larry Silverman, that he considered the information obtain by Scarpa very valuable. According to author Peter Lance in his book, *Cover Up*, Kallstrom told Silverman that the information obtained by Scarpa was very valuable and said, "Don't let Scarpa stop now."

Private Investigators Provided Evidence That the 9/11 Commission Ignored

In an April 5, 2004, letter to the chairman of the 9/11 Commission, former Senator Lee Hamilton, Stephen P. Dresch of the Forensic Intelligence International sought to circumvent the DOJ cover-ups related to the advanced warning of terrorist acts that FBI personnel ignored that Gregory Scarpa Jr. provided to them:

Re: Pre-September 2001 FBI and Dept. of Justice Intelligence on Terrorism (R. Yousef)

Dear Chairman Kean and Vice Chairman Hamilton:

Our monitoring of the Commission's hearings indicates that significant intelligence concerning the terrorist threat to the United States obtained between

1996 and early 2001 by various components of the U.S. Department of Justice has **not** been provided to the Commission.

This intelligence was provided to agents of the New York office of the FBI and senior prosecutors with the offices of the U.S. Attorneys for the Southern and Eastern Districts of New York by an informant, Gregory Scarpa, Jr., who developed a close personal relationship with Ramzi Ahmed Yousef while Yousef and Scarpa were incarcerated at the Metropolitan Correctional Center (MCC) in New York in 1996 and 1997, with supplemental information provided in 2000 by Scarpa to an official of the U.S. Bureau of Prisons after he was transferred to the Administrative Maximum Security (ADMAX) Penitentiary in Florence Colorado, to which Yousef had already been transferred and where both currently remain. In early 2001 another inmate of Florence ADMAX attempted to transmit much of the information developed by Scarpa to the director of the FBI, the President of the United States and the Attorney General.[1]

We first became aware of this intelligence when, for purposes entirely unrelated to terrorism, we met with Scarpa at Florence ADMAX in March 2003. In the course of these meetings Scarpa provided to us his contemporaneous (1996-97) handwritten notes of his conversations with Yousef and his terrorist codefendants[2] and copies of FBI Forms 302 (informant reports) recounting the information which he had provided to agents of the FBI.[3]

1 We cannot, of course, confirm that these mailings, made by Gerard Van Hoorelbeke, in fact left the prison or reached their intended recipients. Van Hoorelbeke remains incarcerated at Florence ADMAX (Reg. No. 10376-029).

2 Scarpa reported conversations with Yousef and with Yousef's codefendants, Wali Khan Amin Shah, Abdul Hakim Murad and Eyad Ismoil. Many of these conversations referenced a person identified by the terrorists as "Bojinga," whom we believe to be Osama Bin Laden.

During his incarceration at the MCC, Scarpa was regularly debriefed by an agent of the FBI who, using the alias "Susan Schwartz," posed as a paralegal employed by Scarpa's attorney, Larry J. Silverman. In addition to these reports, Scarpa, utilizing a mini-camera provided by the warden of the MCC, provided the FBI with photographs of documents ("kites") which Yousef shared with him. Also, with the assistance of Scarpa (acting on behalf of the FBI) Yousef was able to make telephone calls, monitored by the FBI, to active (unincarcerated) members of his terrorist networks via a "patch-through" phone accessed from MCC.

The intelligence provided by Scarpa included specific threats to U.S. airlines, the identification of countries (e.g., England) through which terrorists were entering the United States and testing

U.S. security procedures, instructions for smuggling explosive chemicals and detonators (including hiding these in the heels of shoes), and formulas for explosives and for the production of phosgene and mustard gases. Yousef revealed to Scarpa his strong interest in obtaining blank

U.S. passports which "his people would only use for one trip to board the planes to be hijacked." Further intelligence laid out a plan to videotape the killings of hijacking victims, with distribution of these tapes to the media.[4]

One very serious missed opportunity to disrupt a terrorist network here in the United States prior to September 11, 2001, involved Yousef's agreement to meeting in New York between Scarpa's associates (who would have been disguised FBI agents) and four active (unincarcerated) terrorists. This meeting never took place because the cognizant FBI agents and assistant U.S. attorneys refused to agree to Yousef's demand that $3,000 be provided to the terrorists.

It should be noted that Scarpa provided this assistance to the FBI at considerable risk not only to himself but also to members of his family, whose address he was compelled to provide to Yousef to enhance his credibility.

We have identified the following officials as having been directly involved with Scarpa in his role as an informant, as summarized in the attached "Scarpa-Yousef Intelligence Timeline":[5]

New York Office of the FBI

Susan Schwartz (alias)
Pat White
James Kallstrom

U.S. Attorneys' Offices

AUSA Michael Garcia (EDNY)
AUSA Patrick Fitzgerald (EDNY)
AUSA Valerie Caproni (EDNY)
U.S. Attorney Mary Jo White (SDNY)

Metropolitan Correctional Center (New York)

Warden R.M. Reish

Administrative Maximum Secuity Penitentiary, Florence, Colorado

Mr. Manly (SIS)

4 Scarpa's intelligence anticipates "shoe bomber" Richard Reed, the authorization for the 9/11 attacks given by Yousef's uncle, Kahlid Shaikh Mohammed, Mohammed Atta's and Al Qaeda's English connections, the single-use passports employed to board the airplanes hijacked on 9/11, and the videotaped death in Pakistan of Wall Street Journal reporter Daniel Pearl.

5 The office of the U.S. Attorney for the Eastern District of New York was initially informed of Scarpa's contacts with Yousef at the MCC and his willingness to serve as an informant by his attorney, Larry J. Silverman (46 Trinity Place, New York 10006; 212-425-1616), who remained informed of Scarpa's activities on behalf of the government.

Although the information provided by Scarpa appears to have been fully documented, especially in Forms 302 prepared by the New York office of the FBI, we do not know if this information was disseminated to other agencies with responsibility for the prevention of terrorist attacks on the United States.

We understand that AUSA Patrick Fitzgerald (EDNY), in a later (sealed) court filing, attested to the credibility, accuracy and value of the terrorism intelligence provided by Scarpa. However, at the time of Scarpa's sentencing AUSA Valerie Caproni denigrated Scarpa's credibility as an informant. Apparently, Scarpa's credibility was perceived to pose a threat in the context of serious questions which had been raised concerning the informant relationship of Scarpa's father, Gregory Scarpa, Sr., with FBI Supervisory Special Agent R. Lindley DeVecchio, the revelation of which might place in jeopardy a number of convictions secured by the office of the U.S. Attorney (EDNY). This latter matter, entirely unrelated to terrorism, remains a subject of continuing, independent investigation.

We strongly advise that the Commission fully examine the terrorism intelligence secured by the government through the informant services of Gregory Scarpa, Jr., and assess the extent to which it was appropriately utilized to reduce the terrorist threat to the United States.

Respectfully submitted,

Angela Clemente — Stephen P. Dresch, Ph.D.
Santrea_143.2@juno.com — 706-294-9993

Principal witness: Gregory Scarpa, Jr. Reg. No. 10099-050 ADX
P.O. Box 8500 5880 State Highway 67 South Florence, Colorado 81226
719-784-9464

Attachment: Scarpa-Yousef Intelligence Timeline

Attachment Prepared by Angela Clemente

In this document, "Scarpa" is Gregory Scarpa, Jr. (USBoP Reg. No. 10099-050) and "Yousef" is Ramzi Ahmed Yousef (USBoP Reg. No. 03911-000). Documentation confirming the entries is noted following the date. Documentation includes:

FBI Forms 302 (informant reports)

Scarpa's contemporaneous handwritten notes (originals provided to us in March 2003)

Photos taken with the mini-camera provided by Warden Reish (MCC) Entries for which no source is cited derive from personal interviews conducted with Scarpa at Florence ADMAX in March 2003 and from subsequent telephone interviews. Because neither we nor Scarpa have had access to the full FBI file, FBI Forms 302, photographs and other documentation may exist which provide corroboration for undocumented entries and for other significant intelligence provided by Scarpa.

Approx. February 20, 1996 (Handwritten) (Initiation of Scarpa's contact with Ramzi Yousef at MCC) Yousef began speaking to Scarpa about hurting the judge on his case or other federal judges, prosecutors, or a U.S. ambassador. Yousef stated that he had four of his people in the United States and they are working on and waiting for others. Yousef stated that if he and Scarpa worked together he would show Scarpa secret formulas, chemical mixes and gases that would be able to poison the water in large areas of New York, federal buildings, and courts. Yousef also stated that he would teach him the methods of how to blow up an airplane.

February 27, 1996 (Handwritten) Yousef told Scarpa he would teach him how to make bombs, smuggle them through x-ray machines, assemble the bombs, and how and where to place it in the airplane. Yousef told Scarpa if his people could get military detonators then he would go through teaching him the steps of making massive bombs.

February 29, 1996 (Handwritten) Yousef told Scarpa about three steps for bombing U.S. Airliners:

How to make hydrogen peroxide [sic]
How to make timer devices
How to smuggle the device and assemble it in the airplane

Yousef requested $3,000 for the third step. Yousef spoke of letting Scarpa make contact with the individual terrorists who were here in the United States and on their way to the United States.

March 26, 1996 (Handwritten) Scarpa gave his daughter Maria's address to Ismoil. Ismoil told Scarpa that Yousef was going to hurt someone on his case to cause a mistrial and that he had this person's address. Scarpa tried to discourage him and said that front addresses are used and Scarpa offered Ismoil that he would get the correct address for Yousef.

March 27, 1996 (Handwritten) Yousef later said that Scarpa taught him something new he didn't know that they used "front" addresses and thanked him, then sent Scarpa a kite with AUSA Garcia's name on it.

March 28, 1996 (Handwritten) (Before mini-camera had been provided to Scarpa) Yousef asked Scarpa to have his people (meaning Scarpa's alleged militia group) kill FBI witness Dave Williams and in return he wouldn't have to send him the monies or become a Muslim. Yousef also spoke about teaching Scarpa smuggling techniques and how to blow up airplanes.

[Scarpa reports that the FBI first took him seriously when he reported threats on AUSA Garcia and FBI SA Williams. It was at this point that the mini-camera was provided.]

March 29, 1996 (Handwritten; mini-camera provided and photo taken of this information) Scarpa asked for the name again or whatever information he (Yousef) had on the guy and Yousef gave him a paper with the main FBI witness from Washington. Photo taken of this information.

Approximately April 4 or 12, 1996 (Handwritten; photo taken with mini-camera) Scarpa asked Yousef if he gave him the correct name because his people said there was no such name. Yousef sent a paper back with AUSA Garcia's full name. In addition, Yousef stated that he was sending someone to check on security measures in Atlanta.

April 17, 1996 (Handwritten) Yousef stated to Scarpa that the person who will be sent by Bojinga to see the security measures will be coming from England, otherwise they would attract attention. Immigration is tougher on people coming from Arabic countries than those coming from Europe. Yousef wanted Scarpa's people to either kill FBI Williams or do an attack on a government installation and Yousef wanted to be informed ahead of time because he hasn't seen anything happen yet by Scarpa's people.

April 22, 1996 (Handwritten) $500.00 was placed into Yousef's account. It took approximately 2 1/2 months to release it out of MCC. Approximately two weeks later after the money was released TWA Flight 800 went down in New York.

April 24, 1996 (Handwritten) Yousef questioned Scarpa about a 3-way call. At some point a 3-way call was made out of MCC.

May 1, 1996 302 (Handwritten) Yousef asking about 3-way calling again he said he communicates to Bojinga sometimes through calling his sister and talking in a coded way. Yousef said his sister tells her husband who then passes messages on to Bojinga. Yousef said that he used to receive letters from Bojinga through his paralegal but didn't feel comfortable.

May 7, 1996 (Handwritten) Yousef came back from court. He said that AUSA Garcia was smirking. Yousef said, "This guy's lost his life for sure."

May 8, 1996 (Handwritten; photo shot with mini-camera) Yousef told Scarpa about Marad seeing FBI and Prosecutors about cooperating indicating "a game" saying, "these people are crazy." FBI Susan Schwartz wanted to know who showed Scarpa on paper how to make timing devices and bombs. Scarpa thought about it and thought that it might have been Marad.

May 13, 1996 (Handwritten) Yousef spoke of a person (no name given) that gave up Shah and others. Yousef stated that he sent a coded message to Bojinga and informed him about the guy and that he lives in Qatar. Yousef thought he'd be killed soon. He was not recruited initially by FBI but instead another intelligence agency. He was recruited from a club in his country where he used to hang out. Yousef suggested to Bojinga to attack the U.S. Embassy in Qutar.

May 17, 1996 (Handwritten) A 3-way call took place at 9:45 pm and one on May 16th at 9:10 pm. (Picture shot with mini-camera) Yousef was upset. He had a visit with his attorney and said that the government knew about his tampering with the evidence (taking two ID cards, etc). The judge wouldn't let the information in.

May 19, 1996 (Handwritten) Yousef told Scarpa that he advised his people to start the bombing of airplanes. He told his people that it was to be done by sending a parcel bomb by DHL or any other U.S. Cargo company from Dubai in United Arab Emirates. In addition, if any U.S. airplane should blow up then its origin departure point would be from Dubai. Yousef said it may happen and it may not depend on security measures taken in the cargo offices.

May 19, 1996 (Handwritten) Yousef gave a very detailed paper on how to smuggle explosives into an airplane. He referenced RDX explosives and 747 airliners. He gave detailed information on the weights of explosives and flying heights of airplanes and the types of explosives to be used as well as where they should be placed in the airplane. He detailed smuggling procedures for explosives in the heels of shoes, medicine capsules, baby powder containers, and how TNT- Tetryl can be melted and shaped into a soap or candle. He gave this information two months before TWA Flight 800 went down in New York killing 230 passengers. TWA Flight 800 was a 747 and RDX explosives were found on the remnants of the crash. This flight was not considered a terrorist act.

Month of June papers are all missing from Scarpa's file and no materials are in my possession for June's FBI 302's. On June 22, 1996 I have one document

(Handwritten) stating that Yousef told Scarpa that his people were checking the security measures in Atlanta and then they were on their way back to New York. He further stated that nothing could be done over there (meaning Atlanta). He also said that he would stop the plane explosion for now because his trial was going well and didn't want anything to "dirty up" his trial.

July 2, 1996 (FBI 302, date investigated June 29, 1996) Yousef spoke of Bojinga doing the bombing in Saudi Arabia. Yousef stated that he was originally sent on that mission to check the security measures and that tanker truck was discussed.

[Downing of TWA Flight 800]

July 17, 1996 (FBI 302) TWA Flight 800 crashed killing 230 passengers off Long Island, New York. Yousef asked to use the telephone the night of July 17, 1996 he also had a visit with his attorney until 10:00 pm and still requested use of the telephone which was denied.

July 18, 1996 (FBI 302) Jerry Koupakis a former U.S. Customs Agent that was corrupt told Scarpa that he told his father not to travel TWA or American Airlines on the morning of July 18, 1996. Yousef told him this information prior to July 18, 1996.

July 23/24, 1996 (FBI 302 & Handwritten) Ismoil told Scarpa, "I told you this is going to happen." He was also referencing a conversation Scarpa and he had months prior where Ismoil said that "nothing would be left of New York just give it some time."

July 28, 1996 (FBI 302 & Handwritten) Yousef was questioned by Scarpa about the Atlantic Park bombing. Yousef said that his friends left Atlanta to come to New York.

August 5, 1996 (FBI 302, investigation occurred July 28, 1996) Yousef refused to speak about the TWA Flight 800 because he was afraid that the government would link him to it.

August 7, 1996 (FBI 302 & Handwritten w/o date) Yousef spoke of knowing the address of a U.S. Ambassador from the Philippines. His name was something like Neoponti. In addition, Yousef told Scarpa that he placed his blood on two Casio watches, which were in evidence. He placed blood over the bands of the two watches to show he was tortured and wanted to request to bring in a blood expert. He said no one saw blood on the watches and he's told no one about it.

August 26, 1996 (FBI 302) Scarpa suggested to the FBI that Bin Laden is Bojinga because of the money and his location.

August 28, 1996 (FBI 302) Ismoil stated to Scarpa that Yousef has the brains but Shah has friends all over the country and they will be freed one way or another.

September 4, 1996 (FBI 302 & Handwritten) Yousef wanted $4,000 sent by Scarpa to an address overseas. He said he would then have that money forwarded to his (Yousef's) people here in the United States.

September 7, 1996 (Handwritten) Yousef was upset about tight security on AUSA Garcia and stated that two weeks prior to the trial ending Garcia was seen going to court without anyone near him.

September 8, 1996 (Handwritten) Yousef spoke of hijacking more than one plane and it would be forced to land in either Afghanistan, Sudan, or Yemen. Yousef spoke of Scarpa getting passports for Bojinga. He said Bojinga would get an address for Yousef to send the passports to in Iran or Libya.

September 13, 1996 (FBI 302 & Handwritten) Yousef spoke of how he sent messages out through writing other inmates names and numbers on the envelopes then mailed them out, that way prison staff wouldn't know it was coming from him.

September 14, 1996 (FBI 302 on 9-19-96 & Handwritten) Yousef spoke to Scarpa about wanting to take a hijacked plane to Sudan, and building a temporary runway for the plane to land. Most of Bojinga's followers are in Sudan.

September 17, 1996 (Handwritten) Yousef spoke about sending two bags with cargo in two separate flights to blow up two U.S. airplanes.

September 19, 1996 (FBI 302, investigation on 9-15-96) Yousef said that Sudan has a lot of Bojinga followers. Afghanistan is under authority of Afghan leaders, which are held by Mujahidin. Shah used to work in shipping weapons for Bojinga from Afghanistan and other countries. Bojinga uses Afghanistan as a refuge from other countries looking for him. Muslim fighters have certain areas in those countries under their control in deserts and mountains with all kinds of weapons where no one will be able to reach them without being killed. Women and children would be sold to Muslim fighters in Algeria, Libya, and Sudan. Yousef also spoke again of a U.S. Ambassador by the name of Neoponti from the Philippines who is a target of a kidnapping.

December 8, 1996 (FBI 302 transcribed on 12-16-96) Yousef stated that Bojinga wanted 5 U.S. Passports with no picture or writing on them and one without any picture on it. Yousef advised that Bojinga's people would use all the passports for the hijacking and 1 as a sample to make others. Yousef further stated that the passports are for 1 trip to board the planes to be hijacked.

December 18, 1996 (FBI 302 & Handwritten) Yousef has been visited recently by a new Imam and Yousef and Imam have been speaking for an extended period of time in English and in Arabic.[1] Yousef spoke to Scarpa about an address he would give Scarpa in Iran where the blank passports would be sent and spoke of a way he communicates (sends and receives messages) to outside of the prison. Yousef also stated that the government would never go after Bin Laden because the government knows that within one week 12 U.S. planes would be blown up.

December 27, 1996 (Handwritten) Yousef spoke to Scarpa about getting the passports in a hurry. He wanted them within two days.

December 28, 1996 (FBI 302 & Handwritten) Yousef began bragging to Scarpa about a new formula for gas (Phosgene Cocl and Mustard) that he invented that could be used to harm thousands of people and all countries could use it and could be sold for lots of money and it's inexpensive and easy to use. Yousef advised that a gas mask with oxygen must be worn when making this formula. Yousef sent Scarpa a kite showing him how to make that gas with the equation and diagram. (Scarpa turned this information over to FBI Susan Schwartz)

December 29, 1996 (FBI 302 & Handwritten) Yousef stated that he decoded a message from Bojinga and told Scarpa that after his release (Yousef's release) he (Yousef) would contact Scarpa to meet with him either in Pakistan or Afghanistan. Then later he wanted to meet with Scarpa's people to train them in Guerilla warfare. Yousef wanted to make deals with Scarpa's people in selling counterfeit money, drugs, etc. If Yousef isn't released during the hijacking (because the government doesn't give into their demands then they will kill the passengers 1 by 1 and video tape it then release it to the media.) They would release one tape each week. Yousef also spoke of doing something to the Pakistani government or pertaining to the Pakistani government before the hijacking occurs. Yousef spoke of Afghanistan being isolated from the world and the U.S. government. Yousef also spoke of selling the pretty women passengers for as much as $10,000 per person. Yousef spoke of training all Muslim militants groups around the world about how to hijack planes.

December 29, 1996 (FBI 302) Yousef said they had a "alternative plan" however if it doesn't work they will proceed with the hijacking and demand the release of WTC and the "Sheiks" case defendants. Scarpa felt that Yousef might be getting his messages also through the newspaper.

Imam-The caliph who is successor to Muhammad as the leader of the Islamic community. On January 2001 the FAA issued a warning that terrorist might try to hijack or destroy American aircraft. On January 24, 2001, Italian authorities record an Islamic Imam discussing fake ID's for "The brothers going to America." (See book *1000 Years for Revenge* by Peter Lance)

January 10, 1997 (FBI 302 & Handwritten date also 1-15-97) Yousef showed Scarpa components of the way he sends and receives messages outside of the prison. It was a component equipped with a microphone, transmitter (walkman), electronic board, gas lighter. He showed Scarpa his voice on the radio. Yousef told Scarpa he sends and receives messages similar to Morse code. Yousef stated that he received his last message and said that "everything is a go."

Final Report

That information was kept out of the final report that was released to the public, along with my declarations as a former federal airline safety investigator and inspector. In that way, the 9/11 commissioners protected the large number of FBI-DOJ personnel whose misconduct made possible the series of forewarned terrorist attacks that killed about 3,000 people and set in motion two unwinnable wars.

In another book, I provide evidence of FBI agents planting evidence, bribing witnesses, and other crimes to shift attention from the actual parties responsible for placing the bomb on Pan Am Flight 103, and the catastrophic ripple effects from that culture. And the usual U.S. media cover-up: *Lockerbie to 9/11: Massive Fraud and Consequences*.

CHAPTER TWENTY FIVE

FBI-DOJ As a RICO Criminal Enterprise

Federal statutory and case law requirements for a group to be guilty of a RICO criminal enterprise is repeatedly met by the corruption that I have reported of the people and culture in the FBI and other Department of Justice offices, and as clearly shown within these pages. The following statutes and case law define a criminal racketeering enterprise, including a government body, courts, or judges.

Title 42 USC § 1961. Definition. As used in this chapter-(1) "racketeering activity" means:

(A) any act or threat involving ... relating to 1503 (relating to obstruction of justice), section 1510 (relating to obstruction of criminal investigations), section 1511 (relating to obstruction of State or local law enforcement), section 1951 (relating to interference with commerce, robbery or extortion), section 1952 (relating to racketeering, ...

Title 42 USC § 1962. Prohibited Activities.

(b) It shall be unlawful for any person through a pattern or racketeering activity or through collection of an unlawful debt to acquire or maintain, directly or indirectly, any interest in or control of any enterprise which is engaged in, or the activities of which affect, interstate or foreign commerce.

(c) It shall be unlawful for any person employed by or associated with any enterprise engaged in, or the activities of which affect, to conduct or participate, directly or indirectly, in the conduct of such enterprise's affairs through a pattern of racketeering activity or collection of unlawful debt.

(d) It shall be unlawful for any person to conspire to violate any of the provisions of subsections (a), (b), or (c) of this section. ...

Case Law:

In 1999, the U.S. Department of Justice filed charges against the major tobacco companies charging them with a racketeering enterprise based upon their repeated lies about the harm resulting from the use of their tobacco products. The charges were filed under the Racketeering Influenced & Corrupt Organizations Act (RICO). a federal judge in the District of Columbia issued a judgment on May 22, 2006, upholding the charges by the Department of Justice prosecutors. On May 22, 2009, the judges of the U.S. Court of Appeals in the District of Columbia upheld the lower court's ruling.

Referring to that appellate court ruling, an editorial in the *New York Times* (May 31, 2009) stated:

The unanimous ruling by three-judge panel of the United States Court of Appeals for the District of Columbia upheld major elements of a 2006 lower court decision that found big tobacco companies guilty of racketeering and fraud as part of a prolonged campaign to deceive and addict the public. The 1,742-page opinion, rendered by Judge Gladys Kessler, laid out in painstaking detail how the tobacco companies made false statements and suppressed evidence to deny or play down the addictive qualities and the adverse health effects of smoking.

Judge Kessler found that the companies manipulated the design of cigarettes to deliver addictive doses of nicotine, falsely denied that secondhand smoke caused diseases and falsely represented that light and low-tar cigarettes presented fewer health risks.

The appeals court not only upheld her decision as legally sound, it seemed deeply impressed by the "volumes of evidence" and "countless examples of deliberately false statements" underlying many of Judge Kessler's findings.

Case Law Defining Government Bodies as RICO Participants

Controlling case law holds that government bodies whose conduct meets the definitions as applied to non-government entities also applies to government bodies. That would include state judges, federal judges, and government agencies. A line of cases hold that <u>any</u> governmental agency, court, political office or the like could serve as a RICO "enterprise."

United States v. Thompson, 685 F.2d 993, 999 (6th Cir. 1982)(en banc) *cert. denied*, 459 U.S. 1072 (1983). Among the government units that have been held to be "enterprises" are offices of governors and state legislators, courts, court clerks' offices. See e.g., *United States v. Stratton*, 649 F.2d 1066, 1072-75 (5th Cir. 1981); *United States v. Clark*, 656 F.2d 1259, 1261-67 (8th Cir. 1981) Office of county judge); *United States v. Frumento*, 405 F. Supp. 23, 29-30 (E.D. Pa. 1975), *affd*, 563 F.2d 1083 (3d Cir. 1977). *cert, debued,* 434 U.S. 1072 (1978).

In referring to the RICO liability of government offices the court thought it inconceivable that "in considering the ever more widespread tentacles of organized crime in the nation's economic life, Congress intended to ignore an important aspect of the economy [simply] because it was state operated and state controlled ...." (563 F.2d at 1091.)

Accepting defendants' contentions would mean that "business organizations legitimately owned and operated by the states, even though their activities substantially affect interstate commerce, would be open game for racketeers. [The court refused] to believe that Congress had such 'tunnel-vision' when it enacted the racketeering statute or that it intended to exclude from the protective embrace of this broad statute, designed to curb organized crime, state operated commercial ventures engaged in interstate commerce, or other governmental agencies regulating commercial and utility operations affecting interstate commerce."

Decisions after *Frumento* expanded government activity to every conceivable government agency, court, or political office. *United States v. Thompson*, 669 F.2d 1143 (6th Cir), *revd* 685 F.2d 993 (6th Cir. 1982)(en banc), *cert. denied,* 459 U.S. 1072 (1983)

Judges and Their Courts as Criminal Racketeering Enterprises

In the case of *U.S. v. Harry O. Stratton,* the court defined a RICO enterprise that consisted of two Florida judges:

> The Court of Appeals held that: (1) the indictment properly alleged the "enterprise" to be Florida's Third Judicial Circuit, properly charged a single conspiracy, and properly alleged requisite connection to interstate commerce.
>
> A Florida state court judge—a man charged with upholding our nation's laws—together with his bailiff and two other individuals, has been convicted of converting his office into a nest of bribery and corruption.
>
> 1. Birds of a Feather?
>
> The indictment in this case at bar charges that each of nine defendants participated in "a pattern of racketeering activity" involving the "court and law enforcement system of the Third Judicial Circuit of the State of Florida," and that several of the defendants also obstructed justice and criminal investigations in an effort to cover up the racketeering activities. With a broad brush, the indictment paints a picture of unscrupulous state court judges surrounded by equally unscrupulous court employees, attorneys and citizens, all of whom engaged in the practice of buying and selling "justice."
>
> "To be convicted of conspiracy to violate RICO there must be proof that the individual, by his words or actions, objectively manifested an agreement to participate, directly or indirectly, in the affairs of the enterprise, through the commission of two or more predicate crimes." *United States v. Bright*, 630 F.2d 804, 834 (5th Cir. 1980); ...
>
> The agreements which were part of the alleged conspiracy, the "overt acts" in furtherance of the conspiracy, and the substantive racketeering offenses are all related in great detail. With painstaking particularity, the indictment makes it clear that the alleged conspiracy and substantive offenses centered around the Third Judicial Circuit as an arm of the Florida court system, and not as a mere "geographical designation" as argued by appellants. Moreover, the indictment alleges that the offenses were all part of a single scheme to use the Third Judicial Circuit for illicit profit-making activities and to cover up these illegal activities.

Count One of the indictment alleges that Florida judges Samuel S. Smith ("Smith") and William Arvel Drury ("Drury"), court bailiff Loy Zell Harrell ("Harrell"), public defender investigator Grover Lamar Lee ("Lee"), attorneys Terry R. McDavid ("McDavid") and Arthur K. Black ("Black"), and Florida residents William D. Riggs ("Riggs"), Harry O. Stratton ("Stratton"), and Conlon St. John Wilmott ("Wilmott"), conspired to participate in "a pattern of racketeering activity" involving Florida's Third Judicial Circuit in violation of the Racketeer Influenced and Corrupt Organizations Act (RICO), 18 U.S.C. § 1962(d).

Counts Three, Four, Five and Twelve charge Riggs with obstruction of justice for his attempt to cover up the racketeering conspiracy.

18 U.S.C.A. § 1510 (West Supp. 1981) provides: (a) Whoever willfully endeavors by means of bribery, misrepresentation, intimidation, or force or threats thereof to obstruct, delay or prevent the communication of information relating to a violation of any criminal statute of the United States by any person to a criminal investigator; or:

Whoever injures any person in his person or property on account of giving by such person or by any other person of any such information to any criminal investigator; or:

Whoever injures any person in his person or property on account of giving by such person or by any other person of any such information to any criminal investigator shall be fined not more than $5,000, or imprisoned not more than five years, or both. (b) As used in this section, the term "criminal investigator" means any individual duly authorized by a department, agency, or armed force of the United States to conduct or engage in investigations of or prosecutions for violations of the criminal laws of the United Sates.

The indictment in the case at bar properly alleged the RICO enterprise to be Florida's Third Judicial Circuit, properly charged a single conspiracy, and properly alleged the requisite connection to interstate commerce.

In another example, the case of *United States v. Bill R. Clark*,[54] the court also upheld a decision holding a court to be a criminal enterprise

The Court of Appeals held that: (1) office of country judge was an "enterprise" under the RICO Act, and (2) evidence was sufficient to support defendant's conviction for violating the Travel act.

[2] We are persuaded that the term "enterprise" as used in RICO includes governmental agencies or offices. Webster's Third New International Dictionary 757 (P. Grove ed. 1966), defines "enterprise" as (1) a plan or design for a venture or undertaking, (2) venture, undertaking, project, especially an undertaking that is difficult, complicated, or has a strong element

[54] U.S. Court of Appeals, Eight Circuit, No. 80-1978..

of risk, (3) a unit of economic organization or activity, especially a business organization, and … Congress defined "enterprise" to include "any individual, partnership, corporation, association, or other legal entity, and any union or group of individuals associated in fact although not a legal entity."

The statutory language does not differentiate between government or public "legal entities" and private "legal entities." A government agency or office is a "legal entity." [55]

[3] Thus, we conclude that the language of the statutory definition of "enterprise," in particular the term "legal entity," includes government agencies or offices.[56]

Because we have resolved the question whether a government agency or office can be a RICO "enterprise" on the basis of the language of the statute itself, we have no occasion to turn to other rules of statutory construction. Or legislative history. Our conclusion is supported, however, by other parts of the RICO statute and in part, by the legislative history.

The plain meaning of the definition of "enterprise" given in the statute [and the criminal violations] lead to the conclusion that a governmental agency is a RICO enterprise, and nothing in the legislative history indicates an intention to the contrary.

We are led to the same conclusion if we look at the overall purpose of the statute and the harm it intends to counteract. The legislative history repeatedly says that the statute is designed to stop the "infiltration" of legitimate enterprises by persons who use the enterprise for the commission of certain crimes. This harm can occur just as easily in a police department, a licensing bureau or other governmental agency, as in a company or union. The harm to be counteracted is equally applicable to both public and private institutions.[57]

A Rico offense does not require an agreement to be part of the enterprise. In *United States v. Fabio Alonso,*[58] it was held that conviction of substantive Racketeer Influenced and Corrupt Organizations Act offenses is not an absolute prerequisite for conviction under the RICO conspiracy provisions. The requisite agreement [conspiracy] may be proved without any substantive RICO convictions. To make out a pattern of racketeering activ-

---

[55] *See United States v. Frumento*, 405 F.Supp. 23, 29-30 (E.D.Pa 1975), aff'd, 563 F.2d 1083, 1089-92 (3d Cir. 1977). ….

[56] *See United States v. Brown*, 555 F.2d 407, 415 n.15 (5th Cir. 1977) (RICO is "plain on its face" and covers government agencies), cert. Denied, 435 U.S. 904, 98 S.Ct. 1448, 55 L.Ed2d 494 (1978). We hold that the office of county judge is an "enterprise" under RICO."

[57] See also *United States v. Frumento*, supra, 563, F.2d at 1090-92; and others.

[58] United States Court of Appeals, Eleventh Circuit, 1984, 83-5072)

ity in a RICO conspiracy, the government must either show the defendant agreed to participate in an enterprise with the objective of violating a substantive RICO provision, or prove that he personally agreed to commit two or more predicate acts.

Examples of multiple predicate acts by people in the FBI and other Department of Justice offices that I detail and document in this and my other books:

- Coalition of FBI agents and members of the Bulger criminal group in Boston involved in murders for years, with the knowledge and approval of higher DOJ personnel in Boston and with top officials in Washington, including FBI Director J. Edgar Hoover.
- Coalition of FBI agent Lindley DeVecchio in the New York office with Colombo Mafia capo Gregory Scarpa, Sr. in murders and other crimes.
- The felony cover-ups of these crimes by other DOJ officials.
- The conspiracy to silence or discredit present or former government agents, or witnesses seeking to report federal crimes, that are described in this book and in *History of Aviation Disasters: 1950 to 9/11*, includes, for instance:
- Joseph Occhipinti, the INS agent.
- FBI Special Agent Richard Taus.
- FBI Special Agent Nancy Floyd.
- Gregory Scarpa, Jr.
- Me, by charging me with criminal contempt of court for attempting to report the continuing corruption in key government positions resulting in a continuing series of aviation disasters, terrorist successes, and other harmful consequences.

The Definition of a Conspiracy

A conspiracy is a felony, and includes conduct that many people would hardly consider a conspiracy. The conduct of most of the people in government described within these pages, and particularly the employees of the U.S. Department of Justice, far exceeds the legal requirements of a conspiracy. As used here, the conspiracy has resulted in the deaths of thousands of people and harm to the United States and its people that will continue far into the future. A conspiracy is when two or more people secretly join to do a wrongful or unlawful act

Title 18 U.S.C. § 241. Conspiracy against rights of citizens

If two or more persons conspire to injure, oppress, threaten, or intimidate any citizen in the free exercise or enjoyment of any right or privilege secured to him by the Constitution or laws of the United States, or because of his having so exercised the same; ... They shall be fined ... or imprisoned ... or both.

Legal Definition of a Criminal Enterprise

A criminal enterprise is a group of individuals with an identified hierarchy engaged in significant criminal activity. The Racketeer Influenced and Corrupt Organizations (RICO) statute, or Title 18 of the United States Code, Section 1961(4), defines an enterprise as "any individual, partnership, corporation, association, or other legal entity, and any union or group of individuals associated in fact although not a legal entity." Criminal acts include those found in Title 18 of the United States Code, Section 1961 (1) and include obstruction of justice. Federal case law has held that a government entity can be considered a criminal enterprise.

Definition of Criminal Acts that Apply to Certain Government Personnel Described Within These Pages

The following is a definition of criminal offenses that apply to many of the government personnel described within these pages. Government personnel, FBI agents, prosecutors, other Department of Justice personnel, are just as guilty as a non-government person who engages in these acts. Actually, a government person, in a position of trust, should be subject to an even harsher punishment if he or she violates any of these laws.

Accessory Before and After the Fact

An accessory is a person who in some manner is connected with a crime, either before or after its perpetration, but who is not present when the crime is committed. (21 Am J2d Crim L § 115.) Title 18 U.S.C. § 3. An accessory *before* the fact is a person who contributes to a felony committed by another, but is too far away to aid in the felonious act. In some jurisdictions the accessory before the fact is also charged with the crime of those committing the actual act. An accessory *after* the fact is a person who knows a felony has been committed and who *comforts or assists the felon in any manner to avoid prosecution.* (21 Am J2d Crim L § 126.)

An attorney in the Justice Department, a judge, a member of Congress, someone in the print or broadcast media, who knows of a crime and has the duty to expose it, but doesn't, would be guilty of this criminal offense. As will be seen, the list of groups and individuals guilty of this crime is endless.

Accomplice

An accomplice is a person who knowingly, voluntarily, and with a common interest with others participates in the commission of a crime as a principal, as an accessory, or aider and abettor. That would include a government official who refuses to perform a duty to prosecute someone guilty of a federal crime.

Aiding and Abetting

Any person who "commits an offense against the United States or aids, abets, counsels, commands, induces or procures its commission, is punishable as a principal." Any person who joins any conspiracy, even if they are unaware of the actual act committed by others, or why, become equally liable with the others. Title 18 U.S.C. § 3. This is another crime that has been and is being perpetrated by officials in all levels of government.

Conspiracy

Conspiracy is an agreement between two or more persons to accomplish an unlawful act. Conspiracy is a separate offense over and above whatever other acts the parties conspired to accomplish. The existence of a conspiracy is usually determined from circumstantial evidence, looked at collectively.

This is usually the only means of determining a conspiracy,[59]and is generally established by a number of indefinite acts, each of which, standing alone, might have little weight. But taken collectively, they point unerringly to the existence of a conspiracy.[60]

The existence of a conspiracy may be proven by inference from conduct, statements, documents, and facts and circumstances which disclose a common design on the part of the accused persons and others to act together in pursuance of a common criminal purpose. This offense is rampant throughout these pages. It is a common tactic to ridicule anyone claiming a conspiracy exists, even though conspiracies are possibly the most common offense committed, being simply an agreement between two or more people to commit some act.

Corruption

The term corruption covers a multitude of official wrongdoings, and especially anything that adversely affects the administration of justice; or subverts the instrumentalities of government; or impedes justice and the administration of justice. (*United States v Polakoff*, 121 F2d 333.)

Corruption applies to many of those involved in the activities described earlier and those activities yet to be described.

Double Jeopardy Doctrine

Double jeopardy is a procedural defense that prevents a defendant from being tried twice for the same crime on the same set of facts. If this issue is raised and evidence presented that the defendant had already been acquitted or convicted of the same offense, a second trial is barred. The double jeopardy procedural defense does not apply if the prior trial resulted in a mistrial, or if the charges were dropped before all the witnesses were presented and the judge or jury made no decision as to the guilt or innocence of the party.

---

[59] *United States v. Calaway* (9th Cir. 524 F.2d 609).

[60] *State v. Horton*, 275 NC 651, 170 SE2d 466.

False Statements to Government Agency

Making false statements to or within a government agency is a felony under several government statutes. (Title 18 U.S.C. §§ 35, 1001, 2071.) It is a crime under section 1001 to make a false statement in a "matter within the jurisdiction of a department or agency of the United States." Under the Federal Aviation Act it is also a crime to make a false statement, verbally or in writing, to a federal air safety inspector.

Fraud

Fraud is deceit, deception, or trickery operating prejudicially to the rights of another, and so intended by inducing him to surrender some legal right. It is anything calculated to deceive another to that person's prejudice. It is an act, a word, silence, the suppression of the truth, or any other device contrary to the plain rules of common honesty. (23 Am J2d Fraud § 2)

FBI's Informant Program

The FBI employs general informants, called criminal informants (CI), and also top echelon informants (TE). A top-level informant is a person in a position to provide highly sensitive information concerning activities involving an organized crime family. Normally, one agent is assigned to a criminal informant (CI). An FBI 209 report contains information received from informants. The FBI 302 form is a document that is submitted in court proceedings.

Misprision of Felony

Misprision of a felony is a criminal offense and arises from failure to inform a federal court or other federal authority of a federal offense that has been witnessed or that has come to the person's knowledge. It is also the failure to prevent a felony from being committed. (21 Am J2d Crim L § 7.) It is also the failure to disclose a felony coupled with some positive act of concealment, such as suppression of evidence, harboring of criminal, intimidation of witnesses, or other positive act designed to conceal from the authorities the fact that a crime has been committed. (Title 18 U.S.C. The statute addressing failure to report a federal offense is Title 18 U.S.C. § 4. This criminal offense was repeatedly perpetrated by federal judges and Justice Department attorneys who had an even greater duty to report and receive reports of federal offenses.

Obstruction of Justice

Obstruction of justice is the criminal offense of knowing of a crime and interfering with the administration and due course of justice. This statute was repeatedly violated by corrupt federal judges and Justice Department attorneys.

Mail and Wire Fraud

Under Title 18 U.S.C. § 1341 and 1343, mail and wire fraud is any scheme to harm another by false or fraudulent pretenses, dishonest methods, tricks, deceit, chicane, overreaching, or other wrongful acts, using the mail or wire.

Malfeasance

Malfeasance is the doing of an act which is positively unlawful or wrong, and which causes injury to another's person or property. It is the performance by a public official of an act in an official capacity that is wholly illegal and wrongful.

Misfeasance

Misfeasance is the improper doing of an act, which a person can lawfully do, but done in an unlawful and injurious exercise of lawful authority. This would include a federal judge or Justice Department official who prosecutes informants in retaliation for reporting federal crimes.

Nonfeasance

Nonfeasance is the failure to act where duty requires, such as when a public officer neglects or refuses, without sufficient excuse, to do that which it is the officer's legal duty to do, whether willfully or through malice or ignorance.

Perjury

Perjury is making false statements under oath. Anyone who subscribes or signs any material matter which he does not believe to be true is guilty of perjury.

Treason

Treason is that act committed by a citizen who gives aid and comfort to the enemy; who betrays a trust or a confidence; who commits a breach of faith; who betrays his or her country.[61] Within these pages this offense will arguably apply to various CIA activities yet to be described and to others.

Vicarious Liability

Vicarious civil or criminal liability exists when a person performs a wrongful act, or refuses to perform a duty, such as an employer or management. Where an employee is the proximate cause of the harm, his or her superior is liable on the theory of vicarious liability.

Where an employer, or the government, exercises control over an employee, that employer or government agency has vicarious liability. Where an employer gives a federal employee substantial or complete control over certain acts, an agency relationship exists. As it relates to federal judges, for instance, the federal government pays the salaries of the judges, provides the courts, and provides instructions for administrative duties. The same principle applies to Justice Department attorneys and other government checks and balances.[62]

---

[61] *United States v. Wiltsberger* (US 5 Wheat 76, 5 L Ed 37. A criminal attempt to destroy the existence of the government. *Republica v Chapman* (Pa) 1 Dall 53, 1 L Ed 33. Breaching an allegiance to one's country. Also shown under Article III, § 3 of the U.S. Constitution.

[62] Cases relating to vicarious liability includes *Crinkley v. Holiday Inns, Inc.*, 844 F.2d 156 (4th Cir. 1988); *Cislaw v. 7-Eleven, Inc.*, 92 Daily Journal D.A.R. 4136 (March 30, 1992); *Beck v. Arthur Murray, Inc.*, 245 Cal.App.2d 976 (1966); *Nichols v.*

Federal Sentencing Guidelines

The federal sentencing guidelines recommend certain periods of incarceration for certain offenses. A longer prison term is prescribed for government officials who betray their trust as they commit offenses under civil rights and criminal statutes.

FEDERAL STATUTES

Title 18 U.S.C. § 2[63] provides that any one becomes a principal to a criminal act who in any way aids or covers up for an offense. This could include federal judges, Justice Department attorneys, members of Congress, and the media.

Title 18 U.S.C. § 3. Accessory after the fact.[64] It is a felony for any person, who knows that an offense against the United States has been committed, to obstruct justice by assisting the perpetrators through blocking the reporting of the crimes by an informant or victim. This felony would include federal judges and Justice Department attorneys, members of Congress, media personnel, who knew about the criminal activities described within these pages and either refused to make the crimes known, or worse, who engaged in a cover-up.

Title 18 U.S.C. § 4 (misprision of felony).[65] It becomes a felony if any person who knows of a federal crime does not promptly report it to a federal judge or other federal officer.

Title 18 U.S.C. § 34 Penalty when death results.[66] If death results from violation of a related criminal statute, it becomes a capitol offense.

Arthur Murray, Inc., 248 Cal.App.2d 610 (1967); *Porter v. Arthur Murray, Inc.*, 149 Cal.App.2d 410 (1967); *Wickham v. Southland Corp.*, 168 Cal.App.3d 49 (1985).

[63] Title 18 U.S.C. § 2. Principals. (a) Whoever commits an offense against the United States or aids, abets, counsels, commands, induces or procures its commission, is punishable as a principal. (b) Whoever wilfully causes an act to be done which if directly performed by him or another would be an offense against the United States, is punishable as a principal.

The legislative intent was to punish as a principal not only a person who directly commits an offense, but a person who "aids, abets, counsels, commands, induces or procures" another to commit an offense, and anyone who causes the doing of an act which if done by him directly would render him guilty of an offense against the United States. Case law decisions include *Rothenburg v. United States*, 1918, 38 S.Ct. 18, 245 U.S. 480, 62 L.Ed. 414, and *United States v. Giles*, 1937, 57 S.Ct. 340, 300 U.S. 41, 81 L.Ed. 493.

[64] Title 18 U.S.C. § 3. Accessory after the fact. Whoever, knowing that an offense against the United States had been committed, receives, relieves, comforts or assists the offender in order to hinder or prevent his apprehension, trial or punishment, is an accessory after the fact.

[65] Title 18 U.S.C. § 4. Misprision of felony. Whoever, having knowledge of the actual commission of a felony cognizable by a court of the United States, conceals and does not as soon as possible make known the same to some judge or other person in civil or military authority under the United States, shall be fined not more than $500 or imprisoned not more than three years, or both.

Title 18 U.S.C. § 35. Imparting or conveying false information.[67]

Title 18 U.S.C. § 111. Impeding certain officers or employees.[68] It is a felony to resist, impede, intimidate, or interfere with any person designated in section 1114 of this title.

Title 18 U.S.C. § 153. Embezzlement by trustee or officer.[69] This felony is rampant in federal Chapter 11, 12, 13 courts, with the knowledge of federal judges, Justice Department officials, and many others.

Title 18 U.S.C. § 241. Conspiracy against rights of citizens.[70] This felony applies to anyone, including judges and Justice Department attorneys, who intimidate, threaten, or inflict harm upon any person in retaliation for exercising federal defenses against acts taken to silence him or block him from defending himself.

Title 18 U.S.C. § 371 Conspiracy to commit offense or to defraud United States.[71] There are many ways to commit an offense against, or to defraud the United States. As a matter of law, the word "defraud" is broadly used to include obstructing the lawful operation of any government agency by any "deceit, craft or trickery, or at least by means that are dishonest."[72] To convict someone, including a federal official, under Title 18 U.S.C. § 371, it is only necessary to

---

[66] Title 18 USC § 34. Penalty when death results. Whoever is convicted of any crime prohibited by this chapter, which has resulted in the death of any person, shall be subject to the death penalty or to imprisonment for life...

[67] Title 18 U.S.C. § 35. Importing or conveying false information. (a) Whoever imparts or conveys or causes to be imparted or conveyed false information, knowing the information to be false...

(b) or with reckless disregard for the safety of human life, imparts or conveys or causes to be imparted or conveyed, false information, knowing the information to be false...shall be subject to a civil penalty...or imprisonment....

[68] Title 18 U.S.C. § 111. Impeding certain officers or employees. Whoever...intimidates, or interferes with any person...while engaged in...the performance of his official duties shall be fined...or imprisoned...

[69] Title 18 U.S.C. § 153. Embezzlement by trustee or officer. Whoever knowingly and fraudulently appropriates to his own use, embezzles, spends, or transfers any property or secretes or destroys any document belonging to the estate of a debtor which came into his charge as trustee, custodian, marshal, or other officer of the court, shall be fined not more than $5,000 or imprisoned not more than five years, or both.

[70] Title 18 U.S.C. § 241. Conspiracy against rights of citizens. If two or more persons conspire to injure, oppress, threaten, or intimidate any citizen in the free exercise or enjoyment of any right or privilege secured to him by the Constitution or laws of the United States, or because of his having so exercised the same;...They shall be fined...or imprisoned...or both;

[71] Title 18 U.S.C. § 371. If two or more persons conspire either to commit any offense against the United States, or to defraud the United States, or any agency thereof in any manner or for any purpose, and one or more of such persons do any act to effect the object of the conspiracy, each shall be fined not more than $10,000 or imprisoned not more than five years, or both.

[72] *Hammerschmidt v. United States*, 265 U.S. 182, 188 (1924).

show that the person (1) entered into an agreement (2) to obstruct a lawful function of the government (3) by deceitful or dishonest means and (4) had committed at least one overt act in furtherance of the conspiracy.[73] Obstructing the lawful safety functions of the FAA and the NTSB, for instance, would constitute a felony under this statute. Obstructing the lawful functions of the federal courts, or the Justice Department, would also cause violation of this statute. Prosecuting a citizen seeking to report government corruption would be a crime.

Title 18 U.S.C. § 1001. Statements or entries generally.[74] It is a federal crime for anyone within the jurisdiction of any department or agency of the

---

[73] *United States v. Boone*, 951 F.2d 1526, 1543 (9th Cir. 1991).

[74] Title 18 U.S.C. § 1001. Statements or entries generally. Whoever, in any matter within the jurisdiction of any department or agency of the United States knowingly and willfully falsifies, conceals or covers up by any trick, scheme, or device a material fact, or makes any false, fictitious or fraudulent statements or representations, or makes or uses any false writing or document knowing the same to contain any false, fictitious or fraudulent statement or entry, shall be fined not more than $10,000 or imprisoned not more than five years, or both.

Case law relating to Title 18 U.S.C. § 1001 holds that falsifying any record that reduces the effectiveness of the government agency, causing the agency to wrongfully act or not act on such writings or acts, or decreasing the public confidence in such agency.

Just the mere filing of a false statement within the jurisdiction of any government department or agency constitutes a section 1001 offense. Loss or damage to government is not an essential element of the crime. *U.S. v. Godel*, 361 F.2d 21 (C.S. Va. 1966); *Morgan v. U.S.* 301 F.2d 272 (C.A. Ariz. 1962); Test for determining materiality of false statement is whether the falsification is calculated to induce action or reliance by an agency of the United States. *U.S. v. East*. 416 F.2d 351 (C.A. Mont. 1969);

Section 1001 makes it a crime to knowingly and willfully falsify documents within jurisdiction of government department or agency. It is immaterial whether the false statement actually influenced or caused the government department or agency to act, but rather, whether capable of influencing decision of tribunal making determination. *Robles v. U.S.* 279 F.2d 401 (C.A. Ariz. 1960); a section 1001 violation occurs when a false writing or document is made in any matter within the jurisdiction of a government department or agency, knowing that it contains a false statement or entry, and intending that it shall bear a relation or purpose as to some matter which is within the jurisdiction of the government department or agency, and with the false statement having a materiality on the department or agency matter. *Ebeling v. U.S.*, (C.A. Mo. 1957) 248 F.2d 429.

Section 2071 was to protect the government against false statements that might impede the exercise of federal authority. *U.S. v. Leviton,* C.A.N.Y. 1951, 193 F.2d 848; protect the government against those who would cheat or mislead it in administration of its programs (*U.S. v. Johnson*, D.C. Mo. 1968, 284 F. Supp. 273; affirmed 410 F.2d 38); includes all false and fraudulent statements or representations which are knowingly and willfully used in documents or affidavits in any manner within the jurisdiction of any department or agency of the United States. *U.S. v. Coastal Contracting & Engi-*

United States to knowingly and willfully falsify, conceal or cover up by any trick or scheme a material fact or to make any false, fictitious or fraudulent statement or representation.

Title 18 U.S.C. § 1341. Frauds and Swindles.[75] This statute relates to using the mail to defraud another person.

Title 18 U.S.C. § 1343. Wire fraud.[76] This section applies to anyone who defrauds another while using the telephone or other communications.

Title 28 U.S.C. § 1361. Action to compel an officer of the United States to perform his duty. This statute permits any citizens to invoke federal court jurisdiction to report government misconduct and to obtain a court order compelling a government official to halt the wrongful acts or to perform a lawful duty. A federal judge lacks jurisdiction to void, or to punish a citizen, for exercising this right.

Title 18 U.S.C. § 1505. Obstruction of proceedings before departments, agencies, and committees[77]

Title 18 U.S.C. § 1512. Tampering with a witness, victim, or an informant.[78] It is a crime to interfere or retaliated against a person seeking to report a crime. This would apply especially to Justice Department employees or judges.

---

neering Co., D.C. Md. 1959, 174 F. Supp. 474. See, also, *U.S. v. Allen*, D.C. Cal. 1961, 193 F. Supp. 954.

[75] Title 18 U.S.C. § 1341. Frauds and swindles. Whoever, having devised or intending to devise any scheme or artifice to defraud, or for obtaining money or property by means of false or fraudulent pretenses, representations, or promises,....for the purpose of executing such scheme or artifice or attempting so to do, places in any post office or authorized depository for mail matter, any matter or thing whatever to be sent or delivered by the Postal Service, or takes or receives therefrom, any such matter or thing, or knowingly causes to be delivered by mail according to the direction thereon, or at the place at which it is directed to be delivered by the person to whom it is addressed, any such matter or thing, shall be fined...or imprisoned....or both.

[76] Title 18 U.S.C. § 1343. Fraud by wire, radio, or television. Whoever, having devised or intending to devise any scheme or artifice to defraud, or for obtaining money or property by means of false or fraudulent pretenses, representations, or promises, transmits or causes to be transmitted by means of wire, radio, or television communication in interstate or foreign commerce, any writings, signs, signals, pictures, or sounds for the purpose of executing such scheme or artifice, shall be fined not more than $1,000 or imprisoned not more than five years, or both.

[77] Title 18 U.S.C. § 1505. Obstruction of proceedings before departments, agencies, and committees. Whoever corruptly...influences, obstructs, or impedes or endeavors to influence, obstruct, or impede the due the proper administration of the law under which any pending proceeding is being had before any department or agency of the United States...shall be fined not more than $5,000 or imprisoned not more than five years, or both.

[78] Title 18 U.S.C. § 1512. Tampering with a witness, victim, or an informant.

(a) Whoever...prevents the attendance or testimony of any person in an official proceeding;

(b) prevents the production of a record...in an official proceeding;

Title 18 U.S.C. § 1513. Retaliating against a witness, victim, or an informant.[79] This criminal statute applies to anyone, including judges and Justice Department officials, who retaliate against anyone for reporting federal crimes.

Title 18 U.S.C. § 1515 (a)(3)(A). Misleading conduct means knowingly making false statements.[80].

(c) prevents the communication by any person to a law enforcement officer or judge of the United States, of information relating to the commission or possible commission of a federal offense...(2)(b) Whoever knowingly uses intimidation...or threatens another person, or attempts to do so, or engages in misleading conduct toward another person, with intent to (1) influence, delay or prevent the testimony of any person in an official proceeding; (2) cause or induce any person to (A) Withhold testimony, or withhold a record, document, or other object, from an official proceeding; (3) hinder, delay, or prevent the communication to a law enforcement officer or judge of the United States of information relating to the commission or possible commission of a federal offense...(c) Whoever intentionally harasses another person and thereby hinders, delays, prevents, or dissuades any person from (1) attending or testifying in an official proceeding; (2) reporting to a law enforcement officer or judge of the United States the commission or possible commission of a federal offense...(3) arresting or seeking the arrest of another person in connection with a federal offense; or (4) causing a criminal prosecution...to be sought or instituted, or assisting in such prosecution or proceeding...shall be fined...or imprisoned...

[79] Title 18 U.S.C. § 1513. Retaliating against a witness, victim, or an informant. (a) Whoever knowingly engages in any conduct and thereby causes...injury to another person...or threatens to do so, with intent to retaliate against any person for (1) the attendance of a witness or party at an official proceeding, or any testimony given or any record, document, or other object produced by a witness in an official proceeding; or (2) any information relating to the commission or possible commission of a federal offense...shall be...fined or...imprisoned...

[80] Title 18 U.S.C. § 1515. Definitions of terms in criminal statutes (as used in sections 1512 and 1513). (a)(2) the term "physical force" means physical action against another and includes confinement; [including prison.] (a)(3) the term "misleading conduct" means□□(A) knowingly making a false statement;

(B) intentionally omitting information from a statement and thereby causing a portion of such statement to be misleading, or intentionally concealing a material fact, and thereby creating a false impression by such statement; (C) with intent to mislead, knowingly submitting or inviting reliance on a writing or recording that is false...or otherwise lacking in authenticity; (D) with intent to mislead, knowingly submitting or inviting reliance on a ... object that is misleading in a material respect; or (E) knowingly using a trick, scheme, or device with intent to mislead; (4) the term "law enforcement officer" means an officer or employee of the Federal Government, or a person authorized to act for or on behalf of the Federal Government or serving the Federal Government as an adviser or consultant□□(A) authorized under law to engage in or supervise the prevention, detection, investigation, or prosecution of an offense; (5) the term "bodily injury" means□□(E) any other injury to the body, no matter how temporary. (a)(1) the term "official proceeding" means...(C) a proceeding before a Federal Government agency which is authorized by law. [FAA included.]"

Title 18 U.S.C. § 1515 (a)(3)(A). Misleading conduct means knowingly making false statements.

Title 18 U.S.C. § 1515 (a)(3)(B); Intentionally omitting information from a statement and thereby causing a portion of such statement to be misleading, or intentionally concealing a material fact.[81]

Title 18 U.S.C. § 1515 (a)(3)(C). With intent to mislead, knowingly submitting or inviting reliance on a writing that is false or otherwise lacking in authenticity.[82] Same as other section 1515 violations. Title 18 U.S.C. § 1515 (a)(3)(D). With intent to mislead, knowingly submitting...material that is misleading in a material aspect.[83]

Title 18 U.S.C. § 1515 (a)(3)(E). Knowingly using a trick or scheme to mislead. Misleading statements made by government personnel throughout these pages were violations of this statute.

Title 18 U.S.C. §§ 1621. Perjury generally.[84]

Title 18 U.S.C. § 1622. Subornation of perjury.[85] This felony was repeatedly perpetrated by FAA management during the FAA Denver hearing.

Title 18 U.S.C. § 1623. False declarations before grand jury or court.[86]

Title 18 U.S.C. § 2071. Concealment, removal, or mutilation generally.[87] This criminal statute was violated by the FAA and NTSB in covering up for behind the scene facts in several air disasters described in detail in *Unfriendly Skies*.

---

[81] Title 18 U.S.C. § 1515 (a)(3)(B); Intentionally omitting information from a statement and thereby causing a portion of such statement to be misleading, or intentionally concealing a material fact.

[82] Title 18 U.S.C. § 1515 (a)(3)(C). With intent to mislead, knowingly submitting or inviting reliance on a writing that is false or otherwise lacking in authenticity.

[83] Title 18 U.S.C. § 1515 (a)(3)(D). With intent to mislead, knowingly submitting ... material that is misleading in a material aspect.

[84] Title 18 U.S.C. § 1621. Perjury generally. Whoever (1) having taken an oath before a competent tribunal...willfully and contrary to such oath states...any material matter which he does not believe to be true, he shall be fined...or imprisoned...

[85] Title 18 U.S.C. § 1622. Subornation of perjury. Whoever procures another to commit any perjury is guilty of subornation of perjury, and shall be fined...or imprisoned...

[86] Title 18 U.S.C. § 1623. False declarations before grand jury or court. (a) Whoever under oath ... or statement under penalty of perjury...before or ancillary to any court or grand jury of the United States knowingly makes any false material declaration, or makes or uses any other information...knowing the same to contain any false material declaration, shall be fined...or imprisoned...

[87] Title 18 U.S.C. § 2071. Concealment, removal, or mutilation generally. (a) Whoever willfully and unlawfully conceals, removes, mutilates, obliterates, or destroys, or attempts to do so, or, with intent to do so takes and carries away any record, proceeding, map, book, paper, document, or other thing, filed or deposited with any clerk or officer of any court of the United States, or in any public office, or with any judicial or public officer of the United States, shall be fined not more than $2,000 or imprisoned not more than three years, or both.

Title 18 U.S.C. § 2075. Officer failing to make reports; felony omission of a duty to act.[88] Fraud arising in misleading government reports. It is a federal offense to prepare a report that omits material information that as a result of the omission results in a different inference. Those especially guilty of this offense would be officials within the FAA, NTSB, Justice Department, and members of Congress. This offense is described in many federal decisions, including *Branch v. Tunnel*, 937 F.2d 1382 (9th Cir. 1991) and *Olson v. Tyler*, 771 F.2d 277, 281 (7th Cir. 1985). In these cases the courts held that deception exists when material omission in writing exists, wherein less than the total story is described, and where a different inference is drawn.

Legal Definition of Outrageous Government Conduct

A Ninth Circuit court of appeals decision made reference to what constitutes "outrageous government conduct." In that decision the Court of Appeals stated:

E. Outrageous government conduct.

The appellants argue that the district court should have dismissed the indictments against them because of the allegedly outrageous conduct of the government. This argument may rest upon one of two grounds. First, the court may dismiss the indictment if the government's investigatory conduct violated due process. *Hampton v. United States*, 425 U.S. 484, 489 (1976) (Powell, J., concurring); *United States v. Russell*, 411 U.S. 423, 431-32 (1973).

Second, the court may dismiss the indictment pursuant to its general supervisory powers. *United States v. Simpson*, 813 F.2d 1462, 1465 n.2 (9th Cir. 1987). In evaluating these arguments, we focus on the government's behavior and ignore the appellant's predisposition to commit the crime. *See Lafave & Israel, Criminal Procedure* 247-59 (1985). Unlike the defense of entrapment, the defense of outrageous government conduct is available even if a defendant was predisposed to commit the crime. *United States v. Gonzales*, 539 F.2d 1238, 1239-40 (9th Cir. 1976).

As an example of government conduct that satisfied outrageous government conduct, some courts cite *Rochin v. California*, 342 U.S. 165 (1953). 8 Am. J. Crim. L. 139, 148 n. 35 (1980).

---

[88] This criminal statute was repeatedly violated, commencing with the refusal of FAA and NTSB management to report the air safety and criminal acts, and then omitting key data from the final reports. This criminal offense would also apply to the Justice Department personnel who failed to report the criminal activities made known to them, including the CIA drug activities.

CHAPTER TWENTY SIX

Parallel Corrupt And Murderous Culture in NYPD

The culture in the FBI has spread throughout law enforcement. The roles of two NYPD detectives, Louis Eppolito and Steven Caracappa, turned out very differently from the way it started. Eppolito was one of the most highly decorated officers in the NYPD and the recipient of over 100 medals. He even received two Presidential Citations. Caracappa, who retired in 1992, helped establish the city police department's unit for Mafia murder investigations. Eppolito was the son of a Gambino crime family member, Ralph Eppolito.

Despite the praise, there were suggestions that some of their arrests resulted from mobster tips. And they came under suspicion in 1983 in a case involving mob member Rosario Gambino, but were then cleared.

Eppolito retired in 1990 and co-authored an autobiography[89] called, *Mafia Cop*, portraying himself as an honest and respected law enforcement officer that had grown up in a Gambino Mafia family. In his autobiography, "Mafia Cop," he portrayed himself as an honest cop from a crooked family.

Eppolito also played a bit part in the mob movie "GoodFellas," had small roles in several movies including Predator 2, and unsuccessfully tried his hand at Hollywood script-writing. Eppolito also wrote a screenplay called *Murder in Youngstown*, for which he sought money for the project. Both Eppolito and Caracappa moved to Las Vegas shortly after their retirement.

Providing Public Support To Gain Release of Convicted Murderer

While living in Las Vegas, Eppolito provided public support for Sandy Murphy, who had been convicted of murder in the death of Las Vegas casino owner Ted Binion. This support may have altered the jurors' judgment when Murphy was retried for the murder and held innocent by the jury.

So-Called Hero Arrested in Las Vegas

In 2005, Eppolito and Caracappa were arrested in Las Vegas by federal authorities on the basis of drug crimes in that city and crimes in New York while they were on the New York Police Department force. A *New York Times* article (April 22, 2005) titled, "Retired Detectives Plead Not Guilty in Mafia Killings," stated:

[89] The autobiography, Mafia Cop, was written with author Bob Drury.

Two retired city detectives accused of betraying their badges to become paid Mafia killers were formally arraigned in Brooklyn yesterday pleading not guilty to committing at least eight murders for the mob.

The arraignment of the two, Louis J. Eppolito and Stephen Caracappa, struck the opening note in what promises to be a spectacular trial, Kings County style. The charges in the case include, for example, murders and conspiracy, as stated in the following indictment, filed in the U.S. District Court, Eastern District of New York, which stated in part:

UNITED STATES DISTRICT COURT
EASTERN DISTRICT OF NEW YORK

UNITED STATES OF AMERICA INDICTMENT Against STEPHEN CARACAPPA and LOUIS EPPOLITO	Cr. No. Title 18 U.S.C. §§ 1962(d), 1963, 2 and 3551 et seq.; T 21, U.S.C. § 846 and 841(B) 91 (B)(viii)

THE GRAND JURY CHARGES:

INTRODUCTION TO ALL COUNTS

At all times relevant to this Indictment, unless otherwise indicated:

The Enterprise:

La Cosa Nostra ("LCN") was a nationwide criminal enterprise also known as "the mafia" and "the mob" that operated in the Eastern District of New York, other parts of the United States and Canada. LCN operated through entities known as "families." The five New York City-based LCN families were the Bonanno, Colombo, Gambino, Genovese, and Luchese organized crime families. LCN constituted an "enterprise," as defined in Title 18, United States Code, Section 1961(4), that is, a group of individuals' associated in fact. LCN engaged in, and its activities affected, interstate and foreign commerce.

Each LCN family operated through groups of individuals headed by "captains," who were also referred to as "skippers," caporegimes" or "capodecinas." These groups, which were referred to as "crews," "regimes," or "decinas," consisted of "made" members of LCN. The made members were known as "soldiers, "friends of ours," "good fellows," and "buttons." Persons who were not inducted into an LCN family but who committed criminal activity with, on behalf of, or under the protection of LCN family were known as "associates."

Each captain was responsible for supervising the criminal activities of his crew and providing crew members and associates with support and protection. In return, the captain received a share of the earnings of each of the crew's members and associates.

Above the captains of each LCN family were the three highest ranking members of the LCN family. The head of each LCN family was known as the "boss." He was assisted by an "underboss" and a counselor, who was known as the "consigliere." With the assistance of the underboss and consigliere, the boss was responsible for setting policy and resolving disputes between members and associates of his own LCN family and members, and responsible for approving all significant actions taken by members and associates of his respective family.

The boss, underboss and consigliore of an LCN family, who were sometimes referred to collectively as the "administration," supervised, supported, protected and disciplined the captains, soldiers and associates within the family and regularly received reports regarding the activities of the members and associates of each crew. In return for their supervision and protection, the boss, underboss and consigliere received part of the illegal earnings of each crew.

The ruling body of LCN is known as the "Commission," the membership of which at various times included the bosses of the five New York City-based families, to wit: the Bonanno, Colombo, Gambino, Genovese and Luchese organized crime families.

At all times relevant to this Indictment, the defendants STEPHEN CARACAPPA and LOUIS EPPOLITO were LCN associates. Specifically, they were associated with the Luchese organized crime family of LCN and, at times, they provided sensitive law enforcement information to the Luchese Family that was utilized by various New York City-based LCN families.

LCN was an ongoing organization, whose members functioned as a continuing unit for the purpose of achieving the objectives of the enterprise. The principal purpose of LCN was to generate money for its members and associates. This purpose was implemented by members and associates of LCN through various criminal activities affecting interstate commerce, including arson, credit card fraud, drug trafficking, extortion, kidnapping, illegal gambling, interstate transportation of stolen goods, loansharking and robbery. The members and associates of LCN also further LCN's criminal activities by threatening economic injury and using and threatening to use physical violence, including murder.

Although the primary purpose of LCN was to generate money for its members and associates, members and associates at times used the resources of their respective families to settle personal grievances and vendettas, sometimes with the approval of their respective families. For those purposes, members and associates of the enterprise were asked and expected to carry out, among other crimes, acts of violence, including murder and assault.

The members and associates of LCN engaged in conduct designed to prevent government detection of their identities, their illegal activities and the location of proceeds of these activities. That conduct included attempting to determine the identities of persons who were cooperating with law enforcement authorities or potential witnesses against members and associates of LCN. That conduct also included murdering and attempting to murder members or associates of LCN families who were perceived to be informants or potential witnesses against members and associates of LCN.

The organized crime families within LCN shared information and coordinated criminal activities. This included but was not limited to the following:

Promotion and carrying out joint ventures between and among LCN families to obtain money through illegal activities;

Conduct and control of illegal activities including interference with interstate commerce through extortionate extensions of credit and the collection of debts by extortionate means, commonly referred to as "loan sharking," infiltration and control of labor unions and labor organizations, illegal gambling, money laundering, fraud and narcotics trafficking;

Sharing information regarding government witnesses and potential or perceived government witnesses;

Taking steps to preserve order in, between and among the LCN families, including authorizing acts of murder;

Approving or disapproving the ignition of new members or soldiers in LCN families;

Controlling relations between LCN and members of the "Sicilian Mafia," an enterprise distinct from LCN in the United States.

Establishing certain rules governing the families, officers and members of LCN;

Keeping persons inside and outside LCN in fear of LCN by identifying LCN with threats, violence and murder; and

Extending formal recognition to newly-elected bosses of LCN families, and, from time to time, resolving leadership disputes within LCN families.

COUNT ONE

(Racketeering Conspiracy)

The allegations contained in paragraphs 1 through 11 are realleged and incorporated as if fully set forth in this paragraph.

On or about and between March 1, 1983 and March 22, 2005, both dates being approximate and inclusive, within the Eastern District of New York and elsewhere, the defendants STEPHEN CARACAPPA and LOUS EPPOLITO, together with others, being persons employed by and associated with LCN, an enterprise that engaged in, and the activities of which affected, interstate and foreign commerce, knowingly and intentionally conspired to violate Title 18, United States Code, Section 1962(c), that is, to conduct and participate, directly and indirectly, in the conduct of the affairs of that enterprise through a pattern of racketeering activity, as defined in Title 18, United States Code, Sections 1961(1) and (5).

The pattern of racketeering activity through which the Defendants STEPHEN CARACAPPA and LOUIS EPPOLITO, together with others, agreed to conduct the affairs of the enterprise consisted of the racketeering acts set forth below as racketeering acts one through sixteen of this Indictment. The defendants STEPHEN CARACAPPA and LOUIS EPPOLITO agreed that a conspirator would commit at least two acts of racketeering in the conduct of the affairs of the enterprise.

RACKETEERING ACT ONE

(Obstruction of Justice)

On or about and between December 13, 1983 and March 18, 1984, both dates being approximate and inclusive, within the Eastern District of New York and elsewhere, the defendant LOUIS EPPOLITO, together with others, did knowingly, intentionally and corruptly obstruct, influence, and ….. the due administration of justice to …, … …disclose ……identify is known to the Grand Jury, in violation of Title 18 United states Code, Sections 1503 and 2.

The defendants STEPHEN CARACAPPA and LOUIS EPPOLITO, together with others, committed the following acts, any one of which alone constitutes racketeering act two:

Kidnapping Conspiracy

On or about and between September 14, 1986 and October 31, 1986, both dates being approximate and inclusive, …. Knowingly and intentionally conspired to abduct James Hydell, in violation of New York Penal Law Section 135.20 and 105.15.

Kidnapping.

On or about and between September 14, 1986 and October 31, 1986, …, together with others, knowingly and intentionally abducted James Hydell, in violation of New York Penal Law Sections 1355.20 and 20.00.

Murder Conspiracy.

On or about and between September 14, 1986 and October 31, 1986, together with others, knowingly and intentionally conspired to cause the death of James Hydell, in violation of New York Penal Law Sections 125.25(1) and 105.25.

Murder.

On or about …., together with others, under circumstances evincing a depraved indifference to human life, recklessly engaged in Conduct which created a grave risk of death to James Hydell, and thereby caused his death, in violation of New York Penal Law Sections 125.25(2) and 20.00.

The remainder of the indictment charged the Eppolito and Caracappa with additional murders, including those of Nicholas Guido, John "Otto" Heidel, Salvatore "Sammy" Gravano, Anthony Dilapi, James Bishop, Bruno Facciola, Bartolomeo "Bobby" Boriello, John Doe # 1, John Doe # 2, John Doe # 42; and "together with others, did knowingly, intentionally and corruptly endeavor to influence, obstruct and impede the due administration of justice, to wit, by disclosing sensitive law enforcement information regarding the imminent arrest of John Doe Luchese, Family Member # 2, an individual whose identity is known to the Grand Jury.

Federal Prosecutors' Selective Prosecution

The indictment was filed in federal court by a U.S. attorney, and charged the two former NYPD detectives with numerous crimes that included providing confidential police information to the Luchese organized crime (OC) family of La Cosa Nostra (LCN), and particularly the Luchese Mafia; multiple murders, drug dealings, and money laundering. These were similar crimes that the same DOJ prosecutors covered up when perpetrated by FBI agents.

Prosecutors charged that they used their official positions to catch and then turn over to the Luchese group individuals who were then tortured and murdered. In one instance, prosecutors charged, "Eppolito and Caracappa followed Lino from a social club, pulled him over as he drove down the Belt Parkway, and shot Lino dead."

The prosecutors charged that the Luchese Mafia group paid Eppolito and Caracappa $4000-a-month and also paid them $35,000 for bringing to them a victim, James Hydell in 1986.

Caracappa Forming Unit That Helped Provide Information to Mafia Crime Families

While employed by the NYPD, Caracappa helped bring about the Organized Crime Homicide Unit, which brought together information acquired by the different police districts—enabling Caracappa to have access to more information concerning crime elements—which he then provided to the Luchese Mafia family.

Eppolito Knew the Horror Resulting From His Betrayal

Louie Eppolito knew the horror and suffering that came with the murder of a loved one. His father was a soldier in the Gambino Mafia family, and his grandfather was associated with mobster Lucky Luciano. His brother, James Eppolito and his son were murdered by members of the Gambino Mafia family on October 1, 1979. That didn't stop Louis Eppolito from corrupting his position with the New York Police Department, as he himself, or with his help, was involved with nearly a dozen murders.

Informant Provided Inside Information on Eppolito and Caracappa's Ties to the Mob and Murders

Lucchese crime family mob figure Anthony Casso became an informant for the government and started revealing information on Eppolito and Caracappa to crime figures and to several murders in which they were involved.

Among the information he provided was that while the two were officers with the New York Police Department they kidnapped and murdered, on orders from rival mobsters, Gambino family member James Hydell. It was also learned that they attempted to murder the informant who helped convict John Gotti: Sammy Gravano.

Casso, known as one of the most brutal mobsters in the city, is suspected of involvement in 36 murders himself. Both sides considered calling him as a witness but ultimately decided Casso came with too much baggage. According to testimony, the detectives "arrested" a mobster named James Hydell in 1986, but instead delivered him to Casso for torture and execution.

That same year, the pair furnished the underboss with information on where to find Nicholas Guido, a mobster involved in a planned hit on Casso. Their inaccurate tip led to an innocent man with the same name, who was killed after Christmas dinner at his mother's house.

Frank Santora arranged to have Eppolito and Caracappa to be paid $4,000 a month, plus bonus with the Lucchese Mafia family. Santora was the connection to Burton Kaplan in the Lucchese Mafia family, who arranged for this financial arrangement. So when Santora was killed, Eppolito was furious, thinking that his financial connection might be in peril.

Also providing information was Buton Kaplan, a career criminal and businessman. Their information led to the arrest of Eppolito and Caracappa in March 2005 by federal authorities.

Media-Dubbed "Heroes" Found Guilty of Multiple Murders

On April 6, 2006, after only a few hours of deliberations, the jury rendered a verdict holding Eppolito and Caracappa guilty as charged in the indictment. An *Associated Press* article (April 7, 2006), titled "Jury Convicts N.Y. Detectives of Murders While on Mob Payroll," stated:

> New York. Two highly decorated former detectives were convicted Thursday of moonlighting as hitmen for the mob in one of the most sensational cases of police corruption in New York history.
>
> Louis Eppolito and Steven Caracappa, ... for their roles in eight murders committed between 1984 and 1990 while they were simultaneously on the payroll of both the NYPD and Luchese crime family underboss Anthony "Gaspipe" Casso.
>
> Federal prosecutor Daniel Wenner described the case as "the bloodiest, most violent betrayal of the badge this city has ever seen."

Prosecutors said the two men carried out two hits themselves—in one case after pulling a mobster over in a phony traffic stop—and delivered up some of the other victims to the Mafia to be killed.

Prosecutors said the two used their law enforcement positions to help the Mafia at a price of $4,000 per month—more if they personally handled a killing. They earned $65,000 for the phony traffic stop slaying, prosecutors said.

The two officers also supplied Casso with inside information on law enforcement interest in the mob, prosecutors said. Casso was said to have referred to the two men as his "crystal ball."

They were convicted of charges that included racketeering, conspiracy, witness tampering, witness retaliation and obstruction of justice.

A *New York Post* article (April 8, 2006),[90] titled, "Full Medal Racket: Dirty Cops Keep Their Decorations," stated:

Murderous mob detectives Stephen Caracappa and Louis Eppolito sullied their badges, but they can hang onto their racks of medals, including one of the department's highest commendations, officials said yesterday. And the disgraced NYPD cops will also get to keep their annual five-figure pensions because of city laws, experts told *The Post* yesterday.

"They shouldn't get to keep anything," said Elizabeth Hydell, a sister of one of the mob cops' victims, James Hydell, who was kidnapped by the duo and delivered to mob chieftain Anthony "Gaspipe" Casso, who tortured and killed him. His body has never been found.

Hydell said the detectives who bloodied their badges with their secret lives of crime shouldn't be allowed to hold onto any of their honors—because it takes away their meaning. "They're disgraced," she said. "Those medals should go into the garbage." The news also angered Mary Ann Dilapi, the daughter of Anthony Dilapi, whose 1990 murder was among those attributed to the cops.

"Do I think it's wrong? Of course I think it's wrong. I think it sucks. It's wrong and absurd," Dilapi said, adding that the law should be changed. "It says a big thing about the New York City Police Department."

During the mob cops' sensational two-week trial, Eppolito lawyer Bruce Cutler introduced into evidence a long list of commendations and honors earned by his client during 20 years on the job. Those medals included the NYPD Medal of Valor, the service achievement award in 1990, a Cop of the Month award in 1987, several honorable mentions and a Community Council Cop of the Month award in November 1974. Cara-

[90] Written by Murray Weiss, Philip Messing and Zach Haberman.

cappa also garnered a few medals throughout his career, but his lawyer would not detail the commendations.

Detective Anthony Senft, a deserving winner of the Medal of Honor, the department's highest award, said he had no pity for the highly decorated detectives turned dirty. "Personally, I don't think someone who does something like this deserves anything," he said. "They put a blemish on everyone."

An NYPD spokesman yesterday said stripping the men of their medals "is not being contemplated at this moment," adding: "It's uncertain whether there is a precedent for it."

Ed Hayes, Caracappa's lawyer, said he doubted NYPD officials would strip the men of their medals or the $70,000-a-year pensions each has been collecting. Eppolito retired in 1990, Caracappa in 1992. "I can't imagine they can take their medals," he said. "I don't think they'll strip them of their medals or their pensions."

In his book, *Mafia Cop*, Eppolito claimed he was the 11th most decorated officer in NYPD history. Prosecutors said there was no proof to back up that claim.

Honest cops said that no matter the honors they captured during their careers, the pair have brought shame on the NYPD. "We go out there trying to be the best we can be, and then these guys think they can do whatever they want. It's a disgrace," said one cop at the Times Square precinct.

Some cops, although disgusted by the criminal acts, believe the medals are something that ought to be left standing. "They can't do that [take away the medals]," said one plainclothes detective at the Midtown North Precinct. "You can't take the medals away. They earned them in the line of duty. That's not a punishment."

All said, the rogue cops' crimes were unacceptable, other members of the Finest said. "Killing is killing. Mobsters have family, too," said one of the cops from the Midtown North.

If it's still up in the air what will happen to their medals, the men's pensions are strictly off-limits, experts say. "They can't touch it," said one expert on cop pensions and benefits, prompting some honest cops to call foul. "It doesn't matter whether they keep [the medals] or lose them. They don't mean anything, anyway. The fact that they get to keep their pensions is even worse," said one Midtown cop.

New York City cops, firefighters and correction officers who receive regular retirement pensions are also awarded annual lump-sum payments, known as variable supplements, that now top out at $12,000 yearly, sources said. The fund is not taxed by the state, and candidates forced to retire because of line-of-duty injuries - whose pensions are free of city, state and federal taxes - don't get the supplement.

In an effort to retain police officers who become eligible for retirement after 20 years of service, the city set up a plan in which cops can "bank" their variable supplement in an interest-bearing account. Eppolito retired on three-quarters disability, he suffers from a heart condition. Both mob cops moved to Las Vegas, where they were neighbors on the same block until their arrests.

The city and NYPD are now ripe to be sued by families of the mob cops' victims, and the convictions are likely to strengthen their case. "The verdict clearly paves the way for justice for all the families," said Michaelangelo Matera, lawyer for the family of slain Gambino capo Eddie Lino, who was handed over by the rogue cops for his torture and eventual killing.

The family of victim Israel Greenwald also has filed a notice of claim. The mother of Nicholas Guido, an innocent victim who was mistaken for a mobster and fingered for assassination by the rogue cops, has a federal civil suit pending and also plans a state claim.

"We purposely waited until the completion of the trial so that the filing of the lawsuit would not compromise the right of the defendants to a fair trial," said Benjamin Brafman, lawyer for the Greenwald family. "Now that they have been convicted, however, they personally, and the City of New York, must be held financially responsible for the grave harm their actions caused to the family of Israel Greenwald."

The two cops face sentencing May 22 [2006].

Life Sentence

Eppolito and Caracappa were sentenced to life in prison. After the sentence, newly hired lawyers filed a motion for a new trial (June 23, 2006), claiming that the trial lawyers, Bruce Cutler and Edward Hayes, two of New York's most prominent lawyers, had mishandled their defenses.

Judge Overturning Jury Verdict

Eighty-four-year-old U.S. District Judge Jack Weinstein, overturned the jury verdict of guilty and ruled (June 30, 2006) that the five-year statute of limitations on racketeering and conspiracy charges had expired and that the killers could be set free. State law has no statute of limitations for murder.

Weinstein was the judge that rendered a decision stated that the information on terrorist activities by Gregory Scarpa Jr. from the al Qaeda terrorist, Ramzi Yousef, was not credible. By discrediting Gregory, Weinstein helped protect FBI agent DeVecchio, and the FBI-DOJ involvement.

By discrediting Gregory, the information about the terrorist plans was ignored, and numerous subsequent catastrophic events were inflicted upon the United States and the American people.

Getting Away with Murder: Thanks to Federal Judge

"Getting away with Murder" was the entire front page title in the *New York Daily News* (July 1, 2006) as U.S. District Judge Jack Weinstein voided the jury verdict of guilty for Steven Caracappa and Louis Eppolito on the basis of a technicality:

> In April [2006], a jury convicted Louis Eppolito and Stephen Caracappa on all counts in a wide-ranging criminal conspiracy that prosecutors say dated to their days *as* decorated NYPD detectives. They were found guilty of participating in eight murders, one kidnapping and an attempted murder, as well as leaking the names of informers to the mob, and warning Luchese crime family gangsters when they were about to be busted.
>
> Brooklyn Federal Judge Jack Weinstein threw out the racketeering conviction because he found prosecutors failed to show the cops participated in a continuing conspiracy into 2000, the statute of limitations cutoff. [They continued their crimes in the Las Vegas area after retiring from the New York police department. Weinstein didn't consider that a continuing crime conspiracy!]
>
> Despite having murdered, maimed and sold out informants to bloodthirsty mobsters, the Mafia cops' racketeering conviction was stunningly overturned yesterday.
>
> Brooklyn Federal Judge Jack Weinstein acknowledged there was no doubt the disgraced duo were hit men for the mob—guilty of being the most corrupt cops in NYPD history. Yet, he still threw out the conviction, which carried life sentences on a technicality.
>
> "The evidence at trial overwhelmingly established the defendants' participation in a large number of heinous and violent crimes," Weinstein, 84, wrote. [Was it sanity, or outside influence or bribes?]
>
> The racketeering indictment charged that Eppolito and Caracappa went on the payroll of the Luchese crime family in the 1980s in Brooklyn. It specified that the duo committed or helped commit the slayings between 1986 and 1990.
>
> Despite a lull in their criminal activities in the late 1990s, their criminal enterprise resumed last year in Las Vegas, where they had settled after their retirement, the indictment charged.
>
> Prosecutors noted yesterday that the jurors "specifically found that the defendants' heinous crimes were committed within the statute of limitations," according to a statement from Robert Nardoza, a spokesman for Brooklyn U.S. Attorney Roslyn Mauskopf. But Weinstein concluded that the conspiracy ended when both detectives retired from the force.
>
> To make a racketeering charge stick, there must be an illegal act committed as part of the defendants' continuing criminal enterprise within five

years of the date of the indictment. [The crimes committed in Las Vegas were within that period.]

In the Mafia Cops case, the indictment charged ex-detectives Louis Eppolito and Stephen Caracappa with a wide-ranging conspiracy that began in the early 1980s in Brooklyn and continued years later in Las Vegas, after their retirement from the NYPD—all the way until the time of their arrest in 2005. But Weinstein held that the money laundering and drug charges in Las Vegas were not evidence of continuing racketeering activities. [They obviously were..] Weinstein preferred to describe them as "sporadic acts of criminality" unrelated to their previous ties to the mob.

Eppolito and Caracappa had been suspected of being mob hit men since former Luchese underboss Anthony (Gaspipe) Casso ratted them out in 19894, revealing they had been leaking secret information to him for years. [Casso also identified in the early 1990s that FBI agent DeVecchio was also involved in murders with Colombo capo Gregory Scarpa, Sr.]

Casso self-destructed as a witness, and it took authorities 10 years to flip jailed Luchese associate and Mafia cops go-between Burton Kaplan. The feds, rather than the Brooklyn district attorney, prosecuted the case because the rules of evidence would permit uncorroborated testimony by Kaplan and other cooperating witnesses.

Fortunately, a federal court of appeals panel reinstated the conviction and prison sentence on September 17, 2008.

A Friend and Retired NYPD Detective Described NYPD Corruption

A retired NYPD detective, Jim Rothstein, with whom I had been in contact for many years, told me about the corruption that he found in the New York Police Department. He described the reports that he had filed of CIA drug sales to the blacks in New York City, naming some of those who were involved. His reports described how CIA operatives sold drugs directly to black distributors from about 1967 to 1972, after which time organized crime groups took over the distribution. The CIA then concentrated on supplying drugs to the crime groups. Rothstein described his contacts with a key black that acted as an intermediary between the CIA and minor drug dealers.

Rothstein described how a package of evidence exposing the CIA drug and Mafia links was put into the safe of New York district attorney Robert Morgenthau, and how the evidence disappeared by the following morning. He described how New York City and county authorities refused to prosecute high-level drug bosses while concentrating on low-level street vendors.

"Take a disability retirement or suffer the consequences"!

Rothstein's supervisors didn't want Rothstein's reports of CIA activities that threatened to expose high-level people in the New York Police Department

(NYPD) and local politicians. His NYPD supervisors gave him a choice: take a disability retirement or suffer the consequences. He took the disability retirement in 1981.

Before his forced retirement, Rothstein was given the assignment to protect Maurita Lorenz, the girl friend of Fidel Castro, who bore a son for Castro. She was hiding out in New York City and Rothstein conducted a 24-hour surveillance because CIA asset Frank Sturgis was expected to carry out a contract against her. Rothstein arrested Sturgis when he arrived at her apartment.

Another Friend, the Daughter of Mafia-CIA Insider

Another one of my sources for many years was Dee Ferdinand, whose information dovetailed with Taus' information. She was the daughter of a Mafia-CIA figure. Dee provided me additional information about some of the crime figures Taus described. Dee Ferdinand, the daughter of Albert Carone, described the bizarre and complex relationships between her father, the Mafia, and the CIA. Al Carone was a member of the Gambino family with connections to other crime groups in the eastern United States. He was also a detective on the New York City vice squad, a member of the military, and a CIA operative.

Carone was a white-shield detective in the 42nd and 81st precincts while working with the New York City police department. He took frequent leaves of three or four months at a time to carry out operations for the CIA, using military cover. His connections with the NYPD ended in 1966, after which he concentrated on Mafia related activities with the CIA.

Dee said that her father was in the OSS during World War II (the predecessor to the CIA), working in military intelligence (CIC). After the war, he returned to New York, continued his relationship with the Mafia families, and also became a member of the New York Air National Guard, 27th brigade of the 42nd Infantry division. His earlier army rank was Sergeant, which eventually was raised to the rank of Colonel when he died in 1991. He is buried in the national cemetery at Santa Fe, New Mexico.

Activities with Sicilian and American Mafia

Dee described some of the Mafia's meeting places and front-operations. She referred to a restaurant and catering place in New Jersey called "The Tides" and the "Riviera Club" in the Bronx. She said Cosmo Fish and Shrimp Company in Nevada had connections to organized crime.

She described some of the drug trafficking names that she heard in her home, including Shavey Lee's in Chinatown, New York, where her father frequently visited. Dee said that Shavey Lee had drug connections in Hong Kong. She described the relationship between the Sicilian and American Mafia, and how the Sicilian Mafia first got started working with the CIA during World War II. She said that it was the Sicilian Mafia in Italy that controlled the American Mafia. She described how Vito Genovese kind of adopted her father when her father was growing up in Brooklyn, and that relationship eventually got him into key positions within the Mafia families. Her father called Genovese, Uncle Vito.

JFK Assassination Ties

Referring to what her father and Marita Lorenz had told her (Marita Lorenz worked for the CIA and was a girl friend to Fidel Castro and bore a son from their short relationship. She played a little-publicized role in the JFK assassination), Dee said:

My father knew Frank Fiorini, the alias for Frank Sturgis. One and the same person. Frank Fiorini was there also [Dallas]. Jack Ruby was the payoff man involved with the JFK assassination. Marita had given me information about traveling by car with three Mafia-CIA figures from New Orleans to Dallas, arriving in Dallas the day before the assassination, and facts that strongly implicate this group with the assassination of President John F. Kennedy.

Dual CIA-Mafia Ties

Dee described her father's concurrent relationship with the Mafia, the New York City police department, and the CIA. Key points that she described were confirmed by independent sources, including Jim Rothstein of the New York Police Department and CIA operatives Gunther Russbacher and Oswald LeWinter. She filled in missing Mafia and CIA links that FBI Special Agent Richard Taus had suspected during his FBI investigations.

Having grown up in a Mafia family and being friends with top Mafia bosses, Dee was very helpful in explaining the complex relationship between the Mafia and the CIA. She explained details of her father's activities as a CIA paymaster, moving money to and from the Mafia families in New York, New Jersey, and Pennsylvania, the CIA, the Mossad's involvement, and payoffs to the New York City police department.

Comparing Notes Between FBI and Mafia Families

Taus had given me a list of some of the Mafia figures that he investigated, and I asked Dee what she knew about them. She said that some of the people were her family. She said, "Angelo Ruggiero was my father's cousin." Neil Dellacroce was related to her father. Referring to Joe Percillia by his alias, Joe Pickle, Dee said that he was with the Genovese family and the Gambino family as they merged. He was also with the Colombo family.

Dee said that her father's primary connections were originally with the Genovese and then with the Gambino family, and also the Colombo family through Joe Percillia. She said her father also had lesser connections to other Mafia groups.

Growing Up in a Mafia Family

During one of many conversations, Dee described life growing up in a Mafia family, explaining:

You have to understand when I was growing up, there was no such thing as organized crime being spoken. It was a way of life with certain people in your home, or you were in their home, or whatever. You didn't know what these people did. Everybody's dad was like everybody else. They went to work every day and that's it.

Would they talk about killing people? No. Nothing seemed dysfunctional. It was just a family. You didn't think anything odd. What you saw in your home and how you were treated by these people was not how they were on the outside. You didn't think about it. You didn't know what these people did. It came out after a while as you got older. You wouldn't talk about something like that. What is spoken in the home never goes beyond the home.

Referring to Santos Trafficante, Dee said, "He was a good friend of my dad. He was at my wedding. Uncle Sonny. That's what I called him." Referring to Sam Giancana, she said, "Giancana was a good friend of my dad."

Drugs and the New York Police Department

Dee said her father was a detective and "bag man" in the New York City police department, collecting money that was distributed to captains and inspectors as payoffs for "looking the other way" where drugs were involved. Dee explained that her father, while a plain-clothes detective in the New York City police vice squad, paid money to the captains and inspectors of different precincts, and paid off mob figures. Referring to Inspectors Jack Lustig and Vince Nardiello, Dee said, "They were involved in the payoffs, and these are the people my father worked with."

CIA Paymaster

"My father was not only part of organized crime, but also a CIA paymaster." When I asked where that money came from, she replied, "The monies always came from the agency or the mob, in cash." When I asked what crime families were paid off, she said, "All the families."

Mob Boss Castellano as Frequent Breakfast Guest

She described how Paul Castellano, the boss of the New York crime families, was a frequent breakfast visitor at her home, and how she knew him as Uncle Paul. (Castellano was later murdered on orders of John Gotti.) Dee explained that Castellano was a brother-in-law to the former mob boss, Paul Gambino, and got the job because his wife was Gambino's sister.

Assassins for the CIA

Dee described how the Mafia handled assassinations in the United States that were requested by CIA personnel, explaining, "When the Agency needed people assassinated in the United States, the mob was used." (The CIA does its own assassinations overseas. Deep-cover operatives Gunther Russbacher and

Russell Bowen had reluctantly described their role in assassinations many years earlier.)

Drug Deals Between the Mafia, CIA, and Mossad

Dee said that her father started in drug trafficking in the Vietnam days, for the CIA and the Mafia. Explaining other aspects of the Mafia's drug dealings, Dee said, "Sam Giancana did a lot of drug deals with the Agency." She added that organized crime and the CIA had regular drug dealings with Noriega and the Mossad, and that former Mossad operative Michael Harari was routinely involved. "A lot of this money was split with the Mossad and the Agency. They had to use the mob; there isn't too much difference between the CIA and the mob. They worked together."

Frequent Contacts with CIA Agent Shackley

Dee described the frequent contacts that her father had with CIA agent Theodore Shackley relating to drug trafficking. (Several CIA operatives described Shackley's drug involvement to me over the past ten years.) Dee described how she called Shackley several years ago, demanding that her father's grave marker be changed, showing him as colonel instead of staff sergeant. (Sergeant was Carone's permanent military status and colonel was his temporary commission status.) Within two weeks, the marker was replaced, showing his rank as Colonel.

Operation Amadeus:
Joint CIA-Mafia Drug Smuggling Operation

Referring to the CIA-Mafia drug trafficking relationship, she said she knew from what her father said that the drugs coming from South America went to the Colombo, Genovese, and Gambino families, and that it was a joint CIA-Mafia drug operation under the code name Operation Amadeus. She said that during World War II, Operation Amadeus was involved in transporting Nazi officers from Germany into South American countries. According to her father's notes, Operation Amadeus split into several other operations, including Operation Sunrise and Operation Watchtower. In my books, *Drugging America* and *Defrauding America*, I go into considerable detail about the CIA operation in drug smuggling.

CIA-Mafia Drug Money Trail

Repeating what she learned from her father, Dee said that the money trail went through a bank in England to the Bahamas, and the Bank of Zurich in Switzerland, among others. She said her father carried cash between Mafia figures and the CIA.

Targeting the Blacks in Harlem

I told Dee that Rothstein had told me about CIA drug sales to the blacks in Harlem, and Dee gave me another side to that operation. She confirmed that the CIA and the Mafia did target the blacks in Harlem for drug consumption, adding:

> In Harlem, the blacks, definitely. It was their [CIA-Mafia] mainstay. That's how their money came, but it backfired on them. They really didn't think it would get into the white communities as much as it did. They targeted blacks and Puerto Ricans. My father was always saying, "Who gives a shit about the niggers!"

Dee told me about calling Congresswoman Maxine Waters' office and explaining who she was and about the drug trafficking, including the targeting of the blacks, and the lack of interest shown by Waters' staff. That reflects similar lack of interest shown by Waters' office when some of my drug trafficking sources also volunteered information about their CIA-DEA drug trafficking knowledge.

False Sexual Charges

Dee explained how internal politics within the NYPD resulted in her father being falsely charged with child-molestation offenses, causing him to be sent to the psychiatric unit of South Oaks Hospital. He was then given a choice of retiring or being prosecuted. "My father wound up with a full pension. Charges were dropped. This is how they set them up." Other CIA operatives, including long-time CIA veteran Gunther Russbacher, had told me years earlier about the CIA's use of pornographic and prostitution services used to get incriminating evidence on key political figures for blackmail purposes.

"I'm not long for this world; it's over."

After being ousted from the New York City police department, Carone moved his family to New Mexico (August 1980). He continued his military and CIA connections, traveling frequently to various military bases, including Kirkland Air Force Base, Fort Bliss (El Paso), and others. Eventually Carone fell out of favor with the CIA. Following a trip made to Mexico in 1984, Carone told Dee that he "wasn't long for this world; it's over." Dee said her father felt the CIA had poisoned him, which prompted him to start revealing other CIA-Mafia secrets to her, asking that she eventually make the information known. Before his death, Carone was diagnosed with chemical toxicity of unknown ideology by doctors who were unable to determine the cause of his medical symptoms.

Oliver North's Involvement with CIA-Mafia Activities

Dee described how her father made frequent reference to a John Cathey and his contacts with Cathey involving drug trafficking activities in the Contra operation. Cathey was the alias frequently used by Oliver North.

Input from CIA Operative Gunther Russbacher

Another of my long-time contacts with covert agents in the CIA was Gunther Russbacher, whose covert activities I describe in great detail in my book, *Defrauding America*. Russbacher had a varied CIA background and dealings with organized crime families; I once called him in England and asked if he knew Al Carone. He did, and started giving me additional information, including the fact that Carone was known as "Big Al," and that one of his aliases with the Chicago mob was "Pincheron." Russbacher said that Carone was working with the Delente and Bufalino crime groups.

Military Involvement with Organized Crime

Referring to Army Colonel Edward Cutolo, described in my book, *Drugging America*, Jimmy Rothstein said that he had seen Cutolo's involvement with the Mafia in drug trafficking. He explained that Cutolo, like other military people involved in the drug trafficking, would often have second thoughts and seek to extricate themselves from the operation. That desire may have ended deadly for Cutolo.

Input from CIA Operative Oswald LeWinter

Oswald LeWinter, another long-time CIA operative with whom I had been in contact for years, said he also knew Carone. During that conversation, LeWinter told me that in the Pizza Connection cases, Justice Department prosecutors filed charges against certain Mafia figures such as Gaetano "Don Tanino" Badalamenti, while protecting higher figures in the drug trafficking organization. This coincided with what Taus had told me. LeWinter described how Tomasso Buscetta, the mob witness used by Justice Department prosecutors in the Pizza Connection cases, was a CIA operative who would testify, and who would cover up, as desired by government prosecutors. LeWinter said that New York Senator Alfonse D'Amato was heavily involved with the Mafia.

CHAPTER TWENTY SEVEN

Scarpa Secretly Rewarded with Prison Release

An event happened in November 2011 that to the uninformed was of no consequence. However, it was further support of the criminality that made possible several major terrorist attacks against U.S. targets, including 9/11, and the deaths resulting from the reaction to those multiple hijackings. That was the unpublicized release of former New York City Mafiosi Gregory Scarpa, Jr. from prison—24 years prior to the scheduled release date of October 17, 2035. Scarpa and I had been in continual contact for about 11 years prior to his release. The following information is based on these contacts.

Scarpa's lawyer, New York City attorney Georgia J. Hinde, filed legal papers seeking a court order for Scarpa's early release from prison, basing the request upon promises made by FBI agents in response to the ultra-valuable information Scarpa was obtaining as a mole in the al Qaeda cell headed by Ramzi Yousef. Yousef was a mastermind behind the 1993 bombing of the World Trade Center and the planner behind the planned simultaneous bombings of a dozen airliners departing Far East airports.

Hinde included in her filings the copy of the letter previously sent to U.S. District Judge Edward R. Korman in New York, recommending Scarpa's early release. That recommendation was based upon Scarpa's help in providing information to FBI agents about the plans for the series of deadly terrorist attacks and also for the reliability of the testimony Scarpa was *prepared* to give in the murder trial of FBI supervisor Lindley DeVecchio.

Repeated objections by high officials in the U.S. Department of Justice personnel blocked a decision on earlier release for several years. In a May 19, 2011, letter to Hinde, I offered to send a friend-of-the-court letter to Judge Korman in an attempt to force action the matter, and sent a copy of the proposed letter to Scarpa and his attorney, Georgia Hinde. That letter was never sent, and a copy follows:

From the desk of Captain Rodney Stich
P.O. Box 4, Alamo, CA 94507; phone: 925-944-1930; FAX 925-295-1203
Author of numerous books on government intrigue
International Society of Air Safety Investigators: Assn. of Former Intelligence Officers
E-mail: stich@rodneystich.com www.rodneystich.com www.defraudingamerica.com

May 19, 2011

Georgia J. Hinde
1133 Broadway, Suite 304
New York, NY 10010 FAX 212-727-2627

Ref: Scarpa and proposed letter to Judge Korman

To Georgia Hinde,

It was a pleasure talking to you a short time ago. The purpose of this letter and the enclosed copy of a draft to Judge Hinde is to obtain your comments or suggestions as I try to provide help to your client, Gregory Scarpa, Jr. My *latest* effort would be via a friend-of-the-court brief that provides information on additional matters relating to his and your efforts to obtain a sentence reduction that appears to be blocked.

Several times in the past I have sent friend-of-the-court letters either to federal judges or parole boards relating to incarcerated former CIA-related personnel. In each case, whether I played a role or not, I don't know, but the people were either released or the additional criminal charges were dropped.

I have been in contact with Gregory Scarpa Jr. for many years, and have combined the valuable information he provided with information that I and a coalition of other former government agents and insiders discovered during the past 40 years. Most of these well-concealed matters are probably unknown to you.

There have been grave consequences to what was done—or not done—with the ultra-important information that Scarpa obtained from al Qaeda operative Ramzi Yousef. This relationship is discussed in the enclosed draft of a friend-of-the-court letter to Judge Korman. These serious matters are simply the latest of that type of conduct that I and my group have discovered during several decades.

Based on many years of experience, I think the best way for me to proceed is for *me* to send the attached friend-of-the-court letter (with any changes or suggestions that you might make) to Judge Korman. I understand that it has been over a year since you filed the motion for sentence reduction, and that the judge has not taken any action. Based upon the gravity of the matter, I can see where every effort is being made to keep Gregory Scarpa out of circulation.

In the past, I'm encountered lawyers that acted to protect the system rather than their client, or to protect themselves against retaliation. I don't know your position, but I believe it best, to protect you from any unfavorable judicial or Justice Department reaction, that I submit the enclosed draft without your involvement. However, if you are willing to risk it and enclose my friend-of-the-court letter with your filing, that would be fine. However, I wonder if it would get greater significance if it were sent by someone not related to your office.

I obtain no benefit whatsoever from this effort. I have more than enough material to continue my efforts that are solely to achieve the seemingly unreachable goal that I started in the 1960s while a federal airline safety inspector trying to expose the deadly politics related to a series of horrific aviation disasters.

Gregory's efforts—if they had not been blocked—probably could have prevented several catastrophic national events were it not for the scheme to protect a key FBI supervisor. His efforts should be recognized and credit given for his efforts, especially since many people in key government offices whose documented corrupt acts were major enablers to these terrorist successes.

Sincerely,

Rodney Stich

cc: Gregory Scarpa Jr.

It was decided that the best approach would be to continue waiting for the judge to make a decision. My last letter from Scarpa was dated November 10, 2011. He was pleased to know he was being transferred to a prison where the living conditions were less confining. Part of that letter stated:

> *I think the news I have for you—you will smile. (s) Your Buddy Greg (me) has now finally been designated to another prison. (Should be a lot less restrictive) I am waiting as we speak to be picked up. (c)*
>
> *When I hit the new spot I'll get in touch with you. Till then, Rodney, please keep this news on the down low.*

I never again heard from Gregory. This was unusual. I checked the federal prisoner locator on the Internet and the answer appeared. Gregory didn't know it at the time he wrote that letter, and I'm sure he was told to halt all correspondence with me. If it became widely known that the son of the infamous "killing machine" was released 24 years before his time, questions would arise as to why that occurred.

Gregory's release date was October 17, 2035. But he was transferred to a halfway house. Under federal criminal practices, a prisoner is not released, or sent to a halfway house, until within 12 months of the original sentencing release date. In Gregory's case, that was 24 years away!

Gregory was probably required by Department of Justice personnel to cease contact with me, since I had done many things to make known to many key people what Gregory had tried to do to prevent the attacks, and the names of s the people that criminally blocked his efforts. My letters simply expanded the number of people criminally aiding and abetting the original offences by covering up.

The 24-year-sentence-reduction in federal prison sentence indicated something highly unusual and unprecedented. Gregory was properly given an early release date for the services he provided.

The public would learn that Scarpa had been a mole in al Qaeda's primary terrorist cell and had repeatedly provided information on several major terrorists attacks that killed nearly 4,000 people; and that Department of Justice officials had deep-sixed the information so as to cover up for a key FBI supervisor involved in murders. Actions could have been taken to prevent the success of the terrorist attacks, and in turn the invasions of Afghanistan and Iraq would not have happened, if Scarpa's information had been acted upon rather than deep-sixth.

Federal Home Detention

The following is a published description of the federal release program:

Some federal inmates are placed on home detention at the end of their prison term. Home detention is a generic term used to cover all circumstances under which an inmate is required to remain at home during non-working hours of the day. They serve this portion of their sentences at home under strict schedules and curfew requirements.

Electronic monitoring equipment is sometimes used to monitor compliance with the program's conditions. This program provides an opportunity for inmates to assume increasing levels of responsibility, while at the same time providing sufficient restrictions to promote community safety and convey the sanctioning value of the sentence. Statutory provisions limit the length of home detention to the last six months or 10 percent of the sentence, whichever is less. Ordinarily, an inmate is placed in an RRC prior to placement on home detention.

Under 18 U.S.C. § 3624 (c), home detention is limited to six months or the final 10 percent of the term of imprisonment, whichever is less. The BOP's CCM is the final approving official for home detention placements.

If a policy or older document uses the term CCC, it is referring to an RRC. CCC refers to a community corrections center, but that term was replaced by residential reentry center (RRC) several years ago to more accurately convey the mission of the facility - facilitating reentry into the community.

A halfway house is a residence located in the community where people are placed to either (1) serve all or part of a sentence, or (2) serve a period of time after being released from federal prison, in order to prepare for reentering the community. They are also called "community corrections centers" (CCCs), but several years ago, the Bureau of Prisons (BOP) renamed them "residential reentry centers" (RRCs). This new name shows that the BOP views a halfway house as a place reserved for people leaving prison, as opposed to a place where a person can serve his entire sentence.

The prisoner's unit team should make a release preparation plan, which should include halfway house placement, 11 to 13 months prior to the prisoner's projected release date.

The practical reality is that people being released from prison are not given more than a total of 12 months of reentry programming, either in a halfway house or on home confinement (and time on home confinement cannot be greater than 6 months or 10% of the person's sentence, whichever is less.

Media Silence Required to Prevent Public from Learning Of the Multiple Calamities Arising from Deep-Sixing Crime

Department of Justice officials vigorously opposed Scarpa's release. Unless mainstream media personnel covered up for Scarpa's release and the reason for his release, danger existed of the monumental and calamity-related misconduct being recognized by the American people and other countries.

Scarpa's Concern My Other Half—Glenda

In early 2008, my other half, Glenda, was diagnosed with Stage IV esophagus cancer, and had a very rough first year. In all subsequent letters, Gregory asked about Glenda, how she was doing, and wished her well.

Shortly after Gregory's last letter to me, while Glenda's cancer was in remission, and living quite comfortably having gone three years beyond the normal one-year maximum survival from that diagnosis, I had to take her to the hospital for a treatable shortness-of-breath condition caused by a fungus infection.

Since the mid-1960s, I had uncovered one area of corruption after the other, which I detail in my many books. I never thought I would encounter the pockets of corruption that would bring about Glenda's death. Medical homicide! As in the prior 50 years of providing evidence of corruption, I encountered the same culture that is deeply embedded in the culture within the United States.

I write about this in the book, and an Internet web site:

- *Medical Industry's Death Panels: Greek Tragedy of a Lady Named Glenda.*
- Also, at an internet site: www.defraudingamerica.com/Glenda.html.

CHAPTER TWENTY EIGHT

Suitcase Nuclear Attack Next?

Another example of incompetence by FBI agents involved Mohammed Atta, the ringleader of the al Qaeda terrorists that hijacked four airliners on September 11, 2001. FBI agents had the last opportunity to halt the 9/11 hijackings by passing up the opportunity to learn about the plans directly from Atta himself. FBI personnel had paid Elie Assaad, an FBI informant, to infiltrate the Masjid al Hyrah mosque in Miramar, Florida, the imam of which was Sheikh Gulshair Shukrijumah. Gulshair was formerly the head of the Al Farouq Mosque in Brooklyn that harbored some of the terrorists linked to the 1993 World Trade Center bombing.

Several members of that mosque were arrested on June 24, 1993, and charged with a plot to bomb New York City area targets, including the George Washington Bridge, Holland and Lincoln tunnels, and the United Nations building. In 1996, the nine defendants were convicted and sentenced to prison. Gulshair then left the New York area in that same year to become imam heading the Miami area mosque. His prior association with a band of known terrorists should have put him on a top FBI surveillance list.

Two Infamous Members of the Mosque

Among the members of that Miramar mosque were two Muslims that would become famous: Mohammed Atta and his close associate, Adnan Shukrujuman, the son of imam Sheikh Gulshair. Atta would be known as the ringleader of four groups of terrorists that hijacked four airliners on September 11, 2001. Adnan became famous for his desire to explode nuclear bombs in major U.S. cities. Adnan Shukrujuman worked closely with Atta. He also conspired with such al Qaeda terrorists as Jose Padilla to blow up bridges and tunnels in the New York City area.

FBI Mole Infiltrated *Another* Hotbed of Terrorists

After Assaad infiltrated the mosque he became friends with two of its members, Mohammed Atta and Adnan Gulshair el-Shukrujuman. In an attempt to bring Assaad into their terrorist scheme, Adnan invited Assaad to his home for further discussions. That was a golden opportunity to infiltrate the al Qaeda cell headed by the ringleader that was to carry out the greatest terrorist attack in the history of the United States.

Instead of embracing that opportunity, FBI agents ordered Assaad not to accept that invitation. That refusal caused Atta and Adnan to lose confidence in Assaad. The opportunity to save 3,000 lives was lost by the stupid actions of

FBI agents, adding to seemingly endless other examples that proved deadly for many people. Referring to Shukrujuman, FBI Director Robert Mueller stated Adnan was "the next Mohammed Atta." Adnan Shukrujuman was reportedly a nuclear technician and computer scientist.

Another Al Qaeda Terrorist Revealed Nuclear Attack Planner

The March 2003 arrest and subsequent interrogation of al Qaeda member Khalid Sheikh Muhammad revealed that Adnan el-Shukrujuman was planning nuclear attacks on major cities in the United States. The most likely means to accomplish that would be with suitcase nuclear bombs. Upon learning this, FBI personnel issued an arrest warrant for Adnan Shukrujuman. That arrest warrant had a major loophole. The arrest warrant was issued on the basis of him being a *material* witness, instead of a person charged with a crime.

If Adnan el-Shukrujuman was discovered in another country that material witness warrant would not result in an arrest and taking him into custody and extraditing him to the U.S.

When that fault was brought to the attention of Department of Justice personnel, they claimed that under the Patriot Act a material witness arrest warrant was sufficient. The fallacy with that argument was that a material witness warrant is not sufficient for another country to arrest and deport the person to the United States.

Another Indication of FBI Incompetence

It had been reported that after the material witness warrant was issued, the manager of a Denny's restaurant in Avon, Colorado, Samuel Mac, recognized him and called FBI headquarters in Washington. Samuel reportedly stated that he was told to call the FBI's office in Denver, and then when he did that, he encountered an automated phone answering system instructing him to leave a message. Five hours later a seemingly uninterested FBI agent returned his call, taking notes, and then stated another agent would call back when that agent was available.

Adnan was also reportedly seen in 2006 by a security group in Hamilton, Ontario. They immediately called an FBI office, and three years later, in 2009, that group reportedly still had not heard back from any FBI employee. A similar experience was that of a former Israeli intelligence official who also reportedly saw Shukrujuman in Toronto. He contacted FBI officials at several different FBI offices, and encountered indifference to what he was reporting.

Former FBI Special Agent Richard Taus, described to me over the years that indifferent reaction and incompetence was rampant in the FBI, and that FBI agents were more interested in pursuing and often fabricating false charges against ordinary people.

FBI Personnel Fabricating Crime Schemes and Paying Victims To Become Unwitting Part of the Justice Department Scheme

Where FBI employees really "shine" is in setting up crime schemes and then enticing people who would never have become involved, to tag along, usually lured by money. In this way, Department of Justice employees obtain favorable media attention with exaggerated claims of the severity of the national threat. In this way, the FBI-manufactured crime scenarios promote the image of the U.S. Attorney General, the FBI director, and the individual employees who then shared in job promotion and pay.

Another common ploy by Department of Justice employees to increase their conviction record and job status is to file criminal drug charges against innocent people in schemes that are too numerous to list here, but are described in my book, *Drugging America*. One example was the FBI use of Assaad to fabricate a crime scenario that would not have existed but for the FBI.

Setting Up Scheme to Fabricate a Threat Rather Than Go to Heart of Threat

After barring Elie Assaad to accept the invitation by Adnan Shukrijumah' s invitation to join their group (that subsequently carried out the 9/11 hijackings), FBI employees used Assaad in an FBI scheme to set up a fake terrorist plot and then pay people to unknowingly become "terrorists." In this way, Department of Justice employees could claim that they were competent in preventing terrorists attacks upon the United States.

That scheme ensnared seven people that were paid to attend meetings during which FBI plans were made to engage in criminal acts—that would never occur. Three Jury Trials Were Needed to Obtain Jury Convictions

For Five of the Seven Victims of FBI Entrapment

It took three trials before the DOJ prosecutor could get a jury to hand down convictions to five of the seven defendants. One of the defendant that was found innocent, Naudimar Herrera, stated that he and others played along with Assaad because of the financial incentives promised and given to them. He stated:

> He [Assad] was like, "Oh, your name here. You say your name here" It was more like, it was more like a movie script .... Anyone would be vulnerable to Assad's intelligence.

An ABC Television program focused on this DOJ Scheme

An ABC program described this scheme, in which FBI employees provided the plan, the money, and the evidence for the eventual crime to be conceived. These easily-accomplished schemes target people who often would never have thought or planned such an operation, and who tag along for the money being paid to them to become targets of the sting.

Richard Houlihan, an attorney for Herrera, stated to *ABC News*: "Without Assaad's performance, none of this would have happened. He's dealing with seven basically inner-city kids from Liberty City. Poor, uneducated, looking for money."

Adnan's Reputation as al Qaeda's "Hiroshima" Planner

Going back to the subject of suitcase nuclear bombs, I had provided considerable information on suitcase nuclear bombs being smuggled from Russia's arsenal in Volume Two of *Defrauding America* that I wrote several years ago. I learned about this grave danger to the United States from a source that was training and advising Lithuanian and Russian military and police personnel. The following is a condensed version of what is in that book:

Exploding Suitcase Nuclear Bombs in U.S. Cities

Very little attention had been given in the United States to what may be the most terrifying weapon in the hands of terrorists and the next blowback from the conduct of our illustrious leaders and policies: suitcase nuclear bombs.

These so-called "suitcase" nuclear devices can be easily carried like a suitcase, or backpack, and easily hidden. They can cause personal and property destruction and hysteria unlike anything ever seen in the United States. The explosion of even one such easily concealed nuclear device in a major U.S. city would result in calamitous consequences.

J. Keith Idema had been highly trained in the U.S. Army's Green Berets and Special Operations sections. Although Idema denied it, inside sources confirm that in the 1980s Idema was sheep-dipped, acting as a civilian but actually still connected to the Army's Special Operations Forces, being used in a covert role. In this clandestine capacity, he operated a private training school for counter-terrorism and hostage rescue, operating under the group name of Counter Group Academy.

His students came from U.S. agencies and from foreign governments. They included persons from the U.S. Agency for International Development, Navy SEALs, Department of the Interior, the SWAT teams for the Statute of Liberty rededication, and the elite guard group for the U.S. Mission in Haiti. He later conducted counter-terrorist conventions called Spec-Ops Expo, which had frequent enrollments by military and intelligence personnel from throughout the world.

His expertise in counter-terrorism caused military and intelligence people to invite Idema to conduct teaching seminars in Moscow and Lithuania. They wanted to learn more about western style police, military, and counter-terrorism techniques. During the Lithuanian revolution Idema developed close friendships with several Lithuanian government and military officials, and they invited him to visit them in Vilnius, the capitol of Lithuania, to train their police commandos.

Nuclear Material and Suitcase Nuclear Devices Sold to Terrorists

During these visits and training sessions Idema became friendly with Russian and Lithuanian dignitaries, who looked upon Idema as a celebrity because of his Special Forces background and counter-terrorism expertise. This friendship caused several of them to provide Idema with information about nuclear weapon sales by Russia's KGB and Russian Mafia figures. Idema learned from these sources that Russia's suitcase nuclear devices were disappearing and were being sold by Russian intelligence and crime groups to terrorist groups.

Smuggling of Suitcase Nuclear Bombs

The Lithuanian officials who provided this information to Idema first learned about the shipment of Russian nuclear material and suitcase nuclear devices after eight Lithuanian border guards were shot dead, execution style, on August 1, 1991.

The senior commissar of the Lithuanian Interpol and Criminal Police, Juozas Rimkevicius, conducted an investigation with Idema. Idema believed that the guards were killed because they stumbled upon a shipment of nuclear material being shipped from Russia through Lithuania. Further, that the guards were killed by Russian security forces known as OMON, and that they were protecting or directly involved in the smuggling operation. The nuclear material and the portable nuclear devices were being taken from Russian nuclear storage areas and sold to terrorists.

Several months later, Lithuanian police arrested two men who had in their possession a Russian made AKS-74 rifle that had the serial number belonging to one of the murdered Lithuanian guards. The men claimed to be part of the Communist underground, but Rimkevicius believed they were part of OMON.

The two arrested men revealed that the shipment was one of many that had gone through Lithuania in recent months and that another shipment was scheduled for April 1991. A Lithuanian anti-terrorist commander of its top counterterrorism unit (ARAS) then waited for the scheduled shipment. When they spotted two trucks crossing the border with Russia they followed until reaching a designated point where the trucks were halted.

Upon investigating the truck's contents, they found crates filled with hundreds of pieces of a shiny bright metal (beryllium), tubes, cylinders and undistinguishable parts, some of which contained parts of four disassembled Soviet portable nuclear bombs (SADMs) and uranium (U-235) for detonating them.

Rimkevicius discovered from his informants in OMON and the Russian Mafia that the smuggling operation had continued after the Soviet Union began disintegrating, and that KGB officials and GRU operatives were key players in the smuggling operations, and working with Russian mobsters.

Developing Information about Terrorist Activities

Rimkevicius and Idema became good friends. Over a period of years Rimkevicius spoke at Idema's high-level Special Operations conferences in the United States and Europe. This friendship caused Rimkevicius to reveal a smuggling operation in the Baltic republics that he was about to crack. Simultaneously, other sources were providing Idema information about the Abu Nidal and Hezbollah terrorists, and the assistance provided to these two groups by the Russian KGB. Rimkevicius discovered that OMON was working with the

KGB, organized crime, and such terrorist groups as the Iranian-backed Hezbollah.

KGB Providing Evidence of Nuclear Weapon Sales

While Idema was in Moscow in the summer of 1992, he was approached by a high ranking KGB officer in the Soviet ministry who showed Idema several dozen highly classified documents revealing the removal of several dozen SADMs from the Soviet nuclear inventory under Russian Army control and transferred to the KGB 12th Directorate. This source described to Idema how the smuggling operation worked and how the nuclear weapons were sold to terrorist states like Iran, Iraq, and North Korea. This source told Idema that he would pass the documents to a Lithuanian friend who would then give them to Rimkevicius.

At the same time, Rimkevicius was learning about other parts of the smuggling operation from additional sources. In April 1993 Rimkevicius was informed of another shipment of nuclear material that had already crossed the Byelorussian border into Lithuania and that it had been delayed in Lithuania. The following month, Rimkevicius discovered its location at the Stock Innovation Bank in Vilnius.

Rimkevicius, and a Lithuanian Commando squad Idema trained, discovered 27 crates containing beryllium pieces, cylinders, and uranium plugs, similar to what he had discovered a year earlier in April 1992. These were parts of portable nuclear devices. The bank claimed it was holding the material as collateral for a loan VEKA was seeking to obtain, and it could be assumed that the bank was aware of the nuclear material in the crates and possibly that the material was for portable nuclear devices. But, Idema felt the bank could have been involved and merely one more front company the KGB was using.

It was learned that the nuclear material came from a Russian nuclear research facility at Obninsk, Russia, and had been sold to the A.M.I. Trading Company in Yekinterinberg, located east of the Ural Mountains on the fringes of Siberia. A.M.I. had shipped the nuclear material to another company, the VEKA Trading Company in Lithuania.

The packing list enclosed with the shipment did not list the ultimate destination. International law requires that dual use material such as beryllium must have an approved end user certificate.

In the fall of 1993, Idema and Rimkevicius discovered from a KGB source in Moscow that the KGB source had documents showing the trail and eventual destination of the stolen nuclear weapons and materials. Idema met with the source in a country outside of Russia and Lithuania and examined the documents. They revealed the logistics of the nuclear bomb smuggling activities and the sources willing to sell them.

Key KGB officials would authorize the removal of SADMs from the Soviet 12th Directorate, supposedly for shipment to nuclear research facilities for dismantling purposes. The KGB officials used phony trading companies that worked with the Russian Mafia to transport the stolen material. The trading companies bought beryllium and other needed material from Russian research facilities.

Under this arrangement, the records showed the nuclear weapons as being properly disposed of, rather than missing or stolen. Idema and Rimkevicius discovered documents revealing that several shipments of nuclear explosive material, and suitcase nuclear bombs, went through Turkey and on to Saddam Hussein in Iraq and terrorists in Qom, Iran. Of the 12 nuclear shipments they knew were sent through Lithuania by 1997, two were intercepted.

The KGB officials arranged for the SADMs and U-235 to be packed inside the crates of beryllium. A combination of Russian criminal groups, KGB officials, and Soviet Special Forces, then shipped the material through Lithuania via surface transportation to terrorist groups or foreign governments.

DOJ Personnel Filing False Charges against Idema

Idema's problems with Department of Justice personnel occurred after Idema refused to reveal to them the names of his contacts in Lithuania. Idema did not trust Department of Justice employees with information that could have revealed the identify of his sources to the Soviets. Among the FBI employees seeking that information was FBI agent Earl Edwin Pitts, who was later discovered to have been providing information on FBI sources to the Soviets, resulting in many of them being killed. The criminal charges involved a business partnership that Idema had, involving fraud, which Idema claims was perpetrated by his partner and then used by Department of Justice personnel against Idema.

A *Christian Science Monitor* article (April 2002) described the failure of FBI personnel to recognize the obvious indications that a key FBI agent has a large income greatly exceeding his government salary:

> The Federal Bureau of Investigation missed multiple warnings about spy Robert Hanssen … Russia complained that a "disaffected agent," later identified as Hanssen, tried to sell US secrets in 1993, eight years before his arrest. In 1990, Hanssen's brother-in-law, also an FBI agent, warned that he had suspiciously large sums of money at home.

> A *Washington Post article* (April 7, 2002), headlined, "FBI says spy ratted out 50 informants," stated:
>
> A preliminary damage assessment by the FBI of the impact of convicted spy Robert Hanssen's treachery determined that the identities of more than 50 people who were providing confidential intelligence information to the bureau or were being recruited to do so were disclosed to the Russians.
>
> It has been reported that Hanssen's disclosures played a part in the execution or jailing of at least three Russians who had spied for the United

States, this is the first indication that his activities put in jeopardy a far larger number of other people working clandestinely for the bureau, according to a report released last week by a special commission headed by former FBI and CIA director William Webster.

When CIA spy Aldrich Ames was uncovered in 1994, it was learned that he had disclosed the names of CIA and FBI recruited Soviet and Warsaw Pact agents and that about 10 were executed.

Overwhelming Support for Idema

Many people came forward showing that Idema did not commit the crime. Others wrote letters in support of Idema. U.S. District Judge Terrance Boyle, who was acting to insure the success of the Justice Department scheme, ignored their letters and the newly discovered evidence.

In Lithuania, Rimkevicius, learning of the charges against Idema, tried to get the charges dropped by refusing to allow any cooperation between the U.S. and his Lithuanian commandos regarding the smuggling of nuclear devices. Idema continued to provide additional information about terrorist activities to his Pentagon contacts. But Pentagon officials believed that the information was too sensitive and involved national security issues, and should only be made known to the CIA.

Letters Sent to Sentencing Judge on Idema's Behalf

Colonel William I. Chadwick, Director, Combat Development Division, Headquarters, U.S. Army Special Operations Command, wrote in a March 31, 1994 letter to Judge Terrence W Boyle, U.S. District Judge, at Elizabeth City, North Carolina:

> Keith is an honorable man… I trust his judgment and value his advice. I have pursued his counsel in matters concerning national defense…

In a letter to me on April 20, 1997, talkshow host Barry Farber provided more information:

> After following his story (Idema) now I'm convinced he needs to be on the outside telling what he knows of the traffic in weapon-grade nuclear materials from Russia plus other information he acquired in the service of our country; particularly in reference to the sieve-like leakage from our topmost intelligence agencies.

From Lithuania, Juozas Rimkvicius, Commander and Chief, National police/ARAS Commandos and Interpol, Lithuanian Republic Ministry of Internal Affairs, wrote in a May 26, 1994 official letter to Judge Boyle:

> In this country…Keith is an American hero… He helped our country when we were young and needed assistance… We came to judge most of what we know of America and her ideals by Keith.

Major, now Colonel, Ricky D. Lester, U.S. Special Operations, Task Force 160 (the US's most classified helicopter unit), wrote:

> Keith has dedicated his life to the service of his country, and, on several occasions, was prepared to give his life for his fellow man so they could enjoy the gift of freedom. Keith Idema, a man who has walked the moral high ground, and has lived according to the creed "Duty, Honor, Country…

Ted Kavanau, who spent three decades in journalism, was a CNN Vice President, who won the Emmy Award numerous times for top journalist, wrote in a September 30, 1995, letter:

> *As one of the key founders of Cable News Network and Headline News and as a multiple Emmy Award winning journalist of three decades experience, I know a major story when I see one. Right now "60 Minutes" is working on such a major story, based on information supplied by J. Keith Idema.* Idema has also made several lengthy appearances on the "Barry Farber" national radio program.
>
> Several full-length articles have also been printed in magazi*nes about Mr. Idema*'s situation. This is because, in addition to his significant military, police and civil contribution to our nation, Mr. Idema has made a highly significant contribution to our nuclear security. I think it is worth po*inting out that his contribution is playing an important role in helping to save my family, your family, and all American families from some of the immediate and long range dangers of nuclear terrorist. That which Mr. Idema has told me about his work on these issues has been verified by top investigative journalists. ...*

Retired U.S. Army Special Forces Major Jim Morris sent a September 22, 1995, letter to Senator Arlen Specter (the same senator who repeatedly covered up for the many criminal activities that were described to him in letters that I and some of my other sources wrote to him). Included in that letter were the following comments:

> I am writing to acquaint you with another gross miscarriag*e of justice resulting from FBI hubris and with profound consequences for the nation. This is the story of a young man who came forward with vital intelligence relating to nuclear terrorism. He was more than willing to share this material with the U.S. government, but was not at liberty to divulge his sources.*

That was not good enough for the FBI. He has been in confinement now for almost four years, and his wife has been in confinement for just under one year, all in an effort to make him break his word, *and to do something that he believes, with good reason, would be disastrous for the nation.*

Justice Department Prosecutors
Continued Protecting Its Culture

There were many other letters, but the federal judge ignored them. He also ignored one of the most compelling letters ever sent in connection with a FBI criminal case. Asking for Idema's release, The Deputy Assistant Secretary of Defense for Special Operations and Low Intensity Conflict, the Honorable Timothy A. Connolly wrote to Judge Boyle on official Department of Defense letterhead the following comments:

Keith Idema may be one of the last individuals for whom the phrase "I give you my word" still has meaning. To Keith, honor is everything. And his word is the manifestation of that honor. It is never offered lightly, but once given, its recipient can proceed, confident in the knowledge that Keith will do what he has pledged to do, no matter how difficult... His word. I have accepted it frequently in the past; I have never been disappointed.

Federal Judge Supporting Corrupt
Justice Department Prosecutors

Not only did U.S. District Judge Terrence W. Boyle[91] ignore these letters, and the obvious obstruction of justice tactics by his legal compatriots in the Justice Department, but he sentenced Idema to 20 years in prison. Keith said the federal sentencing guidelines call for 6 to 12 months for similar offenses. The draconian prison sentences imposed to silence those who expose corruption in federal government is a common tactic to keep the information from the public.

Confirming the Existence of Operation Peregrine

Idema had learned of my attempts to expose corrupt government personnel and we started to correspond. Idema wrote in one letter that "my loyalty is to the military; my enemies are the Department of Justice, especially the FBI. I consider the CIA neutral." He confirmed in a June 1997 letter one of the operations that I had described several years earlier in *Defrauding America*:

> Regarding Peregrine, I'm not so sure I want to see any more info about Peregrine, Counter Group, or the IDDC, etc., in print. I believe that what they/we were doing was the right thing to do, and we were soldiers, at war, and righteous. Wrong is things like the FBI's COINTELPRO. I'll only confirm their existence.

In an April 2, 1997, letter, Idema wrote, "It has been my dream to walk into the U.S. Senate and testify before them the real story of nukes, Iraq, and KGB/FBI, and how [Soviet mole] Pitts was really discovered."

---

[91] U.S. district judge Terrence W. Boyle, Elizabeth City, North Carolina.

No Trust in America's Media

Idema felt that government officials control the mainstream media, a discovery that I made over many years, and which has been the subject of several books by media insiders. Before the FBI acted to silence him, Idema briefed many people on the dangers of the ongoing theft of nuclear material and the suitcase nuclear devices.

In letters commencing in early 1997 Idema told me that in March and April of 1992 he briefed Pentagon personnel, and in December 1992 and January 1993, he briefed CIA personnel. He directly informed President Bill Clinton's legal counsel, Bernard Nussbaum, in 1993. He briefed the Special Operations community in June 1993. And he met with ex-Special Forces associates, now working for the FBI, numerous times in 1993, warning them of FBI double agents.

One was FBI Agent Gary Rohen, Idema's old team leader, who remained silent, receiving a promotion and job as head of the Bureau's Emergency Management & Disaster Preparation Office. Idema hand-carried secret messages from Moscow to Top Secret people in the U.S. intelligence community revealing terrorist activities, the existence of Soviet spies in the FBI, and KGB sales of portable backpack nuclear weapons (SADMs) to Iraq, Iran, and North Korea. None showed any reaction or interest, even after Justice Department prosecutors later acted to silence him.

Further Corroboration of Information Provided to Me Earlier

Idema's April 15, 1997, letter referred to the book that I sent him, the second edition of *Defrauding America*: "I received your book. Thanks very much. I didn't plan on reading it for a few days, but when I started to glance through it I was so enthralled that I could not put it down—it's great! Especially for people like us (intelligence community)." Referring to my reference to Peregrine International, Idema wrote in his April 15, 1997, letter of the sister organizations: Counter Group Associate (aka Counter Group Academy—aka The U.S. Counter Terrorist Group):

> The first paragraph on page 605 was fairly accurate b*ut it was a much bigger operation than that. I was the director of the organiz*ation (CGA) for about five years. Counter is still operating. I only tell you this so you may check out my bonifides with whoever your source was for that information. I do not t*ell you for the purpose of exposing Counter—since I still believe in it s purpose, men, mi*ssion (although we were frequently misused).
>
> Understand that my enemy is the DOJ and not the U.S. military to whom I remain totally loyal, as they have remained tota*lly loyal to me...*
>
> I still have extensive contacts and sources in the Special Operations and intelligence community that trust me and will give me anything because I did five years in prison and never sold out any of them, as did my

good friend (but I don't blame him for doing it) Dick Marcinko—he had his reasons for what he did exposing; I have mine for the way I will handle it.

Media Sources Confirmed Idema's Credibility and Truthfulness

Among the people who knew Idema and his activities, with whom I was in contact, was Gary Scurka. He had worked as a television producer for CBS. During a May 18, 1997, conversation, he confirmed much of what Idema wrote to me, that Idema ran special operations exposition shows twice a year to which U.S. and foreign military dignitaries enrolled; that Idema clandestinely operated for the military, yet appeared as a private citizen and businessman; and that he was falsely prosecuted by Justice Department prosecutors.

He explained being very familiar with Idema, his activities, and his European sources, and how his television investigators had traveled to Lithuania, met people who knew Idema, who were trained by him, and confirmed what Idema told me. Scurka stated:

> I heard from a very high up person in the Pentagon (the Assistant Secretary of Defense) several years ago at one of the meetings that was held in July 1992 in the Pentagon. In attendance also were the CIA and the FBI. Keith refused to provide information to them, stating he would provide information only to Pentagon personnel. When Keith refused to cooperate with anyone but Pentagon personnel, there was bad blood.
>
> After the meeting was over, this senior official who I am in contact with told me that CIA personnel came up to him and said, "This guy's full of shit." And the Pentagon guy said, "Well, how do you know?" The CIA really tried to downplay his information. But my source told me, a few weeks later, that the CIA then "flooded Lithuania with agents," rousting Keith's sources trying to find out information. Were people's lives put in danger? Lo and behold, here is this former sergeant in the Green Berets talking to Lauren Fausbit (sp?) and talking to Interpol and talking to organized crime people. I don't think the CIA and FBI liked that very much.
>
> One of my first meetings with Keith in North Carolina, while I was working for CBS, this would have been April or May of 1994, he identified for me that the New York Counter Intelligence & Terrorism Office was compromised. There is obviously a lot to Idema's story. I haven't confirmed it all, but an awful lot of it I have. And I've been to Lithuania twice. Keith supplied all of the information to me that ran on CBS 60 Minutes.
>
> He did link organized crime and officials to the nuclear trade smuggling. He did take this information to the Pentagon; the CIA and FBI were indeed aware of this. They did go to Lithuania, caused some trouble there. And there's a great deal of evidence now that strongly suggests that Keith was set up for the charge that he's now in prison for. Those things I'm quite sure of. Keith's very sensitive about being in Black Ops and he will not

comment on that. But it sure looks like it. He dislikes people who kinda just came out and spilled their guts.

Mr. Idema arranged for Lithuanian Intelligence sources to brief the Department of Defense at the Pentagon in July of 1992 on Russian terrorist activity. After Idema's portion of the briefing Department of Justice personnel requested his assistance. US State Department personnel requested he terminate his activities inside Lithuania and the former Soviet Union. This was the result of a turf war between the FBI, CIA, and US State Department.

Senior officers of the Federal Bureau of Investigation, including Larry Potts and Danny Coulsen, met with Idema and Russian diplomats in December 1992. Shortly thereafter FBI requested his assistance again. Mr. Idema made it clear he would only work with the Department of Defense agencies. The FBI began concerted effort to "squeeze" Idema for the names of the intelligence sources he had sworn to protect.

Special Agent William Zinnikas of the FBI's New York Counter Intelligence Office continued to pressure Idema, and used Judge Boyle to make it stick and increase his punishment.

[Double Agents Were Later Discovered in the FBI]

Scurka told how the New York FBI office of counter-intelligence and counter-terrorism particularly went after Idema to learn the names of his covert sources. One of these agents was special agent Pitts, formerly of the FBI's New York Russian Squad, who later pled guilty to spying for the Russians, and that Pitts was an influencing force in the conviction against Idema.

While Idema was in prison on the bogus Justice Department charges, he provided important information to several of the broadcast and print media concerning the suitcase nuclear bombs, in order to expose the FBI's wrongful actions. This information included top secret Russian documents and referrals to Russian and Lithuanian personnel who had provided Idema with insider information on the theft of the suitcase nuclear devices.

As a result of Idema's information, in June 1996, the Investigative Reporters and Editors Association (IRE) awarded CBS 60 Minutes, U.S. News & World Report, and Gary Scurka of Enterprise Telefilms, the top award for the most outstanding story and investigative report of the year.

On the letterhead of the television program, *Eye To Eye*, dated October 4, 1994, Gary Scurka sent to Idema's wife, Dawn, a letter about the story that that would eventually air on CBS *60 Minutes* in October 1995.

Connie Chung *Eye-To-Eye* Broadcast

The broadcast story, known behind closed doors as *The Vilinus Brief*, was based upon information and documentation provided by Idema and a key official in the Lithuanian Criminal police agency. The broadcast made reference to Idema and the Lithuanian official and their clash with the FBI and CIA as it related to the nuclear devices.

The *Vilnius Brief* stated, "According to a source in the U.S. Army Special Operations, the most common SADM deployed in Europe had an explosive yield of 6.5 thousand tons (kilotons) of TNT." According to a report prepared by the International Strategy Associates, the *Eye-To-Eye* report stated that Soviet SADMs have a destructive yield of between one to ten kilotons and contains about two kilos (less than five pounds) of highly enriched uranium.

The *Eye-To-Eye* report stated that during this time, Idema, who was supposed to be in the Army reserves, was assigned to various positions at active duty units, including the Army's top secret SOT course at the classified installation where "blue light," the forerunner to the Delta Forces was founded. SOT is where the Special Forces trained their elite Ninja-type commando teams. In 1983, Idema's job was evaluating the instructors at the most classified counterterrorism school *in the world.*

An article in the *San Francisco Chronicle* (July 1, 1997) titled, "Pair Allegedly Tried to Sell Soviet Nukes," stated:

Miami. Two Lithuanians have been accused of trying to sell Soviet-era nuclear weapons to federal agents posing as arms brokers for drug smugglers. No weapons changed hands, but the pair were caught on audio and video tape negotiating the sale of nuclear weapons and Bulgarian-made non-nuclear surface-to-air missiles, investigators said Monday. Compiled from Examiner wire reports.

The Perfect Terrorist Weapon

CBS's *60-Minutes* show on September 7, 1997, addressed the suitcase nuclear bombs under the heading, "The Perfect Terrorist Weapon." The program omitted all reference to Idema, who had provided much of the information, documentation, and referrals to Russian and Lithuanian military personnel. Despite the gravity of the subject, the program was limited to the standard few minutes, and centered on the statements made by General Alexander Lebed, who *60-Minutes* described in the following manner:

> The former senior Russian official is none other than General Alexander Lebed, a national hero who commanded Russia's 14th Army, was highly decorated in Afghanistan and, as Boris Yeltsin's national security adviser, was widely credited with ending the Chechnan War.
>
> General Lebed, who has had tactical nuclear weapons under his command, says he was so concerned about the small one-kiloton nuclear demolition devices that while he was national security adviser, he began an inventory to guarantee that all of those weapons were safe and accounted for.

The producers of the CBS *60-Minutes* show were Andrew and Leslie Cockburn. They later sold Idema's story to Steven Spielberg and it became the first film released by Spielberg's newly formed DreamWorks Studios. The blockbuster film was called *The Peacemaker*, and starred George Clooney as a renegade Green Beret chasing backpack nuclear weapons and terrorists in Eastern Europe.

Clooney's character, Tom Devoe, appeared in his opening scene testifying in a Congressional hearing about his alleged illegal activities. Spielberg's film, which did not acknowledge being based on Idema, differed from Idema's story and painted the Clinton administration as being competent in the war on nuclear smuggling.

More Support for Theft of Suitcase Nuclear Bombs

A *Los Angeles Times* article (September 9, 1997) titled, "Ex-general says Russia lost 100 portable nuclear bombs," stated:

> MOSCOW—Alexander Lebed, the former Russian general and presidential hopeful, has been broadcasting his claim over the past week that Russia has lost track of 100 nuclear bombs the size of suitcases. "A very thorough investigation is necessary," Lebed reiterated Monday. "The state of nuclear security in Russia poses a danger to the whole world."

In an interview with CBS *60-Minutes*, aired Sunday, Lebed said:

> The suitcase bombs were ideal weapons for terrorists because they could be armed and detonated by a single person within half an hour. One of the one-kiloton bombs could kill 100,000 people, he said. Of 250 suitcase devices made by the Soviet Union, he said, 100 are unaccounted for.
>
> On Monday, Lebed told *Interfax News Service* in Moscow that he had learned of the existence of the bombs 11 months ago when he was Yeltsin's security adviser.
>
> Lebed said the suitcase bombs, measuring about 23 inches by 16 inches and 8 inches wide, were deployed by the Soviet Union in special brigades in some of the empire's remote regions. After the breakup of the Soviet state, many of the suitcases vanished in what became independent republics, where they could fall into the hands of terrorists, he said.
>
> Lebed's American broadcast brought denunciations from a host of officials, including Prime Minister Viktor Chernomyrdin, who called his contention "absolutely impossible."

Russian General Confirming Stolen Suitcase Nuclear Bombs

A September 14, 1997, newspaper article described the disappearance of suitcase nuclear bombs from Russian military arsenals:

> Alexander Lebed, the former secretary of the Russian security council, had suggested recently that such [nuclear weapons] might be missing from

Russia's military arsenal. That same night on CBS *60 Minutes*, General Lebed confirmed his belief that Russian nuclear weapons *were* missing.

Idema Filed Federal Lawsuit

Idema filed a lawsuit in the U.S. District Court in the Southern District of New York (96 CV-2841) in October 1995, detailing the cover-up and abandonment he experienced from CBS *60-Minutes*, *Eye-To-Eye*, and *U.S. News and World Reports*. The complaint alleged breach of contract and fraud, under the Racketeer Influenced and Corrupt Organizations Act (RICO).

In that lawsuit, Idema explained how he provided these media personnel with confidential information and secret Russian documents from which they then published articles and television presentations, but left out any information that might reflect badly upon government officials in the FBI, the CIA, and Congress. By this slanted presentation of the facts, viewers were unaware of how Justice Department employees and Clinton Administration officials prevented discovery of the logistics involved in the theft of the nuclear material and devices and the people receiving them

Idema's lawsuit explained how his information and contacts were sabotaged by Justice Department officials, preventing discovery of the logistics of the nuclear smuggling conspiracy and what groups had acquired nuclear devices. Also, that the media defendants had violated their agreement to tell the complete story and how Idema uncovered the nuclear smuggling operations.

The lawsuit explains the agreement that he had, that they were to include, as consideration for the material, his role in these activities, without which the published and broadcast description of the suitcase nuclear devices would either have not occurred or much of the supporting material would not have been available to them.

The lawsuit stated how Idema and his wife were improperly convicted as a result of FBI misconduct and witness perjury, that he was an ex-member of the US Army Special Forces, that he and his wife, Dawn Glosson, operated a trade show for the special forces community under the name of Special Operations Expositions and Conference (Spec Ops). He explained how in 1991, while traveling inside the former Soviet Union he came in contact with high ranking members of the Lithuanian and Russian counter intelligence community, gained their trust, and received from them information concerning activities of the KGB, OMON, and various terrorist groups in Lithuania, Russia, and surrounding territories. He stated in this federal court filing that:

> Members of the KGB were engaged in the "theft" of nuclear materials from the Russian Federation, and smuggling these devices to locations in the Middle East and North Korea. These devices and nuclear materials were available for sale to foreign countries and terrorist groups. …
>
> Members of the intelligence community in Lithuania advised Mr. Idema to be very discrete in revealing information about these activities within

the United States because United States intelligence sources and the Federal Bureau of Investigation had been compromised by the KGB.

FBI Incompetence Shown by FBI Agents Openly Spying for the Soviet Union

That was long before Pitts and Hanssen were arrested as KGB spies in the FBI. Idema described in the lawsuit how FBI Special Agent William Zinnikas, Sr., of the FBI's Counter-Intelligence Unit specializing in Russian information and assets, had agreed with Idema, in front of Scurka, that Idema's wife, Dawn, would be released from prison after Idema and Gary Scurka provided a document relating to the sale, transfer, and smuggling of nuclear material. Scurka turned the document over to the FBI, the promised release did not occur.

In fact, not only did the FBI violate the release agreement, but within 72 hours the document was in the hands of the KGB in Russia and Russian officials were frantically trying to find out where their leak was and identify Idema's covert sources in Russia. Idema's worst fears were validated. Idema included in the lawsuit seven sealed copies of documents relating to the theft of the nuclear material that caused the court to place the documents under seal. He also provided these documents to me.

Reminders of Prior Justice Department Calamities

In my books and my 40 years of discovering and exposing corrupt government personnel, a few stand out as they relate to Justice Department lawyers:

Justice Department lawyers covering up the documented corruption that I discovered, initially while a federal air safety inspector. This cover-up enabled the corruption and the crashes to continue, year after year, with the most recent consequences occurring on September 11, 2001.

Justice Department lawyers engaging in conduct that insured the transfer of several dozen surface-to-air missiles to terrorists, and which occurred about seven months prior to the missile downing of TWA Flight 800.

Justice Department lawyers covering up for the people who actually placed the bomb on board Pan Am Flight 103, and the Justice Department retaliation against a covert DIA agent and a former Mossad agent for exposing the people who actually placed the bomb on board the aircraft.

Justice Department lawyers covering up for the decades of CIA and DEA drug smuggling into the United States, which continues in a cover-up status, with grave consequences upon matters of national importance.

Justice Department lawyers covering up for other criminal and subversive activities that are detailed in some of my books, including *Defrauding America, Drugging America*, and *History of Aviation Disasters: 1950 to 9/11*.

Idema Working With Northern Alliance's General Dostum

In early 2001, I heard from Idema's current wife, Viktoria Robertson. She wrote:

> Keith kept a pretty low profile for a few years and rebuilt his life. He had returned to absolutely nothing except the clothes on his back. He then found himself in a whirlwind again, fighting with the DOJ about Waco (he exposed the now famous secret documents that showed the army did NOT want to assault the compound and recommended to the FBI and Reno not to do it)
>
> After that, he moved on to a new mission, finding a Czech spy in the US government, finding the real killer of a famous Green Beret Colonel's wife. (He won the National Press Club Award in Washington, DC last summer for his story, "Spies, Lies, and Serial Killers," a one year investigative report, which I helped co-produce).
>
> Then, comfortable in our home and enjoying life, September 11th happened. Within a month, Keith was in Afghanistan fighting the Taliban and al Qaida. That was six months ago and he has still not returned. There have been hundreds of stories about his deeds in Afghanistan; many of the stories simply refer to him as "Jack, the senior military advisor for the Northern Alliance." Jack is how he is known throughout Afghanistan.

My Early Reference to Northern Alliance's General Rashid Dostum

I first made reference to General Rashid Dostum several years earlier in the third edition of *Defrauding America* and *Explosive Secrets of Covert CIA Companies*. A friend of mine, Ronald Rewald, who had been the head of a secret CIA financial operation based in Honolulu, had played a role in negotiations between General Dostum and CIA and FBI personnel in Los Angeles. The negotiations involved Dostum's offer to provide nearly 100 surface-to-air missiles to the United States, which FBI and CIA personnel refused. The missiles were then reportedly conveyed to Middle East terrorists–about one year prior to the downing of TWA Flight 800.

Post 9/11 Actions of Keith Idema

After 9/11, Idema formed a crew and went to Afghanistan, hunting for Osama bin Laden. Among the crew was journalists Gary Scurka, Kevin Sites, and Ed Caraballo. One reason for going was to produce a film for *National Geographic* and to carry out missions for humanitarian groups.

Once in Afghanistan, Idema fell out with the two humanitarian organizations he was supposed to accompany. Their version is that he violated the agreement (which I have) he signed before accompanying them by wearing a military uniform and carrying weapons. Idema later sued both of these organizations. The group had allegedly lacked the necessary visas to enter several of the countries that they visited. For reasons not clear, the Department of Justice and the Department of Defense issued arrest warrants for Idema

Arrested in July 2004 Under Questionable Conditions

Idema was eventually arrested in Afghanistan. Newspapers in the United States reported the arrest of Idema and his crew, claiming they had their own jail containing Afghans that they had capture, and that the captives had been tortured. Idema claimed he was acting with the approval of the Department of Defense and other Washington officials, and was in frequent contact with the office of Secretary of Defense Donald Rumsfeld.

A *New York Times* article (July 23, 2004) stated:

> American military officials in Afghanistan said that they had accepted but later released an Afghan prisoner handed over to them in May by an American [Idema] now accused of running his own freelance antiterrorism campaign.
>
> Jonathan K. Idema, a former Green Beret who has said he was working in Afghanistan with the approval of senior Pentagon officials. Mr. Idema and two other Americans are being tried by the Afghan government on charges of hostage-taking, operating a private jail, entering the country illegally and illegal weapons possession.
>
> Before his court appearance in Kabul on Wednesday, Mr. Idema told reporters that he had been in direct contact with Defense Secretary Donald H. Rumsfeld's office "five times a day." Mr. Idema said he had correspondence, tape recordings and e-mail messages to prove this.
>
> On July 5, Afghan police raided the house Mr. Idema rented in Kabul and found eight Afghan men being held prisoner.
>
> Mr. Idema is well known among journalists in Afghanistan. After he arrived in 2001, he offered his services as a security expert and produced videos of training camps of Al Qaeda.

Radio Appearance from Afghan Detention Facility

During a radio talkshow appearance (January 25, 2005) from his Kabul detention facility with host Chris Chaos of WFNC-FM in Fayetteville, North Carolina, Idema blamed the charges and his incarceration on the FBI, saying:

> The Afghans didn't do this to me. The FBI did this. Because we were beating them at every step of the way. We were beating them in the investigation on the bombers; these guys were going to kill Marshal Fahim, who was the only guy that could successfully oppose Karzai, for the presidency. Marshall Fahim was the Minister of Defense.
>
> The U.S. didn't want him as Minister of Defense anymore. Because he wasn't willing to let the Taliban come back into power. He wasn't willing to do this Department of State power sharing broker deal. And that's what this is all about. It's about the Department of State saying, "Why fight the

Taliban when we can just assimilate them into the new Government?" You know, the same old thing of appeasement. Well, that's not gonna work. It's gonna work for about six months and then all hell is gonna break loose.

The FBI came in July and confiscated all our documents, all of our video, and an Armada laptop computer. They confiscated our MARSAT phones, our encryption; everything they confiscated. They did this because they didn't want anyone to know we had that stuff, which we would not have if we weren't working with the government.

They also took, more importantly, all the videos and all the documents, including the authorization letters signed by Vice President, the Minister of Interior, and the National Security Council here.

They took 200 tapes; they had erased more than twenty tapes. And they completely confiscated all the tapes that had conversations with high-level Department of Defense people. So now we are left with no evidence. But they were stupid enough to do what the Afghans made them do; which was sign for it.

On one hand you have the American government trying to screw us completely. On the other hand, the Department of Defense is trying not to screw us. And the Afghans, they are caught in between both sides.

Same Team Protecting America from Suitcase Nuclear Bombs

The same people, groups, and culture are in place to protect the American people from the probable nuclear explosion in American cities from the hundreds of suitcase nuclear bombs that were produced by the United States and the Soviet Union–and possibly other countries that possess nuclear capability, such as Pakistan and North Korean.

Starting in the mid 1960s when I held key positions in government, I repeatedly saw–and reported–the existence of corruption of people in key government positions, and a continuing repeat of steadily worsening consequences. We now have nuclear capabilities throughout the world, with American politicians continuing arrogant policies that have created millions of people wanting to kill Americans. here are so many ways in which this can be done, especially by people whose hatred is so strong for Americans that they are willing to kill themselves in the process.

Idema's Problems in Afghanistan

After the U.S. invaded Afghanistan, Idema became involved in one way or another in that war. In September 2004, Idema was convicted in Afghanistan of running a private prison and torturing Afghan citizens—similar to many secret U.S. operations. Idema had been identifying himself as a Special Forces operative on a mission to apprehend terrorists.

In the spook world of U.S. convert operations, it is difficult to know the truth. However, his early release in April 2007, ordered by Afghanistan president Hamid Karzai, after having served three years of a ten-year sentence, suggests Idema was no ordinary prisoner.

CHAPTER TWENTY NINE

Frightful Self-Made Future for Americans

The American public has a right to expect people in positions of trust in government, who are paid to perform a duty and responsibility, to carry out those responsibilities in an honest manner. There are people in multiple checks and balances that are paid and in a position of trust to act when others perform in a corrupt manner. And there are media people and media corporations that have a duty to report when any of these people are not carrying out their responsibilities or are acting in a corrupt or criminal manner.

Unfortunately, the system has been so thoroughly corrupted that rarely are these responsibilities carried out. And so thoroughly corrupt is the system that anyone who does attempt to report corrupt activities, especially when they pass a certain point of gravity, suffers some form of retaliation. Much of the public is unaware of these matters, partly due to the withholding of information by the media, which appears to dumb down the public—or assume that most of them are already there! In addition to the problem of keeping the public uninformed or illiterate about these matters, other segments of the public are complicit. For instance:

- Books and articles have been written for decades about some area or other of corruption in government, and the sometimes deadly consequences suffered by people.
- Many people don't read sufficient numbers of books and other publications to even know there is corruption adversely affecting them. Constant reading is necessary to receive even an initial basic understanding of these matters. And today, the public is obsessed with the most trivial matters possible, at a time when the corruption and the dire consequences are worse than possibly at any time in history.
- And those who do know, are either too lazy, too apathetic, too cowardly, and devoid of the character necessary for our type of government to function as intended.

The information in this book is serious beyond comprehension. The gravity of the information would be recognized even more if the reader read the other books that I have written over the past 30 years with the help and contribution of dozens of other insiders. The contents in this book will help the readers understand several of the many areas of Trojan-horse corruption in and out of government.

In these days of unprecedented distortion of the news by media people and political pundits, the unprecedented lying politicians and their shills in the media, the public urgently needs access to this type of information. Unfortunately, the public today is even *less* interested in the corruption in government, less interested in reading books by insiders, and more interested in trivial activities that appear to be an extension of baby pacifiers.

Any U.S. Interest Can be Sold Out For a Price

As the information here shows, any vital U.S. interest, or the interest of any person, can and is being sold out for a price. There is no absence of people, especially of politicians, that will not use their position, for a price, to sell out American interests.

Only the Tip of Widespread Corruption in the Various DOJ Offices

What has been described about law enforcement corruption within these pages is only a small part of what has been reported over the years. My other books, all of which are based upon what I and other government agents had discovered provide a broader picture of the extent of the corruption.

The harm already inflicted upon America is enormous, and steadily increasing. This cannot continue much further without a total collapse of our society, our government, and the national solvency. Someday, historians may write and wonder why the American public was so indifferent, so illiterate about what was being done to them. If enough responsible people, who recognize their obligations under the form of government in the United States, will become informed and take actions that they *can* take, there may be time remaining.

Can These Things be True?

Can the things stated in this book be true? They are not only true, but the areas of misconduct are only a fraction of the areas of corruption that are detailed in the various books that I have written with the help of dozens of insiders. And the incidents described in these pages are only a minute fraction of similar incidents related to the issues stated here.

The corruption is mutating throughout government, and throughout society. The United States is in deep trouble, and the younger people are going to suffer increasing hardships and tragedies. The best that can be hoped for, is that a sufficient number of them start becoming informed and exhibit some courage in fighting the literal Trojan horses subverting the nation. Much of the factual information stated here is based upon the following:

- What I have actually seen, experienced, and documented as a federal investigator.
- What I discovered and documented in judicial records during the past 40 years.

- What was discovered by government agents and other insiders who have for many years provided me with hundreds of hours of recorded information in deposition-like question, and hundreds of documents. They had nothing to gain, and much to lose, by providing me with this evidence. These sources include, among others, people from the CIA, ONI, DIA, DEA, INS, Customs, FBI, FAA, Secret Service, and local and state investigators. They also include former drug traffickers and Mafia family members. Some have even provided me with sworn affidavits, some of which I have entered into federal court proceedings.
- What I learned as a victim of powerful forces seeking to halt my exposure activities.
- Copies of secret transcripts of testimony given in closed-door congressional hearings.
- Government investigative reports.
- Government documents and newspaper investigative reports.

People must recognize that they, or their families, can be tragically affected, directly and indirectly, by the corruption and its ripple effects.

Those with a Vested Interest in Continuing the Status Quo

Certain groups that will block any effort to expose these matters include, for instance:

- People in control of the Department of Justice, who are or were guilty of the corruption, or knew of it and remained silent.
- Federal judges who were corruptly involved in the cover-ups and obstruction of justice, either actively or passively.
- Members of Congress who have for decades known of the corrupt activities and who either actively or passively covered up for the crimes and the catastrophic consequences.
- Media people and organizations that for decades have covered up for corruption in government when the corruption had serious political consequences.
- Lawyers who have known of the corruption for decades and who have remained silent, and especially those 50 or more that were directly involved in sham attacks against me as they sought to halt my exposure activities.

Breakdown in Constitutional Protections

Only a small percentage of the population is alive today that remember and recognize the constitutional protections that existed years ago. Today, paramilitary attacks upon homes and families, seizing assets without any conviction, long prison sentences for relatively minor offenses, are only a few of the constitutional violations. The generation born after World War II grew up as the constitutional rights and protections were slowly eroded.

The protections of the Constitution disappear when the checks and balances are corrupted as they are today. Certain changes to the Constitution are needed to halt the erosion of these protections.

Changes must be made in the statutes to eliminate the self-serving immunity judges and prosecutors have given themselves. Federal judges and government prosecutors, among other government employees, must be subject to civil and criminal damages when they engage in corruption that inflicts harm upon innocent people. The offices of the Attorney General and the Department of Justice must be removed from the control of the president of the United States, and serve the nation rather than the corrupt acts of a president.

Ombudsmen Needed at Every Level of Government

One answer to this sordid culture is either a constitutional amendment or legislation for an impartial panel of ombudsmen at every level of local, state, and federal government that have the power to take action against those involved in misconduct.

An "ombudsman" group is badly needed that is totally separate from any other government agency or official, with ample staffing to come to the aid of any citizen suffering harm from arrogant and corrupt government personnel. A nationwide system of ombudsmen with the power to take action against any corruption in government, including state or federal, and take action to protect anyone victimized by someone acting under cover of government office.

Without public awareness of the gravity of the problems, and pressure to create the legal or constitutional provision, nothing will be done. And with the worsening interest in such matters by the public, that is unlikely to occur

***Real* Patriots and Heroes Are Badly Needed**

America refers to ball players as "heroes," or those who perform an expected duty, making a mockery of the word. Never has America needed real heroes more than now. Our form of government *requires* its citizens to be patriots. The true patriots are those few people who have the courage to fight the epidemic corruption in government, and they are virtually non-existing. Never has there been such a low percentage of them in the general population. Americans don't seem to know the meaning of the word.

Will the Public Ever Meet Its Responsibilities?

Most of the public remains unaware and indifferent to the harm made possible by their ignorance of important matters. Today, the emphasis is on a constant blaring of what they call "music," or their obsession with videos games or social pursuits. I witnessed this apathy for the past 30 years as I appeared as guest and expert on over 3000 radio and television shows, seeking to inform the people of the great harm being inflicted upon them by corruption in government.

Many listeners expressed concern—and then did nothing. Even relatives of people killed in fraud-related air disasters that I had exposed did nothing, and none offered to help me expose the corruption. Their only interest appeared to be rushing to a law firm for financial enrichment. Those who say the public will *never* wake up and react are probably correct.

Unless a large enough segment of the American people develop the habit of heavy reading of books and articles written by people with a background and expertise in matters affecting their lives, they will continue to be naïve victims of political pundits, and continue to suffer the consequences.

Can America Survive These Deteriorated Values?

Those of us who fought in World War II and saw what America was like in the mid-1900s, have seen the deterioration of constitutional rights, the deterioration of values, the increasing arrogance of government officials, the lying, virtually everything.

Even children are taught violence and contempt for others as they watch violent movies, violent television programs, listen to violent noise they consider "music." Years ago the movies and the music had an uplifting quality. The vulgarity and violence in movies and "music" today have the opposite effect. The April 1999 murder of 13 students by two school students who later committed suicide shows the effect of this violence-prone entertainment that goes on year after year with the American public unable to understand why their children have violent thoughts! Rather than face the real problem, and face a formidable foe, the public goes after the gun manufacturers.

In most American cities the brutal murder of innocent people, contrasted with the relative absence of crime in pre-invasion of Iraq. Although Saddam Hussein was brutal to those who threatened his pro-western government, the streets were far safer in Iraq than they are in the United States.

Fools and Their Freedom are Soon Parted

Fools and their freedom are soon parted was a statement made two centuries ago. That statement is probably truer today than it was then. The following warning message is reportedly attributed to Cicero, 42 B.C.

> *A nation can survive its fools and even the ambitious. But it cannot survive treason from within. An enemy at the gates is less formidable, for he is known and he carries his banners openly. But the traitor moves among those within the gates freely, his sly whispers rustling through all the alleys, heard in the very halls of government itself*
>
> *For the traitor appears not traitor: He speaks in the accents familiar to his victims and he wears their face and their garments and he appeals to the baseness that lies deep in the hearts of all men. He rots the soul of a nation. He works secretly and unknown in the night to undermine the pillars of a city; he infects the body politic so that it can no longer resist. A murderer is less to be feared.*

In a quotation attributable to Martin Niemoeller that is even more applicable today then when first written:

In Germany they came first for the Communist, and I didn't speak up, because I wasn't a Communist. Then they came for the Jews, and I didn't speak up, because I wasn't a Jew. Then they came for the trade unionists, and I didn't speak up, because I wasn't a trade unionist. Then they came for the Catholics and I didn't speak up, because I was a Protestant. Then they came for me, and by that time no one was left to speak out.

The Record of Public Response and Courage is Pathetic

For decades, much information was available showing the arrogance and corruption affecting the people. Pathetically uninformed, partly due to the media and political pundits, the public in many cases couldn't recognize the obvious. Those who did recognize some small part of the corruption remained in denial.

It takes courage to speak out and do something about corruption in government, or to come to the aid of a victim. For years, newspapers have been reporting the specter of people watching and doing nothing to help someone being beaten up. Typical is the headline in the *San Francisco Examiner* on July 16, 1998, "Bystanders Watch Woman's Beating." That is a common event.

The paper reported, "150 people watched and did nothing" as a young woman was being beaten in the heart of San Francisco. Similar headlines have appeared over the years in newspapers in Massachusetts, New York, New Orleans, and other places, showing that cowardice is rampant in America. (One problem with fostering cowardice is the refusal of some states or counties to issue gun permits to law-abiding people.)

"If you don't like what is going on in the United States, leave!"

Some like the country as it is, as shown by talk show host Larry King, who stated during one of his television shows, "If you don't like what is going on in the United States, leave!" With that type of mentality, is it any wonder the United States is in such a state of decline? Americans have the right to expect honest government, and the alternative is not for honest Americans to leave the country

The Ugly American

A little self-evaluation might also help in understanding America's deteriorated morals, culture, and character. Many years ago authors William J. Lederer and Eugene Burdick wrote a novel based on conduct by Americans in Southeast Asia: *The Ugly American*. The book's introduction said:

The Ugly American is about men and women in Southeast Asia-people making mistakes, people being a little corrupt, people trapped by the beauty of a land or of a woman, people being bought cheap with champagne and caviar.

This unflattering conduct has certainly escalated to an unprecedented degree today. Because the United States is a government of, by, and for the people, that means the people approved this misconduct in government. Let's look at some of the conduct that the American public, as a whole, approved, which surely justifies the modern version *Those Ugly Americans: 20th & 21st Centuries* that I wrote. Among the actions by U.S. leaders that justify that title were the following examples:

Inflicting war upon impoverished people throughout the world, killing millions in the process, including men, women, and children. The United States has incinerated thousands of these people, machine gunned them as they huddled in terror of the overwhelming military power of the United States. These were plain simple people defending their country, including women and children, as in the Mai Lai massacre. The United States tortured and killed over 40,000 Vietnamese in the CIA's Operation Phoenix program, while our military gunned down women and children. The excuse for these atrocities? U.S. leaders were not satisfied with the form of government the poor people of this third world country selected, and on the simplistic "domino theory" excuse.

Undermining duly elected governments throughout the world.

Invading Panama and killing hundreds of people to capture the head of Panama on a charge he was trafficking in drugs (while the CIA, the National Security Council, the President and Vice President, were doing the same, often *with* Noriega).

- Invading Granada and killing defenders on the excuse that an airstrip was being enlarged to accommodate Russian bombers. That airstrip today is enlarged, and used for its original purpose: tourist flights.
- CIA teaching, funding, and arming torture squads throughout Central and South America, resulting in tens of thousands of tortured and killed people, and instilling this culture where it has not previously existed.
- Undermining governments throughout Central and South America, providing arms and money, which resulted in many governments being toppled, and many people killed.
- Firing missiles into foreign countries, such as in Sudan where the United States blew up a pharmaceutical plant on the flimsy, and thoroughly discredited claim, that it was producing terrorist chemicals; blowing apart a residence of the Libyan head of state and killing his child on the unproven claim that Libya was responsible for a bombing in Europe; blowing apart the Chinese Embassy in Belgrade, and much more. Eventually, one of these acts will result in missiles blowing apart U.S. cities, something that is sure to come. The United States has made enemies of large segments of Moslem countries, China, Russia, and many other countries, any of which will surely applaud when the United States gets what *it* inflicted upon people of other nations.

- CIA involvement in killings, including the involvement by presidents of the United States in planning the murders of foreign leaders, including Fidel Castro.
- Starting a war against the Iraqi people on the basis of serial lying, lying that anyone except a moron could recognize. Even as the country was reduced to rubble, and hundreds of thousands of Iraqi men, women, children, and infants, were brutally murdered, most of the American people arrogantly supported what they helped bring about.
- Routine murders of Iraqis, including children and infants, by U.S. military personnel and corporate mercenaries.
- Carpet-bombing of Afghanistan, knowingly killing innocent people.

Not sufficiently placated by these killings, most Americans supported their lying president in seeking to start a war with Iran.

If You Think *This* FBI-DOJ conduct is Bad, Read Lockerbie to 9/11

Inform others of the corruption that you learn about

First, get informed. Read *books* written by insiders. Unfortunately, these books by insiders are rarely found in bookstores. With the coming of the Internet, there are unprecedented opportunities for anyone to publicize this information.

- Make repeated phone calls to radio and television shows describing what you have learned.
- Recommend to people that they read books written by knowledgeable insiders concerning corruption in government.
- Stay away from wild conspiracy theories stated by people with no professional background or ability.
- Recognize the pattern of lying by most political pundits, and especially pundits such as Russ Limbaugh and those with similar zero credibility.
- Demand—don't ask—your members of Congress to investigate certain of the areas of corruption. Don't accept their off-the-shelf evasive responses. Send certified letters to each of your U.S. senators and representatives, demanding that they immediately take the following actions, reminding them of their responsibilities, but realizing that their answers will in most cases be off-the-shelf meaningless responses.
- Pressure Congress to provide legislation and ample funding for an ombudsmen division in government that is staffed by people totally isolated from political influence and with the power to fully investigate and recommend prosecution.
- Pressure Congress to pass legislation eliminating the immunity of government prosecutors, federal and state judges, and other government employees whose actions are obviously illegal, unconstitutional, and/or retaliatory.

Anyone who acts under color of state or federal law, acting in violation of settled law and constitutional protections, inflicting harm upon any person, should be subject to being sued for financial damages.

- Pressure Congress to pass legislation subjecting members of Congress and state and federal judges to investigation and punishment by a body not subject to political influence when they commit crimes for which a citizen would be subject to prosecution and imprisonment. This would include cover-ups and obstruction of justice.
- Pass legislation giving to every person the right to file a lawsuit for financial damages, with a jury trial, to sue federal and state judges and prosecutors that violate clearly stated statutory or constitutional law. This protection exists in statutes but judges have held themselves immune.
- Pass legislation permitting people whose assets have been corruptly taken from them in Chapter 11 courts to sue the government and the Judges, Trustees and law firms, in jury trials. Have the statute of limitations start to run from the day the legislation is passed, and have an adequate period of time to file administrative claims under the Federal Tort Claims Act and time to initiate RICO or civil rights violation actions.
- Pass legislation barring seizure of assets on the pretense that the person violated some particular law.

You Can Either Help, Or
Do Nothing, and Be Part of the Problem!

Everyone has a responsibility under our form of government to stay intelligently informed about government misconduct and react within his ability to do whatever is needed. Most of the harm inflicted upon people described in my books continues to occur for various reasons, one of which is the continued ignorance of future victims. None of the American people can ever say, "I didn't know about these things." The information was in many places.

For those few who have read this far, a strong suggestion is made to get an even more complete picture of the extent of the corruption and the harm upon the American public and national security by reading my other books, all based upon insider information.

INDEX

Made in the USA
Monee, IL
04 November 2026

67377000R00344